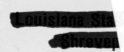

BLUE GUIDE   SCOTLAND

THE BLUE GUIDES

ATHENS AND ENVIRONS
AUSTRIA
BELGIUM AND LUXEMBOURG
BOSTON AND CAMBRIDGE
CATHEDRALS AND ABBEYS OF ENGLAND AND WALES
CHANNEL ISLANDS
CRETE
CYPRUS
EGYPT
ENGLAND
FLORENCE
FRANCE
GREECE
HOLLAND
IRELAND
ISTANBUL
LITERARY BRITAIN
LONDON
MALTA
MOSCOW AND LENINGRAD
MUSEUMS AND GALLERIES OF LONDON
NEW YORK
NORTHERN ITALY
OXFORD AND CAMBRIDGE
PARIS AND ENVIRONS
PORTUGAL
ROME AND ENVIRONS
SCOTLAND
SICILY
SOUTHERN ITALY
SPAIN
VENICE
WALES

BLUE GUIDE

SCOTLAND

JOHN TOMES

Maps and plans drawn by John Flower

A. & C. Black
London

W. W. Norton
New York

Published by A & C Black (Publishers) Limited
35 Bedford Row, London WC1R 4JH

© A & C Black (Publishers) Limited 1986

Published in the United States of America by
W W Norton & Company, Inc
500 Fifth Avenue, New York, NY 10110

Published simultaneously in Canada by
Penguin Books Canada Limited,
2801 John Street, Markham, Ontario L3R 1B4

ISBN 0-393-30370-5   USA

British Library Cataloguing in Publication Data
Scotland.—9th ed.—(Blue guide)
   1. Scotland—Description and travel—1981–
   —Guide-books
   I. Tomes, John
   914.11'04858   DA870

   ISBN 0–7136–2783–2

PREFACE

This, the Ninth Edition of 'Blue Guide Scotland', is the latest in a long and distinguished lineage. The original work was published in 1927 under the editorship of Findlay Muirhead and itself drew upon the resources of Murray's 'Handbook for Scotland'. L. Russell Muirhead followed as editor for thirty years until, with the Sixth Edition, the responsibility as author passed to John Tomes who broke new ground with a much revised and enlarged book. This Ninth Edition—virtually wholly rewritten, considerably expanded, with several additional town plans, and, for the first time, with illustrations—though technically another edition can justifiably claim to be in fact a new book.

John Tomes is also author of the Blue Guides to 'Wales and the Marches', 'Belgium and Luxembourg' and 'Holland'. Both Tom Neville, series editor and editor of this book, and John Flower, cartographer, have enjoyed a long and responsible professional association with the Blue Guides.

The author and editor wish to express their gratitude to the several users who have taken the trouble to send constructive criticism and also suggestions regarding new material and sites. All suggestions have been carefully considered, most have been acted upon, and users of this current edition may rest assured that criticisms and suggestions, and particularly those based on personal discovery, are most welcome.

Acknowledgement is due first to all those who in one way or another have contributed to the compilation and high reputation of this book over the many years since its first appearance, special and most recent appreciation going to the late Stuart Rossiter, long associated with the Blue Guides as both editor and author. Particular thanks also go to the Scottish Tourist Board, whose headquarters in Edinburgh, office in London, and information centres of all levels throughout Scotland have been generous with advice and published material. Much help, too, has been given by many local authority offices and information centres; by those responsible for museums and art galleries; by the owners, administrators and curators of both official and private sites, many of whom went out of their way to explain detail and draw attention to special features; and by several organisations, these including the National Trust for Scotland, the Scottish Development Department (Historic Buildings and Monuments), the Highlands and Islands Development Board, the Nature Conservancy Council, the North of Scotland Hydro-Electric Board, and the Forestry Commission.

The help received from the Chelsea Public Library has, as always, been unfailing, as has also been the support of the author's wife who so successfully combines the roles of navigator, researcher, typist and perceptive critic.

Background sources. From the many reference and other books constantly used, the author would in particular like to record the following: 'Mary, Queen of Scots' by Antonia Fraser (Weidenfeld and Nicolson). 'Portrait of the Border Country' by Nigel Tranter (Robert

Hale). 'Ancient Stones of Scotland' by W. D. Simpson (Robert Hale). 'The Highland Clearances' by John Prebble (Secker and Warburg). 'The Burrell Collection' by John Julius Norwich, Richard Marks, Rosemary Scott, Barry Gasson, James K. Thomson and Philip Vainker (Collins, in association with Glasgow Museums and Art Galleries). 'A Concise Guide to Historic Shetland' by G. A. Points (Shetland Tourist Organisation). 'Guide to Prehistoric Scotland' by Richard Feachem (Batsford). The 'Encyclopaedia Britannica'.

Illustrations. The drawings in this edition of 'Blue Guide Scotland' are by Marcus Lutyens. Those on pages 255 and 283 are based on photographs by Joanne Tomes. The engravings are reproduced from an edition of Walter Scott's 'Tales of a Grandfather', published in Edinburgh by A & C Black in 1860.

NOTES ON USING THIS GUIDE

This guide is in two parts. The first gives background and practical information. The second comprises ten geographic sections, each with an Introduction followed by a number of Routes. For the overall scheme of the Routes, see Atlas 16.

History and Antiquities. Throughout any tour of Scotland prehistory and history always accompany the traveller, usually in the visible form of monuments, ruined or still intact. To avoid repetition the first part of this guide includes an outline *History of Scotland* and also an essay describing the background to Scotland's *Antiquities and Later Buildings*. Also to avoid repetition the first part provides *Biographical Notes*. It would of course be impracticable to cover all the men and women who crowd Scotland's long history, and these notes aim only to identify selected personalities who make a particular, frequent or perhaps confusing appearance and who are not covered in the History or Routes texts.

In the second part, an *Introduction* at the beginning of each geographical section outlines the main features—historical, scenic and other—and a plan sketches that section's *Routes*, these designed, of course, to cover all places of tourist interest. Since some Routes inevitably merge with or run close to others, it is as well to be aware of neighbouring Routes, thus ensuring that places within easy reach but perhaps described under another Route are not missed.

Abbreviations. In addition to generally known and self-explanatory abbreviations, the following are used:

AM	Ancient Monument (site administered by the Scottish Development Department)
Dec	Decorated
ECl	Early Closing (of shops)
EE	Early English
FC	Forestry Commission
NCC	Nature Conservancy Council
NTS	National Trust for Scotland
Perp	Perpendicular
RSPB	Royal Society for the Protection of Birds
SSC	Scottish Sports Council
STB	Scottish Tourist Board

Opening Times. Few sites are willing to commit themselves for even a year ahead, Easter and public holidays add to the uncertainty, and far too often there can be a capricious gap between intent and achievement. Nevertheless the opening times given are believed to have been substantially correct at the time of compilation. Often, of course, sites will be visited simply on an opportunist basis. However, where a site is a definite objective, to avoid possible disappointment intending visitors are advised to consult Tourist Information or to telephone. Telephone numbers are given for most sites (the numbers may in some cases be those of Tourist Information). However, no individual numbers are given for sites controlled by certain organisations which prefer to receive queries centrally. These are the *National Trust for Scotland*, Tel: (031) 2265922; the *Scottish Development Department (AM)*, Tel: (031) 2262570, Ext. 211 or 212; the *Forestry Commission*, Tel: (031) 3340303: in some places, the *Nature Conservancy Council* (see Practical Information, Organisations).

No firm rule can be given regarding public holidays. As a generalisation, though, the larger and more popular sites are likely to be open, the more modest ones closed. It should also be remembered that Scotland celebrates New Year rather than Christmas and that many if not most sites will be closed over the New Year period.

It is also worth noting that larger sites tend to sell their last admission tickets up to 45 minutes prior to published closing times.

In the case of *Scottish Development Department (AM)* sites the opening times are given as Standard or as a variation from Standard. Standard opening times are (but with closure of at least three days over New Year):

April–Sept: Mon.–Sat., 09.30 to 19.00 Sun., 14.00 to 19.00.
Oct–March: Mon.–Sat., 09.30 to 16.00. Sun., 14.00 to 16.00.

Asterisks draw attention to places of special attraction or interest.

Distances. In the case of most Routes the preamble gives both its total distance and a breakdown of distances between principal places. In both the preambles and the texts italicised distances are those between points along the Route, i.e. each italicised distance represents the distance from the previous one. Other distances (e.g. along diversions) are in Roman print. For a number of obvious reasons distances can only be approximate.

Hotels. In response to requests, especially from overseas visitors wishing to plan and book their tour well ahead, the names of a few hotels are, as a convenience, given at the start of each Route. Although these are believed to be good—as a generalisation they are in the middle to higher category—it must be emphasised that these hotels have not necessarily been inspected by the author. It is equally important to emphasise that they are no more than a small selection from the choice available and that the omission of a name certainly does not imply any doubt or criticism. In the larger towns the aim has been to name hotels which are central and, whenever possible, with car parking.—See also Practical Information, Accommodation.

Maps. The Atlas provided with this guide shows principal places mentioned in the text and indicates main physical features. The maps, designed for broad reference and planning, have deliberately not been overcrowded and are not intended to take the place of motorists' maps. Of such there is a huge choice, but special mention may be made of Michelin 'Scotland', sheet 401, covering the whole country, while for detailed exploration most visitors will probably choose the Ordnance Survey 1:50,000 Landranger series.

CONTENTS

MAPS AND PLANS

A NOTE ON BLUE GUIDES

Before the First World War the editors of the English editions of the German Baedecker Guides—marketed from 1908 by T. Fisher Unwin—were Finlay and James Muirhead. During 1915 the editors acquired the copyright of the majority of the famous 'Red' Handbooks, formerly published by John Murray. Muirhead also bought the copyright of a series published by Macmillan, and the first publications by Muirhead Guide-Books Limited appeared in 1916, marketed by Macmillan. In the following year an agreement was made with Hachette et Cie of Paris. This French house had previously published the blue cloth-bound Guides Joanne, named after their first editor Adolphe Joanne (1813–81). Hachette et Cie agreed to handle a translation of a guide to London—the first 'Guide Bleu'. This, and the other guides produced by Muirhead were entitled **The Blue Guides**. Collaboration with the French house also resulted in an adaptation—published in London—of Hachette's Guide Bleu to 'Paris et ses Environs'. In 1927 a new agreement was made and lasted six years. Meanwhile, in 1931, the Blue Guides had been bought by Benn Brothers. In 1934 L. Russell Muirhead (1896–1976), Finlay Muirhead's son, became editor. From 1954 he was assisted by Stuart Rossiter (1923–82), who then became editor in 1963, also taking responsibility for the revision and compilation of several volumes. For the decade 1975–85, Paul Langridge was House Editor, after which he was succeeded by Tom Neville. The series has continued to grow with over 30 titles currently in print.

In April 1984, a year after Benn Brothers had itself been taken over by Extel, their book-publishing subsidiary, Ernest Benn Ltd, was bought by A & C Black. Blacks themselves have a long history of guide-book publishing, beginning, in 1826, with 'Black's Economical Tourist of Scotland', and including several written by Charles Bertram Black, eldest son of the firm's founder. During the 1890s, Blacks had more than 55 titles in their guide-book series in print.

BACKGROUND INFORMATION

Introduction to Scotland

Although constitutionally part of Great Britain ever since the union of the parliaments in 1707, Scotland in the minds of most people still ranks as a country in its own right, particularly since it has its own legal, educational, and ecclesiastical systems. Additionally the banks issue their own notes and the postage stamps carry the Scottish lion, two among the many indications of Scotland's individual identity that will strike visitors once they have crossed what is, significantly, still known as the border.

The name Scotland derives from that of the Irish people (Scoti) who came across during the 6C, but it was not generally used until the formation of a single kingdom during the 11C. To the Romans the northern lands had been known as Caledonia. The broad division of the country into Highlands and Lowlands (roughly either side of a line between Dumbarton and Stonehaven) has no formal significance. But for most of Scotland's history, the two, separated by race, language and geography, had little in common, and it has really only been in recent times that the differences, however artificially still maintained, have in fact begun to fade.

As a holiday choice Scotland can hold its own against most competition. It boasts scenic variety which ranges from the pastoral lands of the Borders with their woods and rippling rivers, through the open down and moorland expanses stretching across much of the South and far North, to the lonely grandeur of the true Highlands, whose mountains towards the North West pile up to a wild and fretted coast. Beyond are the largely unspoilt island groups of the Hebrides in the West and Orkney and Shetland to the North. Within this scenery crowds the visible legacy of Scotland's long and romantic history: a wealth of prehistoric remains, beautiful though ruined medieval abbeys, castles (some ruined, some still inhabited), great houses with superbly decorated and furnished interiors and surrounded by fine parks.

In the sphere of holiday sport Scotland offers, to name only some of the possibilities, golf and fishing (both at a cost far below that in England); water sport, including swimming, underwater, sailing and water-skiing; pony trekking, walking and climbing, gliding, wildlife study and skiing.

With so much scenic grandeur and variety, sport and stirring history, all to be found in a country which is easily accessible, has good internal communications and good accommodation, and which is populated by an attractive and friendly people, it is scarcely surprising that Scotland's holiday popularity is growing so rapidly.

Scotland's weather, sometimes maligned, is not that much more uncertain than that of England, due allowances being made for the country's northerly geography and the effect of mountains which meet the weather systems moving in from the Atlantic. Nevertheless, superb though the weather can often be, the term 'Scots mist' was not born of nothing and the visitor must be prepared for days that can be as wet as others can be hot and dry. The NW coast, in the direct path of the Gulf Stream, can be surprisingly mild, and along it there are several sub-tropical gardens.

The main tourist season is from about Easter to the end of September, and outside this period many though by no means all facilities and some sites are closed. In July and August the more popular districts can be overcrowded, but even at this time there are still remote and lonely corners to be found by those willing to explore the smaller roads. Undoubtedly the best times for touring are May, June and September. While October can also be a good touring month, there can be a chill in the air and the evenings start to shorten.

Aspects of Scotland

Bagpipes, kilts, Highland dancing—these are just some of the things instinctively associated with Scotland and which the visitor will expect to see and hear. Any visitor staying only a day or two is likely at least to meet a kilt. For the whole scene, though, the best course is to arrange to attend a Gathering (see below), of which there are a large number, especially in summer, their dates being listed in the STB's annual publication 'Events in Scotland'. Many hotels and local tourist centres also organise Highland Evenings and suchlike, where, if no cabers are tossed, at least there is a good chance of eating haggis.

Bagpipes, though perhaps most associated with Scotland, are not peculiar to that country. The instrument is one of great antiquity and can be traced in early forms to ancient Persia, Egypt, and Greece, where it was certainly known by AD 100. It was introduced to Britain by the Romans (a bronze figure excavated at Richborough is playing bagpipes), becoming popular in Ireland and Scotland and in the latter developing into something of a status symbol (clan chiefs all had their hereditary pipers by the 16C) as well as a military instrument that inspired the warlike Highlanders, so much so in fact that together with Highland dress it was banned after Culloden.

The instrument itself comprises an airtight bag and pipes of three kinds, a blow-pipe, a chaunter for melody, and drones producing the continuous note which is the bagpipes' main characteristic. The bag may be inflated either by blowing or by small bellows worked by the arm.

Ceilidh is Gaelic for 'visit'. Remote communities were forced to rely for entertainment on their own resources, and it was the custom for groups to meet in one another's homes, each person in turn contributing music, a song, a poem, or whatever else he had to offer. The ceilidh today tends to be more commercial and to be held in halls or hotels, although the occasion is still informal and the entertainment traditional. Visitors should consult their hotel, the local press, or Tourist Information.

Clans. In Gaelic 'clann' means 'children' or 'family'. The start of the clan system may perhaps be traced to the 6C when, after establishing themselves at Dunadd, the Scots began to spread out, dividing the lands between their leaders. A similar process would have been going on elsewhere, and from now on for many centuries the powerful who acquired land acquired also the people living there. Such landowners, though, and especially in the Lowlands, were by no means necessarily Scots and indeed several clans and names have Norman roots, not least that of the great Bruce.

A principal characteristic of the system that developed was the absolute and (an important feature) the willing subservience to the chief. Below the chief there was a recognised hierarchy, descending through the lesser chieftains and the gentlemen (both these being kinsmen of the chief) down to simple clansmen, who did most of the manual work and were the main strength when it came to fighting. Fighting was of course frequent, not only because of clan rivalry, largely over land and cattle, but because loyalty to chiefs ran counter to loyalty to kings, who all the time sought to impose their authority, no easy task with many of the clans living on islands or in remote valleys. Often this was achieved by the king (notably James IV) receiving allegiance in return for formally confirming the chiefs' position by charter (parchment documents known as 'sheepskin grants'). This in turn led to further fighting among the clans, with one chief claiming land by tradition and another by virtue of his royal grant. The Statutes of Iona (1609), signed under duress by nine chiefs 'of the Isles', did much to discourage such fighting, but it was not until 1688 that the last clan battle was fought (at Keppoch).

Culloden killed what was left of the Highland way of life and with it the clan system, but around the turn of the century came the birth of the Highland and clan cult (largely a matter of costume, games, piping, and an urge to 'belong') that on an international scale still flourishes today.

James Pringle Archive Computer, Edinburgh (Rte 18F).

Museum of Scottish Tartans, Comrie (Rte 25B).

Clan Centres: Donald (Rte 62). Donnachaidh (Rte 27). Gunn (Rte 59). Macpherson (Rte 50). Menzies (Rte 24).

The Scottish **Flag**, a white St. Andrew's cross on a blue background, is first recorded as the national emblem at the end of the 13C and derives from St. Andrew being the country's patron saint. St. Andrew was crucified in c69 and buried at Patras in Greece; he is said to have asked for a cross of diagonal beams (saltire) because he considered himself unworthy to die on an upright cross as Christ had done. According to legend St. Regulus, hearing in 370 that the saint's bones were to be removed to Constantinople, took some relics, fled by sea, and was wrecked in Scotland at the spot which is now St. Andrews. More probably the relics came to Scotland in the 8C, and it was at this time (736) that Angus, son of the king of the Picts, adopted St. Andrew as his patron saint.

Another legend is that of the white St. Andrew's cross seen against the blue sky when in the 10C the Picts defeated the Northumbrians at what is now Athelstaneford (Rte 1).—Scotland's other emblem, the **Thistle**, is said to date from an incident at the battle of Largs (1263). One of Hakon's men, barefooted and advancing in the dark to surprise the Scots, trod on a thistle, letting out such a cry that the Scots were alerted and the day was saved. The battle of Luncarty, fought against the Danes in 990, is credited with the same incident.

Highland Dances, though now all in relatively modern form, have ancient origins. The Romans reported that the Caledonians danced wildly around their swords, stuck upwards in the ground, and certain characteristics—sudden high leaps, clockwise movement, chains— allow Celtic origins to be claimed. It has been suggested that the patterns of some dances reflect both ancient sun worship ritual and, more recently, the shape of the Celtic High Cross, and that the circle of the reel symbolises the circle of life.

In 1561 Mary, Queen of Scots, arrived, with her French custom of having musicians and dance-masters to organise court entertainment, and from this date on began a continuous process by which the old dances were tamed and formalised, while others were introduced. Change accelerated with the enthusiasm for everything Highland which followed the repeal in 1782 of the Act of Proscription, new development being to a great extent military as the pipers and dance-masters of the 20 or so Highland regiments became increasingly competitive and inventive.

Highland Dress. Although the word 'tartan' does not appear until 1471, the Romans referred to the Caledonians' 'chequered garments'. There are similar references in later centuries, and in 1578, writing about the ancient customs and dress of the Highlanders, a bishop records that everyone in Scotland wore mantles of the same kind though the nobles favoured many colours.

These mantles would have been plaids, which served both as a single garment and as a blanket. Dressing in a plaid (described as 16 yards of tartan) seems to have been a rather complicated business, involving spreading it on the ground, folding it into pleats, then lying on it, crossing it over the body, and finally belting it. By the 16C, the clan territories were well defined and varied tartan plaid designs developed, to some extent probably as a means of identification.

The kilt is one of the earliest known forms of dress; it appears for instance in the Bronze Age frescoes of Knossos in Crete and was also the dress of the ancient Egyptians. In Scotland, however, the kilt seems to date only from the early 18C when, presumably for reasons of convenience and comfort, the plaid was divided into two halves.

After Culloden Highland dress was forbidden by the Act of Proscription, but with the repeal of the act in 1782 and the explosion of the Highland cult came the development of more or less official tartans, a trend confirmed in 1822 when George IV appeared wearing the Royal Stuart. Today's tartans are defined by sets (which may be registered at the Court of the Lord Lyon), the principal ones being those distinguishing clans, these in turn in many cases sub-dividing into hunting and dress tartans. But it is no longer only the clans who boast tartans. There are sets individual to chiefs and their immediate families, regimental sets, district sets, a clerical set, and even a general set for those with no specific claim.

Scottish Tartans Society, Museum of Scottish Tartans, Comrie, with the largest collection in existence of information on Highland dress.

Canongale Tolbooth, Edinburgh, with a collection of Highland dress and tartans.

Highland Games (Gatherings) probably originated as fairs organised in very early times by kings and chiefs. There seems also, at least on occasion, to have been a military purpose, Malcolm Canmore being credited with the first Braemar Gathering, when he summoned the clans to contests which would enable him to select the best men to be his warriors. Ceres, in Fife, held a Gathering after Bannockburn to honour the village's returning bowmen, and today claims that their games have since been held annually without a break, other than during the two world wars. Like everything else Highland, Gatherings became of widespread popularity after the repeal of the Act of

Proscription, and Queen Victoria's patronage of Braemar ensured that Gatherings became the important feature in the Scottish calendar that they remain today.

Among the features of Gatherings are competitions in Highland dancing; tossing the caber (the largest Braemar caber is 19ft 3 inches long and weighs 120lbs); putting the stone (weighing up to 22lbs); throwing the hammer (weighing up to 22lbs); wrestling; and all manner of piping events.

For dates of Gatherings, see STB annual booklet, 'Events in Scotland'.

Deer Forests. Deer are as much valuable stock as are cattle and sheep, but, being wild, have not until recently been herded on farms and normally have to be culled only in their natural habitat. Deer forests (mostly open mountain and moor) should therefore be regarded as deer farms and are not, as often thought, merely sport shooting lands.

History of Scotland

Prehistoric Period (BC). From midden excavations, tombs and settlements, it is known that Scotland was inhabited in Middle and New Stone Age times, say 5000 and more years ago, these people probably originating from coastwise maritime movements which over millennia brought early man northward along Europe's western shores. Stone circle ritual sites, fortified hill camps and finally earth-houses and brochs continue the story through the Bronze and Iron Ages down to about the time of the birth of Christ, by when the inhabitants must have been many tribes of diverse origins.

The Romans (82–208). The Romans made their first appearance in 82 under Agricola, penetrating into the North East and defeating the tribes at the battle of Mons Graupius (84), the site of which may have been near Stonehaven. The Romans mention one Calgacus, a tribal chief, the first Scot to appear by name in history. Withdrawal soon followed. A second invasion lasted from 142– 185, the area up to the Firth of Forth being occupied and the Antonine Wall built from Forth to Clyde. There followed another withdrawal, after which, apart from a punitive expedition by Septimius Severus in 208, Scotland did not again see the Romans.

Christianity, the Four Kingdoms and the Birth of Scotland (208–1034).
(Kenneth I, Macalpine, 843–860. Constantine I, 863–879. Donald I, 892– 900. Constantine II, III and Donald II, 900–943. Malcolm I, 943–954. Kenneth II, 954–994. Malcolm II, 1005–1034)

In 397 the Christian Church was founded at Whithorn by St. Ninian, and in the following two centuries other missionaries, of whom the best known are St. Columba and St. Mungo (or Kentigern), were spreading the Faith.

Gradually the tribes, original inhabitants and new arrivals, formed into four kingdoms. These were the Scots, Celtic Christians (amongst them, Columba) who crossed from Ireland in the early 6C and settled in Argyll to found the Kingdom of Dalriada; the Picts in the North, of uncertain origin but probably mixed Celtic and aboriginal (Pictland); the Britons, Welsh people who had moved into the South West (Strathclyde); and the Angles, who in the late 6C colonised the E Lowlands (Bernicia, or Lothian, much of the time subject to the neigbouring English Kingdom of Northumbria). The Norsemen appeared around the end of the 8C, soon occupying the Hebrides, Orkney and Shetland, and establishing settlements around the mainland coasts.

Under Kenneth Macalpine the Scots and Picts merged, forming the Kingdom of Alba, later Scotia. He and his successors were constantly engaged with both the Norsemen and Northumbria, and it was not until 1018 that Malcolm II finally defeated the latter at Carham, near Coldstream, and thus joined Lothian to his kingdom. In 1034 Malcolm II was succeeded by his grandson, Duncan I. Duncan had already inherited the remaining independent Kingdom of Strathclyde and thus the single Kingdom of Scotland was born. The Norsemen, though, still held the islands and parts of the mainland.

Development of English Influence (1034–1286).
(Duncan I, 1034–1040. Macbeth, 1040–1057. Malcolm III, Canmore, 1057– 1093. Donald Bane, 1093–1094. Duncan II, 1094. Donald Bane and Edmund, 1094– 1097. Edgar, 1097–1107. Alexander I, 1107–1124. David I, 1124–1153. Malcolm IV, 1153–1165. William I, the Lion, 1165–1214. Alexander II, 1214–1249. Alexander III, 1249–1286)

Duncan I was murdered by Macbeth, himself killed in 1057 and succeeded by Malcolm III (Canmore). Malcolm III's reign was important less because of himself than because of his queen, the English princess, Margaret, to whom, for a man of those times, he seems to have given remarkably free rein. A determined and pious woman, later canonised, she was staunchly English. She started the anglicisation of the Church, till then essentially Celtic, she introduced an English-speaking court and English-speaking clergy, and she brought up her six sons in the English tradition. Three of these, all as pious and as English in outlook as their mother, subsequently reigned and continued her work, which could be said to have changed Celtic Scotland into a feudal kingdom like Norman England. In this task their strongest influence was the Church, and David I, the last son to reign, was particularly active in founding abbeys and granting land to Norman nobles. At this time, too, towns or burghs, as opposed to villages, began to grow; those founded by kings or later granted charters enjoyed the title of Royal Burgh.

Nevertheless relations with England remained uneasy, with the Scots determined to annex Northumbria and the English kings, relying on the wording of a 10C alliance against the Danes, claiming feudal authority over Scotland. William I, the Lion, defeated and captured at Alnwick in 1174, was forced to do homage, but 15 years later the English Richard I (Coeur de Lion), in return for a Scottish contribution to his crusade, annulled this. Then in 1236 Alexander II renounced claim to Northumbria. The long reign of his son, Alexander III, sometimes called the 'Golden Age', was stable and prosperous. It also saw the expulsion of the Norsemen from the Hebrides as the result of Alexander's victory at Largs in 1263. (They had already withdrawn from the mainland 70 years earlier and remained therefore in occupation only of Orkney and Shetland.)

Alexander III's death in 1286 marks a watershed. He was the last of the old line of kings; Border warfare was about to erupt and would continue on and off for three centuries; and from now on English influence would gradually yield to that of France.

Wars of Succession and Independence (1286–1371).

(Margaret, Maid of Norway, 1286–1290. Interregnum, 1290–1292. John Balliol, 1292–1296. Interregnum, 1296–1306. Robert I, The Bruce, 1306–1329. David II, 1329–1371)

Alexander III's heir was his infant granddaughter, Margaret (The Maid) of Norway, but there were rival claimants, John Balliol and Robert Bruce. Scotland's choice thus lay between an infant girl, not even in the country, or civil war between Balliol and Bruce. The Grand Council (barons and clergy) opted for Margaret and her succession was guaranteed by Edward I of England, who, set upon the union of the two countries, arranged for her betrothal to his son. But four years later (1290), on her way to Scotland, Margaret died. Edward I then declared himself feudal overlord and chose John Balliol as his vassal king. Foolishly, but probably egged on by Scottish opinion, Balliol soon revolted, whereupon Edward started to earn his reputation as 'Hammer of the Scots'. He claimed total sovereignty, easily defeated the Scots at Dunbar, and went on to destroy the Great Seal and remove to London the Stone of Destiny, the sacred stone, brought from Ireland to Dalriada and thence to Scone, upon which Scottish kings had been crowned since the 6C. The following year (1297) saw the uprising by Sir William Wallace.

Born about 1270, **William Wallace** lived for some years at Dunipace near Stirling. Being declared an outlaw, for killing an Englishman who had insulted him, he gathered many adherents and frequently attacked the English, perhaps his best known early exploit being the burning of the barracks (barns) of Ayr. Later, when confronted by an English army at Irvine, many of his supporters deserted him, whereupon Wallace gathered a new army in the North. He won outright victory at Stirling Bridge, expelled the English and ruled Scotland as 'guardian'. Edward I retaliated in force, defeating Wallace at Falkirk (1298). Wallace escaped, but was betrayed in 1305 and put to death as a traitor.

In 1306 the rival Scots factions met in Greyfriars Church, Dumfries, to concert plans for resistance to the English. But a quarrel broke out and Bruce slew Comyn ('the Red'), the representative of the Balliols, and then had himself crowned Robert I.

Robert Bruce was born at either Lochmaben or Turnberry in 1274. Of Norman ancestry and owning lands in England, he probably spent his youth at the court of Edward I. As Earl of Carrick he supported Wallace, but later deserted him at Irvine. After the incident at Dumfries, Bruce declared himself unequivocally for Scotland and was crowned at Scone. Defeated at Methven and Dalry, proclaimed an outlaw, excommunicated, and with his wife and daughter in English hands, Bruce's cause seemed hopeless. He spent 1306–07 as a fugitive (some of the time on the island of Rathlin off Ireland, probable scene of the legendary encounter with the persistent spider). But in 1307 Edward I died, being succeeded by his incompetent son, Edward II. There followed seven years of struggle (during which Bruce defeated all rivals, especially the Comyns in the North East), culminating in the defeat of Edward II at Bannockburn in 1314. Only in 1323, though, was Bruce's title as King of Scotland recognised by the Pope. In 1327 the Treaty of York with Edward III declared Scotland's independence. Bruce died, probably of leprosy, at Cardross in 1329. He was buried at Dunfermline, but his heart, after being taken on a crusade by Sir James Douglas, is believed to lie at Melrose Abbey.

Bruce was succeeded by his infant and weak son, David II, whose reign was marked by revolts of the Balliols and other nobles disinherited by Bruce, wars with Edward III and the birth of Scottish French alliances against the English. Captured in battle, David II was held in London from 1346–57, and it was in order to raise his ransom that the constitutional change was made under which representatives of the royal burghs were invited to join the barons and clergy on the Grand Council. David II was succeeded by his nephew, Robert II, the first of the Stewarts.

The Early Stewarts (1371–1542).
(Robert II, 1371–1390. Robert III, 1390–1406. James I, 1406–1437. James II, 1437–1460. James III, 1460–1488. James IV, 1488–1513. James V, 1513– 1542)

From the accession of Robert II to the abdication of Mary, Queen of Scots, in 1567, Scotland's story is a complicated one of wars with England, and the internal intrigue, rebellion, and anarchy resulting from the constant endeavours of kings to impose their authority on people who recognised only that of their chiefs and on chiefs who recognised none. Though at times threatened, the monarchy nonetheless prevailed, notable landmarks being the wholesale execution of the powerful Albany family by James I in 1425, the defeat of the equally powerful Douglases by James II, the introduction by James IV of land grants ('sheepskin grants') in return for formal allegiance, and the assumption for the crown by the same king of the title Lord of the Isles. Also on the positive side, Orkney and Shetland were given to James III in 1469, as a pledge for the dowry of his wife, Margaret of Denmark. The pledge has never been redeemed, and the islands were in any case formally annexed by Scotland in 1472.

James IV, set on helping the French, unnecessarily went to war with England and suffered disastrous defeat at Flodden in 1513. He was followed by James V, who made two French marriages, the second being to Mary of Guise. During his reign the Reformation, encouraged by pressure by Henry VIII in England, began to make progress in Scotland, but James refused to follow Henry's lead and dissolve the Scottish monasteries. Henry then invaded Scotland, and James, little supported by his nobles, who resented the French influence and who also, more realistically than their King, had their eyes on the wealth of the Church, was defeated in 1542 at Solway Moss. He died soon after, leaving as his heir his six-days old daughter, Mary.

Mary, Queen of Scots (1542–1567; died 1587). The reign opened with an uneasy balance between the regent, Arran, who was inclined towards the Reformation, and the court and the Church. However the savage ravaging of southern Scotland in 1544–45 (the 'English' or 'rough wooing') by the Earl of Hertford, consequent upon the Scots' refusal to ratify a treaty of marriage between the infant Mary and Henry VIII's son, pushed Scotland towards France. Hertford (now Lord Protector Somerset) invaded a third time, winning the battle of Pinkie (1547), whereupon the Scots sent Mary, aged 5, to France. She stayed there 13 years, marrying the French boy heir in 1558. The following year her husband became King.

But in Scotland it was the beginning of the end for Catholic power and the French alliance. The Protestant leaders (Lords of the Congregation as they styled themselves) increasingly resented the French influence. Mary of Guise, now regent and backed by French troops, reacted by denouncing the Protestants as heretics. In reply the Protestants, fired by John Knox's sermon in Perth, started to destroy the religious houses and in 1559 deposed the regent queen, seeking the protection of Elizabeth of England for so long as 'the marriage shall continue between the Queen of Scots and the French King'. The next year they formally abolished Roman Catholicism and forbade the celebration of Mass. In that year, too, Mary's husband died.

Such was the situation to which Mary, not yet 20, a devout Catholic and a widow, returned in 1561. Although barely seven years were to elapse between her return and her flight to England, these were so charged with intrigue and violence and have left such a mark on Scotland that this period, with its romantic and tragic heroine, demands more detailed description than either its length or its historical significance warrants.

Mary's principal home was Holyrood and it was here, only a month after her return, that she had the first of her interviews with the reformer, John Knox, and started her unsuccessful struggle for toleration for Roman Catholicism. This apart, the early years were not unhappy and Mary saw something of Scotland. In 1562 she made a royal progress through the North East, combining this with suppressing a revolt by the Earl of Huntly (see Introduction to VI North East), and in 1563 there was another progress, this time through the South West. In 1565 she married Henry, Lord Darnley, with whom she was infatuated. Elizabeth of England's attitude was equivocal—she was always very conscious that Mary was her heiress presumptive—and she halfheartedly supported a rebellion by the Earl of Moray, Mary's half-brother. This failed, and Moray fled. Darnley, a youth as weak as he was ambitious, then set his heart on the Crown Matrimonial, a device which would have given him personal royal status. But when Mary, encouraged by her Italian secretary, Rizzio, refused this, Darnley went over to Mary's enemies, personally taking part in the brutal murder of Rizzio before Mary's eyes at Holyrood in March 1566. Moray and other banished lords then returned to Scotland. However Darnley promptly betrayed his fellow conspirators and fled with Mary to Dunbar, whence, escorted by the Earl of Bothwell and a small army, they returned three days later to Holyrood. Rizzio's murderers fled to England, but Darnley was allowed to protest that he was an innocent dupe. Three months later Mary gave birth to her son, James.

Not only was Bothwell now in the ascendant, but it was also becoming increasingly obvious that the marriage with the impossible Darnley, who had made enemies of everyone, could not last. Although in January 1567 Mary visited him in Glasgow when he was seriously ill (possibly poisoned), and although he then accompanied her to Edinburgh, their brief stay there at the house called Kirk o'Field was their last time together. In early February, when Mary was at Holyrood, Kirk o'Field was mysteriously blown up and Darnley's body, showing evidence of strangulation, found in the garden.

Whether or not Mary had any hand in this murder plot, hatched at Craigmillar Castle, is unproven, but Bothwell was undoubtedly a ringleader, although he successfully overrode all accusations and even achieved formal acquittal by the Privy Council. He virtually abducted Mary to Dunbar, speedily arranged a divorce from his wife, and then married Mary in Edinburgh in May 1567. For Mary, the marriage was the beginning of the end. There was immediate rebellion and, under suspicion for Darnley's murder and discredited by the marriage, she had to flee with Bothwell first to Borthwick, then to Dunbar. In June she surrendered at what was a farce of a battle at Carberry Hill, Bothwell galloping away never to be seen by her again. Five days later, imprisoned in the island castle of Lochleven, she abdicated in favour of her infant son, Moray being appointed regent.

The following year Mary escaped with the aid of the Douglas family. She rode W through Niddry and Hamilton, but suffered final defeat in May 1568, at Langside, whence she fled to England. Not yet 26 years old, she was to face nearly 20 years imprisonment before being executed in 1587.

The Union of the Crowns (1603) to the Union of the Parliaments (1707).
(James VI/I, 1567–1625. Charles I, 1625–1649. Charles II, 1649–1651. Commonwealth, 1651–1660. Charles II, restored, 1660–1685. James VII/II, 1685–1688. William III of Orange and Mary, 1688–1694. William III to 1702. Anne, 1702–1714)

In 1603, on the death of Elizabeth, James VI of Scotland became also James I of England. But this union of the crowns did not mean the union of the two countries and for a century and a half longer Scotland's story continues as a complicated and violent one, its main features being bitter quarrels about the Church, the English and later Scottish civil wars, and Scottish support of Charles II and the Stuart pretenders. (Mary had changed the spelling from Stewart to Stuart.) In simplest terms the Church quarrels sprang from two sharply opposed views. One was the extreme Protestant Presbyterian belief, personified by the Covenanters, which stood for pure Reformation simplicity, the Church's separation from the civil power, the equality of all ministers and little formal worship. The other party believed in more formal liturgy and a hierarchy with bishops (episcopacy), possibly holding authority from the crown. Again in simplest terms, the former were Lowlanders and tended to be supporters of parliament; the latter Highlanders, who, since the Stuarts were by preference episcopalian, tended to be royalist and Jacobite.

The Covenants. James VI/I succeeded in grafting episcopacy on to the Presbyterian Church, but Charles I went too far, particularly in attempting to introduce a new prayer book, the result being the National Covenant, signed with great enthusiasm at Greyfriars, Edinburgh (1638). This stood firm on the principles of the Reformation and led to the abolition of the bishops appointed by James VI/I. Charles I's attempts to impose his will failed, and, under the Solemn League and Covenant (1643; confirmed 1646), Scotland, led by the Earl of Argyll, sided with parliament during the crucial period before and at the start of the English civil war, parliament, for its part, undertaking to introduce Presbyterianism in England.

This turned out to be only a brief alliance, and Cromwell's inability to fulfil parliament's side of the bargain, followed by his execution of Charles I, led to deep divisions within Scotland. Scotland now defied Cromwell's Commonwealth, proclaiming Charles II as King (but only after he had signed both Covenants), and there were

Covenanter.

abortive invasions of England: in 1650 when Cromwell defeated the Scots at Dunbar, and in 1651 when another venture in support of Charles II ended in defeat at Worcester.

A prominent figure during the above period was James Graham, **Marquess of Montrose**, who achieved romantic fame as a betrayed and tragic hero. Montrose found himself having to play a double role. At heart a Covenanter, he was active in suppressing the initial opposition in the North East, but later, in 1640, largely because he could not accept the personal ambition of the dominant Earl of Argyll, he supported Charles I rather than the Solemn League and Covenant. When the Civil War broke out in England, Montrose won several minor battles in the North. But with Charles' defeat at Naseby, Montrose's Highlanders deserted him and he was himself defeated by the Covenanter general, Leslie, at Philiphaugh. Montrose escaped abroad, returning in 1650 when Scotland accepted Charles II. But the latter soon disavowed him, finding it more expedient to become King on Argyll's terms, and Montrose, after failing to rouse the clans, was routed near Bonar Bridge, afterwards being surrendered by MacLeod of Assynt and hanged in Edinburgh in 1650. His enemy, Argyll, suffered the same fate ten years later.

For nearly nine years (1651–1660) Scotland was under Commonwealth military occupation. With the restoration (1660), the Scottish parliament surprisingly annulled all Church legislation since 1633 and appointed bishops. Bitterness deepened until the extreme Covenanters rebelled, first in 1666 when they were defeated at Rullion Green in the Pentland Hills, then again in 1679. Initially successful, they held the Highlander Royalist Claverhouse at Drumclog, but, lacking support from the majority of Scotsmen, were themselves soon defeated at Bothwell Bridge. There followed years of suppression of the Covenanters, so savage that the period became known as 'the killing time', ended only by the English revolution against James VII/II (1688). His successor, William of Orange, agreed to the abolition of bishops. What was left of Scottish episcopalianism became Jacobite (i.e. supporting the Stuarts), but effectively died with its leader Claverhouse (now Viscount Dundee) on the field of Killiecrankie a year later. But the Highlanders continued unwilling to take the oath to William of Orange and Mary, so the last day of 1691 was set as the final date for submission. All the chiefs eventually swore, except Macdonald of Glencoe who delayed. The result was the notorious Massacre of Glencoe.

1707 brought the Treaty of Union, under which the parliaments of England and Scotland were united into that of the United Kingdom, Scotland receiving guarantees on the Presbyterian Established Church and on the maintenance of Scottish law and courts.

After Union.
(George I, 1714–1727. George II, 1727–1760. George III, 1760–1820. George IV, 1820–1830. William IV, 1830–1837. Victoria, 1837–1901. Edward VII, 1901–1910. George V, 1910–1936. Edward VIII, 1936. George VI, 1936–1952. Elizabeth I/II, 1952–)

Despite the Treaty of Union, the Highlands were far from subdued and Jacobite sentiment clung on, erupting in the rebellions of 1715 and 1745. The '15, led by the Earl of Mar on behalf of the Old Pretender, failed to get either Lowland or the promised French support and ended in defeat at Sheriffmuir. To bring the Highlands under control General Wade was then given the task of building a network of military roads, but, despite this, there was another and more serious rising in 1745, this one led by Prince Charles Edward (the Young Pretender or Bonnie Prince Charlie). General Scottish support was patchy and after initial success at Prestonpans and an advance as far S as Derby the Prince had to withdraw until finally defeated by Cumberland at Culloden. After adventurous wanderings he escaped to France, while in Scotland Cumberland set about earning his nickname of 'butcher'.

The **Pretenders** were the end of the Stuart line. The son of James VII/II was James Francis Edward, James III to the Jacobites and the Old Pretender to the Hanoverians. A worthy but uninspiring man, he made three attempts to win his crown. In 1708 he came by sea and was defeated in the Firth of Forth by Admiral Byng; the '15 ended at Sheriffmuir; and a final attempt in 1719 collapsed when the supporting Spanish fleet was lost in a storm and the Highland rising broke in Glen Shiel. He died in 1766. His son, Prince Charles Edward (born 1720), is a better known figure, and, as the Bonnie Prince Charlie of the '45 helped during his adventurous wanderings by Flora Macdonald, briefly even a romantic one. After the '45 he had long years of pathetic exile. He died in 1788, leaving no legitimate male issue, and with the death in 1807 of his celibate brother the Stuart male line ended. These last three Stuarts lie in the crypt of St. Peter's in Rome, unaware that their marble monument was in part paid for by the Hanoverian George III.

Culloden signalled far more than the end of Jacobite hopes. It signalled too the end of a centuries-long Highland way of life. The Lowland Scots and the English were determined to tame the Highlanders, and the Act of Proscription (1747; repealed 1782) formally banned Highland dress, etc., but the Act was scarcely necessary for complete change was inevitable. For centuries the clansman crofter had paid his rent to his chief in warrior service; now, with fighting a thing of the past, and with the chiefs increasingly attracted by the glitter and comforts of London, the latter required

The Stuart Monument at St. Peter's, Rome. Here lie the last of the Stuarts—the Old and Young Pretenders and the latter's prelate brother—their memorial in part paid for by the Hanoverian George III.

rent in cash. But this their tenants did not have, so instead the chiefs turned to Lowland and English sheep farmers only too anxious to buy or lease Highland land, provided always that the crofters were first removed. In the evictions that followed (between about 1780 and 1860, now known as the Highland Clearances), the Highland people were dispossessed and dispersed. Some disappeared into city slums, others died trying to scratch a living from the miserable coastal sand plots allotted to them, thousands emigrated to Canada and Australia. By 1860 the Highlands had been virtually emptied.

In the South, though, during much the same period, Edinburgh took on new life, flourishing as a centre of the arts. Then in 1822 George IV made a State Visit, the first by the sovereign since the Stuarts. Instigated and organised by Sir Walter Scott, Holyrood was brought back to life and the trapping of the occasion included Highland dress, bagpipes, weapons and banners, even the King wearing the Royal Stuart tartan. This occasion, followed thirty years later by the royal purchase of Balmoral, marked the birth of the Highland cult which is today so much a part of what the tourist expects of Scotland.

The Victorian era saw medical landmarks, such as Simpson's use of chloroform in Edinburgh in 1847 and Lister's introduction of antiseptic surgery in Glasgow in 1865, and also great industrial expansion, this bringing far-reaching social change, with at one extreme mass poverty and slums, and at the other a personal and civic prosperity that encouraged noteworthy architectural movements (Scottish Baronial and Neo-Classical) and the founding of some of Scotland's most famous art collections. The era has left such an interesting and varied legacy that 'Victorian Scotland' has become an official theme of Scottish Tourist Board promotion.

Within the first part of the present century belong the gallantry of the Scottish divisions during two world wars, and the inauguration in 1947 of the Edinburgh Festival, quickly to earn international artistic renown. More recent years have seen the exploitation of North Sea oil, the debate on devolution (the Scots showing no great enthusiasm), and, in 1975, the local government reorganisation.

Biographical Notes

Adam. Renowned family of Scottish-born architects, consisting of William and his four sons, John, Robert, James and William. Robert (1728–92) is the best known. The Adam style was basically Roman and Italian rather than native and extended beyond architecture to everything that went with the interior decoration of a gracious building. Adam achievements will be met throughout Lowland Scotland.

Adamnan, Saint (c 624–704). 9th Abbot of Iona. Important as author of the 'Life of St. Columba'.

Albany, Dukes of. 1. Robert Stewart (c 1345–1420). Natural son of Robert II. Became Regent of Scotland and retained this position even after the accession of his brother as Robert III. In 1398 his nephew, David, Duke of Rothesay and heir to the throne, became Regent. Uncle and nephew soon quarrelled and in 1402 the latter died in prison at Falkland. Although parliament recorded that Rothesay died from natural causes, Albany is generally held to have been responsible. Albany became Regent again and was succeeded by his son, Murdoch. 2. Murdoch Stewart ruled feebly on behalf of James I, captive in England. James, on his return to Scotland, resolved to curb the power of the great nobles and started by executing (1425) Murdoch, his son and his father-in-law. 3. John Stewart (c 1481–1536). Regent of Scotland (1515–23). He was active in furthering alliances with the French and negotiated the marriage between James V and Mary of Guise.

Angus. See Douglas (Red).

Argyll, Earls and Dukes of. 1. Archibald Campbell, 5th Earl (1530–73). Although an adherent of John Knox and a Lord of the Congregation, he later sided with Mary, Queen of Scots, but was nevertheless probably concerned in the murders of both Rizzio and Darnley. Commanded Mary's troops after her escape from Lochleven. 2. Archibald Campbell, 8th Earl (1607–61). A Covenanter, he became the most powerful man in Scotland. He sided with parliament in the Civil War and opposed Montrose on both personal and political grounds, their bitter rivalry leading to the latter's final defeat and death. Later Argyll supported Charles II, whom he crowned at Scone. At the Restoration, however, his earlier collaboration with Cromwell was proven and he was executed. 3. Archibald Campbell, 9th Earl (1629–85). Staunchly Protestant he fell foul of James VII/II, supported Monmouth's rebellion, was defeated and executed.

Balliol. Important Norman-Scottish family, of whom the best-known are: 1. John (d 1269). Regent during minority of Alexander III, but was accused of treason and lost his lands. Went to England, fought for Henry III and established several scholarships at Oxford. 2. Devorguilla (d 1290). Daughter of Alan, Earl of Galloway, and wife of the above John Balliol. She founded Balliol College, Oxford, Sweetheart Abbey and several other religious houses. 3. John (1249–1315). Son of John and Devorguilla. Chosen by Edward I to be King of Scotland, in preference to the rival claimant, Robert Bruce.

Barrie, Sir James (1860–1937). Scottish novelist and dramatist. Among many works are: 'A Window in Thrums' (Kirriemuir), 'Quality Street', 'Peter Pan' and 'Mary Rose'.

Beaton. 1. James (d 1539). Archbishop of Glasgow and St. Andrews. Regent during minority of James V and chiefly responsible for the alliance with France. Burned many heretics, including Patrick Hamilton. 2. David (c 1494–1546). Nephew of James. Cardinal and Archbishop of St. Andrews. Strongly supported the Scottish-French alliance, and was a notorious persecutor of Reformers, his best-known victim being George Wishart. Murdered, in revenge, in St. Andrews Castle. 3. James (1517–1603). The last Roman Catholic archbishop of Glasgow. Nephew of Cardinal Beaton. From 1560 he lived in Paris, acting as ambassador for Scotland.

Bell, Henry (1767–1830). Scottish engineer who placed the first steamboat on the Clyde ('Comet'. 25 tons. 3 H.P. engine). He gave much assistance to the American engineer, Fulton.

Bothwell, James Hepburn, Earl of (1536–78). Powerful and turbulent noble during the reign of Mary, whom he married in 1567 after taking the lead in the murder of her husband, Darnley. At Carberry Hill Bothwell offered to fight any of Mary's enemies single-handed, but Mary forbade this. After Carberry Hill Bothwell became leader of a

Cardinal Beaton. A notorious and enthusiastic persecutor of Reformers, he burnt George Wishart but was soon afterwards himself murdered in St. Andrews Castle.

band of pirates. In 1570 Mary was granted a divorce. Bothwell went to Scandinavia where he was held in solitary confinement in the Danish castle of Dragsholm, eventually dying insane.

Brahan, Seer of (Coinneach Odhar). Early 17C Scottish seer. After sleeping on a fairy hillock he awoke to find his head resting on a small stone with a hole in it. He put the stone to his right eye, which from then on was blind to everything except the truth and the future. He gained considerable fame, but was cruelly murdered by the Countess of Seaforth (at Fortrose) for telling her about her husband's infidelity.

Buchanan, George (1506–82). Best-known Scottish 16C humanist. Anti-clerical, he satirised the religious houses and was forced by Cardinal Beaton to flee to France. Returning to Scotland, he became openly a Reformer. He was tutor both to Mary and James VI.

Burns, Robert (1759–96). Generally accepted as Scotland's greatest poet. His early years were spent in some poverty, he, his brother and his father together failing to make a success of farming at Lochlea, near Tarbolton. His first volume was published in 1786, and was so successful that he cancelled the passage he had booked to take up a job in Jamaica. At about this time he was in love with Mary Campbell of Dunoon. She inspired poems such as 'The Highland Lassie' and 'Highland Mary' and, after her early death, 'To Mary in Heaven'. After a period in Edinburgh, where he was lionised but continued to have little financial success, he again tried farming, this time at Ellisland. In 1791 he accepted a post as excise officer in Dumfries, where he remained until his death. He married Jean Armour, by whom, both before and after marriage, he had several children. Among his many works were 'Tam o'Shanter', 'The Twa

Brigs', 'Auld Lang Syne' and 'Hallowe'en'.

Chantrey, Sir Francis (1781–1841). English sculptor; well-known for his portrait-busts, notably one of Sir Walter Scott. Principal works include Washington (State House, Boston); George III (Guildhall, London); George IV (Brighton).

Claverhouse. See Graham of Claverhouse.

Cochrane, Robert (d 1482). Low-born favourite of James III, important also as an architect (Auchindoun Castle; Parliament Hall, Stirling). He became too powerful and was murdered by hanging (at Lauder) by jealous nobles led by Archibald Douglas, henceforth known as 'Bell-the-Cat'. (Some modern authorities suggest Cochrane may never have existed.)

Columba, Saint (c 521–597). A member of the Irish royal house, he founded a number of churches and monasteries in Ireland before in 563 settling in Iona with 12 companions. From here, by his preaching and holy life, he converted much of northern Scotland. As chief churchman of Dalriada, he gave formal benediction to his kinsman Aidan, thus officiating at what was probably the first Christian 'coronation'.

Crichton, William (d 1482). On the murder of James I, he seized the

Oliver Cromwell. Parliamentarian, soldier, man of God, regicide.

infant James II, took over the revenues, became Lord Chancellor and for long enjoyed absolute power. To secure his position (and that of the king) he arranged the judicial murder of William and David Douglas at the Black Dinner in Edinburgh Castle, and he was also present in 1452 when James II treacherously stabbed William Douglas to death at Stirling.

Cromwell, Oliver (1599–1658). Of yeoman stock, he became a member of parliament (England) in 1628. During the Civil War he rose to become parliament's leader and as such bore much of the responsibility for the execution of Charles I. After the execution he ruled as Lord Protector of England (Commonwealth period) until his death.

Cumberland, Duke of (1721–65). Son of George II. Best-known for his defeat of the Young Pretender at Culloden, after which his savage repression earned him the title of 'Butcher'.

Douglas. Ancient Scottish family which divides into the Black and Red Branches. Of the *Black Douglases* the best known are: 1. Sir James, the Good (1286–1330). A staunch supporter of Bruce, he gained the name of 'black' from his savage excesses in raids along the border. (One of his exploits was so barbaric that it became known as the 'Douglas Larder'.) He took Bruce's heart on a crusade, but fell fighting the Moors in Spain. 2. Archibald, the Grim (1328–c1400). Natural son of 'good' Sir James. Became Lord of Galloway, and built Threave Castle, whence he ruled his lands as absolute master. Black Douglas power overshadowed that of the crown during the weak rule of Robert III, and Douglas's daugher, Marjorie, married Robert III's son and heir, the Duke of Rothesay. 3. William and David (d 1440) were sons of the 5th Earl. When little more than boys they were treacherously executed in Edinburgh Castle (the Black Dinner). This murder, arranged by Chancellor Crichton, broke the Douglas power. 4. William (c 1425–52), 8th Earl, temporarily recovered Black Douglas power, but, although under safe-conduct, was murdered by James II at Stirling, Castle. 5. James (1426–88) rebelled to avenge his brother, but was defeated (losing Threave) and the lordship of Douglas passed to the Red Douglas, 4th Earl of Angus. Of the *Red Douglases* (Earls of Angus) the best-known are: 1. Archibald (c 1450–c1514), 5th Earl, who earned the title of 'Bell-the-Cat' for taking the lead in hanging several low-born favourites of James III. 2. Bishop Gavin (c 1474–1522). Third son of the 5th Earl. Churchman, diplomat and poet. Abbot of Arbroath, Bishop of Dunkeld and of St. Machar, Aberdeen. 3. Archibald (c 1489–1557), 6th Earl, who married Margaret, sister of Henry VIII and widow of James IV. He became very powerful and was hated by his stepson (James V), whom for a while he held and controlled. In 1528 Margaret got a divorce, James freed himself and Douglas fled. James then avenged himself by burning Douglas's sister (Janet, Lady Glamis) at the stake, as a witch for conspiring against him. By Margaret this Douglas became grandfather to Darnley, husband of Mary, Queen of Scots.

Dundee, Viscount. See Graham of Claverhouse.

Duns Scotus, John (c 1265–1308). A Franciscan, born at Duns, he became a leading divine and the greatest medieval philosopher. Known as 'Dr Subtilis'. He lived in Oxford, Paris and Cologne.

Fingal. In origin probably a 3C Irish warrior called Finn MacCumhael. Finn attracted much legend to himself and became a mythological figure dominating Gaelic folklore. When not busy with the chase, he and his band of warrior heroes (the original Fenians) defended Ireland against foreign invaders. Traditionally father of Ossian.

Graham of Claverhouse, John (c 1649–89). Viscount Dundee ('Bonnie Dundee' of ballad). Scottish soldier, royalist, and notorious persecutor of the later Covenanters. After the revolution against James VII/II, he placed himself at the head of the Stuart cause in Scotland, but was killed at Killiecrankie.

Hamilton, Patrick (1504–28). Titular Abbot of Ferne, he studied in Paris, was attracted by the teaching of Erasmus and became a convinced Protestant. A member of the university of St. Andrews, he had to flee the persecution of James Beaton. After visiting Luther and studying in Germany, he returned to Scotland, but Beaton had him burned for heresy. He is regarded as the Scottish proto-martyr of the Reformation.

Hertford, Edward Seymour, Earl of (1506–52). Also Duke of Somerset and brother of Jane Seymour, third wife of Henry VIII. In 1544 and 1545 Henry appointed him Lieutenant General of the North, with instructions to punish the Scots for their repudiation of the marriage treaty between the infant Mary and Henry's son, Edward. Hertford carried out his instructions with great savagery. After the death of Henry VIII, Hertford (Somerset) became Lord Protector of England, but was toppled by his rival, Warwick, and executed.

Hogg, James (1770–1835). Scottish poet, known, from his calling, as the 'Ettrick shepherd'. Protégé of Sir Walter Scott.

Jones, John Paul (1747–92). Son of John Paul, a gardener near Kirkbean, he went to sea, at first on slavers and then getting his own ships. In 1773 he changed his name to Jones, after killing the leader of a mutinous crew, an act he always deeply regretted. He received a commission in the new American navy and was the first to raise the Union flag on a warship (the 'Alfred'). Thereafter he spent several years in European waters harassing the English, but usually acting with chivalry. In 1788 he entered Catherine the Great's Russian navy as an admiral, but soon retired disillusioned. He died in France. A century later his body was brought back to the USA and laid in the naval chapel at Annapolis.

Keith. Ancient NE Scottish family whose leaders bore the hereditary title of Mariscal of Scotland. 1. Robert (d 1346) had the title confirmed and made hereditary by Bruce. He commanded the Scottish cavalry at Bannockburn. 2. William (d c 1407) built the great Keith stronghold at Dunnottar. 3. Another William (d 1581) was a guardian of Mary, Queen of Scots, and later became an adherent of the Reformation. He retired to Dunnottar and became known as William of the Tower. His daughter married the regent, Moray. 4. George (c 1553–1623), 5th Earl Marischal, was a highly cultured man. He arranged the marriage between James VI and Anne of Denmark. In 1593 he founded and endowed Aberdeen's Marischal College. 5. William (c 1617–61), 7th Earl Marischal, was a leading Covenanter. It was to his safe-keeping at Dunnottar that the Scottish regalia were entrusted. 6. George (c 1693–1778), 10th Earl, was a Jacobite, took part in the '15, fled to the continent and lost the family estates and titles. 7. James (1696–1758) is best known as Marshal Keith. Like his brother he fled abroad after the '15, but returned to take part in the even more abortive (Glen Shiel) rising of 1719. He thereafter served in the Spanish, Russian and Prussian armies, being given the rank of Field Marshal by Frederick II of Prussia. He had a distinguished career in

Frederick's army during the Seven Years War before he was killed in battle.

Kelvin, William Thomson (1824–1907). Distinguished physicist. For 53 years he held the chair of natural philosophy at the University of Glasgow, during which period it became a source of inspiration for advanced research.

Kirkcaldy of Grange, Sir William (c 1520–73). Determined opponent of Cardinal Beaton whom, with the help of others, he murdered. He was a leader of the Lords of the Congregation; was accessory to the murder of Rizzio, but not to that of Darnley; he received Mary's surrender at Carberry Hill and was mainly responsible for her defeat at Langside. Later he sided with her (although she was by now imprisoned in England) and held Edinburgh Castle in her cause; here he was forced to surrender and hanged.

Knox, John (c 1505–72). Scottish reformer. In 1547, when in St. Andrews, he was taken prisoner by the French, spending 19 months in the galleys. Returning to Scotland he preached (1559) in Perth and St. Andrews the fiery sermons which led to the destruction of the monasteries. As minister of St. Giles in Edinburgh (1561) he held four Dialogues with Mary. Absent in England during the latter part of Mary's reign, he returned to Scotland in 1567 to preach at the coronation of James VI. In character Knox was dogmatic, yet had a sense of humour and tenderness belied by sermons which sparked an orgy of destruction well beyond anything he intended.

Lauder, Sir Harry (1870–1950). Mill boy and miner who became a famed writer and interpreter of Scottish songs.

Leighton, Robert (1611–84). Bishop of Dunblane and Archbishop of Glasgow. A scholarly and meditative man, he is best-known for his efforts to reconcile the Episcopalian and Presbyterian points of view, and for his representations against the persecution of the Covenanters.

Leslie, David (1601–82). Scottish Covenanter and general. After being a colonel of cavalry in the army of Gustavus Adolphus, he fought for parliament during the English Civil War and defeated Montrose at Philiphaugh. He led Scotland's army (in support of Charles II, 1650), but was defeated by Cromwell at Dunbar. The following year he accompanied Charles II to defeat at Worcester, thereafter being imprisoned in the Tower of London until the Restoration when he was made Lord Newark.

Macdonald, Flora (1722–90). After assisting the Young Pretender (see Rtes 62 and 66), Flora was arrested and imprisoned in the Tower of London. Freed under the 1747 Act of Indemnity, she married (1750), later (1773) emigrating to America. Her husband served the British government during the War of Independence and was taken prisoner. Flora returned to Scotland in 1779.

Macpherson, James (1736–96). Scottish poet and 'translator' of the Ossianic poems. He certainly collected a quantity of Gaelic material, but his so-called translations have been much questioned and are probably his own compositions based on Gaelic fragments.

Melville, Andrew (1545–1622). Scottish scholar, theologian and reformer. He studied at St. Andrews (classics), Paris (oriental languages) and Poitiers (civil law). In Scotland his academic appointments were Principal of Glasgow University (1574), raising the university from ruin to prosperity; and Principal of St. Mary's College, St. Andrews, in 1580. He became Rector ten years later. Melville at all times defended the Church against government encroachment, and spent four years in the Tower. His last years were passed in France as a professor at the University of Sedan.

Monk, George (1608–69). Parliamentary general, first against the rebels in Ireland and then in 1650 in Scotland at Dunbar. From 1653 until Cromwell's death in 1658 he governed Scotland. He then became commander-in-chief of the parliamentary forces and marched to London where, after devious manoeuvres, he engineered the Restoration and became Duke of Albemarle.

Monmouth, Duke of (1649–85). Natural son of Charles II by Lucy Walters. Married Anne Scott, Countess of Buccleuch. A Protestant, he claimed that Charles II had been married to Lucy and raised a revolt against James II. The revolt was easily crushed and Monmouth was executed.

Moray, Regent (c 1531–70). James Stuart, illegitimate son of James V, and half brother to Mary, Queen of Scots. He sided with the Lords of the Congregation and opposed Mary's marriage to Darnley, thereupon being declared an outlaw and fleeing to England. Pardoned, he returned to Scotland and became Regent on Mary's abdication. In 1570 he was shot while riding through Linlithgow.

Morton, Regent (?1525–1581). James Douglas, 4th Earl. Led the soldiery which secured Holyrood when Rizzio was murdered. Fought against Mary, Queen of Scots, at Langside. Elected Regent (for James VI) in 1572, but had many enemies and was executed in 1581 for connivance in the murder of Darnley.

Ossian. Shadowy 3C Gaelic bard, possibly son of Fingal. See Macpherson, James.

Queensberry, 'Old Q' (1724–1810). 4th Duke. Notorious as a gambler, as also for other extravagances.

Ramsay, 1. Allan (1686–1758). Scottish poet, who tried to reawaken interest in the older national literature. Perhaps his best-known work is 'The Gentle Shepherd'. In 1736 he unsuccessfully opened a theatre in Carrubber's Close, Edinburgh. 2. Allan (1713–84). Well-known portrait-painter son of the poet.

Rob Roy (1671–1734). Robert MacGregor, known as Rob Roy (Red Robert) from the colour of his hair. Although represented by tradition and Sir Walter Scott as a romantic and genial outlaw akin to Robin Hood, Rob Roy was simply a cattle-lifter and free-booter. He was present at Sheriffmuir, as a Jacobite, but abstained from active help to either side. He submitted to General Wade in 1722, was imprisoned in London and pardoned in 1727.

Rothesay, Duke of (d 1402). Eldest son of Robert III. See Albany.

Scot, Michael (c 1117–1232). 'The Wizard'. Although appearing in Scottish history mainly as an astrologer, alchemist and dealer in the occult, Scot was a scholar, mathematician and linguist. He was a scholar at the court of the Holy Roman Emperor, Frederick II, for whom he translated Aristotle and Arabic commentaries. The legends grew after his death and will be met in many places in Scotland. The opening of his tomb (Melrose Abbey) is a striking episode in Sir Walter Scott's 'Lay of the last Minstrel'.

Scott, Sir Walter (1771–1832). Scott's fame rests not only on his achievements as a prolific poet and novelist, telling the stories of Scotland's romantic past, but also on the way in which he publicised Scotland and restored something of the spirit that had been lost after the Act of Union and Culloden. It was he who instigated the successful search for the Regalia (1817), and it was he who organised the State Visit (1822) by George IV (see History). In 1825 Scott found that in the financial confusion following the collapse of his publisher he was personally responsible for £130,000 and his toil and determination to pay the debt are a famous chapter of literary history. (For Scott generally, see STB booklet, *Land of Scott*.)

Sharp, James (1618–79). Archbishop of St. Andrews. He played a devious role in Scottish Church negotiations with England, but when in 1661 Episcopacy was restored he came into the open and accepted the see of St. Andrews. When in 1666 the Covenanters rose, Sharp acted with cruelty towards the prisoners of Rullion Green. He was murdered by Covenanters at Magus Muir, near St. Andrews.

Stevenson. 1. Robert (1772–1850). Scottish engineer, well-known for his lighthouses, the most important being Bell Rock. 2. Robert Louis (1850–94). Grandson of the engineer, Robert, and son of another engineer, he tried to follow the family profession but had to give up due to ill health, and instead became a famed and prolific literary figure. ('Treasure Island', 'Dr Jekyll and Mr Hyde', 'Master of Ballantrae', etc.)

Telford, Thomas (1757–1834). Scottish civil engineer, especially known for his canals (Caledonian), roads and many still surviving bridges.

Thomas the Rhymer (c 1220–97). Thomas Learmont of Erceldoune (Earlston). Scottish seer and poet associated with numerous fragments of prophetic verse, from which he has gained the name of True Thomas. Traditionally he had a romance with the fairy queen, spending three years with her in the Eildon Hills.

Wade, George (1673–1748). Distinguished English officer sent (as a major-general) to Scotland in 1724 to begin a system of metalled roads and stone bridges, of which he built 40. He tactfully disarmed the clans and is remembered by the couplet:

> Had you seen these roads before they were made,
> You would lift up your hands and bless General Wade.

Warbeck, Perkin (d 1499). Son of a boatman, he was put forward by the English Yorkist faction, the Scots and others as one of the princes murdered in the Tower and thus as rightful claimant to the English throne, rather than Henry VII. He made three futile invasions of England, one from Scotland being supported by James IV. After the third he was caught and executed.

Wishart, George (c 1513–46). Scottish reformer. Accused of heresy in 1538, he fled to England and then to Germany. Returning to Scotland in 1543, he began to preach, but was seized and handed over to Cardinal Beaton who had him burned at St. Andrews.

Wolf of Badenoch (d 1394). A natural son of Robert II, the Wolf was Alexander Stewart, Earl of Buchan. Also known as Alisdair Mor mae an Righ (Big Alexander, son of the King). Turbulent and vicious, he brooked no opposition and from his castles of Ruthven and Lochindorb terrorised and devastated the countryside, notably in 1390 after a quarrel with the Bishop of Elgin resulting in his excommunication.

Scotland's Antiquities and Later Buildings

Ranging from burial cairns and standing stones to castles, abbeys and mansions, the ruins and other evidence of Scotland's past cover a period of 4000 and more years. These notes try to relate these antiquities to their place within this period.

It is impossible to be precise about the dates of cultures which overlapped one another both geographically and in time by perhaps many hundreds of years. This is particularly so of prehistory. In this Guide, whenever the description Stone Age is used it means New Stone Age (Neolithic), the time when man began to change from wandering food gatherer to crop-raising farmer, thus having to settle and build. As a very rough guide, in Scotland this New Stone Age stretched from 3000 BC or earlier to 2000 BC. It was followed by the Bronze Age, lasting to about the date of the birth of Christ and merging with the Iron Age, starting in Scotland around 200 BC and representing the period when prehistory shades into history.

Hill forts, brochs, and also later defensive points, especially in the Highlands and Hebrides, all frequently appear on maps as 'Dun', with or without a name.

Chambered Cairns *(Stone and Early Bronze Age).* Generally, chambered cairns are the oldest structures to be found in Scotland. Of varying shapes, both interior and exterior, the cairns are piles of stones covering well constructed corbelled burial chambers, these often having a number of side cells. Entrance is nearly always by way of a long, low and narrow passage. The four main cairn types are Circular, Stalled, Horned and Heel. Circular cairns are found all over Scotland, the supreme example being the huge *Maes Howe* in Orkney. Although on the mainland there is nothing to compare in size, the *Clava Cairns* (near Inverness) are of considerable interest, both as cairns and because they are encircled by standing stones. Stalled cairns, so called because of their interior partitions, are found largely in Orkney, the best being *Midhowe* on the island of Rousay. Horned cairns, with their strange crescents, are rare and unique to Scotland; a good example is the *Grey Cairns of Camster*, S of Wick. Heel cairns are special to Shetland.

Most cairn tombs seem to have been used over many generations, possibly for a community but more likely just for the ruling families who would have had the necessary organising skill and call on labour. The cairn builders may be pictured as people with some social structure, able to make pottery and having both domestic animals and a developing agriculture.

Stone and Bronze Age Settlements. Scotland's most easily recognisable Stone Age settlement is that at *Skara Brae* in Orkney. Other Stone Age structures are *Knap of Howar* on Papa Westray (Orkney) and *Stanydale* on Shetland's Mainland. The outstanding Bronze Age settlement is *Jarlshof* in Shetland.

Stone Circle Ritual Sites *(Late Stone and Bronze Age).* Ritual sites are of three main types. These are a single ring or concentric circles (*Ring of Brodgar*, Orkney); a ring enclosing a burial cairn (*Clava*); or parallel lines of stones (*Hill o' Many Stanes*, near Wick). A fourth group, confined to the district around Aberdeen, includes a recumbent stone between uprights. The builders were mainly Bronze Age people, who must not only have had skill and the ability to command a large labour force, but also some compelling motivation to erect sites as massive as these. What rituals these monuments saw will probably never be known, but the honouring of the dead certainly played a major part. The sites are often laid out with precision, both in themselves and in relation to conspicuous landmarks, a feature which has prompted some archaeologists to suggest an astronomical significance. Many lone standing stones date from this same period, as do also the mysterious but presumably ritual cup, ring and other markings found on so many stones and natural rocks.

Hut Circles *(Bronze and Iron Age).* Found all over Scotland, often within hill forts, a typical hut circle is a ring of earth and stone about 3ft thick and rarely more than 2ft high enclosing an area of 20 to 30ft in diameter. An entrance can sometimes be traced, and occasionally the interior is in part paved. As huts in use the walls would of course have been higher and a frame would have supported a roof of perhaps wattle or skin. Such primitive huts were probably in use until well into historic times; the age of any particular site can normally only be determined from the relics found there.

Hill Forts *(Late Bronze and Iron Age).* Hill forts is a loose description for a variety of enclosures, such as earth ramparts, dry-stone walling or a combination of both. In large part these were defended villages, evidence of a growing knowledge of metals and competence with tools as well as of how the tribes in the increasingly populated Lowlands were beginning to organise themselves to combine domestic life with defence both against their neighbours and later against the Romans. Hill forts are, in fact, the earliest evidence of military architecture. While some go back to the Bronze Age, relics excavated place most within the Iron Age. Forts vary greatly. Some, on mountain tops and without water supply, would have been occupied only in emergency. Others, such as the complex on *Traprain Law* near Dunbar, would have been permanently occupied villages, while that at *Dunadd* in Argyll was the capital of the Kingdom of Dalriada. It was to hill villages such as these that the early Christian missionaries would have made their way.

A defensive and strengthening feature of the walls was the use of timbers. These were however liable to catch fire, the intense heat then partially melting some types of stone. This, with the impression of burnt timbers, can still be seen today, such forts being called vitrified. About 50 of these are recorded.

The Brochs *(Iron Age).* The defensive round towers known as brochs are unique to Scotland. Although the name is Norse, the brochs were built many centuries before the arrival of the Norsemen and for a long period must have overlapped with the hill forts. Typically, a broch is a hollow round tower, some 40ft high, enclosing an interior of about 40ft diameter at ground level but tapering towards the top. The ingenious double walls are the unique feature. Standing on a solid base, the outer and inner walls are bonded at roughly 5ft vertical intervals by continuous stone lintels forming a series of galleries. Also within the walls is at least one stairway to the top of the broch. This construction, entirely dry-stone, ensures the combination of lightness and strength essential for such a tower, and it seems

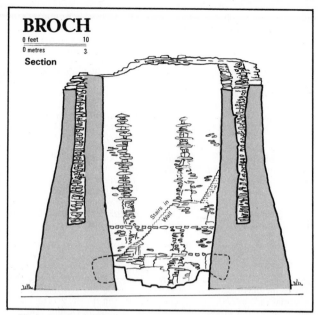

BROCH

0 feet   10
0 metres   3

Section

Stairs in Wall

unlikely that the galleries had any purpose other than structural. The only entrance is narrow and low, with a stone door secured by a drawbar and beside it one or more guard cells. Features in the courtyard often include a hearth and a cistern or well.

The size of the brochs suggests that they were intended for the households of chiefs, though in times of danger doubtless many others would have crowded in. Eventually, around perhaps 200, there seems to have been less demand for the security the brochs provided and they became centres of farming and other settlements. There are some 500 broch sites in Scotland, most now no more than mounds and stones. Some, though, still stand, the finest being *Mousa* in Shetland. On the mainland the best preserved are a pair in *Glen Beg*, near Kyle of Lochalsh.

Wheel-Houses *(Iron Age).* These are round dry-stone dwellings, with curious radial partitions off a common central area. Found in the North they are often built within or alongside brochs (*Gurness*, in Orkney, and *Jarlshof*, Shetland). Wheel-houses are thought to have remained in use until about the time of the first Christian missionaries.

Earth-Houses (Souterrains) *(Iron Age, or earlier).* Neither the purpose nor the age of these strange underground structures has been satisfactorily decided. A typical earth-house is reached by steps down to a long, narrow passage which gradually descends in a curve to an underground chamber, usually with well-built walls and roof and measuring perhaps 12ft by 6ft and over 6ft in height. As to date, some in southern Scotland incorporate Roman stonework; on the other hand those at *Jarlshof* are within a complex of Bronze Age buildings. Earth-houses may have been used as refuges, stores, or even as winter dwellings. Among good and accessible examples are *Culsh*, near Tarland (Deeside); three near Dundee (*Tealing, Ardestie* and *Carlungie*), all now unroofed; one by *Loch Eriboll* in the far N; and two (*Grain* and *Rennibister*) near Kirkwall, Orkney.

Crannogs *(Iron Age and later).* Crannogs are man-made islets on which stood usually single defended dwellings. They were built up in shallow water, simply by sinking a wooden base (normally circular) and then piling stones on to it. Access was either by boat, or by sunken causeway. A large number of small, round islets in lochs are crannogs, an easily seen example being *Cherry Island* in Loch Ness at Fort Augustus.

Roman Period *(80–200).* Scotland's Roman remains are all military, the best being the *Antonine Wall*, several stretches of which can be well seen along the line linking the Forth to the Clyde. This was turf or earth on a stone foundation, with a ditch, a military road and forts at intervals. Other Roman sites are all fortified camps, these being either permanent bases (*Cramond*, Edinburgh; *Ardoch*, between Stirling and Crieff), or marching camps (*Lyne*, near Peebles).

Early Christian *(5–12C).* The first evidence of Christian presence is in the form of grave-slabs, the earliest being in the South West, where St. Ninian preached Christianity about the year 400. Notable collections are at *Whithorn* and *Kirkmadrine*, at the former being the Latinus (or Barrovadus) Stone of 450, probably the oldest Christian memorial in Scotland. St. Columba's mission in the 6C was of wider and more lasting effect than that of St. Ninian. His Celtic Church was monastic in organisation, its early small buildings being circular and thus known as beehive cells, remains of which can still be seen in the more inaccessible Hebrides (*Garvellach Islands*). Later years saw the construction of Celtic churches and monasteries, but with the 7C the Roman Church began to displace the Celtic influence, this process accelerating as between about 850 and 1050 Scotland coalesced into a single kingdom. It is from the end of this period that the Round Towers, of which there are three in Scotland, can be dated. These are on *Egilshay* (Orkney) and at *Abernethy* and *Brechin*, this last being the oldest (probably 10C). These round towers, serving as belfries, landmarks and refuges, are typical of the Celtic Church in Ireland and can be considered as eastward late Celtic intrusions.

The main reminders of Scotland's Early Christian period are the variety of sculptured stones and crosses, these broadly being of Celtic origin in the West and of Northumbrian in the East. The latter, often bearing the knotwork patterns common on the continent, are generally the older, the supreme example being *Ruthwell Cross* (first half 8C). Of mixed Northumbrian and Pictish origin are slabs carved with a cross in relief, knotwork pattern, foliage, human and animal figures and Pictish symbols of unknown but presumably Christian meaning. Crosses or slabs are also common in the West, but the more typical monument here is the free-standing cross, or High Cross, its arms frequently linked to form a ring. Both in form and in their often rich ornamentation these crosses are essentially Irish. They served many purposes (to commemorate the dead, to mark boundaries or preaching sites) and they continued to be erected throughout the W Highlands down to the Reformation. Of the really early crosses two intact examples are *St. Martin's* (10C) on Iona, and *Kildalton* (8C) on

Islay. To this general period also belong stones bearing Ogham inscriptions, the oldest written form of Celtic Gaelic. The writing

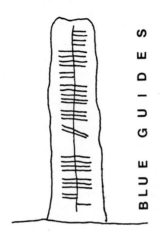

BLUE GUIDES

An example of Ogham writing.

takes the form of strokes or notches along a base-line. The oldest examples are in Argyll (*Dunadd*), and there are later, Pictish Ogham stones in the North East (e.g. *Brandsbutt Stone*, Inverurie).

Holy wells, still found near many Early Christian sites, recall the baptismal and also often healing activities of the early missionaries.

Norse Remains *(9–14C)*. If one discounts a monument such as St. Magnus Cathedral in Kirkwall (built by a Norse earl, but Norman in style), true Norse remains are few and largely confined to Orkney and Shetland. At *Brough of Birsay* there survives something of Earl Thorfinn's Christ Church and Hall, and here also, as at *Jarlshof* and a few other places, there are the outlines of long-houses, the buildings most commonly associated with the Norsemen. Although over the long period of Norse occupation there must have been change, a typical long-house may be imagined as perhaps 100ft long and 20ft broad, built of earth within dry-stone facing and having a turf and wood roof. There would have been two or more rooms, each with its hearth. Perhaps the most interesting Norse remains are their carefully executed graffiti, notably within the chambered cairn of *Maes Howe*.

In the 11 and 12C Malcolm III (Canmore), his queen, Margaret, and the three of their sons who became kings, changed Celtic Scotland into a feudal kingdom of the Anglo-Norman pattern. The change was felt as much in architecture as in other fields, and the period of the 12 and 13C marks the start of large architecture in the form of monastic houses, their associated church buildings, and increasingly formidable castles. This period, which includes first Romanesque, or, as often called in Britain, Norman architecture, and then, by gradual transition, Gothic, continued through to the outbreak of the wars of succession and independence in the 14C. These wars ended two centuries of freedom of movement between Scotland and England, thus opening the way for developments in local style, to some extent influenced by the continent; the 15C can claim to be the second and the more individual of Scotland's great building periods.

Monastic Houses. The monasteries suffered severely from the Reformation and in consequence their remains (that is of the domestic buildings as distinct from their churches) are few and fragmentary. Though there were variations to meet the requirements of each Order, the monasteries were of a more or less standard pattern: the whole was enclosed by an outer wall, often with an imposing gatehouse, within which the nucleus was the cloister, an arrangement of buildings around a central court, usually on the S and thus more protected side of the church. Around the court stood the abbot's lodging, the guest house (hospitium) and various domestic buildings, while the infirmary usually stood to the E of the church. The E range buildings were normally of two storeys, the lower rooms serving various administrative purposes and including the chapter-house which, as the general meeting place, was often the most handsomely built. Above was the monks' dormitory (dorter) with a sanitary provision (reredorter), and, at the end abutting the church, a night stair by which the monks descended to night worship. The S side of the cloister contained the dining hall (refectory or frater), a kitchen and a warming house, this last a common living room with a fireplace. The cloister walk in most cases ended at a door at each end of the S wall of the church.

Some good portions of outer wall can be seen at *Sweetheart Abbey* and the best gatehouse is at *Crossraguel*. The best surviving domestic buildings are at *Dryburgh*.

Cathedrals and Churches. Among the characteristics of Norman architecture are great length of church plan; rounded arches; broad and shallow buttresses; arcading and massive round columns. Bell towers, later absorbed into their churches (as at *Dunblane*), became square and apses angled rather than round. There is also a distinct if crude decorative richness, in which geometric designs such as zigzags are popular. Examples of this period abound in Scotland, though nearly always combined with later styles. The nave of the abbey church at *Dunfermline* is outstanding, with round columns and arches, blind arcading and zigzag decoration, while at *Kirkwall Cathedral* the contrast between Norman and later work can be well seen. Of many smaller churches, probably the most visited is Edinburgh's *St. Margaret's Chapel*, while *Dalmeny* and *Leuchars* rank among Scotland's best Norman work.

Although there was a Transitional (mixed styles) period, the Gothic (or Pointed) style was taking over by the latter part of the 12C. Generally the first phase is known as Early English, others following being Decorated (so called because of the increasing use of rich stone carving) and Perpendicular; in Scotland, though, the later stages of Gothic were characterised more by borrowings from French Flamboyant and earlier Romanesque or Norman styles. The basis of Gothic architecture is structural, arising from the wish to build churches completely vaulted in stone, the main feature for this purpose being the general use of the pointed arch. Other features are ribbed vaults; large areas for stained glass; the use for decorative purposes of what had previously been essentially structural, e.g. buttresses and arcades; and an increasing lavishness in carving.

Generally there was an urge towards soaring height in preference to the squat solidity of the Norman style. Most of the great abbeys are good examples of the Transitional period and after, the long nave at *Jedburgh* being one of the best, while *Glasgow Cathedral*, mainly Early English but with other periods, is outstanding among Gothic buildings.

When from the 15C on Scotland's builders found themselves freed from Anglo-Norman influence, they both looked back to the past and also innovated to meet the needs of their age. From the past they resurrected round-arch doorways and apse, the latter now three-sided as in *Crossraguel Abbey*. Sometimes the need was to fortify church buildings, this explaining the castellation of *Torpichen Preceptory* and the turreted gatehouse at *Crossraguel*. But the most important innovation of this period, arising from the declining interest in monasteries, was the founding instead of collegiate churches (originally chantries), where a 'college' or group of clergy was bound by deed to sing masses and pray for the souls of the wealthy founder and such relatives and friends as he might require. Such churches might be either new or simply older parish churches converted to collegiate status. Later, collegiate churches often became parish churches, as at *Corstorphine*. Many collegiate churches are still in use today, the best known being *Roslin Chapel*, with its unsurpassed richness of carved stone.

Church Architecture

Nave	Main body of the church from the W door to the choir.
Aisles	Almost any division of a church, but usually the areas parallel to and separated by pillars (piers) from the nave, transepts or choir.
Transepts	The transverse (N and S) parts of a cruciform church.
Crossing	Where the transepts cross the nave-choir; usually supports the tower.
Choir (Chancel)	E part of the church reserved for the clergy, choir etc. Often railed off. Strictly the chancel is that part beyond the choir and nearest the altar, the word coming from the altar screens ('cancelli').
Apse	Small extension, usually of the choir and often containing the altar and sedilia (stone seats).
Chapels	Dedicated to saints and others, chapels may be anywhere around the church interior. A Lady Chapel is dedicated to the Virgin and is normally E of the altar.
Sacristy	Repository for vestments, vessels, etc.
Sacrament House (Aumbrey)	Wall recess in which the Sacrament, holy vessels etc, are placed. Often richly carved. Most found in the NE.
Triforium	Gallery (usually arcaded) above the arches of the nave, transept and chancel.
Clerestory	(Clear storey). Part of the upper wall, with windows, above the aisle roofs.

Castles. The feudal castle came to Scotland in the 11 and 12C, with the new Norman ruling class, although during these early centuries few bore much resemblance to the massive structures that were to follow. The castle started as a ditch surrounding an earth mound on which stood a timber tower. Annexed to this mound, and protected by a palisaded rampart and ditch, there was often an enclosure with further timber buildings. The mound was called a 'motte' or 'mote', this being the same as 'moat', the word meaning equally a ditch or what had been heaped out of it. The annexed enclosure was the 'bailey'. Numerous remains of these motte-and-bailey castles survive, though only of course in the form of their earthworks. Good examples are *Peel of Lumphanan, Hawick* and *The Bass* near Inverurie.

Stone castles appeared as early as the mid 12C, though there are now few remains as old as this. Exceptions are *Castle Sween*, with Scotland's only Norman keep and generally accepted as the oldest 'real' castle, and *Kisimul Castle* on Barra, whose tower probably dates from 1120. It was not until the 13 and 14C that stone castles became general, at first being essentially stone versions of the motte-and-bailey pattern, the stone towers (also called keeps or donjons) often rising on the same mottes as had supported the earlier timber towers. *Duffus Castle* well illustrates this.

Throughout this time defensive tactics were based on these massive keeps, regarded as the last line of defence and therefore usually in the remotest or safest corner of the enclosure. But a departure from the strict motte-and-bailey plan came towards the middle of the 14C as the belief grew that defence should be forward on the enclosure rather than within or to the rear. At *Tantallon* and *St. Andrews*, for instance, the chief tower or keep is placed forward of the courtyard and the castle's main entrance is carried through the base of the tower. Another and more significant design change is apparent at *Doune*, where a two-storey building of the kind known as the 'hall', hitherto always an independent building within the enclosure, is now placed alongside the main tower. Indeed with the 15C the hall, together with its kitchen and other domestic rooms, increasingly determined the plan of new castles and of alterations to older ones, the result being that enclosure walls became buildings and, with warfare becoming more mobile, towers decreased in importance. In Scotland, structures where the emphasis was on the hall became commonly known as 'palaces', regardless of whether the owner was a king, a church dignitary, an earl or a mere laird. Later, though, the description 'palace' was reserved for larger places, more modest ones being described as 'mansions' or 'houses' or reverting to the old style of 'castle'. On the grand scale *Linlithgow* superbly illustrates the gradual development from a tower of 1302 to a 16C palace, while of smaller, part-fortified houses there are many.

With the shift from defence to residence came also structural artistic taste, Renaissance styling being a favourite source of inspiration. When for instance, to complete the quadrangle, the N side of *Crichton Castle* was erected in 1585, it was given an elaborate, embossed, Italianate inner stonework decoration. Another example is *Caerlaverock* where a formidably defensive exterior contrasts with the Renaissance elegance of the courtyard. This development of taste was apparent also in the new castles built in the late 16 and 17C, especially in Scotland's North East. Increasingly, defensive features were treated as ornamentation and turreted projections became popular, so that castles such as *Crathes* and *Craigievar*, often with fine internal plasterwork, became as much works of art as defensive strongholds. This style, known as Scottish Baronial, was to be revived during the 19C at Balmoral and many other places.

A type of castle special to Scotland and spanning the 14 to the 17C is the Tower-House, typically a tower to which was normally attached an enclosure (barmkin) for service buildings. In the Borders district these are called 'Pele' towers, the word coming from the Latin 'palus' meaning a stake or palisade. For the most part tower-houses, the majority being built later than the 14C, were the defended homes of the lesser nobility. An early development was the addition of one or two towers built on to the corners of the original (L-plan or Z-plan). Initially this was a defensive requirement to meet the tactical changes of the early 16C when the increasing power of artillery was shifting defence from the parapet to ground level: square or round towers on opposite corners, provided with ground level gunloops, enabled all four sides of the main tower to be covered. Later, as the demand for private accommodation grew, these wings, particularly if square and of several storeys, were used for this purpose. However, original tower-houses onto which extensive additions have been grafted, must rank, according to their development, as full castles, palaces or mansions. The more pleasing tower-houses are those which have retained their tower character, often embellished with the many turrets which were to lead to the Scottish Baronial style already referred to. Examples of all kinds of tower-houses are many. The oldest is probably *Threave Castle*; *Borthwick Castle* has typical massive wings; *Craigmillar* and *Crichton*, both starting as tower-houses, received so many additions that they became complex castles. Of tower-houses still retaining their original character, *Smailholm*, free of any additions, best represents the essentially military Borders pele tower, while *Claypotts* is turreted.

The word 'castle' has become somewhat overworked in Scotland today and will be found describing almost anything from a massive feudal stronghold to a modest country mansion.

Dovecots (Doocots). Dovecots are an attractive and interesting minor form of older architecture. It was only in the 18C that turnips and swedes were introduced, thus making it possible to feed livestock throughout the winter; before this only breeding stock could be kept, the remainder being slaughtered and salted. Pigeons then provided fresh winter meat. The most distinctive types of dovecot are round-domed (beehive) structures with a circular hole in the roof for the birds (*Northfield* at Old Preston and *Phantassie* at East Linton); square plan, with a slated, sloping roof with entry holes part way down (a pair may be seen at *Tantallon Castle*); incorporated in towers (*Hailes Castle*).

17 and 18C Military Works. Something survives of the military works erected by the English in the 17 and 18C, first by Cromwell and later by the Hanoverian governments. Of what Cromwell built most was destroyed at the Restoration, but his great fort at *Lerwick* (Shetland) still stands, though reconstructed in 1781. Rather more can still be seen of the Hanoverian works, notably the intact *Fort George* near Inverness and, near Kingussie, the shell of *Ruthven Barracks*, standing on an ancient motte.

Building after the Union of the Parliaments. Presbyterianism had triumphed at the revolution of 1688, and Culloden in 1746 was the last battle to be fought on Scottish soil. The former meant simple yet dignified churches to match a simple form of worship, the latter the end of major military building. Activity turned to the erection of fine civic buildings and, in the country, great mansions. In both spheres

the Adam family were pre-eminent, their work embracing achievements as diverse as *Culzean Castle*, Glasgow's *Trades' House*, the
splendid mansions of *Hopetoun, Haddo* and *Mellerstain*, and the N
side of Edinburgh's *Charlotte Square*. The Georgian elegance of
Edinburgh's New Town grew between 1767 and the early 19C, to
be followed by the Victorian era, with, roughly in succession, the
grandiose revival of the Scottish Baronial, Neo-Classical solidity,
probably still best seen in Glasgow despite much demolition and the
steady intrusion of modern tower blocks, and Art Nouveau, of which
the principal exponent was C.R. Mackintosh of Glasgow.

The Church in Scotland

The Celtic Columban Christianity brought to Scotland in the 6C was
soon displaced by the Roman forms favoured by the powerful kings
of Northumbria, and from the early 8C until the Reformation Scotland
was Roman Catholic. The 16 and 17C saw first the strife between
the Roman Catholics and the reforming Protestants, and then the
struggles within the Protestant faith between the covenanting
Presbyterians and the Episcopalians. This struggle ended with the
revolution of 1688, the triumph of Presbyterianism and the formal
establishment of the Church of Scotland.

Church of Scotland. The Presbyterian and national *United Established Church of Scotland* is the Church to which the overwhelming
majority of Scottish Presbyterians belong today. This Church has
emerged only after a long and confusing history of secessions and
unions which began soon after the establishment of the Church of
Scotland and continued until 1956. Throughout this period of some
250 years all the seceding groups remained strictly Presbyterian,
their differences with the Established Church being not on points of
faith but rather on aspects of the relationship between Church and
State, and between congregations and elders or the assembly. The
main events are summarised below.

1688. James VII/II deposed in favour of William and Mary. Presbyterianism
established, with the *Church of Scotland* administered by an assembly. Abolition
of patronage. (The right of the crown, local landowner or other patron to
nominate or 'present' the minister.)

1706. Secession of the *Cameronians* (originally followers of the fanatical
Covenanter, Richard Cameron). An extremist group, they rejected any
supremacy of the State in ecclesiastical matters.

1712. The Act of Toleration allowed Episcopalian dissenters to use the English
liturgy, and the same parliament restored patronage, an act which led to much
subsequent trouble.

1733–45. The *Secession Church* founded by Ebenezer Erskine; largely in
opposition to an assembly decision that, when patrons failed to present a
minister, then the minister would be chosen, not by the local congregation, but
by the elders.

1743. The Cameronians assumed the name *Reformed Presbyterian Church*.

1747. The Secession Church split into the *Burghers* and the *Anti-burghers*. This
split arose out of a religious clause in the oath required of burgesses in
Edinburgh, Glasgow and Perth. ('I profess and allow with my heart the true
religion presently professed within this realm and authorized by the laws

thereof'.) The anti-burghers condemned the swearing of such an oath as sinful.

1761. The *Relief Church* seceded. Adherents objected to patronage and any other lay interference and stood for 'the relief of Christians oppressed in their Church privileges'.

1799 and 1806. The Burghers and the Anti-burghers each split into the *Old Light* and *New Light* groups. The split was basically one between the views of conservative and other elements on the issue of the jurisdiction of the civil authority in ecclesiastical affairs.

1822. The two New Lights merged to form the *United Secession Church.*

1841. The two Old Lights merged to call themselves the *Original Seceders.*

1843. The Disruption. 451 ministers (of a total of 1203), headed by Dr Thomas Chalmers, resigned their livings, largely on the issue of patronage, and formed the *Free Church.*

1847. The United Secession Church joined with the Relief Church to become the *United Presbyterian Church.*

1874. The Patronage Act, conferring on congregations the right of electing parish ministers, removed a long-standing grievance.

1876. The Free Church absorbed the Reformed Presbyterian Church (formerly Cameronians).

1900. The Free Church and the United Presbyterian Church united to become the *United Free Church.* But a few Free Church congregations, chiefly in the Highlands, remain outside this union and retain the name of Free Church; colloquially these are called the *'Wee Frees'.*

1929. The United Free Church joined the Church of Scotland, the two becoming the *United Established Church of Scotland* under a General Assembly, presided over by a Moderator.

1956. The Original Seceders (Old Lights) joined the United Established Church of Scotland.

Episcopal Church of Scotland. After 1688 Episcopalian incumbents who took the oath of allegiance were allowed to retain their benefices, and an Act of 1712 protected the Episcopal Communion. Although suspect at the time of the '15 and the '45, an independent Episcopal Church survived. The Church has seven bishops, direct successors of those consecrated at the Restoration, and all the sees (except Edinburgh, founded by Charles I) are pre-Reformation. The sees are Aberdeen and Orkney; Argyll and the Isles; Brechin; Edinburgh; Glasgow and Galloway; Moray, Ross and Caithness; St. Andrews, Dunkeld and Dunblane. The bishops constitute the synod and elect their own Primus.

Roman Catholics. At the Reformation a considerable part of the population, especially in the Highlands and Hebrides, remained faithful to the 'old religion' which, strengthened by the immigration of Irish and others, still flourishes today. A new RC hierarchy was established in 1878 and now includes two archbishops (St. Andrews and Edinburgh; Glasgow) and six bishops (Aberdeen; Argyll and the Isles; Dunkeld; Galloway; Motherwell; Paisley).—Modern Scotland's first saint, John Ogilvie, a priest hanged in Glasgow in 1615, was canonised in 1976.

PRACTICAL INFORMATION

Organisations

Local Government. Under the 1975 local government reorganisation the counties of Scotland disappeared as such. Instead the country is now administered as nine Regions and three Island Areas (see Atlas 16). Sub-divisions comprise 51 Districts, many of these bearing the names of the former counties. The nine Regions are: Highland, Grampian, Tayside, Fife, Lothian, Borders, Central, Strathclyde and Dumfries-Galloway. The three Island Areas are Western Isles, Orkney and Shetland.

The **Scottish Tourist Board** (STB) has its headquarters in Edinburgh at 23 Ravelston Terrace, EH4 3EU. Tel: (031) 3322433. The next level comprises some 36 Tourist Areas, below these being the town and other centres' Tourist Information Offices, many of the smaller of which are open only during the summer. STB also has a London office and information centre at 19 Cockspur Street, SW1Y 5BL (just off Trafalgar Square). Tel: (01) 930 8661.—A wide range of attractive and informative publications (many free) is provided by all levels.

The **National Trust for Scotland** (NTS), with its headquarters in Edinburgh (5 Charlotte Square, EH2 4DU. Tel: 031–2265922), was formed in 1931 with the purpose of promoting the preservation of places of historic interest or natural beauty. Currently the Trust has in its care around 100 properties covering some 100,000 acres. The Trust is not a government department, but a charity supported by the subscriptions of its members, the entrance fees charged at the larger sites and the voluntary contributions received at others. Membership (quickly arranged at most sites) is well worth considering as much for the merit of the cause as for the practical reason that it affords free entry to all NTS sites as also to those in the care of the National Trust in England, Wales and Northern Ireland.—The Trust offers many general and local publications (some free), a summary of properties being in the annual 'Guide to Properties'.

Ancient Monuments (AM) officially in the care of the nation are the responsibility of Historic Buildings and Monuments, Scottish Development Department, 3–11 Melville Street, Edinburgh, EH3 7QD. Tel: (031) 2262570. Ext. 211. For principal sites there is an entrance fee, but a season ticket (obtainable at most sites and through some Tourist Information centres) giving access to all sites and valid for one year could be a considerable saving. For opening times of sites, see 'Notes on using this Guide'.

Forestry Commission (FC), 231 Corstorphine Road, Edinburgh, EH12 7AT. Tel: (031) 3340303. In Scotland the Commission owns some two million acres, about half of which are plantation. The Commission aims to produce as much home-grown timber as possible, both through its own forestry enterprises and through encouragement and financial incentives to private landowners. At the same time it has to meet other important objectives, regarding amenity and landscape design, wildlife conservation and the provision of facilities for public access and recreation.

For the tourist the Commission provides several superb forest parks, as well as information centres, picnic areas, forest cabins and holiday houses, outstandingly attractive caravan and campsites, and waymarked forest trails. All forest roads are open to walkers, but cars are not permitted other than along designated Forest Drives.—Publications, notably the admirable Forest Park Guides and the map 'See your Forests', are obtainable from local booksellers, FC information centres and local district offices, and often from Tourist Information.

Nature Conservancy Council (NCC). Scottish Headquarters: 12 Hope Terrace, Edinburgh, EH9 2AS. Tel: (031) 4474784. The Council is the official body which promotes a national policy for the conservation of flora, fauna, and geological and physiographical features. Its work falls into three main categories—the establishment and management of National Nature Reserves; advice on nature conservation; and the support and conduct of research. Several of Scotland's National Nature Reserves are mentioned in the Routes texts. Access to some is restricted and in such cases permission should be requested from the appropriate Regional Office.

NCC Regional Offices. *South East*: 12 Hope Terrace, Edinburgh, EH9 2AS. Tel: (031) 4474784. *South West*: The Castle, Loch Lomond Park, Balloch, G83 8LX. Tel: (0389) 58511. *North East*: Wynne-Edwards House, 17 Rubislaw Terrace, Aberdeen, AB1 1XE. Tel: (0224) 642863. *North West*: Fraser Darling House, 9 Culduthel Road, Inverness, IV2 4AG. Tel: (0463) 239431.

Countryside Commission for Scotland, Battleby, Redgorton, Perth PH1 3EW. Tel: (0738) 27921. The Commission was established in 1967 and has five main aims: Protection (the conservation and enhancement of the natural beauty of Scotland's countryside); Recreation Provision (provision and development of facilities for the enjoyment of the countryside); Conservation Education (increasing public awareness, and promoting proper use of the countryside); Research and Development (provision of a practical base for determining policies and for field work); Review (updating of policies and practices).

The Commission is essentially an advisory and promotional body, which seeks to influence official policy. It has the responsibility for advising the Secretary of State and planning authorities on planning matters and is able to channel funds in the form of grants for the provision of a wide range of countryside recreational facilities. It has published proposals, which have been agreed in principle, for a park system for Scotland, and has undertaken a survey of scenic resources, identifying 40 areas considered to be of national scenic importance.

Highlands and Islands Development Board, Bridge House, Bank Street, Inverness. Tel: (0463) 234171. The Board has two main functions—to help the people of the Highlands and Islands to improve their social and economic conditions; to enable the Highlands and Islands to play a more effective part in the economic and social development of Scotland. Financed by the government, the Board has a wide range of powers, these including land acquisition; factory construction; the provision of equipment and services; the establishment of businesses; the granting of financial assistance and advisory services etc.

Scotland's Gardens Scheme, 26 Castle Terrace, Edinburgh EH1 2EL. Tel: (031) 2291870. The scheme promotes the occasional opening, in aid of charity, of about 300 gardens. A programme can be obtained from the above address, and local Tourist Information offices will advise on gardens open in their areas.

Scottish Sports Council, 1 St. Colme Street, Edinburgh EH3 6AA. Tel: (031) 2258411. See under Sports Holidays.

Getting around Scotland

Visitors planning to make extensive use of public transport—rail, sea, air or road—should ask about the selection of discount tickets on offer (most Tourist Information offices should have up-to-date information on these).

'Getting about the Highlands and Islands', published twice yearly in association with the Highlands and Islands Development Board, details all forms of transport in the Highlands and Islands.

Road. Main road motoring in Scotland is generally little different from elsewhere in Britain. What is different is that many roads in mountain and moorland districts and on the islands are single track and often winding, with the additional hazards of humpbacked and thus blind bridges and loose sheep and cattle. Surfaces are nearly always good and gradients long rather than steep, and there are frequent passing places, normally well marked and clearly visible from a distance. Motorists are asked to remember, though, that these are passing and not parking places, and also that, if travelling slowly, it is courteous to draw in and allow others to overtake. It is also worth remembering that in the remoter districts, and on the islands, petrol stations can be far apart and unlikely to be open late or on Sundays.

Automobile Association, Fanum House, 18–22 Melville Street, Edinburgh, EH3 7PD. Tel: (031) 2258464. *Royal Automobile Club*, RAC House, 200 Finnieston Street, Glasgow, G3 8NZ. Tel: (041) 2484444.

Public Transport. For those with the time it is possible to see much of Scotland by using the network of scheduled bus services, the obvious generalisation being that the more inhabited the district the better the service. Nevertheless dependence on public transport must limit the choice of sites that can be visited, as also the length of time spent there, and in some remoter areas where buses may run only once a day, or even only once or twice a week, the practicability of breaking a journey at sites along the way is small.—*Coach Tours*, lasting anything from a few hours to several days and covering all the more popular areas, start from many of the larger Scottish towns during the season; also from London and other English towns.

Rail. Scotland's mainland is quite well covered by rail, the principal routes coming in from the S to Edinburgh and Glasgow and serving the populated areas around and between these cities. Main lines continue to Perth and Dundee, with a direct mountain route from Perth to Inverness (at Drumochter reaching the highest level of any railway in Britain, 1484ft), and an eastabout route linking Dundee, Aberdeen and Inverness.

Smaller lines run down the SW coast to Stranraer; from Glasgow to Oban, and via Fort William to Mallaig; from Inverness N to Wick and Thurso; from Inverness W to Kyle of Lochalsh. Services on the smaller lines, especially in the N, can be infrequent, and restricted on Sun.

Some of the rail routes are very scenic, notably Glasgow to Mallaig (with, on certain days, a steam service from Fort William) and Inverness to Kyle of Lochalsh.

Information on services and discount travel from British Rail, Buchanan House, 58 Port Dundas Road, Glasgow, G4 0HG. Tel: (041) 3329811.

Air. A network of services covers the mainland centres of Edinburgh, Glasgow, Aberdeen, Inverness, Wick and Campbeltown, and there are also services to and within the Hebrides and the Orkney and Shetland groups. The principal operators are British Airways and Loganair, the emphasis of the latter being on the islands for which the company operates virtually all the inter-island services. *British Airways*, 85 Buchanan Street, Glasgow, G1 3HQ. Tel: (041) 3329666. *Loganair*, Glasgow Airport, PA3 2TG. Tel: (041) 8893181.

Sea. For ferries, see the relevant Routes.

Accommodation. Food and Drink

Scotland offers **Accommodation** of all kinds, ranging from luxury hotels (some in mansions or castles) to simple bed-and-breakfast premises, these latter increasingly also providing an evening meal. The more sophisticated hotels serve dinner in the evening; many others provide the rather earlier high tea, a usually excellent meal with fish or meat course and very likely a selection of local breads and cakes. It should be remembered that in summer, and particularly in popular districts, there is considerable pressure on accommodation and that booking, if only a few hours ahead, is virtually essential; also that accommodation may be sparse in some remote areas and that some hotels are directly associated with fishing or other sporting facilities. Some country hotels close during the winter.

For the traveller without sophisticated demands bed-and-breakfast establishments, whether in town or country, can be recommended. They are clean, comfortable and surprisingly cheap, the food is usually generous, and they offer the opportunity to meet local people.

STB publish annually four books (charge) covering all aspects of accommodation and filled with comprehensive information on prices and facilities. The books are: 'Where to Stay: Hotels and Guest Houses'. 'Where to Stay: Bed and Breakfast'. 'Self-catering Accommodation'. 'Camping and Caravan Sites'. Additionally all area Tourist Boards provide comprehensive booklets, a welcome feature of these being that most premises are illustrated.

All Tourist Information centres will help over finding local accommodation, and at many a telephone or telex advance booking service (Book-a-bed-ahead) is operated, well worth using for the cost of a small fee and the telephone charge.

See also Notes on using this Guide, Hotels.

Food and Drink. While in most hotels and restaurants the food served is of standard, international type, Scotland does have its own specialities which have evolved locally or from long French or Scandinavian association. Among many specialities are Scotch Broth and Cock-a-leekie, soups that are a meal in themselves; trout and salmon from local rivers and lochs; sea fish cured and smoked in the Norse tradition (Arbroath Smokies, Finnan Haddies); from the moors, venison and game. Haggis, a minced mixture of animal organs with suet and oatmeal, looks and tastes better than it sounds. From the bakers come Selkirk bannocks and a whole delicious range of oatcakes, scones and baps, while for the sweet-toothed there are Edinburgh rock and butterscotch. Scotland's cheeses, notably Islay, are becoming increasingly better known; and Scotch beef, Dundee cake and Dundee marmalade are as world famed as is also of course Scotland's whisky.

A free leaflet, 'A Taste of Scotland', lists hotels and restaurants (identified visually by a stockpot plaque) participating in a Taste of Scotland scheme.

Sundry Information

Banking and Currency. Main banks are open Mon., Tues., Wed., 09.30 to 12.30. 13.30 to 15.30. Thurs., as above but also 16.30 to 18.00. Fri., 09.30 to 15.30. Some city banks do not close over lunchtime; equally some banks may do so on Fri. Holders of English bank cashpoint cards will only rarely find machines that will accept them. Traveller's Cheques should be carried or personal cheques cashed with a Cheque or other card.—Scotland uses British currency, but locally issued bank notes circulate as well. Scottish notes are not always willingly accepted in England but can always be exchanged without loss at banks.

Credit cards. The major credit cards are widely accepted, but may well be refused in remote districts or modest establishments.

Events. Coming events of all kinds are listed in the annual publication 'Events in Scotland'.

Licencing Hours are currently standard throughout Scotland, pubs being open Mon.–Sat., 11.00 to 14.30. 17.00 to about 23.00. Increasingly, also, licences are being granted for Sun. opening. Hotel bars conform to the same hours and are open on Sun., 12.30 to 14.30. 18.30 to 23.00. Residents in licensed hotels may order drinks at any time. Persons under the age of 18 may not drink in licensed premises.

Postal Services. Scottish stamps attractively carry a lion but the postage rates are the same as in England. Main Post Office hours are normally Mon.—Fri., 09.00 to 17.30. Sat., 09.00 to 12.30.

Public Holidays. The Bank Holidays, which are also general holidays in England, do not apply as such in Scotland. In Scotland, in principle, these bank holidays are for banks only, though they often also apply to some professional and commercial offices. Christmas Day and a period of two or three days over New Year are treated as general holidays. Additionally most towns and districts have local public, trades' and other holidays which vary from place to place and year to year but are usually in Spring or Autumn.

Early Closing days are given in the Routes texts. There can, though, often be a gap between theory and practice and in main tourist centres in summer much will be found open.

Shopping. Normal shopping hours are 09.00 to 18.00, though, in the case of smaller establishments, with a break over lunchtime.

Sports Holidays

Scotland abounds in opportunities for holiday sport, much of which is sponsored by the Scottish Sports Council, 1 St. Colme Street, Edinburgh, EH3 6AA. Tel: (031) 2258411. For all activities STB will also, on request, provide specialist information, accommodation lists and suchlike.

The Council operates *Inverclyde* (at Largs), established in 1958 as a memorial to King George VI. This is the National Sports Training Centre, with facilities for most indoor and outdoor sports; it also administers the National Water Sports Training Centre (see below) on the island of Great Cumbrae. Both the above facilities are largely used by education authorities, youth groups and suchlike, but in addition to such closed courses SSC runs its own courses which are open to the general public. SSC also operates the *National Outdoor Training Centre* at Glenmore Lodge (residential) near Aviemore. Here there are open courses in canoeing, sailing, hill walking, rock climbing and field studies, while winter courses include skiing, winter mountaineering, snow and ice climbing.

Climbing and Hill Walking. The climbing and walking attractions of Scotland are obvious, the possibilities ranging from skilled rock climbing on the Cuillins of Skye down to simple upland walking along well defined paths. Yet too many people still get lost, in most cases through inexperience, lack of correct clothing and equipment and an unwillingness to believe how suddenly the weather can close in. The rule is always to ask local advice, and also, in the case of anything perhaps venturesome, to ensure that the police or somebody else responsible know what is planned. Hill walkers should also seek local advice before venturing far during the shooting seasons.—STB's 'Scotland: Hillwalking' describes the more arduous walks and scrambles, while 'Scotland: Walks and Trails' lists over 200 waymarked easy walks. FC also provide a map ('See your Forests: Scotland') showing forest walks and including brief descriptions.

Curling, although traditionally Scotland's national winter game, is today mostly played on indoor rinks, notably at Edinburgh, Perth (museum), Stranraer and Aviemore. The game, which may very roughly be described as bowls played on ice, has been popular in Scotland for approaching 500 years, the oldest dated curling stone bearing the date 1511, though yet older stones have been found in rivers and lochs.

Dry Skiing. The largest artificial slope in Britain (almost ¼m and with a chairlift) is at Hillend on the Pentland Hills just S of Edinburgh. There are also slopes at a number of other places.

Fishing. Scotland is famed for its salmon and trout fishing, but what is less well known is how cheaply fishing may be enjoyed. Salmon fishing, admittedly, is usually, though not necessarily, expensive, but trout fishing permits are reasonably priced and sometimes free. Coarse fishing can also be inexpensively enjoyed, particularly in southern Scotland, permits being obtainable from local owners or leasing clubs, or sometimes simply through Tourist Information.

Sea Angling as a sport is governed by the Scottish Federation of Sea Anglers, 18 Ainslie Place, Edinburgh, EH3 6AV. Tel: (031) 2257611. The federation sponsors shore and open boat championships and publishes an annual list of festivals and competitions.

Gliding. For information apply Scottish Gliding Union, Portmoak Airfield, Scotlandwell, Kinross. Tel: (059284) 243.

Golf is Scotland's national game and courses will be found almost everywhere, the great majority of them accepting visitors without introduction. The cost is small compared to most other countries, England included, and Sunday play is now the rule rather than the exception.

Pony Trekking and Riding holidays may take the form of ordinary riding instruction, pony trekking or, for more experienced riders, trail riding. Trekking is becoming increasingly popular as a means of exploring tracts of wild country, not otherwise easily accessible, and most centres providing trekking offer accommodation which may range from hotel to simpler farmhouse standard. STB will, on request, provide lists of establishments.

Water Sport. SSC's Cumbrae National Water Sports Training Centre offers facilities for sailing and sub-aqua, both for beginners and the experienced.

Canoeing of all kinds is popular and can be well combined with bird and even seal watching and other nature study. Among fast rivers the Spey and Tay are well known, the Grandtully rapid on the latter being used for slalom competitions.

Winter Sports. Skiing facilities are most developed at four places: the Cairngorms (Rte 50), Cairnwell (Rte 28), Glen Coe (Rte 44) and the Lecht (Rte 38). At or near all these will be found accommodation, après ski, instruction, equipment hire, access roads to lifts and tows.

Language

The language of Scotland is English, spoken with the distinctive Scots accent, itself having local variants clear enough to the expert ear. But the virtually universal use of English dates from comparatively recent times, and over its history Scotland has used at least three other languages. These were the original Pictish in the North East; Gaelic, brought across by the Irish who in the 6C settled in what is now Argyll and carried far and wide by Christian missionaries; and Norn, the language of the Norsemen. As the Irish, or, as they became, Gaelic-speaking Scots, spread across Scotland, the three languages mixed, with Gaelic predominating and becoming the main language of all Scotland other than the Lowlands and Orkney and Shetland. Pictish disappeared early but Norn held on until about 1800 when it finally died, last being used on the Shetland island of Foula. Gaelic remained in common use throughout the Highlands until after the Clearances in the 19C. It is still spoken by many people, mainly in the Hebrides and remoter districts, although the number of these who have no English is negligible.

So far as the visitor to Scotland is concerned Pictish, Norn and Gaelic survive mainly as the whole or part of place names and, although intermixed, it is still possible to identify origins. Places, for instance, beginning with *Pit* or *Pet* may be Pictish, the word meaning a plot of land or a homestead, while from Norn come such words as *by* (village), *lybster* (farmstead), *vick* or *wick* (bay), *thing* or *ding* (council), and *brough* (same word as broch, a fortified place).

Where English was Scotland's language, it developed local dialect forms, generally known today as Lowland Scots.

The glossaries below may both interest and help the visitor.

Gaelic (with some Norn and Pictish)

Aber, mouth or confluence of a river.
Aird, ard, height, promohtory.
Allt, ault, stream.
An, of the.
Aros, dwelling.
Auch, ach, field.
Auchter, see *Uachdar*.
Ay, island.

Ba, bo, cow.
Bal, baile, town, homestead.
Ban, white, fair.
Barr, promontory, top.
Beag, beg, little.
Bealach, balloch, mountain pass.
Bean, woman.
Ben, beann, beinn, mountain.
Bhlair, blar, plain.
Bhuidhe, bui, vuie, yellow.
Bister, busta, bost, dwelling.
Bo, ba, cow, cattle.
Brae, braigh, bread, upper part.
Breac, vrackie, speckled, variegated.

Cailleach, nun, old woman.
Cam, cambus, crooked.
Caolas, a strait, a firth.
Car, a bend or winding.
Carn, cairn, heap of stones.
Ceann, ken, kin, head, end.
Cil, kil, church.
Clach, cloich, stone.
Clachan, place of stones, helmet.
Cladach, shore, beach.

Cnoc, hill, knoll.
Coillie, killie, wood.
Coire, corrie, hollow.
Creag, craig, rock, cliff.
Cruach, rick, stack.
Cul, coul, back, recess.

Dal, dail, field.
Dalr, valley.
Damph, damh, ox, stag.
Darach, an oak.
Dearg, red.
Dour, water.
Droichead, drochit, bridge.
Druim, drum, ridge, back.
Dubh, dhu, black, dark.
Dun, hill fort.
Dysart, desert (i.e. hermitage).

Eaglais, church.
Eas, esh, waterfall, ravine.
Eilean, island.
Ey, island.

Fada, long.
Fail, rock, cliff.
Fear, fir, fhir, man.
Fetter, fothir (for), field or wood.
Fionn, fyne, white, shining.
Fraoch, heather.

Gabhar, gower, goat.
Garbh, garve, rough, rugged.
Gart, an enclosed place.
Gearr, gair, short.

Geo, gia, gio, chasm, rift.
Gil, ravine.
Gille, lad; pl. *gillean.*
Glass, grey.
Gleo, gloe, mist.
Gobha, gowan, blacksmith.
Gorm, blue or green.

Holm, uninhabited island.
Hope, small bay.
How, haugr, burial mound.

Inch, innis, island.
Inver, inbhir, mouth of a river.

Ken, kin, head, promontory.
Kil, church, burying-place.
Knock, knoll.
Kyle, a strait, a firth.

Lag, laggan, hollow.
Larach, site of an old ruin.
Larig, pass, mountain track.
Leac, flagstone.
Leana, a plain.
Learg, pass, hill-slope.
Liath, grey.
Linn, linne, pool.
Lis, lios, fortress, now a garden.
Loch, lake; *lochan,* lakelet.

Machar, plain by the sea.
Maol, meal, mam, bald headland.
Mon, monadh, moorland.
Mor, more, great, extensive.
Moy, a plain.
Muc, muic, sow.
Muli, mull, promontory.

Na, nam, nan, of the.

Ob, oba, oban, bay.
Ochter, high-lying.

Pit, pet, homestead, hollow.
Poll, pool.

Quoich, cuach, cup.

Rath, fort.
Reidh, smooth.
Riach, riabhach, brindled.
Ross, peninsula, forest.
Ru, rhu, row, rubha, point.

Sgeir, skerry, sea, rock.
Sgor, scuir, sgurr, sharp rock.
Slochd, sloc, hollow, a grave.
Spideal, spittal, hospice.
Stob, point.
Strath, broad valley.
Strone, sron, nose, promontory.
Struan, sruth, stream.

Tarbert, tarbet, isthmus.
Tigh, tay, house.
Tir, land.
Tobar, well.
Tom, hillock, bush.
Torr, round hill, heap.
Tulloch, tilly, tully, knoll.

Uachdar, high-lying, upper.
Uamh, cave, 'weem'.
Uig, nook, sheltered bay.
Uisge, esk, water.

Voe, narrow bay.

Wick, vik, bay or creek.

Lowland Scots

Aiblins, perhaps.
Arles, earnest-money.
Ashet, meat-dish.

Bailie, alderman.
Bairn, child.
Bannock, flat cake, generally of oatmeal.
Bap, breakfast roll.
Bawbee, halfpenny.
Beadle, church officer, verger.
Ben, see *But and Ben.*
Bien, well-to-do, prosperous.
Biggin, a building; *big,* to build.
Bing, slag-heap.
Birk, birch-tree.
Blate, shy, timid.
Blether, to talk nonsense.

Bothy, farm-hands' barrack.
Brae, rising ground, hill.
Bramble, blackberry.
Branks, scold's bridle (comp. 'jougs').
Braw, fine, handsome.
Breeks, trousers.
Brig, bridge.
Bubblyjock, turkey.
Burn, stream.
But and Ben, two-roomed cottage.
Byre, cowhouse.

Ca', to be set in motion; also to call;
ca'canny, be cautious.
Caller, fresh, cool (of air).
Canny, cautious, gentle.
Clarty, dirty.

Close, common entry to a tenement-house.
Clout, to patch, a cloth.
Clype, a tell-tale.
Corbie, a crow.
Coup, to upset; a rubbish-heap or dump.
Crack, to converse.
Creel, basket, usually large.
Croft, small-holding, often with a common grazing, peat-bog, fishery, etc.
Cuddy, donkey.
Cutty, short; *cutty-stool,* stool of repentance.

Daft, mentally deranged, silly.
Daunder, to stroll.
Ding, to smash, to worst.
Doo, dove.
Douce, sober, quiet, prudent.
Dreigh, tedious, dull.
Drumly, muddy (of water).

Factor, bailiff, land-steward, agent.
Farl, segment of oatcake.
Fash, to trouble, to vex.
Feu, to let (house or land).
Fey, under mystic influence.
Flesher, butcher.
Flype, to turn a stocking inside out.
Forbye, besides.
Fou, intoxicated.
Fushionless, insipid, weak-kneed.

Gab, the mouth, incessant talk.
Gey, very, 'pretty'.
Gigot, leg of mutton.
Girdle, round iron baking-plate.
Glaur, mud.
Gleg, ready, sharp.
Gowan, daisy.
Gowk, cuckoo, foolish person.
Greet, to weep.
Grieve, farm-overseer.
Grozet, gooseberry.

Haar, drizzling rain; hoar-frost; mist.
Handsel, gift for luck.
Hantle, a small amount.
Harl, to roughcast a wall.
Haugh, alluvial plain.
Haver, to talk nonsense.
Heugh, a low hill.
Hog, unshorn lamb.
Hogmanay, New Year's Eve.
Howe, a hollow or sheltered place.
Howff, meeting place, resort.
Howk, to dig.
Howm, a dell

Huntygowk, fool's errand (April 1st).
Hurl, to wheel (a barrow).

Ilk, the same; 'of that ilk' indicates that a landowner's surname and the name of his property are the same.
Ilka, each, every.

Jink, to dodge.
Jougs, scold's bridle (comp. 'branks').
Jouk, to duck (e.g. to avoid a blow).

Kail, cabbage.
Keek, to peep.
Keelie, street-arab.
Kelpie, water-sprite; river-horse.
Kenspeckle, conspicuous.
Kitchin, relish, or seasoning.
Knowe, a knoll, head.
Kye, cows.

Laigh, low, south.
aird, landed proprietor.
Land, a tenement-house.
Lave, the rest, remainder.
Law, conical hill.
Leal, loyal.
Lift, the sky.
Limmer, rogue.
Links, sand-dunes.
Lith, section (of an orange).
Loan, loaning, lane.
Lug, ear.
Lum, chimney.

Mair, more; *maist,* most, almost.
Manse, clergyman's official residence.
March, boundary.
Mavis, song-thrush.
Meikle, great, much.
Minister, clergyman.
Muckle, large.

Neeps, turnips.
Nieve, fist.

Outwith, outside.

Partan, crab.
Pawky, shrewd, sly, arch.
Philabeg, kilt.
Pickle, small quantity.
Pig, earthenware pot.
Plenishing, furniture.
Ploy, enterprise, something to do.
Poke, a bag.
Policies, private grounds.
Provost, mayor.

Puddock, frog.

Quaich, drinking-up.

Reek, smoke.
Rig, a ridge.
Roup, auction-sale.

Sark, shirt.
Saugh, willow.
Scunner, dislike.
Sheriff, county court judge.
Sheiling, hut.
Shinty, hockey.
Siccar, sure, certain.
Siller, money, silver.
Skail, dispersal of a meeting.
Skelp, to whip.
Smeddum, mettle, sense.
Sneck, *snib*, latch, hasp.
Sonsie, jolly, good-looking.
Sort, to arrange, to put right.
Soutar, shoemaker.
Speir, to ask.
Spunk, a match (for lighting).
Steek, to shut.
Stey, steep.
Stour, dust.
Stravaig, to wander aimlessly.
Sumph, dunderhead.
Sweer, averse.
Swither, to vacillate, to hesitate.

Syne, ago, since.

Tassie, small cup.
Tawse, leather strap used for corporal punishment.
Teinds, tithes.
Tent, heed; *tak' tent*, take care.
Thole, to bear; to put up with, bear with.
Thrang, crowded, busy.
Thrawn, stubborn, misshapen.
Threap, to assert.
Tine, to lose; *tint*, lost.
Tocher, dowry, marriage-portion.
Tod, a fox.
Toom, empty.
Tow, a rope.
Twine, to part.

Unco', strange, monstrous; very.
Usquebaugh, whisky.

Vennel, an alley.

Wale, to choose.
Wame, belly.
Wean, child.
Whaup, curlew.
Wight, *Wicht*, strong, powerful.
Wynd, an alley.
Wyle, blame.

Yett, gate.

I SOUTH EAST

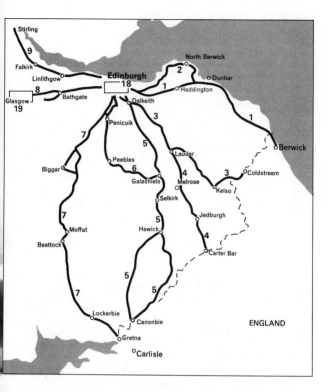

South East Scotland divides itself into two parts. The district loosely known as The Borders (roughly the modern Borders Region) lies S of the line of the Lammermuir, Moorfoot and Pentland hill ranges and E of Annandale and the upper valley of the Tweed. The other and much smaller part, Lothian, is sandwiched between the hills to its S and, to the N, Edinburgh and the Firth of Forth. During the Dark Ages (say 600–1000) most of this South East, colonised by Angles from the Continent, grew to become the 'Kingdom' of Lothian, which was though for much of the time subject to Northumbria to the S. In 1018 Malcolm II decisively defeated Northumbria at Carham, just S of the Tweed near Coldstream, but despite this there were still some 650 years to follow during which the South East, and especially The Borders, would be under frequent English threat and occupation.

The Borders

The Borders is thus a land fought over with little respite from Roman times until the mid 17C. Of the Romans there remains little beyond earthworks and occasional foundations, but of the savage centuries that followed the evidence is everywhere in ruined towers, castles and abbeys (these last also of course suffering the neglect following the Reformation) as well as in the stories that still live on in the pageantry of local festivals. The towns today are prosperous, but it should not be forgotten that scarcely one did not several times change hands, on most such occasions being razed then rebuilt by the surviving citizens. With the more peaceful times starting in the mid 17C came the stable growth of the towns, the construction of great mansions, and of course, in the 19C, the era of Sir Walter Scott, man of letters and publicist for Scotland, who, from his years spent at Ashiestiel and Abbotsford, and from his writings so intimately concerned with that area, has left such a mark that a whole district centred on *Abbotsford* is known as the *Scott Country*. This indeed is the heart of The Borders and, a little extended, includes all four of the great abbeys (*Kelso, Jedburgh, Dryburgh* and *Melrose*) as well as towers and castles such as *Smailholm, Greenknowe* and *Hume* and the Adam mansion of *Mellerstain* (Rtes 3, 4 and 5, while Rte 6 extends as a westward arm up the Tweed to historic *Traquair House* and *Peebles*).

The Borders is also Scotland's horse country, with roots going back to the marauding freebooters (or reivers or moss-troopers) of medieval times. Today the tradition continues with breeding and sales and the growing popularity of holiday trail riding and pony trekking, while more picturesque links with this past are provided by the Common Ridings which are a central feature of several towns' summer festivals. (In the past, as a guard against encroachment, towns carried out periodic rides around their bounds. Today's Common Ridings, with sometimes 300 or more riders, are a re-enactment of this precaution, the rides also often being accompanied by pageantry recalling some brave skirmish with the English.)

Scenically The Borders offer in the E rolling wooded and pastoral country, threaded by famous fishing rivers such as Tweed and Teviot. West of a line through Galashiels, Selkirk and Hawick lie the moors, often lonely upland, with rounded mountains, some over 2000 feet. Throughout this area, even in summer, the many small roads can be surprisingly uncrowded.

Many visitors will associate The Borders with weaving, tweed and knitwear, the practical and profitable result of the fortunate union of lush sheep pasture and soft river water. But, contrary to widely held belief, the word 'tweed' has no proper link with the river of that name. The Borders weavers called their product 'tweel', a local variant of course of 'twill', and it was a London merchant who jumped to the conclusion—in this case happy enough—that what was really meant was 'tweed'. And then it was Sir Walter Scott, ever the publicist, who by sporting chequered trousers in London sparked an enthusiasm that would spread around the world. In the Borders today *Galashiels* and *Hawick* are the main, though by no means only centres. Some firms can be visited, and shops selling their work will be found throughout most of The Borders.

Lothian

Lothian is a shallow strip some 50m long and 10m deep between the Firth of Forth and the succession of hill ranges to the S. Partly, though not only because of the relationship to Edinburgh, the district includes more sites likely to attract the visitor than its size might suggest. The closeness to Edinburgh also means that the visitor has the choice between being based in Edinburgh, thence making excursions into Lothian, or alternatively choosing one or more of Lothian's attractive small towns as bases from which both to tour around and to visit the city.

History in Lothian visibly spans some 4500 years. *Cairnpapple Hill* is Stone, Bronze and Iron Age, and the Roman period is represented by their fort at *Cramond* near Edinburgh and the remains of the *Antonine Wall* at Falkirk (Central Region). Medieval times live on in the humble 15C *Soutra Aisle*, the triangular plan of *Dirleton* village and, above all, in castles (*Hailes, Tantallon* and *Dirleton* in the E, *Craigmillar* and *Crichton* to the S of Edinburgh, and to the W the great palace of *Linlithgow*); while, travelling on in time, *Hopetoun House* reigns as the supreme example of 18C palatial elegance. But it is the brief but stirring seven years of Mary, Queen of Scots, that tend to dominate Lothian's past. She was born at *Linlithgow*; the plot to murder Darnley was hatched at *Craigmillar*; three times she took refuge in *Dunbar*'s castle; from *Borthwick* she had to escape disguised as a man; *Carberry Hill* was the scene of her defeat and of the last time she saw Bothwell; and the following year, after her escape from Loch Leven, she experienced a brief but last encouragement at *Niddry*.

Lothian is not outstanding scenically, and in fact the west, with slagheaps, urban spread, motorways and the petro-chemical works around Grangemouth in adjoining Central Region, is not inviting, although here are some of the more interesting sites, such as Cairnpapple Hill, Linlithgow and Hopetoun House. But the *Pentlands* offer good upland, and the wooded slopes of the *Lammermuirs* with Stenton, Nunraw Abbey and Gifford, are quiet, lost country. There is also a particular charm to the Forth coast E of Edinburgh with its links and dunes. Much of this shore is controlled by public authorities who have made it a model of conservation planning with coastal parks, picnic areas, camping sites, and seabird sanctuaries at *Aberlady* and on the islands.

1 Berwick-upon-Tweed to Edinburgh via Dunbar and Haddington

A1 to Burnmouth. A1107 to Cockburnspath. A1 to Edinburgh.—Agricultural and pastoral with coastal views. Alternatives touch the Lammermuir Hills, part open upland and part wooded, with quiet roads and valleys.

SOME HOTELS. **Berwick-upon-Tweed**. *King's Arms*, Hidehill; Tel: (0289) 307454. **Dunbar**. *Battleblent*, West Barns. Tel: (0368) 62234. *Bayswell*, Bayswell Park. Tel: (0368) 62225. *Bayview*, Bayswell Road. Tel: (0368) 62778. **Gifford**. *Tweeddale Arms*, EM41 4QU. Tel: (062081) 240. **Haddington**. *George*, 91 High Street. Tel: (062082) 3372. **Musselburgh**. *Drummore Motor Inn*, North Berwick Road. Tel: (031665) 2302.

Total distance 50m.—*6m* **Burnmouth**.—*2m* **Eyemouth**.—*3m*
Coldingham.—*9m* **Cockburnspath**.—*7m* **Dunbar**.—*10m*
Haddington.—*13m* **Edinburgh**.

Berwick-upon-Tweed (see also 'Blue Guide England'), for all its
tentative feel of Scotland, is wholly in England, for the border, which
from well to the W of Coldstream has run with the Tweed, loops
sharply northward as soon as the river comes in sight of the town.
That there is nevertheless an anticipation of Scotland here is hardly
surprising, for not only is Scotland a mere 3m away but also, over
centuries, Berwick belonged first to one country, then to the other,
until it was finally ceded to England in 1482. Even then Berwick was
not allowed to forget the Scots as it saw itself both fortified and
administered as a bastion against them, and the virtually complete
Tudor *Ramparts, begun in 1558 but not completed until 1747, still
stand as the town's most distinguished feature. They are best
appreciated as the town is approached from the S across one of the
impressive Tweed bridges. Of the castle in which in 1291 Edward I
concluded the assembly begun at Norham (see below) and
pronounced in favour of John Balliol's claim to the Scottish crown
only fragments survive, near the station.

Before setting out northward along A1, two alternative and quieter
entries to Scotland are worth considering.

BERWICK TO COLDSTREAM (A698, SW. 13m). This road remains in
England, but short diversions N reach places of interest in or closely
associated with Scotland, such as *Union Suspension Bridge*, ap-
proached by a minor road off A698 about 2m W of Berwick. This
Tweed bridge, linking England and Scotland and built by Samuel
Brown in 1820, was the first of its type in Britain designed for road
traffic. It was in the church at *Norham*, N off A698 some 7m from
Berwick, that Edward I opened the assembly called to weigh the
contesting claims to the Scottish throne of Bruce and Balliol, later, at
Berwick Castle, ruling in favour of the latter. *Norham Castle* (Mid
March–mid Oct: Mon.–Sat., 09.30 to 18.30. Sun., 14.00 to 18.30. Mid
Oct–mid March: Mon.–Sat., 09.30 to 16.00. Sun. 14.00 to 16.00. Fee),
a huge Norman keep of c 1160 and long a stronghold of the
prince-bishop of Durham, was the place in which· Scott set the
opening scenes of 'Marmion'. At *Ladykirk*, in Scotland just N of
Norham, the church was built by James IV in 1500 in gratitude for
an escape from drowning; his bust (19C) is on the interior W wall of
the nave, near it being a small blocked window used by the priest
whose room was behind (steps). Of the tower at the W end only the
lower part is original, the upper levels having been added in 1743
from a design by William Adam. For **Coldstream**, 6m SW of Norham
by A698, see Rte 3.

BERWICK TO DUNS (A6105, NW. 14m). Before entering Scotland the
road runs below *Halidon Hill* on which in 1333 a Scottish army
marching to raise the English siege of Berwick was defeated with
great slaughter. At *Foulden*, across the border, there is, beside the
road, a most attractive two-storeyed tithe barn with an outside stair,
while at *Chirnside*, 3m farther, the tower of the parish church
incorporates a Norman doorway. But the Norman doorway at *Edrom*,
another 3m W, is perhaps more noteworthy; for here it has been
rebuilt on its own in the churchyard. *Manderston* (Mid May–Sept:

Thurs., Sun., 14.00 to 17.30. Also Bank Hol. Mons. Tel: 0361-83450.
Fee), off A6105 2m E of Duns and ranking among the best of
Scotland's Edwardian country mansions, boasts a silver staircase,
believed to be unique. Also of interest are the spacious domestic
quarters and the splendid stables and dairy. **Duns** is a modest market
town which first stood on the SW slope of nearby Duns Law, until
wholly destroyed by the English in 1545. It was rebuilt on its present
site 43 years later. The town claims (as do also Down in Northern
Ireland and Dunstane in Northumberland) to be the birthplace in c
1266 of John Duns Scotus, the medieval philosopher, and a statue to
him stands in the public park. A very different native was Jim Clark,
the motor racing champion killed in 1968, a collection of whose
trophies is displayed in the *Jim Clark Memorial Room* at 44 Newtown
Street (Easter–Sept: Mon.–Sat., 10.00 to 13.00. 14.00 to 18.00. Sun.,
14.00 to 18.00. Tel: 0361-82600. Fee). On the summit of Duns Law
the *Covenanters' Stone* commemorates that Leslie's army camped
here in 1639. *Fogo Church*, 3m SW of Duns, has an unusual outside
staircase of 1671 leading up to the laird's loft.

Along the A1 the border is crossed *3m N* of Berwick-upon-Tweed at
Lamberton Bar where once, as at better known Gretna, the toll-keeper
performed marriages for runaway couples. The now ruined church
in the hamlet is mentioned in the marriage contract of 1502 between
James IV and Margaret, daughter of Henry VII of England.—*3m*
Burnmouth, where this Rte temporarily leaves A1, forking right for
Eyemouth and Coldingham. However some motorists may prefer the
Lammermuir alternative suggested immediately below.

LAMMERMUIR ALTERNATIVE. A1 is followed past *Ayton Castle*
(May–Sept: Wed., Sun., 14.00 to 17.00. Tel: 03902-212. Fee), a
conspicuous red sandstone Scottish Baronial edifice of 1846, as far
as Grantshouse, 10m from Burnmouth. Here A6112 leads S towards
Duns, in about 3m reaching a sign for *Edin's Hall Broch*, for those
interested in Iron Age antiquities a worthwhile objective at the end
of a long mile's walk. On a commanding crest above a wooded valley,
this substantial broch-like structure, one of few of its kind in southern
Scotland, stands within a complex of earthworks which may represent
both hill fort and settlement. The broch remains comprise a thick
base wall 4 to 5ft high, parts of side chambers and a few steps of the
stairway between the walls. After returning to the car, a pleasant
circuit can be made by continuing S 2m to Preston, there bearing
NW along B6355 before in another 3m turning N along a minor road
for **Abbey St. Bathans**, a lost little place on a lovely stretch of the
Whiteadder Water. Here the village church incorporates part of the
walls, and the tomb of a prioress, of a 13C church dedicated to St.
Bathan, a successor to St. Columba. And here, too, there is a *Trout
Farm* (May–Sept: Daily, 11.00 to 17.00. Oct–April: Sat., Sun., 11.00
to 17.00 Tel: 03614-242. Free), doubling as an interpretive centre of
the life of this valley from prehistoric to modern times. Roads N from
here rejoin A1 in 7m at Cockburnspath. Alternatively B6355 traverses
the heart of the Lammermuir Hills on its way to Gifford and
Haddington.

2m (from Burnmouth) **Eyemouth** is an incidental small town combining the activities of minor seaside resort, with angling festivals and
competitions, and the business of commercial fishing. The harbour

stretching up the river is both picturesque and lively, and the *Eyemouth Museum* in Market Place, telling about the fishing and farming industries of this district, serves also as a memorial to what has become known as the Great East Coast Fishing Disaster of 1881 in which 129 local men lost their lives (Easter, May–Oct: Mon.–Sat., 10.00 to 18.00. Sun., 14.00 to 18.00. Tel: 0390-50678. Fee).—*3m* **Coldingham** lies just inland from Coldingham Bay which, with St. Abb's and West Loch, forms a popular summer holiday corner. In the village are the remains of a 13C *Priory* founded in c 1098 by King Edgar as successor to a nunnery founded in the 7C on St. Abb's Head by Ebba (a Northumbrian princess saved from a shipwreck here) and burned by the Norsemen in c 870. The priory was much damaged by Hertford in 1545, and its domestic buildings were largely demolished by Cromwell in 1648, but some features survive, notably the N and E walls of the choir, with their Gothic EE arcade, all now embodied in the parish church. *St. Abb's Head*, a sheer headland with cliffs 300ft high, ranks as a National Nature Reserve (managed by NTS and the Scottish Wildlife Trust), known for its nesting and migrating seabirds. *Fast Castle*, 4m NW of Coldingham, although little more than battered fragments, stands stark and dramatic on its lonely crag above the sea at the foot of high grassy cliffs. The approach road, off A1107, ends at the clifftop, along which a short walk brings the ruin into sight at the end of the path far below. Of uncertain origin, Fast was by the end of the 14C a stronghold of the Homes and later held by the Logans. Margaret of England, aged only 14 and on her way to marry James IV, stayed here, but left her retinue of 1500 people to overnight under what must have been somewhat overcrowded conditions at Coldingham.

9m (from Coldingham) **Cockburnspath**, where the church has a distinctive 16C round beacon-tower, was the birthplace of John Broadwood (1732–1812), the pioneer piano craftsman. About 1m N, and delightfully sited in the grounds of Dunglass House, will be found the partially restored *Dunglass Collegiate Church*, a typical mid 15C example of its kind, with much rich detail both inside and out. The arched tomb niches suggest that the founder, Sir Alex Hume, intended the church to serve as his family burial place. A1 continues N between coast and railway, passing on the W *Innerwick*, with castle remains, and, in contrast on the E, *Torness Nuclear Power Station*.

6m **Broxburn**, the fork where A1 bears W to bypass Dunbar, is the place near which anyone interested in battles should stop, for it was here, in 1650, that Cromwell decisively defeated the Scottish supporters of Charles II under Leslie. Leslie had the advantage for he was massed around Doon Hill (582ft), 1m SW of this road fork, while Cromwell's army, enfeebled by hunger and disease, was strung across the low ground towards Dunbar. However, urged on by fanatical Covenanting clergy, Leslie came down, pushing forward his right wing to occupy the low ground at what is now Broxburn, whereupon Cromwell, quick to seize his opportunity, sent in his cavalry which drove the Scots back in total disorder. About 3000 Scots lost their lives and 10,000 were made prisoner.

1m **Dunbar** (4500 inhab. *ECl.* Wed. *Inf.* Town House, High Street), historic fortress port and royal burgh, has in modern times developed as a holiday town.

History. In 1295 Dunbar saw the defeat of the Scots by England's Edward I, when suppressing the revolt unwisely launched by his protégé, John Balliol. Nineteen years later, Edward II, fleeing from his defeat at Bannockburn, ignominiously escaped by sea from here. In 1339 'Black Agnes', Countess of Dunbar, successfully defended the fortress for six weeks against the English until it was relieved by supplies brought in by sea. Over two centuries later, in 1566, Mary, Queen of Scots, and Darnley found refuge here during the dangerous days following the murder of Rizzio. Within a month, though, Mary made Bothwell governor of the castle, and the following year twice visited it with him, the first occasion being after he had carried her off from Edinburgh, the second after their interrupted honeymoon and flight from Borthwick. After Mary's defeat at Carberry Hill, the castle was razed by the regent, Moray. Oliver Cromwell was here in 1650, totally defeating the supporters of Charles II (see above) and later further destroying the castle by using its stones to improve the harbour.

After being razed by Moray and used as a source of building material by Cromwell it is hardly surprising that of the historic and once formidable *Castle* all that now remains are fragments picturesquely clinging to the small headland which forms one abrupt arm of the entrance to the harbour. The other arm is a string of rocks, and this harbour area, with the castle headland, the cobbled quays and some mellow warehouses, is the most attractive part of the town. The contrastingly busy upper town stretches the length of the broad High Street, midway along the E side of which is the steepled 17C *Town House*, claiming to be the oldest civic building in Scotland in continuous use. At the N end of High Street stands *Lauderdale House* (Robert Adam), now owned by the local authority. John Muir (1838–1914), the American naturalist, writer and father of America's National Parks, was born in Dunbar where he is remembered by *John Muir Country Park*.

From Dunbar there is a choice of three approaches to Edinburgh. This Rte follows the main A1, but, immediately below, first suggests a meandering southerly alternative through Gifford, only 3m longer and running below the northern slopes of the Lammermuir Hills. The coastal road through North Berwick is described as Rte 2.

DUNBAR TO EDINBURGH VIA GIFFORD. Approaching **Stenton**, the curious small conical structure beside the N side of the road marks the site of an ancient pilgrims' well. The village, which has never quite lived down its notoriety for the burning of witches, is now a quiet little unspoilt place, protected as a conservation area and with some cottages still showing traces of their original external stairs. On the green stands the *Wool Stone*, or tron, used for weighing wool at the wool fair, while behind there is a dovecot with crow-step gabling, once the tower of a now ruined church.—In 3m B6370 reaches Garvald, above which stands *Nunraw Abbey*, built by Cistercian monks in 1948, their first Scottish foundation since the Reformation. What in fact happened was that the monks bought the property in 1946, building this large new abbey and leaving the old Tower-House (15C with additions) to serve as a guest house (Mon.–Sat., 09.30 to 11.00. 14.00 to 17.00. Tel: 062083-228. Free). In origin Nunraw (Nuns' Row) was a grange belonging to the convent at Haddington, founded in c 1158, the nuns accepting the bizarre obligation to maintain a four-gun fortification for use in case of invasion. During the 16C the property became first the preserve and then, after three Hepburn prioresses, the residence of the Hepburn family. In 1548 the Scottish parliament met here and took the decision to send their five-year-old queen, Mary, to France to marry the heir to the French throne. Today the most important interior feature is the painted ceiling of 1610, bearing the initials of the then owner and his wife, Patrick and Helen Hepburn, and the arms of medieval monarchs. In the grounds there is a 16C dovecot with 450 nests.

Gifford, 4m farther, is a neat 17–18C village, specially laid out to meet the needs of the many people who had settled around Yester House at that time. A plaque on the church wall commemorates the birth in Gifford in 1723 of the Rev. John Witherspoon, one of the signatories of the American Declaration of Independence and first president of what is now Princeton university. At *Pencaitland*, 6m W of Gifford, the church preserves a 13C N choir aisle, while at the pleasant village of *Ormiston* (2m W) a 15C cross adds to the charms of the tree-lined street. The main A1 can be rejoined in 2m at *Tranent*, some 7m short of central Edinburgh.

5m (from Dunbar) **East Linton**, with a part 13C church and a 14C bridge, is however best known for *Preston Mill and Phantassie Doocot* (NTS. April–Oct: Mon.–Sat., 10.00 to 12.30. 14.00 to 17.30, or 16.30 in Oct. Sun., 14.00 to 17.30, or 16.30 in Oct. Nov–March: Sat., 10.00 to 12.30. 14.00 to 16.30. Sun., 14.00 to 16.30, Fee). On a quiet river bank where there may have been a mill from the 11 or 12C, Preston as seen today dates from the 16C and is one of the oldest watermills still working in Scotland and was even in commercial use until as late as 1957. Although the machinery has been regularly renewed, the system remains unchanged and the technical ingenuity of the past can be appreciated in something like its original setting. *Phantassie Doocot*, a beehive type once with 544 nests, is a short walk away. John Rennie (1761–1821), the engineer and architect, was born at the mansion, an event commemorated by a memorial on A1 East Linton bypass. For *Tyninghame House Gardens*, just NE, see Rte 2.

Hailes Castle (AM. Standard. Fee), S of A1 and 1½m SW of East Linton, is the place to which Bothwell, the then owner, brought Mary, Queen of Scots, on their way to Dunbar. Architecturally the castle is notable for the substantial amount of its 13C masonry, to this period belonging much of the lower structure E from and including the central tower, while that extending W and S is of the following century. But for many people the most lingering memory will be of the two grim pit prisons, one in each tower, with narrow air and lavatory shafts angling away through the massive walls. Today ladders enable visitors to descend into these and sense what being lowered, or perhaps even thrown in must have meant to a medieval prisoner.

Traprain Law (734ft), the distinctive whale-back hill to the S, may have been occupied during the Stone Age and certainly was an Iron Age fortified site, the city of the Votadini, spreading over some 40 acres. The Votadini are thought to have been in some form of alliance with the Romans, so much of the defensive surrounds may date from later, Dark Ages, times and it seems that the site continued in use until perhaps as late as the 11C. A treasure of 4C Christian and pagan silver, excavated here in 1919, is now in the Edinburgh Royal Museum of Scotland (Queen Street).

Within a 2m-wide belt paralleling A1 on the N between East Linton and Haddington there are various places worth either looking at or visiting. As a start, in a field just W of East Linton and just N of A1, a lone standing stone is thought to have been a Bronze Age route marker. Beyond, B1347 leads N to *Athelstaneford*, a place associated with the origin of Scotland's flag. Tradition tells that the Pictish Scots, fighting a battle here in the 10C against the Northumbrians under Athelstane, saw a white St. Andrew's Cross against the blue sky and, thus encouraged to victory, made a banner which became the Scottish flag. A flag now flies beside the church where a pictorial plaque tells the story. At nearby East Fortune airfield the *Museum of Flight* (July, Aug: Daily, 10.00 to 16.00. Also several annually changing special days, such as Easter, May Day and local holidays. Tel: 031–2257534. Free) is an outstation of Edinburgh's Royal Museum of Scotland. Aircraft on display range from a Comet airliner and a Vulcan bomber to a 1930 De Haviland Puss Moth, and include also a Lightning and a Spitfire. Additionally there are a Blue Streak rocket and several varieties of aero engine dating from 1909 onwards. The airfield itself has its notch in history as the starting point of the airship R34 when it made the first double crossing of the Atlantic in 1919, and the museum shows contemporary material. To the NW of Athelstaneford rises the hill fort of *Chesters*, posing something of a riddle because, although obviously a defensive complex with multiple banks and ditches, it nevertheless stands in a tactically ridiculous situation below a high ridge. The *Hopetoun Monument*, 1m N of Haddington and as conspicuous today as its erectors always intended it to be, commemorates the 4th Earl who fought with distinction in the Napoleonic wars.

5m (from East Linton) **Haddington** (6500 inhab. *ECl.* Thurs), noted today for its dignified 17–19C streets, in fact dates from at least the 12C when it was made a royal burgh by David I. At that time what are now Market, Court and High streets marked the town's triangular plan around an open centre which was not built on until some 400 years later. Alexander II was born here in 1198 and John Knox in 1505. The town was several times burned by the English, and was held by them against the Scots and French in 1548–49.

A tour of Haddington's buildings of architectural and historic interest can best follow the route suggested and explained in a booklet called 'Walk around Haddington', obtainable in local shops and also shown on a plan on the wall of the *Town House* (William Adam, 1748 but enlarged 1830). The *Court House* (William Burn, 1833) stands on the site of the royal palace, and the *Knox Memorial Institute* (1879), with a statue of the reformer, is the successor to the school at which Knox was educated. The *Church of St. Mary*, near the river and perhaps the town's most important building, though renovated, dates from the 13–15C. The nave and tower, the latter once carrying an open masonry crown, are intact, but the choir and transepts are roofless. Near the E end of the choir is the tomb of Jane Welsh (1801–66), wife of Thomas Carlyle and a native of Haddington. From the church Pleached Alley leads to *St. Mary's Pleasance*, the garden of Haddington House now restored as a 17C garden (rose, herb, cottage and sunken gardens). *Haddington Museum* (Mon., Tues., Thurs., Fri., 10.00 to 13.00, 14.00 to 19.00. Sat., 10.00 to 13.00. Tel: 062082–4161. Ext 346. Free), in the 19C public library in Newton Port, displays local historical material. The names Abbey Bridge and Nungate Bridge, both 16C in origin, recall a Cistercian nunnery founded by the Countess of Northumberland in c 1159.

Lennoxlove House (April–Sept: Wed., Sat., Sun., 14.00 to 17.00. Tel: 062082-3720. Fee), 1m S of Haddington on B6369, is now the

Maitland of Lethington, 'Secretary Lethington' to Mary, Queen of Scots.

home of the Duke and Duchess of Hamilton. Originally called Lethington, this was the seat of the Maitlands, one of whom (William Maitland, 'Secretary Lethington') was secretary to Mary, Queen of Scots. Acquired by the Richmond and Lennox family in the 17C, the house was renamed Lennoxlove after the celebrated beauty known as 'La Belle Stuart'; daughter of a physician, she became mistress of Charles II, but in 1667 eloped with Charles Stuart, Duke of Richmond and Lennox. The house now shows the Hamilton Palace collections of portraits, furniture and porcelain.

6m. The mining and industrial town of **Tranent**, an outlier of the Edinburgh conurbation, has two niches in history—as the place from which the Highlanders advanced to their victory of Prestonpans (see Rte 2), and as one of the two stations of the first railway in Scotland; built in 1722, the railway's purpose was to carry coal the 2m N to ships berthed at Cockenzie and its course is now a popular walk.—*3m* **Musselburgh** earned the title of the 'Honest Toun' as long ago as 1332 when Bruce's nephew, the Earl of Moray, died here and the citizens disclaimed any reward for honouring his body. Golf has been played since 1672 on the Links Course and the town also boasts the oldest racecourse in Scotland. Although for the most part a busy, modern place, Musselburgh still has attractive corners. For instance, *Pinkie House* (Mid April–mid July and mid Sept–mid Dec: Tues., 14.00 to 17.00. Tel: 031-6652059. Free), off A1 at the E end of the town, is known for its plaster ceilings and painted gallery of c 1620, while the old *Esk Bridge* and nearby *Tolbooth* (the latter built partly with the stones of a once famous pilgrim chapel, Our Lady of Loretto) are both of the 16C.

Inveresk, immediately S of Musselburgh, once the Roman station at the N end of Dere Street and today a contrastingly quiet suburb, has several pleasing Georgian houses. Here *Inveresk Lodge Garden* (NTS. Mon., Wed., Fri., 10.00 to 16.30. Also Sun., 14.00 to 17.00 when house is occupied. Fee) specialises in plants for the small garden. Rather over 1m farther S is the site of the battle of Carberry Hill at which in 1567 Mary, Queen of Scots, and Bothwell were defeated by the rebel lords.—*4m* central **Edinburgh**, see Rte 18.

2 Dunbar to Edinburgh via North Berwick

A198 to Musselburgh. A1 to Edinburgh.—Pastoral and coastal, with cliffs and islands around North Berwick; links and dunes along the Firth of Forth.

SOME HOTELS. **North Berwick**. *Golf*, Dirleton Avenue. Tel: (0620) 2202. *Marine*, Cromwell Road. Tel: (0620) 2406. *Nether Abbey*, Dirleton Avenue. Tel: (0620) 2802. **Gullane**. *Greywalls*, Muirfield. Tel: (0620) 842144. **Aberlady**. *Kilspindie House*, High Street. Tel: (08757) 319.

Total distance 32m.—*12m*. **North Berwick**.—*7m* **Aberlady**.—*9m* **Musselburgh**.—*4m* **Edinburgh**.

Dunbar, see Rte 1, is left by A1, a turn N on to A198 being made after 2m.—*5m* (from Dunbar) **Tyninghame House Gardens** (June–Sept: Mon.–Fri., 10.30 to 16.30. Tel: 0620-860330. Fee), extending to the E of the road, merit a visit as much for herbaceous borders and terraces as for the neat little ruin of St. Baldred's Chapel, built in the 12C and still with pleasing Norman arches. This 8C saint, said to have lived and died near here, certainly made his mark because he is remembered also by two rocks on the shore bearing his name, St. Baldred's Cradle here near Tyninghame and St. Baldred's Boat farther N below Tantallon Castle. The first of these, we are told, was originally between Bass Rock and the shore and thus a danger to shipping; however in response to Baldred's prayers God obligingly shifted the rock a couple of miles southward.—At (*2m*) **Whitekirk** there is a large 15C church beside which is a two-storeyed 16C tithe barn, long ago used by the monks of Holyrood Abbey for the storage of their grain. At that time, and during preceding centuries, Whitekirk boasted a miraculous crucifix and a holy well, possessions which attracted several thousand pilgrims a year during the 15C, amongst them being the later Pope Pius II who is reputed to have walked here barefoot from Dunbar, thus contracting the rheumatism which plagued the rest of his life.

3m *****Tantallon Castle** (AM. Standard, but in Oct–March closed Tues. and alternate Wed. Fee) is a massive red sandstone ruin, occupying a breathtaking position, long impregnable, on a towering cliff promontory. On three sides defence is assured by sheer drops to a rock-strewn sea, on the fourth by a double moat. A notorious lair of the Douglases, the main ruin now comprises a central tower, flanking towers and linking ramparts, the walls being 14ft thick and the well plunging 100ft deep into the rock. Dating from c 1375, Tantallon was never taken until 1651 when Cromwell's general, Monk, destroyed it, though only after 12 days of bombardment.

Bass Rock, prominent about 1½m out to sea, is a precipitous basalt island 350ft high and a mile in circumference. There was a castle here from early times (its building must have been a daunting undertaking), and traces still remain of fortifications and a chapel, the latter tenuously associated with St. Baldred, who may indeed have lived here. The rock was used as a prison for Covenanters after 1671, one of these being 'Prophet' Peden, (see Rte 11, Cumnock and Sorn), and, soon after, for Jacobite prisoners who in 1691 dramatically seized the fort and successfully held it until 1694 when they were granted an amnesty. Today Bass Rock is the home of huge colonies of noisy seabirds, including several thousand gannets. Boat trips round the rock from North Berwick.

2m **North Berwick** (4500 inhab. *ECl.* Thurs. *Inf.* Quality Street), a royal burgh of Robert III, was developed during the 19 and early 20C as a holiday and golf resort, and the confident Victorian and Edwardian architecture of that period seems still to set the tone in this continually fashionable and popular place. The most interesting area of the town is around the rocky spit with the small harbour and bays on either side. On the spit stands the ruin of the notorious *Auld Kirk*, with 12C foundations and a 16C porch; notorious because it was here in 1591 that a gathering of witches and wizards negotiated with the Devil to bring about the death of James VI. North Berwick's other antiquity is the so-called *Abbey*, in fact a fragment of a 12C nunnery. The ruin is in the grounds of the house called The Abbey, owned by Edinburgh corporation, but its relics in the *Borough Museum* in School Road are perhaps more interesting (Easter–May: Sat., Mon., 10.00 to 13.00. 14.00 to 17.00. Fri., Sun., 14.00 to 17.00. June–Sept: Mon.–Sat., 10.00 to 13.00. 14.00 to 17.00. Sun., 14.00 to 17.00. Tel: 0620-3470. Free).

Behind the town rises *Berwick Law* (613ft; path). At the top there are a view indicator; a watchtower from Napoleonic times, when the Law was one of a chain of beacons ready to warn of the approach of French invaders; concrete buildings used for a similar purpose against the Germans in 1914–18; and a curious arch made of a whale's jawbones. The origin of this arch seems to be unknown, but one was erected in about 1709 and there have been a number of replacements.—Seawards, in addition to Bass Rock, there are four islands, all alive with seabirds. From E to W these are *Craigleith* with puffins, then *Lamb*, *Fidra* and *Eyebroughty* with eider duck and terns.

2m ***Dirleton**, with its castle, two triangular greens and the way in which its buildings are grouped in the traditional style of a medieval feudal township, is often, and with good reason, described as the prettiest village in Scotland. The ruined *Castle* (AM. Standard. Fee) was started in about 1225, but later centuries saw many additions to this ancient keep, notably a 15C hall and a 17C Renaissance mansion. In 1298 the castle held out for Wallace against England's Edward I, and it was finally demolished by Cromwell in 1650. Within the walls there are a garden and a 17C bowling green, while a 17C dovecot, built with 1100 nests, stands at the E corner.—2m **Gullane** is a name almost synonymous with golf, here being five courses including the championship course of Muirfield. *Heritage of Golf* (By appointment. Tel: 08757-277. Free), on West Links Road, is an exhibition telling the story of golf after the game's arrival in Scotland from Holland in the 15C. Gullane Bay, with extensive sands and many parking and picnic places, is the focus of a major sand dunes control scheme.

Approaching (3m) **Aberlady** are Luffness Castle and Myreton Motor Museum. *Luffness Castle* (By appointment. Tel: 08757-218), with its foundations on the site of a Norse camp, centres on a 13C keep. *Myreton Motor Museum* (Daily, 10.00 to 18.00, or 17.00 in Nov–April. Tel: 08757-288. Fee) shows vintage cars, cycles and commercial vehicles. Aberlady once enjoyed maritime status as the port of Haddington, but the bay in which so many ships once anchored is now a silted nature reserve, the haunt of some 200 recorded species of birds, including all five types of tern.

4m **Seton Collegiate Church** (AM. Standard, but closed Tues. afternoon and Wed. Fee) dates from the 15–16C but followed a church of 1242. The oldest portion of the present church are the foundations (in the transept) of a south aisle added to the original church of c 1410 but demolished a century later. The choir is of c 1460; the 4th Lord Seton added the Sacristy and in 1492 established the church as collegiate (ruins of the domestic buildings can be seen); the 5th Lord Seton, killed at Flodden, probably lies in the choir to which he had added glazed windows and paving; his widow built the transept and spire, in so doing demolishing the south aisle wall of c 1410. External features are the truncated stone spire and the stands for statues on the buttresses. Worth noting inside the church are, in the south transept, a Renaissance monument with a delightful inscription; the crossing's vault with a hole for hoisting the bells; and, in the choir, sedilia set at a curiously awkward height, and what are probably the effigies of the 5th Lord and his wife.

Seton Castle (1790; no adm.), nearby, stands on the site of Seton Palace, home of the Lord Seton who was such a staunch supporter of Mary, Queen of Scots. It was to Seton Palace that Mary and Darnley fled after Rizzio's murder, and the following year Mary was here again, this time with Bothwell after Darnley's murder.

Prince Charles charging at the head of the clans at Prestonpans. 'The sun broke out, and the mist rose from the ground like the curtain of a theatre' (Scott).

Approaching (*2m*) **Preston**, a cairn beside A198 at a road fork commemorates the Battle of Prestonpans of 1745 when the Young Pretender's Highlanders, approaching from Tranent across a morass,

in a ten-minute dawn charge routed the government forces under
General Cope, losing only 30 men and killing 400 of the enemy. The
village is known for its magnificent 17C *Market Cross*, complete
with unicorn, lockfast chamber and crier's platform, as also for its
compact and elegant group of 15–17C buildings. These include the
part-ruined 15C tower, with a 16C addition perched on top and an
attached lectern dovecot; turreted 16C Northfield House; 17C
Hamilton House; and, beside A198, a 16C beehive dovecot.—
Prestonpans, immediately N of Preston, is a straggling industrial
community which traces its name back 700 years to the time when
monks from Newbattle Abbey, near Dalkeith, extracted salt here by
using local coal to heat sea water in metal pans. *Scottish Mining
Museum: Prestongrange Site* (Mon.–Fri., 10.00 to 16.00. Sat. and
Sun., 12.00 to 17.00. Tel: 031–6659904. Free) makes use of a former
colliery site (now closed after some eight centuries of activity) just W
of Prestonpans on the coast road. The main exhibit, in its 5-storey
shed, is a huge beam engine, Cornish-built in 1874 and in operation
until 1954. The mine's former power house now serves as an exhibition
hall, while other attractions here include steam locomotives and a
colliery winding engine.—*3m* **Musselburgh**, see Rte 1.—*4m* central
Edinburgh, see Rte 18.

3   Coldstream to Edinburgh via Kelso and Lauder

A698 to Kelso. A6089 and A697 to Lauder. A68 to
Edinburgh.—Tweed valley to Kelso, followed by gently rising
pastoral country to Lauder. Beyond Lauder, upland moor across the
W flank of the Lammermuir Hills (1130ft) with views northward
over Edinburgh and the Firth of Forth.

SOME HOTELS. **Coldstream**. *Majicado*, 71 High Street. Tel: (0890)
2112. **Kelso**. *Cross Keys*, 36–37 The Square. Tel: (0573) 23303.
Ednam House, Bridge Street. Tel: (0573) 24168. **Lauder**.
Lauderdale, 1 Edinburgh Road. Tel: (05782) 231. **Dalkeith**. *County*,
High Street. Tel: (031663) 3495.

Total distance 52m.—*6m* **Kelso**.—*9m* **Gordon**.—*9m* **Lauder**.—*20m*
Dalkeith.—*8m* **Edinburgh**.

Coldstream (2000 inhab. *ECl*. Thurs. *Inf*. Henderson Park.
Easter–Oct), a small Border town above a wooded curve of the Tweed,
today with a bridge built by Smeaton in 1766, was earlier known for
a ford which all too frequently provided military passage during the
long years of Border warfare. Edward I crossed here in 1296, as did
also Bruce several times when fighting Edward II. In 1513 James IV
forded the river on his way to defeat and death at Flodden, 3m SE,
where today there is a monument to the brave of both nations.
Montrose, too, crossed here in 1640 and, 20 years later, General
Monk, on his way southward to play his devious part in the business
of the Restoration. Monk was accompanied by a regiment, soon to
become famous as the Coldstream Guards, which he had personally
raised in Coldstream in 1659, and the site of the original headquarters
of this regiment, in Market Square, now houses the *Coldstream*

Museum (Whitsun–Sept: Tues.–Fri. and Sun., 14.00 to 17.00. Sat., 10.00 to 13.00. Tel: 0890-2630. Fee). At the E entrance to the town an obelisk honours Charles Marjoribanks, the first Member of Parliament for Berwickshire after the Reform Bill of 1832.

Wark, S of the Tweed just W of Coldstream, still shows fragments of a castle defended in 1344 against David II by the beautiful Countess of Salisbury; according to Froissart, England's Edward III, having relieved the castle, fell in love with its defender and may have here founded the Order of the Garter. The battle of *Carham*, in which in 1018 Malcolm II defeated the Northumbrians and annexed the kingdom of Lothian, was fought immediately E of Wark.

A mile to the W of Coldstream, A697 forks N, a short way along this road being the entrance to *The Hirsel*, seat of the Douglas-Home family. The grounds are open daily, dawn to dusk (donation), and include an Estate Exhibition Centre in an old farm by the loch.

   6m **Kelso** (5000 inhab. *ECl.* Wed. *Inf.* 66 Woodmarket. Easter–Sept), a compact market town at the confluence of the rivers Teviot and Tweed, has as its two main features its famed ruined abbey and its spacious, elegant Georgian square.

History. Known in the 12C as 'Calkou' (Chalk Hill), Kelso was never a fortified place, optimistically relying for its defence on its status as an abbey town, and, earlier, on the neighbouring great castle of Roxburgh. Nevertheless it was repeatedly sacked by the English, notably in 1522, 1544 and 1545, and also became an accepted assembly place for Scottish armies on their way south. James III was crowned here in 1460. In 1715 the Old Pretender was proclaimed James VIII in the main square, and in 1745 his son, retreating N, stayed here for two days.

Two minor curiosities merit a glance. One is a horseshoe set in the road in Roxburgh Street marking the spot where the Young Pretender's horse shed a shoe; the other, two lamps on Rennie's bridge of 1803, these being from London's Waterloo Bridge, modelled by Rennie on this Kelso bridge but demolished in 1935.

   As seen today, ***Kelso Abbey** (AM. Standard. Free) probably represents no more than the W end of what was one of the greatest of the Borders abbeys.

History. The original foundation was by Alexander I at Selkirk in 1113, but the monks (from Picardy) moved to Kelso when David I founded his abbey in 1128. For several centuries the abbey enjoyed great wealth and influence, its abbots at one time claiming precedence over even St. Andrews, but the end came in 1545, when Hertford, finding the place garrisoned, slaughtered the 100 defenders, including 12 monks, and razed the buildings. From 1649 to 1771, when the roof collapsed, the transept was used as parish church.

Architecturally the abbey as seen today—that is, what is left of the great church—is mixed Norman and Gothic EE, surviving being the W facade, transepts and tower and two bays of the nave. By far the most striking aspect is the facade of the NW transept, unaltered for 800 years. Here, mounting one above the other over the fine doorway, are an ornamental arcade and a gable with diamond patterning; two levels of Norman windows; a round window; and at the top two turrets with, between them, another gable. The tower was supported by four great arches, of which two remain.

   The massive earthwork with fragments of masonry just outside Kelso beside the Selkirk road (A699) is all that remains of *Roxburgh Castle*, below which once clustered the town of the same name, an important walled royal burgh which became so large that, as early as the 12C, some of its inhabitants had to be dispersed to the medieval equivalent of a satellite town near the site of the present village of Roxburgh 2m to the S. In 1460 the town and castle, both long in English hands, were being besieged by James II, who, however, was killed by the bursting of a cannon he was inspecting. A yew tree in the grounds of Floors Park (see below) marks the spot. When the Scots finally took Roxburgh, they wholly destroyed both castle and town.

At *Ferneyhill*, 1½m N of Kelso by B6461, an obelisk remembers James Thomson (1700–48), born at nearby Ednam and author of the words of 'Rule Britannia'.

B6352 wanders SE to *Town Yetholm* and *Kirk Yetholm*, twin villages divided by the Bowmont Water, the latter once noted as the home of the Scottish gypsies. Kirk Yetholm is also at one end of the Pennine Way, a 250m path running S into Derbyshire. The round can be continued on B6401 to *Morebattle*, 2m beyond which a minor road leads S past 14C *Cessford Tower.*

Kelso is left by A6089 which soon passes **Floors Castle** (Easter. May, June and Sept: Sun.–Thurs. July, Aug: Sun.–Fri., 11.30 to 17.30. Tel: 0573-23333. Fee), seat of the Duke of Roxburghe. Built by William Adam between about 1721–25, the mansion was added to and given most of its present aspect by W.H. Playfair in 1849. It was in the park that James II was killed (see above), a yew tree now marking the spot.

Although A6089 for the present remains the axis of this Rte, smaller roads can conveniently be chosen first to the W to visit Smailholm Tower followed by the mansion of Mellerstain, then to the E for Hume Castle.

*****Smailholm Tower** (AM. Standard. Fee) is 7m W of Kelso off B6404. Perched on an isolated green hillock with rocky outcrops beside a small loch, and with unspoilt all-round vistas, this must surely be the most satisfying of all the Borders towers, of which it is a typical and exceptionally well preserved 16C example. The interior construction can be readily enough understood, and a neat domestic touch is provided by a small privy with seat, window and niche for a lantern. Nearby Sandyknowe Farm, the home of Sir Walter Scott's paternal grandfather, was often visited by the poet, and Smailholm houses an exhibition on the theme of his 'Minstrelsy of the Scottish Border'.

*****Mellerstain House** (Easter. May–Sept: Sun.–Fri., 12.30 to 17.00. Tel: 057381-225. Fee), 7m NW of Kelso off A6089, was begun by William Adam in 1725 (he built both wings) and completed in 1778 by his son, Robert—an architectural partnership which resulted in what is arguably the most attractive 18C mansion in all Scotland. The elegantly proportioned front is approached through a park rich in superb and varied trees, while the rear overlooks contrastingly formal Italian terraced gardens below which the grounds slope to a lake. The interior, with exquisite Robert Adam ceilings and decoration, is a treasure-house of antique furniture, with work by Chippendale, Sheraton and Hepplewhite. There are two libraries, one accepted as among the finest of Adam's creations, and the notable collection of paintings includes works by Gainsborough, Allan Ramsay, Constable, Veronese, Bassano, Van Goyen and Nic. Maes.

Due NE across A6089, and prominent on a hilltop, stands the

dramatic if somewhat bogus outline of **Hume Castle** (key at reasonable hours from The Smiddy, Hume). Reaching back to the 13C and once the seat of the earls of Home, the castle fell to Cromwell in 1651, after which it was neglected until 1794 when the Earl of Marchmont not only patched up the ruin but for good measure added sham medieval battlements.

9m (from Kelso) **Gordon** recalls through its name a long if distant association with the Gordon family, who moved to NE Scotland in the 14C when Bruce presented the fortress of the Comyn at Huntly to his supporter, Sir Adam Gordon. *Greenknowe Tower* (AM. Standard. Free), on A6105 just W of Gordon, is a well preserved and warmly attractive fortified house of 1581, possibly unique for still having its iron gate.

9m **Lauder** is a quiet little royal burgh, known today for its *Church* (William Bruce, 1673), curious for having an octagonal spire and a ground plan in the shape of a Greek cross with the congregation occupying all four aisles. The 17C *Town Hall* was once the tolbooth, the cellar gaol of which remained in use as such until 1840. The town's annual Common Riding (July, Aug) is one of the older such, although it was discontinued from 1841 to 1911.

But for many visitors Lauder tends to be overshadowed by **Thirlestane Castle** (Mid May–June, Sept: Wed. and Sun. July and Aug: Daily, except Fri., 14.00 to 17.00, but grounds open 12.00. Tel: 05782-254. Fee), which has long been the home of the Maitland family, whose earlier tower is represented by a ruin some 2m E, and just S of the Kelso road (A697). It was during the time of this earlier castle, in 1482, that Archibald Douglas earned his title of 'Bell-the-Cat' by taking the lead in seizing and hanging from a bridge a group of humbly-born favourites of James III of whom he and the other nobles were jealous. Among those hanged was Cochrane, the king's architect. The present castle, notable for its sumptuous state rooms, represents stages of building between c 1595 and the 19C. In the grounds will be found the *Border Country Life Museum* (April–Oct: Mon.–Fri., 10.00 to 17.00. Sat. and Sun., 14.00 to 17.00. Nov–March: Mon.–Fri., 10.00 to 16.00. Tel: 05782-560. Fee), admirably illustrating, through both displays and demonstrations, the development of country life in these Borders lands from prehistoric to modern times.

A68 now ascends Lauderdale, beyond (*4m*) *Oxton* breasting the open western slopes of the Lammermuir Hills to reach (*4m*) *°Soutra Hill* (1130ft), a noted viewpoint sweeping Edinburgh and the Firth of Forth. Just N, up B6368, there hides a modest and roofless little stone building, possibly of the 15C or earlier, said to be *Soutra Aisle*, a hospice for the poor founded in 1164 by Malcolm IV.

The road now drops sharply, in some *4m* reaching minor roads which lead W for 2m to *°Crichton Castle* (AM. Standard, but open only Sat. and Sun. in Oct–March. Fee). Crowning a hillock on the steep flank of a quiet valley, Crichton is important as an example of how a once plain 14C tower-house grew into an elegant mansion with elaborate 16C Italianate decoration; earlier rooflines, walls and other details can be well seen, enabling much of the sequence of structural change to be appreciated. Originally owned by Sir William Crichton, chancellor to James II, the castle passed to the Bothwells, and it was the 5th Earl, who had visited Italy, who was responsible for the decorative work (c 1585) of which the most striking feature is a high wall with diamond bosses. Equally, if very differently striking is the contrast provided by the castle's grim oubliette. The building alongside the castle is also worthy of attention, for this was a defended stable, with an unusual trefoil gunport and a double-horseshoe door.—Nearby *Crichton Collegiate Church*, in continuous use since built in 1449, is known for its barrel-vaulting.

6m **Dalkeith**, which owes its origins to the 12C or earlier castle now represented by *Dalkeith Palace* (no adm.), is a place of some historical interest in the context of the 17C. Dalkeith has been a seat of·the Scotts of Buccleuch since the 2nd Earl purchased the castle from the Douglases of Morton in 1651. His surviving heiress daughter, Anne, had Cromwell's General Monk for a guardian at the time when, here at Dalkeith, he was plotting the Restoration. At the age of 12 Anne was married to Charles II's natural son James (he himself was only 14), later made Duke of Monmouth and Buccleuch and executed in 1685 after the failure of his Protestant rebellion against James VII/II. Later, in c 1700, Anne commissioned James Smith to build the présent palace around the old castle. Although the palace does not admit visitors, *Dalkeith Park* (Easter–Oct: Daily, 11.00 to 18.00. Nov: Sat. and Sun., 11.00 to 18.00. Fee) is open and offers woodland walks beside the river Esk, as well as nature trails, a Robert Adam bridge and, for the children, an adventure play area. In the town the *Church of St. Nicholas*, made collegiate in 1406, contains the tomb of Duchess Anne as also of the 1st Earl of Morton and his deaf and dumb wife Joanna, daughter of James I.

In a little under *4m*, and now in the outskirts of Edinburgh, A68 passes (right) a group of houses known as *Little France*, recalling that here was the home of some of Mary, Queen of Scots', French attendants. Here also, beside the road, is the stump of a tree planted by Mary in 1561.

Above stands ***Craigmillar Castle** (AM. Standard, but closed Thurs. afternoon and Fri. Fee), one of Mary's favourite residences and the place where, with or without her connivance, the murder bond was signed that Darnley, 'sic ane young fool and proud tirrane', should be 'put off by one way or uther'. The castle still impresses as a formidable pile, despite the modern development which has crept towards it. The heart is the L-shaped tower-house of about 1374, with, on the first floor, a great hall served by four stairways, the way in which one of these changes direction at a landing being one of the castle's several defensive features. The year 1427 saw the addition of the strong wall with round corner towers, the gunports in the NE tower being among Scotland's earliest examples of this kind of defence. Destruction in 1544 by Hertford was followed by the building of the three-storeyed E side courtyard buildings, this probably resulting in the Craigmillar Mary would have known. Interesting features are the kitchen with drain and service hatch, and a dungeon in which in 1813 a skeleton was found. The outer wall with its defended dovecot dates from about this same period, but the W courtyard buildings belong to the mid 17C when the emphasis was no longer on defence.

4m central **Edinburgh**, see Rte 18.

4   Carter Bar to Edinburgh via Jedburgh and Melrose

A68.—Much of this Rte runs with the general line of the Roman
Dere Street which, after leaving the Cheviots near Woden Law,
crossed the Tweed near Melrose and the large camp of Trimontium
(today Newstead) then ascended Lauderdale to reach the Firth of
Forth at Inveresk. After descending from Carter Bar this Rte crosses
the pastoral and wooded valleys of the Teviot and Tweed before
gradually rising with Lauderdale (see Rte 3).

SOME HOTELS. **Jedburgh**. *Glenbank*, Castlegate. Tel: (0835)
62258. *Jedforest Country House*, 3m S of Jedburgh on A68. Tel:
(08354) 274. **Newton St. Boswells**. *Railway*, TD6 0PW. Tel: (0835)
23797. **Melrose**. *Burts*, Market Square. Tel: (089682) 2285. *George
and Abbotsford*, High Street. Tel: (089682) 2308. **Earlston**. *White
Swan*, The Square. Tel: (089684) 283.

Total distance 60m.—*10m* **Jedburgh**.—*12m* **Melrose**.—*4m*
Earlston.—*6m* **Lauder**.—*28m* **Edinburgh**.

Carter Bar (1371ft), at the lofty SW end of the Cheviot range, is one
of the best known and scenically most exciting gateways into
Scotland. The Reidswire Stone here reminds of the Raid of Reidswire
of 1575, the last true Borders skirmish between the Scots and the
English, but somehow—and especially on a clear day when their
earthworks can be picked out—the Roman presence seems stronger.
Their great camp of *Ad Fines* spreads across lonely border moorland
6m to the E, and from it Dere Street started northward past unmistak-
able *Woden Law* (1388ft), with Iron Age and Roman earthworks, the
latter perhaps constructed as part of their training by the garrisons
at *Pennymuir* between Kale Water and Oxnam Water at the hill's
NW foot. And it is easy to get closer, for 2m N below Carter Bar a
minor road ambles E for 5m to a point where it crosses Dere Street.
Northward, from this point, there is no more than a track, but
southward a little road, actually named Dere Street, aims straight at
Woden Law, beside the road being clear traces of those Pennymuir
camps mentioned above.

Approaching Jedburgh, 1m S of the town, A68 passes the *Capon
Tree*, reputedly 1000 years old and perhaps once the local hanging
tree.

10m (from Carter Bar) **Jedburgh** (4000 inhab. *ECl.* Thurs. *Inf.*
Murray's Green. Easter–Nov), once known as Jedhart, is a royal
burgh of c 1300, most visited today for its abbey and Queen Mary's
House. Also of interest are the Castle Jail Museum and medieval
Canongate Bridge.

Jedburgh's history is essentially that of its abbey and castle, for both of which
see below.—Jedburgh Festival (Callants Festival) lasts over a period of two
weeks, usually in June–July.—'Jedhart Justice' was to hang a man first and try
him afterwards. The expression seems to have grown out of a single incident
involving a gang of thieves during the reign of James IV.—A 'Jedhart Staff', a
well-known Borders weapon, was an 8ft-long shaft with a head shaped as a
hook or an axe.

Jedburgh Abbey (AM. Standard, but closed Thurs. afternoon and
Fri. in Oct–March. Fee) survives as a mainly 12–15C red sandstone
ruin, standing above the Jed Water down to which once spread the

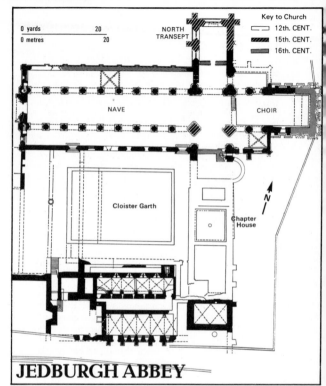

Key to Church
- ☐ 12th. CENT.
- ▨ 15th. CENT.
- ▬ 16th. CENT.

0 yards   20
0 metres   20

NORTH
TRANSEPT

NAVE

CHOIR

Cloister Garth

Chapter
House

N

JEDBURGH ABBEY

domestic buildings, reduced now to the foundations of the cloisters and the chapter house.

This has long been a Christian site. A 9C chapel gave place to the priory founded in c 1138 by David I for monks from Beauvais, this being raised to abbey status in 1147. In 1285 Alexander III was married here to Yolande, daughter of the Count of Dreux. Later the abbey suffered the usual Borders cycle of sacking, rebuilding and neglect, the worst destruction being by Hertford in 1544–45. After the Reformation part of the nave served as parish church until 1875.

The 12C Norman West Front is particularly fine, with, above the door, three gables, above these arcading and a large window, and, higher again, a 14C wheel-window. Beyond this doorway stretches away the length of the Nave of nine bays, one of the leading examples in Scotland of the Transitional period, features to note being the unbroken ranges of windows and the three stages or storeys. First there is a lofty main arcade resting on solid piers; next a triforium (where round arches enclose pointed arches), from which there would have been access to the space under the aisle roof; and, on top, the clerestory has pointed arch windows. On the S side of the nave there is another Norman door, with elaborate though worn exterior decoration (repeated in facsimile on a modern door farther W. The Choir rises to a triforium, in a semicircular arch embracing two smaller arches, and a clerestory above. The Tower, rebuilt in 1500, should be pictured as completed by a spire.

The *Castle Jail Museum* (Easter–Oct: Mon.–Sat., 10.00 to 12.00. 13.00 to 17.00. Sun., 13.00 to 17.00. Tel: 0450-73457. Fee), in Castlegate up the hill from the abbey and town centre, is on the site first occupied by Jedburgh's castle and later by the prison built here in 1825. This latter was designed to meet the requirements of the penal reform thinking of the early 19C, and the rooms have been imaginatively reconstructed to illustrate this prison period.

The *Castle*, roughly contemporary with the abbey, was one of five fortresses surrendered by the Scots to England under a treaty of 1174 as surety for the ransom of William the Lion after his defeat and capture at Alnwick. Later the castle became a favoured royal residence, and it was here, at Alexander III's wedding feast in 1285, that the appearance of a spectre was interpreted as a warning of early death; and correctly, because in the following year Alexander was thrown from his horse and killed. Later the castle became such a magnet for English attacks that the Scots demolished it in 1409.

When Mary, Queen of Scots, came to Jedburgh in 1566 for the assizes, she lived in what is now known as *Queen Mary's House* (Easter–Oct: Mon.–Sat., 10.00 to 12.00. 13.00 to 17.00. Sun., 13.00 to 17.00. Tel: 0835-63331. Fee), reached from High Street by way of Smith's Wynd. Built less than 20 years earlier, and thus a modern house, Mary chose it, or so it is said, because it was the only house in Jedburgh with indoor sanitation. It was from here that she rode in one day to Hermitage Castle and back—a good 40 miles in all—to visit the wounded Bothwell, on her return falling dangerously ill and nearly dying. The Queen's stuffy little room, and the even more cramped space in which her ladies, the four Marys, slept, can be seen. The house is also arranged as a museum with many relics, these including a death mask (restored); one of the very rare portraits (1565) of Bothwell; and Mary's watch, found 200 years after she had lost it in what is now known as the Queen's Mire, close to Hermitage.

Canongate Bridge (15C), one of the few medieval three-arch bridges still in use in Scotland, survives as something which readily conjures back the past. Mary almost certainly rode across these arches; the Young Pretender certainly did. Well received in Jedburgh, the latter lodged in a house in Castlegate.

A68 crosses the Teviot, in *4m* from Jedburgh reaching the intersection with B6400. At *Ancrum*, a secluded village immediately to the W, there is a 13C cross on the village green. Just E of the crossroads will be found the *Woodland Centre* (July, Aug: Sun.–Thurs., 13.00 to 17.30. Otherwise, between Easter and Oct, Sun. and Bank Holiday Mon. only. Tel: 0835-62201. Fee), a pleasant and original interpretation centre, the main theme of which is timber and the care and use of woodland. The *Waterloo Monument*, to the N on Penielheugh Hill (741ft), was erected by the Marquis of Lothian and his tenants shortly after the victory.

Ascending N, A68 in just over *2m* reaches the spot known as *Lilliard's Edge*, on Ancrum Moor, where in 1545 an English force, returning laden with booty from a raid, was attacked and defeated with great slaughter. The name perpetuates the memory of the legendary Maid Lilliard who fought here, her courage told in the spirited lines:

Fair Maid Lilliard lies under this stane
Little was her stature, but great was her fame:
Upon the English loons she laid many thumps,
And when her legs were cuttit off, she fought upon her stumps.

All the way since Jedburgh the Romans' Dere Street has been angling
in on the E, and at Forest Lodge, less than 1m N of Lilliard's Edge,
it merges with A68 which now enters what is sometimes known as
the 'Scott Country'. Centred on Sir Walter Scott's home at Abbotsford,
the district (quartered roughly by Selkirk and Galashiels and
Dryburgh and Melrose) has many associations with both Scott's life
and his works.—*2m* (from Lilliard's Edge) **St. Boswells** derives its
name from one Boisel, a prior of Old Melrose, a monastery founded
in the 7C within a loop of the Tweed 2m N of here, below what is
now known as Scott's View (see below).

*Dryburgh Abbey (AM. Standard. Fee) is reached by car by
following B6404 E from St. Boswells to cross the Tweed, and then
returning along the other bank. An alternative is to walk, using a
lane off A68 just S of Newtown St. Boswells and then a footbridge.
Within a lovely pocket of the river and amid handsome trees,
Dryburgh is of outstanding interest because of the exceptional
completeness of the 12 and 13C monastic buildings. Here, better
than at any other Scottish abbey, it is possible to get reasonably close
to the day-to-day life of the monks. The abbey church shelters the
tombs of Sir Walter Scott and of Earl Haig, the Allied commander
during the 1914–18 war.

History. On a site once occupied by the 6C sanctuary of St. Modan, the abbey
was founded in 1150 for Premonstratensians, probably by Hugh de Morville,
Constable of Scotland. In 1322, 1385 and finally in 1544 it was destroyed by
the English, after the last occasion never to be rebuilt. In about 1700 the abbey
lands belonged to the great-grandfather of Sir Walter Scott, but they soon
passed from the family who retained only the quaint right to 'stretch their bones'
there.

The *Church* is badly ruined, but the remains still include parts of the
nave, transepts and choir. Especially to be noted are the moulded W
door of the nave, with, strangely, a semicircular Norman arch despite
the date being as late as the 15C; and the processional doorway
(which, though Transitional, also has a semicircular arch) leading
from the nave into the cloister. The tombs of Scott and Earl Haig, as
also of members of their families, are by the N transept. From the S
transept a night stair, used for attending night worship, descends
from the remains of the dormitory which once stretched as an upper
floor along the length of the E side of the cloister.

The **Monastic Buildings* are for the most part on the E and S
sides of the cloister. Nearest the church is the vaulted Vestry (or
sacristy or library), later converted into a chapel dedicated to St.
Modan. Next comes the Parlour, or slype, the only place where the
monks were permitted to receive visitors. The Chapter House,
virtually intact and entered through a fine doorway with another
semicircular arch, was the main place of formal assembly. The room
is surrounded by a stone bench, the abbot occupying the E end with
its arcade, and the large openings on either side of the door enabled
the lay-brothers to listen to the discussions and readings inside. A
day stair beside the chapter house gave access to the dormitory. The
next room is the Calefactory, with a large fireplace and remains of

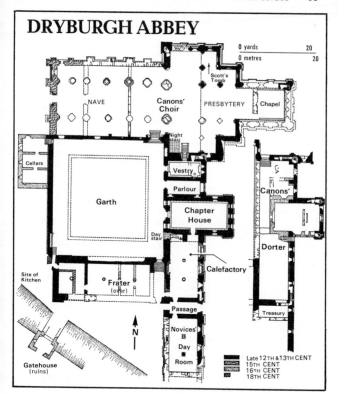

DRYBURGH ABBEY

elegant vaulting columns, best considered as the medieval monastic equivalent of an academic common room. Beyond, a passage leads into the Novices' Room, above which would have been their dormitory. The Refectory, the W·gable of which has a large rose window, stretches the length of the S side of the cloister, the kitchens being just beyond. Just S of the cloister are the remains of a gatehouse.

From the hill N of the abbey a huge statue (1814) of William Wallace surveys the scene.—B6356, beside the abbey, in 1m passes *Bemersyde*, seat of the Haigs since 1162 (no adm. Relics of Earl Haig are in Huntly House Museum, Edinburgh). The mansion's 16C tower-house can be seen from the road. Beyond is *Scott's View*, overlooking Old Melrose where once stood the monastery in which Boisel was a prior (see above), the Tweed and the Eildon Hills. Here, at this spot so loved by Scott, the cortege taking his body to Dryburgh paused a while.

Melrose is approached by A6091 out of Newtown St. Boswells, a road which curves across the NE slopes of the **Eildon Hills**—for challenging walking and a touch of prehistory and the Romans. For romantic legend, too, for Arthur and his knights lie below this turf in enchanted sleep, and it was here also that Thomas the Rhymer (see Earlston below) was given his power of prophecy by the Fairy Queen—an event marked, anything but romantically, by the *Rhymer's Stone* on the N verge of A6091 about a mile short of Melrose. The hills lift as three volcanic summits, the central one of which is the highest (1385ft, with an orientation table). The N summit shows traces of a prehistoric or Iron Age settlement and was probably also used as a signal station by the Roman garrison of Trimontium near today's Newstead (see below).

4m (from St. Boswells) **Melrose** (2000 inhab. *ECl.* Thurs. *Inf.* Priorwood Garden, near the Abbey. Easter–Oct) is a compact small town, known perhaps more for its abbey than for itself. Yet with its Cross of 1642 and several attractive old houses, some with carved stones pillaged long ago from the abbey, the town as such merits at least a glance. *Priorwood Garden*, near the abbey and with a visitor centre and picnic area, specialises in flowers suitable for drying (NTS. April, Nov–Christmas: Mon.–Sat., 10.00 to 13.00. 14.00 to 17.30. May, June, Oct: Mon.–Sat., 10.00 to 17.30. Sun., 13.30 to 17.30. July–Sept: Mon.–Sat., 10.00 to 18.00. Sun., 13.30 to 17.30. Donation). *Melrose Motor Museum* (April–Oct: Daily, 10.00 to 18.00. Nov–March: Sat., Sun., 10.00 to 17.00. Tel: 089682-2624. Fee), also near the abbey, is primarily concerned with the period between 1914 and the late 1930s.

*Melrose Abbey (AM. Standard. Fee) is of architectural and artistic interest for its elaborately carved stonework, and of possibly more popular and romantic curiosity as the burial place of Bruce's heart and of that legendary all-rounder, Michael Scot, the Wizard.

History. The abbey was founded in 1136 by David I for Cistercian monks from Rievaulx in Yorkshire and also as successor to the 7C monastery of Old Melrose. Alexander II was buried here in 1249, probably in the choir. Lying in the path of the English invasions, the abbey was repeatedly destroyed, notably in 1322 and 1385. Bruce restored Melrose in 1326, following the first English destruction, and bequeathed his heart to the abbey, but, apart from the short N wall of the sacristy, the present remains are a mixture of the rebuilding after 1385 together with work of the mid 15C. After Hertford's passage in 1545 there was no real restoration, and for a long time the ruins were pillaged as a source of building material.

What stands today represents the E part of the nave of the church, into which projects the unusual monks' choir; the transepts, with remains of the tower; the main choir; and much of the S nave aisle. As indicated above, perhaps the abbey's finest feature is its elaborate stonework, in particular the bosses and capitals of the columns with intricate and delicate foliage in which the leaves of curly kale stand out as typical of the skill and fancy of the Scottish stone carvers of the time.

The S Nave Aisle was flanked by a row of chapels, of which eight remain, each one the burial place of an important family. By comparison, the N Nave Aisle, because it abuts on the cloister, is narrow, undistinguished and without chapels. A stone screen separates the central aisle from the Monks' Choir, the elegant pointed arches of which are hidden on the N side by piers and arches erected in 1618 as part of conversion to a Presbyterian church, a role which it played until 1810. The Tower still preserves its two W piers, the capitals of the clustered shaft on the SW pier bearing particularly fine examples of curly kale carving. The S Transept provides the best window in the abbey, with five lights, 24ft high and 16ft wide, and a wealth of lovely tracery. A tablet in this transept mentions one John Morow as master mason (mid 15C). Off the N Transept opens the Sacristy, with its 12C N wall representing the oldest part of the whole abbey. An inscription on the threshold commemorates Joan, wife of Alexander II and sister of Henry III of England.

The Choir still shows its fretted stone roof, and the windows retain their early Gothic design of c 1387, though with later mid 15C tracery, perhaps the work of Morow. Below the E window is the traditional resting place of the heart of Robert Bruce, buried here when brought back from Spain whither Sir James Douglas had carried it on his way (cut short because of his death in battle) to the Holy Land. An embalmed heart found in a casket here in 1920 and reburied could well have been Bruce's. Also in the choir are Douglas tombs, and possibly that of Alexander II, while what may be the tomb of Michael Scot, the Wizard, is in a chapel off the S side of the choir.

North of the church are the Cloisters, the S walk of which has some good shallow arcading, while the earlier arcade on the E is also attractive. Excavation in 1921 exposed the whole ground plan and identified also the foundations of the chapter house (on the E) and other parts of the monastic buildings.—The *Abbey Museum* (across Cloisters Road) is housed in what was the Commendator's House, built in 1590 on the site of the abbot's palace but since much altered. Relics include material from Roman Trimontium, and in the museum area further foundations have been exposed, as also the course of the great drain.

MELROSE ABBEY

0 yards   30
0 metres   30

12TH CENT
13TH CENT
15TH CENT

N

Frater

Dorter (over)

Reredorter

Kitchen   Calefactory

Cloister lavatory

Parlour

Cloister Garth

Chapter House

Sacristy

1. Tomb of Michael Scot.
2. 'Curly Kale' Shaft.
3. Bruce's Heart.

North Transept

NAVE   Monks' Choir   Tower

3

2

1

Chapels   South Transept

Abbotsford House (Late March–Oct: Mon.–Sat., 10.00 to 17.00. Sun., 14.00 to 17.00. Tel: 0896–2043. Fee), Sir Walter Scott's flamboyant creation and home for the last 20 years of his life, is 2½m W of Melrose.

Scott bought the farm here in 1811, renaming it Abbotsford, because the monks of Melrose formerly crossed the river here. Five years later he added an armoury, dining room, study, conservatory and some bedrooms. In 1822 he demolished the old farmhouse, replacing it with the main block of today's Abbotsford. (The W wing and the entrance lodge were added after Scott's death.) When financial disaster overtook Scott, the house was presented back to him by his creditors, since when it has remained in the family, though sometimes through the female line.

Abbotsford, together with its park, is essentially Scott's personal achievement, a place which, however it may strike the modern visitor, was as much in sympathy with 19C taste as it reflected its builder's unfettered romantic imagination. A mock baronial complex of turrets and gables, Abbotsford is part original and part copied from elsewhere. The garden screen wall, for instance, reflects the cloister at Melrose, the porch that at Linlithgow Palace, and the library ceiling has designs from Roslin Chapel.

Today Abbotsford is a museum not only of Scott but also of the many and curious historical relics he so enthusiastically collected. The Study, surprisingly small and dark and with a restricted view, is little altered. The Library and the Drawing Room both offer views along the river. The former contains a bust of Scott (Francis Chantrey, 1820), a portrait of him by Raeburn, and oddities such as Napoleon's cloak-clasp, Rob Roy's purse, Burns's drinking glass and a lock of The Young Pretender's hair. The Armoury is a museum of Scottish and other weapons of various periods, these including Scott's own blunderbuss, Claverhouse's pistol and Rob Roy's sword; here also are an interesting contemporary portrait of James IV, and a bizarre painting of the head of Mary, Queen of Scots, made by Amyas Cawood the day following her execution. The Dining Room, with family portraits, is the room in which Scott died, his bed near the window within sight of the Tweed.—Outside, in the South Court, five medallions in the S wall are from the old Edinburgh Cross, pulled down in 1756; and, above the porch, there is a more macabre souvenir, the door of the upper floor of the Edinburgh tolbooth through which condemned prisoners emerged for execution.

Returning to Melrose, A68 can be reached by way of *Newstead*, close to the site of Rome's Trimontium, so called of course from the triple peaks of the Eildon Hills. Nothing visible remains, but an inscribed stone beside the road E of the village outlines the history of the camp.

4m **Earlston** was the home of Thomas Learmont (c 1220–97), known as Thomas the Rhymer, or True Thomas, because of his famous verse prophecies, a gift which he claimed to have received from the Fairy Queen (see Eildon Hills above). It is a measure of his fame that a stone on the church wall still records 'Auld Rhymer's race lies in this place', and that a small ruin, which may have been his tower home, continues to be known as Rhymer's Tower.

For (*6m*) **Lauder**, and for Lauder to (*28m*) **Edinburgh**, see Rte 3.

5   Canonbie (Carlisle) to Edinburgh via Hawick, Selkirk and Galashiels

A7 (alternative B6399 to Hawick).—As far as Selkirk, much lonely
open moor with heights approaching 2000ft. Included also along
this stretch are diversions such as Eskdale and the Ettrick and
Yarrow valleys, all providing a scenic mix of valley and upland
moor broken by afforestation. Between Selkirk and Edinburgh the
road ascends the Gala Water and touches the comparatively modest
Moorfoot Hills.

SOME HOTELS. **Canonbie**. *Riverside Inn*. Tel: (05415) 295.
Langholm. *Crown*, High Street. Tel: (0541) 80247. *Eskdale*, Market
Place. Tel: (0541) 80357. *Hawick*. *Elm House*, 17 North Bridge
Street. Tel: (0450) 72866. *Kirklands*, West Stewart Place. Tel: (0450)
72263. *Selkirk*. *County*, High Street. Tel: (0750) 21233. *Philipburn
House*. Tel: (0750) 20747. **Galashiels**. *Douglas*, Channel Street. Tel:
(0896) 2189. *Kingsknowes*, Selkirk Road. Tel: (0896) 3478.

Total distance 78m.—*7m* **Langholm**.—*22m* **Hawick**.—*11m*
Selkirk.—*6m* **Galashiels**.—*20m* **Borthwick Castle**.—*12m*
Edinburgh.

The border is 12m N of **Carlisle** (see 'Blue Guide England'), A7
initially following the line of a Roman road and crossing the Esk at
Longtown, just W of which is *Solway Moss*, scene of the defeat of
James V in 1542. The border is more or less marked by *Scotsdyke*,
the remains of an earth and stone wall defining the border (as agreed
in 1552) where it crosses between the Esk and Sark rivers (see also
Rte 7, Sark Bridge).
    Canonbie is 2m N of the border. From here there is a choice of
roads to Hawick, similar scenically and in distance: either A7 through
Langholm, whence Eskdale and the moors across to Ettrick can be
reached, or B6399 up Liddesdale, passing Hermitage Castle and
providing approaches to Border Forest Park.

Canonbie to Hawick via Langholm

2m Hollows Tower, also known as Holehouse and dating from the
16C, was one of the lairs of Johnnie Armstrong of Gilnockie, a
dashing Borders bandit who, despite a reputation for never molesting
a Scotsman, was nevertheless eventually taken by James V and
hanged near Teviothead (see below) together with some 36 companions.—*5m* **Langholm** (2500 inhab. *ECl*. Wed. *Inf*. Town Hall.
Easter–Oct) is a long, enclosed small town at the confluence of the
Esk, Ewes and Wauchope waters and of the roads which run with
their valleys. Historically it is known for the battle of 1455 in which
James II finally crushed the Douglases. The obelisk on a hill to the
E is a memorial to Sir John Malcolm, an 18C Indian administrator.

ESKDALE (B709), ascending NW out of Langholm—at first pastoral,
then forest, then sweeping upland moor—provides an ever-changing
scenic cut across to the Ettrick Valley, some 28m away. In 2m comes
the rather misleadingly named *Scottish Explorers' Museum* (Tel:
0541–80137. Fee), housed in a 19C mansion and showing curiosities
such as oriental carved coral, prehistoric North American Indian
artefacts, and a collection of African masks. Beyond, the road bends
sharply W, across the river here being *Burnfoot*, the home of that Sir

John Malcolm whose monument stands above Langholm. *Bentpath* comes next, with, 1m N opposite Westerkirk school, a memorial (1928) to Thomas Telford, born in 1757 near here. Beyond, B709 crosses the river before plunging into Castle O'er Forest to meet (in 2m) the White Esk, beside which are two groups of standing stones, first the battered stone circle known as the *Girdle Stanes*, then, just beyond, the *Loupin' Stanes*, a more scattered and shapless group which does, however include a small circle. From *Eskdalemuir*, some 13m now from Langholm, a track up the left bank of the river in 1m reaches *Raeburnfoot*, an important Roman fort on the road to Trimontium, while, in startling contrast beside B709 beyond Eskdalemuir, suddenly appears a *Tibetan Monastery*, complete with pagoda, prayer wheels and perhaps even a glimpse of a monk. Beyond *Eskdale Observatory*, an important meteorological station, the watershed is crossed at 1095ft, the road then dropping beside the afforested valley of Tima Water to reach Ettrick (see below).

From Langholm A7 ascends the Ewes Water and the Mosspaul Burn to (*10m*) *Mosspaul Hotel* before starting to descend to (*4m*) *Teviothead* with, in its churchyard, a memorial stone to the bandit Johnnie Armstrong, hanged by James V at Caernlanrig, ½m to the SW; the stone, set in the wall of the part of the cemetery across the road from the church, bears an inscription which leaves little doubt where local loyalties lay. Now dropping with the upper Teviot, A7 in *8m* reaches **Hawick**.

Canonbie to Hawick via Hermitage

B6399 ascends Liddesdale, to the E of which spreads the huge *Border Forest Park*, virtually the whole of which however is in England. The heart of the park can be reached by taking B6357 from just N of (*10m* from Canonbie) *Newcastleton*, this road reaching Saughtree and then curving away to the lovely expanse of man-made Kielder Water.

6m (from Newcastleton) ***Hermitage Castle** (AM. Standard. Fee), beside Hermitage Water and in bleak, lonely open plain, impresses as a grim place of defiant impregnability.

History. The original 13C castle belonged to the Soulis family, of unsavoury reputation and one of whom, William (the 'Wizard'), is said to have forfeited his lands in 1320 for conspiring against Bruce. The Douglases took Hermitage in 1341, and the following year the castle was the scene of the cruel fate of Sir Alexander Ramsay, whom Douglas starved to death, although the unfortunate but determined man survived for 17 days on corn trickling through from the granary above (the pit prison can still be seen). In 1492 the Douglases exchanged Hermitage for Bothwell Castle near Glasgow, and in 1566 it was fleetingly visited by Mary, Queen of Scots who, in residence for the assizes at Jedburgh, rode the 40 miles round journey to Hermitage and back in one day in order to visit Bothwell who had been wounded in a foray against the English. This ride is still remembered by the map entry 'Queen's Mire' 3m NW of the castle.

Much restored on the outside, today's ruin is mainly of the late 14C and comprises a keep and corner towers, joined by great arches at the E and W ends, the whole having a corbelled parapet. The SW tower was extended during the 15C. In the much ruined interior survive remains of the original Soulis 13C tower. Here, too, the bakehouse merits attention, while the curious may scramble above it to a lavatory shafting directly to the cesspit outside below.

Continuing N, B6399 skirts a hill known, because of its stone circle, as *Nine Stane Rig*, where, it is said, the cruel Lord Soulis was

boiled alive, though the more prosaic truth is that he died as a
prisoner in Dumbarton Castle. Beyond, and now in lonely countryside,
a patch of woodland is crossed (Wauchope Forest, a Scottish outrider
of Border Forest Park) immediately beyond which (*5m* from
Hermitage), at a spot called Robert's Linn Bridge, the road meets the
mysterious *Catrail*, a wide ditch and embankment which runs from
Peel Fell on the border NW to Borthwick Water and thence towards
Galashiels but the purpose of which must remain a matter for
individual guesswork.—*8m* **Hawick**.

Hawick (pron. Hoik. 16,000 inhab. *ECl.* Tues. *Inf.* Common Haugh.
Easter–Sept) is important as a main Scottish textile centre. Of early
Hawick all that remains, near the town centre, is the *Mote*, a high
mound which was once the base of a Norman defensive work and
later became the meeting-place of the Manor Court; and of 16C
Hawick there is just (merged with other building in High Street) a
tower which managed to survive the destruction of the town by the
English in 1570. The English were here a few years earlier, too, in
1514, when the local youths (callants) defeated a marauding force at
Hornshole, 2m E, and captured their banner. This skirmish is recalled
both by a monument in High Street and also annually as part of the
Common Riding pageantry (June).

It was in the predecessor of *St. Mary's Church* (1764; restored)
that in 1342 Douglas seized Sir Alexander Ramsay, carrying him off
to Hermitage and death by starvation in the pit. In the W outskirts
of the town are the grounds of *Wilton Lodge*, now a public park along
the banks of the Teviot. The estate originally belonged to the
Langlands, friends of Wallace, who is said to have visited here in
1297 and to have tethered his horse to a tree near the house (memorial
stone). Also outside the house stand the reconstructed remains of
Hawick's mercat cross, removed from the town in 1762. The house
is now *Wilton Lodge Museum* (April–Oct: Mon.–Sat., 10.00 to 12.00.
13.00 to 17.00. Sun., 14.00 to 17.00. Nov –March: Mon.–Fri., 10.00 to
12.00. 13.00 to 16.00. Sun., 13.00 to 16.00. Tel: 0450–73457. Fee),
exhibiting material relating to the knitwear industry, Borders history
and archaeology and natural history. *Trow Mill* (Mon.–Sat., 09.00 to
17.00. Sun., 10.00 to 17.00. Tel: 0450–72555. Free), 2m E on A698,
offers visitors the opportunity both to watch tweed being made and
to buy it. Opened in the 1750s as a meal-grinding mill powered by
water, Trowmill converted to textiles production in c 1880 but
continued to use water power until 1965.

11m **Selkirk** (5500 inhab. *ECl.* Thurs. *Inf.* Halliwell's House,
Market Place. Easter–Oct) sprawls over a hillside high above the
Ettrick river.

History. Selkirk was declared a royal burgh by David I in 1113, and it was here
in the late 13C that Wallace was proclaimed Guardian of Scotland. After
Flodden the town was burned by the victorious English. In 1645 Montrose slept
here (in West Port) the night before his disastrous defeat by Leslie at nearby
Philiphaugh.

The town centre is the dignified, triangular Market Place, where a
statue of Sir Walter Scott, county sheriff for 27 years, stands in front
of his spired Court Room. Here too is *Halliwell's House Museum and
Gallery* (April–Sept: Mon.–Sat., 10.00 to 12.00. 14.00 to 17.00. Sun.,
14.00 to 17.00. Tel: 0750–20096. Free), housed in a neat row of
restored 18C dwellings and devoted to local history. The Gallery

mounts changing exhibitions. At the other end of High Street there is a particularly fine statue, with African figures, of the explorer Mungo Park (1771–1806), born at nearby Foulshiels (see below), while a more martial memorial, with a virile standard-bearing man-at-arms, commemorates Flodden, whence of the 80 townsmen who fought only one returned. But he came back with honour and a banner, and the parading of the banner (shown in Halliwell's House Museum) is a highlight of Selkirk's Common Riding (June), with its many riders one of the Borders' most colourful, and celebrated for five centuries without a break.

From Selkirk tours can be made up the quietly lovely pastoral and moorland Ettrick and Yarrow valleys. Although each is described separately below, a circuit of c 30m is possible, at least in part, by using B709 between Tushielaw on the Ettrick and Gordon Arms Hotel on the Yarrow. This upland area was once the great Ettrick Forest, rich with game and secure refuge for Wallace, and perhaps also for Bruce, as well as for the Borders freebooters and indeed for any man on the run. In 1528 James V, with a retinue of, it is said, 12,000, hunted here (thieves, it appears, as much as game), but it seems also to have been he who later so increased the number of sheep that eventually the forest became the peaceful moor and downland hills that it is today. Both Ettrick and Yarrow were long the subject of ballads—which, in these valleys, tend to get confused with reality—and they also inspired poets such as Scott, Wordsworth and Hogg.

ETTRICK VALLEY (B7009. 17m to Ettrick). *Oakwood Tower* (16C), above the road on the left 4½m from Selkirk, is said to be successor to a 13C home of Michael Scot, the Wizard. On the hillside 1½m NW of Ettrick Bridge stands *Kirkhope Tower*, a lair of the freebooter, Wat of Harden, and perhaps the tower to which he brought his bride, Mary of Dryhope, the 'Flower of Yarrow' of ballad. *Tushielaw*, 7m farther W, was the home of another freebooter, Adam Scott, hunted down and hanged by James V during his foray of 1528. From here B709 climbs NW high across wild moorland to drop down to the Yarrow at Gordon Arms Hotel, while the valley road (now B709) continues SW to reach (in 2m) *Ettrick*, perhaps best known as the home of James Hogg (1770–1835), the poet called the 'Ettrick Shepherd' and protégé of Sir Walter Scott. A monument marks his birthplace and his grave is in the churchyard. From Ettrick B709 bears S to climb across the moors to Eskdale, while a smaller road accompanies the river towards its source.

YARROW VALLEY (A708. 17m to Tibbie Shiel's Inn on St. Mary's Loch). Below Selkirk the road crosses the Ettrick and bears W, here traversing the site of the battle of Philiphaugh (1645) at which Leslie decisively defeated Montrose. **Bowhill**, just beyond and across the river, has long been the home of the Scotts of Buccleuch. The present house (Tel: 0750-20732. Fee), started by the 3rd Duke of Buccleuch in c 1795, contains an outstanding collection of French furniture, as well as pictures by, amongst others, Leonardo da Vinci, Gainsborough, Reynolds, Claude, Canaletto, Guardi and Raeburn. There are also relics of the Duke of Monmouth and Sir Walter Scott. In the grounds there are nature trails and, for the children, an adventure woodland play area. Nearby *Newark Castle* (for entry

apply Bowhill), now a ruined 15C oblong tower-house, stands on the
site of an earlier royal hunting lodge. It was in the courtyard here in
1645 that Leslie shot in cold blood 100 of Montrose's supporters who
had been made prisoner at Philiphaugh.

Newark Castle can also be seen across the river from A708 at
Foulshiels, where beside the road are the remains of the cottage in
which the explorer Mungo Park born in 1771. From here the
road gently ascends beside Yarrow Water, leaving woodland for bare
country and reaching first *Yarrow*, with a church of 1640 and a bridge
(Deuchar) of 1653, and then *Gordon Arms Hotel*, from where B709
provides a remote moorland link across to Tushielaw in the Ettrick
valley. James Hogg must have known this crossroads well, for he
farmed unsuccessfully for nearly ten years (1821–30) at Mountbenger,
immediately N. In just over another 2m the E end of St. Mary's Loch
is reached at Dryhope, where *Dryhope Tower*, visible N of the road,
dates from c 1600 and, at that time four storeys high, was the home
of Mary, the 'Flower of Yarrow' (see also Ettrick Valley, Kirkhope,
above). *Tibbie Shiel's Inn*, on the spit separating St. Mary's Loch
from Loch of the Lowes, perpetuates the name of the lady who was
the innkeeper here for many years after 1823 (born in 1783, she lived
until 1878). Her inn was a favourite meeting-place of such men of
letters as Scott, Carlyle, Stevenson and James Hogg, the last of whom
now sits as a statue beside the road here.

For the motorist not wishing to retrace to Selkirk there are now two choices,
both scenically outstanding. One is to continue along A708 to cross the
watershed at 1100ft, beyond dropping steeply towards Moffat (see Rte 7), on
the initial descent passing *Grey Mare's Tail Waterfall* hurling itself 200ft down
a bare mountain cleft. This dark and remote country is under the care of the
National Trust for Scotland who maintain a path to the foot of the waterfall.—The
other choice is the minor road, surely one of the loneliest in southern Scotland,
which breaks away westward from St. Mary's Loch to hug Megget Reservoir
and climb to nearly 1500ft before—and with breathtaking views—winding
abruptly down to dark *Talla Reservoir* and the hamlet of *Tweedsmuir* (see Rte
7).

Leaving Selkirk A7 curves down to the confluence of the Ettrick and
Tweed, here crossing the latter, though B6360 along the right bank
should be taken if Abbotsford (see Rte 4), 2m from the bridge, is the
objective.

6m (from Selkirk) **Galashiels** (12,000 inhab. *ECl.* Wed. *Inf.* Bank
Street. Easter–Sept.), a long, rather grey town, was founded as a kind
of staging camp for pilgrims to Melrose; hence the name, meaning
Huts on the Gala Water. That Galashiels also played its part in the
constant struggle against the English is recalled by its arms, a fox
reaching for plums, the origin being a successful skirmish with a
body of English surprised when gathering wild plums. The annual
Braw Lads Gathering in June, though dating only from 1930, lacks
little in spirit.

Today Galashiels is known for its textile manufacture and as the
home of the internationally important Scottish College of Textiles,
and visitors interested in this field may visit the *Peter Anderson
Woollen Mill* (Oct–May: Mon.–Sat., 09.00 to 17.00. June–Sept:
Mon.–Sat., 09.00 to 17.00. Sun., 12.00 to 17.00. Tel: 0896-2091. Free).
Here not only can the manufacturing process of tweeds, tartans and
suchlike be followed, but the mill also serves as a museum of the
local past, both industrial and social.

A7 now accompanies the Gala Water, reaching (*7m*) *Stow*, where, beside A7 to the S of the village, there is a battered packhorse bridge of 1655, before climbing along the E flank of the modest and rather dull Moorfoot Hills.—*13m* *Borthwick Castle*, to the E of A7 at North Middleton, although not open to the public can be well seen from the outside. And the short diversion is worthwhile on two counts—architecturally because, built in c 1430, this castle with its twin towers and two wings is the strongest and most massive of all Scotland's tower-houses; historically because it was to Borthwick that Bothwell brought Mary for a brief and dramatic visit after their wedding. When almost at once the place was surrounded by their enemies, Bothwell slipped away to Dunbar and Mary, disguised as a page, followed two days later. The village of *Temple*, 3m W, is so named because this was the Scottish seat of the Knights Templar, suppressed in 1312; there survives a roofless 13–14C church.—*6m* (just beyond Eskbank) *Edinburgh Butterfly Farm* (April–Oct: Daily, from 10.00. Tel: 031–6634932. Fee) shows exotic free-flying butterflies from worldwide habitats.—*6m* central **Edinburgh**, see Rte 18.

6   Galashiels to Edinburgh via Peebles

A72 to Peebles. A703 to Edinburgh.—As far as Peebles along the largely wooded valley of the Tweed, A72 following the N bank while a smaller and quieter road follows the other. From Peebles northward, below generally bare rounded hills, with the Pentlands to the W and the Moorfoot Hills to the E.

SOME HOTELS. **Walkerburn**. *Tweed Valley*, EH43 6AA. Tel: (089687) 220. **Peebles**. *Park*, Innerleithen Road. Tel: (0721) 20451. *Peebles Hydro*, Innerleithen Road. Tel: (0721) 20602. *Cringletie House*, Eddleston. Tel: (07213) 233. **Roslin**. *Original*, Main Street. Tel: (031440) 2384.

Total distance 41m.—*11m* **Innerleithen (Traquair)**.—*6m* **Peebles**.—*13m* **Penicuik**.—*3m* **Roslin**.—*8m* **Edinburgh**.

A72 curves westward out of Galashiels, on the right at the curve, *2m* from the town centre, being *Torwoodlee House* (May–Sept: By appointment. Tel: 0896-2151. Fee), a small Georgian mansion of 1783 with Victorian modifications on an estate which has been the home of the Pringle family for approaching 500 years. *Torwoodlee Broch and Fort*, just N of the house, is one of southern Scotland's rare examples of this kind of structure and one also about which, unusually, a little seems to be known, or at any rate deduced. The native fort seems to have been built first, only however to be destroyed by the Romans during their first penetration in c 82. With the Roman withdrawal soon afterwards, Picts may have moved in from the N to build the broch, in which they seem to have stored Roman pottery and glass, perhaps abandoned at Trimontium. However, the Romans were back by 140 and seem soon to have destroyed the broch, perhaps also killing the woman whose skeleton was found here.—In another *2m* A72 reaches the Tweed and bears W, opposite across the river being *Ashiestiel*, the house tenanted by Sir Walter Scott for several years before moving to Abbotsford.—*5m* **Walkerburn**, where the *Scottish Museum of Wool Textiles*, adjacent to a large shop, has imaginative displays illustrating the rearing of sheep, how a weaver once lived and worked, dying and spinning, the origins of knitting and other themes. (Mon.–Fri., 10.00 to 17.00. Also, between Easter–Sept: Sat., 11.00 to 16.00. Sun., 14.00 to 16.00. Tel: 089687-281. Fee).—*2m Innerleithen.*

*Traquair House (Week before Easter–mid Oct: Daily, 13.30 to 17.30 but open from 10.30 July–mid Sept. Tel: 0896-830323. Fee), beyond the river 1m S of Innerleithen, claims to be the oldest continuously inhabited home in Scotland, and certainly the impression today is of a mature home rather than of a formal mansion. It was the residence of William the Lion, who held court here in 1209, and it is further claimed that 27 Scottish and English monarchs (including Mary, Queen of Scots, Darnley, and their baby, the future James VI/I) have visited here. The 2nd Earl is said to have betrayed Montrose's plans to Leslie before the battle at Philiphaugh and then denied Montrose entry after his defeat, the latter having ridden from Philiphaugh in a direct line across Minch Moor (1856ft). The 5th Earl, however, received the Young Pretender, and when the latter departed through the avenue's Bear Gates swore that they should not open again until a Stuart regained the throne; so, they remain closed. The house is largely of the 17C, but with a very ancient tower, and many relics are on view in its historic rooms and passages, which include a priest's room and escape stairway. Other attractions are an 18C brewhouse, still producing ale, five craft workshops and a maze.

Peebles may now be approached either by A72 N of the river, or by the pleasanter, quieter and wooded B7062 along the S bank, the latter passing *Kailzie Gardens* (Daily, 11.00 to c 17.30. Tel: 0721-20007. Fee), with a walled garden of 1812, greenhouses, etc., and, beyond, affording a pleasing view of Peebles across the river. The main road runs immediately S of *Glentress Forest*, with an information room and several trails, some of which visit forts and towers and reach the highest viewpoint in the Tweed valley.

6m (from Innerleithen) **Peebles** (6000 inhab. *ECl.* Wed. *Inf.* Chambers Institute, High Street. Easter–Oct) is a country town set among gentle wooded hills on a broad stretch of the Tweed.

History. Legend insists that St. Mungo visited Peebles in the 6C. Be this as it may, it is known that its castle, now vanished, was a favourite hunting lodge of the early Scottish kings, and particularly of Alexander III, and that David II granted royal burgh status in 1367. More than once sacked by the English, Peebles was later occupied by Cromwell in 1649 and, briefly, by the Young Pretender in 1745. The home of the Queensberry family, it was the birthplace of 'Old Q' (1725–1810), the notorious gambling 4th Duke, as also of the publishers, William and Robert Chambers, born here in 1800 and 1802.

The Beltane Festival (June) is probably of Celtic origin. Revived in 1899, it now lasts a week, the highlights being the Common Riding and the crowning of the Beltane Queen.

Only fragments of the old town wall remain, near the former railway station. In High Street the *Tweeddale Museum* (Mon., Tues., Thurs., Fri., 09.00 to 19.00. Wed., 09.00 to 17.30. Tel: 0721-20123. Free), with material of local interest, is housed in the Chambers Institute, once the town house of the Queensberry family. The *Tweed Bridge*, though widened at least twice, is basically of the 15C, but Peebles's oldest site is the ruin of *Cross Kirk* (AM. Standard. Free), on the W edge of the town. Built by Alexander III in the 13C, the church was associated with a Trinitarian friary, the foundations of which can still be seen.

Neidpath Castle (Easter–mid Oct: Mon.–Sat., 10.00 to 13.00. 14.00 to 18.00. Sun., 13.00 to 18.00. Tel: 08757-201. Fee), 1m W of Peebles on A72, stands dramatically amid woods on a green hillock immediately above the N bank of the Tweed. Built through the 13–15Cs, and with later additions, this was the stronghold first of the Frasers and then of the Hays. The castle held out for Charles II, but the old tower, which had only recently been raised a storey, was soon battered by Cromwell's cannon and the castle surrendered after a long siege. Later, in 1686, Neidpath was bought by the 1st Duke of Queensberry, whose worthless successor, 'Old Q', was denounced in a sonnet by Wordsworth as a 'degenerate Douglas' because he cut down the timber. For today's visitor perhaps Neidpath's main interest lies in the way in which it developed from grim fortress complete with pit prison into a (for the times) comfortable 17C residence.

At *Lyne*, 3m W of Neidpath, there are the remains of a Roman camp, contained within a loop of A72 immediately E of the river bridge. Belonging to the first foray into Scotland, the camp was built in c 84 but survived only until 117. In the tiny church of Lyne (c 1645) there are a contemporary pulpit and two good canopied pews.

From Peebles this Rte continues N by A703 up the valley of the Eddleston Water. The road can either be taken direct out of Peebles, or, if Lyne has been visited, joined at Eddleston, the minor cross-country road to which affords a good view across the valley to the earthworks of the large Iron Age fort of *Milkieston Rings.—13m* (from Peebles) **Penicuik**, below the Pentland Hills, marks the S limit of the Edinburgh conurbation. Here the *Edinburgh Crystal Works* (Mon.–Fri., 09.00 to 11.15. 13.00 to 15.30. But first telephone 0968-75128. No children under 10. Fee) arrange conducted tours for visitors interested in the glassmaker's craft and, in particular, the production of high-grade crystal.

3m ***Roslin (or Rosslyn) Chapel** (April–Oct: Mon.–Sat., 10.00 to 17.00. Tel: 031-4402159. Fee), to the E of A703, houses within its comparatively small space the most lavish, most intricate and in its themes most intriguing stone carving in Scotland, if not in Britain.

History. Founded in 1446 by William Sinclair, 3rd Earl of Orkney, the chapel was made collegiate in 1521. It was the burial place of the Sinclairs, reputedly interred in full armour until 1650 when the widow of that year broke the ancestral custom, 'thinking it beggarly to be buried in that manner'. The chapel was damaged by the Edinburgh mob in 1688, partly repaired during the 18C, and thoroughly restored in 1862 by the Earl of Rosslyn for Episcopalian use.

Architecturally the chapel represents the choir of a church of which the nave was never built and the transepts only begun. The central aisle, of five bays, is separated from the side aisles by clustered columns, all with extravagantly carved capitals. It is barrel-vaulted with transverse ribs, and the roof of each bay is worked with a different flower. The side aisles are crossed by transoms covered on both sides with elaborate bas-reliefs. On one are the Seven Deadly Sins and the Seven Cardinal Virtues; on another is a Dance of Death; on a third the opinion 'Forte est vinum, fortior est rex, fortiores sunt mulieres, super omnia vincit veritas'.

The *Prentice Pillar, entwined by particularly complex flowers and foliage, is at the E end of the S aisle. The not very original story is that the pillar was carved by an apprentice in the absence of his

master, and that the latter, on his return, killed the apprentice in a
fit of jealousy. The story is rounded off by the suggestion that the
three heads at the end of the nave are those of the apprentice, his
master and his sorrowing mother.

At the E end of the N aisle a slab in the pavement showing a
knight in armour with a dog at his feet is said to represent the founder
of Roslin Castle, but is probably of later date. This story tells that Sir
William Sinclair wagered his lands against the lands of Pentland that
two of his hounds would pull down, before it reached a certain burn,
a deer that had often escaped the royal huntsmen. The deer was
killed exactly at the burn and Robert Bruce at once awarded the
estate to Sinclair. In gratitude Sir William built the church of St.
Katherine in the Hopes, now drowned beneath Glencorse reservoir
in the Pentlands.

Behind the altar, a Lady Chapel shows carved pendants descending
from the central ribs. At the SE angle of the choir steps descend to
a chamber projecting beyond the E end of the chapel. The altar and
piscinae show that this was a chapel, while the fireplace and other
secular conveniences suggest use also as a vestry or perhaps priest's
room.

Roslin Castle (apply to the caretaker), below the chapel to the S
and perched on the edge and against the face of a cliff overhanging
the North Esk, was perhaps built by an earlier Sir William Sinclair
than the founder of Roslin Chapel; perhaps, even, it was that Sir
William who earned his lands from Bruce by means of the wager
described above. More certain is that the keep was enlarged by the
founder of the chapel. Destroyed by Hertford in 1544, the castle was
gradually restored and converted to a 16–17C fortified house, and it
is this rebuilding that is most in evidence today. Of the original little
remains, bar some sections of 14C wall, and rooms, dungeons and
passages part wedged into the cliff. One intriguing feature is an
escape slide from the lower part of the castle to below the water level
in the moat.

3m Burdiehouse is thought to derive its name from 'Bordeaux
House', a settlement of the French attendants of Mary, Queen of
Scots.—*5m* central **Edinburgh**, see Rte 18.

7   Gretna to Edinburgh via Lockerbie and Moffat

A74 to Lockerbie. A709 to Lochmaben. B7020 to Beattock (Moffat).
A701 to Broughton. B7016 to Biggar. A702 to Edinburgh.—As far as
Lockerbie a rather dull and busy main road, followed, after
Lochmaben, by a smaller parallel road a mile or two to the W of the
main road. Beyond Moffat, a climb to the watershed at 1330ft,
followed by moorland down the valley of the upper waters of the
Tweed. North of Biggar A702 runs below the bare Pentland
Hills.—*Note*: A74 is a dual-carriageway trunk road and as such
bypasses the places along it mentioned below. Care must therefore
be taken to choose the relevant exits.

SOME HOTELS. **Gretna Green**. *Royal Stewart Motel*. Tel: (04613)
210. **Ecclefechan**. *Kirkconnel Hall*, DG11 3JH. Tel: (05763) 277.
Moffat. *Ladbroke Mercury Motor Inn*, Church Street. Tel: (0683)
20464. *Moffat House*, DG10 9HL. Tel: (0683) 20039. **Biggar**. *Hartree
Country House*. Tel: (0899) 20215. **West Linton**. *Medwyn House*,
Medwyn Road. Tel: (0968) 60542.

Total distance 89m.—*15m* **Lockerbie**.—*4m* **Lochmaben**.—*14m*
Moffat.—*28m* **Biggar**.—*12m* **West Linton**.—*16m* **Edinburgh**.

The bridge over the river Sark marks the border as agreed in 1552.
Prior to this the tract between the Sark and Esk rivers, roughly 8m
by 4m, was simply known as the Debatable Land, the lair of Borders
freebooters. *Gretna* is on the border, but it is **Gretna Green**, just
beyond, that is instantly associated with elopements and anvil
marriages at the smithies. Today the *Old Smithy* (Reasonable hours.
Tel: 0671–2549. Fee), immediately N of A74, has a museum and
marriage room.

For a long period English people seeking secret marriages had to resort to
London's Fleet Prison where imprisoned clerics, having nothing to lose from
breaking a law which was in any case ill defined, were happy to oblige for a
fee. A law of 1573, however, required banns, a licence and marriage in a church,
so from then on couples had to go to Scotland where marriages by declaration
before two witnesses were legal. At Gretna Green the ceremony was performed
by the blacksmith, the ferryman, the tollgate keeper or almost anyone else
convenient. After 1856 immediate marriage by declaration became illegal and
one of the parties had to have a residential qualification, and in 1940 marriage
by declaration ended altogether.

3m **Kirkpatrick Fleming**, where signs direct to *Bruce's Cave*
(Reasonable hours. Tel: 04618–285. Fee), in which Bruce was hidden
for about three months by Irving of Bonshaw, then owner of the
adjacent house from which there was a passage to a small tower
above the cave. At that time the only access was by swinging down
by rope over the cliff, but today's visitor has a path. Whether it was
here, or on Rathlin in Ireland, or at a choice of other places, that
Bruce took new heart from watching the persistence of a spider must
be a matter of personal judgement, but, Bruce apart, this cave
half-way down the cliff face is interesting for having been hollowed
out by prehistoric men whose tools have been found by the river
below.—*3m Kirtlebridge*, 1m short of which stands the *Merkland
Cross*, a 9ft-high cross of 1494 believed to have been set up to
commemorate the death of a Maxwell in battle.
  3m **Ecclefechan** was the birthplace in 1795 of Thomas Carlyle, the
essayist and historian. The *'Arched House'* (NTS. Easter–Oct:
Mon.–Sat., 10.00 to 18.00. Fee), in which he was born (built by his
father and uncle, both master masons), is now a museum with letters
and relics. His tomb is in the churchyard. *Hoddam Castle*, 2m SW, a
mainly 15C Maxwell stronghold, stands below Repentance Hill (with
a watchtower), a name said to commemorate the remorse of a Lord
Herries for having pulled down a church in order to build the castle.
An alternative story is that he repented for having thrown his
prisoners overboard during a storm while returning from a sea raid
on the English coast. *Blatobulgium*, 2m E, was a Roman station
occupied with breaks from 80 to 180; the visible remains (virtually
crossed by a minor road leading S out of Middlebie) date from c 152,
after the construction of the Antonine Wall.
  Between Ecclefechan and Lockerbie A74 runs below *Burnswark*

(920ft), scarred from summit to foot by a confusion of earthworks representing a native fort and Roman camps. The approach is by a small road from the S (off B725) which, deteriorating into a track, reaches the base of the hill more or less at the point at which the Romans' road angled NW. It is thought that the Romans may have besieged the fort, afterwards using Burnswark, or Birrenswark as it is sometimes called, as a kind of battle-practice area. Some eight centuries later, in 937, a greater battle may have been fought here, for this place is one of many claiming to be the site of the battle of Brunanburh at which the English King Athelstane decisively defeated an army of Scots, Norsemen and Irish.

6m **Lockerbie**, a small market town important since the 17C for its lamb fairs, is historically notorious as the focus of bloody feuding between the Maxwells, who held the lower end of Annandale, and the Johnstones who controlled the central reaches. So savage indeed was the fighting and the feeling that the Johnstones adopted the custom of slashing the faces of defeated Maxwells, a practice which became known as the 'Lockerbie Lick'. Much of this feuding took place beside the Dryfe Water which angles down from the NE to join with the Kinnel Water and flow through a sandy, marshy tract to the N of A709 between Lockerbie and Lochmaben. Here in 1593 the Johnstones decisively defeated the Maxwells (the latter losing 700 men including their chief) in revenge for the burning by the Maxwells the previous year of the Johnstones' Lochwood Tower (see below). And here, too, it is said, a lady of the Johnstones, while pretending to surrender, brained a Lord Maxwell with her castle key.

Approaching *(4m)* **Lochmaben**, A709 skirts the N shore of Castle Loch with, on a promontory on the S shore, *Lochmaben Castle* (Reasonable hours. Free), the early 14C successor of a castle of the Celtic-Norman De Brus (Bruce) family in which Robert Bruce may have been born (but see also Turnberry, Rte 15). The huge castle, once a place of great importance and strength covering some 16 acres and standing within four encircling defensive layers, was a favourite residence of James IV and was also visited in 1565 by Mary, Queen of Scots, and her husband Darnley. Castle Loch is only the largest of a group bordering this quiet, small town in which, in the main street, a statue of Bruce recalls a more violent past. *Rammerscales* (Easter, May and Spring holiday periods. Summer, June or July–Aug: Tues.–Thurs., 14.00 to 17.00. Also some Sun. Tel: 038781-361. Fee), 2½m S of Lochmaben on B7020, is a manor house begun in 1760 and today offering modern works of art and, in the park, woodland walks. The house was built for Dr James Mounsey, some-time physician to the tsarina of Russia.

The **Forest of Ae**, some 7m NW of Lochmaben, forms a large irregular triangle measuring roughly 7m from N to S and the same from E to W. The map shows a scatter of intriguing names, such as Souter's Grave, Bruce's Well, King's Well, Glenae Tower and, at the SE corner of the forest, Wallace's House, said to be the ruin of a tower held by Wallace in 1297. *Ae Village* is half-way along the forest's S fringe, just over 1m N of here being a FC parking and picnic area from which start two forest walks.

B7020 followed N in *6m* reaches the minor crossroads of *Springwells*, 1m E of which on A74 the name Johnstonebridge recalls those who once held power here.—*3m Lochwood Tower*, just W of a crossroads and dating from the 15–16C, was long the principal centre of the Johnstones, and it was its destruction by the Maxwells in 1592 that

led to the bloody Johnstone revenge beside the Dryfe in the following
year (see above). Abandoned by the Johnstones in 1710, Lochwood
has since been partially rebuilt. Immediately N of the tower there is
a 12C motte. *4m* **Beattock**, where Rte 10 continues NW on A74 while
this Rte takes A701 due N.

1m **Moffat** (2000 inhab. *ECl.* Wed. *Inf.* Church Gate. Easter–Oct),
lying well clear of A74 with its heavy traffic, is a quiet small town,
probably best known for its main street, notable for being the broadest
in Scotland, for the trees which break the street's centre line, and for
the Colvin Fountain which with its pleasing figure of a ram
emphasises the long-standing importance here of sheep farming. But
Moffat was perhaps better known during the 18C when its sulphur
spring gave it the status of minor spa, visited by, for instance, Hume,
Boswell and Burns. And it was during the 18C, too, that James
Macpherson lived here, working as a tutor in Moffat House (now a
hotel) and in 1759 publishing his controversial translation of the
Ossianic fragments. A708 penetrates NE up the dark glen of Moffat
Water to reach (10m) *Grey Mare's Tail* waterfall (see Rte 5, Yarrow
Valley).

Beyond Moffat A701 climbs N to reach (*6m*) a sharp loop in the
road which here skirts the precipitous rim of the **Devil's Beef Tub**,
so named because it was in this vast, gloomy hollow which forms the
head of Annandale that the Johnstones hid the cattle they had lifted
in raids on their neighbours, notably the Maxwells. In 1746, it is said,
a follower of the Young Pretender here escaped his guards by diving
into the Beef Tub's mists, but the roadside stone near here recalls
one who was less fortunate, John Hunter, who in 1685 was shot as
a Covenanter and whose body now lies in the churchyard at
Tweedsmuir. About 1m farther on there is another memorial, this
one at the spot where in 1831, and in a blizzard, the mail coach lost
the road and overturned, killing both the driver and his companion.

A short way beyond, the road breasts the watershed with, just to
the E, *Tweed's Well* (1500ft), the source of the Tweed, then, accompanied now by the quickly maturing stream, begins to fall to
(*10m*) the hamlet of *Tweedsmuir*. From here it is just 1m SE, and a
very worthwhile diversion, to *Talla Reservoir*, a long artificial loch
filling a sombre narrow cleft of a valley overhung by steep bare
mountains gashed by rocky corries. The small road skirting the N
shore of the reservoir scrambles steeply through remote and wild
country to drop down to St. Mary's Loch (see Rte 5, Yarrow
Valley).—*6m* (from Tweedsmuir) *Rachan Mill*.

B712, leading E, almost at once crosses the Tweed at a spot called Merlindale,
one of the many legendary sites of Merlin's grave but one strengthened in its
claim by Thomas the Rhymer who foretold that 'when Tweed and Powsail meet
at Merlin's grave, England and Scotland shall one monarch have'. And, it
seems, on the day of the coronation of James VI/I, the Tweed did here overflow
into the little Powsail stream. *Tinnis Castle*, just beyond and reached by a short
path, is the ruin of an early 16C stronghold of the Tweedies. Two miles E again
are *Dawyck House Gardens* (Easter–Sept: Daily, 10.00 to 17.00. Fee), with rare
trees and shrubs and woodland walks. A chapel in the grounds was designed
by William Burn.

The Tweed now curves away eastwards while this Rte continues N
for just over *1m* to reach **Broughton** in which is the *John Buchan
Centre* (Easter–mid Oct: Daily, 14.00 to 17.00. Tel: 0899-21050. Fee).
Housed in what was the United Free Church, the centre is devoted

to this distinguished Scottish statesman (1875–1940) who as John Buchan thrilled a generation and more with his gripping fiction, and then, as the 1st Lord Tweedsmuir, went on to become Governor General of Canada.

At Broughton this Rte bears W along B7016 for (*5m*) **Biggar** (2000 inhab. *ECl.* Wed. *Inf.* Main Street. May–Sept), where, thanks in large part to the vigour of the Biggar Museum Trust, the attractions awaiting the visitor well exceed what might be expected of a town so relatively small. First there is the *Gladstone Court Museum* (Easter–Oct: Mon.–Sat., 10.00 to 12.30. 14.00 to 17.00. Tel: 0899-21050. Fee), in which the visitor can wander around the shops, a bank, a schoolroom, a telephone exchange, a library and much else of the 19C. Nearby, in Burn Braes, *Greenhill Covenanters' House* (Easter–mid Oct: Daily, 14.00 to 17.00. Tel: 0899-21050. Fee), once a sadly neglected 17C farmhouse, decaying some 10m away from Biggar, was rescued, re-erected and restored here to serve as a museum of local life during the 17C, some emphasis being placed on Covenanting times. Also nearby, the *Moat Park Heritage Centre* (for opening times apply Gladstone Court), occupying a now redundant church, is, as its name implies, a museum of local history, this embracing that of the Albion Commercial Vehicle Company, the archives of which (including some 164,500 job sheets dating from 1899) are in the care of the Biggar Museum Trust. Lastly there is the *Gasworks Museum* (open on several special days in summer, 11.00 to 17.00. Tel: 031-225 7534, Dept. of Technology. Free), site of the Biggar Gas Light Company which served the town from 1839 to 1973. Now classified as an Ancient Monument and operated as an outstation of Edinburgh's Royal Museum of Scotland, the buildings (essentially major reconstruction of 1914) serve as a museum of the gas industry.

Beside the *Church of St. Mary*, the last pre-Reformation foundation in Scotland (by Lord Fleming, 1546), are the graves of Gledstanes or Gladstones, ancestors of William Gladstone, the statesman, whose grandfather left Biggar for Leith in c 1756. Only one small tower remains of *Boghall Castle* (½m S), one time seat of the Flemings. On A72, 1½m SW of Biggar, there is a particularly good motte.

Generally following the course of a Roman road, A702 in *12m* arrives at **West Linton** below the SE slopes of the Pentland Hills. Although today something of a lost little place, West Linton was once the rough and lively gathering place for drovers accompanying their herds across the Pentlands' pass of Cauld Stane Slap (1500ft), a period celebrated today by the annual Whipman festivities in June. But West Linton was also once famed for the skill of its masons, two interesting examples of whose work survive, both associated with the Gifford family. *Lady Gifford's Well*, with the lady's figure on top, was carved in 1666, while, roughly opposite, a curious bas-relief (1660 and 1678) on a house shows figures representing 'the six progenitors of James Gifford, his awne portract and eldest sone'.

A702 continues NE immediately below the **Pentland Hills**. Running for some 16m SW from Edinburgh, these hills are four to five miles wide and, with their streams and reservoirs, many signed paths and wide views, offer some exhilerating upland walking. The highest point is Scaldlaw (1898ft), and the higher ground generally is easily reached either by car to Castlelaw, by various paths on foot, or by means of the chairlift at Hillend.

The more gradual and less interesting W slopes can be seen from A70, the direct road between Edinburgh and Lanark. Along this road, at Balerno, 8m from Edinburgh, the garden of *Malleny House* (NTS. May–Sept: Daily, 10.00 to dusk. Fee) is best known for its shrub roses. The house (no adm.) dates from c 1635.

6m (from West Linton) *Silverburn*, just beyond which a path climbs between Scaldlaw and Carnethy Hill to reach Loganlea Reservoir, thence dropping to Balerno and Malleny House, some 6m from Silverburn.—*2m* The name *Rullion Green*, a farm off the left of the road, recalls the battle here of 1666 at which General Tam Dalyell (See Rte 9, The Binns) decisively defeated the Covenanters who were marching on Edinburgh. Less than a mile beyond, a small road ascends to *Glencorse Reservoir*, the water of which covers the ancient church of St. Katherine in the Hopes, perhaps built by Sir William Sinclair in gratitude for his successful wager with Bruce (see Rte 6, Roslin Chapel). Beyond, again, another small road is the approach to *Castlelaw* (AM. Standard. Free), an Iron Age hill fort of three concentric ramparts, within which there is an earth-house.—*4m* (from Rullion Green) *Hillend*, with the longest dry-ski slope in Britain and a chairlift (open to non-skiers) to a point offering views over Edinburgh.—*4m* central **Edinburgh**, see Rte 18.

8   Edinburgh to Glasgow via Bathgate

There are four main approaches to Glasgow from Edinburgh, these being, from N to S:

1. Via Linlithgow and Falkirk. See Rtes 9 and 22.

2. Via Bathgate. Described below as this Rte 8. (A8. A89).

3. Motorway M8. Of no interest.

4. Via Mid Calder (A71). The few places of interest are included below as diversions from this Rte 8.

SOME HOTELS. **Uphall**. *Houston House*, EH52 6JS. Tel: (0506) 853831. **Bathgate**. *Golden Circle*, Blackburn Road. Tel: (0506) 53771. **Airdrie**. *Staging Post*, Anderson Street. Tel: (02364) 67525.

Total distance 40m.—*10m* **Broxburn**.—*8m* **Bathgate**.—*22m* **Glasgow**.

Edinburgh is left by A8 through *Corstorphine* (see Rte 18), 1m beyond which, at Gogar, a road drops 1m S for *Suntrap* (NTS. Garden: Daily, 09.00 to dusk. Advice Centre: March–Oct: Mon.–Fri., 09.30 to 17.00. Sat. and Sun., 14.30 to 17.00. Nov–Feb: Mon.–Fri., 09.30 to 17.00. Fee), a gardening advice centre catering primarily for owners of small gardens. After passing, both to the N, *Edinburgh Airport* and then *Ingliston*, the latter the site of the Royal Highland Show and with an Agricultural Museum (May–Sept: Mon.–Fri., 10.00 to 16.00. Tel: 031-332 2674. Free), A8 crosses the motorway to reach (*10m* from central Edinburgh) **Broxburn**. From here B8020, followed by a minor road E just S of Winchburgh, reaches *Niddry Castle* (no adm. to interior), now only a forlorn and blackened keep, but once the setting for a scene hard to picture in today's drab setting. For it was to this castle of Lord Seton's that Mary, Queen of Scots, rode after her adventurous escape from Loch Leven, the story being that next morning she came out to receive the acclaim of the local people with her long auburn hair flowing undressed in the breeze, so eager was she to show herself.

2m **Uphall**, from where A767 runs 3m S to **Mid Calder** (on A71) with a church in which the choir dates from 1541. It was at *Calder House* that the first Protestant Communion was administered by John Knox in 1556 (see picture in John Knox House, Edinburgh), and here also Chopin rested during his tour of Britain in 1848. *Almondell Country Park*, 1m E on A71, is a wooded and riverside country park with a network of paths and bridges built by Enterprise Youth, and a visitor centre with aquaria. *Limefield House*, 3m SW on the E edge of West Calder, was the home of J. 'Paraffin' Young, son of a Glasgow joiner, who (at Bathgate, see below) established the world's first commercial oil works, using oil-shale and starting an industry (Young's Paraffin Light and Mineral Oil Company) which sold oil lamps all over the world.

6m (from Uphall) **Bathgate**, a pleasantly sited small industrial town, was the birthplace of James Simpson, pioneer of anaesthesia, who first used chloroform in 1847, and the place also in which in 1851 James 'Paraffin' Young established his first works. Immediately N of the town rise the Bathgate Hills (1017ft, and rewarding for their views) which have to be crossed to reach two objectives of very real interest—Cairnpapple Hill and Torpichen Preceptory.

*Cairnpapple Hill (AM. Standard, but closed Mon. morning and throughout Oct–March. Fee), 2m N of Bathgate, is reached by B792 and a minor road leading off NE at Ballencrief Toll just clear of Bathgate. Here, on this isolated open hill with superb all-round views, primitive man worshipped his god or gods and buried his dead over the immense span of perhaps 2500 years, from around 2500 BC to the 1C AD. Five archaeological phases have been identified. Ritual of some probably never-to-be-known form, but probably associated with cremation and observed within a henge with boulders, ditch and bank, seems to have been the primary purpose of the Neolithic people of the first two phases, say 2500 to 1650 BC. Then in the third phase (Bronze Age, c 1600 BC) a large cairn was erected and the emphasis shifted from ritual to burial, this continuing down through the Bronze and into the Iron Age centuries. This great cairn was built within and on top of the earlier complex, the original henge stones being either removed or perhaps incorporated. A fourth phase (c 1300 BC) saw urn cremations built into the by now enlarged cairn, while a fifth (possibly early Iron Age) saw four elongated graves cut into the stone mass.

Today, while much of the original can still be seen, the site (archaeologically perhaps the most important in Scotland) has been imaginatively reconstructed, the whole being made clearer to the visitor by means of a model and a taped commentary.

Torpichen Preceptory (AM. Standard, but closed Fri. and alternate Weds. Fee), 1m NW of Cairnpapple, was founded in 1153 by the Knights of St. John of Jerusalem as the preceptory (or community) that was to be their Scottish centre. With all the air of an elegant small castle, what remains today is partly ruin dating from the 13–15C and partly the 18C parish church built over the original Norman nave. This site is not only an outstanding and attractive example of the way in which during the 15C defensive features had to be incorporated even in church architecture, but it also provides an interesting exhibition illustrating the history of the founding Order. Torpichen village was the birthplace of Henry Bell (1760), pioneer of the steamboat.—From Torpichen A89 may be rejoined in 10m at Caldercruix by way of B8047, B8028 and B825. Central Glasgow is then 12m farther.

10m (from Bathgate by A89) *Caldercruix.—2m* **Airdrie**, marking the start of Glasgow's eastward industrial spread.—*10m* central **Glasgow**, see Rte 19.

9 Edinburgh to Stirling via South Queensferry (Forth Bridge), Linlithgow and Falkirk

A90 and B924 to South Queensferry. A904 and A803 to Linlithgow. A706 to Bo'ness. A904 to Grangemouth. B904 and A803 to Falkirk. A9 to Stirling.—Flat and agricultural mixed with a central core of urban driving between Linlithgow and Larbert to the N of Falkirk. Some views along and across the Firth of Forth.

SOME HOTELS. **South Queensferry**. *Forth Bridges Moat House*, EH30 9SF. Tel: (031) 3311199. **Linlithgow**. *St. Michael's*, High Street. Tel: (0506) 842217. *Star and Garter*, High Street. Tel: (0506) 845485. **Falkirk**. *Stakis Park*, Camelon Road, Arnothill. Tel: (0324) 28331.

Total distance 38m.—*8m* **South Queensferry**.—*10m* **Linlithgow**.—*5m* **Grangemouth**.—*5m* **Falkirk**.—*10m* **Stirling**.

Edinburgh is left by Queensferry Road (A90) which in rather over *4m* reaches a roundabout (*Barnton*), feeding in A902 from the S. Here the smaller road N in 1m reaches the quiet and most attractive village of ***Cramond**, standing beside the Firth of Forth at the mouth of the little river Almond; a place for Roman and medieval remains, restored 18C houses, and pleasant walks up the Almond and in both directions along the Forth, to the W through Dalmeny Park to the Forth Bridges, to the E to Lauriston Castle. The *Roman Fort*, of which the foundations are laid out, is by the church of 1656. Built in c 142 to guard the harbour, this fort may well have been used by Septimius Severus as a base for his punitive expedition of 208 against NE Scotland. A good display plan and some admirable illustrations bring this place to life, and objects excavated here are on display in Edinburgh's Huntly House Museum. Just E of the fort stands a 15C tower, thought once to have belonged to the bishops of Dunkeld.

A short way beyond the roundabout A90 crosses the Almond by Cramond Bridge, just downstream of which is *Cramond Old Bridge* (1619), which, standing on the site of an older bridge, has a curious link with James V who was attacked here by footpads. The local miller, Jack Howieson, rescued his king and brought him water, the king in gratitude granting land to the family on the quaint condition that they always had a basin and ewer ready whenever a sovereign should pass. Such were in fact offered to George IV in 1822, to Queen

Victoria in 1842, to George V in 1927, and in 1952 to the present Queen.

In a little under 2m beyond Cramond Bridge B924 forks right, just beyond the fork and to the W being *Dalmeny Church*, dating from the 12C and one of the most satisfying examples in Scotland of a small Norman church. Of special note are the S door with its arch of double mouldings and interlaced arcade of five arches; the stone-vaulted choir and apse, both in their original state and showing two sculpted circular arches: and the round-headed windows with their typical chevron mouldings. The W tower, which collapsed in the 15C, has been rebuilt, and on the N side of the nave an addition has been made for the Rosebery Aisle built in 1671 by Sir Archibald Primrose. The Primrose (Rosebery) family have for over three centuries been the owners of **Dalmeny House** (May–Sept: Sun.–Thurs., 14.00 to 17.30. Tel: 031-331 1888. Fee) standing in its park beside the Firth of Forth. Built in 1815 by William Wilkins, the house is not only the first but also one of the grandest examples of Scottish neo-Gothic, a style and splendour represented inside by a fine hammerbeam hall. The paintings, furniture, tapestries, porcelain and much else are in keeping, especially notable being the Rosebery Collection, reflecting the many interests—historical, literary, artistic, racing and political—of the earls of Rosebery; the collection of 18C portraits by Reynolds, Gainsborough and Lawrence; the Mentmore Collection of 18C furniture, porcelain and other works of art; and a Napoleon room, with some interesting relics, including the furniture the Emperor used when in power and the simpler pieces he had to accept on St. Helena.

2m **South Queensferry**, since the demise of the ferry in 1964 increasingly known simply as Queensferry, somehow manages to retain a character of its own despite the dominating presence of the

The famed Forth Bridge of 1890 contrasting with the modern (1964) Road Bridge behind.

two great bridges far above. The town owes its name to Queen Margaret, wife of Malcolm Canmore, who frequently passed through here when journeying between Edinburgh and her palace and abbey across the Forth at Dunfermline. This was in about 1070, so there was a ferry here for at least 900 years, until the opening of the rail bridge in 1890 sounded the first warning and that of the road bridge in 1964 finally closed the long chapter. Today, inevitably, it is the two lofty bridges which first force themselves on the visitor's attention, though something of the town's past can be learnt from a visit to the small *South Queensferry Museum* in the Burgh Chambers (May–Sept: Thurs., Fri., 14.30 to 16.45. Tel: 031-3311590. Free).

The *Rail Bridge*, the achievement of Sir John Fowler between 1883–90, was one of the great engineering feats of its day. The length of the bridge proper is just over one mile; the railway track is 157ft above the water; there are two spans of 1710ft each and two of 690ft; and the painted surface represents 135 acres. Below the bridge, in mid Firth, the island of Inchgarvie has a 15C fort which held out against Cromwell in 1650 and was rebuilt in 1779 when the American privateer John Paul Jones was in the offing.—In 1964 the Queen opened the *Road Bridge* (toll, but free for pedestrians and cyclists). The bridge proper is almost 2000 yards long, the central span 3300ft and the side spans 1340ft each. The towers are 512ft high.

3m *Hopetoun House* (Easter. May–mid Sept: Daily, 11.00 to 17.00. Tel: 031-3312451. Fee), superbly situated in parkland beside the Firth of Forth, can be reached from Queensferry by way of the small shoreside road, or from A904 by a turn N 2m W of that road's departure from A90. If the two Forth bridges represent the constructive genius of the 19 and 20C, then this, one of the most splendid of Scotland's mansions, surely represents that of the 18C; more particularly that of William Adam and his son John, who between 1721 and 1754 rebuilt and enlarged the original structure of about 1700 which had been put up by William Bruce for the 1st Earl of Hopetoun, ancestor of the present Marquis of Linlithgow. And it was John Adam who was largely responsible for the interior decoration of the main state apartments (especially noteworthy being the yellow drawing room and the ballroom) which today house a distinguished collection of paintings by, amongst others, Rubens, Titian and Canaletto as well as portraits by Gainsborough and Scottish artists. Additionally the house offers a museum of china, costumes and other bygones; a roof platform with Forth views; and in the stables, an exhibition devoted to 'Horse and Man in Lowland Scotland'.

In the park will be found a flock of rare four-horned black St. Kilda sheep, and also two deer herds; red deer in the North Park, reached by a woodland nature trail, and fallow deer in the South Park in which there is also a picturesque ruined 17C tower.

From Hopetoun it is convenient to visit the secluded church of *Abercorn*, ½m W of the house and reached by an unclassified road. Founded in the 5C, and later (681–85) the seat of a short-lived Northumbrian bishopric, the church as seen today dates in part from the 12C (a blocked Norman doorway), but suffered from over-restoration which amounted almost to reconstruction in 1579 and 1893. To be seen here are a splendid 8C Anglian cross-shaft with interlaced pattern, an ancient hog-backed tombstone, and the burial place of the colourful Thomas (Tam) Dalyell of the Binns, though those who prefer legend to fact will argue that his body was in reality carried off by the Devil.

3m The **House of the Binns** (NTS. Easter. May–Sept: Daily except Fri., 14.00 to 17.00. Park open all year, daily, 10.00 to 19.00 or dusk. Fee), just N of A904, derives its rather curious name from the old Scots word 'bynnis', meaning twin hills, a reference to two such hills which slope up to the E. This old Scots name well reflects the antiquity of this estate, documentary evidence of whose existence reaches back to 1335, although it was not until 1612 that house and lands were bought by Thomas Dalyell, a cadet of an ancient family, the senior line of which later achieved the earldom of Carnwath. This Thomas Dalyell accompanied James VI/I to London, made his fortune and returned to build this house, then as now a fine example of a comfortable 17C home developed from a 15C nucleus. A western range was added later in the 17C, and the main fronts were remodelled in the 19C, at which time also (1826) the tower on the hill was erected (paid for with money won in a wager), but, despite these changes, the house remains essentially the creation of the man whose initials still so ubiquitously intertwine with those of his wife, Janet Bruce. Fine carpets, antique furniture and valuable china are all on display here, but far and away the most notable feature is the elaborate *plasterwork, much of it dating from 1630 in anticipation of a visit by Charles I.

The most colourful member of the Dalyell family was 'General Tam' (1599–1685), son of Thomas. A staunch Royalist, he was captured at Worcester, escaped from the Tower of London, and then served the Tsar in Russia until recalled by Charles II at the Restoration. In 1666 he soundly defeated the Covenanters at Rullion Green on the Pentland Hills, and in 1681 he raised the Scots Greys. Though legend insists that his body was carried off by the Devil, his tomb, with or without contents, is in Abercorn church.

Blackness Castle (AM. Standard, but closed Mon. afternoon and Tues. in Oct–March. Fee), occupying a Forth promontory 1m N of the House of the Binns, could scarcely provide a greater contrast in situation, appearance or purpose. Built in the 15C, this was once one of the most important fortresses in Scotland and one of the four which under the Articles of Union (1707) was to be left fortified. In Covenanting times Blackness served as a prison, and during the 1870s as a powder magazine.

4m (from the Binns) **Linlithgow** (5500 inhab. *ECl.* Wed. *Inf.* Burgh Halls, The Cross), chartered by David I and probably from at least that time a royal residence, is today best known for the well-preserved ruins of Scotland's most splendid fortified palace, as also for one of the country's most interesting churches.

History. The history of the town and palace are interwoven. After David I's charter Linlithgow became a place of some importance. England's Edward I camped here in 1298 before the battle at Falkirk against Wallace, wintered here in 1301, and in 1302 built a tower, later to become incorporated into the palace planned and partly built by James I over 100 years later. The capture of this tower in 1313 by a handful of Scots concealed in a load of hay is one of the many romantic feats that abound in Scottish history. Here in 1513 Queen Margaret waited in vain for her husband, James IV, to return from Flodden. James V was born in the palace the year before this, and his daughter, Mary, Queen of Scots, in 1542. Edinburgh University moved temporarily to Linlithgow in 1545–46 when the plague was raging in the capital. Charles I was the last monarch to sleep in the palace, in 1633 at a time when he was considering making Linlithgow the Scottish capital, and from 1651–59 the town was

garrisoned by Cromwell. The Young Pretender visited the palace during the
'45, and the following year, when occupied by government troops, it was
burned, probably accidentally. In 1914 George V held a court here.

***Linlithgow Palace* (AM. Standard. Fee) is approached through a
Gateway erected by James V in c 1535. On the 19C parapet are the
badges of four orders of knighthood to which James belonged: the
Garter of England (three lions), St. Andrew of Scotland (one lion),
the Golden Fleece of Spain (castle and lions), and St. Michael of
France (fleur de lys).

Of any residence David I may have had here there is now no trace,
the oldest visibly surviving part of the palace being the tower at the
SW angle built by Edward I in 1302. For over a century this was
probably all there was, until in 1425 James I laid out the plans from
which would grow the great palace beside the loch. The W side of
the quadrangle dates partly from this time, but the S and E sides,
architecturally the richest, are mid 16C (James V), while the N, which
collapsed in 1607, is a reconstruction of 1618–30.

The Quadrangle is the heart of the palace, with round towers at
the angles and an octagonal tower of 1620 on the N side. Above the
modern entrance (S side) can be seen part of an Annunciation, while
to the E is the palace's earlier massive entrance across the moat,
which should of course be pictured with a drawbridge. Above this
entry there are three canopied niches, once housing statues. In the
centre stands an ornate fountain, a wedding present from James V
to Mary of Guise, said on that glittering occasion to have run with
wine.

Around the quadrangle everything is on the grand scale, the chief
apartments being on the first floor. Here, along the E, stretches the
Great Hall, 94ft long with tall windows, a huge fireplace and
ornamental mantelpiece, and a curious kind of side-passage within
the inner wall. Elsewhere halls and rooms, notably their fireplaces,
are in proportion and, though roofless, intact enough to enable
something of the life of their times to be imagined. In the S wing are
the Chapel, which has five lancets, and another hall. The Royal
Apartments, along the W side, include the King's Hall, the Presence
Chamber with a curious horizontal window, and the Bedchamber.
Two recesses in the N wall represent the royal oratories. The room
in which Mary of Guise gave birth to Mary, Queen of Scots, was
probably in the N wing, later rebuilt; and at the top of the NW tower
a little octagonal turret known as Queen Margaret's Bower may have
been the place where Margaret, doubtless all too well aware of the
ghostly warning conveyed to her husband in St. Michael's church
(see below), so anxiously awaited the news from Flodden.

The **Church of St. Michael* (June–Sept: Daily, 10.00 to 12.00.
14.00 to 16.00. Oct–May: Mon.–Fri., 10.00 to 12.00. 14.00 to 16.00.
Donation), adjacent to the palace, is the largest pre-Reformation
parish church in Scotland and a good example of the Scottish Dec.
style.

Consecrated in 1242, the church was largely rebuilt in 1424 after
a fire. The nave is the oldest part, the choir (c 1497) and tower being
of later date and the apse not completed until 1531. Until 1821 the
lofty, pinnacled tower carried an open stonework crown, added by
James IV, this being replaced in 1964 (by helicopter) by a modern
work (Geoffrey Clarke). Beneath the tower there is a notable doorway,

and there is another entrance on the S side under an elegant porch with a priest's chamber and an unusual oriel above it. The image of St. Michael at the SW angle is the only image to have survived the Reformation.

Inside the church the broad, handsome nave comprises five bays, with pointed arches resting on clustered pillars. The triforium and clerestory, each with a main arch enclosing two smaller lights, deserve attention, as does also the church's varied and graceful window tracery, especially that of the Flamboyant window in the S transept. It was in this transept, known as St. Catherine's Aisle, that, just before Flodden, an apparition warned James IV against war with England. At the end of the church is a three-sided apse of tall windows and tracery that is surprisingly severe.

Within Linlithgow town there are a few 17C houses, notably *West Port House* (c 1600) at the W end of High Street, while, near the town hall, the *Cross Well* with its quaint figures is an 1807 reproduction of an earlier fountain said to have been here during the reign of James V.—The Union Canal, opened in 1822 and originally running 13½m from Edinburgh to join the Forth–Clyde Canal (see below), crosses the southern part of the town. Here, today, the *Canal Museum* (April–Sept: Sat. and Sun., 14.00 to 17.00. Donation), housed in stables of 1822, shows records and relics and provides an audio-visual display, while for those in search of a closer nostalgia there are cruises on the 'Victoria', a replica of a 19C boat. (Tel: 0506–842528).

From Linlithgow A803 provides the direct approach to (7m) Falkirk, but this Rte takes a northerly loop through Kinneil, not to be missed by anyone with an interest in James Watt's engineering research, and the petro-chemical town of Grangemouth.

3m **Bo'ness** is a contraction of Borrowstounness. *Kinneil House* (AM. Standard, but closed Tues. afternoon and Fri. Fee), on the W of the town and just S of A904, is the tall shell of a 16–17C fortified seat of the dukes of Hamilton. The building shows outstanding contemporary wall and ceiling paintings, but, apart from these, is perhaps less interesting than its grounds, now a public park containing a small Roman fort and the remains of the outhouse in which in 1765 James Watt developed his steam engine (by arrangement with the then occupier of the house, the owner of the Carron Ironworks, who was financing Watt's research). Alongside, an iron cylinder, cast to Watt's design for a local mine pump, was set up in 1946 as a memorial. The *Bo'ness Museum* (May–Sept: Mon.–Sat., 10.00 to 17.00. Nov–April: Sat., 10.00 to 17.00. Tel: 0324-27703. Free), nearby in converted 17C stables, is devoted mainly to local industrial history, but also tells about the Roman fort, while, appropriately enough here, the *Scottish Railway Preservation Society* has a site in Bo'ness (off Union Street). Here there is a working steam railway system (Sat., Sun., 11.00 to 17.00. Tel: 0506-822298. Donation) and steam trains run on summer weekend afternoons (12.00 to 17.00).

2m **Grangemouth** (24,500 inhab. *ECl.* Wed.), a large industrial complex with extensive docks and oil-refining and chemical works, would never claim to be a tourist's town. Yet with its massed oil tanks and often pervasive petro-chemical atmosphere it has an individual character and sense of purpose that can hardly be ignored. Founded in 1777 at the E end of the Forth–Clyde Canal (see below), Grangemouth grew during the 19C but remained relatively unimportant until the 1940s when its expansion really began. Today

Scotland's principal petro-chemical centre, Grangemouth's oil tanks
are fed by North Sea oil pipeline. The *Grangemouth Museum*
(Mon.–Sat., 10.00 to 17.00. Tel: 0324-27703. Free), in the Victoria
Library, Bo'ness Road, is mainly concerned with the story of the
canals of central Scotland, but also displays material on the 'Charlotte
Dundas' (see immediately below) and on modern Grangemouth.

The **Forth–Clyde Canal**, now long disused, was built by John Smeaton in
1768–90 and in large part still runs for some 38m roughly below the line of the
Romans' Antonine Wall (see below). The canal started at Grangemouth, crossed
Falkirk (from where the opening of the Union Canal in 1822 provided a link
into Edinburgh), and ended on the Clyde at Bowling where its basin is now a
marina. The tug 'Charlotte Dundas', engined by William Symington and the
world's first practical steamboat, appeared on the canal in 1802.

From Grangemouth there is a choice of approaches to Falkirk, but
this Rte takes B904 which crosses the M9 motorway to join A803 at
Polmont. A short way to the W, and immediately S of A803 between
the road and a high-rise housing estate (Callendar Park), a good
length of Antonine Wall ditch will be found.

5m (from Grangemouth) **Falkirk** (37,500 inhab. *ECl.* Wed.) is an
industrial town, known historically for two battles. In the first, fought
on the S side of Callendar Wood in 1298, Edward I, advancing from
his encampment at Linlithgow, defeated Wallace. In the second
(January 1746), at Bantaskyne, just 1m W of the first, the retreating
Young Pretender inflicted a severe repulse on the pursuing government forces. *Falkirk Museum* (Mon.–Sat., 10.00 to 17.00. Tel: 0324-
27703. Free), in the town centre, covers the archaeology and history
of the district, with some emphasis on local pottery and foundry
products.

The Romans' **Antonine Wall**, four good sections of which are in
or close to Falkirk, was built between the Firth of Forth at Bridgeness,
1m E of Bo'ness, and Old Kilpatrick on the Clyde, a length of 37m.
Its date is c 140, its building resulting from a decision by the Emperor
Antoninus Pius to abandon Hadrian's Wall across northern England,
built only ten years earlier, and adopt a more forward policy towards
Scotland. The work was entrusted to the II, VI and XX Legions under
the orders of Quintus Lollius Urbicus, governor of Britain. Unlike
Hadrian's Wall, which is of stone, the Antonine was a turf rampart
on a stone base, with a ditch to the N and a military road along the
S side. Spoil from the ditch was tipped to form an outer obstacle, and
there were forts about every 2m. The wall was abandoned by the
end of the 2C, possibly as early as 163. Inscriptions, sculptures,
distance slabs (erected by the legionaries to mark the completion of
their length) and other finds can be seen in the Edinburgh Royal
Museum of Scotland (Queen Street) and in the Hunterian Museum
in Glasgow. Sections of the wall survive at several points along its
length.

The two sites in Falkirk are the ditch at *Callendar Park* mentioned
above, and another particularly well preserved length of ditch known
as *Watling Lodge*. This latter, in the W suburbs of Falkirk, is reached
by turning S off A803 through Camelon to cross the Forth–Clyde
Canal for Tamfourhill Road (B816).

Rough Castle, by far the most extensive and best preserved
fortified site, is on the hills 1½m from Bonnybridge (4m W of Falkirk)
from where there are signs. The road reaches the wall, the line of

which it follows to a car park, 300 yards E of which is the complex
of earthworks of about one acre which makes up the fort. The fort's
rampart abutts that of the wall itself, and the military road runs
through the fort. Although little else is now recognisable, the barracks
are known to have been to the N of the road, while to the S lay, in
succession, the commander's house, the granary and the headquarters
buildings. Earthworks well seen just E of the fort are the remains of
an annexe with baths.—*Seabegs Wood*, beside B816 2½m W of Rough
Castle, shows a stretch of rampart, ditch, mound and military road.

For some other good and accessible Antonine Wall sites, see Rte 20, *Duntocher*;
Rte 21, *Bearsden*; Rte 22, *Castlecary*.

Leaving Falkirk A9 passes to the W of *Stenhousemuir*, a name
recalling the great days of droving when cattle fairs were held on
the 'muir' monthly between spring and autumn. Immense herds of
livestock crowded here from far and near, including cattle from the
Western Isles, sheep from Ross and Sutherland, even ponies from
Shetland, and after sale found their way farther S by the great drove
roads.

  8m **Bannockburn**, a name as resounding in Scotland's history as
it is inglorious in England's. The actual site of the battle (1314) in
which Robert Bruce so spectacularly defeated Edward II is disputed,
but most maps seem agreed on an area, about 1m N of today's town,
between the railway and A905. For the *Bannockburn Memorial and
Information Centre*, 1m W, see Rte 23.—*2m* **Stirling**, see Rte 23.

II SOUTH WEST

Lying to the side of the popular through-roads, and thought to have little to offer scenically, the South West is a district relatively little visited. Yet much of Scotland's story has its roots here and the visitor willing to make the detour will be the richer for it. Those heading for Highland Scotland may then use the interesting and scenic island of *Arran* as a stepping-stone across the Clyde estuary to Kintyre. Alternatively the island of *Bute*, with its unique round castle at Rothesay, or the car ferry from *Gourock* to *Dunoon*, can both serve as gateways to the North by way of the Cowal peninsula.

Scenically much of the inland South West may be unexciting moorland, but *Galloway Forest Park*, the nearest approach in southern Scotland to Highland grandeur, is a superb 200 square miles with 10 summits of over 2000ft, and along the *Solway* coast there is a rolling, wooded and pastoral countryside, which with its neat small towns, many of them 17–18C in character, offers pleasant and undemanding touring; and the Firth itself, a shallow estuary of sandy flats, bays and beaches, for much of its length untouched by a main road, has many lost and unspoilt corners. The *West Coast* is bolder and more incidental, with views across to the Clyde islands. But though superficially more scenic than Solway, this coast loses through being hugged by a busy main road linking a string of sometimes undistinguished resorts.

The South West enters history as the Kingdom of Strathclyde to the N and independent Galloway to the S, while the coasts were subject to Norse raiding and settlement. In 1034 Duncan of Strathclyde succeeded Malcolm II as king of the rest of Scotland and Strathclyde was thus absorbed as the single Kingdom of Scotland was born.

Today's traveller will hear many references to Galloway, the name still used for the ancient territory which once embraced virtually the whole of the S part of the South West. He will also soon become aware that the South West was the cradle of Christianity in Scotland; the cradle too, through the early struggles of Wallace and Bruce, of Scotland's fight for independence; the land through which Mary, Queen of Scots, made a royal progress in 1563 and a desperate flight five years later; and the scene, during the following century, of the strife into which Christianity slid and under which the Covenanters so bitterly suffered. Finally, in the mid 18C, the South West was the home of Scotland's national poet, Robert Burns.

Galloway. Until the end of the 12C Galloway comprised the whole of the South West roughly W of Nithsdale and S of the river Doon (Loch Doon to Ayr). The district immediately S of the Doon, then, as now, known as *Carrick*, broke away at the end of the 12C, leaving, as Galloway, what would later become the counties of Wigtown and Kirkcudbright. The name derives from 'Gallwyddel' ('stranger Gaels'), a term anciently applied to the Celts of this region. These were an independent people, who fraternised with the Norse raiders when they began to settle towards the end of the 9C, and who refused formal allegiance to any Scots crown until the reign of Malcolm Canmore (c 1060). Even then Galloway maintained a partial independence under its own lords until the death of the last of these in 1234, and thereafter the tradition still lived on in the power and lawlessness of the great families. In the 14C the chief such families were the Balliols and Comyns, bitter enemies of the Bruces, earls of Carrick. In c 1370 the lordship of Galloway was obtained by the Douglas family who exercised a haughty dominion until 1455 when, by reducing *Threave Castle*, James II crushed their power. Galloway then passed fully to the crown, though, as elsewhere in Scotland, there were hereditary sheriffs until 1747.

Christianity. Christianity was brought to Scotland in c 400 when St. Ninian built his church at *Whithorn*, and its story in the South West can be followed in stone from soon after then until modern times. Although traces have been found of what may have been St. Ninian's church, these can no longer be seen. What can be seen are Early Christian memorial stones, surviving as evidence of how Christianity established itself and spread. Examples are the *Latinus Stone* (450) at Whithorn; the *Kirkmadrine Stones* (5–12C) on the Rhinns of Galloway to the W, and the cross at *Ruthwell*, near Dumfries, important for showing the influence by the 8C of several new strands.

Possibly the earliest church building still surviving, though only as foundations, is the 10 or 11C *Chapel Finian*, but of the work of the immediately following centuries there are many examples, starting with humble chapels and flowering into the great medieval abbeys. Of the first category, mention may be made of the 12–13C *Chapel of St. Ninian* at Isle of Whithorn and the fragment of 12C *St. Kentigern's* at Lanark, where Wallace may have been married. Of the great abbey churches, though, there is more to be seen and the South West is rich in these. The best are *Sweetheart*, with its touching story of Devorguilla Balliol and her husband's heart; *Dundrennan*, where Mary, Queen of Scots, last slept in Scotland; *Whithorn Priory*, built on the site of St. Ninian's church; *Glenluce, Crossraguel*, and *Paisley* with its early Stuart tombs. There followed the Reformation and the building of Greenock's *West Kirk*, the first post-Reformation church to be built in Scotland, now known also for its Burne-Jones and Rossetti stained glass.

Wars of Independence. Wallace and Bruce both started their patriotic struggles in Scotland's South West and, though few physical remains are to be seen, the visitor is constantly reminded that these heroes were active here. A monument at *Elderslie*, near Paisley, commemorates Wallace's birth there, and it was at *Lanark* that he took up arms after the death of his wife at the hands of the English. A fragment survives of the church where he may have been married, and *Cartland Crags*, where he hid, can be visited. In 1297 *Ayr* was the scene of one of his most famed exploits, the burning with all the occupants of the English barracks known as the Barns of Ayr. The same year, though, at *Irvine*, Wallace was deserted by his supporters and thus forced to flee to northern Scotland.

Bruce was born in c 1274 at either *Lochmaben* or *Turnberry*, both strongholds of his powerful Norman-Celtic family. In 1306 he killed Comyn at Greyfriars, *Dumfries*, and thus rekindled the war of independence. Two places can be seen where he may then have hidden: *Bruce's Cave*, near Gretna, and the fort on *Tynron Hill*, near Moniaive. He next appears in the wild country that is now *Galloway Forest Park*, where two memorial boulders mark the sites of his successful skirmishes. A plaque at *Girvan* records the granting of a charter, but after 1307 Bruce was mostly elsewhere in Scotland. He returned towards the end of his life when he made a pilgrimage to *Whithorn* and then, sick with leprosy, founded a hospital for lepers at Prestwick, beside *Bruce's Well* where he had been refreshed; the well and the hospital chapel can be seen.

Mary, Queen of Scots. Mary was twice in the South West. The royal progress of 1563 started at *Seagate Castle*, Irvine, then made a sweep S and E to finish at *Drumlanrig* in Nithsdale. Many of the places at which she stayed can be seen, amongst them *Dunure* and *Ardstinchar* castles, the abbeys of *Glenluce* and *Whithorn*, and *Kenmure Castle*. She is reported to have had 18 horses and six baggage mules and to have been escorted by barons and local lairds. Five years later, after the defeat at Langside, this pomp had been replaced, to use her own words, by having 'to sleep upon the ground and drink sour milk'. Her exact path is uncertain, but she seems to have ridden S across *The Glenkens*, continuing past *Kenmure* down the W bank of the Ken to cross the Dee near *Tongland*. From here she made for *Terregles*, near Dumfries, on the way stopping at *Corra*. The decision taken to leave Scotland, she then retraced the route to *Dundrennan* and embarked to cross Solway.

Covenanters. The Covenants were obstinately supported in the South West, this support being recalled today mainly in the form of numerous memorials either to victories or more often to martyrs. Notable early victories were the taking in 1640 of *Caerlaverock* and *Threave* castles. Another, later, was the defeat of Claverhouse in 1679 at *Drumclog*, though this was soon followed by defeat at *Bothwell Bridge*, near Hamilton. *Sanquhar* twice became famous, in 1680 and 1685 when the first and second Declarations of Sanquhar were affixed to the town cross. The leader on the first occasion, Richard Cameron, was killed at *Airds Moss* and that of the second, James Renwick, had the dubious distinction of being the last Covenanter to be executed (1688). His monument is at *Moniaive*. The worst period for the Covenanters was 1684–88 (the 'killing time') and the majority of the South West's memorials, most of them carrying stirring words, are to the victims of these years. Three may be mentioned as particularly poignant: the bleak and lonely site of the *Wigtown Martyrs'* stake on the estuary flats where two women were left to drown; the little stone tomb in *Galloway Forest Park*, with engraved upon it the names both of the six Covenanter martyrs and of the men who killed them; and at *Douglas* the stone carved in protest by a Covenanter tailor who had had his ears cut off with his own shears.—For those wishing to trace the Covenanter story more closely, Tourist Offices will provide a leaflet entitled 'In Covenanting Footsteps'.

Robert Burns. The poet spent his life in the South West, he and his work being most associated with two areas; that around *Ayr*, and *Dumfries*. At most places there is a monument or a museum. Burns was born at *Alloway* in 1759, and the scene of his famous poem 'Tam o' Shanter' is laid between Ayr and Alloway Brig o'Doon. *Ayr Auld Brig* has been made famous by the poem 'The Twa Brigs'. In 1777 his family moved to Lochlea Farm near Tarbolton. At *Tarbolton* he founded the Bachelors' Club and at nearby *Mauchline*, the scene of 'The Holy Fair', he was married. The first edition of his poems was published at *Kilmarnock*. In 1788 Burns tried farming at *Ellisland* in lower Nithsdale', but three years later he accepted a post as an excise officer at *Dumfries* where he died in 1796.—A Burns Heritage Trail (leaflet) traces the poet's life in more detail.

Castles. Of the South West's many castles, six (other than Lochmaben and Turnberry as possible birthplaces of Bruce) merit particular mention. These are *Caerlaverock*, for its triangular shape and elegant Renaissance interior; *Threave*, for its grim aspect; *Craignethan*, for defensive features; *Bothwell*, as perhaps the finest 13C castle in Scotland; *Culzean*, as an 18C masterpiece of Robert Adam; and *Rothesay* (Bute), for its unique round shape.

10 Gretna to Glasgow via Beattock (Moffat) and Lanark

A74 to Douglas. A70 and A73 to Lanark. A72 to Hamilton. Choice
of roads into Glasgow.—As far as Douglas, a busy arterial road
across varying moorland, with high passes westward through the
Lowther Hills; A74 closely follows the line of the Roman Watling
Street. Around Lanark, woods and orchards, in places gashed by
river ravines.—*Note*: A74 is a dual-carriageway trunk road and as
such bypasses the places along it mentioned below. Care must
therefore be taken to choose the relevant exits.

SOME HOTELS. **Beattock**. *Auchen Castle*, DG10 9SH. Tel: (06833)
407. *Beattock House*, DG10 9QB. Tel: (06833) 403. **Douglas**.
Douglas Arms, 54 Ayr Road. Tel: (055585) 322. **Lanark**. *Cartland
Bridge*. Tel: (0555) 4426. **Hamilton**. *Avonbridge*, Carlisle Road. Tel:
(0698) 420525.

Total distance 100m.—*32m* **Beattock** (for **Moffat**).—*29m*
Douglas.—*11m* **Lanark**.—*18m* **Hamilton**.—*10m* **Glasgow**.

For **Gretna** to (*32m*) **Beattock** (**Moffat**), see Rte 7. Beyond Beattock
A74 ascends for some 7m before reaching the watershed at 1029ft
and starting its descent into the upper valley of the Clyde.—*13m*
(from Beattock) *Elvanfoot*, whence two roads angle SW across the
Lowther Hills to reach Nithsdale (Rte 11). One of these (A702) ascends
the Powtrail Water to cross the long, bare and winding Dalveen Pass
(1105ft), but first, 2m S of Elvanfoot, throws off a minor road to Daer
Reservoir with its long dam. The other road (B7040, becoming B797)
climbs up to **Leadhills** (1350ft) and **Wanlockhead** (1380ft), curiously,
despite being in the Lowlands, the bleakly sited highest villages in
all Scotland, once prosperous through mining lead, gold and silver.
Local gold went into the crowns of James V and his queen and, in
our century, provided a ring for George V's Queen Mary and a brooch
for Elizabeth, the Queen Mother. In these somewhat unpromising
surroundings, at Leadhills to be precise, were born William Symington
(1763–1831), pioneer of marine steam engines, and Allan Ramsay
(1686–1758), the poet. The latter's name is here perpetuated in that
of the *Allan Ramsay Library* (By arrangement. Tel:06594–243.), a
lead miners' library founded in 1741 and showing rare books and
mining documents. At Wanlockhead the *Museum of the Scottish
Lead Mining Industry* (Easter–Sept: Museum: Daily, 11.00 to 16.00.
Mine: Daily, 13.00 to 15.30. Tel: 06594–387. Fee.) offers both indoor
and outdoor sections, the latter including beam engines and a visitor
mine, worked from the early 18C until 1860.

2m Crawford, where there is a fragment of Tower Lindsay, once
seat of the Lindsays, earls' of Crawford. Here Wallace fought a
skirmish with the English, and here too James V pacified foreign
ambassadors, disgruntled by a poor day's hunting, by presenting
them with gold 'bonnet' pieces. The gold came from Leadhills and
the pieces bear a portrait of the king wearing a Scottish bonnet.

14m **Douglas** was long a Douglas centre, and it was here in 1307
that the misnamed 'Good' Sir James destroyed his own English-
occupied castle, using such barbarity that to this day the exploit is
known as the 'Douglas Larder'; knowing that the English would soon
return in strength, he made a great pile of all the grain and other
foodstuffs, poured on all the wine and ale, killed all his prisoners,

Douglas Castle, scene in 1307 of the notorious 'Douglas larder'.

throwing their corpses onto the mix, filled the well with slaughtered horses and, finally, fired the castle. The later castle, a rebuilding of the 18C, in 1938–48 suffered a less bloody if by some standards perhaps less dignified demolition as the result of undermining by a coal seam.

What has survived is the ancient part-ruined *St. Bride's Church* (AM. Standard. Free), founded in the 12C and still sheltering the Douglas mausoleum, less sombre than many such and interesting for the canopied tombs and effigies below which lie some historically colourful if, even by the custom of their day, often brutal characters (see also under Biographies). Among the tombs is that of 'Good' Sir James (1286–1330) of 'Douglas Larder' infamy; the man, too, who earned the title of 'Black' from his English victims, but that of 'Good' from the Scots because in 1330 he undertook to carry Bruce's heart to the Holy Land, in so doing losing his life in Spain in battle against the Moors (since then a heart has always been part of the Douglas arms). Here too lies a later James (died 1443) beside his wife Beatrice Sinclair, daughter of the Earl of Orkney, their tomb attracting attention not so much for its rather undistinguished occupants as for the appealing frieze of their ten children. On the floor, under glass, rest caskets with the hearts of 'Good' Sir James and of Archibald 'Bell-the-Cat', another who thought nothing of hanging those lesser men who incurred his displeasure (died 1514: see Rte 3, Thirlestane Castle). The clock (1565) on the tower, said to have been a gift from Mary, Queen of Scots, is reputedly the oldest still-working public clock in Scotland; it chimes three minutes before the hour, thus keeping faith with the Douglas motto of 'Never Behind'.

Beside the road leading to St. Bride's, what must surely be a unique monument—a stone with carved scissors and a human ear—provides a reminder, as sharp as it is poignant, of the hazards of 17C life. In 1684 James Gavin, a Covenanter tailor who lived here, had his ears cut off with his own shears before being transported to the West Indies. On his return, years later, he erected this stone in protest against the outrage he had suffered.

Lesmahagow, 5m N on A74, takes its name from St. Machutus, a 6C Culdee missionary. A priory, dedicated to the saint, was founded in 1144 and its foundations can still be seen close to the present 19C church.

A70, followed NE, skirts the NW flank of *Tinto* (2320ft), an isolated hill mass famous for its views and easily climbed by a path up the E side from near Thankerton. To have to carry a stone to Tinto's summit was long a recognised penance, and today some people still take up a stone to add to the ever-growing cairn.

11m (from Douglas) **Lanark** (9000 inhab. *ECl.* Thurs. *Inf.* Horse-market. May–Sept). Standing above the Clyde and today a busy market town, Lanark is historically associated with the start of Wallace's rebellion as also, in more recent times, with the social experiments (at New Lanark) of Robert Owen.

History. By the 10C Lanark was already sufficiently important for Kenneth II to have held a parliament here in 978. The town was made a royal burgh by David I in 1140, and later Wallace is thought to have lived in Castlegate. He is said to have killed an English soldier during a brawl, then fled to Cartland Crags, whence, on learning that his wife had been murdered, he returned with a band of supporters, overthrowing the English garrison, killing its commander and thus committing himself to rebellion. Three centuries later Lanark was a Covenanter centre (the Declaration of Lanark of 1682 was a confirmation of that of Sanquhar), this period now recalled by a monument in the churchyard.

Lanark's traditional festival is the Lanimers (Land march), lasting throughout the first week in June and in origin going back to the granting of the status of royal burgh in 1140. The highlight is the Lanimer Day procession which includes the riding of the marches or bounds.

Architecturally about all that remains of ancient Lanark are some EE pointed arches of what was once the 12C *Church of St. Kentigern*, the church in which Wallace may have been married. This church's ancient bell (recast in 1659, 1740 and 1836) also survives, although it now hangs and still tolls in the tower in front of the *Church of St. Nicholas* (1774). Here too, above the door to this tower, Wallace is remembered by a statue (1822), the work of Robert Frost, a Lanark man who claimed to have taken the likeness from an authentic old print.

*New Lanark, beside the Clyde, was founded in 1784 as an industrial village by David Dale, a merchant, and Richard Arkwright, pioneer in cotton spinning, and soon developed into a large complex involving some 2000 people. Later (1800–25), the village became the scene of the early social experiments of Robert Owen, Dale's son-in-law and mill manager over this period. Convinced that better living conditions meant better output, he, amongst other things, opened a free school, provided a club and operated a co-operative store. Today the principal buildings have been accurately restored and converted for use as modern housing and shops, including craft shops, and a descriptive leaflet enables visitors to make a self-guided tour (New Lanark Conservation. Tel: 0555–61345).—The former dyeworks now house a *Scottish Wildlife Trust Visitor Centre* (Daily, 10.00 to 17.00. Tel: 0555–65262. Donation), telling the story of the nearby *Falls of Clyde Nature Reserve*, a wooded gorge with waterfalls.

Blackhill (NTS), 3m W of Lanark between A72 and A74, is a hill fort offering views over the Clyde valley.—*Castledykes*, 3m E of Lanark and just E of A70, was a Roman fort; and at *Carnwath*, on A70 4m farther E, there is a motte and also, abutting the W end of the parish church, an attractive and intriguing survival in the form of the transept of a collegiate church of 1424.

6m **•Craignethan Castle** (AM. Standard. Fee) will be found 2m W of Crossford on A72, and for anyone even slightly curious about medieval defensive ingenuity few castles can be as rewarding as this, or, because of the intactness of the ruins and the careful restoration, as easy to understand. Its defensive aspect apart, this site is particularly attractive with its spacious open court and its surrounds of parkland and wooded river defile.

Built in the 15–16C, Craignethan was a stronghold of the Hamiltons, staunch supporters of Mary, Queen of Scots. Inevitably, as with so many others, the castle suffered after Mary's flight to England, but about a century later, in 1665, a new mansion was built in the court by the Hay family. The castle is generally accepted as the original of Tillietudlem of Scott's 'Old Mortality'.

But despite dismantling and change of ownership Craignethan has preserved its main and most fascinating defensive feature, its caponier, possibly the earliest example in Britain of such a structure. The castle was built at the time when the ever-increasing power of artillery was shifting the target of siege attack away from the soldiery manning the ramparts and down to the vulnerable base of the walls, and the caponier—a large, vaulted chamber set solidly across the floor of a broad, dry moat—was the defensive reply to these new tactics. This chamber was, and still is reached by a stair in the castle wall (this proving that the caponier was integral with Craignethan's original design), and from inside it can at once be seen how effectively gunports on both sides commanded the moat and thus the length of the base of the keep—the defenders' task of course made simpler by the fact that on the remaining three sides the keep stood above steep cliffs. Photographs in the custodian's office further explain the caponier as well as other defensive features.

12m **Hamilton** (52,000 inhab. *Inf.* Roadchef Service Area on M74. May–Sept) owes its industrial growth to the discovery and mining of coal, but, with the closing of the pits, has now much diversified.

History. There was a settlement here in prehistoric times, and later this area became known as Cadzow, a name which stuck until 1445 when a charter from James II to the first Lord Hamilton officially changed the name to that of the family. This early township (Netherton) clustered around Mote Hill, still a name on modern Hamilton's northern edge. In 1568 Mary, Queen of Scots, came here to confer with her supporter the 4th Marquis of Hamilton before the battle of Langside. Cromwell set up his headquarters here for a short while in 1651, and in 1679, after their defeat at Bothwell Bridge, many of the fleeing Covenanters sought refuge in the woods of Hamilton Palace where they were protected by Anne, the then duchess, who pressed the victorious Monmouth not to disturb the game in her coverts.

The Hamilton family dominated the town from as early as the 14–15C, their palace standing in the area later known as the Low Parks and now absorbed by Strathclyde Country Park. The palace was pulled down in the 1920s because of the subsidence resulting from coal workings; however, incongruously, the slabs of its basement flooring now pave the choir of Paisley Abbey.

In the town, beside the *Old Church* built by William Adam in 1732, stands the Netherton Cross, certainly pre-Norman in date and for long the Cross of the township around Mote Hill. The macabre 'Heads Memorial', on the churchyard E wall, commemorates four local Covenanters beheaded in 1666. The text gives a grim insight to the viciousness of the times. *Hamilton District Museum* (Mon.–Sat., 10.00

to 17.00. Tel: 0698–283981. Free), at 129 Muir Street in the N part of the town, occupies an interesting building that was originally a coaching inn (1696) but was enlarged in 1790 to provide an assembly hall. The museum records the social and industrial development of Hamilton and includes a reconstructed Victorian kitchen, a section devoted to transport, and material on Sir Harry Lauder who is buried in the town's Bent cemetery. The nearby *Cameronians (Scottish Rifles) Regimental Museum* (Mon., Tues., Thurs., Fri., 10.00 to 12.00. 13.00 to 17.00. Wed., 10.00 to 12.00. Sat., 10.00 to 17.00. Tel: 0698–285382. Donation.), telling the story of this Covenanter regiment (see also Rte 11, Sanquhar), is housed in the Duke of Hamilton's former stables in Mote Hill.

Strathclyde Country Park (Free, but fees for facilities and official tour. Tel: 0698–66155.), completed in 1978, occupies both sides of the M74 motorway between the Hamilton and Bothwell interchanges (A723 and A725). Described as a major advance in recreational and environmental terms, the park has absorbed the formerly unsightly coal-working subsidence area known as Hamilton Low Parks, itself once the gracious park—that same park in which Duchess Anne sheltered the Covenanters—of imposing Hamilton Palace. A major feature is the 200-acre loch (formed by diverting the Clyde) which is a national watersports centre. Other amenities include a nature reserve (entry by permit), a caravan and camping site, many sports facilities and even some Roman remains. Within the park bounds stands the strange *Hamilton Mausoleum*, a square edifice with a cupola built in 1840 by David Bryce for the 10th Duke who died in 1852 (Guided tours. Easter–Sept: Daily at 15.00, but also Sat. and Sun. at 19.00 in July and Aug. Sept–Easter: Sat. and Sun., 14.00. Tel: 0698–66155). The interior is a solemn octagonal chapel, notorious for producing an echo so resounding that the chapel could not be used as such. The huge original bronze doors, now kept inside, bear mouldings illustrating Bible stories and are facsimiles of panels on Ghiberti's doors at the Baptistry in Florence.

In *Hamilton High Parks* (Country Park), beyond the S of the town, are the ruins of Cadzow Castle, a royal residence until the time of Bruce when it passed to the Hamiltons and was eventually destroyed by Moray after Langside, and also Chatelherault, a mansion of 1732 recalling that the dukes of Hamilton also bear the title of Duke of Chatelherault. The ancient oaks in the High Parks are said to have been planted by David I to replace yet older trees, formerly part of the Caledonian forest.

EAST OF HAMILTON. *Carfin*, 2m N of Motherwell E of the motorway and river, once with a population largely of Irish and Polish origin, is visited for its Grotto, dedicated in 1922 to Our Lady of Lourdes and still much visited by pilgrims. The original shrine is modelled on that at Lourdes and there are a number of other shrines within the grounds.

WEST OF HAMILTON. *East Kilbride*, 5m W, was Scotland's first satellite town, built in the 1950s and 1960s and with some interesting architecture of that period, such as St. Mark's Episcopal Church, of triangular elevation (Noad and Wallace, 1956), and the seven-sided Church of Scotland (Robert Rogerson, 1964). The new town sprawls generally to the S of the site of the original village, in which, in 1653, the first Scottish meeting of the Society of Friends was held. A memorial in the town commemorates the brothers John and William Hunter, the 18C anatomists, both born in this parish.—*Calderglen Country Park*, off A726 to the S of East Kilbride, stretches for some 3m along the wooded cut of Calder Water and offers nature trails, waterfalls, picnic areas, a children's zoo, and a visitor centre telling the story of the local environment (Zoo: Daily, 10.00 to dusk. Visitor Centre: Mon.–Fri., 11.00 to 17.00. Sat. and Sun., 11.00 to 21.00. In winter, Visitor Centre open only Sat. and Sun., 11.00 to 17.00. Tel: 03552–23621. Free).—It was near *Eaglesham*, 4m SW of East Kilbride, a 'model' village laid out in 1769 by the Earl of Eglinton, that the Nazi leader, Rudolf Hess, made his sensational parachute landing in 1941.

Leaving Hamilton northwards A74 passes the racecourse and then dips to *Bothwell Bridge* (spanning the Clyde), where a monument recalls the battle here in 1679 in which the royal troops under Monmouth and Claverhouse, marching down from the N, routed the Covenanters on the S who lost 500 killed and 1000 as prisoners. This bloody affray can be more easily pictured if today's bridge is ignored in favour of one which was barely 12ft wide, with a steep hump at the centre where it was barred with a gate.

2m (from Hamilton) **Bothwell**, where the *Church of St. Bride* was founded in 1398 by Archibald, 3rd Earl of Douglas ('The Grim', whose daughter Marjory was married to the unfortunate Duke of Rothesay; see Rte 33, Falkland). The original choir with stone-slab roof and generous buttresses is well seen from outside, while inside the church the sedilia are noteworthy, as are also some capitals from an earlier (Norman) church, the grave-slab of Walter de Moravia, builder of Bothwell Castle, and the Burne-Jones E window. A door beside an elaborate monument to the 3rd Duke of Hamilton (died 1694) leads into the 14C sacristy.

David Livingstone (1813–73), the explorer, was born at Blantyre, immediately W of Bothwell, and today the mill tenement in which he was born, in a 'one-room' dwelling, and the adjoining houses have been restored as a ***Livingstone National Memorial** (Mon.–Sat., 10.00 to 18.00. Sun., 14.00 to 18.00. Tel: 0698–823140. Fee). Here, in these almost unbelievably cramped and dingy surroundings, he spent his youth—going to school, working long hours in the mill, and studying until he achieved the qualifications which enabled him to escape to London to become a doctor and missionary. This Memorial is not only an instructive museum of Livingstone's career as mill 'piecer', missionary, explorer and fighter against the slave trade, but the section devoted to his birth and early years also gives a fascinating if sobering insight into the life of the poor during the Industrial Revolution in the early 19C. Livingstone's last journey, when his body was carried by his devoted African bearers 1500 miles from the interior to the coast (and eventual burial in Westminster Abbey) is movingly captured in sculpted wood by Pilkington Jackson. Other features here are a pavilion devoted to modern Africa, and a museum illustrating the history of local agriculture, cotton spinning and mining.

*Bothwell Castle (AM. Standard, but closed Thurs. afternoon and Fri. in Oct–March. Fee) is 1m NW of Bothwell church. A sprawling red ruin amid woods high above the steep-sided Clyde, this is held by many to be the finest 13C castle in all Scotland.

During its first 200 years Bothwell's story was rarely free of blood and drama. It all started in c 1270 with Walter de Moravia (later the name became Moray and then Murray) who in that year probably began to build his castle here. Soon afterwards, in 1289–90, the castle was held for Edward I, but eventually carried by the Scots after a siege lasting 14 months. But only 11 years later, in 1301, Edward I was back again and Bothwell remained in English hands until Bannockburn when the governor, Fitzgilbert, had no choice but to surrender both the castle and the many important English who had taken refuge here to Robert Bruce's brother Edward. Although then dismantled, Bothwell was occupied again by the English from 1331–36, during which period it was rebuilt by the master-mason John de Kilburn—only to be destroyed a year later when taken by the Scots, led by Sir Andrew Moray, to whom the castle by right belonged and who under the 'scorched earth' policy of the day was obliged to dismantle his own property. In 1361 Bothwell passed by marriage to the 'black' Douglases, who rebuilt it, only to lose it in 1445 after the Douglas defeat by James II. Patrick Hepburn, created Earl of Bothwell, became the new owner, but four years later he exchanged the castle for Hermitage, the property of Archibald, Earl of Angus, the 'red' Douglas.

Towards the end of the 17C a mansion (demolished 1926) was built beside the castle, the latter suffering yet further destruction in the process.

After some 700 years of war, destruction, rebuilding and neglect these ruins are inevitably very complicated and visitors in serious search of structural detail are advised to buy the site booklet which helps out with plans and photographs. Below, however, is an outline of the main features.

Along the N curtain wall, crudely built and with buttresses at either end, a gap indicates the position of the main entrance. The great 13C *Keep*, the oldest part of Bothwell, stands half-wrecked at the castle's SW corner, a notable feature here being the way in which the moat which separates the keep from its own court has in part been hacked out of the rock. Designed not only for defence but also as a residence, the keep's interior was of several levels—cellar, the lord's hall, the garrison's hall, the lord's private room, and a defensive top. From this keep a massive curtain wall, running SE to the prison tower and postern, was extended in the early 15C as far as the SE tower. At the SE corner of the court are the remains of the *Chapel*, with aumbrey and piscina, while at the court's E end, on the first floor, was the *Great Hall*, rebuilt in c 1500. Two interesting features here are the absence of a fireplace, this indicating that there would have been a central hearth, and the arrangement for a drawbridge on the square tower; the rectangular recess into which the small door is set would have housed the drawbridge when raised, and above can be seen the channels into which slotted the bar and hoop by which the bridge was lifted.

8m central **Glasgow**, see Rte 19. This approach to the city passes *Calderpark Zoo*.

11   Gretna to Glasgow via Ruthwell, Dumfries and Kilmarnock

A75 to Annan. B724 and B725 to Dumfries. A76 to Kilmarnock. A77 to Glasgow.—As far as Dumfries, agricultural countryside with views across Solway Firth. Nithsdale, gently ascended after Dumfries, is cultivated and lightly wooded with moor and downland rising behind. After Nithsdale, generally open and cultivated countryside.

SOME HOTELS. **Annan**. *Queensberry Arms*, High Street. Tel: (04612) 2024. **Dumfries**. *Cairndale*, English Street. Tel: (0387)

54111. *Station*, 49 Lovers Walk. Tel: (0387) 54316. **Thornhill**.
Buccleuch and Queensberry, 112 Drumlanrig Street. Tel: (0848)
30215. **Sanquhar**. *Mennockfoot Lodge*, DG4 6HS. Tel: (06592) 382.
Blackaddie House, Blackaddie Road. Tel: (06592) 270. **Cumnock**.
Royal, 1 Glaisnock Street. Tel: (0290) 20822. **Kilmarnock**. *Burnside*,
18 London Road. Tel: (0563) 22952.

Total distance 104m.—*8m* **Annan**.—*6m* **Ruthwell**.—*13m*
Dumfries.—*26m* **Sanquhar**.—*16m* **Cumnock**.—*7m* **Mauchline**.—*8m*
Kilmarnock.—*20m* **Glasgow**.

Gretna, see Rte 7.—*8m* **Annan**. A75 here provides the direct road to
Dumfries, in 4m passing *Kinmount Gardens* (Easter–Nov: Daily, 10.00
to 17.00. Tel: 05763–251. Fee) where there is a picnic area and
waymarked walks meander through woodland and around lakes.
This Rte, though, leaves A75 for B724 to reach (*6m*) **Ruthwell** (pron.
Rivvel), a village famous for the *Ruthwell Cross* which stands in its
church. Shaped and carved in the early 8C and one of Europe's most
important Early Christian monuments, the cross long lay virtually
unnoticed under the church floor but was set up in its present position
in the 19C. The lofty shaft, 18ft high, is original, but the cross-arm is
restoration, although a detached piece of the original can be seen.
The carving is work of Northumbrian Christianity and important for
the glimpses it affords of that faith's mixed ancestry: the Roman
lettering is Celtic in style, the vineleaf ornamentation and the figures
suggest an early Roman Catholic influence, and the runic characters
express an English (Northumbrian) text. The carving on the main
faces is of scenes from the life of Christ, with Latin inscriptions, while
on the sides there is foliage interlaced with birds and animals feeding
on fruit. Around the margin, in runic characters but Northumbrian
speech, unfolds a poem on the Passion in which the Cross describes
the part it played in the tragedy of the Crucifixion.

The *Henry Duncan Cottage Museum* (Custodian on call at all
reasonable times. Free), in Ruthwell village, is on the site of the first
Savings Bank, founded here in 1810 as one of his pastoral initiatives
by Henry Duncan who was minister at Ruthwell in 1799–1843.
Although philanthropic and not operated for profit, the bank was run
on firm principles and imposed what must have been an almost
unbearable discipline on its usually impoverished members who, for
example, could be fined if they defaulted on the regular deposits to
which they had hopefully committed themselves. So successful was
Duncan's venture that within 15 years similar societies had sprung
up all over Britain.—*Brow Well*, an ancient mineral well on B725 1m
W of Ruthwell, deserves mention as a spot visited by Burns when
sea-bathing here on medical advice.

4m ***Caerlaverock Castle** (AM. Standard. Fee). With its unusual
triangular plan, its Renaissance carving and its moat still full of water,
Caerlaverock ranks among Scotland's best both for structural interest
and visual satisfaction.

This stronghold of the Maxwells, later earls of Nithsdale, dates from c 1290
when it succeeded an earlier castle which lay to the S. It was taken by Edward I
in 1301, but by 1312 was back in the hands of Sir Eustace Maxwell, a supporter
of Bruce. Later, once more with an English garrison, it was assaulted and taken
by Sir Roger Kirkpatrick who seems to have destroyed much of the building.
Repaired by Lord Maxwell in 1593, and elegantly extended and modified in
1634 by the 1st Earl of Nithsdale, Caerlaverock eventually capitulated to the
Covenanters in 1640 after a siege lasting 13 weeks.

The castle's symmetry, and particularly that of the massive gateway at the triangle's apex with its formidable drum towers, is immediately striking, as is also the contrast between the wholly defensive 14–15C exterior and the 1st Earl's elegant Renaissance interior of 1634. Here, around a triangular courtyard, are what must have been exquisite rooms, incidental in shape, with large windows on two sides, and most with generous fireplaces. This, at the time known as 'Lord Nithsdale's dainty fabrick'—and the adjective is not ill-chosen—was enjoyed by its owner, a supporter of Charles I, for a mere six years before his achievement was largely destroyed by Covenanter rebels. However, the Maxwell crest and motto still obstinately survive above the gateway.

Caerlaverock National Nature Reserve (Open, except for sanctuary area. Free) embraces 13,594 acres of saltmarsh, tidal mud and sand extending along six miles of coastline along the Nith estuary and Solway Firth. The reserve is noted for its winter wildfowl, especially many thousands of geese, these including the entire Spitsbergen barnacle goose population. The unreclaimed saltmarsh, the largest such in Britain, is the most northerly breeding site of the natterjack toad, remarkable for having legs so short that it runs rather than hops.

9m **Dumfries** (32,000 inhab. *EC*1. Thurs. *Inf*. Whitesands. Easter–Oct), with a historic and violent past typical of a Borders town, is today a lively centre, of interest to visitors mainly because of the associations with Robert Burns, for the picturesque Nith waterfront with its 15C bridge, and for ruined Lincluden Abbey in the N suburbs.

History. Probably originating as a settlement on the Roman road up Nithsdale, Dumfries became a village protected by the early castle (now vanished, but its site recalled by Castle Street). The town was made a royal burgh in the 12C, possibly by William the Lion, and of subsequent charters the best known is Robert III's of 1395. In 1301 Edward I seized the castle, but perhaps the town's most historic date is 1306 when Bruce and Roger Kirkpatrick here murdered Balliol's man Comyn and thus started the long war of independence. Later, Dumfries was burned or sacked by the English in 1448, 1536 and 1570. In 1745 the Young Pretender passed through here on his northward retreat from Derby, treating the town with some severity because of the hostility shown to him on his southward march. During the 1939–45 war Dumfries was the headquarters of the Norwegian forces in Britain (tablet in St. Michael's Church).

Robert Burns lived in Dumfries from December 1791 until his death in 1796, working as an excise officer and here writing over 100 of his poems. His first home was a three-room flat in the Wee Vennel (now Bank Street), but in May 1793 he moved to a better house in Mill Vennel (now Burns Street) where he died.

The town motto, A' Loreburn!, derives from the Saxon. Meaning 'To the muddy burn', it was a rallying cry for the weakest part of the defences, recalled today by the name of a street to the NE of Greyfriars.—Guid Nychburris Week (Good Neighbours Festival), held in June, is the town's annual festival, centred on the granting of Robert III's 1395 charter. A part of the festival is the competition to win the 'Siller Gun', a miniature firearm presented by James VI in 1617 to encourage marksmanship. The trophy is held in the museum and the winner receives a replica. The festival's quaint name stems from a local medieval court which compelled the quarrelsome to become friends.

The best of Dumfries can be seen by walking the length of High Street from Greyfriars Church southward to St. Michael's Church, a distance of about half a mile, and then returning northward along the waterfront (Whitesands).

Greyfriars Church, with a statue of Burns in front, is a prominent

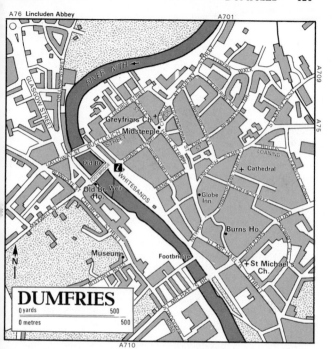

red building of 1867 within the angle of Academy and Castle streets.
The church occupies the site of the ancient castle but should not be
confused with the 13C Franciscan Greyfriars Friary, founded either
by Alan of Galloway or his daughter Devorguilla Balliol. This stood
on the W side of today's Castle Street and it was here (plaque) that
Bruce and Kirkpatrick murdered ('the Red') Comyn. Tempers rose
while Bruce was conferring with Comyn, who had come here as the
representative of John Balliol, the rival claimant to the crown. Bruce
stabbed Comyn, then ran out of the friary, crying 'I doubt I have slain
the Comyn', whereupon Bruce's supporter, Roger Kirkpatrick, reply-
ing 'I'll mak siccar', went in and finished Comyn off.

Midsteeple (1707), the former tolbooth, marks the town centre. On
it there is a plan in relief showing how Dumfries was in Burns's time,
and also a distance table which includes the distance to Huntingdon
in England, once the end of the road for the Scots cattle drovers.
Farther S, Bank Street, dropping W off High Street, was formerly the
Wee Vennel in which Burns found his first home (plaque). Burns
gave this street yet another name, Stinking Vennel, because an open
culvert here carried blood and offal from the meat market down to
the river. It was in the County Hotel, just S on High Street and then
called the Commercial Hotel, that the Young Pretender held a council.
Farther S, off the E side of High Street, Burns's favourite tavern (or
howff), the *Globe Inn*, with the poet's chair and other relics, still
welcomes those in search of atmosphere and a drink. *Burns House*,
in Burns Street a short distance beyond, was the poet's second and

last home in Dumfries, and the home also of his wife, Jean Armour,
until her death in 1834. Admirably refurbished, the house now serves
as a Burns museum (April–June, and Sept: Tues.–Sat., 10.00 to 13.00.
14.00 to 17.00. Sun., 14.00 to 17.00. July and Aug: Daily 10.00 to
17.00. Oct–March: Tues.–Sat., 10.00 to 13.00. 14.00 to 17.00. Tel:
0387–55297. Fee).

St. Michael's Church, a few yards farther S across a main road,
was built in 1750. A tablet on a pillar near·the entrance marks the
Burns family pew, and in the churchyard stands the *Burns
Mausoleum,* an elaborate Grecian edifice to which his body was
moved in 1815 and within which also rest his wife and several of his
children. The monument contains a sculptured group by Peter
Turnerelli depicting the Muse of Poetry finding Burns at the plough.
But Burns is not the sole focus of interest in this melancholy
churchyard which contains many weird tombs, one being the mass
grave of the hundreds who died in the cholera outbreak of 1832. And
here, too, near the mausoleum, a grey·granite pyramid marks the
tomb of three Covenanters, executed (two in 1667, one in 1685) on
Whitesands beside the river (see also below).

The waterfront (Whitesands) with its part 15C six-arched *Old
Footbridge* is the most attractive part of Dumfries. The first bridge
here was a wooden one put up by Devorguilla Balliol in the 13C, this
being succeeded by a stone bridge of 1431, a part of the W arch of
which is said to have survived. This bridge was wrecked by floods
in 1620, but was rebuilt to much the same design and using much of
the original stone. The *Old Bridge House* (April–Sept: Mon./Sat.,
10.00 to 13.00. 14.00 to 17.00. Sun., 14.00 to 17.00. Tel: 0387–53374.
Free) dates from 1662 and contains a delightful sequence of period
rooms. Below the bridge the river is broken by a weir (or caul) built
during the 18C to provide power for the grain mills, and just beyond
the weir, in the road centre, a paving stone commemorates one James
Kirko, a Covenanter shot in 1685, the last of the three remembered
on the memorial in St. Michael's churchyard.—*Dumfries Museum* is
at the Observatory, on the river's W bank 300 yards S of the footbridge
(April–Sept: Mon.–Sat., 10.00 to 13.00. 14.00 to 17.00. Sun., 14.00 to
17.00. Oct–March: Same times but closed Sun. and Mon. Tel:
0387–53374. Free). Incorporating an 18C windmill and with a camera
obscura, the museum serves as regional museum for the Solway
district.

This Rte leaves Dumfries northward by A76 which in *1m* reaches
Lincluden Abbey (AM. Standard, but closed Thurs. afternoon and
Fri. Fee). Founded in the 12C for Benedictine nuns, the house was
made collegiate (the site is sometimes called Lincluden College) by
Archibald the Grim in 1389. Of this early structure little if anything
remains, what survives today being mainly the choir and part of the
S transept of the small but exquisite 15C church. Of particular note
are the carvings from the life of Christ on the stone screen at the
entry to the choir; the effigy and decorated canopied tomb (c 1430)
of Margaret, daughter of Robert III and Countess of Douglas; and,
beside the tomb, the carved doorway bearing the Douglas heart (see
also Rte 10, Douglas). Of the domestic buildings little survives other
than garden terraces to the E. A motte stands beside the site.

5m **Ellisland Farm** (All reasonable times, but please first telephone
0387–74426. Free), on the E side of A76, is where Burns, as always
unsuccessfully, experimented with new farming methods in 1788

(display showing Burns as a farmer). As a poet, though, he was more successful since it was during his time here that he wrote 'Tam o' Shanter', 'Auld Lang Syne' and 'Mary in Heaven'. *Craigenputtock*, some 10m W of Ellisland through Dunscore, is the bleak moorland farm which was Thomas Carlyle's home from 1828–31; it was the property of his wife's mother and it was here that he wrote most of 'Sartor Resartus'.

7m **Thornhill**, where the Buccleuch and Queensberry Hotel stands on the site of a cobbler's shop to which Burns brought his shoes for repair. *Keir*, 2m SW, was the birthplace of Kirkpatrick Macmillan who in 1840 here built the first real bicycle; he rode his machine all the way to Glasgow and was fined for 'furious driving' and knocking down a girl. *Tynron Doon*, a hill fort 2m W of Thornhill, is said to have been the refuge to which Bruce fled after the murder of Comyn at Dumfries.—The village of **Moniaive**, 7m SW of Thornhill, was the birthplace of James Renwick, son of a weaver (1662–88; see also Sanquhar below), hanged in Edinburgh and the last of the Covenanter martyrs; his monument stands above the village. *Maxwelton House*, on B729 2m E of Moniaive, was the birthplace (1682) and home of Annie Laurie, subject of the haunting ballad. The original song was written by William Douglas of Fingland in c 1700; the more modern version by Lady John Scott in 1835. The early 17C house incorporates part of a 14–15C castle, originally a stronghold of the earls of Glencairn. Annie Laurie's boudoir is shown, and there is also a museum of early kitchen, dairy and farming implements (May–Sept: Wed. and Thurs., 14.00 to 17.00. Also fourth Sun. in July and Aug. Tel: 08482–385. Fee).

2m (from Thornhill) **Carronbridge**, where A702 forks NE to cross Dalveen Pass, a long and bare ascent to 1105ft following the line of a Roman road traversing the Lowther Hills. About 1m along A702 a minor road bears SE across the railway for *Morton Castle* (AM. View from outside), a small ruin of c 1480 beside a loch. A castle here was occupied during the 14C by Randolph, 1st Earl of Moray, as regent for David II; it later passed to the Douglases, a branch of whom became earls of Morton. At *Durisdeer*, off A702 4m after leaving Carronbridge, the small 17C church contains a particularly fine black-and-white marble monument (by Van Nost) to the 2nd Duke of Queensberry (died 1711) and his duchess (died 1709).

*Drumlanrig Castle is set in glorious parkland just NW of Carronbridge (Easter: Fri., Sat., Mon., 13.30 to 17.00. Sun., 14.00 to 18.00. May and June: Mon.–Sat., except Fri., 13.30 to 17.00. Sun., 14.00 to 18.00. July and Aug: Mon.–Sat., except Fri., 11.00 to 17.00. Sun., 14.00 to 18.00. May close before end Aug. Times may change. Tel: 0848–30248. Fee). This home of the Duke of Buccleuch and Queensberry, occupying the site of a 15C Douglas stronghold and close to that of a Roman fort, is a huge palace of local pink sandstone, forming a central courtyard with corner towers, built (probably by James Mylne) between 1679–90 for the 1st Duke of Queensberry. Among the superb paintings are works by Rembrandt ('Old Woman Reading'), Holbein, Murillo, Ruysdael and Rowlandson, while family portraits are by Kneller, Reynolds and Ramsay. The collection of outstandingly fine French furniture includes a cabinet given by Louis XIV to Charles II, who in turn presented it to his natural son the Duke of Monmouth and Buccleuch, and there are also some interesting relics of the Young Pretender, displayed in the bedroom in which he spent a night while on his retreat from Derby. The old kitchen now serves as a tea room, there is a gift shop in a vaulted basement, and the grounds provide formal gardens, nature trails, woodland walks, and, for the children, an adventure woodland play area.

. 5m beyond Carronbridge A76 reaches *Enterkinfoot* where the Enterkin Burn, descending from the NE, flows into the Nith. It was up this burn, along its short, narrow and steep-sided cut into the flank of the Lowther Hills, that Covenanters holding the heights forced a party of English Dragoons to hand over prisoners they were escorting, an incident well described by Daniel Defoe in his 'Memoirs of the Church of Scotland'.—*4m Mennock* is at the foot of the pass of the same name (B797) which ascends to 1409ft to reach Wanlockhead and Leadhills, for both of which see Rte 10.

2m **Sanquhar**, the southern entry to which is marked by ruined *Sanquhar Castle*, built in the 15C and in 1630 bought by Sir William Douglas of Drumlanrig whose grandson, the 1st Duke of Queensberry, lived here while the present Drumlanrig Castle was under construction, and until his death in 1695. The 2nd Duke—the one honoured by that marble monument at Durisdeer—abandoned Sanquhar when he moved into Drumlanrig.

Sanquhar is famous in the story of the Covenanters, for it was here in 1680 that Richard Cameron, a schoolteacher born in Falkland, with a band of armed supporters, affixed to the town cross the first 'Declaration of Sanquhar', renouncing allegiance to Charles II. Soon afterwards, and with a price on his head, he was killed in a skirmish on Aird's Moss NE of Cumnock, but the survivors of his band were later amnestied by William III and became the nucleus of the regiment, the Cameronians. The year 1685 saw the second Declaration, affixed by James Renwick (see Moniaive above), a young man who, fired by his theological studies in Holland, returned to his native Scotland to become a field preacher. Sadly, Sanquhar's historic cross has not survived, though its site is now marked by a monument. But something else, equally historic if very different, has survived, namely Britain's oldest *Post Office* which was providing service as long ago as 1783, a year before the introduction of the mail coach service. Another survival is the *Tolbooth* (William Adam, 1735) which houses the local museum (apply Local Government Offices, High Street. Tel: 06592–347).

16m **Cumnock** (10,000 inhab. *ECl.* Wed. *Inf.* Glaisnock Street. April–Sept) was for most of his life the home of James Keir Hardie (1856–1915), the early Socialist leader. Already at work in the coal mines at the age of ten, he later (1888) helped in the founding of the Scottish Labour Party and was elected to parliament in 1892. His bust, the work of Benno Schotz, stands outside the town hall, and here too is a monument to Alexander 'Prophet' Peden (c 1626–86), a leading Covenanter divine who, after burial at nearby Auchinleck, suffered the indignity of being exhumed by the English soldiery and re-interred in unconsecrated ground here at Cumnock.

CUMNOCK TO MUIRKIRK (A70, NE. 9m). Bello Mill, at *Lugar*, was the birthplace of William Murdoch (1754–1839), pioneer of coal-gas lighting. Beyond Lugar, A70 skirts *Aird's Moss*, a dreary moor which was the scene of the skirmish in which Richard Cameron (see Sanquhar above) lost his life, and then reaches *Muirkirk* where a cairn marks the site of John McAdam's tar works.

2m **Auchinleck**, associated with James Boswell (1740–95), lawyer and man of letters, best known as the close friend and biographer of Dr Johnson. Boswell's father, the Edinburgh lawyer Alexander Boswell, on being raised to the bench took the title of Lord Auchinleck, a place in which his family had long had roots. The ancient parish church, reaching back to Early Christian origins, was enlarged in the 12 and 17C, on the latter occasion by a Boswell, and now serves as a *Boswell Museum* (Tel: 1290 20757. Donation), which also contains a memorial to William Murdoch (see above), together with documents and relics. James Boswell, a man who described himself as '... pleasant and gay, For frolic by nature designed', is buried in the adjoining Boswell mausoleum, built by his father in 1754.

5m **Mauchline** is a village which, with Dumfries and Alloway, will surely be an obligatory stop for all Burns enthusiasts. Here in 1788 the poet was married to Jean Armour, daughter of a local mason, in Gavin Hamilton's house near the 15C Mauchline Tower, and the cottage at which he afterwards lived is now the *Burns House Museum* which includes Jean Armour's upper floor room, furnished in the style of her time (Easter–Oct: Mon.–Sat., 11.00 to 12.30. 13.30 to 17.30. Sun., 13.30 to 17.30. Tel: 0290–50045. Fee). *Poosie Nansie's Tavern*, inspiration and setting for part of 'The Jolly Beggars', is still a public house, and in the churchyard, scene of 'The Holy Fair', are buried four of the poet's children and several of his friends.

Nor are Burns associations confined to the village. *Mossgiel*, just NW, was the site of the farm (since rebuilt) at which between 1784–88 the poet and his brother Gilbert lived and farmed, as always unsuccessfully, while *Lochlea*, farther NW, was the Burns family home before this, another disastrous farm and the place where Burns's father died. Yet more will be found along or close to A758 linking Mauchline with Ayr. At *Failford* a monument marks the place where, it is popularly accepted, Burns bade farewell to Mary Campbell, his 'Highland Mary'—his betrothed for the few months she had yet to live and, after her death, the subject of the poignant 'To Mary in Heaven'. Then comes Tarbolton, associated with the youthful Lochlea period and particularly with the *Bachelors' Club*, a 17C house in which Burns and some friends founded their literary and debating society; in which, too, Burns was initiated as a freemason (NTS. April–Oct: Daily, 10.00 to 18.00. Fee). To the W of Tarbolton, 2m S of A758 and 4m E of Ayr, there is *Leglen Wood* (on some maps *Laighland*) in which Wallace is believed to have hidden before burning the Barns of Ayr. Burns, to whom, understandably, Wallace was a hero, often visited here 'with as much devout enthusiasm as ever pilgrim did the shrine of Loretto' and a cairn of 1929 now commemorates his visits. The *Barnweil Monument* of c 1860, 2m N of Tarbolton, marks the height from which Wallace is thought to have watched Ayr burning.

Sorn, 3m E of Mauchline, is a straggling village with, at its W end, a most attractive bridge and a 17C church with jougs hanging on the wall. Alexander Peden (see Cumnock above) ended his days as a fugitive in a cave near here.

8m **Kilmarnock** (52,000 inhab. *ECl.* Wed. *Inf.* Civic Centre), today a confusing, largely industrial town, was in its quieter 18C days well known to Burns, for here in 1786 was published the first edition of his poems—an event which brought the poet fame and £20, and a century later (1879) led to the erection of the *Burns Monument* in

Kay Park in the NE part of the town. The monument, an ugly red sandstone structure with an 80ft tower and a statue of Burns by W.G. Stevenson, houses material on the poet's life and work (By arrangement. Tel: 0563–26401).

Kilmarnock's perhaps more important other museum is the *Dick Institute*, in Elmbank Avenue off London Road (April–Sept: Mon., Tues., Thurs., Fri., 10.00 to 20.00. Wed. and Sat., 10.00 to 17.00. Oct.–March: Mon.–Sat., 10.00 to 17.00. Tel: 0563–26401. Free). Here are a good geological collection, local archaeological material, a natural history section, a display of Scottish weapons, and an art gallery with changing exhibitions. *Dean Castle*, in Dean Road off Glasgow Road (Mid May–mid Sept: Mon.–Fri., 14.00 to 17.00. Sat., and Sun., 12.00 to 17.00. Tel: 0563–26401. Free), in turn 14C stronghold and 15C palace, was the seat of the Boyds, lords Kilmarnock, the last of whom lost his head after Culloden. Arms and armour, tapestry and musical instruments are among the collections here, while the grounds have been designated a Country Park.

ENVIRONS OF KILMARNOCK. To the N., *Kilmaurs* (3m by A735) has a delightful, almost miniature tolbooth, still with jougs hanging from its wall. *Rowallan Castle*, NE of Kilmaurs off B751, is an outstanding example of a 16–17C mansion (AM. View from outside until opened).—For *Dundonald Castle*, 5m W, see Rte 16.—Wallace is thought to have spent much of his youth at his uncle's farm at *Riccarton*, 1m S.

KILMARNOCK TO STRATHAVEN (A71, E. 18m). *Cessnock Castle*, just S of Galston, was visited by Mary, Queen of Scots, soon after her defeat at Langside. Sir Alexander Fleming (1881–1955), discoverer of penicillin, was born at *Darvel*. *Louden Hill*, 11m from Kilmarnock, a prominent rocky knoll immediately N of the road, is the spot where in 1306 Bruce, with only 600 men, defeated the Earl of Pembroke's six thousand. To the N of *Drumclog*, 2m farther E, an obelisk commemorates 1 June 1679 when Claverhouse (Dundee), leading Lifeguards and Dragoons, was routed by a mere 200 Covenanters. **Strathaven** (pron. Strayven) offers the visitor ruined 15C *Avondale Castle*; the *John Hastie Museum* of local history in Strathaven Park (May–Sept: Mon.–Fri., 14.00 to 17.00 or 16.00 on Thurs. Sat., 14.00 to 19.00. Free); and the *Town Mill and Granary*, abandoned as such when the dukes of Hamilton moved out of the

The Battle of Drumclog (1679). Claverhouse's Dragoons are defeated by a modest force of Covenanters.

castle in the early 18C and now restored and put to good use as a club, theatre and arts centre.

20m central **Glasgow** (see Rte 19), the approach to the city passing close to Pollock Park with *Pollock House Art Gallery* and the *Burrell Collection, Queen's Park* (Battle of Langside), and (until c 1988) the Glasgow *Museum of Transport*

12 Dumfries to Newton Stewart via Kirkcudbright

A710 to Dalbeattie. A745 to Castle Douglas. A75 and A711 to Kirkcudbright. A755 and A75 to Newton Stewart.—Mainly rolling pastoral country, rounding first Criffel (1868ft) and, later, Cairnharrow (1496ft). Views along the Solway coast, with many small roads down to a shore with shallow, sandy bays.

SOME HOTELS. **New Abbey**. *Abbey Arms*, 1 The Square. Tel: (038785) 215. *Criffel Inn*, 2 The Square. Tel: (038785) 244. **Castle Douglas**. *Douglas Arms*, King Street. Tel: (0556) 2231. *King's Arms*, St. Andrew's Street. Tel: (0556) 2097. **Kirkcudbright**. *Selkirk Arms*, Old High Street. Tel: (0557) 30402. **Gatehouse of Fleet**. *Murray Arms*, High Street. Tel: (05574) 207.

Total distance 67m.—*6m* **New Abbey**.—*5m* **Kirkbean**.—*15m* **Dalbeattie**.—*6m* **Castle Douglas**.—*10m* **Kirkcudbright**.—*10m* **Gatehouse of Fleet**.—*15m* **Newton Stewart**.

From **Dumfries** (see Rte 11) there is a choice of roads to Dalbeattie; the direct A711, or (this Rte) the more scenic and more interesting A710. Those who choose the A711 will nevertheless pass two historic sites, both close to Kirkgunzeon, 9m from Dumfries. One of these is *Corra Castle*, on A711 immediately S of Kirkgunzeon; once a Maxwell stronghold but today a mere fragment half lost among farm buildings, Corra was one of a number of places which afforded shelter and rest to Mary, Queen of Scots, during her flight from Scotland. The other site is *Drumcoltran Tower* (AM. Standard. Free), just over 1m N of Corra; also once belonging to the Maxwells, Drumcoltran survives as a typical example of a sternly simple mid 16C tower-house.

6m **New Abbey** is a modest village, visited for its ruined abbey, its costume museum and its corn mill.

Sweetheart Abbey (AM. Standard. Fee), an unfortunate modern elision of this place's Latin name of Dulce Cor, is so called because of the touching devotion of its founder, Devorguilla Balliol, to the memory of her husband. After his death she not only founded this abbey (in 1273; for Cistercians from Dundrennan) but also carried his heart around with her wherever she went until her own death in 1290, when she and the heart were buried together in front of the high altar. Fragments of her tomb have been incorporated in a reconstruction in the S transept, while a memorial slab (1966; from Balliol College, Oxford, which she founded) marks the original site.

Architecturally the red sandstone ruins are essentially those of the abbey church (largely EE) and include all the main arches, part of the clerestory of the nave (oddly combined with an inside passage to form a triforium), much of the transepts and choir, and a tall central

tower. The fine wheel above the three lights of the great W window
is of particular note. Only the aisle of the S transept still carries its
roof, groined and with shields at the intersections. On one of these
can be seen two pastoral staffs and a heart, while another bears the
enigmatic injunction 'Chus tim of nid' (Choose time of need). Of the
domestic buildings little remains bar the W door of the cloister, such
wholesale destruction perhaps explained by the fact that the last
abbot, Gilbert Brown of Carsluith who died in 1612, was such a
doughty opponent of the Reformation. Finally, and perhaps the most
impressive feature of this site, there is the great boulder precinct wall
which encloses some 30 acres.—In the village an amusing note is
provided by a small stone, once part of the abbey but now set into a
house, depicting a boat carrying three ladies who, the story goes,
ferried stone for the abbey across the Nith.

New Abbey Corn Mill (AM. Standard, but closed Wed. and Thurs.
afternoons. Fee) is a still functioning 18C water-powered mill.
Shambellie House Museum of Costume (May–Sept: Mon.,
Thurs.–Sat., 10.00 to 17.30. Sun., 12.00 to 17.30. Tel: 031–2257534.
Free) is housed in an unpretentious mid 19C manor designed by
David Bryce. An outstation of Edinburgh's Royal Museum of Scotland,
Shambellie displays material from that museum's Charles Stewart
Collection of European Fashionable Dress, donated by the collector
in 1977.

A710 rounds the conspicuous mass of Criffel (1868ft) to reach in
5m **Kirkbean** where the church contains a memorial font presented
by the US Navy, a reminder that *Arbigland*, 1m SE, was the birthplace
in 1747 of John Paul Jones whose father was an estate worker here.
The woods, and formal and water gardens, are open May–Sept:
Tues., Thurs., Sun., 14.00 to 18.00. Tel: 038788–213. Fee.—*9m*
Rockcliffe, a village by the shore 1m SW of White Loch on A710, is
associated with a number of nearby NTS properties, notably several
acres of coastline beside Rough Firth, and also *Mote of Mark*, a large
earthwork fort overlooking *Rough Island*, also NTS and a bird
sanctuary (because of ground-nesting birds, please do not try to visit
in May and June).

6m **Dalbeattie** (*Inf.* Car Park. Easter–Oct) is a small town built
largely of a local grey granite which until a century ago was widely
exported. *Woodside Studio* in William Street (Daily, 09.30 to 19.00.
Tel: 0556–610117. Free) exhibits and sells craft gifts and paintings.
Mote of Urr, just over 2m N beside B794, is a notable example of
mixed Saxon and early Norman fortification, in which an almost
circular mound, surrounded by a deep trench, rests on a massive
platform measuring 500 by 216ft. *North Glen Gallery* (Daily, 10.00
to 18.00. Tel: 0556–610117. Fee), at Palnackie 3m S by A711, offers
the opportunity to see crafts such as glass blowing, sculpture assembly
and steel working, while *Orchardton Tower* (AM. Standard. Free),
1m farther S, is a rare and most attractive circular tower-house built
in the mid 15C by John Cairns.

A745 now leads westward, in 1m passing the entrance to Buittle
Place, close to which stood Buittle Castle, still marked on some maps,
where John Balliol was born in 1249 and where his mother,
Devorguilla, in 1282 signed the charter founding Balliol College,
Oxford.

6m (from Dalbeattie) **Castle Douglas** (3400 inhab. *ECl.* Thurs. *Inf.*
Markethill. Easter–Oct), standing above the W end of Carlingwark

Loch, is a town which has known three names. Originally, or at any rate as far back as can be traced, this was Causewayend, from an ancient causeway which led to one of the wooded islets in the loch. Next it took the name of its loch, retaining this until 1789 when its purchase by a merchant called Douglas resulted in the present name. Long before this, though, this place was subject to the Douglases of nearby Threave, and the name Gallows Plot, still sometimes used for the S end of the loch, is a reminder of what their rule was like. The ruined Douglas castle (Threave), together with Threave gardens and wildfowl refuge, are the three attractions here for today's tourist.

Threave Castle (AM. Standard. Fee for ferry) is a tower stronghold, stern and daunting enough as such and even more so for its island situation. Built between 1369–90 by Archibald the Grim, 3rd Earl of Douglas, who died here in 1400, it was the last Douglas castle to surrender to James II in 1455 during the struggle between the crown and that family, and then only after James had brought against it the cannon Mons Meg (see also Rte 18, Edinburgh Castle). Repaired after Flodden, Threave was seized in 1640 by Covenanters who finally wrecked the interior. The tower, some 70ft high and now but a shell, once sheltered five storeys, each a single room—store, kitchen, great hall and two domestic levels—while from the kitchen a stair spiralled within a corner turret. The curtain wall represents addition during the 15C, and the 'gallows knob' still projecting over the doorway survives as a grim reminder of owners who boasted that it 'never wanted its tassel'.

Threave Gardens (NTS. Daily, 09.00 to sunset, but walled garden and glasshouses close at 17.00 and Visitor Centre is open only April–Oct: 09.00 to 18.00. Fee). The park and gardens of over 600 acres include peat, rock and water gardens, and in April and May there is a superb display of naturalised daffodils. The Victorian house (no adm.) is the NTS School of Practical Gardening.—*Threave Wildfowl Refuge* (NTS. Access Nov–March, but to controlled points only. Fee), on the Dee, attracts many species of geese and duck.

This Rte leaves Castle Douglas by A75 and in just under 4m forks left along A711 to reach (*8m* from Castle Douglas) *Tongland Power Station*, a unit of the Galloway Hydro Electric Scheme (see Rte 13, New Galloway. The power station is open to visitors mid May–mid Sept: Mon.–Sat., 10.00 to 15.30. Tel: 0557–30560. Free).

2m **Kirkcudbright** (pron. Kir-coo-bree. 2500 inhab. *ECl.* Thurs. *Inf.* Harbour Square. May–Sept.) owes its name to the Kirk of Cuthbert, an ancient church here which for a while sheltered that saint's bones. A small royal burgh (of 1455) and stewartry capital on the Dee, Kirkcudbright's open waterfront, long quay and wide, dignified 18C streets have rightly earned it the distinction of being the most attractive of the Solway towns and a place popular with artists.

The term 'stewartry' is a survival from the time when the overlordship of the Balliols, followed by that of the Douglases, was annulled in the mid 15C and their lands were placed under a royal steward. From 1526 onwards the office of steward became the hereditary right of the Catholic Maxwells, one of whom is said to have offered Kirkcudbright harbour to Philip II of Spain for use by the Armada of 1588.

Of ancient Kirkcudbright only two traces survive. One is the name Castledykes, beside the river on the W edge of the town and marking the site of the 13C castle. The other is a fragment in 19C *Greyfriars*

Church of the 13C Franciscan friary church, thought to have survived into the 16C and to have been host to Mary, Queen of Scots, in 1563. Greyfriars preserves a 16C aisle of its predecessor, in this being the tomb and effigy (1597) of Sir Thomas Mclellan who, in 1582 and using stones from the old friary, built himself the elegant castellated and turreted mansion which today, under the name *Mclellan's Castle* and long a ruin, still overlooks the harbour (AM. Standard. Fee).

Also of interest in Kirkcudbright are the *Market Cross* of 1610, standing beside the 16–17C *Tolbooth* in which John Paul Jones was once imprisoned, having been charged with the manslaughter of his ship's carpenter who had died after a flogging; the *Stewartry Museum* in St. Mary Street (Easter–Oct: Mon.–Sat., 11.00 to 13.00. 14.00 to 16.00 or 17.00 in July and Aug. Tel: 0557–30494. Fee) with a good collection of Galloway historical, domestic and crafts material as also a section devoted to John Paul Jones; *Broughton House* in High Street (Easter–Sept: Mon.–Sat., 11.00 to 13.00. 14.00 to 17.00. Oct–Easter: Tues. and Thurs., 14.00 to 17.00. Tel: 0557–31217. Fee), an 18C mansion showing the paintings of the landscape artist E.A. Hornel, who on his death in 1933 bequeathed his home and its contents to the town; and *Harbour Cottage Gallery* (March–Dec: Mon.–Sat., 10.30 to 12.30. 14.00 to 17.00. Occasional Sun., 14.00 to 17.00. Fee), a whitewashed riverside cottage showing paintings and crafts.

Beyond the S of the town, Paul Jones Point at the foot of the peninsula called St. Mary's Isle, recalls that in 1788 this marauding seaman looted the plate from the nearby house but later for some reason returned it to its owner, the Countess of Selkirk.

A visit to Kirkcudbright would scarcely be complete were it not to include *Dundrennan Abbey (AM. Standard. Fee), just under 6m SE and quickly reached by A711. Certainly no one who, be it historically or geographically, has followed the tragic story of Mary, Queen of Scots, would wish to miss this place where it all ended, at least so far as Scotland was concerned.

Founded in 1142 for Cistercians by either David I or Fergus, Lord of Galloway, Dundrennan achieved its poignant footnote in history on 15 May 1568 when Mary came here, in all probability to sleep her last night in Scotland though possibly only to rest, having already slept at Lord Herries's mansion at Terregles near Dumfries. In sharp contrast to Niddry (Rte 8) less than two weeks before, when she could scarce wait to show herself, she arrived here in secret and with her hair shorn for disguise. She wrote a letter to Queen Elizabeth asking for sanctuary, then descended the burn to the little bay now called Port Mary, whence she crossed to England.
    In 1606 the abbey came into the possession of the Earl of Annandale, thereafter being neglected and used as a quarry. Dundrennan village is partly built of the abbey's stones.

The ruins are those of the abbey church, the W door leading into all that remains of the nave, off which the transepts, with roofless aisles on the E side, are the abbey's most beautiful remnants. Here the pointed arches in the N transept are surmounted by blind arcading, and those in the S by a triforium. An exquisite 13C pointed doorway, with elegant windows on either side, was the entrance to the chapter house. Of the choir, with plain round windows, only the N and S walls remain. In the N transept there is a monument to Alan, Lord of Galloway, father of Devorguilla Balliol. On the W side of the ruins

A711, followed E, in 4m reaches *Auchencairn*, at the mouth of the bay of the same name being *Hestan Island*; once a home of Edward Bruce, this was also the 'Isle Rathan' of Crockett's 'The Raiders' (see Rte 13, Raiders' Road Forest Drive).

Kirkcudbright is left by A755 for (*10m*) **Gatehouse of Fleet** (*Inf.* Car Park. Easter–Oct), a small place at the head of the estuary of the Water of Fleet. *Fleet Forest*, with a visitor centre and forest walks, lies to the S, while 1m to the W beside A75 will be found *Cardoness Castle* (AM. Standard. Fee), a ruined 15C tower-house of four storeys above a vaulted basement, particularly interesting on account of its original stairway, stone benches and elaborate fireplaces. Cardoness—and hence its name—belonged originally to the De Cardines, but by 1450 ownership had passed to the McCullochs of Galloway. In the churchyard at *Anwoth*, just N of Cardoness, there is an 8C Christian cross.

A75 skirts Cairnharrow (1496ft) and runs above wooded and rocky Ravenshall Point before crossing Kirkdale Burn (*5m* from Gatehouse of Fleet). On the shore, a short way E of the burn's mouth, is *Dirk Hatteraick's Cave*, the largest of several here, while the woods to the NE hide the remains of *Barholm Castle*, a 16–17C McCulloch stronghold. And it is worth driving half a mile up the glen to find the two chambered cairns together known as *Cairn Holy*. At the first a stone cist can be clearly seen, as can also standing stones in front of which funerary rites would have been celebrated. The more modest cairn just to the N is interesting for its double chamber.—*2m Carsluith Castle* (AM. Standard. Free), a roofless 16C tower-house built to the L-plan, was the home of Abbot Brown who at Sweetheart Abbey so staunchly opposed the Reformation.—*3m* **Creetown** enjoys the odd distinction of having supplied the granite for the building of Liverpool's docks. A turning opposite the clock tower leads to the *Gem Rock Museum*, displaying a large collection of gems, rocks and minerals of worldwide provenance. Cutting, shaping and polishing can all be viewed, and there is also a shop (Daily, 09.30 to 19.00 or 17.00 in winter. Tel: 067182–357. Fee).—*2m Palnure*, where a sign directs to the FC Daltamie picnic site, starting place for forest trails to Bruntis lochs. At *Kirroughtree Forest Garden* (sign on A75 just S of Palnure) paths lead through 60 different species of trees.—*3m* **Newton Stewart**, see Rte 13.

13 Dumfries to Stranraer and Rhinns of Galloway via New Galloway and Newton Stewart

A75 to Crocketford. A712 to Newton Stewart. A75 to Stranraer.—Pastoral and downland countryside as far as New Galloway, between which and Newton Stewart A712 skirts the S edge of Galloway Forest Park with the finest 'Highland' scenery in southern Scotland.

SOME HOTELS. **Crocketford**. *Galloway Arms*, DG2 8RA. Tel: (055669) 240. **New Galloway**. *Ken Bridge*, DG7 3PR. Tel: (06442)

211. **Newton Stewart**. *Bruce*, 88 Queen Street. Tel: (0671) 2282.
Stranraer. *George*, 49 George Street. Tel: (0776) 2487. *North West
Castle*, Royal Crescent. Tel: (0776) 4413. **Portpatrick**. *Fernhill*,
Hough Road. Tel: (077681) 220. *Knockinaam Lodge*, DG9 9AD. Tel:
(077681) 471.

Total distance 64m.—*9m* **Crocketford**.—*15m* New Galloway.—*17m*
Newton Stewart.—*14m* Glenluce Abbey.—*9m* **Stranraer**.

Dumfries, see Rte 11.—*6m* Deanside is little more than a name on
the map, but it is from here that a minor road leads N through
Shawhead to reach in 3m *Glenkiln Reservoir* where sculpture by
Henry Moore, Epstein and Rodin stands around the reservoir.—*3m*
Crocketford where this Rte forks NW along A712 to reach (*6m*)
Corsock House Gardens with rhododendrons and a water garden
(May: Sun., 14.30 to 18.00. Tel: 06444-250. Fee).

9m **New Galloway**, a place which, though no more than a village,
nevertheless enjoys the distinction of being a royal burgh. It also
stands at the heart of the Galloway Hydro-Electric Scheme and on a
crossroads offering the motorist a choice of diversions.

Galloway Hydro-Electric Scheme. Using the waters of the Dee and Ken, this
was the first of Scotland's large-scale power schemes (1929–36). There are five
generating stations. Kendoon, Carsfad and Earlstoun, in the hills between Dalry
and Carsphairn, are supplied by reservoirs created by damming the Ken;
Glenlee is fed from Clatteringshaws Loch, 6m W of New Galloway, whence the
water is piped through a tunnel; Tongland (see Rte 12), above the Dee estuary,
utilises its own headpond and storage water from Loch Ken, raised by a dam
at Glenlochar (2m N of Castle Douglas) to form a reservoir. Loch Doon, at the
N end of the system, serves as an extra storage reservoir. Fish-passes for salmon
have been built at Tongland, Earlstoun and Carsfad, and there is a regulated
level pass at Loch Doon.

SOUTHWARD DIVERSION. Two pleasant roads run S from New Galloway.
A713 to Castle Douglas skirts the nearly 10m straggling length of
Loch Ken along its E shore.—A762 soon passes *Kenmure Castle*
(15–17C), long the seat of the Gordons of Lochinvar. The family was
host to Mary, Queen of Scots, in 1563 during her western tour, and,
after Langside, it was Lochinvar who gave her the clothing in which
she disguised herself. The 6th Viscount Kenmure was executed for
his part in the '45. Beyond, this road (to Kirkcudbright) skirts part of
Loch Ken's W shore below the fir-clad slopes of Cairn Edward Forest,
and at Bennan, 4m S of New Galloway, it passes the E entrance of
Raiders' Road Forest Drive (see below).

NORTHWARD DIVERSION (To Dalmellington. A762 and A713. 20m.
B7000 and B729 offer a lonelier and hillier alternative to the E of
Lochs Earlstoun, Carsfad and Kendoon). This diversion crosses the
empty mixed pastoral and moorland district known as *The Glenkens*,
with the heights of the Rhinns of Kells (c 2600ft), marking the SE
flank of Galloway Forest Park, away to the W. It is generally accepted
that it was across this lonely country that Mary, Queen of Scots, fled
S after Langside. *St. John's Town of Dalry*, just N of New Galloway,
is so named because here was once a church (St. John's) of the
Knights Templar; also because tradition insists that St. John the
Disciple once sat on the neat stone, shaped as a seat, which can be
seen beside a bench at the road fork at the N end of the town. Three
miles E of Dalry a gated road off A702 leads to *Lochinvar*, with an
islet and fragments of a castle, the home of Young Lochinvar of ballad
fame.—From Dalry A713 continues N through Carsphairn to reach

(17m from Dalry) a little road which angles away SW to reach *Loch Doon*, once a small loch but now a long and narrow reservoir. Here, beside the loch near the road's end, stands a ruined 14C castle, interesting less for itself than for the fact that it once occupied the islet which can still be seen when the water is low. In danger of drowning when the loch was converted to a reservoir, the castle was taken down and then re-erected on this new site. *Dalmellington*, 1m N of the road junction, has a motte.

Between New Galloway and Newton Stewart, and especially along the stretch W of Clatteringshaws Loch, this Rte traverses its most scenic miles; miles, moreover, which were known to Mary, Queen of Scots, who in 1563 travelled this road on her way from Alexander Stewart's house at Garlies near Newton Stewart to the Lochinvar castle of Kenmure.—*5m* (from New Galloway) **Clatteringshaws Loch**, site of the *Galloway Deer Museum* (FC. April–Sept: Daily, 10.00 to 17.00. Free) with attractively displayed and instructive material covering not only deer (information on the nearby Red Deer Range) but also feral goats, trout (live exhibit) and the history, botany and mineralogy of this wild district. *Bruce's Stone*, adjacent, marks the site of the Battle of Rapploch Moss (1307), a successful skirmish by Bruce against the English. The W entrance to *Raiders' Road Forest Drive* (FC. June–Sept: Daily, 09.00 to 21.00. Fee) is a short distance beyond the Deer Museum. The drive takes its name from S.R. Crocket's novel 'The Raiders' (1894), set in the period immediately following the '15 and describing a raid by the Faas and Marshalls who, following the line of today's drive, lifted cattle from the Maxwells' Solway lands and drove the herds back along the Black Water of Dee and into the hills around Loch Dee, 3m W of Clatteringshaws Loch. Crocket knew this land well, for Little Duchrae, just N of Kirkcudbright, was his birthplace. The drive (10m) is mainly through woodland planted in the last 30 or so years, but at the E end the Sitka spruce and Douglas fir were planted some 55 years ago. Many species of birds may be seen, including buzzards.

Farther W, beyond the dam marking Clatteringshaws' end, A712 skirts a *Wild Goat Enclosure*, in which the animals, feral rather than wild, can normally be seen close to the road, and reaches *Murray's Monument*, an obelisk to Alexander Murray (1775–1813) who, reared as a shepherd boy in these remote hills, and despite his living only to the age of 38, nevertheless became Professor of Oriental Languages at Edinburgh University. A short easy walk leads to the partially restored cottage in which Murray was born, while a tougher trail (Talnotry, leaflet from campsite shop) offers 4m of walk and some superb views.

12m (from Clatteringshaws Loch) **Newton Stewart** (2000 inhab. *ECl.* Wed. *Inf.* Dashwood Square. Easter–Oct) is less important for itself than as a base for visiting Galloway Forest Park to the N and the interesting Machars district (Rte 14) to the S. The town is relatively modern, having been built in the late 17C by William Stewart, a son of the then Earl of Galloway, as the result of a charter granted in 1677 by Charles II. A long main street runs above the W bank of the river Cree, which is crossed by a bridge with, at its W end, a memorial to the 9th Earl of Galloway. *Minigaff*, just NE, has a good 19C church by William Burn, as also does *Penninghame*, 2m NW, while the map entry Garlies Castle, 2m N, recalls the visit here in 1563 by Mary, Queen of Scots.

Galloway Forest Park (FC), rising immediately N of Newton Stewart, embraces some 150,000 acres of varied forest, moor, bog, loch, burn and mountains of which ten are higher than 2000ft. *Merrick*, at the centre of the park and its highest point, rises to 2766ft, and the wild, high wastes of moor hold the headwaters of at least six rivers: Stinchar, Girvan, Doon, Dee, Fleet and Cree. The reserve shelters much wildlife, such as red and roe deer and feral goats, while among the many birds are species, including the golden eagle, normally associated only with the Highlands. Only the walker can enjoy the remote best of the park, and the Forestry Commission has opened up many miles of trails far removed from any road.

The motorist can enjoy two areas. The southern area traversed by A712 and including Clatteringshaws Loch has already been described above, but the heart of the park (*Loch Trool*, 10m from Newton Stewart) is almost equally easily reached by A714 ascending the Cree up to Bargrennan where a right fork leads first to *Glentrool Village* (for forest workers) and then up the glen to Loch Trool. This loch, with its steep wooded banks and backdrop of mountains, is superbly spread below the road which climbs its N flank and commands views across a wild and remote country which successively provided refuge for Bruce and, centuries later, Covenanters. Both are commemorated. Here, on a bluff high above the loch, the *Bruce Stone* recalls a skirmish of 1306 when Bruce defeated the English by rolling boulders down on to them. Below, a path from the camp and caravan site near the foot of the loch leads to the sad little *Memorial Tomb* of six Covenanters murdered here while at prayer; a stone records their names and those of their killers.

From Newton Stewart A75 runs W to reach (*14m*) **Glenluce Abbey** (AM. April–Sept: Mon.–Sat., 09.30 to 19.00. Sun., 14.00 to 19.00. Oct–March: Sat., 09.30 to dusk. Sun., 14.00 to dusk. Fee). Founded in 1192 by Roland, Earl of Galloway, as a daughter-house of Dundrennan, Glenluce will surely appeal as much to the romantic as to the connoisseur of abbatial architecture. In these surroundings the former will readily enough accept that this was the home during the 13C of Michael Scot the Wizard; that it was to these walls that he lured the plague, and then imprisoned it in a vault; that, moreover, his books on alchemy and the occult lie buried here. Others, though, will enthuse over the intact vaulted Chapter House of 1470, entered by an ornamental round-arched doorway and having within an elegant central pillar and some Dec. windows. Also worth noting are the possibly unique interlocking red-clay water pipes. The abbey's cloister walls still stand, but of its EE church little remains save the foundations and a gable of the S transept.—*Castle of Park* (AM. View from outside), just W of Glenluce, is a castellated tower-house of the Hays, built in 1590. To the SW stretch *Luce Sands*, with dunes which once threatened the fertile land behind, but are now held by the planting of Corsican pine.

6m **Castle Kennedy Gardens** (April–Sept: Daily, 10.00 to 17.00. Tel: 0776–2024. Fee) are those of *Lochinch Castle* (1867; no adm), the stately home of the Earl of Stair. Long neglected, the gardens were restored in about 1847 to their original 17C form. The notable pinetum was the first such in Scotland, while one of the main attractions here today is the broad avenue of monkey puzzle trees, now about 100 years old and 70ft high. Within the grounds, on an isthmus between the White and Black Lochs (with a crannog), stand the ivy-clad ruins of *Castle Kennedy*. Built during the reign of James VI, the castle was the seat of the earls of Cassillis before passing to the Stair family during the 17C, only to be destroyed by fire in 1715. Park features such as Mount Marlborough and Dettingen Avenue recall the campaigns of the 2nd Earl of Stair (died 1747) who became a Field Marshal; he was also ambassador to France and, inspired by Versailles, it was he who first laid out the grounds round the old castle, unashamedly using soldiers of the Royal Scots Greys and Inniskilling Fusiliers, officially supposed to be hunting down Covenanters.

3m **Stranraer** (10,000 inhab. *ECl.* Wed. *Inf.* Port Rodie) is important as a market centre, as a holiday resort and base from which to tour the Rhinns, and, together with Cairnryan on the E side of Loch Ryan, as a port for car ferry and passenger sailings to Larne in Northern Ireland. The crossing takes just over two hours and specially priced day excursions are popular. Stranraer's only historic survival is a fragment of the *Old Castle of St. John*; over the years it served many purposes and in 1632 it was occupied for a while by Claverhouse during his persecution of the Covenanters. *North West Castle*, opposite the pier and now a hotel, was the residence of Sir John Ross (1777–1856), the Arctic explorer. In London Road the *Wigtown District Museum* (Mon–Fri., 09.30 to 13.30. 14.00 to 17.00. Sat., 09.30 to 13.00. Tel: 0776–2151. Ext. 250. Free) offers exhibits on dairy farming and Sir John Ross.

Rhinns of Galloway
Rhinns of Galloway is the name given to the hammer-shaped double peninsula that marks the SW corner of Scotland. The Rhinns are sometimes incorrectly called the Mull of Galloway, this in fact being only the S extremity.

NORTH ARM. *The Wig*, a scoop of a bay along the W shore of Loch Ryan, was used during the 1939–45 war as a repair base for flying boats. The explorer, Sir John Ross, was born at Balscalloch, some 3m NW. On the N shore stands *Corsewall Lighthouse*, built by Robert Stevenson; the view can embrace Ireland and the island of Ailsa Craig (Rte 15).

SOUTH ARM. **Portpatrick**, 5m SW of Stranraer, is a thriving if small holiday resort and the only town of significance on the Rhinns. During the 17–19C, however, it was of wider importance since between 1661 and 1849 the little harbour with its narrow entrance handled all regular sailings to Northern Ireland. Then came steam and with it the transfer of the service to Stranraer; and Portpatrick's new harbour works, constructed only six years previously, were abruptly abandoned. The ruins of early 15C *Dunskey Castle* stand on a promontory (dangerous cliff area) immediately to the S.

B7042 angles across to Sandhead on the E coast, rather over 1m SW of which, in the ancient churchyard of a little church, will be found the *Kirkmadrine Stones*, generally accepted as being among the earliest Christian memorials in Britain (5–12C). Some of the stones bear Latin inscriptions and the 'Chi-Rho' symbol, formed by combining the first two letters of Christ's name as written in Greek, and it is interesting that the stones suggest the successful presence of Christianity in this remote corner only a few years after the arrival of St. Ninian at Whithorn in c 400.—*Ardwell House Gardens*

(March–Oct: Daily, 10.00 to 18.00. Tel: 077686–227. Donation), 2m farther S, offer daffodils and rhododendrons, while *Logan Botanic Garden* (April–Sept: Daily, 10.00 to 17.00. Tel: 077686–231. Fee), another 2m S, shows sub-tropical plants flowering in a district which enjoys the mildest climate in Scotland. Cabbage palms and tree ferns are among the southern hemisphere species to be seen here. One mile S, on the N shore of Logan Bay, will be found a tidal *Sea Fish Pond* (Easter–Sept: Mon., Wed.–Fri., Sun., 10.00 to 12.00. 14.00 to 17.30. Tel: 077686–300. Fee). Built in 1800 as a larder for Logan House, but closed 1939–55 due to war and damage by a mine, the pond now contains fish (mainly cod) sufficiently tame to be fed by hand.

Mull of Galloway is a bold headland with cliffs 200ft high and a lighthouse. Double Dykes, two earthworks across the W end of the Mull, was traditionally the site of the last defence of the Picts against Scots pressing down from the N.

14 Newton Stewart to Wigtown, Whithorn and Glenluce

A714 to Wigtown. A746 to Whithorn. A750 to Isle of Whithorn. A747 to Glenluce.—Farmland and modest coastal scenery.

SOME HOTELS. **Wigtown**. *Fordbank Country House*, DG8 9BT. Tel: (09884) 2346. **Whithorn**. *Castlewigg*, DG8 8DL. Tel: (09885) 213. **Isle of Whithorn**. *Queen's Arms*, 22 Main Street. Tel: (09885) 369. **Port William**. *Monrieth Arms*, DG8 9SE. Tel: (09887) 232.

Total distance 44m.—*7m* **Wigtown**.—*10m* **Whithorn**.—*4m* **Isle of Whithorn**.—*23m* **Glenluce Abbey**.

Newton Stewart, see Rte 13.—*7m* **Wigtown**, a little royal burgh (1457) with a dignified, spacious square, is known for the Wigtown martyrs; Margaret Lachlan, aged 62, and Margaret Willson, a girl of 18, two Covenanters who in 1685 were tied to a stake in the estuary and left to drown in the rising tide. Together with other Covenanter martyrs they now rest in the churchyard. The *Martyrs' Monument*, on high ground above the town, was erected in 1858, but the *Martyrs' Stake*, standing lone by the traditional site on the bleak estuary flats, is a great deal more moving. The small town, sprawled over a hill, boasts two Burgh Crosses (1738, 1816), and, lower down the hill, the church incorporates a ruined Gordon chantry. To the N of the river mouth, once with a harbour, a grassy mound marks the site of the old castle, but of a Dominican priory founded here by Devorguilla Balliol there survives no trace. *Torhouse Stone Circle*, 3m W beside B733, comprises 19 stones forming a circle 60ft in diameter with three individual stones in the centre.

5m A746 runs through *Kilsture Forest* with a 1m-long trail starting from the Forest Office.—*1m* **Sorbie**, from where B7052 leads E for 2m to reach *Galloway House Gardens* (Daily, at any reasonable time. Tel: 09886–641. Fee), with ancient beech and other trees, spring flowers and a walled garden. The house (no adm.), now owned by Help the Aged, was built by the 5th Earl of Galloway in 1740. *Cruggleton Church* (keys from nearby farm), between B7063 and the

sea a mile or so S of Galloway House, is one of the few examples of
Norman architecture in this part of Scotland. By the shore an arch is
about all that remains of what was once a Comyn coastal defence
fortress.

4m (from Sorbie by A746) **Whithorn**. Although a royal burgh since
the time of Bruce, this little place enjoys a more ancient and, some
would say, more important past as the place where in 397 St. Ninian,
a local man who had made a pilgrimage to Rome and studied there,
introduced Christianity to Scotland, building a small stone church
which he covered with white plaster. This stone and plaster, contrasting with the dark wattle of the peasant huts, earned the building
the Anglo-Saxon name 'huit aern' (becoming Whithorn) meaning a
white house (also called in Latin the 'Candida Casa').

According to Bede, writing centuries later, St. Ninian dedicated his church to
his master in Rome, St. Martin of Tours, who is also reputed to have sent masons
to help shape the walls after the Roman fashion. (Excavations of c 1895 and
1948–63 revealed the walls of an ancient building, with a coat of light-coloured
plaster over the masonry, making it reasonably certain that here indeed was
the site of St. Ninian's 'huit aern'. For preservation, these remains are now
covered.) Christianity throve here, Whithorn becoming an important missionary
centre and shrine. The bishopric—first Celtic, and then in the 8–9C
Northumbrian—was revived in c 1125, and in c 1160 a Premonstratensian priory
was founded here to serve the shrine. For many generations Whithorn was
visited by pilgrims of all ranks and many nationalities, some of the better-known
pilgrims being Bruce (1329) and James III, IV, and V, James IV being particularly
devoted and coming here almost annually. After 1560 the nave of the church
served as a cathedral for the now Protestant bishop, and from 1689 to 1822 it
was the parish church.

Priory and Museum (AM. Standard. Fee). Today's site is approached
through what is known as The Pend, a 17C arch flanked by 15C
pillars with sculpted coats-of-arms and surmounted by a panel with
the Scottish arms as borne before the Union. Of the Priory all that
remains above ground is the 13C nave of the church, with some
17–18C alterations. On the S side of the church are two doorways,
that at the W end, with fine mouldings, dating from the 12C; the
other is 13C, with a rich outer archway of c 1500. Inside the church,
on the N side, there are two canopied tombs of c 1300 and a 17C
arched recess. The choir and E chapels have disappeared, but the
crypts (c 1200) beneath the latter have survived, in them being late
medieval tombs overlying an early Christian cemetery.—The
*Museum is of its kind outstanding, with graphic and admirably clear
explanations of local history and an important collection of Early
Christian crosses and stones. The *Latinus (or Barrovadus) Stone of
450, the earliest Christian memorial in Scotland, records the burial
of one Latinus and his daughter (very probably members of St.
Ninian's flock) and the fact that the stone was set up by Latinus's
grandson, Barrovadus. The St. Peter Stone (7C) is also of particular
interest as bearing lettering of a type normally found only in Gaul.
   Rispain Camp (1m SW of Whithorn, off A746), an enclosure within
earthworks, may have been a medieval farm.
   4m **Isle of Whithorn** is not in fact an island, but a little port within
a rather desolate coast of low rocks. It is a popular centre for tope
and shark fishing. Ruined *St. Ninian's Chapel*, dating from c 1300
and on the foundations of an even older building, was probably used
by pilgrims to Whithorn arriving from overseas. A late 17C tower-

house overlooks the village.

Isle of Whithorn is left by A750, this Rte soon forking left along A747. One mile beyond the fork a minor road drops seaward for *St. Ninian's Cave* (short walk), said to have been used by the saint as an oratory. Small votive crosses on the wall and on the rocks outside date from about the 8C. For much of the next 20m the road runs along a coast of low rock, with several small sites of interest either beside the road or within 4m of the shore.

8m (from Isle of Whithorn) *Barsalloch Fort*, on the inland side of A747 by Barsalloch Point, is an Iron Age fort sprawled over a bluff some 60ft high and surrounded by a wide and deep ditch.—*2m* **Port William**, whence A714 in 3m reaches *Drumtrodden Stones*, two groups of exceptionally clear Bronze Age cup-and-ring markings on natural rock. Four hundred yards S there is an alignment of three standing stones.—*Mote of Druchtag*, just N of Mochrum less than 2m NW of Drumtrodden, is a typical early medieval earthwork, with some traces of stone buildings.—*5m* (from Port William) *Chapel Finian*, beside A747, although now little more than foundations, a wall and traces of a well, was once a 10–11C chapel dedicated to St. Findbarr. An evocative, modest ruin, standing beside an inlet in the rocks, the chapel may be pictured as serving pilgrims landing here on their way perhaps to Glenluce, perhaps to Whithorn.—*Old Place of Mochrum* (4m inland off B7005. No adm. but seen from the road) is a 15–16C castle with two towers.—*8m* **Glenluce Abbey** , see Rte 13.

15   Stranraer to Ayr

A77, with alternatives after Turnberry.—A coastal road offering access to a rocky and often seaweedy shore; some sandy bays. Views across the water to Ailsa Craig and Arran. The road runs through the former territory of the Kennedys, successors to the earls of Carrick (a title held by Bruce) and later earls of Cassillis. Of this once powerful family—the ruins of whose castles and watchtowers will be found crumbling along the coast and up many glens—doggerel asserts:

'Twixt Wigtown and the town of Ayr,
Portpatrick and the Cruives of Cree,
No man may think for to bide there,
Unless he court St. Kennedie.

SOME HOTELS. **Girvan**. *Westcliffe*, 15 Louisa Drive, Tel: (0465) 2128. **Turnberry**. *Turnberry*. Tel: (06553) 202. **Alloway**. *Burns Monument*. Tel: (0292) 42466. **Ayr**. *Ayrshire and Galloway*, 1 Killoch Place. Tel: (0292) 262626. *Caledonian*, Dalblair Road. Tel: (0292) 269331. *Horizon*, The Esplanade. Tel: (0292) 264384. *Stakis*, Burns Statue Square. Tel: (0292) 263268.

Total distance 45m.—*15m* **Ballantrae**.—*10m* **Girvan**.—*5m* **Turnberry**.—*15m* **Ayr**.

Leaving **Stranraer** (see Rte 13), A77 runs northward skirting the E shore of Loch Ryan, once used as an anchorage by the Romans who knew it as Rerigonius Sinus. In just under 2m the hamlet of *Innermessan* is reached, with a motte by the shore, while just beyond, to the E of the road, ruined *Craigcaffie Castle* provides an example of 13C architectural ingenuity, for this late 16C keep rests on 13C foundations, laid, or so it is said, on bags of wool because the ground was so boggy.—*5m* (from Stranraer) **Cairnryan** is the port for a car ferry service to Larne in Northern Ireland. During the 1939–45 war the harbour facilities here were of some importance, latterly controlled by the Americans, and components of the 'Mulberry Harbour' used in the 1944 Normandy invasion were made here.

Briefly leaving the shore the road now ascends wooded Glen App to return to the coast at (*10m*) **Ballantrae** which is not, as might be thought, the scene of R.L. Stevenson's 'The Master of Ballantrae', (this was Borgue, SW of Kirkcudbright). Stevenson did, though, visit here in 1876 and, with his usual good humour, recorded that people threw stones at him because of the eccentricity of his dress. Above the village stands the shell of *Ardstinchar Castle*, host to Mary, Queen of Scots, during her royal progress of 1563 and coastal (Ard) guardian of the Stinchar valley, today ascended by B7044 (becoming A765); roads which pass fragments of Kennedy strongholds and, above Colmonell, a monument to John Snell (1629–59) who, despite his short life, founded exhibitions to help Scottish students at Balliol College, Oxford.—*5m* **Carleton Castle**, now a ruin but once one of a line of proud Kennedy watchtowers along the coast, has achieved a more lasting fame in ballad, for this, we are told, was the seat of a baron who rid himself of seven wives by pitching them over the cliff, but was finally himself similarly disposed of by his eighth, a redoubtable lady called May Cullean. Beyond, another reminder of this coast's former lords, the road reaches first Kennedy's Pass and then 16 and 18C Ardmillan Castle, despite its name a Kennedy possession until 1658.

5m ***Girvan** (8000 inhab. *ECl.* Wed. *Inf.* Bridge Street. April–Oct) is a sizeable resort, typical of this coast, with a spacious waterfront and good sands. A touch of history can be found in the public gardens on Knockcushan Hill above the harbour where a stone records that Bruce presented a charter and held his court on this hill, the name of which means the Hill of Justice. *Penkill Castle* (April–Sept: By appointment. Tel: 046587–261. Fee), 3m NE at Old Dailly, traces its origin to c 1420 and was until recent years the seat of the Boyds, one of whom, Spencer Boyd, in 1857 castellated his by then largely 16–17C mansion. But it is for its Pre-Raphaelite association that Penkill is best known for in the 19C this was the home of William Bell Scott (1811–90) who here welcomed Rossetti and several of his contemporaries and even built a gallery to house their works. Sadly, Penkill's Pre-Raphaelite collection has been dispersed, but visitors can still see some paintings as also antique furniture and tapestry.

*Ailsa Craig, also sometimes known as 'Paddy's Milestone' for being half-way between Belfast and Glasgow, is a solid 1114ft-high mountain island 10m offshore from Girvan. In Gaelic the name means Fairy Rock—singularly inappropriate for such a lump of granite—and Burns surely showed a finer perception when, in 'Duncan Gray', he wrote that 'Meg was deaf as Ailsa Craig'. In medieval times the rock belonged to Crossraguel Abbey, and it is no surprise to learn that it may have been used as a place to which the abbot exiled his less tractable monks. Later, during the Reformation, Ailsa Craig became a refuge for Catholics, some of whom at one time openly declared that they were holding it on behalf of Philip II of Spain. Once famed

as provider of the best granite curling stones, today the island is part
bird sanctuary (gannets, puffins, guillemots and other seabirds). In
summer there are boat excursions from Girvan, time being allowed
for a walk around the rock (c 2m) at low tide or for a climb to the
top, on the way passing a medieval tower.

B741, ascending Girvan Water, offers two scenic northern approaches to
Galloway Forest Park (Rte 13). The first road is from Crosshill, the second from
Straiton, the two merging in the heart of Carrick Forest to follow the lovely
course of the Water of Minnoch.

5m **Turnberry** is an internationally recognised golf centre with two
courses overlooked by a huge hotel. *Turnberry Castle*, fragments of
which adjoin the lighthouse, which probably stands on the medieval
courtyard, claims (as does Lochmaben, see Rte 7) to be the birthplace
of Bruce. But, whether he was born here or not, Turnberry was long
the centre of intrigue to put him on the throne, a role which was
probably the cause of the castle's destruction in 1307, the year in
which, lured it is said by a mystic fire, Bruce came across from Arran.

*A lighthouse marks the site of Turnberry Castle, closely
associated with Bruce.*

At Turnberry a choice must be made between the coastal and
inland roads to Ayr, the former passing Robert Adam's elegant
Culzean Castle, the latter the equally elegant but ruined abbey of
Crossraguel. There are several linking roads enabling a criss-cross
course to be planned.

Coastal Road to Ayr

4m ***Culzean Country Park and Castle** (pron. Cullane. NTS and
others. Grounds always open. Fee for cars. For Castle and Visitor
Centre, see below). The showplace along this part of the coast, the
Culzean complex comprises the fine mixed woodland park, a visitor
centre, and the great Robert Adam castle sprawled above the sea.

The estate, the seat of the Kennedys since the 14C, was given to the National Trust for Scotland in 1945.

Visitors are rightly encouraged to go first to the *Visitor Centre* (April–Sept: Daily, 10.00 to 18.00. Oct: Daily, 12.00 to 17.00. Free), a most successful and pleasing conversion of the 1777 Robert Adam Home Farm. The centre is the base for the park's ranger service, the starting point for guided walks and the venue for talks and films. Facilities include an auditorium, exhibition, shop and restaurant. The *Country Park*, of 560 acres and the first (1970) in Scotland to be declared such, includes a beautiful and mellow walled garden established since 1783, an adventure playground, a deer park and some 17m of woodland walks through rare trees and shrubs.

Culzean Castle (April–Sept: Daily, 10.00 to 18.00. Oct: Daily, 12.00 to 17.00. Fee), one of Robert Adam's outstanding achievements, was built between 1772–92 for the 10th Earl around an ancient Kennedy tower. Particular features are the handsome Oval Staircase, the Round Drawing Room, and the plaster ceilings now restored to Adam's original colouring. A flat in the castle was presented to General (later President) Eisenhower for his use during his lifetime and an Eisenhower Presentation now illustrates the General's link with Culzean.

Beyond Culzean A719 soon passes a road (B7023) to Maybole on the inland route to Ayr and then reaches (*5m*) *Dunure Castle*, the stark cliffside ruin of a castle in which in 1563 Mary, Queen of Scots, spent one of the first nights of her royal progress. Here, too, some seven years later in 1570, the then Earl of Cassillis is said to have roasted in soap the lay-abbot of Crossraguel in an attempt to persuade him to surrender the rich abbey lands. Whether or not this treatment succeeded does not seem to be recorded, but the abbey's days were in any case numbered and by 1592 it had succumbed to the Dissolution.—*6m* **Ayr**, see below.

Inland Road to Ayr

From Turnberry A77 angles NE to reach in *3m* **Kirkoswald**, a village where Burns went to school. Here *Souter Johnnie's Cottage* (NTS. April–Sept: Daily except Fri., 12.00 to 17.00. Fee) was the home of John Davidson, the original of the Souter (cobbler) Johnnie of Burns's 'Tam o' Shanter', Tam being Douglas Graham of nearby Shanter Farm. The cottage shows Burns material, contemporary furniture and the tools of a village cobbler, while in the restored ale-house are life-size stone figures (by James Thom) of Souter, Tam, the innkeeper and his wife. Both Davidson and Graham are buried in the village churchyard.

2m ***Crossraguel Abbey** (AM. Standard, except closed Thurs. afternoon and Fri. Fee) was founded in 1244 by Duncan, Earl of Carrick, for Cluniac monks from Paisley, these remaining in occupation until 1592, probably later than at any other abbey in Scotland. The abbots enjoyed the convenient privilege of minting their own coins. More intact and extensive than many of their kind, these ruins allow a clearer picture than is usual of abbey life as it may have been. This is especially so of the 16C turreted *Gatehouse*, each floor complete with its window seats and garderobe; of the *Dovecot*, now merely decorative but once so essential to the community's economy; and of the *Abbot's House*. The gatehouse and keep, both products of the increasing militarisation of Scottish life around the 15–16C, may have been built by the same lay-abbot, Allan Stewart, who was roasted in soap at Dunure (see above). Another monastic remain is the handsome rectangular *Chapter House*, with beautifully groined vaulting sweeping from a slender central pillar. The ruined *Church* consists of nave and choir, ending in a 15C three-sided apse in which the sedilia are, unusually, of four seats. Part of the foundations of the original transepts can be seen, and the Sacristy, entered from the choir, retains its 15C vault.

2m **Maybole** (5000 inhab. *ECl*. Wed.), sprawled over a hill, is a lively town which has long been the centre for the district of Carrick. The *Tolbooth* preserves the 17C tower of a town mansion of a branch of the Kennedys, and the *Castle*, restored now and used for offices, was that of the earls of Cassillis. Below the main street are the ruins of the 15C *Collegiate Church* (college founded 1373), the sacristy of which was early enlarged as a Kennedy burial place, while, adjacent, the old graveyard is on the site of a 12C church founded by Duncan, Earl of Carrick.

B7024 is now followed N for (*5m*) **Alloway**, the village in which Burns was born in 1759 and lived his first seven years and, more even than either Dumfries or Mauchline, today a focus of Burns pilgrimage. The local tour is best started at the adjacent *Interpretation Centre* and *Burns Cottage* (April, May, Sept., Oct: Mon.–Sat., 10.00 to 17.00. Sun., 14.00 to 17.00. June–Aug: Daily, 09.00 to 19.00. Nov–March: Mon.–Sat., 10.00 to 16.00. Tel: 0292–41215. Fee, which includes Burns Monument). Originally a clay hut, this thatched cottage was rebuilt by Burns's father with his own hands and served as the family's home between 1757 and 1766 when they moved to Mount Oliphant, a farm about a mile to the SE. The cottage and interpretation centre mark the start of the Burns Heritage Trail, and facilities here include a shop and tea room.

A short distance to the S will be found *Alloway Kirk* which was a ruin even before Burns's time. The poet's father is buried here, and it was through the E window that Tam o' Shanter watched a witches' orgy. Opposite the church is the *Land o' Burns Centre* (Daily. Spring and Autumn: 10.00 to 18.00. Summer: 10.00 to 21.00. Winter: 10.00 to 17.00. Tel: 0292–43700. Free, but fee for audio-visual display) with an exhibition and an audio-visual presentation. Just beyond stands the startling *Burns Monument* (April–mid Oct: Daily, 09.00 to 19.00. Tel: 0292–41215. Fee, which includes Burns Cottage), a most inappropriate Grecian round temple showing yet more Burns material. Below, and in pleasing contrast, the river is spanned by *Brig o' Doon*, a single arch, possibly of the 13C, which features in 'Tam o' Shanter' as the means by which Tam escaped from the witches who dared not cross running water.

The *Maclaurin Gallery*, at Rozelle House just N of Alloway and just E of the Ayr road, offers a change from Burns. Both the gallery proper, in the servants' quarters and stables, and the main house are used for exhibitions of fine art, sculpture, crafts and local history (Mon.–Sat., 11.00 to 17.00. Also in April–Oct: Sun., 14.00 to 17.00. Free).

2m **Ayr** (50,000 inhab. *ECl*. Wed. *Inf*. 39 Sandgate) is a large, busy town which with its extensive sands and many amenities ranks as the principal resort along this coast. The amenities include three golf-courses, town-owned river fishing, one of Scotland's leading racecourses, swimming baths with three heated pools, and three fine

Alloway, Burns Monument. Incongruous today, but in 1820 imperatively Classical.

parks offering a total of 489 acres of open space. And for visitors with interests more literary than recreational there is a strong, almost ubiquitous Burns connection.

History. A settlement as far back as the 8C, Ayr received its first charter in c 1202 from William the Lion. Less than a century later Wallace was active here, one of his earliest, best known and bloodiest exploits (1297) being the burning, with 500 English soldiers, of the 'Barns of Ayr', a collection of temporary wooden barracks erected by Edward I. A year later, to prevent its occupation by the English, the castle near the river mouth was demolished by Bruce. In 1315 the parliament which settled the succession of the Scottish crown in the event of Bruce's death met in the (old) church of St. John, a church which later was absorbed into the great fort covering 12 acres built by Cromwell in 1652. In medieval times Ayr harbour saw Perkin Warbeck sail in 1497 to his final defeat, and James IV berthed and anchored his fleet here in 1513.

Alloway Street, extended by High Street, forms Ayr's curving main axis, most places of interest lying close either side over a distance of roughly half a mile between the station in the S and the New Bridge in the N.

Burns extolled Ayr as unsurpassed 'for honest men and bonnie lasses' and thus earned himself the statue (George Lawson, 1891) in front of the railway station. The *Tam o' Shanter Museum*, on the right of the road by the start of High Street, is generally accepted as the starting point of the wild ride so vividly described. Today a museum, in Burns's time this was a brewhouse to which Douglas Graham of Shanter, the real life Tam, supplied malted grain (April, May, Sept: Mon.–Sat., 09.30 to 17.30. June–Aug: Mon.–Sat., 09.30 to 17.30. Sun., 14.30 to 16.00. Oct.–March: Mon.–Sat., 12.00 to 16.00. Tel: 0292–269794. Fee). Beyond, Burns yields place to Wallace, commemorated by the *Wallace Tower* built in 1828 on the site of an ancient tower in which, tradition holds, Wallace was imprisoned and from which he made a daring escape. A statue of the hero, by the local sculptor James Thom, looks out from a niche.

Farther on, and again on the right, an alley (Kirk Port) off High Street leads through an arch (with mort-safes, once placed over new graves to prevent body-snatching) to *Auld Kirk*, also known as the New Church of St. John because both the church and its gateway were built in 1654–56 using money given by Cromwell in compensation for the old Church of St. John which he had absorbed into his great fort (see below). Here Burns was baptised. Restored in 1952 as a war memorial, the church preserves the panelling of the original pulpit and is particularly interesting for its three lofts—merchants', traders' and sailors'. The churchyard, beside the river and a haven away from the traffic of High Street, allows a pleasant and detached view of the *Auld Brig*, dating from the 13C and for 500 years Ayr's only bridge—and an indifferent one, too, according to Burns, who in his dialogue, 'Twa Brigs', writes scornfully of a 'poor narrow footpath of a street where twa wheelbarrows tremble when they meet'.

Opposite the S end of Auld Brig once stood the Fish Cross, symbol of the town's main market centre; today the site is remembered by a cobbled cross and a plaque. Beyond, where High Street meets a T-junction, are the spired *Town Buildings*, built by Thomas Hamilton in 1820–28, and, to the right, the *New Bridge*, first built in 1788 and the other participant in Burns's dialogue. The new bridge's abutments, adorned with allegorical figures, roused the ire of the Auld Brig which prophesied that this newcomer would not last, a prediction which came true when a newer bridge was built in 1877. *Loudoun Hall* (mid July–Aug: Mon.–Sat., 11.00 to 18.00. Tel: 0292–284196. Free), nearby in Boat Vennel, is the oldest house in Ayr. Dating from the turn of the 15– 16C and beautifully restored, the house, once the home of a wealthy merchant, is a fine example of the better type of domestic architecture of the period.

Fort Street, running S from Loudoun Hall, is a reminder that it was in this corner of Ayr that Cromwell built his huge fort, using, it is said, stones from the medieval castle and incorporating the 12C Church of St. John as an armoury. Citadel Place, another reminder of the fort, leads W out of Fort Street to *St. John's Tower*, the restored tower of the militarised church. From here Eglinton Terrace and Cassillis Street drop S to Wellington Square in which are the *County*

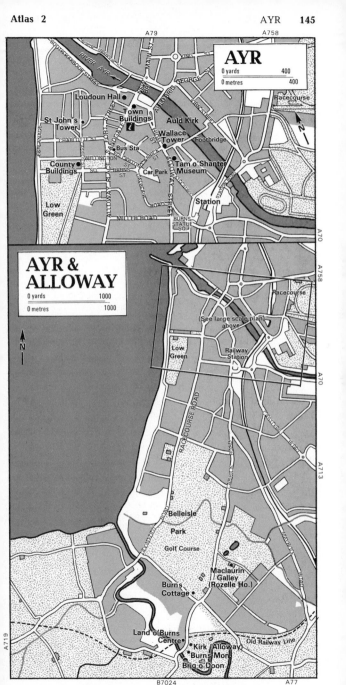

A79

A758

AYR

0 yards   400

0 metres   400

River Ayr

Racecourse

Loudoun Hall

St John's Tower

Town Buildings

Auld Kirk

Wallace Tower

Footbridge

Bus Sta

County Buildings

Car Park

Tam o'Shanter Museum

Low Green

MILLER ROAD

Station

BURNS STATUE SQ.

N

A70

A758

AYR & ALLOWAY

0 yards   1000

0 metres   1000

N

Racecourse

(See large scale plan above)

Low Green

Railway Station

A70

RACECOURSE ROAD

A713

Belleisle Park

Golf Course

Maclaurin Galley (Rozelle Ho.)

Burns Cottage

A719

Land o' Burns Centre

Kirk (Alloway)

Burns Mon.

Brig o' Doon

Old Railway Line

A77

B7024

Buildings (Robert Wallace, 1820–22 but later extended) and a monument to John McAdam, the road builder, who was born in Ayr in 1756.

16   Ayr to Paisley and Glasgow Round the Coast

A78 to Greenock and Port Glasgow. A761 via Paisley or A8 via Renfrew to Glasgow.—As far as Ardrossan, generally flat with golf courses and resorts, the last few miles industrialised. After Ardrossan, improving, with coastal scenery, good Clyde views and moorland inland. East from Gourock increasingly built-up and industrial. There is a large area of empty upland (Clyde-Muirshiel Regional Park) within the N loop of this Rte.

SOME HOTELS. **Prestwick**. *Carlton*, 187 Ayr Road. Tel: (0292) 76811. *Kincraig*, 39 Ayr Road. Tel: (0292) 79480. *Parkstone*, Esplanade. Tel: (0292) 72286. **Troon**. *Craiglea*, South Beach. Tel: (0292) 311366. *Sun Court*, 19 Crosbie Road. Tel: (0292) 312727. **Irvine**. *Annfield House*, Castle Street. Tel: (0294) 78903. **Largs**. *Elderslie*, John Street. Tel: (0475) 686460. *Mackerston*, Mackerston Place. Tel: (0475) 673264. **Skelmorlie**. *Manor Park*. Tel: (0475) 520832. **Gourock**. *Stakis Gantock*, Cloch Road. Tel: (0475) 34671. **Greenock**. *Tontine*, 6 Ardgowan Square. Tel. (0475) 23316. **Paisley**. *Stakis Watermill*, Lonend. Tel. (041) 889 3201.

Total distance 66 or 62m.—*9m* **Irvine**.—*18m* **Largs**.—*6m* **Wemyss Bay**.—*7m* **Gourock**.—*2m* **Greenock**.—*2m* **Port Glasgow**.—*22m* **Glasgow** via **Paisley**, or *18m* **Glasgow** via **Renfrew**.

THE CLYDE AND CLYDE CRUISING. The *Clyde* rises in the hills of Tweeddale, some 80m above Glasgow. Below the moors the river's course to the city is known as Clydesdale, a district of orchards and market gardens interspersed with industry. Along this course the Clyde is used for hydro-electric purposes near Lanark, and near Hamilton it has been diverted and canalised as part of the planning of Strathclyde Country Park (Rte 10). At Glasgow the river is broadish and fairly shallow, and it is interesting that up to about the close of the 18C it was still fordable here. Below Glasgow all changes as the river suddenly reaches maturity—wide, navigable, and, as far as Greenock on the S and Dumbarton on the N, its banks in large part lined by industry. Further W the river becomes the Firth of Clyde, at Gourock curving S to open as a broad and scenic estuary stretching across to hilly Kintyre and embracing the islands of Arran, Bute and Cumbrae. To the N, sea lochs pierce deep into Cowal (Rte 47) and Argyll. The combination of islands, sea lochs and many cheerful summer resorts makes these waters popular for day cruising.

Cruising may be by either one or a combination of the scheduled routes, or in summer by taking a cruise as such. The principal scheduled routes are those to the islands (see Rte 17), day round-trips, often including an island coach tour, being popular; and those from Gourock across the Clyde to Dunoon and Hunter's Quay on Cowal, to Kilcreggan on the Rosneath peninsula, and to Helensburgh on the E side of Gare Loch. The services to Kilcreggan and Helensburgh do not carry cars. Gourock, Wemyss Bay, Largs and Ardrossan all have connecting train services with Glasgow.

Visitors in search of a unique cruise will choose the PS 'Waverley', the last paddle steamer to be built for use on the Clyde and now the world's only surviving sea-going paddle-steamer (operated by the Paddle Steamer Preservation Society). During summer there is a variety of Clyde cruises from Glasgow, as also sailings much farther afield—for instance, the Isle of Man, Stranraer, Irish ports, South Wales, the English S coast and even London. Information from Waverley Excursions Ltd, Anderston Quay, Glasgow G3 8HA. Tel: (041) 221 8152.

The principal Clyde operator is Caledonian MacBrayne Ltd, Gourock PA19 1QP. Tel: (0475) 33755. Others include Western Ferries, 16 Woodside Crescent, Glasgow G3 7UT. Tel: (041) 332 9766 (for Gourock-Hunter's Quay): Clyde Marine Ltd, Princes Pier, Greenock PA16 8AW. Tel: (0475) 21281 (for cruises, and services from Gourock to Helensburgh and Kilcreggan).

The northern suburbs of **Ayr** (see Rte 15) merge with the southern suburbs of Prestwick, and it was to this, then very different corner that Bruce came towards the end of his days; to the spot now called *Bruce's Well*, today within a bungalow estate at the southern approach to Prestwick (sign W off Ayr Road). Tradition tells that Bruce, in sombre mood and fearing that he had leprosy—which he probably had for he is thought to have died of it—sank down here exhausted, at the same time striking his spear into the ground. Water miraculously welled up, which Bruce drank, at once feeling restored. Be this as it may, Bruce did endow a leper hospital here and the ruin beside the well may be that of its Chapel of St. Ninian.

1m (from Ayr) **Prestwick** (13,500 inhab. *ECl.* Wed. *Inf.* 2 The Cross), although noticeably overshadowed by Ayr, remains a resort in its own right, particularly for golf, for which, together with its international airport, it is probably best known. The town's origins go back to at least the 12C, at which time it was held by Walter Fitzalan of Dundonald (see below), Lord High Steward. But of Prestwick's remoter past there is but one remain, its c 15C *Cross*, and even this was rebuilt in 1779 and moved to its present central position in 1963.

Prestwick Airport was started up in 1935 by the Duke of Hamilton and Group Captain D.F. McIntyre, the first men to fly over Everest (1933). At first just the grass field of Scottish Aviation Ltd, Prestwick's fog-free record led to rapid development during the war when it became the headquarters of RAF Ferry Command and of the USAF Transport Command. After the war the same fog-free characteristic ensured growth to international civil airport status.

At *Monkton*, just N of the airport, there is a monument to James Macrae (died 1744), a poor local boy who went to India and became Governor of Madras. He returned a wealthy man and is said to have begun this monument himself. His tomb is in Monkton churchyard, though there is a local belief that his bones were disinterred and placed within the monument. At *Symington*, a short way NE on A77, the small church preserves three 12C Norman windows.

3m **Troon** (11,000 inhab. *ECl.* Wed. *Inf.* Municipal Buildings, South Beach) is a summer and golf resort, refreshingly smaller and quieter than the Ayr-Prestwick complex. There are good beaches, as also several golf courses in the neighbourhood. The place derives its name from the Troone (nose), the rocky arm of land which hooks seaward. *Lady Island*, 3m offshore, is a bird sanctuary.—*Dundonald Castle*

(AM. View from outside), 3m NE of Troon, a rough but striking ruin on a hill above its village, is a place which demands to be visited by anyone with a feel for Scotland's history, for this was the cradle of the Stuart line. This came about because the castle was held by the Fitzalans, Lord High Stewards, one of whom married the daughter of Bruce, their son becoming Robert II, the first of the Stewarts or Stuarts. Both Robert II and his son Robert III lived and died here (1390 and 1406), but after their time the castle fell into neglect. The early structure (13C) seems to have been a keep-gatehouse with two towers. This, however, was largely destroyed during the wars of independence, afterwards being rebuilt as a large tower-house by Robert II. The great hall was on the third floor, its upper part, however, being removed in 1644 by the 1st Earl of Dundonald to provide material for his castellated mansion of *Auchans*, a mile to the S and also now a ruin.

5m **Irvine**. Despite its modern industrial setting with large chemical works and a coal port, Irvine is nevertheless a royal burgh which has played its part in Scotland's history. It was here in 1297 that Wallace was deserted by his supporters (who signed the Treaty of Irvine with the English), thus being forced to flee to the North and gather fresh allies. Here also, in August 1563, Mary, Queen of Scots, visited during her western royal progress, being entertained in 13C Seagate Castle, today but a drab shell. It was a visit which obviously touched a local chord, for today, over 400 years later, the occasion is celebrated each August with Marymass, a week or more of festivity which includes a procession past the castle and the crowning of the queen. Burns was here too, working as a flax-dresser between 1781–84 until the shop was burnt down during New Year revels. Today, the street in which he lodged and worked, Glasgow Vennel, has been restored and there is an audio-visual display at the flax-dressing or *Heckling Shop*, while Burns is also remembered at the Irvine *Burns Club Museum* (Sat. afternoon. Or Tel: 0294-74511. Free) at 28 Eglinton Street.—James Montgomery (1771–1854), the poet and hymn writer, and John Galt (1779–1839), the novelist and traveller who gave his name to the town of Galt in Canada, were both born here. J.B. Dunlop (1840–1921), the vet who in 1888 invented the pneumatic tyre, was born at Dreghorn (plaque), 2m E of Irvine.

2m Eglinton Park, roughly half-way between Irvine and Kilwinning, was the scene of the extravagant 'Eglinton Tournament' of 1839, a romantic if dotty attempt to revive the forms and ceremonies of ancient chivalry. Prince Louis Napoleon (Napoleon III) was one of the knights, as was also, and more appropriately for this district, the Earl of Cassillis; Lady Seymour, a granddaughter of Sheridan, was Queen of Love and Beauty; and the tournament provided Disraeli with material for his novel 'Endymion'. The 17C castle is now derelict.—*2m* **Kilwinning** claims to be the earliest home in Scotland of freemasonry, possibly introduced by foreign workers who came to build the *Abbey*. This, founded about 1150 by Richard de Morville on the site of a church built by the 6C Irish St. Wynin (hence the town's name), was largely destroyed in 1561 and the ruins left today are scanty. Nevertheless they provide the town with an attractive central feature alongside the parish church with its detached tower of 1815. Among the remains are the S transept wall with gable and three lancets, the doorway into the E cloister walk, the chapter house entrance and part of the W front.—*3m* **Saltcoats**, now a harbour and

resort on the depressing fringe of an industrialised district, owes its
name to the saltworks established here by James V. The *North
Ayrshire Museum* (Mon.–Sat., 10.00 to 16.00. Tel: 0294–64174. Free),
in the 18C former parish church, well illustrates the industrial and
maritime development of this region and includes some early 19C
interiors.—**Ardrossan**, another resort and port (sailings to Arran),
although physically joined to Saltcoats, achieves some individuality
through having been laid out to a formal plan by Peter Nicholson in
1806. *Ardrossan Castle*, a small 12C ruin above the town, was taken
by Wallace from the English and finally destroyed by Cromwell.
Horse Island, just offshore, is a bird sanctuary.

The coastal road now clears the industrial belt to reach (*4m*) *West
Kilbride* where there is a late 15C tower (Law Castle). The ruined
castle on the shore at *Portencross*, 2m W, was visited by Robert II in
1372. Continuing N, the road passes Hunterston Nuclear Power
Station (1957–60) and British Steel Corporation's huge deep-water
iron ore terminal (1979) on the way to (*4m*) **Fairlie**, a pleasant modest
resort looking across to Cumbrae, known also for its castle, a small,
creeper-clad 16C keep standing above the town in a pretty glen with
a waterfall. *Kelburn Country Centre* (Easter–Sept: Daily, 10.00 to
18.00. Tel: 047556–554. Fee) is off A78 a short way N of Fairlie. Here
18C farm buildings, forming a kind of village square, are a centre
for exhibitions, nature trails, pony trekking, a children's adventure
course and suchlike. The castle (12C with additions), seat of the earls
of Glasgow, is not normally open to visitors.

3m **Largs** (10,000 inhab. *ECl*. Wed. *Inf*. Promenade). Standing on
its own below green hills and with views across to Cumbrae, Largs
seems to have more style than other Ayr coast resorts and is popular
as much for itself and its holiday amenities as for being the port for
the Cumbrae ferries. Architecturally the star here is the *•Skelmorlie
Aisle* (AM. Standard, but apply to key keeper in winter. Fee) in
Bellman's Close off Main Street. Originally the N transept of the old
church, the aisle was converted in 1636 into a mausoleum by Sir
Robert Montgomerie of Skelmorlie and now ranks as one of Scotland's
most elegant examples of Renaissance work. The handsome monument of Sir Robert and his wife stands below a wooden barrel-vault
elaborately painted by Stalker. The adjacent *Largs Museum*
(June–Sept: Mon.–Sat., 14.00 to 17.00. Tel: 0475–68708. Donation) is
that of the Largs and District Historical Society. That Largs enjoys
an honoured place in Scotland's history is recorded by the 'Pencil',
a monument at Bowen Craig to the S of the town commemorating
the Battle of Largs of 1263, in which year Alexander III fought and
routed Hakon, King of Norway. The battle, part naval and also part
land as a storm drove Hakon's galleys ashore here, was won by the
Scots after two days of fighting, the result meaning that the Hebrides
and the Isle of Man, held by the Norsemen for 400 years, were ceded
to Scotland.

General Sir Thomas Brisbane was born in Largs, in what is now called *Brisbane
Glen*. He was Governor of New South Wales in Australia, which at that time
included present day Queensland, and the city of Brisbane was named after
him. He was also an astronomer, and three stone columns he erected for
astronomical purposes still stand on The Mound, the motte of medieval
times.—The *Prophet's Grave*, 2m up Brisbane Glen, commemorates one William
Smith, the local minister, who died of the plague in the 17C while continuing
to care for his flock who had fled into the glen.

The minor road N up Noddsdale Water climbs over moorland to *Cornalees Bridge*, see below.

For *Inverclyde, National Sports Training Centre*, E of the town, see Sports Holidays.

Clyde-Muirshiel Regional Park (Tel:041–887 2806).
A760, leading E to reach Lochwinnoch in 14m, skirts the southern boundary of Clyde-Muirshiel Regional Park which embraces much of the empty, roadless upland moor enclosed by this road; by B786 and B788 between Lochwinnoch and Greenock; and by the minor road leading S from Greenock past Loch Thom and down Noddsdale Water to Largs. Hill of Stake (1711ft) rises at the heart of the park, which has four visitor centres—Cornalees Bridge at the NW, and, at the SE and close to Lochwinnoch, Castle Semple Country Park, Lochwinnoch Nature Reserve, and Muirshiel Country Park.

On the way to Lochwinnoch, **Kilbirnie** is of interest for the ruin of Kilbirnie Place (above the town off A760), a seat of the Crawfords built in the 14C and burnt down in the 18C and, more particularly, for Kilbirnie Church, dating from 1470–90 (nave and tower) and 1597 (N aisle). Inside the church the striking feature is the Laird's Loft of 1642, adorned in 1703 by the 1st Viscount Garnock with 18 shields of the Lindsay lineage.

Lochwinnoch, with the high 16C tower of Barr Castle, and with a local museum in old school buildings in Main Street, is close to three Clyde-Muirshiel Regional Park centres. *Castle Semple Country Park*, with the loch of the same name as its main feature, was created mainly for sailing, canoeing, rowing and coarse fishing. *Lochwinnoch Nature Reserve* (RSPB. Thurs.–Sun., 10.00 to 17.00. Tel: 0505–842663. Fee) offers an observation tower, exhibition and gift shop. *Muirshiel Country Park*, off B786 4m N of Lochwinnoch, was opened in 1970 as a contribution to European Conservation Year. Here, in an area of upland rolling moor and mixed woodland, the amenities include a visitor centre, ranger services and several trails of varying length.—Beyond the NE end of Loch Semple, on a hill, can be seen *The Temple*, a folly said to have been built to enable a crippled Lady Semphill to watch the hunt. *Castle Semple Collegiate Church* (AM. View from outside), 2m NE of Lochwinnoch, represents a foundation of 1504. The remains include a square tower and a three-sided apse, each side with three Gothic windows.

Leaving Largs A78 keeps to the coast, passing two former Montgomerie strongholds; *Knock Castle* (late 16C), just visible among trees, and, conspicuous·on a rise, *Skelmorlie Castle* of 1502.—*6m* (from Largs) **Wemyss Bay** (pron. Weems) is the port for the ferry to the island of Bute.—*2m* **Inverkip** where there is a nuclear power station. From here a small road climbs to open upland on which is *Cornalees Bridge*, one of the centres of Clyde-Muirshiel Regional Park. Here the interesting 2m-long Cornalees Trail follows first the Greenock Cut, an aqueduct designed and built in 1827 by Robert Thom (after whom the nearby loch is named) to provide Greenock with drinking water and power for its mills; the trail then continues down the wooded glen of Kip Water, to return by the Kelly Aqueduct which once carried water along the hillside from Kelly Reservoir near Skelmorlie.—*3m* *Cloch Lighthouse* (1797) stands on the bend of the Firth of Clyde.

2m **Gourock** (11,000 inhab. *ECl.* Wed. *Inf.* Municipal Buildings, Shore Street). Although on the fringe of the urban and industrial strip stretching E through Greenock and Port Glasgow, Gourock remains essentially a resort. Standing, too, on the bend where the Clyde changes direction, the town enjoys wide views across the estuary and is busy with ferries. There are frequent daily car ferries (20 minutes) to Dunoon on the Cowal peninsula (Caledonian MacBrayne from Railway Pier to Dunoon Pier; Western Ferries from McInray's Point to Hunter's Quay), and passenger ferries (Clyde Marine) also run N to Kilcreggan on the Rosneath peninsula and to Helensburgh on the E side of Gare Loch. On Gourock Pier are the offices (booking) of Caledonian MacBrayne Ltd, the main W coast operators of ferries, both within the Clyde and, from W Highland ports, to the Hebrides.

Gourock also has one curious local antiquity, namely the *Kempock Stone* (or Granny Kempock's Stone), beside A78. Probably prehistoric, the stone was used by fishermen in rites to ensure good weather, and also by couples about to marry who encircled it for good luck. In 1662, one Mary Lamont was burned as a witch after confessing she had intended to throw the stone into the sea and thus cause shipwrecks.

A78 now plunges into a virtually uninterrupted urban and industrial strip, sandwiched between the Clyde and the steep hills behind and extending from Gourock through Greenock to the E edge of Port Glasgow. Yet it could be a mistake to hurry through, for both places have something to offer.

2m **Greenock** (69,500 inhab. *ECl.* Wed. *Inf.* Municipal Buildings, 23 Clyde Street), long connected with shipbuilding, was the birthplace in c 1645 of Captain Kidd, the privateer and pirate, and also of James Watt (1736–1819), engineer and inventor of the condensing steam engine.

Today's visitor should aim first for the E end of the long, elegant Esplanade which runs westward out of the main town. Here stands the *Old West Kirk* of 1591, interesting on three counts. It was the first church built after the Reformation and the first Presbyterian church confirmed by parliament; in 1920, to make room for industrial development, it was removed from its original site and rebuilt here; and it has stained-glass windows by Burne-Jones, Morris and Rossetti. In the main town the *Municipal Buildings*, with their 245ft Victoria Tower, are of 1886. Watt's birthplace is marked by a plaque at the corner of William and Dalrymple streets. Beyond the *Mid Kirk* (1757–87), Hamilton Way runs NW to cross West Burn and Nicolson streets. John Galt (see Irvine, above) died in West Burn Street (plaque) and is buried in the old graveyard in Inverkip Street, its continuation up the hill. In Nelson Street is (new) *West Kirk* (David Cousin, 1841–53), and this same street ascends to the cemetery in which is the tomb of Mary Campbell, Burns's 'Highland Mary', removed from the graveyard of the Old West Kirk.

Argyle Street, parallel with Nicolson Street, reaches George Square and Union Street, in the latter being the building (Blore, 1835), commissioned by Watt's son as a memorial to his father. Here, now, is the *McLean Museum and Art Gallery* (Mon.–Sat., 10.00 to 12.00., 13.00. to 17.00. Tel: 0475–23741. Free) showing, in the art gallery, works by, amongst others, James Guthrie (1859–1930), a native of Greenock; and, in the museum, local and natural history exhibits, model ships and material associated with James Watt.

In 1940–45 Greenock was the chief Free French naval base in Britain, and a great granite *Cross of Lorraine* and anchor, the French memorial to their men who died in the Battle of the Atlantic, stands on Lyle Hill above the town.

2m **Port Glasgow**, built in the 17C as the furthest deep water port up the river and the place where, in 1812, Henry Bell's steamer, the 'Comet', was constructed by John Wood; of about 25 tons and with a 3 horsepower engine, the boat achieved a speed of 7mph. *Newark Castle* (AM. Standard. Fee), beside the Clyde at the E end of the town, is an almost intact turreted mansion of the Maxwells, for the most part of the 16–17C but with a 15C tower. This elegant building, with its dovecot, once solitary and gracious beside the river, today contrasts almost startlingly with the ugly industry which has now engulfed it.

From Port Glasgow to Glasgow there is a choice between the inland road (A761) through Paisley or the faster Clydeside road (A8, M8) through Renfrew.

Inland Road to Glasgow

A761 climbs steeply out of Port Glasgow, offering wide and interesting views before reaching open upland.—*10m* **Kilbarchan**, just S of the main road, was once well known for its tartan weaving, and the 18C *Weaver's Cottage* (NTS, Easter–May, Sept, Oct: Tues., Thurs., Sat., Sun., 14.00 to 17.00. June–Aug: Daily, 14.00 to 17.00. Fee) is typical of those in which home weaving was practised until as recently as 1940. Weaving is demonstrated and the cottage and garden contain looms, contemporary furniture and an eclectic collection of interesting and curious period articles. On the town steeple there is a figure of Habbie Simpson, a famous 17C local piper.—At *Elderslie*, just W of Paisley and the traditional birthplace of Wallace in c 1272, a memorial, with dramatic pictorial plaques, put up by the Clan Wallace Society, stands beside A737 at the W entrance to the town.

5m **Paisley** (85,000 inhab. *ECl.* Tues. *Inf.* Town Hall, Abbey Close) is a large, busy town which, although essentially industrial—it is still the world's leading producer of thread—is nevertheless a place of some spaciousness and character. It is best known for its abbey and for the shawls with their distinctive pattern woven here during the 19C. Born here were Alexander Wilson (1763–1813), poet and American ornithologist, and Robert Tannahill (1774–1810), the weaver poet.

Virtually all that remains of *Paisley Abbey* is its church, the nave of which has long served as parish church. The main architectural phases are Transitional (12C) in the three bays at the E end of the S aisle of the nave; Gothic First Pointed (13C), the W end of the church; Gothic Decorated (15C), nave interior and transepts; and post-Reformation restoration.

The priory of Pasletum was founded by Walter Fitzalan (ancestor through Bruce's daughter of the Stuart kings, see Dundonald Castle) who in 1171 here installed 13 Cluniac monks from Wenlock, in Shropshire, his native home. The relics of St. Mirren or Merinus (c 7C), whose cell had stood here, were transferred to the church and his shrine soon became a place of pilgrimage. The priory rapidly grew to be a wealthy house and was promoted to abbey in 1219. It was destroyed by the English in 1307 and, although favoured by the Stuart kings, was not rebuilt until after 1450, to which date much of the present structure belongs. Further destruction came with the Reformation, at which time the tower collapsed, destroying the choir in its fall. The church, with the exception of the nave and one chapel, then fell into decay and the lower part of the W front and the S wall of the nave are all that survive of the early church. The nave roof was replaced in 1780. The main restoration, begun in 1897 by Rowand Anderson and McGregor Chalmers, was completed by Sir Robert Lorimer between 1922–28.

The West Front has a deeply recessed EE doorway flanked by two blind arches and surmounted by three traceried windows. The Nave is remarkable for a richly developed triforium of broad round arches, and on the left of the W door there is a memorial to John Hamilton, the last abbot, executed in 1571 for alleged complicity in the murder of Darnley. The place of the S transept is occupied by *St. Mirren's Chapel (1499), with a fascinating series of panels (one missing), probably of the 12C, depicting episodes of doubtful authenticity from the life of the saint. The Choir, surprisingly paved with slabs from the basement of Hamilton Palace and with stalls designed by Lorimer, is historically the most interesting part of the abbey, for here are the Stuart Tombs. A recumbent female effigy may be that of either Euphemia Ross, wife of Robert II, or, more popularly, of Marjory Bruce, Bruce's daughter and Robert II's mother. She was killed in 1316 at the age of 23 while hunting at Knock, just N of Paisley. Here also are buried six High Stewards, the first, Walter Fitzalan, being the founder of the abbey and the sixth the husband of Marjory; two wives of Robert II; and Robert III.

Place of Paisley, adjoining the church on the S, was in origin a part of the abbey's domestic buildings dating from c 1475. After the Dissolution the buildings were converted to a mansion (or palace, which word has corrupted to Place) of first the Hamiltons and then the earls of Dundonald, and it was either here, or perhaps in the church, that Jean Cochrane, granddaughter of the 1st Earl, was married to Claverhouse in 1684. In 1764 the Abercorn family bought the mansion, but it was later so neglected that the old kitchen became used as a tavern. However in 1903 the Place returned to Church ownership, since when there has been constant improvement culminating in the 1950s in the conversion of the upper levels to Abbey Manse.

From Place of Paisley, Bridge Street crosses the river, after which a right turn along Orchard Street leads into New Street in which, by the junction with Shuttle Street, stands the *Laigh Kirk* of 1738, of particular interest to Americans because the Rev. John Witherspoon, the only cleric to sign the Declaration of Independence, was minister here for 12 years before emigrating in 1768. Farther along New Street, the *Bull Inn*, built in 1901, is known for its Art Nouveau interior. New Street meets High Street, with, to the W, the *Thomas Coats Memorial Church* (Hippolyte Blanc, 1894), the cruciform church of the Baptist community and perhaps the most conspicuous building in Paisley.

The *Paisley Museum and Art Gallery* (Mon.–Sat., 10.00 to 17.00. Tel: 041–8893151. Free) is in High Street at the opposite end to the abbey. Founded in 1870, but now admirably modernised and with an art gallery, the museum covers local history, archaeology (with excellent explanations of prehistoric dwellings, etc) and natural sciences. Perhaps the most important section is the display of *Paisley Shawls and Plaids, of which the museum has some 700, as well as much other material (design books, looms etc) relating to this former industry.

At the end of the 18C British and French soldiers returning from India brought back Kashmir shawls. These—warm, light and with beautiful designs—were soon copied at several places in both countries, one of these being Paisley, where shawl weaving was started in 1805. The 'pine motif' (virtually synonymous with the term 'Paisley pattern', though in fact there were many other designs) was Kashmiri in origin, there known as 'Baandaam' and deriving from the shape of the native almond in its early green state. It was copied and developed at most weaving centres, but nowhere more efficiently than at Paisley, which soon became as famous for its mass production (after c 1840 boosted by increased use of the Jacquard mechanised loom) as it was notorious for its imitation of others' designs. By the second half of the century Paisley had achieved a virtual monopoly in Britain. Printed shawls date from about the 1840s; reversed shawls, with the pattern on both sides, began to appear in about 1865. The 1870s saw the sudden end of the popularity of the Paisley shawl and plaid, largely because this decade also saw the passing of the crinoline for which the large plaids had been about the only possible over-cover. Fortunately the new demand for cotton thread was ready to provide alternative employment.

The *Coats Observatory and Weather Station* (Mon.–Fri., 14.00 to 17.00. Sat., 10.00 to 13.00. 14.00 to 17.00. Free), an outstation of Paisley Museum, is in Oakshaw Street, N of and roughly parallel to High Street.

7m central **Glasgow**, see Rte 19.

Clydeside Road to Glasgow

This road connects to M8, the quickest way into Glasgow. Also to *Erskine Bridge* (toll) which, built in 1971, superseded a ferry and now provides a main Clyde crossing, particularly useful for traffic heading N and wishing to avoid Glasgow.—The *Blantyre Obelisk*, N of B815 and 2m W of Erskine Bridge, commemorates the 11th Lord Blantyre who lost his life in Brussels in 1830 during the fighting for Belgian independence.

Clear of Port Glasgow A8 passes first *Parklea Farm*, between road and river, a NTS property leased to Inverclyde District Council as a recreational area, and then (*3m*), on the right, *Finlaystone House* (Tel: 047554–235. Fee), with Victoriana, a collection of dolls, gardens and woodland walks. The estate once belonged to Lord Glencairn, a patron of Burns.—In the churchyard at *Inchinnan*, N of A8 and 2m W of Renfrew, there are Celtic stones, Templar graves and mort-safes recalling the days of body-snatching.

9m **Renfrew**, today an industrial town, has also long been a royal burgh which gives the title of baron to the Prince of Wales. Somerled, Lord of the Isles, was defeated and slain here by Malcolm IV in 1164, and it was here too that the 9th Earl of Argyll, who was supporting Monmouth's rebellion, was taken (and later executed) in 1685. —**Govan**, just E of Renfrew, is a shipbuilding suburb of Glasgow. Here the parish church, on the site of a Celtic monastery, claims to shelter the sarcophagus of St. Constantine, a shadowy figure confused between a Cornish king martyred by pirates on Kintyre and one of the early Scottish kings. The S entrance to the Clyde Tunnel (cars) is just N of Govan.—*6m* central **Glasgow**, see Rte 19.

17 The Clyde Islands (Arran, Bute, Cumbrae)

The islands of Arran, Bute and Cumbrae, all lying in the Firth of Clyde, are scenically pleasant, though, with the exception of Arran, not outstanding. Popular family resorts, all are on the whole quiet and with something of an old-fashioned flavour. In summer, accommodation should be reserved in advance.

Car ferries serve all three islands. Timetables are, however, subject to annual and seasonal changes. For latest information, apply to Caledonian MacBrayne Ltd, Gourock, PA19 1QP. Tel: (0475) 33755. Telex: 779318.

Island of Arran

Tourist Information. The Pier, Brodick. Tel: (0770) 2140.

Access. 1. Car ferry from Ardrossan to Brodick, with train connections from Glasgow. Several times daily, but restricted timetable on Sun. and in winter. Advance booking for vehicles essential in summer; passenger embarkation (reservation) tickets also required for some sailings at peak periods. Crossing 55 minutes. 2. Car ferry from Claonaig (Kintyre) to Lochranza. Several times daily, approx mid May to end Sept. No winter service. Small ship; services liable to cancellation in poor weather. Crossing 30 minutes.

Local companies operate coach tours around the island. Self-drive cars are available.

SOME HOTELS. **Brodick**. *Altanna*, KA27 8DW. Tel: (0770) 2232. *Douglas*, KA27 8AW. Tel: (0770) 2155. **Catacol**. *Catacol Bay*, KA27 8HN. Tel: (077083) 231.

History. The many standing stones and burial cairns show that Arran was well populated in prehistoric times. Later the island became a part of the kingdom of Dalriada, but was soon taken by the Norsemen who held it until Somerled, Lord of the Isles, wrested it from them in the mid 12C. Bruce, fired by the example set by the spider while on the Irish island of Rathlin, landed here in 1306 on his way to Turnberry to start in earnest the war of independence. In 1503 Arran was awarded by royal charter to the Hamilton family. The island has been a holiday resort since the early 18C and at one period it was fashionable to come here to drink the allegedly health-giving wild goats' milk.

Arran is about 20m long by 10m wide, much of the island being uncultivated moor and mountain, the latter rising in the N to a serrated range, with Goatfell (2866ft) the highest peak. The island belongs almost wholly to the Hamilton family and the National Trust for Scotland, whose combined successful policy has been the exclusion of offensive development. Among the many recreational possibilities are swimming, boating, fishing, golf (7 courses), climbing and pony-trekking, while for those in search of the past there are medieval castles and a profusion of prehistoric and Iron Age sites.

The description below makes an anti-clockwise circuit of 55m starting from Brodick.

Brodick, the island's capital and with many hotels, straggles around the bay of the same name. The *Isle of Arran Heritage Museum* (Mid May–mid Sept: Mon.–Fri., 10.30 to 16.30. Sun., 14.00 to 16.30. Tel: 0770–2140. Fee) occupies buildings which were once an 18C croft. Local history, archaeology and geology are among the fields covered, and there is also a picnic area.—*2m* **Brodick Castle** (NTS. All Easter period. April: Mon., Wed., Sat., 13.00 to 17.00. May–Sept: Daily, 13.00 to 17.00. Fee) is the ancient seat of the dukes of Hamilton. Built on the site of a Viking fort, the castle dates in part from the 13C (N wing) and was extended in 1652 and 1844. It was held by Edward I, and later by Cromwell's troops, who however were massacred by the islanders. The drawing room has a rich plaster ceiling with coats of arms, and the series of rooms contain silver, porcelain and paintings—Watteau, Turner and Rowlandson are among the artists—from the collections of the dukes of Hamilton, William Beckford and the Earl of Rochford. There are two gardens. The formal walled garden dates from 1710; the woodland garden of some 60 acres was started in 1923 by the late Duchess of Montrose and is now accepted as one of the finest rhododendron gardens in Britain. Both gardens now form *Brodick Country Park* (Daily, 10.00 to 17.00. Fee).

Goatfell (2866ft), rising to the N above Brodick Castle, forms part of a NTS property which includes Glen Rosa to the S and Cir Mhor (2618ft) to the N, an area which provides some superb scenic walking. The walk, of around 11m, from Brodick, up Glen Rosa, across the saddle (1500ft), then down wild Glen Sannox to Sannox Bay is well worth considering. The ascent of Goatfell is best made by a path which starts near Brodick Castle and climbs to the summit by way of the mountain's eastern shoulder.

5m Sannox Bay, from where Glen Sannox cuts across the N flank of Goatfell towards Cir Mhor.—*7m* **Lochranza**, a village below mountain and high moor and strung along the narrow sea loch of the same name, is reputed to be the place where Bruce landed in 1306 or 1307 on his return from Rathlin. It is said, too, that there was a nunnery here which gave shelter to Bruce's sister, but of this, if indeed it ever existed, there is now no trace. What does survive, though, is *Lochranza Castle* (AM. Standard. Free), a ruin with two square towers, built during the 13–14C and enlarged in the 16C. The car ferry to Claonaig on Kintyre sails from Lochranza.

The road S hugs the shore, affording a continuous view across Kilbrannan Sound to Kintyre and passing in *6m* the hamlet of *Pirnmill*, a name recalling the 'pirns', or wooden bobbins, once used at the mill here.—*7m Auchagallon Stone Circle*, a somewhat battered site on the E of the road close to a road junction, comprises a circle of 15 stones around a burial cairn of possibly rather later date. The moor (***Machrie Moor**) within the triangle formed by the main coastal road, the small road leading E from Auchagallon, and B880 heading NE from Blackwaterfoot, is (on the S side of the Machrie Water) exceptionally and visibly rich in prehistoric remains, these including burial chambers and at least six stone circles, some marked by uprights 12–18ft in height. For detailed study some walking is necessary—the normal approach being a path just S of the Machrie Water near Tormore—but much can also be seen from the roads, especially from the slightly higher ground crossed by the small one from Auchagallon.

4m **Blackwaterfoot**, from where B880, a road known as The String and built in 1817, skirts the SE flank of Machrie Moor. *Shiskine*, 1m up this road, claims to be the burial place of St. Molaise, also known as St. Luserian, who, despite deliberately contracting 30 diseases in expiation of his sins, is nevertheless popularly believed to have lived to the age of 120. A rough stone on a wall of the church is said to have once covered the saint's remains. *King's Cave*, reached by a 2m walk along the shore from the golf course at Blackwaterfoot and the largest of a group, was, tradition asserts, used by Fingal and his followers, as also later by Bruce who, needless to say, here watched that spider while his companions drew the rough hunting scenes on the walls. A sign about 1m S of Blackwaterfoot directs to *Kilpatrick Dun* (short walk), an unusual site at which a small Iron Age fort has been surrounded by a turf and stone cashel (enclosing an area of about two acres) which would seem to be of Celtic Christian origin; while at Corriecravie, rather over *3m* from Blackwaterfoot, a second sign suggests another short walk, this time to the Iron Age fort of *Tor Chaistel.*

3m **Kilmory** village, in which, 500 yards down a path, will be found *Torrylin Cairn*. Now no more than a mound, this Stone or Bronze Age tomb once had several compartments in which were found the remains of four adults and two children. And, for those prepared to face a seven-or-so-mile moorland trudge, there is *Cairn Ban* (sign E of Kilmory. 3½m), a large and well preserved chambered cairn lying at 900ft way out on the moors.—At (*6m*) *Kildonan* the ruined medieval keep by the sea is that of a castle first granted in 1406 by Robert III to his bastard son, John.

The road now curves N with the coast, in *5m* reaching **Kingscross**, a name recalling that it was from Kingscross Point that, lured by a mystic fire, Bruce set sail for Turnberry in 1307. Only 44 years earlier Lamlash Bay, of which Kingscross Point marks the southern arm, had witnessed a very different scene as King Hakon here tried to rally his shattered fleet after its defeat at Largs. *Holy Island*, which with its quite impressive 1000ft peak protects the seaward side of the bay, owes its name to St. Molaise (see Shiskine above) who used a cave on the W shore as his meditative cell. Runic inscriptions here were, it is tempting to suppose, left by Hakon's defeated followers.—*3m* **Lamlash** is, after Brodick, Arran's largest village. From here there is a scenic footpath to Brodick (4½m), passing the Iron Age fort of *Dun Fionn.*—*4m* (by road) **Brodick**.

Island of Bute

Tourist Information. The Pier, Rothesay. Tel: (0700) 2151.

Access. 1. Car ferry from Wemyss Bay to Rothesay, with train connections from Glasgow. Several times daily, but restricted timetable on Sun. and in winter. Crossing 30 minutes. 2. Car ferry from Colintraive (Cowal) to Rhubodach. Frequent daily service. Crossing 5 minutes.

SOME HOTELS. **Rothesay.** *Ardmory House*, Ardmory Road, Ardbeg. Tel: (0700) 2346. *Glenburn*, Glenburn Road. Tel: (0700) 2500.

Bute is 15m long by 3m broad, with gentle scenery, mostly farming land with patches of moor. Its northern part is tucked into the Cowal peninsula, from which it is separated by the narrow and beautiful straits known as the *Kyles of Bute*, while the southern island runs out to Garroch Head on the way to which there are various remains of interest. The island's history is essentially that of Rothesay Castle.

The sizeable and popular resort of **Rothesay** is the island's capital, a royal burgh which gives the title of Duke to the Prince of Wales. The first holder of the title—the premier Scottish title of the Heir to the Throne—was the ill-fated David, son of Robert III (see Rte 33C,

Falkland Palace). *Bute Museum* (April–Sept: Mon.–Sat., 10.30 to 12.30. 14.30 to 16.30. Also Sun., 14.30 to 16.30 in June–Sept. Oct–March: Tues.–Sat., 14.30 to 16.30. Tel: 0700–2151. Fee), in Stuart Street, has exhibits illustrating local and natural history and archaeology. The museum also provides information on the island's prehistoric sites, as well as on the several nature trails arranged by the Bute Natural History Society. *St. Mary's Chapel*, on A845 just S of the town, is a ruin beside the High Kirk of 1796. Built in the 16C as the chancel of the parish church, the small ruin houses two canopied tombs (13–14C), probably of the Stewarts of Menteith, and also a recumbent effigy. It is said that here also are buried five 14C bishops of Sodor and Man.

*Rothesay Castle (AM. Standard, except closed Thurs. and Fri. mornings in Oct–March. Fee) is a historic and attractive ruin, of particular interest for being round in shape.

History. The castle dates from at least the early 13C, first appearing in history in 1230 when it was stormed by the Norsemen; the breach then made can still be seen. Only a few years later, in 1263, the Norsemen were here again, but this time only briefly because they were soon routed at Largs. During the Stuart period, Rothesay was a royal residence, much used by Robert II and Robert III. Later, James IV and V both based themselves here during their operations against the Lords of the Isles, and it was these two kings who added the Great Tower. Much battered during the Civil War, the castle was burned by Argyll in 1685, thereafter remaining a neglected ruin until repaired during the 19C by the 2nd and 3rd Marquises of Bute.

Today's still impressive remains include the 12 or 13C Circular Wall (unique in Scotland), with four round towers, and the Great Tower of James IV and V, the forework through which the castle is entered. Within the Great Tower, on the first floor, is the Great Hall which has been restored. Inside the round open courtyard are the well and the roofless Chapel (appropriately dedicated to St. Michael, patron of warriors) in which the piscina and sacrament house can still be seen. Behind the chapel is the Bloody Stair, on which, the story goes, the daughter of a High Steward stabbed herself in order to escape from an unwelcome bridegroom.

NORTH OF ROTHESAY. **Port Bannatyne**, 2m N of Rothesay, is a resort on Kames Bay, at the head of which stands *Kames Castle*, dating in part from the 14C. The writer John Sterling (1806–44), known less for himself than as the subject of a biography by Carlyle, was born here. Two roads branch W for the sands of Ettrick Bay, while A886 followed N runs with the shore of the eastern arm of the Kyles of Bute, with views across to Cowal, and in 5m reaches *Rhubodach* for the ferry to Colintraive.

SOUTH OF ROTHESAY. The coastal road (A844) leads past (at Kerrycroy) the gates of *Mount Stuart* (1877), seat of the Marquis of Bute, to reach *Kingarth*, 5m from Rothesay. Beyond, the small road down the centre of the peninsula links some minor but ancient sites. First (E) come the remains of a stone circle, followed by (W) the *Standing Stones of Lubar*. Farther on (E) are the fragments of a monastery founded in the 6C by St. Blane, a native of Bute who studied in Ireland and preached in Scotland, being best known in connection with Dunblane, while a short way E stands ruined *St. Blane's Chapel*, in origin perhaps of c 1100. On the shore to the W there is a vitrified Iron Age fort. From Kingarth B878 offers a different return to Rothesay and a view across to St. Ninian's Point with traces of another ancient chapel.

Island of Cumbrae

> **Tourist Information**. Guildford Street, Millport. Tel: (0475) 530753. June–Sept.
>
> **Access**. Car ferry from Largs to Cumbrae Slip, with train connections from Glasgow and bus from Cumbrae Slip to Millport. Frequent. Crossing 10 minutes.
> In summer, island-circuit coach tours.
>
> HOTEL. **Millport**. *Millerston*, West Bay Road. Tel: (0475) 530480.

Cumbrae, or more properly Great Cumbrae, although only ten minutes offshore, has a character surprisingly different from that of the busy mainland. One road (about 12m) circles the island, and in summer much of its traffic is made up of families riding hired bicycles.

Millport, the only town, curves round its bay for 1½ miles, and with its pleasantly incidental sandy beach, broken by rocks and a scatter of islets, rightly claims to be a family resort. The episcopal church (William Butterfield, 1849) was in 1876 consecrated as Cathedral of Argyll and the Isles. The *Museum of the Cumbraes* (June–Sept: Tues.–Sat., 10.00 to 16.30. Tel: 0475–530753. Free), in Garrison House, is devoted to the history of the local way of life, a feature being Cumbrae in Victorian and Edwardian times. The *University Marine Biological Station* (universities of Glasgow and London), just N of Millport, is concerned with the study of marine life in Clyde waters and admits visitors to its interesting aquaria (Mon.–Fri., 09.00 to 12.30. 14.00 to 17.00. Also open Sat. in summer. Tel 0475–530581. Fee).

For *Inverclyde, National Water Sports Training Centre*, in the NE of the island, see Sports Holidays.

On *Little Cumbrae*, immediately to the S, the only dwellings are a farm and a lighthouse. The island was maintained as a deer forest by Robert II and Robert III. On an islet off the E shore are the remains of a tower erected in 1527 to control deer poaching and destroyed by Cromwell in 1653.

18 Edinburgh

Tourist Information. Waverley Market, Princes Street (E end). Tel: (031) 5572727.

Public Transport buses are operated by Lothian Regional Transport, North Bridge (corner with Princes Street). Tel: (031) 5565656. A map clearly covers all city and suburban services. *City Tours*. A comprehensive choice of conducted tours of varying length leave Waverley Bridge throughout the day from 09.30. Also full and half day excursions to several places in this part of Scotland.—The *Coach Station*, for scheduled services beyond the city, is off St. Andrew Square N of Princes Street from Tourist Information.

British Rail. Waverley Station, below E end of Princes Street.

Airport. 6m W. City Terminal at Waverley Bridge.

Spectacles. The colourful, traditional ceremony of Beating the Retreat, with pipe bands, is usually staged on the Castle Esplanade once or twice a week in May and June. Between June–Sept there is sometimes Scottish dancing in Princes Street gardens. Daily, except Sun., the 'One o'clock gun' is fired from the castle.

Edinburgh Festival. *Festival Offices*: 21 Market Street, EH1 1BW. Tel: (031) 2264001.—Started in 1947, the Edinburgh International Festival of Music and Drama has now long been accepted as one of the world's leading festivals of its kind. It extends over a period of three weeks (usually the last three weeks in Aug.) and although the emphasis is on music and drama, many other aspects of the arts are included, one of the most popular events being the spectacular military searchlight tattoo staged on the Castle Esplanade with the floodlit castle as a dramatic backcloth.

What has come to be known as *The Fringe* (Offices: 170 High Street, EH1 1QS. Tel: (031) 2265257) is now firmly established as companion to the Festival proper. It may be described as 'that vast range of entertainment available during the Festival period just beyond the official Festival programme... adventurous, irreverent, and invariably intriguing'.

Edinburgh becomes very full indeed during the Festival, and advance booking both for events and accommodation is strongly advised. Information, programmes, bookings and accommodation reservation all through the official Festival offices.

SOME HOTELS. As Scotland's capital Edinburgh offers a generous choice of hotels of all categories; what are missing, though, near the city centre, are hotels with parking. The following three, however, all have parking and are all close to Princes Street (and thus in the more expensive bracket). *Caledonian*, Princes Street. Tel: (031) 2252433. *George*, 19–21 George Street. Tel: (031) 2251251. *King James Thistle*, 7 St. James Centre, Leith Street. Tel: (031) 5560111.

Some other central hotels: *Roxburghe*, 38 Charlotte Square. Tel: (031) 2253921. *Carlton*, North Bridge. Tel: (031) 5567277. *Howard* (with parking), 32–36 Great King Street. Tel: (031) 5573500. *Mount Royal*, 53 Princes Street. Tel: (031) 2257161. *North British*, Princes Street. Tel: (031) 5562414. *Old Waverley*, 43 Princes Street. Tel: (031) 556 4648.

Some suburban hotels, all to the W on the approaches to the airfield and the Forth Road Bridge: *Ladbroke Dragonara*, Bells Mills, 69 Belford Road. Tel: (031) 3322545. *Post House*, Corstorphine Road. Tel: (031) 334 8221. *Crest*, Queensferry Road. Tel: (031) 3322442. *Barnton Thistle*, 562 Queensferry Road. Tel: (031) 3391144.

Routes to and from Edinburgh. Several of the Rtes in this guide run into or out of Edinburgh. To Edinburgh from *Berwick-upon-Tweed, Dunbar* and *Haddington*, see Rte 1; from *North Berwick*, see Rte 2; from *Coldstream, Kelso* and *Lauder*, see Rte 3; from *Jedburgh* and *Melrose*, see Rte 4; from *Canonbie, Hawick, Selkirk* and *Galashiels*, see Rte 5; from *Peebles*, see Rte 6; from *Gretna, Lockerbie* and *Moffat*, see Rte 7.

From Edinburgh to *Bathgate* and *Glasgow*, see Rte 8; to *Linlithgow, Falkirk* and *Stirling*, see Rte 9; to *Aberfoyle* and *The Trossachs*, see Rte 21; to *Dunfermline, Culross, Alloa* and *Stirling*, see Rte 31; to *Perth*, see Rte 32; into *Fife*, see Rtes 33A and 33C.

Justly held to be one of Europe's most distinguished and most dramatic capitals, Edinburgh is a city of style and dignity, a place well aware that Scotland has just about everything to offer and that this, its capital—and for many visitors their introduction—must not disappoint. It is a responsibility the city accepts with confidence and discharges with instinctive flair; a confidence and flair both born of that same vision which shook off the trauma of lost status, of becoming second to London—the incubus, too, of crowded tenements towering above dark wynds—and in the 18–19C exploded into an era of brilliance in the arts and of elegant expansion which set a tone still dominant today.

Yet, for all its sense of style, this is no stuffy city. Festival and Fringe can live together, as can gourmet restaurants with the extrovert cheerfulness of Victorian pubs, the sedate, established shops of Princes Street with the brasher denizens of modern precincts.

History. Edinburgh was probably born in pre-Roman times when Pictish huts would have begun to cluster along the slopes of the rock. Later the Romans were here, building their fort at Cramond, but after their departure from Britain the Angles of Northumbria subjugated Lothian and in the 6C their king, Edwin, rebuilt an earlier fortress whose name of Dun Eadain, the Fortress on the Slope, readily if inaccurately adapted to Edwin's Burgh. For many centuries Edinburgh's story was that of this fortress or castle, the town as such really only starting to develop during the 11C when markets began to spring up in the area where High Street now runs. On accession in 1124 David I moved his capital from Dunfermline to Edinburgh, founding his abbey at Holyrood four years later, and the progress in the town's growth is marked by the granting of a charter by Bruce in 1329.

The reigns of James II to IV (1437–1513) marked an outstanding period in Edinburgh's history. It saw the construction (1436) of the first effective town wall, Wellhouse Tower at the N foot of Castle Rock being about the only surviving trace; the start in c 1500 of the construction of Holyrood Palace; much patronage of the arts and education, including the granting of a charter (1506) to the Royal College of Surgeons and the setting up in 1508 of Scotland's first printing press; and, finally, with the disaster of Flodden in 1513, the hasty building of the Flodden Wall, a part of which can still be seen S of Grassmarket.

But Flodden ushered in what was to prove a century or more of darkness and disaster. In 1544, and again in 1547, the years of the 'rough wooing' (see History of Scotland), England's Henry VIII, baulked in his plan of marriage between his son to Mary, the infant Queen of Scots, devastated the city. Then in 1561 Mary returned from France, and Edinburgh and the surrounding district became the stage on which was played much of the tragedy and turbulence of her seven years in Scotland—years which presaged that day in 1603 when Mary's son, James VI, becoming James I of England, moved with his court to London, leaving Edinburgh as a deserted capital of secondary importance. Not that this new status brought any compensating tranquility, for the city was now to experience much of the bitter religious and associated struggle that, born in Mary's short reign, reached its climax during the 17C. Among the events of these years were the signing of the National Covenant at Greyfriars in 1638; Cromwell's occupation of the city in 1650 and the execution here of Montrose in the same year; the continued burning of witches on the castle esplanade;

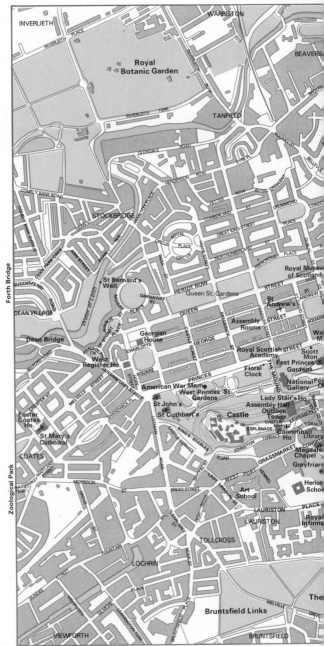

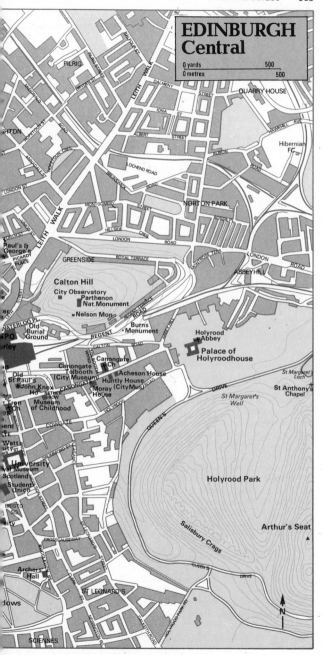

EDINBURGH
Central

0 yards   500
0 metres   500

QUARRY HOUSE

PILRIG

LEITH WALK

DALMENY   STREET

IONA ST

ALBERT   STREET

HAWKHILL AVE

Hibernian
FC

LOCHEND ROAD

MONTGOMERY   STREET

NORTON PARK

HILLSIDE

LONDON   CRES   ROAD

LONDON ST

LEITH WALK

Paul's &
George's
PICARDY
PLACE

GREENSIDE   ROYAL TERRACE

MONTROSE TERR

LONDON   ROAD

ABBEYHILL

Calton Hill
City Observatory
Parthenon
Nat.Monument
Nelson Mon

WATERLOO PL
Old
Burial
Ground

REGENT   CALTON   ROAD

Burns
Monument

Holyrood
Abbey

Palace of
Holyroodhouse

St Margaret's
Loch

St Paul's
John Knox
Ho
Tron
Ch
Museum
of Childhood

Canongate
Tolbooth
(City Museum)
Acheson House
Huntly House
Moray (City Mus)
House

Ch
Canongate

NETHER
BOW

CANONGATE

HOLYROOD   ROAD

St Margaret's
Well

St Anthony's
Chapel

COWGATE

QUEEN'S

Watt
sity ST

University
al Museum
Scotland
Student
Union

DRUMMOND ST

Holyrood Park

BRISTO
SQ
sity

CROSSCAUSEWAY

Salisbury Crags

Arthur's Seat

Archers
Hall

ST LEONARD'S

dows

QUEEN'S   DRIVE

SCIENNES

N

and the martyrdom in Grassmarket of over 100 Covenanters.

The 18C got off to a bad start. Although with the Restoration Charles II had rebuilt Holyrood Palace, Edinburgh was soon to become even less of a capital when the Act of Union was passed in 1707, and in 1745 there followed that moment of divided loyalty, when the Young Pretender held court at Holyrood while the castle remained in Government hands. Then, and suddenly, there was that explosion of brilliance referred to above. In the broad field of the arts Allan Ramsay, Adam Smith, Hume, Goldsmith, Sir Walter Scott and R.L. Stevenson are only some of the galaxy of names associated with the 18 and 19C. At the same time, with the bridging of Cowgate, Edinburgh shook itself free of its tenemented rock as buildings began to spread southwards beyond the Flodden Wall and, more significantly (starting in 1767), northwards to become over the ensuing 70 or so years the most distinguished and most extensive area of Georgian architecture in Britain.

Of many important 18 and 19C landmarks, the years 1818 and 1822 are perhaps the most deserving of mention, both closely associated with Sir Walter Scott. In 1818 a search made in the castle at his instigation rediscovered the Scottish regalia, forgotten since 1707; and in 1822 he organised a highly successful visit by George IV, the first royal visit for over a century and one which not only brought Holyrood back to life but, so far as Scotland as a whole was concerned, could be said to have signalled the end of the aftermath of Culloden. The Industrial Revolution brought little visible harm to what had long been an essentially professional rather than industrial city (the railway is well hidden) and, though inevitably there are sores, 20C development is on the whole being kept clear of the best areas of old and Georgian Edinburgh.

Central Edinburgh divides itself into three distinct yet adjacent areas and is thus easy for the visitor. The older city sprawls across a conspicuous, sloping volcanic rock along which stretches historic **Old Edinburgh,** or the **Royal Mile,** linking the Castle, high on its precipitous crag at the W, with Holyrood Palace and Abbey at the slope's foot in the E. On either side of this spine there are roughly parallel valleys, gouged out during the Ice Age. The valley to the N, until 1816 filled by a loch (Nor'Loch), is now the long panoramic sweep of Princes Street, renowned for its dramatic setting and as Edinburgh's main shopping street. From Princes Street there extends northward, up and over the ridge which carries George Street, the spacious and dignified mainly 18C **New Town.** To the rock's S there is a sheer drop to the area of **Grassmarket and Greyfriars,** both of no little historical interest, while beyond spreads a district of only limited attraction for the visitor, where Georgian and Victorian streets and squares are gradually giving way to modern development.

However short the time available most visitors will not fail to see the Castle, the Royal Mile and Holyrood, as well as Princes Street and George Street, with perhaps something of their Georgian neighbours. The Grassmarket and Greyfriars district, though of less immediately obvious interest, retains, despite some development, much of the feel of 17 and 18C and early Victorian Edinburgh and will certainly attract any student of the Covenanter years. Which of Edinburgh's many museums and art galleries are chosen will be a matter of time and taste, but two should perhaps be mentioned here. The Royal Museum of Scotland (Queen Street) shows prehistoric and historic material from all over Scotland and a browse around can be a rewarding accompaniment to sites already visited, or to be visited, throughout the country. The City Museum at Huntly House, on the other hand, is concerned exclusively with Edinburgh and offers invaluable background to anyone wishing to get below the surface of this city's story.

Although Edinburgh divides into the three main areas referred to above (Old Edinburgh, Grassmarket and Greyfriars, and New Town), for descriptive convenience these are covered below as five sections: A. Edinburgh Castle. B. Royal Mile and Holyrood. C. South Edinburgh (Grassmarket, Greyfriars and beyond). D. Princes Street. E. North Edinburgh (New Town). A sixth section (F.) describes other places of interest within the city or its environs. A whole day should be allowed for the Castle, Royal Mile and Holyrood, all conveniently combinable as one walk. South and North Edinburgh can each comfortably be covered in a half day, although this does not of course allow for time spent in the several museums and galleries.

A. *Edinburgh Castle

Visitors may wish to note that this is not just another castle. Indeed, strictly as a castle, Edinburgh can be a shade disappointing, though the bastions and their views are of course breathtaking. These apart, what counts here is what the castle embraces—a rich and varied offering which includes ancient (11C) St. Margaret's Chapel; the deeply impressive Scottish National War Memorial; the old palace, with the Crown Room in which are proudly displayed the regalia of Scotland, and with Queen Mary's Apartments, these including the room in which the future James VI/I was born; the handsome 15C Old Parliament (or Banqueting) Hall, scene of at least two treacherous murders; an ancient and historic cannon; and two military museums.

The Castle (AM) is open April–Sept: Mon.–Sat., 09.30 to 17.05. Sun., 11.00 to 17.05. Oct–March: Mon.–Sat., 09.30 to 16.20. Sun., 12.30 to 15.35. Fee. The above closing times are all last admission times, the castle remaining open for a further 45 minutes. The castle is closed for about four days over the New Year period, and the above times may be altered during the tattoo, state occasions and military events.

During the crowded season a one-way system is sometimes imposed and places may not be visited in the order described below.

History. So natural a defensive position was clearly a fortress from earliest times, and indeed in monkish legends this site is mentioned as Castrum Puellarum, Castle of the Maids, presumably a safe retreat for the daughters of Pictish kings. In the 6C the Northumbrian king Edwin rebuilt the older fortress as a strong northern bastion of his lands, and 500 years later, in the 11C, Malcolm Canmore seems to have lived both here and in Dunfermline, his saintly wife, Queen Margaret, building in c 1076 the simple little chapel which bears her name. She died in the castle in 1093, while it was being besieged by Donald Bane, and her body was secretly let down the cliff beyond the West Sally Port and taken to her priory at Dunfermline. In 1174, after his defeat and capture at Alnwick, the castle was surrendered by William the Lion to England's Henry II, and from 1296 to 1313 it was again in English hands (Edward I) until retaken by the Earl of Moray after a daring climb up the cliff; then, in accordance with Bruce's scorched earth policy, the castle was largely dismantled. David II rebuilt and did much to strengthen the defences, part of his great keep, in which he died in 1371, still surviving, though as a ruin.

It was in the castle that Mary, Queen of Scots, gave birth in 1566 to the future James VI/I, and two years later, when she was captive in England, her former enemy, Kirkcaldy of Grange, held the castle in her cause for an epic five years; he was finally defeated by cannon brought from England and, later, hanged. Cromwell seized the castle in 1650, and in 1745 it declined to open its gates to the Young Pretender, then installed in some state in Holyrood Palace after his victory at Prestonpans. During the Napoleonic wars French prisoners were confined here.

The castle is approached across the spacious sloping **Castle Esplanade**, the dramatic stage for the Festival's Military Tattoo as also for the ancient ceremony of the Beating of the Retreat (see Spectacles, above). Around the Esplanade are a number of military memorials recalling past glories and disasters, and also two other memorials, not military and of more general interest. The first—and not for the squeamish—is against the wall, immediately on the right on entering the Esplanade. Here the *Witches' Well* marks the spot where more than 300 witches were burned between 1479 and as late as 1722, a sharp reminder both of past attitudes and of past spectacles staged here. Nor were the victims all wretched old crones, for one of their number (1540) was the beautiful Janet, Lady Glamis, found guilty of mixing potions but in reality one of the many casualties of James V's implacable hatred of the Douglas family (see Biographical Notes). The well bears a curious if somewhat equivocal design with a wicked head (bad witches), a serene head (witches who may have been benevolent), and a serpent representing both evil and wisdom. The other memorial of general, or at any rate Canadian interest, is at the opposite end of the Esplanade where a plaque commemorates the spot where, at a ceremony in 1625, the Earl of Stirling received formal possession of the lands of Nova Scotia; in other words a gift from the crown of huge tracts of land in what is now Canada (see also Rte 23, Stirling, Argyll's Lodging; and Rte 25C, Menstrie Castle).

The entrance to the castle proper is across the moat and through an outer gateway (1888), flanked by statues of Bruce and Wallace, the path then bearing right for the *Portcullis Gate*, just before which (above, left) there is a memorial stone to Kirkcaldy of Grange. The Portcullis Gate stands below the *Constable's Tower*, later called *Argyll's Tower* because the 8th Earl of Argyll was held in the gateway dungeon before his execution in 1661 (see Biographical Notes). The old prison here, built by David II in 1369, was destroyed by English cannon in 1573 during the closing hours of Kirkcaldy's stand and, though rebuilt in the following year, required reconstruction in 1890. The path curves upward past the *Argyll Battery*, named after the victor of Sheriffmuir (1715) and overlooking Princes Street; past the tourist administration area, with shop etc., beside which a ramp slopes down to the battlement walk known as *Queen Mary's Post*; and on to *Foog's Gate*, just before which is the *Regimental Museum of the Royal Scots and Royal Scots Dragoon Guards* (Mid May–mid Sept: Mon.–Sat., 09.30 to 16.30. Sun., 11.00 to 16.30. Mid Sept–mid May: Mon.–Fri., 09.30 to 16.00). Beyond Foog's Gate the **King's Bastion* is reached, the highest platform of the castle and a spot affording a famous view.

St. Margaret's Chapel was probably built by Margaret in 1076, though some hold that it may have been founded rather later in her honour by her son, David I. Although the chapel early acquired sanctity—that the dying Bruce made provision for restoration work is evidence enough—it was not always treated with reverence and as recently as 1845 it was used for storing the gunpowder with which ceremonial salutes were fired. However, later years brought more enlightened attitudes, starting with a restoration by Sir David Wilson in 1853 when the five small windows were given stained glass, this being replaced in 1921 by figures of St. Margaret, St. Andrew, St. Columba, St. Ninian and Wallace, all by Douglas Strachan. Further restoration in 1929 was sealed by the rededication of the chapel in

1934. However approached, this little place will surely not disappoint. As a link with a remote past, and even allowing for restoration and the modern windows, the simple interior cannot be very different to the chapel that Margaret knew and in which she probably spent her last hours; architecturally this is the oldest building in Edinburgh, an example of humble Norman, complete with zigzag moulding around the chancel arch; and if a sense of piety is sought, then it is surely more present here than in many a more pretentious edifice.

In the S part of this general area are the *Castle Well*, 110ft deep and used since at least 1313, and the remains of *David's Tower* (no adm.), the name given to the keep built by David II in 1367 and battered down by the English cannon during Kirkcaldy of Grange's famous defence. Immediately after the fall of the castle what is known as the *Half Moon Battery* was erected over the ruins, effectively hiding them until, by then almost forgotten, they were found in 1912.

Around Crown Square—the heart of the castle complex—are the Scottish National War Memorial, the Crown Room, Queen Mary's Apartments, the Old Parliament or Banqueting Hall, and the United Services Museum.

The **Scottish National War Memorial**, an inspired achievement by Sir Robert Lorimer (1927), covers a site on which once stood a church, then barracks, part of the walls of which have been incorporated into the present building. The memorial comprises a long Gallery of Honour with bays at either end, and, centrally opposite the entrance, the octagonal *Shrine*, within which, strikingly on an outcrop of natural rock, stands the marble Stone of Remembrance, bearing a wrought-steel casket containing records. The stained glass windows, depicting war as a mysterious element in the destiny of man, are by Douglas Strachan, while below, and perhaps more readily understood, are reliefs by Morris and Alice Meredith Williams portraying types of all who served, men and women, as also animals and birds. The *Gallery of Honour* is divided into recesses devoted to the Scottish regiments. The W Bay commemorates the Women's War Services and the Air Force; the E Bay the Navy, Cavalry, Yeomanry, Artillery and Engineers.

The E side of Crown Square represents the medieval royal palace, dating from the 15C but with additions of 1566 and 1615. Here now is the **Crown Room** in which are shown the Regalia, or, more romantically, the 'Honours of Scotland'—the crown, the sceptre and the sword, generally accepted as the oldest regalia in Europe. After their gallant and romantic rescue from Dunnottar Castle, followed by some years beneath the pulpit of Kinneff church (see Rte 35), the regalia were returned to Edinburgh at the Restoration, but on the union of the parliaments were ignominiously deposited in a chest and virtually forgotten. But not by Sir Walter Scott who in 1818 instigated a search resulting in their discovery here in this then sealed Crown Room.

The Crown, made of Scottish gold and said to incorporate the circlet with which Bruce was crowned at Scone in 1306, is decorated with 94 pearls, ten diamonds and 33 other stones. Refashioned in 1540, when James V added the mound and cross at the top, the crown was last used for the coronation of Charles II at Scone in 1651, nine years before his restoration to the English throne. The Sceptre (1494; refashioned 1536), a gift to James IV from Pope Alexander VI, shows a Madonna, St. James and St. Andrew. The Sword, a sumptuous

Italian masterpiece, was presented to James IV in 1507 by Pope Julius II. The other objects, displayed separately and bequeathed to George IV by Cardinal York, the last of the Stuarts, include the Collar and George of the Order of the Garter presented by Elizabeth to James VI/I, the latter's badge of the Order of the Thistle, and a ring given by him to the future Charles I.

In **Queen Mary's Apartments**, in the SE corner of Crown Square, is the modest little room in which, on 19 June 1566, Mary, Queen of Scots, gave birth to the son who, only a year later, would succeed her as James VI of Scotland and who in 1603 would triumphantly move to London as James I of England. A bizarre scene may be pictured as—with Mary in long and painful labour—the Countess of Atholl resorted to witchcraft in an attempt to transfer the pangs to a seemingly willing Lady Reres lying on a bed nearby.

The **Old Parliament Hall** (or Banqueting Hall), occupying the S side of Crown Square, is of early 15C origin but was extensively rebuilt by James IV. Here, in the predecessor of this handsome hall with its lofty open-timber roof, another bizarre scene, though one with a darker outcome, was played—the so-called Black Dinner of 1440. Chancellor Crichton—self-appointed guardian of James II, then only eight years old, and determined to smash the powerful Douglases—treacherously invited the boy Earl of Douglas and his younger brother to a banquet to meet James. And here they were seized and executed, having first been cruelly warned of their fate by the bringing on of a black bull's head, in the Scotland of the time the customary sign of violent death.

Used as the meeting-place of the Scottish parliament until 1639, and still in good condition in 1648 when Cromwell was entertained here by the Earl of Leven, the hall later declined, at one time being converted into storeys and used as a military hospital, and it was not until 1892 that it was restored, by the effort and purse of William Nelson, the publisher. It now houses a fine display of armour and weapons, together with general material connected with the castle's history.

Below the hall there are dungeons, in one of which the 9th Earl of Argyll—the one who was rash enough to support Monmouth—was held before his execution in 1685, and in which French prisoners were confined during the Napoleonic wars.

Mons Meg, perhaps forged in Belgium in the 15C. Described in a Cromwellian inventory as the 'great iron murderer, Muckle Meg'.

Today, though, the dungeons—or the French Prison as they are commonly called—house *Mons Meg*, a 15C artillery piece of disputed origin but well enough recorded history. One tradition asserts that the gun was made at Mons in Belgium; another, certainly more entertaining, that it was forged in 1455 at Castle Douglas by a blacksmith who, anything but loyal to his cruel Douglas lord in Threave Castle, presented it to James II who was thus able to reduce Threave and finally smash the Douglases. What is certain is that Mons Meg was brought by James IV against the English Norham Castle in 1497, and that a century and a half later it was still formidable enough to warrant inclusion—as the 'great iron murderer, Muckle Meg'—in the inventory of castle guns captured by Cromwell. However the gun's operational life came to an undignified end in 1682 when it burst while attempting to fire a salute in honour of the Duke of York, afterwards James VII/II. In 1754 it was removed to the Tower of London, but in 1829, at Sir Walter Scott's request, restored to Edinburgh. The gun is made of long iron bars looped together, but the carriage is a reproduction of the kind that would have been used at Norham.

The **Scottish United Services Museum** (Tel: 031-2266907) was opened in 1931 as the Scottish Naval and Military Museum, receiving its present title when, after wartime closure, it reopened with an Air Force section. The longest established institution of its kind in Britain, the museum, with its comprehensive reference library, plays an important research and archival role. Additionally a unique collection of some 10,000 contemporary prints provides a valuable pictorial reference to changes in military uniforms from the early 18C to the end of the 19C, while more modern subjects are covered by an equally large collection of photographs.

B. Royal Mile and Holyrood

From those medieval centuries when traders and others gradually began to settle along the track between the castle and David I's abbey of Holyrood, right up until the explosive expansion of the 18 and 19C, this long slope, now popularly known as the Royal Mile, was the busy spine of Edinburgh life; the place where or close to which most of the inhabitants both lived and worked. Today it is paved and clean, relatively quiet, almost staid, but the Royal Mile of the past should be pictured as a narrow way, not too clean and certainly smelly, crowded with stalls and booths, behind which rose the ever taller tenement buildings (lands) inevitable with a fast-growing population and lack of space within the town wall. Off this bustling main thoroughfare a maze of dark wynds and closes or courts (the first a throughway wide enough for a horse, the last two generally blind alleys) led to business or residential courts, many of which, some admirably restored, can still be explored today. A visit to the City Museum in Huntly House will prove a great help towards understanding Edinburgh as it once was.

The distance between the castle and Holyrood is just about the one mile of this stretch's name; a mile surely unique for its crowding sequence of surprising and curious corners, for its kaleidoscope of

associations with a long past, and for the throng of characters—royal,
aristocratic, intellectual, criminal and humble—who in one way or
another have left their mark. It is a mile that must be pottered on
foot.

The Royal Mile leaves the Castle Esplanade as Castle Hill, the
house at the top of Castle Wynd steps, which drop down to
Grassmarket, being known as *Cannonball House* (1630) because of
the ball still embedded in its W gable. Traditionally this was fired
from the castle in 1745 and intended for Holyrood, then occupied by
the Young Pretender. Below, with a fine tower and spire, is the
church of *Tolbooth St. John's*, built in 1842–46 by Gillespie Graham
and A.W.N. Pugin, while across the road is **Outlook Tower**
(April–Sept: Mon–Fri., 09.30 to 18.00. Sat. and Sun., 10.00 to 18.00.
Oct–March: Daily, 10.00 to 17.00. Tel: 031-2263209. Fee), a popular
Edinburgh attraction for close on 150 years; since the 1850s when
an upper level was added to a 17C tower and, equipped with a
viewing platform and a camera obscura, Short's Popular Observatory
began to pull in visitors. This camera obscura—reflecting a living,
moving picture of Edinburgh on a white table while a guide provides
a commentary—remains the principal and most popular feature here,
but, ever since the close of the 19C when the tower gained its present
name, there has been a progressive programme of other features,
such as, today, laser holography and space photography.

Mylne's Court, just below Outlook Tower, recalls Robert Mylne,
Master Mason to Charles II and the man responsible, with William
Bruce, for Holyrood Palace as it now is. Dating from 1690, this court
has been restored by the University of Edinburgh as student accommodation.

Castle Hill now becomes Lawnmarket, the western section of High
Street and once, as its name suggests, the centre for linen merchants.
Here, on the left, is **Gladstone's Land** (NTS. April–Oct: Mon.–Sat.,
10.00 to 17.00. Sun., 14.00 to 17.00. Nov: Sat., 10.00 to 16.30. Sun.,
14.00 to 16.30. Last adm. 30 minutes before above closing times. Fee),
dating from 1620 and a typical example of a lofty (six storeys)
tenement, with an arcaded front, outside stair and stepped gables.
Both externally and internally—with reconstructed booths showing
17C goods, and, inside, painted ceilings and the main rooms
refurbished in the style of the period—this house provides a glimpse,
as accurate as is reasonable to expect after a lapse of some 300 years,
of an Edinburgh that would have been familiar to a comfortable
merchant, such as was Thomas Gledstanes. And *James Court*,
alongside, provides a similar glimpse, both visually and historically,
for here, before becoming one of the first to succumb to the attractions
of the New Town, lived the historian David Hume (1711–66) and
here, too, in the same flat, lived James Boswell who in 1773
entertained Dr Johnson here.

Hume earlier lived opposite in *Riddle's Close*, where he wrote a
part of his 'History of England', while the inner court here, known
as *Macmorran's Close*, was the home of the ill-starred Bailie
Macmorran, a wealthy merchant who was shot in 1595 while attempting to quell a school riot. Three years later his son entertained James
VI and his queen, Anne of Denmark, in this fine late 16C house,
today an adult education centre.

So far all place names have been those of respectable citizens. At
Brodie's Close, however, the pattern changes since here lived the

notorious Deacon Brodie, by day an esteemed town councillor, but by night a thief. Finally caught trying to rob the Excise Office in Chessel's Court (see below), he was hanged in 1788, the mechanism of the 'drop' being of his own design and apparently more successful than the steel collar he wore which was supposed to save his neck. In two things, though, he was, if unwittingly, successful, for he provided the inspiration for R.L. Stevenson's 'Dr Jekyll and Mr Hyde' as also the name for the pub on the corner of Lawnmarket and The Mound.

Opposite, a short close descends to **Lady Stair's House** (Mon.–Sat., 10.00 to 17.00 or 18.00 in June–Sept. Also, during Festival, Sun., 14.00 to 17.00. Tel: 031-2252424. Free), much restored but retaining some features of the house of 1622 which was the home of the beautiful Lady Stair (died 1731), whose story as Lady Primrose (during her first marriage) forms the basis of Scott's story 'My Aunt Margaret's Mirror'. Today the house serves as a museum of all manner of material on Scotland's three great literary figures, Burns, Scott and Stevenson. Below the house, and built over the site of the palace of Mary of Guise, is the *Assembly Hall* of the General Assembly of the Church of Scotland.

Lawnmarket ends at a busy crossroads (Bank Street and George IV Bridge), at the SE corner of which brass strips on the road mark the site of the scaffold, scene of public hangings until 1864. From here the Royal Mile continues as High Street, with, immediately on the right, Parliament Square, not immediately recognised as a square since most of its centre is filled by St. Giles Cathedral.

The heart of Edinburgh until the expansion of the 18C—and still the heart so far as the visitor to Old Edinburgh is concerned—

Old Tolbooth of Edinburgh, built in 1466 and demolished in 1817. Here during the 16 and 17C the citizens gathered to stare at severed aristocratic and humbler heads.

Parliament Square still provides several links with the city's past, starting, on the W near a statue of the 5th Duke of Buccleuch, with the '*Heart of Midlothian*', a cobblestone heart and outline marking the site of the entrance to the Old Tolbooth, built in 1466, extended by the New Tolbooth some time after 1561 and demolished in 1817. Here stood a building which over its centuries met many needs—in turn chapter house for St. Giles, meeting-place of parliament, the law courts, the town council and, in the 1560s, of the General Assembly of the Reformed Kirk—until degraded to the role of prison, the place, too, on which many an aristocratic head was displayed; those of the regent Morton in 1581, of Montrose in 1650, and of the 8th Earl of Argyll in 1661. This site later achieved fame as the scene of the opening of Scott's novel 'The Heart of Midlothian', the author having acquired the tolbooth keys and the great wooden door, all now to be seen at Abbotsford.

The S side of Parliament Square was once the cathedral cemetery, in which, it is thought, John Knox was buried in 1572, probably near the spot which his statue now overlooks. Here too an equestrian Charles II poses as a martial Roman, a statue (of 1685, by an unknown Dutch sculptor) enjoying the esoteric distinction of being the only leaden one in Scotland.

Parliament House (Tues.–Fri., 10.00 to 16.00. Tel: 031-2252595. Free) fronts the S side of Parliament Square. Erected in 1632–40, but given its present Italianate facade in 1808–14, this was the meeting-place of the Scottish parliament from 1639, the year in which it abandoned the castle, until it abolished itself under the Act of Union of 1707, the building then becoming, and remaining to this day, the legal heart of Scotland, the home of the Court of Session and the High Court. For the tourist the main interest will lie in the *Parliament Hall*, now used as a concourse—and a lively one, too, when crowded with gowned and wigged advocates, solicitors and clients—a majestic Gothic place with an open timber roof, a great window depicting the inauguration of the Court of Session in 1532 by James V, and several legal portraits by, amongst others, Kneller and Raeburn. Access to the splendid *Signet Library* (Robert Reid, 1815) is by written application only (to the Librarian).

This circuit of Parliament Square ends on the E side, where the *Mercat Cross* marks the true city centre, the traditional place, today as over a long past, of Royal Proclamations by the Lord Lyon, King of Arms, one such, in 1745, being that of the Young Pretender as James VIII. The tradition, though, is older than this cross which, though incorporating parts of its 14–16C predecessor, is essentially 19C, a gift to the city by the statesman W.E. Gladstone, who also composed the Latin inscription.

*St. Giles Cathedral (Daily, 09.00 to 17.00 or 19.00 in April–Sept. Free, but fee for Thistle Chapel) is a courtesy title for what is more properly the High Kirk of Edinburgh; a courtesy earned because this church was in fact twice a cathedral, albeit over only brief periods. The first was under Charles I who established a bishopric of Edinburgh in 1633; the second under Charles II and James VII/II, this however ending in 1689 when episcopacy was disestablished in Scotland. For today's visitor the cathedral's principal features are, outside, the famous Crown of St Giles atop the square tower, and, inside, the memorials to famous Scots, some the victims of hanging, execution or murder.

History. It is known that there has been a church on this site since at least 854 and that this was replaced by a Norman structure in c 1120, the church at this time being subordinate to the bishopric of St. Andrews which in 1243 authorised the dedication to St. Giles (see below). This Norman church was destroyed by Richard II of England in 1385 (although today's four massive central piers may, if only in part, be survivals), the successor Gothic church then growing over the course of the 15C during which three significant dates were 1454 when Sir William Preston gifted the church a bone from the arm of St. Giles; 1467 when, by achieving collegiate status, the church gained independence from St. Andrews; and 1495 which saw the construction of the tower completed.

At the Reformation, when amongst other damage the church lost its 44 altars (one at each pillar, and one in each side chapel) and its statue of St. Giles was thrown into Nor'Loch, John Knox became minister (1559–72), and it was in this capacity that he had his debates with Mary, Queen of Scots. The two subsequent bishopric periods have already been mentioned, and it was during the first of these, in 1637, that there occurred the incident when Jenny Geddes, incensed at hearing the episcopal service being read, hurled her stool at the preacher, thus launching the first blow of the movement that would be formalised the following year by the signing of the National Covenant at Greyfriars. During the 18 and 19C St. Giles was divided into four separate churches, and also at times in part used for secular purposes, only becoming one again with successful restoration work carried out between 1872–83, largely at the expense of William Chambers, the publisher. The Chapel of the Order of the Thistle, Scotland's highest order of chivalry, was added in 1911.

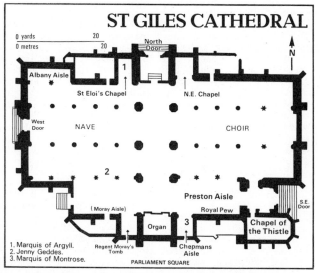

ST GILES CATHEDRAL

1. Marquis of Argyll.
2. Jenny Geddes.
3. Marquis of Montrose.

St. Giles, who died in c 710, seems to have been a Provençal by birth and to have lived his hermit life on land given to him by the local king Wamba. One day Wamba shot at a hind, which Giles was sheltering, missing the hind but crippling Giles with an arrow. St. Giles, by then the patron of cripples and beggars, became hugely popular in medieval times—perhaps simply because there were so many cripples and beggars—and throughout Europe many churches were dedicated to him. Here in the cathedral the story of St. Giles and the hind is portrayed in four places: outside, on the W door, below the archway; and, inside, in a window in the N nave, in a S clerestory window in the central chancel, and in the Chapel of the Thistle.

The description below of the cathedral's interior follows a clockwise course starting from the W door below the Burns Memorial Window of 1985 and first travelling the length of the N aisle. First comes the *Albany Aisle*, said to have been built in c 1410 by the Duke of Albany as a prudent expiation of his murder by starvation of the Duke of Rothesay (see also Rte 33C, Falkland Palace). Rededicated in 1951 as a war memorial, the aisle now houses military memorials and, in a recess the original purpose of which is unknown, the Roll of Honour of the 1939–45 war. *St. Eloi's Chapel*, next to the E, recalls a French saint (c 588–c 660), who, himself a skilled metalworker, became patron of the Guild of Hammermen whose chapel this once was and whose hammer is outlined on the floor. Today the main feature here from the past is the handsome memorial to the Covenanter 8th Earl of Argyll who lost his head in 1661, while modern times are represented by the Queen's Standard of No. 603 (City of Edinburgh) Squadron, Royal Auxiliary Air Force, a squadron which, operating in Gladiator biplanes from the grass field at Turnhouse (now Edinburgh airport) defended both the city and the fleet at Rosyth during the early months of the last war. The *NE Chapel*, beyond the N door, originally a memorial to William Chambers who financed the church's 19C restoration, now serves as a Chapel of Youth, while, as noted earlier, the four central piers near here may be survivals from the earlier Norman church.

The church is now crossed to the SE corner and the *Chapel of the Thistle*, entered through an ante-chapel listing the names of members since the founding of this Most Ancient and Most Noble Order of the Thistle in 1687 by James VII/II. This, Scotland's premier Order, consists of the sovereign and 16 knights and long used Holyrood Abbey as its chapel. The 12th Earl of Leven bequeathed funds for the restoration of Holyrood, but when this proved impracticable the bequest was directed to the construction of this new chapel, designed by Sir Robert Lorimer and opened in 1911. An admirable self-guide board details architectural and other information, the principal features being the lofty groined roof, the elaborate canopies of the carved oak stalls, the heraldic windows, and the floor of Ailsa Craig granite with a memorial slab to George VI; and, for connoisseurs of the quaint, there is that angel playing bagpipes, to be found by the upper right side of the entrance arch.

Back in the church proper, the *Preston Aisle* was founded in 1454 to honour Sir William Preston who died in that year having presented the church with an arm-bone of St. Giles. Two hundred years later (1643) this aisle was the scene of the signing of the Solemn League and Covenant, under which Scotland sided with the Puritan Cromwell—an occurrence which would hardly have pleased the obviously devoutly Catholic Sir William Preston. The main feature here today is the carved Royal Pew, with stalls for the Queen and the Duke of Edinburgh and, below, those occupied on ceremonial occasions by Lord Lyon, King of Arms, and his heralds and pursuivants. *Chepman's Aisle*, off the SW corner of the Preston Aisle, was a gift from Walter Chepman (died 1532) who in 1508 set up the first printing press in Scotland. Although remembered by a plaque here, Chepman is overshadowed by the great Marquis of Montrose, hanged in 1650, whose dismembered remains were collected and buried here in 1661 and whose monument is on the E wall. Here too is an original (Queensferry) parchment of the National Covenant signed at Greyfriars (see below) in 1638.

The original *Moray Aisle* (in which Lord James Stewart, later Regent Moray and leader of the Reformers against Mary of Guise, was buried after his murder in Linlithgow in 1570) was in the S transept, but the name Moray Aisle is now rather loosely given to the whole area W of the S transept. The Regent Moray Memorial (1864) is in the SE corner of this area, in what was once the Holy Blood Aisle, here too being a window (Noel Paton) depicting both the murder and John Knox preaching at the funeral. Roughly opposite, on the floor on the N side of this new Moray Aisle, a tablet marks the traditional spot from which Jenny Geddes launched her stool.

Across High Street from St. Giles Cathedral stand the *City Chambers* (1753–61; entrance archways 1902), originally built to serve as a Royal Exchange but taken over by the city council in 1811. In the quadrangle there is a lively statue of Alexander the Great and his horse, Bucephalus, and the city's war memorial Stone of Remembrance is beneath the central arch. In *Anchor Close*, alongside, once stood the Anchor Tavern, a favourite pub of Burns, and also the printing works of William Smellie who in 1768 published the first edition of the 'Encyclopaedia Britannica' and in 1787 the first Edinburgh edition of Burns's poems. Roughly opposite, at 142 High Street and occupying the restored New Assembly Rooms of 1766, the **Wax Museum** (Daily. Tel: 031-2264445. Fee), illustrates Scotland's past, complete with over 150 wax figures, sound and lighting effects, a children's 'Never Never Land' and, of course, a Chamber of Horrors.

High Street next reaches its second busy intersection, here with the streets known as North Bridge and South Bridge. Here *Tron Church* (1637–47) recalls through its name the tron or public weighbeam which stood nearby, merchants risking being nailed by their ears to the beam if they gave short measure. No longer in use, the church may be converted to house a city heritage centre. Below the intersection, off the N side of High Street, the narrow Carrubber's Close was the site of Edinburgh's first theatre, opened in 1736 'at vast expense' by Allan Ramsay; but Edinburgh was not yet ready for this kind of thing and the place was soon closed by the magistrates. The close leads to *Old St. Paul's Episcopal Church* (1883), standing on the site of a wool store which served as church for those who quit St. Giles in 1689 when the Episcopal Church was disestablished. In the present church a chapel commemorates the contentious Samuel Seabury, who worshipped here while a student and went on to become in 1783 the first bishop of the American Church. By contrast, a sculpted relief over the entrance to nearby *Paisley Close* recalls the cheerful courage of a mere lad who, trapped below a collapsed tenement in 1861, encouraged his rescuers by shouting 'Heave awa', I'm no deid yet'. Blackfriars Street, opposite, was formerly Blackfriars Close, during the 16–18C one of Edinburgh's most aristocratic quarters.

John Knox House (Mon.–Sat., 10.00 to 16.00. Tel: 031-5566961. Fee) next juts into High Street. Dating in appearance from c 1560, the house incorporates in its lower part work of c 1473 and of the early 17C above. Whether in fact John Knox ever lived here can be debated, but it does seem that he may well have occupied the second floor from 1561, when the house was raised a storey, until his death in 1572. In any event the house shows material on Knox, as also some interesting pictures of old Edinburgh, and with its wood panelling

*Edinburgh, Canongate Tolbooth. Long the civic centre of
independent Canongate.*

and hand-painted ceiling is one of the most attractive old houses in Edinburgh.

Opposite, at 38 High Street, is the attractive and unusual **Museum of Childhood** (Mon.–Sat., 10.00 to 17.00 or 18.00 in June–Sept. Also during Festival, Sun., 14.00 to 17.00. Tel: 031-2252424. Free), the world's first museum devoted to the history and theme of childhood. With displays illustrating such aspects as upbringing, clothing, health and education, this is in many respects a museum of more interest to parents than to children. But toys, dolls, books and suchlike are here too, so, however serious the museum's intent, the children tend to swamp the adults in what has been described as the 'noisiest museum in the world'.

Below John Knox House is the site of *Netherbow*, a spot at which to pause for here once stood the lower gate of the city, removed in 1764 but still recalled by a pictorial sign on the Church of Scotland Art Centre and by brass strips on the ground. Imagination can conjure much from the past here, but perhaps no scene as dramatic or dashing as that of the early hours of 17 September 1745. Edinburgh, in a turmoil of terror and ambivalent loyalty with the Young Pretender encamped at Duddingston and faced with a demand for surrender by 2 a.m., sent a delegation to the rebel camp to plead for time. Spurned by the Young Pretender, the delegation returned, its coach passing through Netherbow sometime after midnight. Soon afterwards a force of Highlanders under Lochiel assembled below the gate but, on being refused entry and with dawn not far away, decided to retire. Then, to their amazement, the gate opened—simply to allow out the city deputation's coachman who happened to stable his horses outside the walls—whereupon Lochiel stormed through to take the city.

The Royal Mile now becomes *Canongate*, running through a district which, being outside the Netherbow, enjoyed the status of independent town until absorbed in 1856. The name derives from the canons or clerics of Holyrood Abbey, while 'gait' is a walk or road, and Canongate was for long the smart residential quarter of the aristocracy, anxious to be close to Holyrood Palace. Recent years have seen much successful restoration aimed at reconciling the best of the old with modern requirements. *Chessel's Court*, for instance, on the S and once the Excise Office, the robbing of which was Deacon Brodie's last crime, has now been reconstructed as flats, while *Playhouse Close*, on the same side, recalls an early theatre which, opening 11 years after Allan Ramsay's unsuccessful venture in Carrubber's Close, flourished from 1747–69. Opposite, new buildings incorporate the facades of the 17C Bible Land and the 18C Shoemakers' Land, and there is a reproduction of the 17C Morocco Land.

Built in 1625 by the Dowager Countess of Home, and receiving its name from her daughter the Countess of Moray to whom it passed in 1645, **Moray House** (S), now a college of education, was visited by both Charles I and Cromwell. From its balcony in 1650, while here at his son's wedding party and 11 years before his own execution, Argyll watched Montrose pass in a cart on his way to his death; and in 1707, when Commissioners were discussing the Treaty of Union in a summerhouse in the garden, they were assailed by an angry mob and forced to flee to a cellar in High Street. Part of Moray House is an archway across St. John's Pend where the Knights of St. John once had their quarters.

The ***City Museum** (Mon.–Sat., 10.00 to 17.00 or 18.00 in June–Sept. Also, during Festival, Sun., 14.00 to 17.00. Tel: 031-2252424. Free), devoted to the story of Edinburgh, occupies Huntly House, dating from 1517, bought and restored by Edinburgh Corporation in 1926, and opened as a museum in 1932. The wide range of exhibits—from decorative art to a clay pipe workshop, from an original copy of the National Covenant to material on Earl Haig—is admirably displayed through an attractive, rambling series of rooms. *Canongate Tolbooth*, opposite, is also a part of the museum, used for temporary exhibitions and housing the J. Telfer Dunbar Tartan Collection and the popular Scottish Stone and Brass Rubbing Centre (Tel: 031-2251131) where visitors can make rubbings from replicas of medieval brasses and Pictish inscribed stones. The building (dating from 1591 but successor to a much earlier tolbooth), with its projecting clock, hall used as council room and court, and prison below, long served as the civic centre of independent Canongate.

A switch can now be made from the past to the present, from sightseeing to stylish shopping, for *Acheson House* (1633), next door to Huntly House, is the home of the **Scottish Craft Centre** (Mon.–Sat., 10.00 to 17.30. Tel: 031-5568136. Free), founded several years ago as a charity charged with encouraging the highest standard of Scottish craft work and today offering the widest range of quality products in the country.

Canongate Church, opposite, was built in 1688 by James Smith to serve the parishioners ejected from Holyrood's Chapel Royal by James VII/II, but in 1745 was treated with scant respect by the Young Pretender who found it to be a convenient place in which to hold the several officers he had taken at Prestonpans. The remains of Rizzio are said to lie under a stone in the SE corner of the church, while in the churchyard are the graves of Adam Smith (SW corner) and, N of the church, the poet Robert Fergusson (1750–74), best known for his 'Auld Reekie' but here perhaps of more interest for the fact that his headstone was paid for by his admirer, Robert Burns.

At the foot of Canongate, with Holyrood just beyond, there are four places deserving attention. First, a cobbled circle on the road marks the position of the *Girth Cross*, the western limit of the Sanctuary of Holyrood which, until the abolition in 1880 of imprisonment for debt, offered a refuge to debtors, derisively known as 'abbey lairds'. *White Horse Close*, N off Canongate and possibly so-named after Mary, Queen of Scots' white palfrey, was once a busy coaching station with a long courtyard at the end of which stood the White Horse Inn, in 1745 much frequented by the Young Pretender's officers. Dating from the 17C, the Close, now private homes, has been sensitively restored and, architecturally at least, still conveys the essence of its early character. *Nos 11–15 Canongate* make up a typical 17C tenement building, or land, now restored as flats and a shop. Lastly, round the corner, on the edge of Holyrood grounds, will be seen the curious, small turreted lodge, obscurely called *Queen Mary's Bathroom*. The tradition that Rizzio's murderers escaped by way of this lodge may well be true; another, that Mary habitually bathed here in white wine, seems less likely.

**Holyrood comprises the Palace of Holyrood House, with its State and Historical Apartments, and, behind, the much older and ruined Holyrood Abbey. Thus for the visitor there is a tangible and visible identification spanning from modern state splendour, back through the brief but turbulent and bloody days of Mary, Queen of Scots, down to the ruins of medieval piety and superstition.

Holyrood means Holy Cross, and its use here may stem from that fragment of the True Cross said to have been treasured by Queen Margaret, mother of David I, founder of the abbey. A more stirring tradition is that David, out hunting and in danger of being gored by a stag, was saved by the miraculous intervention of a Cross.

Palace visits are by conducted tours, these being frequent and lasting about 40 minutes. The Abbey ruins are visited on leaving the Palace after the tour. Broadly the opening times of the Ticket Kiosk are April–late Oct: Mon.–Sat., 09.30 to 17.15. Sun., 10.30 to 16.30. Winter: Mon.–Sat., 09.30 to 15.45. Dates and times however may vary and the Palace may at any time in whole or in part be closed at short notice. The Palace is normally completely closed for some two weeks in late May and again for the same time in late June and early July when it is occupied by the Lord High Commissioner and the Queen respectively. For a few days before the start and after the finish of these dates, and for the period in between, only the Historic Apartments are open and the shorter tour lasts 15–20 minutes. Intending visitors should refer to Tourist Information or telephone 031-5567371.

The **Palace of Holyrood House**, or simply Holyrood Palace, has, with varying fortunes, been a royal residence since the reign of James IV, his predecessors having frequently used Holyrood Abbey's guest house for the same purpose. However, except for the NW tower—and even this was altered—the building seen today essentially represents major rebuilding and extension of 1671–80. Today the palace is the Queen's official residence when visiting Edinburgh.

History. Starting in c 1500, and using the abbey's guest house as a nucleus, James IV and James V completed what may be called the first palace, which, however, was burnt by the Earl of Hertford in 1544 and again badly damaged three years later, only the NW tower significantly surviving. Mary, Queen of Scots, spent only six years here at Holyrood—in that NW tower—but they were eventful ones. Hither the young widowed queen came from France in 1561, and here took place her famous disputation with John Knox, her marriage (in the abbey) to Darnley, the butchery before her eyes of Rizzio, and her hasty marriage to Bothwell (in the predecessor of today's Gallery).

But change came in 1603 with the departure for London of James VI/I, since which date, although occupied by royalty from time to time, Holyrood has never been a royal residence in any permanent sense. Cromwell occupied the palace in 1650, even ordering some repairs after a fire, but it was during the reign of Charles II, between 1671–80, that the major work (design by Sir William Bruce, executed by Robert Mylne) took place which converted what was essentially just the NW tower and some ruins into the great palace as seen today.

Despite this major work, the use made of the palace from now on was only intermittent. James VII/II, as Duke of York, resided here on and off between 1679–82; and in 1745, from 17 September to 31 October, the Young Pretender held his court here, beneath the guns of the hostile castle, though he often passed the night with his troops at nearby Duddingston. The Comte d'Artois, afterwards Charles X of France, occupied a suite of rooms for some years after 1795, and again, as an exiled monarch, in 1830–32. George IV held a levée here in 1822, Queen Victoria came from time to time on her way to and from Balmoral, and her son, Edward VII, lived here for some months in 1859 when studying in Edinburgh.

The spacious *Outer Court* is enclosed by wrought-iron gates which, together with a statue, form a national memorial to Edward VII. The fountain in the centre, a Victorian replica of that at Linlithgow Palace, provides a link back to James V and Mary of Guise, as also do their badges on the tower, or wing, projecting to the left, the only significant survival of that king's 16C palace.

The visitor starts his tour of the interior by the Grand Stair, which shows the first of the fine 17C ceilings prominently displaying the Honours of Scotland, from here diverting to the Household Dining Room with its Adam-style green and white decoration.

The *State Apartments*, or Charles II Great Apartments (something of a courtesy name, referring to the rooms' date rather than Charles II, who in fact never came here), are visited next, starting with the Throne Room (Charles II's Guard Hall), converted to throne room use at the time of George IV's visit of 1822. Still used for investitures and dinners, this room shows four works by Lely and one by Wilkie. Beyond come the Evening Drawing Room and the Morning Drawing Room, the latter with particularly fine decoration, both these rooms formerly designated as audience chambers. The tour now turns left (N) to pass through the Ante Chamber, Bedchamber and Closet, all three presented today as they would have been in 1680 when the future James VII/II held court here as Duke of York and Albany, with his wife Mary of Modena and their child, the future Queen Anne. Most of the furniture shown here is original, including the restored State Bed, and what is not original is for the most part contemporary. Finally there are three smaller state rooms, formerly the king's domestic rooms (Wardrobe, Dressing Room, and a room allotted to the Page of the Back Stairs) which today display various relics associated with the palace and its historical users, of particular note being a 15C service book, one of the very few medieval liturgical books surviving in Scotland.

The *Picture Gallery*, extending the length of the northern range of the rebuilt palace, has long been and still is a kind of royal promenade, used for a variety of court events, including, in 1567, though in an earlier form, the marriage between Mary and Bothwell (according to Protestant rite and a sombre occasion compared to the

Queen Mary's Chamber at Holyrood. It was while supping with the queen in an adjoining chamber that Rizzio was attacked, his bleeding body being dragged through this bedchamber before he was finally despatched in the room beyond.

pageantry and festivity of the marriage to Darnley two years earlier),
and, in 1745, a ball given by the Young Pretender, a description of
which will be found in Scott's 'Waverley'. But what will most attract
the attention of today's visitor will surely be the astonishing collection
of portraits of 89 Scottish kings, the prolific and highly imaginative
outcome of a government commission executed in 1684–86 by Jacob
de Wet the Younger.

The tour now moves to the *Historical Apartments* (in what little is
left of the 16C palace of James V), dividing into Darnley's and thence,
by way of a private stair in the wall, Mary's above. Darnley's rooms
(antechamber, bedroom and dressing room), show Mortlake tapestry,
portraits and antique furniture, including a set of contemporary
Turkey-work chairs, but are without the historical association of
Mary's, comprising Outer Chamber or Audience Room, Inner
Chamber or Bedroom and, in turrets opening off the latter, small
North and South Cabinets or closets. The Outer Chamber was
undoubtedly the scene of John Knox's famous interview with Mary
when she arrived in Scotland in 1561, but whether the supper from
which Rizzio was dragged took place in the North or the South
Cabinet is disputed. Either way, it was in one of these two small
rooms that on 9 March 1566 Mary was supping with, amongst others,
her favourite and secretary David Rizzio when a party led by Darnley
and Ruthven burst in. Seizing Rizzio they dragged him through the
bedroom to the outer chamber where he was left dead with 56 dagger
wounds. A plaque on the floor marks the spot where his body lay,
but the alleged indelible stain of blood, if indeed it exists, is concealed
by floor covering.

Holyrood Abbey. Of the once great abbey, with its guest house
large and important enough to serve as a court residence, only the
church survives, and of that only the ruined nave, the remainder
having in part been demolished at the Reformation and again (SW
corner) to make way for Sir William Bruce's enlargement of the
palace in 1671–80. The collapse of the roof in 1768 completed the
process of ruin.

History. The abbey was founded in 1128 by David I, his church however being
replaced in the 13C by a grander edifice. During the 15C the abbey became a
regular court residence of James I, II and III—all of whom doubtless found this
valley site preferable to their bleak quarters up in the castle—James II being
born and crowned here, while he, James III and James IV were all married in
the church. Like the palace, the abbey was burnt in 1544 by Hertford, and
suffered again in 1547, but less than 20 years later, in 1565, the church was in
good enough condition for the wedding of Mary and Darnley, followed a century
later (1633) by the coronation of Charles I, in preparation for which the king
ordered extensive refurbishment. Under Charles II the church became a Chapel
Royal, and under James VII/II the chapel of the Order of the Thistle.

A Norman arch, visible behind the royal vault (SE corner), is about
the sole vestige of David I's church, today's ruins being essentially
those of the 13C replacement. Worth noting are the W Front
(remodelled for Charles I's coronation), the small but richly arcaded
NW tower, and the blind arcading either side of the nave. David II,
James II and his queen, James V and Darnley (as King Henry) were
all buried near the high altar; this, however, was desecrated in the
religious rioting of 1688, and now, by order of Queen Victoria, they
lie together in the royal vault. Rizzio, also, may lie somewhere in the
ruins, though tradition also places his grave in Canongate Church.

For **Holyrood Park** , or Queen's Park, adjoining the palace, see F. Other Districts of Edinburgh.

Buses return up Canongate and High Street. An alternative is to return to Canongate Church, there taking Old Tolbooth Wynd, beyond which a footpath climbs up to Regent Road (with the Burns Monument and Calton Hill), the eastward extension of Princes Street.

C. South Edinburgh (Grassmarket, Greyfriars and beyond)

A pleasant way to start this walk is by the path leading off Princes Street opposite the foot of Castle Street. This crosses the gardens to King's Stables Road, once a tilting ground but now with a large car park.

To the SW of King's Stables Road, within the angle with Lothian Road, are *Usher Hall* (1814), a fine hall for meetings, concerts etc., and the *Royal Lyceum Theatre*, an extensively renovated opulent Victorian theatre (1883).

Grassmarket is soon reached, a drab rectangle, certainly improving but to anyone so attuned still oppressive with echoes from a dark past, bloody, violent, even ghoulish. For long this was the main place of execution, the many victims including over 100 Covenanters who here were martyred, or, in the cynical words of the Earl of Rothes, 'glorified God in the Grassmarket'. Today a cobblestone cross within a railed enclosure at the E end both marks the site of the gallows and remembers those who died. Here too, in 1736, Captain Porteous was lynched. Commander of the guard when the thief Wilson (see Rte 33A, Pittenweem) was hanged, he panicked when the mob—judging the robbing of an Excise officer to be no great crime—got ugly, ordering his men to fire and causing several deaths. Tried and found guilty of murder, Porteous was however reprieved, only to be dragged from the tolbooth and hanged here in Grassmarket from a dyer's pole. And the evil Burke and Hare had their den near here (in Tanner's Close, now gone but once the last close off the N of West Port beside Lady Lawson Street), in 1827–28 enticing at least 18 men and women here so that they could suffocate them and sell their bodies to doctors. Even the disaster of Flodden is recalled here, for in Vennel, reached by steps off the SW of Grassmarket, there survives a section of the *Flodden Wall*, hastily built in 1513 but still serving as the W wall of George Heriot's School (see below). But on Grassmarket's N side a lighter note is struck, for here stands the old *White Hart Inn*, once the convivial haunt of Burns and other writers.

Three streets lead out of the E end of Grassmarket, in West Bow (becoming Victoria Street), the northernmost, being the *Traverse Theatre*, a leading experimental theatre in an 18C building. **Magdalen Chapel** (Scottish Reformation Society, 17 George IV Bridge. Tel: 031-2251836), of unusual interest as a charitable and guild chapel, will be found a short way up Cowgate, the central of the three streets and the one in which in 1508 Scotland's first printing press operated.

The chapel was founded in 1547 by Janet Rynd (buried here; widow of Michael Maquhen, a prominent citizen whose wishes she was carrying out) as a chapel and hospice for seven bedesmen (pensioners). Although well cared for, the pensioners did not have an easy life, amongst other obligations having to attend three lengthy services daily, including repeating the Lord's Prayer five·times and the Creed 50 times before breakfast, and before supper praying for the souls of the founders and their relations. The chapel was placed under the patronage of the Hammermen, the guild of all metalworkers (except gold), and so remained until 1857, though the last bedesman had left in 1665. During the 17 and 18C, probably because of the closeness to the Grassmarket gallows, the chapel was used as a mortuary.

The Hammermen's insignia, with the crests of the founders, may be seen on a panel over the principal door. The main features of the interior are the boards recording charitable gifts for the benefit of the poorer members of the craft; below the dais a wrought-iron railing with the craft insignia; and the stained glass in the central window, the only important pre-Reformation stained glass in Scotland still in its original building.

St. Cecilia's Hall, farther along Cowgate beyond South Bridge, was built in 1763 by Robert Mylne (using the Teatro Farnese in Parma as a model) for the Musical Society of Edinburgh who used the hall until 1802. Later serving as a Baptist chapel and a Freemasons' Hall, St. Cecilia's has since 1960 belonged to Edinburgh University Faculty of Music, and is used, mainly during the Festival, for small musical and óther recitals. The hall houses the *Russell Collection of early Keyboard Instruments*, these including harpsichords, clavichords, fortepianos, spinets, virginals and organs (Sat., 14.00 to 17.00. Also daily a.m. during Festival. Tel: 031-6671011, Ext. 4414. Fee).

Candlemaker Row, the southernmost of the three streets leading out of the E end of Grassmarket, reaches Greyfriars Place at the junction with George IV Bridge, a spot at which dog lovers will surely pause, for here sits the appealing small statue of *Greyfriars Bobby*, a Skye terrier which for 14 years after 1848 kept watch over his master's grave in Greyfriars churchyard opposite. At one time, in danger of being destroyed as a stray, the dog was given a special licence collar (now in Huntly House City Museum) by the then city provost.

Greyfriars Kirk and Kirkyard, as the name suggests on the site of a 15C Franciscan friary, offers history, one of Scotland's most extraordinary collections of weird and pretentious tombs, and even services in Gaelic. This is, of course, a place sacred in Scottish religious history, because it was here that the National Covenant was signed in 1638, some of the names being written in blood. The many consequent martyrs are commemorated by a stirringly worded memorial against the N wall of the kirkyard, while in the S is the enclosure where 1200 Covenanters taken prisoner at Bothwell Bridge in 1679 were held for five months, rigorously guarded, without shelter and poorly fed. Among those buried here are the Regent Morton (1581), George Buchanan (1582), the artist George Jamesone (1644), Captain Porteous (1736), Allan Ramsay (1758), Duncan Ban MacIntyre (the 'Burns of the Highlands', 1812), and, of course, John Gray (1848), owner of Greyfriars Bobby, whose simple grave, with a red granite stone erected by American admirers of Bobby, may be seen to the left of the path leading from the kirkyard entrance to the Martyrs' Memorial.—*Greyfriars Kirk*, dedicated on Christmas Day 1620, was the first to be opened in Edinburgh after the Reformation.

Just SW of Greyfriars, but reached by Forrest Road and Lauriston Place, is ***George Heriot's School**, one of the most handsome and original buildings in Edinburgh (visitors may walk around the exterior and the quadrangle). Endowed by George Heriot (died 1624), jeweller and banker to James VI/I, the building, sometimes ascribed to Inigo Jones, grew between 1628–93, the large quadrangle being particularly pleasing with over 200 windows, said all to be different in decoration. The Vennel, with remains of the Flodden Wall, marks the school's W boundary. The Scottish Baronial *Royal Infirmary* (David Bryce, 1879) is to the S of the school on the other side of Lauriston Place.

To the E of Greyfriars the two places of principal interest are the Royal Museum of Scotland (Chambers Street) and the complex, old and new, of Edinburgh University. A clockwise round, starting along Chambers Street, is suggested, the first buildings on the N being those of Heriot-Watt University. Founded in 1821, this college moved from South Bridge to its present site in 1873 and received technological university status in 1966.

The *Royal Museum of Scotland (Chambers Street)*, until 1985 called the *Royal Scottish Museum* (Mon.–Sat., 10.00 to 17.00. Sun., 14.00 to 17.00. Tel: 031-2257534. Free), on the S side of Chambers Street, is almost as worth visiting for its soaring, airy design (Fowke and Matheson, 1861–66) as for the astonishing variety of its exhibits. The museum was established in 1854, but the foundation stone of the present building, appropriately reminiscent of his Crystal Palace in London, was laid in 1861 by Prince Albert. As its name indicates, this is a Scottish as opposed to city museum, the home of national collections of seemingly limitless scope in both time and subject. The time scale spans from fossils formed in remote ages up to the most modern technology, the principal fields embraced being the decorative arts (the national fine arts collections are in the National Gallery in Princes Street), archaeology, ethnology, natural history in its widest sense, and technology. Additionally there is a programme of specialised temporary exhibitions, while for those in search of more than just a browse around there are lectures, films and gallery talks.

The older buildings (Old College) of **Edinburgh University** occupy the SW angle of Chambers Street and South Bridge, while the new buildings are just to the S and SW, generally along Lothian Street and around Bristo Square.

The youngest of Scotland's historic universities, Edinburgh in large measure owes its origin to the generosity of two brothers, William and Clement Little, and one James Lawson, an associate of John Knox. It was in 1580 that Clement Little presented his collection of 300 books to provide a library, and in 1582 the university was founded as the Town College. In the following year James VI granted a charter, the name then being changed to College of King James. In more recent times Edinburgh was one of the first universities to admit women (1884).

The *Old College* stands partly on ground once belonging to the collegiate Kirk o' Field, where stood the house in which Darnley met his violent and mysterious death. In classical style, the Old College was designed by Robert Adam in 1789 (the portico is judged to be one of his most distinguished achievements) and completed by W.H. Playfair in 1834, the delay being because of the Napoleonic wars. The dome (by Rowand Anderson), surmounted by a figure of Youth (by J. Hutchison), was added in 1884. The *Talbot Rice Art Centre* (Mon.–Sat., 10.00 to 17.00. Tel: 031-6671011. Free) houses, in a fine gallery designed by Playfair, the Torrie Collection of 16 and 17C

European painting and sculpture, while an adjacent gallery is used
for temporary exhibitions. To the SW are the *New University Buildings*, an imposing group designed by Rowand Anderson in 1884,
with, facing Teviot Place, the Medical Centre (1897). The large
Student Centre flanks the NE side of the large open Bristo Square,
off the diagonal corner being the McEwan Hall of 1897. The above
complex, effectively forming a campus, on the S merges with George
Square, dating from about 1770 when the gentry began to move out
of the Old Town (Sir Walter Scott lived his first 25 years here) but
today with much of its former dignity exchanged for functional
modern university buildings.

The Meadows, just S of George Square, were a fashionable 18C promenade,
while James IV is said to have played golf on *Bruntsfield Links*, farther S across
Melville Drive. At one time both Meadows and Links formed part of the Burgh
Muir, a frequent rallying place for Scottish armies.
    Archers' Hall (no adm.), at the NE of The Meadows, built in 1776 and later
extended, is the headquarters of the Royal Company of Archers. Constituted
by the Privy Council in 1676 and chartered in 1704, the Company was formally
appointed as King's Bodyguard in Scotland on the occasion of George IV's visit
in 1822. Enjoying high rights of precedence, the Company consists of some 500
noblemen and gentlemen, commanded by a Captain General, who is invariably
a distinguished Scottish peer. When the monarch holds court in Edinburgh they
are on duty as escort, guards and gentlemen-in-waiting.
    In Leven Street, just W of The Meadows, the *King's Theatre* was opened in
1906 and today, grandly refurbished, still shows its Baroque frontage and
Rococo interior.

The return to Princes Street can be made along George IV Bridge
(from Greyfriars at the W end of Chambers Street), passing on the
left the *Central Library* (Mon.–Fri., 09.00 to 21.00. Sat., 09.00 to 13.00.
Tel: 031-225 5584. Free), with comprehensive reference collections
on Scottish and local history (including an admirable Edinburgh
Room), music and the fine arts. Opposite is the **National Library of
Scotland** (Mon.–Fri., 09.30 to 20.30. Sat., 09.30 to 13.00. Exhibitions
open Mon.–Fri., 09.30 to 17.00. Sat., 09.30 to 13.00. Sun. in April–Sept,
14.00 to 17.00. Tel: 031-2264531. Free), occupying a building (by R.
Fairlie, 1956) the main facade of which carries statues by Hew
Lorimer typifying seven branches of learning. This is one of the
largest libraries in Britain, developed from the Advocates' Library
founded in 1682, formally opened as a law library seven years later,
and since 1710 enjoying the right to claim a copy of every book
published in Britain. In 1922 the library was offered to the nation
(the Faculty of Advocates reserving for themselves the specifically
legal works), and in 1925 it assumed its present name. Books apart,
the library owns an extensive collection of illuminated manuscripts,
specimens of early printing, and historical documents, amongst these
being the last letter of Mary, Queen of Scots, written on the eve of
her execution; the order resulting in the massacre of Glencoe; and
letters and papers of Hume, Boswell, Burns, Stevenson, Scott and
Carlyle. Frequent special exhibitions are also mounted.

D. Princes Street

Completed in 1805 as part of the New Town concept of 1767 (see E.
below), and named after Prince George, later George IV, Princes

Street is Edinburgh's main thoroughfare. With its eastern extension, Waterloo Place, it is just about a mile in length, its N side an architectural and functional hotchpotch of shops, banks, clubs, hotels and suchlike; its S side, by contrast—and it is this that gives the street its exciting character—a panoramic sweep of gardens backed by the steep sided long slope of the Royal Mile rising to the battlemented mass of the historic castle sprawled over its precipitous rock. Add the street's airy width, its unbroken straightness, its several monuments both beside the street and in the gardens, and that astonishing eastern wall provided by Calton Hill and its curiosities, and it is easy to see how Princes Street has earned its fame.

Waverley Market (with Tourist Information), at the street's E end, can be regarded as the modern heart of Edinburgh. The description below therefore starts here, afterwards first looking eastward to Waterloo Place and Calton Hill before travelling westward the length of Princes Street.

Waverley Market, a precinct of the 1980s filling much of the slope within the E angle of Princes Street and Waverley Bridge, is more imaginative than many such and at any rate successfully hides what was once the desolate roofscape of Waverley Station. Here, in the market, *Tourist Information* occupies spacious modern premises. Waverley Bridge descends past *Waverley Station* and over the railway to reach a crossroads at the foot of the slope. From here Cockburn Street winds up to the Royal Mile, while Market Street runs E–W below the slope. To the W, at No. 21, are the *Festival Offices*; to the E, and opposite one another, the City Art Centre and the Fruitmarket Gallery.

The **City Art Centre** (Mon.–Sat., 10.00 to 17.00 or 18.00 in June–Sept. Also, during Festival, Sun., 14.00 to 17.00. Tel: 031-2252424. Free), housing the city's permanent fine arts collection and the focus, too, of a diverse programme of temporary exhibitions, occupies an interesting warehouse of 1899, used in turn for storing newsprint and then fruit and vegetables but now skilfully converted to reconcile architectural integrity with the sophisticated needs of a modern art centre. The city's permanent collection (sometimes withdrawn to allow space for temporary exhibitions) comprises some 3000 works—paintings, drawings, prints, sculpture—mainly by Scottish artists active between the 17C and the present day, and, quite apart from artistic enjoyment, the visitor can, through the many topographical views and portraits, conjure up much of old Edinburgh and its distinguished citizens. The *Fruitmarket Gallery* (Tues.–Sat., 10.00 to 17.30. Also·Sun. and Mon. during Festival. Tel: 031-2252383. Free), opposite at No. 29 Market Street in a 1920s warehouse, mounts temporary exhibitions of modern, and particularly contemporary, Scottish and international fine art, the emphasis tending to be on one artist or one theme.

EASTWARD from Waverley Market Princes Street ends at a major intersection with North Bridge (S) and Leith Street (N), on the SE corner being the *General Post Office* (1861) with the *Philatelic Bureau* (Mon.–Thurs., 09.00 to 16.30. Fri., 09.00 to 16.00. Sat., 10.00 to 12.30. Tel: 031-5568661. Free) with stamp displays and a service for collectors. Opposite, behind a statue (by Steell) of the Duke of Wellington, extends the long, symmetrical facade of *General Register House* (Scottish Record Office), built between 1774–1827 largely to the design of Robert Adam though completed by Robert Reid. Here are housed Scotland's legal and historical public records, some dating from the 13C, and here too, in the entrance hall or in the gallery below Adam's dome, are mounted special exhibitions (Mon.–Fri., 10.00 to 16.00. Tel: 031-5566585. Free.—See also West Register House under E. North Edinburgh). Behind General Register House, within the general angle of Leith Street and York Place and in sorry contrast to Adam's fine taste, sprawls the externally drab and ponderous *St. James Centre*, with a hotel, shops, offices, multi-storey parking etc.

Princes Street is extended E by **Waterloo Place**, off the SE corner of which is *Calton Old Burial Ground*, with the Lincoln Monument (1893), dedicated also to the Scottish-American soldiers who fell in the American Civil War, the tomb of David Hume designed by Robert Adam, and an obelisk honouring five early political reformers, found guilty of sedition (1793–94) and sentenced to transportation by a government nervous of contagion from the spreading and bloody revolution in France.

Calton Hill can be ascended either by steps at the corner of Waterloo Place and Regent Road, or by a road a little farther on. It is an ascent well worth making if only for the views, even though that over the main city is now somewhat blocked by the mass of St. James Centre. This can to some extent be overcome by climbing the *Nelson Monument* (April–Sept: Mon., 13.00 to 18.00. Tues.–Sat., 10.00 to 18.00. Oct–March: Mon.–Sat., 10.00 to 15.00. Tel: 031-5562716. Fee), erected between 1807–15 to honour the admiral. However, even without doing this, grand views can still be enjoyed across to Leith and its harbour, across and along the Forth, and, best of all, over Holyrood and Arthur's Seat. The attempt to honour the Scottish dead of the Napoleonic wars, and their 'glorious naval and military achievements', was less than successful, for the grandiose and ambitious *National Monument*, intended to be a reproduction of the Parthenon—perhaps because this was a temple to Athena, Goddess of War—though begun in 1822 was before long abandoned when funds, and memories too perhaps, ran dry. However the relatively obscure philosopher Dugald Stewart (1753–1828), professor of moral philosophy at the university, was for some reason deemed worthy of a place on this hill where he is remembered by a reproduction of the monument of Lysicrates in Athens. Cannon up here include a Portuguese one of 1624, captured at Mandalay in 1886, while the buildings represent the *Observatory* (see F. Royal Observatory).

Opposite the steps up Calton Hill, the S side of Regent Road is lined by the long block of *St. Andrew's House* (1937–39), while across the road and just beyond stand the *Crown Office Buildings* (Thomas Hamilton, 1825–29), an adaptation of the Temple of Theseus in Athens and long the home of the Royal High School, the pupils of which included such as Robert Adam, Alexander Graham Bell, George Borrow, James Boswell and Sir Walter Scott. A short distance beyond stands the classical *Burns Monument* (Hamilton, 1830), close to which a path leads down to Old Tolbooth Wynd and then Canongate near the foot of the Royal Mile.

WESTWARD from Waverley Market Princes Street runs beside the **East Gardens**, with, beside the road, the **Scott Monument**, a lofty Gothic spire forming a canopy over a statue of Scott with his dog (by Steell) and with niches in which are historical figures and characters from Scott's novels. Erected in 1840–44 the monument is the design of George Kemp who, however, did not live to see his work completed.

(Ascent, 287 steps, April–Sept: Mon.–Sat., 09.00 to 18.00. Oct–March: Mon.–Sat., 09.00–15.00. Fee). Just beyond stands the confident figure of Adam Black (1784–1874), Provost of Edinburgh, Member of Parliament and founder in 1807 of the publishing house of A. and C. Black which in the 19C acquired the copyright of Scott's novels and today the publishers of the 'Blue Guides'. Beyond, the East Gardens end at the two dignified classical edifices, both by W.H. Playfair, of the Royal Scottish Academy (beside Princes Street) and the National Gallery of Scotland, the latter beside the street called The Mound which, built on the dumped debris of the New Town excavations, now curves up to meet the Royal Mile at the foot of Lawnmarket.

The **Royal Scottish Academy** (Mon.–Sat., 10.00 to 17.00. Sun., 14.00 to 17.00. Tel: 031-2256671. Fee), in a building of 1823–36, was founded in 1826. Normally there are two main exhibitions; one, showing the work of the elected members and contemporary artists, running from late April to early August, the other a special Festival Exhibition.

The ****National Gallery of Scotland** (Mon.–Sat., 10.00 to 17.00. Sun., 14.00 to 17.00. During Festival, Mon.–Sat., 10.00 to 18.00. Sun., 11.00 to 18.00.—Print Room, open by arrangement, Mon.–Fri., 10.00 to 12.30. 14.00 to 16.30. Tel: 031-5568921. Free), in a building of 1845–58 (New Wing 1978), shows distinguished collections spanning the 15–19C and including Italian, Flemish, Dutch, French, German and British (especially Scottish) artists.

A radical rearrangement is in hand, involving changes in the numbering of rooms and in the hanging of the pictures. In principle, though, the gallery is in two parts, with the Main Wing, on the ground and first floors, housing the permanent collections of European and British (other than Scottish) paintings, while the New Wing (downstairs) is the home of the Scottish works.

Also in the New Wing are the Library, the Print Room and the Prints and Drawings Gallery.—The extensive collection of drawings and prints, which may on request be seen in the Print Room, includes works by Old Masters (e.g. Tintoretto, Rubens, Rembrandt, Dürer, Goya), by English artists (Blake, Palmer) and, above all, by a range of Scottish artists. Selections from the collection are shown in the Prints and Drawings Gallery, the material being changed roughly every two months.

The *Vaughan Bequest of 38 watercolours by *J.M.W. Turner* is exhibited annually in January, and may at other times be seen by advance request.

The following paragraphs, though mentioning only a fraction of the works shown, may indicate the gallery's level and scope.

EUROPEAN AND BRITISH (OTHER THAN SCOTTISH). *Andrea del Verrocchio* (attrib.): *Madonna and Child. This picture, brought to Britain by John Ruskin and acquired by the gallery in 1975, is an outstanding work of c 1471 by Verrocchio or by one of the artists of his studio, who included Ghirlandaio, Leonardo and Lorenzo di Credi. *Raphael:* *Holy Family with a palm tree. *Bridgewater Madonna. *Filippino Lippi:* Nativity with two angels. *Titian:* Diana and Actaeon. *Three Ages of Man. *Diana and Calisto. *Andrea del Sarto:* Portrait of Becuccio Bicchieraio.

Hugo van der Goes: *Trinity Altarpiece, or the Trinity College Panels (James III and IV. Margaret of Denmark, queen of James III.

Holy Trinity. Sir Edward Bonkil). The Collegiate Church of the Holy Trinity, standing near what is now Waverley Station but demolished in 1848, was founded in 1462 by Mary of Gueldres, widow of James II. Sir Edward Bonkil was its first provost and may have commissioned the artist. The panels were probably the wings of an altarpiece, the centre of which was destroyed at the Reformation.

Tintoretto: •The Deposition of Christ. *Guercino:* St. Peter Penitent. Madonna, Infant and St. John. *El Greco:* •Saviour of the World. *Velazquez:* •Old Woman cooking eggs.

Ambrosius Benson: Madonna and Child with St. Anne. *Gerard David:* Three legends of St. Nicholas. *Quentin Massys:* •Portrait of a man. *Van Dyck:* St. Sebastian. The 'Lomellini' Family. *Rubens:* St. Ambrose. Feast of Herod. Adoration of the Shepherds. *Jan Vermeer:* •Christ in the house of Martha and Mary.

Rembrandt: •Woman in bed. •Self-portrait. Young woman with flowers in her hair. *Jan Steen:* School for boys and girls. *Frans Hals:* Dutch lady. Dutch gentleman. *Goya:* El medico. *Elsheimer:* •Stoning of St. Stephen.

Thomas Gainsborough: Portrait of the Hon. Mrs Graham. Landscape with Cornard village. Rocky landscape. *William Hogarth:* Portrait of Sarah Malcolm. *Joshua Reynolds:* The Ladies Waldegrave. *John Constable:* •Vale of Dedham. On the Stour. *J.M.W. Turner:* Folkestone.

Nicholas Poussin: •The Seven Sacraments. *J-B. Greuze:* Girl with a dead canary. Boy with a lesson book. *Jean Chardin:* Flower piece. *Gustave Courbet:* River in a mountain gorge. *J-B.C. Corot:* The artist's mother. Entrance to the wood. The goatherd. *C. Pissarro:* The Marne at Chennevières. *Edgar Degas:* Diego Martelli. Group of dancers. *Paul Gauguin:* •Vision of the sermon. Three Tahitians. Martinique landscape. *Claude Monet:* Haystacks. Poplars on the Epte. *Paul Cézanne:* Mont Ste-Victoire. *Vincent van Gogh:* Olive trees.

SCOTTISH WORKS. The collection is too large for the space available, so the works on show are changed at intervals. However, some of the artists and pictures which may well be seen are listed below (in alphabetical order of artists). *William Aikman:* Self-portrait. *Andrew Geddes:* Summer. The artist's mother. *James Guthrie:* Oban. Pastoral. *George Jamesone:* Lady Mary Erskine. *Horatio McCulloch:* Inverlochy Castle. *William McTaggart:* Spring. The Storm. The coming of St. Columba. *Jacob More:* Falls of Clyde. *Alexander Nasmyth:* Edinburgh Castle. *Noel Paton:* Oberon and Titania. Luther at Erfurt. *Henry Raeburn:* Several portraits including Sir John Sinclair, •Rev. Robert Walker, and a self-portrait. *Allan Ramsay:* Several portraits including •The Artist's Wife, Mrs David Cunyngham, Lady Robert Manners, and J.J. Rousseau. *David Wilkie:* •Pitlessie Fair. Irish whiskey still. Self-portrait. Distraining for rent. The letter of introduction.

The **West Gardens** spread southward across the railway to the foot of the castle cliff, at the gardens' NE corner, immediately below the angle of Princes Street and The Mound, being the *Floral Clock*, dating from 1903 and believed to be the oldest of its kind in the world. The *Ross Open Air Theatre* is a central feature of the gardens, near here being the ornate Ross fountain and a contrastingly simple and effective boulder to the Norwegian Brigade 'raised and trained in Scotland'. The *Scottish American War Memorial* (by R. Taít McKenzie of Philadelphia), symbolising 'The Call, 1914' and erected by Americans of Scottish blood and sympathies, is in the gardens below the level of Princes Street, while the *Royal Scots Greys Memorial* (Frank Mears, 1952) is beside the street. Others remembered here, by statues, are the poet Allan Ramsay (1686–1758); Sir James Simpson (1811–70), who in 1847 introduced the use of chloroform as an anaesthetic; and Dr Thomas Guthrie (1803–73), apostle of the Ragged Schools (1844) for the education of the poor. Finally, beyond the railway and at the foot of the castle rock, *Wellhouse Tower* survives as the last vestige of the town wall of 1436.

The West Gardens end with two churches, the one beside Princes Street being the 19C *St. John's*, worth entering for William Burn's neo-Gothic nave of 1817. *St. Cuthbert's* , just to the S, is an ancient foundation, perhaps of the 7C, although today's church, except for its tower of 1789, is a rebuilding (1894) by Hippolyte Blanc. In the yard are the graves of the writer Thomas de Quincey (1785–1859) who died in Edinburgh, of George Kemp (1795–1844), architect of the Scott monument, and of the painter Alexander Nasmyth (1758–1840). But the mathematically inclined visitor should head for the church's vestibule where there is a monument to John Napier of Merchiston (1560–1617), inventor of logarithms and of various rules and formulae in spherical trigonometry.

Rose Street, running parallel to and just N of this western section of Princes Street, is known for its pubs, some showing Victorian or Edwardian interiors as opulent as they can be inviting.

E. North Edinburgh (New Town)

In 1767 the decision was reached that Edinburgh—hitherto essentially a confined tenemented maze clinging to its rock ridge between Holyrood and the castle—must breathe. Thinking in enviably bold and radical terms, in which space rather than the lack of it was the key, the authorities sponsored a competition, the winner of which was James Craig, aged only 23. His grand and formal scheme was based on George Street, named after George III, to run along the natural ridge; Queen Street, parallel to the N, named after George's consort; and Princes Street, for the Prince of Wales, along the valley to the S.

Work soon started and was continued by successive planners and architects until well into the 19C. The N and W extension is largely the achievement of Robert Reid (1802); the E that of Archibald Elliot in 1815 and William Playfair in 1819; J.G. Graham planned the NW in 1822, while to Henry Raeburn (up to 1823) must go the credit for much of what lies beyond the Water of Leith. The outcome is a confident and extensive grid of solid wide streets, of spacious crescents and squares, of restrained symmetrical classical buildings, and of elegant urban views, all impeccably combining as a monument to Georgian vision and achievement and as much a part of the character of today's Edinburgh as are the older historical and architectural associations of the Royal Mile.

The New Town is of course an officially designated conservation area, subject to strict planning control. Well aware of the value of this heritage, the City of Edinburgh and the Historic Buildings Council in 1970 embarked on a conservation programme, many interesting aspects of which are explained at the *New Town Conservation Centre*, 13A Dundas Street, which is the northward extension of Hanover Street (Mon.–Fri., 09.00 to 13.00. 14.00 to 17.00. Tel: 031-5567054. Free). Here are an exhibition of conservation work in progress and a library, while for the enthusiast there is a programme of conducted walks.

The fortunate visitor will have the time to explore. Others, inevitably, will have to be content with the essentials which, at their barest, may be pruned to Charlotte Square and a taste of George Street. For the most part, though, the New Town, or Georgian Edinburgh, is professional and residential, with correspondingly relatively light traffic, and the visitor with a car will be able to enjoy a good overall impression simply by driving around.

The description below starts in the E at St. Andrew Square; follows George Street W to Charlotte Square and, beyond, the districts of West End and Dean; then returns E along Queen Street to the National Portrait Gallery and Royal Museum of Scotland.

St. Andrew Square, to many probably best known on account of the Coach Station off the NE corner and architecturally something of a mixture, lacks both the essential character and the dignity of other New Town squares. However, there can be no complaint about the stylish premises of the *Royal Bank of Scotland* on the square's E flank, the bank occupying the mansion built in 1772–74 by William Chambers for Sir Lawrence Dundas who, as owner of the land, insisted on a family town residence here in preference to the church originally planned. Other notable buildings here are No. 26 (by Chambers) and No. 38 (by Bryce, 1851–52), while in the square's centre soars the lofty fluted column of the *Melville Monument*, supporting a statue (Robert Forrest, 1828) of Henry Dundas, 1st Viscount Melville (1742–1811).

The Royal Museum of Scotland and the National Portrait Gallery, both described below, are in Queen Street one block N of St. Andrew Square.

George Street now swathes westward along its ridge from which, at the several intersections, there are glimpses N towards the Forth and S to the spine of the Royal Mile. *St. Andrew's Church* (1782–85, by Andrew Fraser; steeple of 1789 by Andrew Sibbald), on the N just after leaving St. Andrew Square, is of interest not only as the first to have been built in the New Town but also because this was the scene in 1843 of the Disruption when 451 ministers, seceding from the Established Church, marched out to found the dissenting Free Church of Scotland.

Opposite, the Corinthian bank building is by David Rhind (1847), while farther along on this S side the *Assembly Rooms* were designed in 1784–87 by J. Henderson and later added to by William Burn. The bank at No. 25 is by David Bryce (1847), and No. 22 has, since 1909, been the seat of the *Royal Society of Edinburgh*, Scotland's leading scientific society, incorporated in 1783 and numbering Scott and Kelvin among its presidents. Scott lived in this district, too; at No. 107 George Street soon after his marriage in 1797, then successively at Nos. 10 and 39 Castle Street, the latter being his home from 1802–26 and the place at which he wrote many of the Waverley Novels.

**Charlotte Square, the epitome of the New Town, was designed in 1791 by Robert Adam who, however, died soon afterwards. Nevertheless the superb N side, a masterpiece of restrained symmetry and accepted as one of Europe's most distinguished frontages, is entirely his; his 'again', one might write, because thanks to the imagination and drive of the 4th Marquis of Bute during the 1920s and '30s, the depredations of the Victorians—lowered windows, dormers added, doors altered—were largely erased and this N side restored as nearly as possible to its original state. After the death in 1956 of the 5th Marquis of Bute, the three houses (Nos. 5–7) passed to the *National Trust for Scotland*, No. 5 now being the headquarters of the Trust, while No. 6 (Bute House) is the official residence of the Secretary of State for Scotland. No. 7 is now the *Georgian House* (NTS. April–Oct: Mon.–Sat., 10.00 to 17.00. Sun., 14.00 to 17.00. Nov: Sat., 10.00 to 16.30. Sun., 14.00 to 16.30. Last adm. 30 minutes before closing times. Fee), the lower floors of which have been furnished as a typical wealthy New Town home generally of the period 1790–1810; the home, in fact, of the first owner, John Lamont of Lamont, 18th chief of Clan Lamont. As is normal with Trust property, the contents are admirably described and there are knowledgeable guides in each room. The furnishings apart, the house shows several notable paintings, among the artists being (in alphabetical order) Ferdinand Bol, Jan van Goyen, Melchior de Hondecoeter, George Morland and Alexander Nasmyth, as also, for portraits, Dobson, Hoppner, Kneller, Ramsay and Raeburn.—The upper floors of the house are the official residence of the Moderator of the General Assembly of the Church of Scotland.

Two other places in Charlotte Square, both on the W side, may be of interest. The *Scottish Arts Council Centre*, at No. 19, provides detailed information on arts events of all kinds throughout Scotland (Mon.–Fri., 09.00 to 17.30 or 17.00 on Fri. Tel: 031-2266051. Free); and nearby *West Register House*, since 1962 occupying the former church of St. George (Reid, 1810–14), offers a permanent exhibition of documents relating to Scotland's history (Mon.–Fri., 10.00 to 16.00. Tel: 031-5566585. Free. See also General Register House under D. Princes Street).

WEST OF CHARLOTTE SQUARE. Visitors with time and, if on foot and since some climbing is involved, a measure of energy, may now choose a worthwhile and varied meander (in large part also motorable) in the general area to the W and NW of Charlotte Square. Others may descend the short distance S into Princes Street, or perhaps make their way E along Queen Street for the portrait gallery and Royal Museum of Scotland.

Behind West Register House, Randolph Place runs into busy Queensferry Street, across which is Melville Street, a broad and dignified creation of 1820–26 with a monument to the 2nd Viscount Melville (1802–61) and, at the street's end, the triple-spired *Episcopal Cathedral of St. Mary* (1874–1917), designed by George Gilbert Scott and one of the largest Gothic churches built in Britain since the Reformation. The path along the cathedral's N side passes *Easter Coates House*, a gracious small house of about 1615, now St. Mary's Music School.

Queensferry Street, followed NW, soon reaches **Dean Bridge**, built by Telford in 1832 and much acclaimed, not least by coach travellers who hitherto had had to negotiate the steep and sometimes treacherous valley. Today the Water of Leith, over 100 ft below and flowing through a wooded cleft, is scarcely noticed. Yet it should be, for this modest river was once of huge economic importance, turning some 70 mills over its brief course between the Pentlands and the Forth, no fewer than 11 of these being in the neighbourhood of **Dean Village**, just W below the bridge and reached (from the S side) by the street called Bell's Brae. A milling centre for at least four centuries—indeed an active life of twice that length is sometimes claimed—this almost secret jumble of houses and converted mills all cramped within the narrow valley provides a startling contrast to the spacious Georgian elegance above. There is a riverside path here too, bearing back below the bridge to reach *St. Bernard's Well*, a small Doric temple of 1789, popular with 18 and 19C strollers who paused here beside the figure of Hygieia, Goddess of Health, to sip the waters.

From the S side of Dean Bridge the superb sequence of Randolph Crescent, Great Stuart Street and Ainslie Place lead to St. Colme Street, representing the westward extension of Queen Street (see immediately below).

From the NE corner of Charlotte Square, North Charlotte Street quickly reaches the W end of Queen Street, a broad largely residential thoroughfare running along the N face of the New Town ridge and flanked on the N by gardens, across which, at No. 17 Heriot Row, Robert Louis Stevenson lived from 1859–79.

At Queen Street's E end are the **Royal Museum of Scotland (Queen Street)** and the **National Portrait Gallery**, occupying respectively the E and W wings of a red sandstone building (by Rowand Anderson) dedicated by the munificence of J.R. Finlay, a proprietor of 'The Scotsman', to 'the illustration of Scottish history'. And this indeed is just what this museum and gallery do, for here can be seen, in physical or portrait form, much of what to the touring visitor can be no more than a printed historical reference or the mention of a name. What the imagination may have pictured is here brought to reality.

The Museum and Gallery are open Mon.–Sat., 10.00 to 17.00. Sun., 14.00 to 17.00. During Festival, Mon.–Sat., 10.00 to 18.00. Sun., 11.00 to 18.00. Tel. for Royal Museum of Scotland: 031-5573550. Tel. for Portrait Gallery: 031-5568921. Free).

The Museum and Gallery are either side of a central balconied well, below the balcony being a colourful if imaginative frieze of Scottish historical figures, starting with prehistoric man and finishing with Carlyle. And around the first floor balcony are equally colourful and probably equally imaginative battle and other scenes, these including Stirling Bridge (1297), Bannockburn (1314), Largs (1263), and, by way of contrast, the Good Deeds of David I and the Landing of Queen Margaret at Queensferry (1086). If neither the frieze nor the battle and other scenes lay great claim to either artistic merit or historical authenticity, at least it can surely be said of both that they stimulate the imagination.

The *Royal Museum of Scotland (Queen Street)*, until 1985 the *National Museum of Antiquities*, provides a rich and immensely varied background to any tour of Scotland, the material illustrating many aspects of Scottish life from earliest to quite modern times. The museum is arranged on three levels, the Ground Floor being the Historic Gallery (with also Dark Ages sculpture); the 1st Floor, the Prehistoric and Viking Gallery; and the 2nd Floor, the Roman Gallery. The following paragraphs claim only to offer a (roughly chronological) glimpse of the wealth of material exhibited.

1st Floor. Prehistoric and Viking. Cases display palaeolithic to Bronze Age artefacts—articles which, even if in their earliest forms they perhaps strike the layman as no more than stone chips and slivers, nevertheless remind that primitive man had a lifestyle here millenia ago. But gradually the artefacts become recognisable—as ornaments or tools or weapons—later even exciting aesthetic admiration as, for instance, gold jewellery, jet necklaces or sophisticated Pictish silver chains of double rings. And in the same category, if of a later period, there is the *St. Ninian's Isle Treasure, a silver hoard of c 800, the sight of which may tempt the viewer to that fragment of Shetland ruin in which, after perhaps being hidden from Viking raiders, it was discovered in 1958 (Rte 68). Additionally, everyday objects enhance the human aspects (from remote Stone Age to Viking) of sites such as Skara Brae (Rte 67), of which there is an instructive model, and Jarlshof (Rte 68), while pottery, largely from burials, adds meaning to the cairns, cists and suchlike the traveller will meet over so much of Scotland. And examples of cup-and-ring stones are shown too, as unexplained here as they are on their moorland sites.

2nd Floor. Roman. Roman sites in Scotland tend to be little more than earthworks or stone foundations and are thus hard to people. But the many finds displayed here—admirably arranged by themes such as army, cooking, transport, religion, burial, hypocausts—go a long way to suggest what life may have been like along the exposed length of the Antonine Wall (Rte 9); or at, for instance, more comfortable Cramond (Rte 9) beside the Forth; or at Trimontium (Newstead, Rte 4), once a considerable camp but now little more than a notice board; or within the wide defences of 'Ardoch (Rte 25B). And if the sight of those Inchtuthill nails (Rte 28) does nothing to provide an explanation for the abandonment of such a huge store of unused building material, at least the nails' reality is established.

But the highlight in this Roman section is the *Traprain Treasure (Rte 1), a hoard of Christian and pagan silver, largely Roman work of the 4C, found on Traprain Law in 1919 and thought perhaps to represent the loot brought back from an early 5C raid southwards, possibly even into Gaul.

Ground Floor. Historic Gallery. Here the scope of the exhibits greatly broadens, spanning from the Dark Ages through medieval antiquities and on into the 18C. From the Dark Ages there are grave contents, including finds from Whithorn (Rte 14), as also originals and casts of 6–11C sculptured stones, some bearing strange symbols peculiar to Scotland. Weapons of many kinds and periods are shown here too, as are also instruments of law and order, including that grim ultimate, the Maiden, which removed the heads of the Regent Morton in 1581, and of the 8th and 9th earls of Argyll in 1661 and 1685. Additionally there are domestic exhibits of many, and often strange kinds; bagpipes and other musical instruments; and personal relics of, for example, Mary, Queen of Scots and the Young Pretender (his *Canteen, a unique set of Jacobite silver).

The *National Portrait Gallery records Scottish history, from the 15C onwards and in its broadest sense, by means of portraits of men and women who in one way or another have contributed to the whole. Broadly the themes covered are the Early Stewarts, National Revivals, Jacobites, Scots Abroad, Civil War and the Union, Scots at home in the 18C, and Scientific and Industrial Progress. Only a hint can be given below of the artistic and historical scope that here awaits the visitor.

As might be expected, royalty is strongly represented, starting with that tragic sequence of James I to Mary, Queen of Scots, every one of whom—except for James V who is said to have died of heartbreak after his defeat at Solway Moss—met a violent end. Mary is contrastingly shown—in white mourning for her husband Francis II of France and in a *portrait of 1578 by P. Oudry. Her mother, Mary of Guise, is here too (painted it is thought, by Corneille de Lyon), as are also her son James VI/I and his son Charles I, the latter painted with his queen (after Van Dyck) and on the scaffold by an unknown artist. And the royal sequence continues, notably with *Charles II as a boy by William Dobson, James VII/II by Lely, George II by John Shackleton and *George IV by Thomas Lawrence.

From Scotland's deeply scarred 17C many famous faces look down, led perhaps by James Graham, Marquis of Montrose (after Honthorst), and his enemies the Covenanter general David Leslie (by Lely), the man responsible for the massacres of prisoners at Philiphaugh and Dunaverty, and the 8th Earl of Argyll (by David Scougal). The devious General Monk (by Lely) represents the Commonwealth and the Restoration; Claverhouse (or Bonnie Dundee) the final throw, at Killiecrankie, on behalf of James VII/II.

The Pretenders, Old and Young, hang here too—as do the latter's courageous guide 'over the sea to Skye', Flora Macdonald (painted by 'Richard Wilson); Henry, Cardinal York, the last of the Stuarts; and even Charlotte, Duchess of Albany, the Young Pretender's natural daughter, who may or may not have been mother of that self-styled Count Roehenstart who lies in Dunkeld cathedral.

When it comes to portraits of the 18C onwards, the artist increasingly begins to claim as much attention as the sitter. And rightly so, for several of these artists are in themselves a part of Scotland's history. Allan Ramsay portrays David Hume; George Willison, James Boswell; William Aikman, Allan Ramsay the poet; Henry Raeburn, *Sir Walter Scott; Andrew Geddes, Scott and the artist David Wilkie; Alexander Nasmyth, Robert Burns (twice); and William Nicholson, James Hogg the 'Ettrick Shepherd'. And, moving into the present century, a strong Scottish Socialist flavour is provided by J.J. Dobson's James Keir Hardie; A. McEvoy's Ramsay Macdonald (also appearing as a bust by Epstein); and John Lavery's Clydesider James Maxton.

The Gallery's main collection is supported by engravings, water-colours, drawings and other material, the *Print Room* also containing a reference archive of many thousands of engravings and photographs of portraits. There is also the largest existing collection of work by the pioneer photographers D.O. Hill and Robert Adamson (Print Room and Reference Section open Mon.–Fri., 10.00 to 12.00. 14.00 to 16.30).

The eastward extension of Queen Street is York Place, in which No. 32 was the home and studio of Sir Henry Raeburn. *St. Paul's and St. George's* (1816–18), at the NE corner, was built by Archibald Elliot, the man responsible for much of this E part of the New Town. Picardy Place, beyond, recalling in its name a settlement of French weavers, was the birthplace (No. 11) of Arthur Conan Doyle (1859–1930), creator of Sherlock Holmes. In Union Street, just N of Picardy Place off Leith Walk, will be found the *Printmakers Workshop* (Mon.–Sat., 10.00 to 18.00. Also, during Festival, Sun., 14.00 to 17.00. Tel: 031-5572479. Free), representing an Association devoted to promoting all aspects of the art of printmaking. There is a continuous programme of exhibitions, and visitors are welcome to view and, if they wish, buy members' original prints.

F. Other Districts of Edinburgh

This section covers, in alphabetical order, places of interest not already included under the previous five sections.

There are also a number of outlying places which can conveniently be visited from Edinburgh, but which are described along other Routes. The principal such places are: On Rte 1—Musselburgh. Inveresk. Carberry Hill. On Rte 3—Dalkeith. Butterfly Farm. Craigmillar Castle. On Rte 6—Edinburgh Crystal (Penicuik). Roslin Chapel. On Rte 7—Pentland Hills. On Rte 8—Suntrap. Ingliston. On Rte 9—Cramond. Dalmeny. South Queensferry and the Forth Bridges.

The **Caiy Stone** (NTS) is an ancient standing stone, 9ft in height and, on its E face, bearing traces of cup markings. The stone will be found on the N side of Oxgangs Road, about 4m S of Waverley Market and best reached by A702, the road by which Rte 7 enters Edinburgh.

Once the hunting reserve of kings, and perhaps the place where the miraculous Cross saved David I from being gored by a stag, **Holyrood Park**, sometimes called Queen's or King's Park, stretches away southward from Holyrood Palace. Some 4m in circumference, the park is one of hilly and craggy moorland, the most prominent feature of which, with of course a superb view, is *Arthur's Seat* (822ft). The climb to the top, best started from Dunsapie Loch (parking), is less formidable than it may appear. The origin of this hill's name is shadowy; it claims no connection with Britain's legendary king, and no knights slumber here, but the name may relate to a 6C Prince Arthur of Strathclyde. Among other suggestions are a simþle corruption of 'Archer', or 'Ard Thor', Gaelic for the Height of Thor.

Queen's Drive makes the clockwise (one way) circuit of the park, soon after leaving Holyrood Palace reaching St. Margaret's Loch, near which are *St. Margaret's Well* and, higher up the hill, the small ruin of *St. Anthony's Chapel*. Both places are tenuously associated with afflictions of the eyes, the well reputedly brought here during the reign of James IV from Restalrig (see entry below), where a spring was credited with alleviating eye disease. The chapel is thought to date from the 15C, and its dedication may indicate some kind of connection with a hospital for sufferers from 'St. Anthony's Fire' (erysipelas) known to have been founded by James I at Leith in c 1430. Beyond the loch (Restalrig is ½m NE from the exit here) Queen's Drive curves E, then S, to reach *Dunsapie Loch* (see above), beyond slicing between the Lion's Haunch (N) and Samson's Ribs (S) to arrive at the foot of *Salisbury Crags*. Here a road hairpins back to reach *Duddingston* village, beside its bird-sanctuary loch and known for its church with a Norman S door and chancel arch and, near the gate, a horse-mounting block, the village jougs and a small watch-tower for the guard against body-snatchers. It was here at Duddingston that the Young Pretender's army camped for six weeks in 1745.

Inchcolm Island. For detail, see Rte 33A. From Edinburgh there are cruises to the island (two hours, of which one ashore) by the 'Maid of the Forth' from Hawes Pier near the Forth railway bridge (Tel: 031-3311454).

Lauriston Castle, off Cramond Road North (which is off Queensferry Road) some 4m NW of Waverley Market, was built in about 1590 by

Sir Archibald Napier (father of John Napier of Merchiston, the mathematician and inventor of logarithms) and later occupied by John Law (1671–1728), the buccaneering financier who in 1716 established the first Bank of France. Napier's turreted and corbelled tower was later much extended, mainly by William Burn during the 19C, and stands today as a gracious Edwardian mansion showing period furniture, objets d'art and a notable collection of Derbyshire Blue John ware. The fine grounds extend down to the Forth. (Visit by conducted tour only. April–Oct: Daily, except Fri., 11.00 to 13.00. 14.00 to 17.00. Nov–March: Sat. and Sun., 14.00 to 16.00. Last tours leave roughly 40 minutes before above closing times. Tel: 031-3362060. Fee, but grounds free).

Leith, the port of Edinburgh, straddles the Water of Leith which flows into the sizeable harbour, comprising the large, open outer or western harbour, and, running away SE, an inner harbour complex of docks—an area which in recent years has become increasingly popular for its lively restaurants and pubs. These apart, Leith's main tourist attraction, and particularly so for overseas visitors, is the James Pringle Woollen Mill with its Clan Tartan Centre.

History. As the port of the capital, Leith has experienced its touches of history—violent, ceremonial and even sporting, for its Links, on the E of the town, represent one of the world's most venerable golf courses. Vulnerable beside the water, Leith was frequently ravaged by the English, but the year 1561 brought a more welcome landing, when, returning after the years in France, Mary, Queen of Scots, came ceremonially ashore here, to be entertained by a local merchant, Andrew Lamb, whose house in Burgess Street still stands. In the following century, in 1641, Charles I was here, receiving the ominous news of the Irish insurrection while he was enjoying a game of golf; but, only a few years later, in 1650, Cromwell had taken over and was building a great waterside fort. The Jacobite Highlanders seized this fort in 1715, and in 1822 it was the turn of ceremonial again when George IV landed here at the start of his State visit.

The approach from the E end of Edinburgh's Princes Street is by Leith Street and Leith Walk, the latter in rather over a mile reaching a major intersection at the S apex of a triangle of roads—clockwise, Great Junction, North Junction, Commercial, Bernard and Constitution streets—which define central Leith. Great Junction Street, followed NW, in about five blocks reaches Bangor Road (S) in which is the James Pringle Woollen Mill (April–Dec: Daily, 09.00 to 17.00, or 18.00 in high season. Jan–March: Mon.–Sat., 09.00 to 17.00. Buses 10 and 22 from Princes Street. Courtesy coach makes morning circuit of leading hotels. Tel: 031-5535161 or 5100. Free, but fee for reading from Archive Computer). Here, in addition to a huge shop area, there is a Clan Tartan Centre in which an Archive Computer, fed with a surname, will present the applicant with a printed certificate detailing, if there is such, any clan connection, together with information regarding the clan chief, its origins, heraldic emblems, plant badge, tartans and other historic information, including even the clan war cry. Postal applications may also be made to the Clan Tartan Centre Ltd, 70–74 Bangor Road, Leith, Edinburgh EH6.

Visitors wishing to make the round of Leith should continue N along Great and then North Junction streets, at the end of the latter bearing E along Commercial Street which runs beside (N) the site of Cromwell's fort, recalled on the S by the names Cromwell Street and Citadel Street. After crossing the Water of Leith, Commercial Street

CRAMOND ISLAND
CRAMOND
GRANTON
MUIRHOUSE
Lauriston Castle
FERRY
Royal Botanic Garc
DAVIDSON'S MAINS
FORTH BRIDGE A90
QUEENSFERRY ROAD
COMELY BANK
BLACKHALL
Corstorphine Hill
Nat. Gallery of Modern Art
Water of Leith
DRUM BRAE
GLASGOW A8
Zoological Park
Donaldson's Hospital
CORSTORPHINE
CORSTORPHINE ROAD
MURRAYFIELD
Rugby Ground
DALRY ROAD
DALRY
Turnhouse Airport &
ROAD
MERCHIST
Napier Technical College
STENHOUSE
GORGIE
SIGHTHILL
ROAD
CALDER
WESTER
CRAIGLOCKHART
HAILES
ROAD
COLINTON
COMIST
ROAD
LANARK A70
LANARK
JUNIPER GREEN
Caly Sto
OXGANGS

EDINBURGH Environs

| 0 miles | 1 |
| 0 kilometres | 2 |

PORT

NEWHAVEN

DOCKS

Firth Of Forth

LEITH

James Pringle
Woollen Mill

St Mary's

SEAFIELD

RESTALRIG

Meadowbank
Sports Centre

Central Area
(See large scale plan)

Waverley
Station

LONDON

PORTOBELLO

Palace of
Holyroodhouse

St Margaret's Loch

stle

Holyrood Park

Dunsappie Loch

DUDDINGSTON

MILTON

Arthur's
Seat

tsfield
nks

Duddingston
Loch

Braid Burn

NIDDRIE

NETHER
LIBERTON

Craigmillar Castle

Blackford
Hill
Observatory

N

Braid Hills

NORTHFIELD

FERNIEHILL

RMILEHEAD

LIBERTON

GILMERTON

LIN

KAIMES

A701

A7 DALKEITH

A1

A68

becomes Bernard Street which turns S as Constitution Street. Within the angle, in Burgess Street, is *Andrew Lamb's House* (Mon.–Fri., 10.00 to 16.00. Tel: 031-5543131. Free), the house in which Mary, Queen of Scots, was received on her arrival from France in 1561. Typically combining residence and warehouse, the house (now an old people's day centre) is four storeys high and has a projecting staircase-tower. Historic *Leith Links* are to the E for most of the length of Constitution Street which, at its S end, becomes Leith Walk.

Newhaven, to the W of Leith, was founded by James IV in c 1500 as a naval dockyard. *Granton*, farther W, was a creation of the Duke of Buccleuch, who in 1835 began the construction of the harbour, now mainly used by pleasure craft.

Mathematicians may choose to make a pilgrimage to **Merchiston**, some 2m S of Waverley Market, the approach road (Bruntsfield Place) skirting *Bruntsfield Links* (see C. above). Merchiston takes its name from an estate which belonged since 1483 to the family of Napier, their seat being *Merchiston Tower* (15C; now appropriately incorporated into Napier Technical College), in which in 1560 was born John Napier (see also D., Princes Street, St. Cuthbert's Church).

The **National Gallery of Modern Art** (Mon.–Sat., 10.00 to 17.00. Sun., 14.00 to 17.00. During Festival, Mon.–Sat., 10.00 to 18.00. Sun., 11.00 to 18.00.—Print Room, open by arrangement, Mon.–Fri., 10.00 to 12.30. 14.00 to 16.30. Tel: 031-5568921. Free) is housed in the classical former John Watson's School (William Burn, 1823) on Belford Road, rather less than a mile W of Dean Bridge between the Water of Leith and Queensferry Road. The surrounding extensive grounds provide a good setting for some larger sculpture.

Founded in 1960, the gallery has aimed to build up a representative collection of the essential forms of 20C art with works by most of the major European and American artists. Names include Matisse, Picasso, Kirchner, Klee, Hepworth, Moore and Hockney; Braque, Léger and Mondrian; Ernst, Miró, Giacometti and Magritte; and contemporaries such as Lichtenstein, Lewitt, Kitaj and Chia. There is also a programme of temporary exhibitions.

Portobello, on the coast 3m E of Princes Street, owes its exotic name not to topographical beauty, though this is a pleasant enough corner, but to one George Hamilton who built the first house here and named it after Portobello in Panama, at the capture of which he had fought in 1739. Later, and especially during Victorian times, Portobello became a popular resort, a period still echoed by its genteel houses. Sir Harry Lauder was born at 3 Bridge Street in 1870.

Restalrig Church (in an E suburb just N of Holyrood Park), although a 19 and 20C restoration, has ancient and confused roots associated with St. Triduana, a saint who, regrettably, never existed, the name in fact deriving from a three-day fast practised by the old Celtic Church. Founded probably in those Celtic times, the church was destroyed by a Reformist mob in 1560, but restored in 1837 and again in 1910. Adjoining is a small hexagonal chapel, with a groined roof supported by a central pillar, successor and in part survivor of the chapel of a college founded here in 1478 by James III. During restoration in 1908 the new floor paving was suddenly burst by a spring, this enabling the building to be identified as the successor of a hitherto more or less legendary *Chapel of St. Triduana*, famed for a spring once resorted to for diseases of the eye (see also Holyrood Park, St. Margaret's Well, above).

Founded in 1670 on the site of Waverley Station, the **Royal Botanic Garden** moved in 1823 to its present site in the district of Inverleith, a mile to the N of Princes Street. Among the oldest botanic gardens in Britain, the main features here are a magnificent collection of rhododendrons; woodland, heath and rock gardens; plant houses with landscaped exotic plants; and an exhibition hall. (Garden: Daily, 09.00, or 11.00 on Sun., to dusk. Plant Houses and Exhibition Hall: 10.00, or 11.00 on Sun., to 15 minutes before Garden closes. Tel: 031-5527171. Free).

The **Royal Observatory**, today a joint research institution of the Science Research Council and the University of Edinburgh, was built on Calton Hill in the early 19C but moved in 1894 to its present site on Blackford Hill, rather over 2m S of Princes Street. The *Visitor Centre* (1978) is open Mon.–Fri., 10.00 to 16.00. Sat. and Sun., and Hol., 12.00 to 17.00. Tel: 031-6673321. Fee.

The **Scottish Zoological Park** (Daily, 09.00, or 09.30 on Sun., to 18.00 or dusk in winter. Tel: 031-3349171. Fee) is 3m W of Waverley Market, the approach being along West Coates and Corstorphine Road. This road passes (N) *Donaldson's School*, a set-back, dignified building by W.H. Playfair, founded by James Donaldson (died 1830) for the education of poor children and now used for the education of the deaf, and soon afterwards crosses the Water of Leith at *Coltbridge*, scene of the 'Canter of Coltbridge', an incident during the '45 when a body of Dragoons, taking fright at the appearance of the Young Pretender's Highlanders, turned tail and are said not to have drawn bridle until they reached Prestonpans, 9m distant. The Zoo, perhaps best known for its penguins, was established by the Royal Zoological Society of Scotland in 1913 and now spreads over more than 70 acres on Corstorphine Hill.

19 Glasgow

Tourist Information. 35 St. Vincent Place (off George Square). Tel: (041) 2274880.

Public Transport is operated by the Trans-Clyde Integrated Public Transport System (underground, buses, local trains). For information apply Strathclyde Transport, Travel Centre, St. Enoch Square. Tel: (041) 2264826. The *Underground* is a circular system of some 6½m serving 15 stations. From Buchanan Street and St. Enoch in the city centre the circuit crosses the Clyde and turns W to curve N back across the Clyde between Govan and Partick. The circuit then heads E through the northern inner suburbs. Dating from before the turn of the century, the system was completely modernised in 1979.—*Buses*. Extensive and frequent city and suburban services, the latter operating from bus stations at Buchanan Street and Anderston Cross. For city tours, inquire at Tourist Information.

British Rail Stations. There are two main British Rail stations, Central and Queen Street, linked by a special bus service. *Central Station* for services to England (W line) and Wales, and to Scottish destinations in the S and W. *Queen Street Station* for services to the W Highlands; to Loch Lomond; to N and E Scotland; and to Edinburgh and the E line to England.

Airport. Abbotsinch, near Renfrew 7m W. City link bus from both main bus and main railway stations.

Paddle Steamer 'Waverley'. For cruise information apply Waverley Excursions Ltd, Waverley Terminal, Anderston Quay, Glasgow G3 8HA. Tel: (041) 2218152. See also Rte 16, The Clyde and Clyde Cruising.

SOME HOTELS. There is parking at all the following. **Central Area**. *Skean Dhu*, 36 Cambridge Street. Tel: (041) 3323311. *Stakis Ingram*, 201 Ingram Street. Tel: (041) 2484401. *Holiday Inn*, Argyle Street, Anderston. Tel: (041) 2265577.—**West Area** (N of the Clyde; for Art Gallery and Museum and Hunterian Art Gallery and Museum). *Stakis Grosvenor*, Grosvenor Terrace, Great Western Road. Tel: (041) 3398811. *Stakis Pond*, Great Western Road. Tel: (041) 3348161.—**South West Area** (for Pollok Park and Burrell Collection). *Tinto Firs Thistle*, 470 Kilmarnock Road. Tel: (041) 6372353. *Bellahouston Swallow*, 517 Paisley Road West. Tel: (041) 4273146.—**Airport Area**. *Excelsior*, PA3 2TR. Tel: (041) 8871212.

History. Although in the 5C St. Ninian is supposed to have blessed the ground on which the cathedral now stands, Glasgow probably started as a cluster of huts around the church built on the same site by St. Mungo (Kentigern) in the 6C. This site was known in Celtic as 'Glas Cau', the 'Green Place'. St. Mungo is Glasgow's patron, and the attractive city arms represent his miracles. (The tree is the frozen branch with which he rekindled the monastery fire; the bird is the decapitated redbreast he restored to life; the salmon, with a lost ring in its belly, was a miraculous capture to save the honour of a princess; and the bell was brought by the saint from Rome). The city motto—in full, 'Let Glasgow flourish by the preaching of the word'—recalls that it was to convert its inhabitants that St. Ninian came here to Strathclyde.

A charter granted by William the Lion in 1175 marks the official start of Glasgow's history, the cathedral then growing in importance between the 12–15C and with it the adjoining bishop's palace on the site now occupied by the

Royal Infirmary. Thus this district, now roughly Cathedral Square, was long the heart of the town until it gradually shifted S to Glasgow Cross. Some key dates are 1300 when Wallace defeated the English at Bell o' the Brae, now the upper part of High Street; 1451 when the university was founded; 1568 when Mary, Queen of Scots, was defeated at Langside, near today's Queen's Park; 1611 when Glasgow was made a royal burgh; 1615 when a Catholic priest, John Ogilvie (canonised in 1976) was hanged in Glasgow; 1650–51 when Cromwell was here; and 1745–46 when the Young Pretender stayed here, without however receiving significant support. By this time Glasgow Cross had become the town centre, the present centre, George Square, still being only marshland.

Rapid growth came with Georgian times, and then the Industrial Revolution, during which period Glasgow took on the solidly prosperous Victorian face that, despite much bold modern development, is still likely to be a main impression for today's visitor.

For Glasgow to **Edinburgh**, see Rte 8; to **Lanark**, **Moffat** and **Gretna**, see Rte 10; to **Kilmarnock**, **Dumfries** and **Gretna**, see Rte 11; to **Paisley** and **Ayr**, see Rte 16; to **Tyndrum**, see Rte 20; to **Aberfoyle** and **The Trossachs**, see Rte 21; to **Stirling**, see Rte 22.

With a population approaching a million, Glasgow is by far the most populous city in Scotland; a bustling, sprawling commercial and industrial complex, for too long equated with slums and scarcely considered in tourist terms. Yet this is unfair. Admittedly lacking instant aesthetic appeal, Glasgow nevertheless compensates with a purposeful character all its own, and, as proud of its past as it is of its new course, offers the visitor a wealth of places of beauty, cultural distinction and interest. The Cathedral is a superb example of EE Gothic and its Lower Church a gem among interiors of that period; the Theatre Royal is the home of Scottish opera; the Art Gallery and Museum at Kelvingrove Park are world-famous, while the Hunterian Museum and Art Gallery within the imposing 19C University buildings increasingly enjoy a similar distinction; the Museum of Transport is outstanding among the few of its kind; and finally, in Pollok Park, there is the Burrell Collection, as priceless in itself as it is superbly housed.

For the visitor Glasgow can conveniently be divided into three districts: East and Central (A); West (B); and South (C). These are described in turn below, the first as a walk, the other two as rounds by bus. A fourth section (D) covers selected places in other districts, while a fifth (E) introduces the Burrell Collection.

A. East and Central Glasgow

The following tour, for the most part through the busiest part of the city, is only practicable on foot. If all the places mentioned were visited the distance could add up to perhaps 8m. However, a good mile of walking can be cut out, after leaving the cathedral, by taking a bus from Cathedral Square to Jocelyn Square. Also, so much of the round is within the concentrated central area in which perhaps most visitors are likely to be staying that it can conveniently be split into several parts to suit individual preferences. Not much less than a whole day should be allowed if the Cathedral, Provand's Lordship and People's Palace are given the time they deserve.

Dignified **George Square**, laid out in 1781 and named for George III, may be considered the heart of modern Glasgow. However George III has not achieved a statue here, the place on the pillar (80ft high intended for him having been taken by Sir Walter Scott, wearing, as was his custom, his plaid on the 'wrong' shoulder (John Greenshields, 1837). Other statues in the square include equestrian figures of Queen Victoria and Prince Albert, both by the Italian Marochetti; Robert Burns (George Ewing, 1877), with, in his hand, the 'wee modest, crimson tipped flower'; James Watt (Chantrey, 1832); two prime ministers, Gladstone (Hamo Thornycroft, 1902) and Peel (Mossman, 1859); and, the first statue to be honoured with a place here, Sir John Moore (Flaxman, 1819), born in Glasgow and hero of Corunna during the Peninsular War. Also in the square is the *Cenotaph* (John Burnet), unveiled in 1924 by Earl Haig before an immense crowd (an interesting photograph in the People's Palace records the scene).

Of the buildings around the square the most important is the **City Chambers** (guided tours, Mon., Tues., Wed., Fri., at 10.30 and 14.30. Tel: 041-2219600. Free). Built in 1883–88 by William Young, and extended to the E by John Watson in 1923, and occupying the whole of the E side of the square, this imposing mass with a 216ft-high tower and built in Italian Renaissance style, is as impressive inside as it is outside. From the loggia, built to the plan of a Roman Renaissance church, there rise two staircases, one to the Council Chamber, the other to reception rooms and the Banqueting Hall, with murals by Glasgow artists depicting the city's growth. Throughout there is a richness of mosaic, majolica and fine wood.—Other buildings around George Square are the *General Post Office* (1876) on the S; *Queen Street Station* on the N; and, on the W, the *Merchants' House* (May–Sept: Mon.–Fri., 09.00 to 16.00. Tel: 041-2042121. Free), built by John Burnet in 1874 and home of Glasgow Chamber of Commerce, the oldest in Britain.

George Street leads out of the NE corner of George Square, with, on the left, the length of the *University of Strathclyde*, a technological university with roots going back to 1796 but not achieving its present title until 1964. A plaque here commemorates a former student, John Logie Baird, pioneer of television. Beyond, High Street is reached, ascending N towards Provand's Lordship and Glasgow Cathedral. Once, this general area was Bell o' the Brae where in 1300 Wallace defeated Percy, the English governor holding the castle. Here, too, approaching the cathedral, two statues deserve notice; one, equestrian, of William III (H. Cheere, 1735), the other of David Livingstone (Mossman, 1879).

Provand's Lordship (May–Sept: Mon.–Sat., 10.00 to 17.00. Sun., 14.00 to 17.00. Tel: 041-5528819. Free), just opposite the cathedral, is Glasgow's oldest house, built in about 1471 probably for the priest in charge of the then nearby St. Nicholas Hospice, which had been founded for a priest and 12 old men. James II and IV may have stayed here, as very likely also Mary, Queen of Scots, in 1566, when she visited the very ill Darnley prior to taking him to Edinburgh and his murder at Kirk o' Field. The house in which Darnley lay ill may have been in the southern part of Cathedral Square, and in the People's Palace there is a model showing the house and this area as it was at that time.

*Glasgow Cathedral (April–Sept: Mon.–Sat., 09.30 to 19.00. Sun., 14.00 to 17.00. Oct–March: Mon.–Sat., 09.30 to 16.00. Sun., 14.00 to 16.00. Donation), or the Cathedral Church of St. Mungo, is, both historically and architecturally, one of Glasgow's most important buildings. Smaller than most cathedrals, the style is mainly 13C EE, though several other periods are represented. Among striking features are the very modest projection of the transepts, and, because of the sloping ground, the construction of the E end in two storeys, so that the crypt is really the Lower Church. This Lower Church and the Blacader (or Fergus) Aisle are from the visitor's point of view the two most noteworthy parts of the interior.

History. The story goes that in the 6C St. Mungo (or Kentigern), coming from Culross, found a holy man, Fergus, on the point of death. He placed the body on a cart, yoked to it two untamed bulls, and bade them drag the cart to the place determined by God. The bulls halted at a cemetery, consecrated two centuries earlier by St. Ninian, and there the body of Fergus was buried at a spot now covered by the Aisle of Car Fergus or Blacader's Aisle. St. Mungo at the same time founded a church on the same spot. Other churches doubtless followed, until today's cathedral was founded by David I and Bishop Achaius in 1136. Soon destroyed by fire, the church was rebuilt by Bishop Jocelin in 1197. Of this, however, only a fragment remains (visible in the Lower Church). Crypt, choir and tower were completed by Bishop de Bondington (1233–58). Bishop Lauder (1408–25) added the stone spire and also finished the chapter house or crypt below the sacristy. Bishop Cameron (1425– 47) completed the sacristy. The nave, begun early in the 14C, was not finished until 1480. Archbishop Blacader (1483–1508) constructed the stair from the nave to the crypt and founded the Blacader Aisle; he is also generally credited with the beautiful choir screen.

In 1560 James Beaton, the last Roman Catholic archbishop, carried off the treasure and the archives to France, whence they have never returned. At the Reformation the church was purged of 'monuments of idolatry', but the building was saved from destruction by the intervention (1578) of the city trade guilds. Later it was divided into three congregations (in the nave, in the choir and in the crypt). An unusual episode occurred in 1650 when Cromwell sat in the nave and heard himself denounced, in a two-hour-long sermon, as a 'sectary and blasphemer' by Zachary Boyd, rector of the university and minister of the church then occupying the crypt. Cromwell's revenge was to invite Boyd to dinner, after which he subjected him to prayers lasting three hours. When, in 1801, the crypt ceased to be used as a church, it was part filled with earth and used as a cemetery.

Entry is normally by the SW porch, outside which is a monument to Thomas Hutcheson, one of the founders of Hutchesons' Hospital (see below). The *Nave* is stately and well proportioned, with a triforium of two arches to each bay and a clerestory. The clustered columns separating it from the aisles have plain capitals. On the walls are numerous monuments and regimental flags and on the easternmost column on the N side of the nave hangs a 17C Italian Nativity. The Victorian stained glass was of poor quality but good modern glass (1950–58) has replaced it in most of the windows; the great W window, with the Creation, is by Francis Spear (1958). The *Choir*, a beautiful example of EE Gothic, now used as the High Church, is raised 3ft above the nave and is entered by a low elliptic-arched doorway in the fine *Rood Screen*, on the corbels of which appear the Seven Deadly Sins. It is separated from its aisles by clustered columns with flowered capitals, and has a peculiarly fine triforium. The choir pulpit was made c 1600 for use in the lower church. A window in the S aisle shows the arms of the fourteen incorporated trades. The E end has four slender lancet windows instead of the more usual three or five, and its arrangement is interesting. Here is a double aisle, the W half forming an ambulatory, while on the E are chapels, separated by elegant shafts supporting the vaulted roof. In the SE chapel is the tomb of Archbishop Law (died 1632). Adjoining

GLASGOW
Central

0 yards   700
0 metres   700

A803

M8

M8 A8

POSSIL ROAD
NEPOCH HILL ROAD
PETERSHILL ROAD
PORT DUNDAS
KEPPOCHHILL ROAD
STIRLING ROAD
ROYSTON ROAD

M8

BAIRD STREET
STREET

COWCADDENS
DOBBIES LOAN
KYLE ST
PARLIAMENTARY ROAD
ST JAMES ROAD

Theatre Royal
AUCHIEHALL STREET

Bus Station
CATHEDRAL STREET

Royal Infirmary
Cathedral
Provand's Lordship
Necropolis
CATHEDRAL SQUARE

Queen St Sta.
Athenaeum
St George's
Stock Exch
Royal Coll
Univ of Strathclyde
City Chambers
GEORGE SQUARE
GEORGE STREET

Royal Exch
GPO
Hutch Hosp.
INGRAM STREET
Trades House
St David's
City Hall
COLLEGE ST
DUKE ST

Central Station

Royal Bank
ST ENOCH SQUARE
TRONGATE
Tron Steeple
GLASGOW CROSS
HIGH ST

ARGYLE

George V Bridge
Glasgow Bridge
Victoria Bridge
CARLTON PLACE
OXFORD STREET
NORFOLK ST

GALLOWGATE
The Barrows
GALLOWGATE
MILE END

ST ANDREW SQUARE
St Andrew's
JOCELYN SQUARE
GREENDYKE STREET
High Court

Albert Bridge

LONDON ROAD
MONTEITH ROW

GORBALS
People's Palace
Glasgow

HUTCHESONTOWN
CUMBERLAND RD
BEDFORD ST
CROWN ST

Green

King's Bridge
KING'S DRIVE
JAMES ST

RUTHERGLEN ROAD

Richmond Park

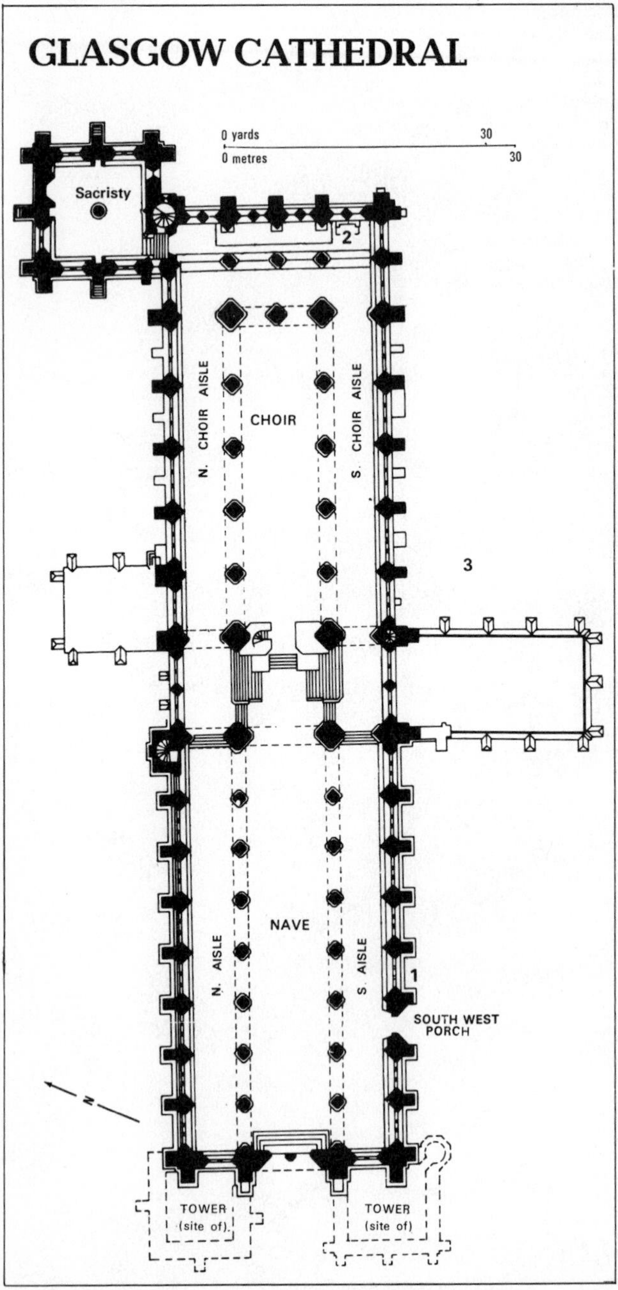

GLASGOW CATHEDRAL

0 yards   30
0 metres   30

Sacristy

2

N. CHOIR AISLE

CHOIR

S. CHOIR AISLE

3

N. AISLE

NAVE

S. AISLE

1

SOUTH WEST
PORCH

N

TOWER
(site of)

TOWER
(site of)

the choir on the NE is the *Sacristy*, a square chamber with its original oak door, and a central shaft on which appear the arms of the founder, Bishop Cameron (died 1446).

From the S transept steps descend to the *Blacader Aisle* a fine vaulted crypt founded by Archbishop Blacader (died 1508). The exquisitely carved ceiling bosses can be appreciated with the help of excellent modern lighting. As related under 'History', this aisle, or chapel, reputedly occupies the site of the cemetery blessed by St. Ninian, to which St. Mungo brought the body of Fergus. A carving over the N pier (visible just above and ahead on entering) shows a body on a cart, surrounded by the inscription 'This is ye ile of Car Fergus'. The *Lower Church, with its rich vaulting, its proportion, the simple tomb of St. Mungo and the row of four chapels, is an outstanding example of medieval Scottish architecture and the chief glory of the cathedral. The date is mid 13C, but a pillar with a capital differing from those of the others (ahead right, on entering by the S steps) is probably a vestige of Bishop Jocelin's church of 1197. On the N side of the Chapel of St. Andrew, one of the row of four, there is an effigy of Bishop Wischard, who gained fame and favour for his support of Bruce, whom he absolved of the murder of Comyn and later crowned.—At the NE angle of the Lower Church is the *Chapter House* (13–15C), founded by Bishop de Bondington and connected by a turret staircase with the sacristy immediately above. Here are preserved a bell of 1594 (recast in 1790) and a gravestone com-

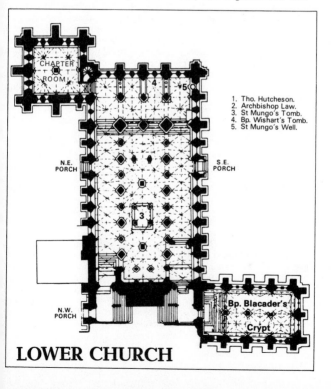

1. Tho. Hutcheson.
2. Archbishop Law.
3. St Mungo's Tomb.
4. Bp. Wishart's Tomb.
5. St Mungo's Well.

LOWER CHURCH

memorating in a quaint rhymed inscription nine martyred Covenanters.

Over the hill behind the cathedral sprawls the *Necropolis*, with many elaborate tombs and memorials, the most conspicuous monument being a Doric column erected in 1825 to the memory of the Reformers and crowned by a statue (by Robert Forrest) of John Knox.

Castle Street and High Street are now retraced, noting that the railway area on the E of the latter, roughly opposite College Street, was the site of Glasgow university from 1632 to 1870. **Glasgow Cross**, a short way beyond, followed Cathedral Square as the town centre and so remained until the 19C. Today this is still a busy crossroads, marked by the *Cross* (a 1929 replica of the medieval original removed in 1629) and the isolated *Cross Steeple*, all that remains of the tolbooth of 1626, alongside which once stood the Tontine buildings, much used by the 'tobacco lords' in the 18C.

This tour continues W along Trongate, but, first, the area to the SE of Glasgow Cross is described. Gallowgate runs E, once the road to the gallows but today known for the 'Barrows', Glasgow's weekend flea-market. Saltmarket, the southward road and once what its name suggests, reaches Jocelyn Square and the river, the former once known as Jail Square and as recently as 1865 the scene of a public hanging watched by some 30,000 people. On the W stands the *High Court* (Stark, 1814), while, opposite, in Turnbull Street leading N off Greendyke Street, *St. Andrew's Church* (1750) is worth a visit for its dignified Corinthian-pillared front and elegant 18C interior. Glasgow Green, dating from 1662 and the oldest of Glasgow's parks, stretches away SE beside the river, here being a monument (1806) to Lord Nelson, of interest for being the first in Britain to be erected to the admiral, and also the **People's Palace** (Mon.–Sat., 10.00 to 17.00. Sun., 14.00 to 17.00. Tel: 041-5540223. Free), so named because it originated (1898) as a cultural centre for the people of the eastern districts of Glasgow. Today it consists of a museum devoted to the story of Glasgow from its official foundation in 1175 through to modern times, and also winter gardens housing some splendid tropical plants and birds. The wide-ranging survey of Glasgow's history—the emphasis being on the 19 to 20C—embraces, among many others, themes such as trade and industry, politics, the press, housing and health, women's suffrage, entertainment and sport, admirable use being made of a rich collection of paintings, prints and photographs to bring home, often startlingly, the changes and developments of the last century and more.

The fourth street out of Glasgow Cross is Trongate which, in an area undergoing much development and with many shops, heads W, passing *Tron Steeple* (1637), all that is left of St. Mary's Church, burned down in 1793 and now in part the home of a theatre club. There is a northward glimpse up Candleriggs to St. David's Church (see below) beyond the City Hall (1841), the home of the Scottish National Orchestra, then another glimpse up Hutcheson Street to Hutchesons' Hospital (see below). On the Royal Bank of Scotland, on the right at the corner of Glassford Street, there is a plaque recording that this was the site of Shawfield House where the Young Pretender stayed during his northward retreat.

A southward diversion may be made along Stockwell Street to reach the Clyde at Victoria Bridge (John Walker, 1851–54), successor to a medieval bridge at the S end of which once stood a leper hospital. Here is moored the *SV 'Carrick'* (no adm.), a three-master clipper of 1864, once named the 'City of Adelaide' and now a Royal Naval Volunteer Reserve headquarters. And here, too, starts the Clyde Walkway, leading nearly 2m westward to reach the *Scottish Exhibition Centre* (1985).

Beyond the junction of Glassford and Stockwell streets, Trongate becomes Argyle Street, in part pedestrian and one of Glasgow's busier shopping stretches. Argyle Street reaches St. Enoch Square (named after St. Mungo's mother, 'Enoch' being a corruption of 'Thenew') with the Strathclyde Transport *Travel Centre* for information on public transport. Just beyond is the *Central Station*, beyond again, another quarter of a mile, being Anderston Cross, site of one of the city's two main bus stations and at the start of the westward running Clydeside Expressway.

Now heading N this walk follows Glassford Street, near the top of which is the domed *Trades House* (Mon.–Fri., 10.00 to 17.00. Tel: 041-5522418. Free), built by Robert Adam in 1794 but today with an interior much altered to meet the modern needs of the city's fourteen incorporated trades who administer large charitable funds. Glassford Street ends at Ingram Street, to the right along which there are three buildings of interest. The first is *Hutchesons' Hospital* (NTS Visitor Centre. Mon.–Fri., 09.00 to 17.00. Sat., 10.00 to 16.00. Tel: 041-5528391. Donation), an attractive and compact spired house built in 1805 to a design by David Hamilton but considerably enlarged and heightened by John Baird in 1876. Originally a charitable institution founded in 1641 in Trongate by two brothers—their statues stand here in niches—for poor old men and orphan boys, the building now not only serves as NTS regional offices, with a visitor centre, but is also used as an elegant setting for concerts, small conferences and suchlike. The *Law Courts*, opposite, date from 1824 and later. *St. David's Church* (Thomas Rickman, 1824), beyond on the N side of Ingram Street, is, curiously, also known as 'Ramshorn', possibly from a monastery which once stood here until its walls reputedly collapsed when threatened by Reformers as did the walls of Jericho before Joshua's rams' horns. Until 1835 the pavement in front of the church was a part of its cemetery and the initials R.F. and A.F. carved into it are over the graves of the Foulis brothers, 18C printers and founders of Glasgow's first School of Art.

Followed W, Ingram Street ends at the *Royal Exchange* (Mon., Tues., Thurs., Fri., 09.30 to 20.00. Sat., 09.30 to 13.00. 14.00 to 17.00. Tel: 041-2211876. Free), in front of which stands a particularly lifelike Marochetti equestrian statue of the Duke of Wellington, with, around the plinth, some vivid action friezes. Today housing Stirling's Library, Glasgow's central lending library and known for its books on music and the pictorial arts, the Royal Exchange building has as its core a mansion of 1780 built as a suburban home by one of Glasgow's prosperous 'tobacco lords' (see Glasgow Cross above). To these were added in 1829 a great hall to the rear and, to the front, an imposing portico, both necessary for the needs and dignity of the Exchange which opened here in the same year.

Buchanan Street, part pedestrian and running behind the Royal Exchange, is now followed N through St. George's Place, surrounded by buildings worth noting. On the S side is the *Stock Exchange* (John Burnet, 1877), with a visitors' gallery open Mon.–Fri., 10.00 to 12.45. 14.00 to 15.30. Tel: 041-2217060; in the centre stands *St. George's Tron Church* (William Stark, 1807); and on the N the *Athenaeum* (John Burnet, 1888), home of the Royal Scottish Academy of Music and Drama, carries statues (by George Mossman) of Reynolds, Wren, Purcell and Flaxman.

Sauchiehall Street, Glasgow's perhaps best known and certainly most 'popular' street, stretches from its junction with Buchanan Street westward for almost 2m across the M8 motorway to Kelvingrove Park and the city Art Gallery and Museum (see next section). At its E end the street is a pedestrian shopping precinct. Here it crosses Hope Street, a short way N up which is the *Theatre Royal* (Tel: 041-3311234), the home of Scottish opera and ballet in a gem of a theatre restored to all its Victorian splendour in 1975. The name Cowcaddens, just N of the theatre, preserves a rather different link with the past, this name recalling that what is now a busy street was once the common pasture. A little farther along Sauchiehall Street, connoisseurs of early 19C architecture will walk S down Blythswood Street to enjoy Blythswood Square; while admirers of Glasgow's perhaps most distinguished architect, C.R. Mackintosh (1868–1928; see also Charles Rennie Mackintosh Society below), will aim N up Scott Street to the corner of Renfrew Street to find his *Glasgow School of Art* (tours when staff available. Mon.–Fri., 10.00 to 12.00. 14.00 to 16.00. Tel: 041-3329797) built in two stages, the first being the E facade to the main entrance (1897–99) and the second, the remainder of the building, 1907–09.

Accommodation of a very different kind can be savoured about 300 yards NW (145 Buccleuch Street) at the *Tenement House (NTS. April–Oct: Daily, 14.00 to 17.00. Nov–March: Sat., Sun., 14.00 to 16.00. Tel: 041-5528391. Fee), a capsule from the past enabling the modern visitor to walk straight into the flat of Miss Agnes Toward, a typist with a shipping firm. The tenement house was built in 1892—at a time when this was a genteel neighbourhood—and Miss Toward lived in this flat (parlour, bedroom, kitchen) from 1911 to 1965, little concerned, it would seem, with modern domestic progress though in 1959 she did exchange her gas lighting for electricity. In 1965 she was taken to hospital, and for ten years, until her death, the flat was unoccupied and time suspended. Today, the gas has been restored, the fire in the cast-iron grate has been rekindled, Miss Toward's heavily-draped table has been set for tea, and a partly finished dress lies across the ancient sewing machine to which she was doubtless devoted.

The *Third Eye Centre* (Tues.–Sat., 10.00 to 17.30. Sun., 14.00 to 17.30. Tel: 041-3327521. Free), at 350 Sauchiehall Street, is a multi-purpose art centre mounting up to four exhibitions monthly, ranging from contemporary art to historical and social documentary. Farther W, at 518 Sauchiehall Street just before the motorway, the Museum of the Royal Highland Fusiliers (Mon.–Fri., 09.00 to 16.30 but 16.00 on Fri. Tel: 041-3320961. Donation) covers the histories of the Royal Scots Fusiliers and the Highland Light Infantry, amalgamated in 1959. Beyond, in Kent Road the other side of the motorway, is the Mitchell Library (Mon.–Fri., 09.30 to 21.00. Sat., 09.30 to 17.00. Tel: 041-2217030. Free), built by W.B. Whitie in 1911 but founded in 1874 out of a bequest by the tobacco merchant Stephen Mitchell. In this, the largest public reference library in Europe, the specialist collections include Robert Burns, Scottish poetry, Music, Celtic literature and Glasgow.

From St. George's Cross, half a mile N of the Mitchell Library, Great Western Road leads NW, soon passing on the right the graceful

Episcopal Cathedral of St. Mary (George Gilbert Scott and J.O. Scott, 1871–93). Half a mile N again, at 866 Garscube Road, the *Charles Rennie Mackintosh Society* has its headquarters and a small exhibition in the former Queen's Cross Church, built by Mackintosh in 1897 (Tues., Thurs., Fri., 12.00 to 17.30. Sun., 14.30 to 17.00. Tel: 041-9466600).

B. West Glasgow

The two places most likely to attract the visitor (the Art Gallery and Museum, and the University with the Hunterian Museum and Hunterian Art Gallery) are either side of Kelvingrove Park, about 1½m W of George Square, while Victoria Park with its unique Fossil Grove is the same distance westward again. The round can conveniently be made by bus, or even by car, and at least a whole day should be allowed if the above are to be given the attention they deserve. A choice of buses run W from the city centre along Sauchiehall Street and Argyle Street to the Art Gallery and Museum.

Kelvin Hall, opposite the Art Gallery and Museum, a large hall formerly used for exhibitions, sports events and similar activities, is to open in 1988 as the new home of the Museum of Transport.

The **Art Gallery and Museum** occupy a palatial red sandstone building of 1901 by J.W. Simpson and Milner Allan. Open Mon.–Sat., 10.00 to 17.00. Sun., 14.00 to 17.00. Tel: 041-3573929. Free. A good ground plan is available free of charge.

The *Art Gallery*, with Britain's finest civic collection of British and European paintings, is spread over two wings on the first floor, the E wing housing British and the W wing Continental works. The balconies are in general devoted to applied art, with sculpture (Rodin, Epstein and several others), ceramics, silver and jewellery, while the corridors show water colours, drawings and prints. In almost all categories the collection is larger than the display space and the exhibits are therefore changed from time to time.

The most publicised and popular painting is Salvador Dali's Christ of St. John of the Cross, normally awarded an individual balcony setting. Painted in 1951 at Port Lligat, Spain, the artist has stated that the picture was inspired by the 16C drawing of the Crucifixion by the Spanish Carmelite friar who became known as St. John of the Cross. The landscape is Port Lligat; the figure on the left derives from a drawing by Velazquez, and that by the boat from the detail of a peasant in a painting by Le Nain. Dali has also stated that his aim was to avoid the usual 'expressionistic and contortionist' portrayal and to achieve instead a Christ who 'would be beautiful as the God that he is'.

The Continental Wing comprises Italian, Flemish, Dutch and French galleries. Among the many outstanding Italian works are Giorgione's The Adultress brought before Christ, with Head of a Man, now separated but once the top right hand figure in the first picture; and Salvator Rosa's romantic landscapes. Flemish works include Nature adorned by the Graces (an interesting joint effort by Rubens and Jan Brueghel the Elder) as also paintings by such names as Jacob Jordaens, Van Dyck and David Teniers the Younger. The Dutch are represented by Rembrandt's A Man in Armour and, contrastingly, also by a good choice of genre works, Benjamin Cuyp's The Quack Doctor being a notable example. Although there are what amount to two French galleries, these are still inadequate for the extensive collection (Barbizon, Impressionist and Post-Impressionist) which includes, to mention only a few artists, works by Courbet, Corot, Millet, Monet and Degas.

The British Wing is split into four galleries: 16 to early 19C; Late 18 to early 20C; Glasgow artists, including Scottish watercolours; and Modern. Among the artists hanging here are Raeburn, Allan Ramsay, George Jamesone, Horatio McCulloch (a dramatic Glen Coe), William McTaggart (a delightful Grandmother's Pet), David Wilkie, Reynolds, Constable and Turner.

The *Museum* occupies the entire ground floor either side of the vast central hall with its organ (recitals). To the W the central gallery shows a collection of Arms and Armour of international repute, two particularly outstanding pieces being the Milanese 'Gothic' armour of c 1450, one of the oldest and most complete armours in Britain, and the unique Greenwich armour for man and horse of c 1550. Around the armour hall the gallery on the S is for Special Exhibitions, those on the W cover History, while that along the N is devoted to Archaeology with some particularly interesting models of Antonine Wall forts and reconstructions of Bronze Age cists, showing their contents as discovered.—In the E wing the theme of the central gallery is the Natural History of Scotland, around this being galleries devoted to Ethnography, Biology, Birds, World wildlife and Geology.

The University may be reached by walking across **Kelvingrove Park** (1852) lying either side of the river Kelvin. Originally laid out by Sir Joseph Paxton, the park has twice been used for international exhibitions (1888, 1901) as well as in 1911 for the Scottish National Exhibition. Within the park are a war memorial to the Scottish Rifles (P. Lindsay Clarke, 1924) and monuments to Carlisle, Lister and Kelvin. The university, spread pretentiously along its hill to the N, dominates the park from that side.

The main building (George Gilbert Scott) of **Glasgow University** is a vast late 19C Gothic edifice with a frontage of over 500ft and a tower and spire reaching to 300ft. (Campus: Mon.–Fri., 09.00 to 17.00. Sat., and Sun., 10.00 to 13.00. Tower: Fri. at 14.00. Tel: 041-3398855, Ext. 252).

The university was founded in 1451 mainly through the exertions of Bishop Turnbull who became the first principal. Classes met first in a crypt in the cathedral, then in a house, but after c 1460 in High Street, where, however, the accommodation was very humble until 1632 when the chief parts of the Old College were begun (see plaque in High Street opposite College Street). Here Adam Smith expounded his doctrines and Watt perfected his scientific discoveries. In 1870 the university moved to its present site, where today there are some 10,000 students.

The main buildings form two quadrangles, separated by a cloister of granite pillars which support the great Bute Hall, used for graduation and other functions. Other buildings of interest are the smaller Randolph Hall, the Tower and the War Memorial Chapel of 1929. Reminders of the Old College are the Lion and Unicorn balustrade in a stone stair opposite the Principal's Lodging in Professors' Square, and Pearce Lodge, at the university entrance, which incorporates stonework of the High Street frontage.

At the N end of the cloister (in which there is a plaque to James McGill, 1744–1813, student here and founder of McGill University, Montreal, Canada), are stairs up to the Hunterian Museum.

The *Hunterian Museum* (Mon.–Fri., 10.00 to 17.00. Sat., 09.30 to

13.00. Tel: 041-3398855, Ext. 221. Free) originated in a bequest by
Dr William Hunter (1718–83), Doctor of Medicine, Professor of
Anatomy in London and Physician Extraordinary to Queen Charlotte.
Opened in 1807, when the university was still in High Street, the
museum is the oldest in Scotland. Now housed here in the main
building of the university, the nucleus of the museum remains
Hunter's ‍collections of coins and medals, paintings, antiquities and
books, but it has since attracted many other and varied bequests.
The archaeological, geological and numismatic exhibits are notable,
as is also one on the history of the university and the achievements
of its staff and students. Special application must be made to see the
collections in the anatomical and zoological departments and in the
University Library Special Collections Department.

The *Hunterian Art Gallery (Mon.–Fri., 10.00 to 17.00. Sat., 09.30
to 13.00. Tel: 041-3398855, Ext. 221. Free, but fee for Mackintosh
House afternoons and Sat.) is entered from Hillhead Street immediately N of the university. Opened in 1980 and the recipient of
several awards, this gallery now houses the university's art collections,
of which William Hunter's bequest, with works by Chardin and
Stubbs, forms the core. Among major holdings are works by James
McNeil Whistler—paintings, drawings and prints, as also furniture
and personal items—and a notable collection of works by Scottish
artists of the 19 and 20C. Here too are the university's print collection,
the largest in Scotland; a sculpture courtyard displaying large modern
pieces; and—a major feature of the gallery—*Mackintosh House, a
reconstruction of three floors of the interiors of the major rooms of
the Glasgow home of the architect and designer C.R. Mackintosh
(1868–1928), incorporating original furniture and other features.

University Avenue skirts the N side of the main university building,
and buses from here run to Victoria Park, home of the Tree Fossil
Grove (Daily, 08.00, or 10.00 on Sun., to dusk). In 1887, when this
area was taken over as a park, the cutting of a path across an old
quarry revealed these erect stumps and other fragments of trees of
the carboniferous period of some 300 million or more years ago. What
is seen is not petrified wood, but casts formed by mud which set
within the bark. That these were trees of a species not known today
can be seen from their symmetrically forking roots; and these were
in fact the trees which after millions of years became the Clydeside
coal of today.—Victoria Park can be left by a small gate at this corner,
and buses from nearby Dumbarton Road return to the city centre.

C. South Glasgow

A comfortable half-day round can be made by bus and foot, visiting Queen's
Park (for the site of Mary, Queen of Scots', final defeat at the Battle of Langside)
and then Glasgow's justly famed Museum of Transport which, however, is
planned to move in 1988 to Kelvin Hall. Buses (for Victoria Infirmary) leave
from St. Enoch Square and at once cross the Clyde.

The Clyde is crossed by **Glasgow Bridge** (also known as Broomielaw
Bridge or Jamaica Bridge), a massive structure opened in its present
form in 1899. The first bridge on this site was erected in 1767–72,
and a second, by Telford, in 1833–36. Just downstream is the railway
bridge serving Central Station, while the bridge immediately below
this is George V Bridge, opened in 1928. The suspension bridge,

upstream, dates from 1871. After crossing the river the bus passes through or close to districts (Gorbals, and, to the E, Hutchesontown) where once notorious slums have been replaced by modern buildings. Here the *Citizens Theatre*, in Gorbals Street, now a repertory theatre, opened originally in 1878 as a music hall.

By *Victoria Infirmary* (in the district of Langside) a plaque on the corner of Battlefield Road and Sinclair Drive reads 'Battlefield. May 13, 1568', and at the top of Battlefield Road, in Battle Place, there is a memorial pillar.

Battle of Langside. Here, 11 days after her escape from Loch Leven and making for the shelter of loyal Dumbarton, Mary, Queen of Scots, was defeated by Moray. Much of the battle was fought in what was then the narrow street of the village of Langside, Mary's defeat being largely caused by disputes among her supporters and the incompetence or, it is sometimes suggested, defection of her commander, Argyll. She probably watched the battle, or at any rate awaited its outcome, from Court (or Queen's) Knowe in Linn Park, over a mile to the S (see also D. Other Districts of Glasgow), though it is known that at one stage she rode forward in a vain attempt to encourage her men. Although not of this actual battle, there is in the People's Palace an exquisitely executed print of 1588 illustrating a typical battle of this time.

A pleasant walk of about half a mile NW across the park reaches *Camphill House*, a costumes and textiles outstation of the Art Gallery and Museum. It is planned to open this as a museum in perhaps 1987, but in the meanwhile entry is restricted to persons with a special interest (Tel: 041-6321350).

Buses running N along Pollokshaws Road which here fringes Queen's Park soon stop at Albert Drive for the ***Museum of Transport** (Mon.–Sat., 10.00 to 17.00. Sun., 14.00 to 17.00. Tel: 041-4238000. Free. Note that in 1988 this museum is planned to move to Kelvin Hall, opposite the Art Gallery and Museum). Opened in 1964, in spacious premises adapted from what were once part of the municipal transport works, size has been no deterrent and most main forms of transport are represented here, ranging from bicycles and a painted, carved caravan of 1900 to six huge railway engines of 1886 to 1920. There is a comprehensive collection of trams, illustrating the whole span of this era of transport, and a generous variety of horsedrawn vehicles, commercial vehicles and motor cars. Other features are a shipping gallery (the Clyde Room), a subway gallery with a reconstructed station and two original coaches, and imaginative displays of old photographs enabling visitors to see in actual use many of the types of transport exhibited.

D. Other Districts of Glasgow

This section covers, in alphabetical order, places of interest not already included under the previous three sections.

There are also a number of outlying places which can conveniently be visited from Glasgow, but which are described along Routes. The principal such places are: On Rte 10—Livingstone Memorial, Blantyre. Bothwell Castle. On Rte 16—Paisley. Renfrew. Govan. On Rtes 20 and 21—Duntocher and Bearsden (Antonine Wall).

Botanic Gardens (Gardens: Daily, 07.00 to dusk. Kibble Palace: 10.00 to 16.45 in summer or 16.15 in winter. Glasshouses: 13.00, or 12.00

on Sun., to 16.45 in summer or 16.15 in winter. Tel: 041-2219600. Free). On the corner of Great Western Road and Queen Margaret Drive, to the N of the university and 2m NW of the city centre.

Founded in 1817 as the Royal Botanic Institute on a site in Sauchiehall Street (now Fitzroy Place), the gardens moved to their present site of 40 acres beside the river Kelvin in 1841 and were acquired by the city 50 years later. They early became famous because of the distinguished work of Sir William Hooker, then Professor of Botany at the university. The main range of *Glasshouses* contains a fine collection of orchids, begonias and tropical plants, while the striking *Kibble Palace*, with an exhibition on the Plant Kingdom, shows tree ferns and temperate plants. There are also a Herb Garden, with culinary and medicinal plants; a Chronological Border showing when common garden plants were introduced to cultivation in Britain; and a Systematic Garden with plants grouped in botanical families.

Calderpark Zoological Gardens (Daily, 10.00 to 17.00 or 18.00. Tel: 041-7711185. Fee) are 6m SE of the city centre, reachable by London Road (A74) and Hamilton Road.

The **Clydebank Museum** (Mon. and Wed., 14.00 to 17.00. Sat., 10.00 to 17.00. Tel: 041-9521416. Free) specialises in shipbuilding and sewing machines, of which there is a remarkable collection of over 600. The museum is in the Old Town Hall, Dumbarton Road, Clydebank, some 6m W of the city centre.

Crookston Castle (AM. Standard, but closed Wed. afternoon, and Fri. in winter. Fee) is 4m SW of the city centre, reached by Paisley Road and Crookston Road, then, after crossing the White Cart Water, Brockburn Road. A 14C stronghold of the Stewarts of Darnley, the ruin preserves walls and a tower and is surrounded by the 12C earthworks of the earlier castle built here by Robert Croc, whose name if little else has survived. The Stewarts of Darnley were ancestors of Henry, Lord Darnley, who married Mary, Queen of Scots, and the couple spent some days at this castle after their marriage.

Greenbank Garden (NTS. Daily, 10.00 to dusk. Garden advice given Thurs., 14.00 to 17.00 at the garden or by telephone. Tel: 041-6393281. Fee) is the garden of a Georgian house (no adm) of 1763. There are 2½ acres of garden and 13 acres of other grounds. Greenbank is 6m S of the city centre, off B767 which is off A77, the Kilmarnock road.

Haggs Castle (Mon.–Sat., 10.00 to 17.00. Sun., 14.00 to 17.00. Tel: 041-4272725. Free) is about 3m SW of the city centre at the SW end of St. Andrews Drive off the NE edge of Pollok Country Park. In origin of 1585 but much converted, Haggs is now a museum and centre 'with children in mind'. The theme here is the ways in which life has changed over the last 400 years, and an 18C cottage in the grounds now serves as an activities workshop, with facilities for spinning, weaving, candle making and suchlike.

Linn Park is 4m S of the city centre and 1m S of Queen's Park. Covering over 200 acres beside the White Cart Water, the park includes at its N tip the ruin of *Cathcart Castle*, abandoned in 1750, nearby being *Court Knowe* (or Queen's Knowe), perhaps the spot from which Mary, Queen of Scots, watched the battle in Langside.

BEARSDEN & MILNGAVIE A81

BISHOPSBRIG

Dawsholm
Park

KELVINDALE

MARYHILL

LAMBSHILL

A82 DUMBARTON

GREAT WESTERN ROAD

MARYHILL ROAD

BALMORE ROAD

Ruchill
Park

SPRINGBU

Royal Botanic
Gardens

Queen's
Cross

PARTICK

DUMBARTON ROAD

• University

Kelvingrove
Park

PORT DUNDAS

M8

KELVINSIDE

Central Area
(see large scale plan)

Cath +

GOVAN

PAISLEY ROAD

IBROX

A8

River Clyde

• Central Station

M8

A737 Crookston Cas M8

Glasgow
Rangers
FC

M8

PAISLEY ROAD

M8

M8

Glasgow
Green

Bellahouston
Park

A77

DRIVE

ST ANDREW'S

POLLOKSHIELDS

POLLOKSHAWS ROAD

AIKENHEAD

• Haggs Castle

Pollok
Country Park

• Burrell Collection

• Pollok House

Camphill
House

Queen's
Park

GOVANHILL

Victoria
Infirmary

• Hampden Park

LANGSIDE

KING'S PARK

BARRHEAD RD

KILMARNOCK ROAD

POLLOKSHAWS

CATHCART

CROFTFO

NEWLANDS

MERRYLEE

THORNLIEBANK

GIFFNOCK

Linn
Park

A77 Rouken Glen & KILMARNOCK   CLARKSTON

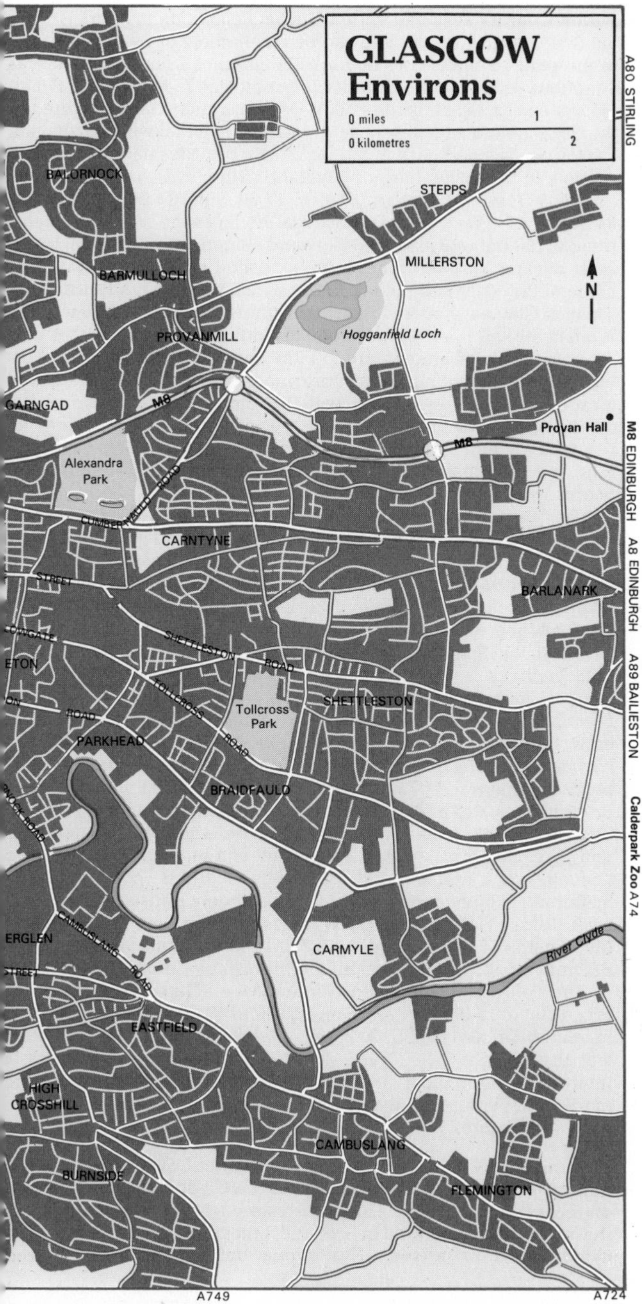

GLASGOW
Environs
0 miles 1
0 kilometres 2
A80 STIRLING
N
BALORNOCK
STEPPS
MILLERSTON
BARMULLOCH
PROVANMILL
Hogganfield Loch
GARNGAD
M8
Provan Hall
M8
M8 EDINBURGH
Alexandra Park
CUMBERNAULD ROAD
CARNTYNE
A8 EDINBURGH
STREET
BARLANARK
SHETTLESTON ROAD
ETON
TOLLCROSS ROAD
Tollcross Park
SHETTLESTON
A89 BAILIESTON
ROAD
PARKHEAD
BRAIDFAULD
Calderpark Zoo A74
CAMBUSLANG ROAD
ERGLEN
CARMYLE
River Clyde
STREET
EASTFIELD
HIGH CROSSHILL
CAMBUSLANG
BURNSIDE
FLEMINGTON
A749
A724

Pollok Country Park and Pollok House. *Pollok Country Park* is some 3m S of Glasgow Bridge and can be reached either by car or by bus to the park's Pollokshaws Road (A77) entrance from where there is a minibus service to the Burrell Collection (see E. below) and Pollok House, beside which is the Pollok Demonstration Garden. Gifted to the city, together with the house, in 1967 by Miss Maxwell Macdonald, the largely wooded park of 361 acres also provides nature trails and is home to the Pollok herd of Highland cattle.

Pollok House (Mon.–Sat., 10.00 to 17.00. Sun., 14.00 to 17.00. Tel: 041-6497547. Free), long an ancestral home of the Maxwells, dates from c 1750 but was extended (Rowand Anderson, 1890–1908) by Sir John Stirling Maxwell. The house is visited both as an interesting home of this style and period, for its stylish plasterwork (possibly by Thomas Clayton, Robert Adam's plasterer), and as the home of the William Stirling Maxwell collection of paintings. These, together with sculptures, are scattered around the several rooms which show furnishings—including musical instruments, books, silver, china and glass—some long associated with the house, others more recent acquisitions. Two useful booklets are available, one detailing the rooms and their contents, another identifying by numbers the paintings and sculptures. Additionally there are self-guide information boards in each room.

The *Paintings make up one of the most representative Spanish collections in Britain, the examples starting with a late 16C work by Jeronimo Cosida (San Ildefonso receiving the Chasuble) and then ranging across much of the field, among the more famous names being two religious works by Murillo, two pictures of boys at play by Goya, and two portraits by El Greco.

But if the Spanish enjoy pride of place, the British and Dutch schools run close, while names such as Hackaert, Signorelli, Guardi, Dughet, Jordaens and De Crayer represent the Germans, Italians, French and Flemish. The British representation is particularly strong in portraits, many of the Maxwell family (by, for example, Etty and Nicholson), while William Blake contributes five works and Hogarth provides a portrait of James Thomson, author of the words of 'Rule Britannia', as also a fascinating historical glimpse into the Tower of London in 1745. From the Dutch, there are landscapes by Jan Both and Claes Berchem, a delightful portrait of a small girl by Johan van Loenen, and a guitarist and listener by Godfried Schalcken.—The Sculpture, of both bronze and marble, is largely British (William Reid Dick, Alfred Gilbert and F.J. Williamson being among the artists), but Canada is represented by R.T. Mackenzie and, outstandingly, Belgium by two typical and striking bronzes by Constantin Meunier.

The *Pollok Demonstration Garden* (Mon.–Thurs., 08.00 to 16.00 Fri., 08.00 to 15.00. Sat., and Sun., 08.00 to 18.30 in summer or 16.00 in winter. Tel: 041-6329299. Free), adjacent to Pollok House in what was the estate's walled garden, offers a wide range of features of interest to both amateur and professional flower or vegetable gardeners. Throughout the year there is a programme of demonstrations and lectures.

Provan Hall (NTS, leased to Glasgow District Council. For opening inquire of Tourist Information) is N of the Clyde, in Auchinlea Park 4m E of the city centre. This well-restored 15C mansion, arguably the most perfect of its kind in Scotland, takes the form of two buildings either side of a courtyard. The original building, with a turret and stepped gable, was added to in the 17–18C, and an attractive wall garden adjoins.

602 (City of Glasgow) Squadron Museum (Wed. and Fri., 19.30 to 21.30. Tel: 041-8826201, Ext. 105. Donation), in Queen Elizabeth Avenue, Hillington, some 5m W of the city centre, is run by the Air Training Corps and tells the story of the local auxiliary squadron which achieved such a gallant and distinguished war record.

E. **The Burrell Collection

The Burrell Collection of decorative and fine art is brilliantly displayed in a specially designed building in Pollok Country Park (see D.), some 3m S of Glasgow Bridge, and can be reached either by car (ample parking) or by bus to the park's Pollokshaws Road (A77) entrance from where there is a minibus service every 20 minutes to Burrell and Pollok House. The walk through the park takes some 25 minutes. The Collection is open Mon.–Sat., 10.00 to 17.00. Sun., 14.00 to 17.00. Tel: 041-649715, Free.

Sir William Burrell (1861–1958) successfully combined the roles of wealthy Glasgow shipowner and compulsive and dedicated art collector, the former a prosperous inheritance, the latter an individual and self-taught passion of astonishing excellence, vision, range and scale. In 1916 he bought Hutton Castle near Berwick-upon-Tweed, a 15–16C keep and extension, the interior of which was during the following two decades sumptuously refurbished both as a home and as a setting for its owner's treasures. In 1944 Burrell and his wife donated the whole collection, by then totalling some 6000 items, to the city of Glasgow, a decision which, however, in no way reined his enthusiasm and by the date of his death in 1958 a further 2000 items had been added. Burrell in fact deliberately devoted his later years to strengthening areas he considered to be weak, notably the field of ancient civilisations, and in acquiring material which would add distinction to the museum he would in fact never see. For in making his gift, which was later accompanied by a large sum for a building, Burrell laid down stringent conditions, the essence of which was that the new museum was to be both close to Glasgow yet also in a rural setting; a seeming impossibility, resolved only in 1967 when Mrs Maxwell Macdonald presented the Pollok estate to the city.

The *Building*, designed by Barry Gasson and associates and opened in 1983, provides a fitting setting. Uncompromisingly yet unobtrusively modern in concept, it avoids all the drilled presentation of more conventional museums. Spacious yet always intimate, this is a place in which inviting vistas alternate with corners and surprises and sudden glimpses through medieval archways—the whole, moreover, set close against woodland, in spring a carpet of bluebells, which, for all that it is beyond a great glass wall, seems nonetheless as much a part of the Burrell experience as are the treasures on formal display.

A mezzanine is set aside for study material, but, this apart, the entire collection is at ground level, arranged, as can be seen from the ground plan, as six principal sections. Physically, though, the divisions are not as precise as might appear, and essentially this is a

BURRELL COLLECTION

Courtyard

Lecture Theatre

Temporary Exhibitions

Mezzanine
(Study Rooms)

- The Hutton Castle Rooms
- Ancient Civilisations
- Oriental Art
- Medieval & Post-Medieval European Art
- Paintings, Drawings & Bronzes
- Period Galleries

place in which to drift from one world into another rather than follow a disciplined path. Everything on display is admirably identified and explained. Nevertheless the paragraphs below visit each section in turn, elaborating modestly where judged helpful and indicating a few representative themes or items.

A service passage (shop, information, toilets) leads into the so-called Courtyard in which stands the massive Warwick Vase (not one of Sir William's acquisitions but a subsequent one by the Burrell trustees), once gracing Hadrian's villa at Tivoli and in more recent times a feature of the gardens of Warwick Castle.

Around the Courtyard are the three **Hutton Castle Rooms**, reconstructions of the drawing room, hall and dining room, the concept well explained by a notice in the Courtyard. It was Burrell's wish that the rooms into which he had worked some of his most valued acquisitions should be reproduced in the museum, and, as much for their size as for their sumptuous decoration and contents, they certainly provide a sobering picture of the castellar life still enjoyed by a magnate of good taste until only a few years ago. Panels, armorial decoration, heavy yet graceful and unfussy furniture, medieval sculpture, and, above all perhaps, priceless medieval tapestries and stained glass are the features here.

Ancient Civilisations here means Egypt, Mesopotamia (modern Iraq and Iran), Greece and Italy, and it was to the strengthening of this field that Burrell devoted much of his effort during his closing years. The *Egyptian* material forms the bulk of the collection—an exquisite small alabaster offering table and, by contrast, the heads of gods ('human' and animal), kings, queens and lesser men may be singled out—while the *Mesopotamian* collection, though relatively small, can in scope claim to be one of the most distinguished in Britain. Seals, always intriguing and always rewarding detailed study, represent workmanship of over 5000 years ago, while bronze work illustrates the 7C BC, amongst this a bull's head which has the added interest of being Burrell's final acquisition. From *Greece* and the eastern Mediterranean come the inevitable vases and jars of various periods, shapes and purposes, some attractive small statuary, and, from the later period (say the last 500 years BC) exquisite objects in gold such as a charming pair of bull's-head earrings. *Italy*, too, contributes pottery, notably a magnificent 4C BC Greek-style wine bowl (or krater) and, from the same period, an elaborate if perhaps inconvenient cup set into a sheep's head. The, later, Roman material includes stone sculpture and some superbly executed decorative mosaic.

The **Oriental Art** collection, the Burrell's largest and accounting for around a quarter of the whole, embraces the ceramic work of China and the Near East (this latter a wide belt of lands extending from Pakistan, Samarkand and Kabul in the E across to Istanbul, Cairo and Saudi Arabia in the W); the bronzes and jades, too, of China; the prints of Japan; and carpets from right across the Near East.

China's Pottery and Porcelain story spans from Neolithic to modern times, over the whole of which period of some 5000 years the country's skill and industry have rarely flagged and examples of most periods of which are shown here. Prominent, and certainly most publicised, is an almost life-size cross-legged Buddhist disciple (or lohan) of 1484, shaven, serene and smug. But from millenia before this there are painted and patterned Neolithic urns, and as the visitor tours the centuries recorded in this part of the museum he will find an impressive variety of subjects and colours and skills. A model storage tower, for instance, remarkable for its architectural detail and with purposeful figures on its external stair (from about the time of the birth of Christ); a sturdy, harnessed dog of about the same date; the inevitable horses and camels (largely Tang funerary, 618–907), as gorgeously decked out as are their human companions; fearsome tomb guardians of the 8C and others rather less intimidating of the Ming 14C era; and much handsome, sophisticated work in copper-red, blue and famille verte representing the later centuries.

The collection of *Near Eastern Ceramics* spans a shorter period, the 900 years between the 9 and 17C, but more than holds its own in deep richness of colour (notably turquoise for the twin practical reasons that it was not only readily to hand but also had a magic significance) and in daring yet distinctive design. Dishes and vessels of great variety predominate here in a dazzling display in which the design of each item repays detailed study, whether of the typically Islamic arabesques, of the gold leaf worked in with the dark cobalt of an elegant 12C Persian jug, or, by contrast, of two almost gaudy 17C Turkish jugs on which arabesques and blue-leafed flowers rest on tightly meshed blue, green and turquoise fish scales.

Aesthetically bronze can be a connoisseur taste and *Chinese Bronzes* are no exception, standing as they do in almost sombre contrast to the coloured exuberance of the ceramic. But if the ever-aging subtlety of the patina is perhaps lost on the layman, he can nevertheless enjoy the more obvious elegance and sometimes ingenuity of design as also the detail of the decoration. It may add interest to a study of the latter to look for specifics, such as dragons and also the masks (taotie) which, in a variety of forms, distinguish much ancient Chinese bronze (normally the masks, best identified by the eyes, are in twin mirrored parts). Eyes, for instance, stare out of the tripod legs which support an ingenious 11C BC food steamer, and also from the surface of what looks like a chamber-pot but is in fact a food vessel called a gui. For decoration perhaps the most important piece in the collection is a large cylindrical container (a lian, 1 or 2C BC), notable on a number of counts, such as the kneeling figures which support it, the masks holding the rings, and the decorative bands of birds in flight, birds walking and a delightful procession of stags and does. Finally, connoisseurs of weapons will note the crossbow mechanism, precisely dated to 147.

Chinese Jades. To the Chinese, jade. (geologically the term is imprecise and jade may turn out to be any of several valuable, hard stones) has long been a favoured medium, and, as was the case with ceramics, the material in this collection spans from Neolithic to modern times. Given the choice of stones, the shades, though always sober, have a subtle range, while the articles made embrace weapons, ornaments, vessels, small figures and ritual and funerary objects, these last because jade was popularly supposed to prevent body decay.

The Burrell's *Japanese Prints* are all of the 18 and 19C and thus represent the art's most mature period. They are perhaps something of an acquired taste, but most visitors will surely find it hard not to smile with the apparently happily inebriated fisherman smoking his long, thin pipe (probably a self-portrait by the artist Hokusai). The *Near Eastern Carpets* shown here in the Burrell span the 16 to 19C and richly reflect the decorative imagination and skill, not to mention infinite patience (frequently the work was, and still is, executed by children), of a broad swathe of lands stretching from India through Persia to Turkey.

The very broad heading **Medieval and Post-Medieval European Art** embraces not only the strongest, and by Sir William most favoured, element in the whole collection but also the widest range of art-forms, extending from imposing sculptured doorways down to delicate silver and glassware and even needlework. Within this bracket of excellence, perhaps the tapestries and stained glass, each allotted its own gallery, can claim the most formal distinction.

Sculpture and Church Art. The large doorways, such as the heraldic portal of Hornsby Castle (early 16C) and the late 12C portal from Montron in France, fantastically carved with foliage and beasts, can hardly be missed. But the emphasis here—and there are over 300 pieces—is on stone and wooden statuary, largely from England, Spain, Germany and the Netherlands, some figures being individual, others once parts of retables (altar backings). Each piece has its own character, and each demands attention, whether, for example, for the naive charm of the painted wooden figures of St. John and the Virgin

(13C, Spanish); or the poignancy of an early 16C German painted Lamentation; or the absorbed dedication expressed by Austrian 16C musician angels; or even the faintly comical, self-conscious group-photograph pose of the members of a late 15C English alabaster Adoration of the Magi.

In medieval times *Tapestries* were, to use the modern idiom, status symbols. Philip the Bold of Burgundy was, we are told, accounted immensely wealth with his 75. The Burrell Collection boasts over 150 (many displayed in the tapestry gallery and the Hutton Castle rooms), a world-famous assemblage ranging in date from a fragment of 1300 up to the 16C and with provenance from most of the major weaving centres, such as Germany, France, Burgundy and the Netherlands. If the heraldic designs hanging in the Hutton Castle rooms perhaps strike one as pretentious, there are plenty of others which can delight and even amuse. The sheer, idyllic innocence, for instance, of two young lovers hunting Fidelity (German, 15C); the purposeful and obviously well planned diligence of a group of peasants after rabbits (Franco-Burgundian, perhaps Tournai, 15C; sadly this tapestry shows only the start of the hunt—the setting of the nets—and journeys to San Francisco and Paris would have to be made to enjoy the actual hunt and the picnic that followed); or, in the Hutton Castle Drawing Room, a fashionably attired lady (Charity), improbably balanced astride an elephant and about to be anything but charitable as she prepares to cut down Envy, a craven little fellow allowed only a dog as a mount.

The Burrell's collection of more than 600 panels of *Stained Glass* is as world-famed as is its tapestry. The emphasis is on northern European work of the 15–16C and the glass is admirably displayed both in the Hutton Castle rooms and in a special gallery. For many people stained glass is perhaps instinctively associated with cathedrals and churches with their often stylised sacred themes. Here, though, the visitor also has the opportunity to enjoy lay themes, some of such panels revealing charming glimpses of contemporary everyday life.

The glass in the Hutton Castle rooms is both heraldic and religious, an interesting example (English) of the former, if only because the oldest, being a Dining Room pair of shields (first window on the left giving on the Courtyard) showing the royal arms and those of the Clares and dating back to the 13–14C. Less ancient (1537–47) are the roundels in the Hall framing several shields of arms, amongst these those of Henry VIII, Jane Seymour and their son the Prince of Wales. In the Hall, too, are three 15–16C German religious panels, one showing an Adoration of the Magi which can interestingly be compared with the alabaster rendering of the same date referred to above. Plenty more rich glass, some heraldic, some religious, graces the Drawing Room, much of this being English, as, for example, two 15C vertical strips showing St. Peter and an archbishop, each watched over by angels.

The subjects in the Stained Glass Gallery are of refreshing variety. Here a seated Solomon receives a kneeling Queen of Sheba (German, late 15C); St. Nicholas, protector of scholars, merchants and sailors, tries to halt a mass execution (Netherlands, early 16C); a prissy Princess Cecily, daughter of Edward IV, shows her displeasure (English, c 1485); a man toasts his toes before his fire (English, late 15C); and a Dutchman is seen busy at his task of making tiles

(Netherlands, 17C).

Burrell's enthusiasm and taste ranged freely over much of the virtually infinite field of *Decorative Art*. His emphasis, though, tended to be on British examples of the 16–17C, a period in which Elizabethan and Restoration verve bracketed the brief years of simpler Commonwealth taste. Decorative Art exhibits, although largely in the Medieval and Post-Medieval area, will also be found in other parts of the museum, notably in the Hutton Castle rooms and in the three Period Galleries (see below). Among the forms represented are silver, ceramics, carved and decorated wood, glass and needlework, with also, to a more substantial physical scale, arms and armour and furniture.

Three **Period Galleries**—Elizabethan, 17–18C and Gothic Domestic—in part separate the Medieval and Post-Medieval European Art area of the museum from **Paintings, Drawings and Bronzes**, a field in which Burrell's tastes were conservative, or at any rate cautious. Here, although the collection's essential strength is 19C French, the total spread in fact is wide, reaching back to 15 and 16C masterpieces by Memling and the elder Cranach and at the other end of the scale touching the present century with the muted works of the Hague School (Anton Mauve and the Maris brothers). In between, the 17C Dutch find a distinguished place, éxemplified by Rembrandt's Self Portrait of 1632 and Franz Hals's confident, patrician Gentleman of 1639.

The French paintings, including Impressionists, embrace a galaxy of names. Le Nain groups his rather surprisingly well dressed peasant children, even if one is without shoes. Géricault is here with his 'romantic' Prancing Grey Horse. Courbet's grotesque Dickensian Charity of a Beggar contrasts with Millet's gentle little shepherdess. Manet's blousy ladies quaff their beer; Boudin, Sisley and Cézanne provide sea and landscapes, Degas his usual horses and always charming young ballet dancers.

As to Sculpture, Burrell's taste in bronzes was as cautious as his attitude to paintings. No abstract compositions will be found here, but there is a place for such as Meunier, Rodin and a disciplined Epstein.

V EAST CENTRAL

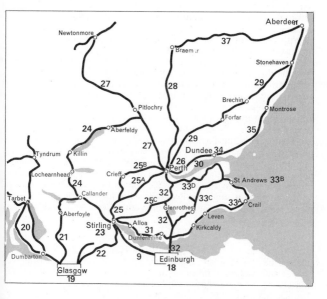

East Central Scotland extends as a broad belt from Loch Lomond in the W clear across the country to the E coast. From S to N, from a narrow, thickly populated urban and industrial base between Glasgow and Edinburgh, it fans out into undulating farming land which in turn shades off into the wooded foothills, or braes, through which lovely valleys climb gradually into empty Highland moor, loch and mountain. Yet, despite this' Highland North, East Central Scotland, as a whole, is essentially Lowland in character.

In ancient times this was the land of the earliest Scotsmen, the Picts, people of unknown origin who had been established here, and in the Highlands behind, long before the Irish, Welsh and Angles began moving into the South West and South East (say, 5 and 6C). The Romans came during the 1 and 2Cs, establishing their great marching camps and defeating the tribes at Mons Graupius, the site of which may have been the high ground above Stonehaven. But they did not stay long in the N, soon withdrawing behind their Antonine Wall between the Forth and the Clyde, and with their departure Pictland began to take shape, with its own kings, one of whom, Brude, in 685 at the battle of Nectansmere near Forfar, decisively defeated the Northumbrians and put a stop to their northward expansion. Christianity began to spread (the evidence is still to be seen in the many sculptured stones), and then in c 843 came the big change when Kenneth Macalpine united his western kingdom of Dalriada to that of Pictland, thus laying the first foundation on which the single kingdom of Scotland would grow. For some six centuries East Central Scotland remained the country's heartland—Perth was the capital and the kings were crowned at nearby Scone—and even after the transfer of the capital to Edinburgh in the mid 15C places such as Dunfermline, Stirling and Falkland remained favourite royal residences, while St. Andrews retained the spiritual primacy of Scotland down to the Reformation, when it became a centre of extreme religious persecution.

With such a background, and bordered by the Highlands, untamed until after Culloden, it is not surprising that this part of Scotland is rich in places of historical and other interest, far too numerous to list. Despite this richness—or perhaps because there is so much, so scattered—East Central Scotland has never really established itself as a touring region in its own right. Rather it is regarded by many as a belt (though an interesting one) to be crossed on the way N to whichever of the 'gateways' to the Highlands has been chosen. Of these 'gateways', the main five are outlined below and suggestions are made regarding principal places of interest—historical, scenic, modern and other—along the way. **Stirling**, central and with its famous castle, is taken as the common starting point. Close to Stirling are the site of the *Battle of Bannockburn*, where Bruce won Scotland's independence from England (NTS Visitor Centre); *Doune Castle* which, more than any other, conveys what life in such a place may have been like; *Doune Motor Museum*; and *Scotland's (Blair Drummond) Safari Park*.

1. **Loch Lomond** (Rte 20). This is the road likely to be chosen by those heading for Glencoe and the W Highlands and islands. At Tarbet, on the loch, an alternative road leads into the attractive Cowal and Kintyre peninsulas, and at Crianlarich, farther N, there is a choice between continuing NW, or instead bearing E for Loch Tay and the Central Highlands. Loch Lomond can be approached by way of Erskine Bridge across the Clyde, through Glasgow, or from Stirling along A811. The famous name 'Loch Lomond' apart, the attraction of this route is mainly scenic. However, if the approach is made from Erskine Bridge or Glasgow, two sites of interest are passed. At *Bearsden*, a NW suburb of Glasgow, some good sections of the Roman Antonine Wall can be seen, and at *Dumbarton* the impressively sited castle is worth a visit.

2. **Pass of Leny and Strathyre** (Rte 24). This is a useful road which, near Killin on Loch Tay, offers a choice between W and E. *Blair Drummond Safari Park* and *Doune*, with its castle and motor museum, can be visited soon after leaving Stirling, and at *Callander* a short diversion leads to *The Trossachs* and *Loch Katrine*, renowned beauty spots, the territory of Rob Roy, the early 18C Robin Hood, and the setting of Scott's 'Rob Roy' and 'The Lady of the Lake'. *Lochearnhead* is a centre for sailing and water-skiing, and on *Ben Lawers*, high above Loch Tay, there is an outstanding National Trust Visitor Centre in a mountain zone of exceptional geological and botanical interest.

3. **Sma' Glen** (Rte 25B). The glen—a pleasant, narrow valley climbing up to moorland—starts just E of Crieff which it links to Aberfeldy, where there is a choice between bearing W along Loch Tay or E for Pitlochry and the main A9. Along or close to the short stretch between

Stirling and Crieff there are several places worthy of attention. *Dunblane* has a superb Norman-Gothic cathedral, and just to the E is *Sheriffmuir*, the site of the battle of 1715 which ended the Old Pretender's hopes. Some other places are the great Roman camp at *Ardoch*; a collection of vintage aeroplanes at *Strathallan*; a 12C Norman tower at *Muthill*; and, at *Innerpeffray*, Scotland's oldest public library (1691).

4. **Pitlochry and Glen Garry** (Rte 27). This road (A9) is Scotland's main S–N artery and carries heavy traffic. From Stirling it runs NE to Perth, after which it heads N for Pitlochry, after which it climbs through wooded Glen Garry on to desolate high moor before descending to meet the Fort William-Spey Valley road (Rte 50) at Newtonmore. Stirling to Perth is described as Rte 25, and the town of Perth as Rte 26. Nearby *Scone Palace*, although 19C, retains medieval parts and has ancient associations, mainly with the crowning of Scotland's kings. North of Perth, places worth noting are *Dunkeld*, with a ruined but beautiful cathedral and a street of restored 17C houses; *Loch of the Lowes*, a nature centre where ospreys may be seen; *Pitlochry*, in lovely surroundings of loch and wood, with a fish-pass (observation chamber) and, at *Killiecrankie*, a National Trust for Scotland Visitor Centre which explains the battle here (1689) which, with that at Dunkeld three weeks later, ended the hopes of James VII/II and assured the position of William and Mary; and *Blair Castle*, the last castle in Britain to be besieged.

5. **Glenshee and Cairnwell Pass** (Rte 28). This is the route for those aiming for Royal Deeside and NE Scotland. *Cairnwell Pass* (2199ft) is the highest main road pass in Britain. *Scone Palace* (see above) is passed just N of Perth, but after this the road's interest is mainly scenic.

There remain two areas of East Central Scotland, the E Coast and Fife, tours through both of which can conveniently be combined by using the Tay bridge from Fife to Dundee. **Fife**, a self-contained touring district in its own right and well worth a diversion of a day or two, is described as Rte 33. Among its many places of interest are *Dunfermline*, where Bruce and other Scottish kings lie buried in the abbey; *Falkland Palace*, a historic Renaissance-style royal dwelling; the string of picturesque small fishing ports between Elie and Crail; and *St. Andrews*, with its famous ruined cathedral and castle, Scotland's oldest university, and the world's premier golf club. The **East Coast**, including the inland road through Forfar and Brechin, though of limited scenic worth unless diversions are made N into the many lovely glens, compensates by having along its roads an almost unbroken succession and variety of places worth visiting. These are covered under Rtes 29 and 35. The choice includes unique collections of Early Christian Pictish sculptured stones at *Meigle*, *Aberlemno* and *St. Vigean*; historic great castles such as intact *Glamis* and ruined *Dunnottar*, as well as the lesser castles of *Claypotts* and *Edzell*, this last with a famous early 17C walled pleasance; earth-houses, unusual for being associated with huts, at *Ardestie* and *Carlungie*, near Dundee; and ancient religious establishments such as the priory at *Restenneth*, the great red sandstone abbey of *Arbroath* and the famous round tower at *Brechin*.

20 Glasgow to Tyndrum

A82 (with A814 alternative).—Beyond Balloch the main road
follows the beautiful W shore of Loch Lomond into increasingly
Highland scenery. This road can be crowded in summer, especially
beside Loch Lomond, and A814 from Dumbarton via Helensburgh
and rejoining A82 at Tarbet offers a highly scenic alternative only
some 4m longer.

SOME HOTELS. **Balloch**. *Balloch*, G83 8QL. Tel: (0389) 52579.
Luss. *Colquhoun Arms*. Tel: (043686) 282. **Garelochhead**.
Garelochhead. Tel: (0436) 810263. **Inverbeg**. *Inverbeg Inn*, G83
8PD. Tel: (043686) 678. **Tarbet**. *Tarbet*, G83 7DE. Tel: (03012) 228.
Ardlui. *Ardlui*. Tel: (03014) 243. **Crianlarich**. *Allt-Chaorain House*.
FK20 8RU. Tel: (08383) 283. **Tyndrum**. *Inverey*, FK20 8RY. Tel:
(08384) 219.

Total distance (A82) 51m.—*10m* **Dumbarton**.—*5m* **Balloch**.—*16m*
Tarbet.—*16m* **Crianlarich**.—*4m* **Tyndrum**.

A82 leaves **Glasgow** (see Rte 19) as Great Western Road, passing
the Botanic Gardens and in *8m* from the city centre reaching the
road complex marking the N end of *Erskine Bridge* (see Rte 16). Here
the elegantly functional bridge, the railway and the skeins of fast,
purposeful traffic combine as a wholly modern ambience, yet the
map entry 'Roman Fort' beside *Old Kilpatrick* just below reminds
that it was here that the Antonine Wall met the river, while the strip
of the *Forth Clyde Canal* (see Rte 9) closely paralleling the shore
survives as a feat of traffic engineering as acclaimed in 1790 as was
Erskine Bridge in 1971. But of the Roman presence at Old Kilpatrick
there are now but scanty traces, the nearest significant Antonine
remain being at *Duntocher*, 2m E, where there is a rampart base. A
short way beyond Erskine Bridge *Auchentoshan Distillery* (Mon.–Fri.,
09.00 to 12.00. 14.00 to 16.00. Tel: 0389-78561. Free) provides a dram
at the end of a guided tour which covers brewing, distilling and
warehousing. The Forth-Clyde Canal joins the Clyde at (*1m*) *Bowling*
where the canal's basin, once busy with industrial barges, now serves
as a recreational marina. A short mile to the W, by a castle ruin on
the shore, the Bell Obelisk honours Henry Bell (1767–1830), engineer
of the 'Comet' which, built across the water at Port Glasgow, was the
first Clyde passenger steamer. And here, abruptly broadening, the
Clyde matures from the river to estuary.

1m **Dumbarton** (23,000 inhab. *ECl.* Wed.) is of interest for its
historic and theatrically sited **Castle* (AM. Standard. Fee), visually
best appreciated from a distance but also rewarding those who climb
the 200ft to the top with far-reaching river and moorland views.

History. The name Dumbarton, a corruption of Dun Bretane, the Fort of the
Britons, establishes the antiquity of this place which was probably the birthplace
of St. Gildas (c 316–70) as also of St. Patrick (c 387–461), the latter being
captured here by raiders in 405 and sold into captivity in Ireland. By the 13C
the British dun had become a royal stronghold, the governor of which in 1305
was that Sir John Menteith who, if the verdict of tradition is accepted,
treacherously captured Wallace and probably brought him here before the long
journey to London and a cruel execution.
    It was from here in 1548 that Mary, Queen of Scots, then a child of five, was
sent to France, escorted by a French fleet all the way to Roscoff in Brittany. In
1571, despite their sovereign's final flight to England, Dumbarton was still held

by Mary's adherents who, however, were overcome by a daring attack by 100 men who, at dead of night, scaled the least accessible face of the rock using ladders and ropes; and when, so the story goes, one of the band took vertigo and froze, he was lashed to the ladder which was then turned round so that his companions could climb past him. So total was the surprise achieved that none of the attackers was killed and only four of the garrison. But John Hamilton, Archbishop of St. Andrews, was less fortunate; taken in the attack, he was accused of complicity in the murder of Darnley and Regent Moray and four days later hanged at Stirling. In 1707, under the Treaty of Union, it was declared that Dumbarton should be maintained as one of the chief fortresses of Scotland.

The castle sprawls over much of a large, isolated basaltic rock which lifts abruptly from the shore of the Clyde and is cleft into two summits, the higher of which is known as Wallace's Seat. It is entered from the seaward side, the landward approach having been destroyed, near the entrance being a sundial presented by Mary, Queen of Scots. From the former Governor's House (1735–1832) a daunting flight of steps climbs within the cleft, passing the so-called Wallace's Guardhouse, on which a gable terminates in a crude head of Sir John Menteith, with his finger in his cheek, the conventional sign of betrayal. Beyond, the steps continue E past two gun batteries to reach the magazine; and W to the site of the White Tower, from which point there is a view (orientation table) which Dorothy Wordsworth, at any rate, judged to be 'sufficient recompense' for the climb.

Of interest in the town, in Church Street, is a tower arch of the collegiate church of St. Mary, founded by the Duchess of Albany in 1454 and re-erected in 1850.

Dumbarton to Tarbet via Helensburgh.

It was at (*4m*) *Cardross* that Bruce died in 1329, probably a victim of leprosy. *Kilmahew Chapel*, ½m N on Darleith Road, beyond the golf course, was dedicated to St. Mayhew, a companion of St. Patrick, as long ago as 535; the present building, dating from 1467 and derelict since c 1840, was restored for parish use in 1955.

4m **Helensburgh** (13,000 inhab. *ECl.* Wed. *Inf.* Pier Head Car Park. April–Sept. Passenger ferry link to Gourock) is a residential and resort town of both dignity and character, named after the wife of Sir James Colquhoun of Luss who laid out the older part on a draughtboard pattern around the end of the 18C. Henry Bell (1767–1830), engineer of the 'Comet', the first Clyde passenger steamer (see also Rte 16, Port Glasgow), who lived and died here, is commemorated by an obelisk as also by the anvil and flywheel of the 'Comet', both of which are preserved in Hermitage Park. J.L. Baird (1888–1946), pioneer of television, was a native (bust) as was also the distinguished Glasgow architect, C.R. Mackintosh, whose memorial here is the *Hill House* (NTS. Daily, 13.00 to 17.00. Fee). Built in 1904 for the publisher W.W. Blackie, the house, which contains Mackintosh furniture and other material, is accepted as perhaps the most outstanding example of Mackintosh's domestic architecture.—In *Rhu*, a northern suburb of Helensburgh, Henry Bell is buried beside the church.

A814 now hugs the shore of Gare Loch which, sheltered and less than a mile wide, was an important Combined Operations base during the last war and today still serves both civil and naval maritime needs with shipbreaking yards at *Shandon* and a submarine base at (*6m*) *Faslane*. From this latter a minor road leading NE in under 2m enters *Glen Fruin*, peaceful and pretty enough today but a valley

long bloodily and legally infamous in the feud between the
MacGregors and the Colquhouns.

The battle fought here in 1603 was a typical example of the disputes that could
arise out of 'sheepskin grants' (see Aspects of Scotland, Clans). The MacGregors
held their lands by clan tradition, but the Campbells, flaunting an official grant,
demanded rent from the MacGregors and, when this was refused, began to
seize land. The impotent MacGregors could only live by cattle stealing, on one
occasion raiding Colquhoun land at Luss on Loch Lomond. The Campbell chief
encouraged the resultant bitterness and on 18 February 1603 the MacGregors
and Colquhouns met here in Glen Fruin. Not only were many of the Colquhoun
men killed, but a number of their onlookers (sons of the gentry of the district),
who had been shut in a barn for safety, were massacred in cold blood by the
victors. Sixty Colquhoun widows appeared before James VI at Stirling, each
with the bloody shirt of her husband in her hand, and the king was so moved
that he outlawed the MacGregors and proscribed their very name. Not until
1663 was the act of outlawry reversed by Charles II, as a reward for services
rendered to Montrose, but it was renewed in 1693 by William III, and full legal
rights were not finally restored until 1755, under George II.

1m **Garelochhead**, from where a road drops S to round the Rosneath
peninsula as far as Coulport. A small road across the centre of the
peninsula completes the circuit, while Kilcreggan, on the S shore, is
linked by passenger ferry with Gourock.—A814 now enters its most
scenic stretch, climbing to the watershed between Gare Loch and
Loch Long, a spot offering wide views which include, to the W, a
glimpse of the entrance to Loch Goil. Loch Long is reached at (*3m*)
Finnart, an oil port where large tankers may be moored close to the
road. Between here and (*7m*) **Arrochar** (see Rte 45) the road runs
with the lovely E shore of Loch Long, above which to the W towers
the lofty and lonely skyline of Argyll Forest Park.—*1m* **Tarbet** where
A82 is rejoined.

Dumbarton to Tarbet via Loch Lomond

Between Dumbarton and Balloch at the S tip of Loch Lomond A82
imperceptibly ascends the valley of the Leven, only 5m long and
mainly given over to light industry. Once this was the land of the
Smolletts, and at (*2m*) **Renton** a monument, bearing a Latin epitaph
by Dr Johnson, commemorates the novelist Tobias Smollett (1721–71),
born at the family home of Dalquharn (pron. Dalwhan), ½m to the
S.—*2m* farther, **Alexandria**, with mill shops and a sheepskin factory,
has neither Greek nor Egyptian links but, less romantically perhaps,
traces its name back to an Alexander Smollett.

   1m **Balloch** (*ECl.* Wed. *Inf.* Car Park. April–Sept.), virtually
continuous with Alexandria, is a popular resort and recreation focus
straddling the outflow of the river Leven from Loch Lomond. The
attractive *Balloch Castle Country Park*, on the E side of the outflow,
offers woodland and lakeside walks, a nature trail and a moated
mound marking the site of ancient Balloch Castle, while at the
modern (19C) castle there is a local Interpretation Centre (Tel:
0389-58216).

   Loch Lomond, 24m long and varying in width between 5m in the
S and well under 1m in the N, is the largest stretch of inland water
in Britain as also one of the most varied and beautiful. To the N the
loch quickly narrows before piercing into the Highlands as a narrow
finger below ranges of high mountains, these including Ben Lomond
(E) and Ben Vorlich (W), both over 3000ft. In the S, by contrast, the
waters are broad and broken by many islands and islets while the

shores—those 'bonnie banks' of ballad (see below)—wash modest pastoral and wooded scenery backed by green hills and more distant mountains. *Inchmurrin* (Isle of Spears) is the largest island, with, at its S end, the ruins of Lennox Castle, retreat of the unfortunate Duchess of Albany after the wholesale execution of her husband, sons and father. Both this island and *Inchlonaig* (Marsh Island), opposite Luss, were once used as places of internment for the chronically drunk and insane. *Inchcailloch* (Island of the Old Women), off Balmaha, was the burial place of the MacGregors who long took their oaths on those that slept 'beneath the grey stone of Inchcailloch'. This island, together with adjacent *Clairinsh* and others, forms a national nature reserve (see below).

Some History. The loch's ancient name was Leven, whence the surrounding lands came to be known as Levenox or Lennox, and the leading clans were the MacGregors and the Colquhouns, who in 1603 met in bloody conflict in Glen Fruin (see above). Magnus, King of Man, son-in-law of Hakon, is said to have dragged his galleys across the narrow isthmus from Arrochar on Loch Long to Tarbet in 1263 and to have harried the startled dwellers around the loch while Hakon was meeting defeat at Largs. Bruce is popularly supposed to have found refuge in Rob Roy's Cave at Inversnaid in 1306, the cave's name recalling that Robert MacGregor (Rob Roy) was the most colourful local figure in the early 18C. At about the same time, in 1715, the MacGregors, ever ardent Jacobites, seized every boat on the loch and assembled them at Inversnaid, where, however, they were speedily repossessed by a Hanoverian force that had dragged some armed boats up the Leven. In 1959 Commander Forsberg swam the length of the loch in 15 hours and 31 minutes.—The popular ballad, 'The Bonnie Banks o' Loch Lomon', the lament of a Scottish soldier dying far from home, recalls the long-held belief that, on death, the spirit returned home underground ('the low road').

Boat Excursions. Operating out of Balloch the 'Countess Fiona' cruises the loch once or twice daily according to season. Cruises last between 4½ and 5 hours, calls being made at Luss, Rowardennan, Tarbet and Inversnaid. Connecting trains from Glasgow Queen Street to Balloch Pier. Further information from Alloa Brewery Ltd, Anderston House, 389 Argyle Street, Glasgow. Tel: (041) 2264271. For recorded information on space availability, timetables etc. Tel: (041) 2482699. Last minute information from Balloch Pier, Tel: (0389) 52044.—Services are also provided by the two ships of Loch Lomond Sailings, Balloch Marina. Tel: (0389) 51481.—For boats from Balmaha see below.

The main A82, followed by this Rte, travels the entire length of the W shore of Loch Lomond, but the small road along the E shore ends at Rowardennan. This latter, providing a rewarding diversion, is described immediately below.

BALLOCH TO ROWARDENNAN (18m). The road (A811) from Balloch to (8m) *Drymen* runs well inland of the loch shore and is of no great scenic or other interest. From Drymen (where, see below, intending visitors to the Loch Lomond Nature Reserve may wish to apply for information) B837 in 4m reaches the loch at **Balmaha**, a prettily situated village looking out to the group of wooded islands (Inchailloch, Clairinsh, Torrinch, Creinch and Aber) which, together with a small area on the mainland on the S bank of the Endrick Water, make up the *Loch Lomond National Nature Reserve* (semi-natural deciduous woodland; aquatic invertebrates; botanical rarities; wintering wildfowl). Access to Inchcailloch, with a nature trail, is unrestricted to the casual visitor. Further information from the Warden, 22 Muirpark Way, Drymen. For mail boat cruises, island cruises and boats to Inchcailloch, apply MacFarlane and Sons. The

Boatyard, Balmaha. Tel: (036087) 214. Balmaha enjoys the additional attraction of being on the western fringe of Queen Elizabeth Forest Park (see Rte 21), two official forest walks of which start from the village car park.

Northward from Balmaha a narrow, minor road keeps close to the loch, passing Forestry Commission picnic sites and waymarked walks, to reach (6m from Balmaha) the road's end at **Rowardennan**. From here one path continues N along the shore, while another, starting from the pier picnic place and car park, climbs the steep, grassy slope to the summit of Ben Lomond (3192ft. 3½ miles, or maybe 3 hours, to the top). There is also a passenger ferry across to Inverbeg.

A82, leaving the W outskirts of Balloch, in *1m* reaches the wildlife park and leisure area of **Cameron Loch Lomond** (April–Oct; Daily, 10.00 to 17.00. Tel: 0389-53533. Fee), a place which owes its name not to the Cameron clan but to a corruption of the Gaelic 'cam sron' (crooked nose), a small peninsula hooking into the loch. The estate, long the home of the Smolletts, now offers bears and monkeys, the largest model train layout in Scotland, boating and other attractions. *Cameron House* (no adm.), on the site of a 14C house, had developed into a mansion by the 18C and was extensively rebuilt and enlarged after a fire in the 19C.—*5m Rossdhu* (no adm.), a name meaning Black Point, was long a seat of the Colquhouns whose 15C castle was replaced in 1773 by a house attributed to Robert Adam.—*2m* **Luss**, a pretty village enhanced by occupying one of the loveliest sites along this side of the loch, preserves in its church a 14–15C effigy of St. Kessog, a local evangelist of the 6C. A scenic road, affording unequalled views of the loch and its islands, ascends for 2m up Glen Luss.

Now close beside the water, A82 in *3m* reaches *Inverbeg*, offering a hotel, a passenger ferry across to Rowardennan, and a small, lonely road westward by way of Glen Douglas to Loch Long.—*15m* **Tarbet**, a modest summer centre, stands at the E end of the 1½m-wide isthmus, today with a main road and a railway, across which Magnus, King of Man, hauled his galleys in 1263. For Tarbet (Arrochar) to Lochgilphead and Kintyre, see Rte 45.—With the loch on one side, and the railway and woodland on the other, A82 in *3m* arrives at *Inveruglas Power Station*, operated by water from Loch Sloy, 2m NW below Ben Vorlich. This Loch Sloy Scheme was the first project of the North of Scotland Hydro-Electric Board, the waters of its loch being doubled in volume by a dam. Across Loch Lomond can be seen Inversnaid and Rob Roy's Cave (see Rte 21).

Eilean Vow, reached in rather less than *3m*, is the next island, seat once of the Macfarlanes, the remains of whose castle still cling on, and the place also, or so it is said, where the far-seeing Bruce planted yew trees to ensure good bows for his descendants.—*2m* The village of *Ardlui* marks the head of Loch Lomond, here less than ½m wide, and the start of the glen of the river Falloch, wooded at first but the road soon entering a bleak mountain district, dotted with a few stunted survivors of the once great Caledonian Forest.—*8m* **Crianlarich**, popular with walkers and wildlife enthusiasts, stands at the junction of three fine Highland glens (Falloch, Fillan and Dochart) as also of the railway lines to Oban and Fort William. A85, bearing E up Glen Dochart, joins Rte 24 shortly before reaching Killin.

Now heading NW along Strath Fillan, and close beside the Oban railway, A82 parallels the Fillan Water, in which (roughly 3m from

Crianlarich) is *St. Fillan's Pool*, a holy pool to which lunatics were brought to be cured by a method which could hardly have been simpler. After being plunged into the water the patient was bound and then left overnight in a corner of *Strathfillan Priory*, still surviving as a ruin on the far bank of the river; if, next morning, the knots were still tied, a cure was judged hopeless, but if he had managed to free himself then he was considered bright enough to be accepted as sane. St. Fillan, of Irish origin, retired to this strath and died here after years spent as a hermit at Pittenweem where his cave can still be seen (see Rte 33A). Centuries later, Bruce took his arm-reliquary to Bannockburn and, attributing his victory to the saint, founded this Augustinian priory in 1314.

A short distance farther, approaching Tyndrum, the railway takes a pronounced SW loop, the area within being known as *Dalry* (King's Field) and providing another, earlier and more dramatic association with Bruce. Fleeing after his defeat at Methven in 1306, Bruce was attacked here by John MacDougall of Lorne, a kinsman of the Red Comyn, at the head of a swarm of Highlanders. One of these seized Bruce's plaid and, though mortally wounded, held on so firmly that Bruce was compelled to abandon the garment together with its brooch fastening. This Brooch of Lorne is still treasured at Dunollie (Oban), but Bruce's sword, lost in the same encounter, is said to have finished up in nearby Lochan nan Arm, the Loch of the Sword.

4m (from Crianlarich) **Tyndrum**, a village in very Highland surroundings, enjoys the distinction of having two railway stations, one for the Oban and one for the Fort William line. Earlier very different travellers passed this way, for Tyndrum was an important stage along the drover route from the N before it split to reach the great cattle markets at Falkirk (Stenhousemuir) and Crieff. Here at Tyndrum the road forks, A82 continuing N (as Rte 44A) to reach Fort William via Glen Coe, while A85 heads W (as Rte 44B), aiming for Oban and Fort William by way of Connel.

21 Glasgow (Edinburgh) to Aberfoyle and The Trossachs

From **Glasgow**. A81 to Aberfoyle. A821 to The Trossachs.—After Strathblane the road runs below Campsie Fells, a tract of moor rising to 1800ft, and then into cultivated country. Beyond Aberfoyle the scenery quickly becomes more wooded and Highland.—From **Edinburgh**, the Trossachs district is reached in 61m via Stirling (by-passed) and Callander. See Rtes 9 and 24.

SOME HOTELS. **Strathblane**. *Country Club*, Milngavie Road. Tel: (0360) 70491. *Kirkhouse Inn*, G63 9AA. Tel: (0360) 70621. **Aberfoyle**. *Covenanters Inn*, FK8 3XB. Tel: (08772) 347. *Forth Inn*, Main Street. Tel: (08772) 372. **Kinlochard**. *Forest Hills*, FK8 3TL. Tel: (08777) 277. **Inversnaid**. *Inversnaid*. Tel: (087786) 223.

Total distance 29m.—*10m* **Strathblane**.—*14m* **Aberfoyle**.—*5m* **The Trossachs**.

Glasgow (see Rte 19) is left by Maryhill Road for (*5m*) the northern suburb of **Bearsden**, near which can be seen good sections of the Roman Antonine Wall and of an associated bath-house. Here, at

Bearsden Cross, the main road is crossed by Thorn Road (W) and Roman Road (E), together tracing the course of the military way which here ran through one of the series of forts. Beyond the end of Thorn Road, at the highest point of Thorn housing estate (steps off Iain Road), will be found a length of rampart base, partly still with its stones, and ditch. East from Bearsden Cross, a few yards along Roman Road, are the remains of a bath-house, for over a century covered by houses until revealed as the result of demolitions in 1973. Roman Road continues E to *New Kilpatrick Cemetery*, where there are two well-cleared lengths of rampart base, complete with stones and considered to be the best examples of rampart base along the whole wall.

A809 out of Bearsden leads via Drymen to (16m) *Balmaha* at the SE corner of Loch Lomond, see Rte 20. On the way (6m) *Queen's View* is reached (Auchineden Hill, 1171ft), so called because it was from here that Queen Victoria had her first glimpse of Loch Lomond. From the car park there is a signposted path to (1m) a curious chasm known as *The Whangie*.

2m **Milngavie** (pron. Milguy) marks the northern limit of the Glasgow conurbation. Here the *Lillie Art Gallery* (Tues.–Fri., 11.00 to 17.00. 19.00 to 21.00. Sat. and Sun., 14.00 to 17.00. Tel: 041-9562351. Free) shows a permanent collection of 20C Scottish paintings, sculptures and ceramics, as also a series of temporary exhibitions, while the *Heatherbank Museum and Library of Social Work* (Tel: 041-9562687. Free) is just what its name implies and includes a reference library of over 5000 volumes. Above the town are the adjoining Mugdock and Craigmaddie reservoirs, together feeding Glasgow, to the N of the former being *Mugdock Country Park*, with the remains of a castle, once a principal seat of the Montrose family. Just E of Milngavie, seen from A807 across a small loch, is mid 16C Bardownie Castle.

Leaving Milngavie A81 rounds Craigmaddie Reservoir and drops into the Blane valley to reach (*3m*) **Strathblane**, lying below the SW shoulder of Campsie Fells, a long, volcanic moorland hump lifting to over 1800ft.

CAMPSIE FELLS. A scenic circuit of some 17m can be made by driving E to Lennoxtown and then N across the centre of the Fells to return to A81 by way of Fintry and Killearn. On the way to Lennoxtown the road almost at once crosses the Ballagan Burn, a short way up which the *Spout of Ballagan* cascades over a fine example of stratification where layers of sandstones, clays and slates succeed each other with an unusual regularity; while, on the other side of the road, the hillock of *Dunglass* provides more geology, here in the form of a volcanic vent with columnar basalt. *Craigend*, 2m E of Strathblane, was the birthplace of Sir Thomas Mitchell (1792–1855), Surveyor General of New South Wales and explorer of the Australian interior. The road across the Fells (B822; sometimes known as the Crow Road) tops 1064ft and affords fine views. And it is an ancient and historic road too, for, if the story is to be believed, it would have been over this Crow Road that St. Mungo and his bulls brought the body of Fergus (see Rte 19, Glasgow Cathedral). From *Fintry*, at the N end of the Crow Road, B818, running between Campsie Fells and the Endrick Water, completes the circuit, towards the end passing close to the village of *Balfron*, said to owe its name (Village of Sorrow) to the bizarre tradition that in some dark past all its children were devoured by wolves.

A81 continues NW along Strath Blane, in *3m* arriving at the junction with A875, ½m beyond which, on A81, *Moss* was the birthplace of George Buchanan (1506–82), humanist, reformer, historian and tutor to Mary, Queen of Scots, and, more significantly, to her son James VI. He is commemorated by a large obelisk in the straggling village of *Killearn*, just NE on A875.—*3m* A small crossroads at which a short diversion E to *Gartness*, where the Endrick Water flows through a ravine with a salmon leap, can be recommended.—*6m* A82 crosses the Kelty Water, then in another *1m* the Forth, beyond which it skirts the E fringe of Queen Elizabeth Forest Park to reach (*1m*) the junction with A821 on the edge of Aberfoyle.

Here, although this Rte now shifts to A821, a 3m-long diversion E along A81 should be considered by anyone with a feel for ancient monastic houses, touched by history and beautifully set. The objective is ruined **Inchmahome Priory**, built on an island in Lake of Menteith (AM. Standard, except closed Thurs. and Fri. in Oct–March. Fee for ferry. There is only one ferry, so some waiting may be necessary. Ferry liable to suspension in winter months).

Inchmahome means Isle of St. Colmoc or Macholmoc. Also sometimes called the Isle of Rest, it is the largest of the islands in the lake. The priory was founded for Austin Canons in c 1238 by Walter Comyn, Earl of Menteith. In 1362 David II was married here to his second wife, Margaret, and in 1547, after their defeat at Pinkie, the Scots here hid Mary, Queen of Scots, then aged five. She stayed until July 1548 when she was stealthily moved to Dumbarton, whence she sailed for France. After the Reformation ownership passed to the Earl of Mar.

Of the original 13C church, in which David II was married, there still remain a part of the choir, the tower arch and two arches of the nave. The deeply recessed mouldings of the W entrance are particularly noteworthy. In the chancel rests the tomb of Sir John Drummond (died 1390), and in the chapter house, partly rebuilt in the 17C, are those of Walter Stewart, Earl of Menteith, and his wife (died 1295 and 1286), presumably both placed here within about 50 years of the priory's founding. As to the spot known as Queen Mary's Bower, romantics will readily enough accept that this was the favoured playground of the little queen; others, that this was simply where the monks grew their vegetables.—The ruined castle on Inch Talla was long (1227–1694) a principal residence of the earls of Menteith.

The pleasant, overgrown and, it must be admitted, sometimes overcrowded village of **Aberfoyle**, with macabre mort-safes flanking the entrance to the ruined church, rightly regards itself as the gateway to a district which—embracing The Trossachs as also lochs Ard, Chon, Venacher, Achray, Katrine and Arklet—has achieved fame partly because of its varied scenery, partly because it was the territory of the early 18C 'Robin Hood' Rob Roy MacGregor, and partly because it provides the romantic setting for Sir Walter Scott's 'Rob Roy' and 'The Lady of the Lake'. Those familiar with Scott's works will readily recognise the many associations; others will enjoy the mountain, woodland, rock and loch scenery, most of which is part of *Queen Elizabeth Forest Park*. Covering 67 square miles of one of the most scenic tracts in central Scotland, and with many recreational facilities, trails and picnic areas, the forest—in fact three, for it divides into Buchanan, Loch Ard and Achray—is the essence of this district and the wise visitor will first make for the admirable Forestry Commission visitor centre *David Marshall Lodge*, 1m N of Aberfoyle (Mid March–mid Oct: Daily, 11.00 to 19.00. Tel: 08772-258. Free, but

fee for car park). Built by the Carnegie Trust, of which David Marshall
was chairman, the Lodge not only provides a wide range of information but includes also a large picnic area, trails and a viewpoint
commanding much of the valley of the upper Forth.

ABERFOYLE TO INVERSNAID (LOCH LOMOND). Before continuing N along
A81 it is worth considering, on the grounds of both scenery and
interest, a longish diversion along B829 to Inversnaid on Loch
Lomond. No circuit is possible (other than the minor road from
Kinlochard through Duchray and the heart of Loch Ard Forest), and
the distance to Inversnaid and back is some 30 slow miles. As will
be seen at the beginning of this Rte, there are hotels at Kinlochard
and Inversnaid. There are also Forestry Commission picnic sites and
waymarked walks at Balleich, just outside Aberfoyle, at Renagour
and Kinlochard on Loch Ard, and at each end of Loch Chon.

B829 runs along the N shore of wooded *Loch Ard* with, on an islet
off the S shore, the foundations of a castle owned by Murdoch, 2nd
Duke of Albany, beheaded in 1425. *Loch Chon*, reached 2m after
Kinlochard, though also wooded, is rockier and wilder than Loch
Ard. *Stronachlachar*, 2m beyond Loch Chon, is the pier at the W end
of Loch Katrine (see below). Rob Roy was born at Glengyle, 2m NW
of here (no cars), and his wife, Helen, is popularly supposed to have
been born in Glen Arklet, now largely filled by *Loch Arklet*, doubled
in size since becoming a reservoir and now hugged by the unclassified
extension of B829. Near the descent to the narrow northern finger of
Loch Lomond a farm, still known as 'The Garrison', incorporates as
a sheepfold the remains of a fort, built in 1713 (and once commanded
by Wolfe, of Quebec fame) to overawe the unruly MacGregors. From
Inversnaid, on Loch Lomond opposite the power station of Inveruglas,
a lochside path wanders N (1m) to Rob Roy's Cave, rock crevices in
which Bruce is said to have hidden in 1306. This path continues to
the head of the loch and joins A82 (Rte 20) in Glen Falloch, while
another path leads S from Inversnaid to (7½m) Rowardennan, there
meeting Loch Lomond's E shore road from Balmaha (see also Rte 20).

Leaving Aberfoyle, and 1½m N of David Marshall Lodge, A821 arrives
at the entrance to *Achray Forest Drive* (March–Oct: Daily 10.00 to
18.00. Coin machine), a glorious 7m-long forest and mountain drive
touching four lochs. A route map indicates parking and picnic areas,
forest trails and a children's play area.

5m In a romantic setting of rocks and hummocks luxuriantly
covered with oak, birch, hazel, rowan and heather, **The Trossachs**
('the Bristly Country') is, properly, simply the short gorge linking
lochs Achray and Katrine. The 'old pass', the one known to Sir Walter
Scott, diverges as a footpath to the N of the present road at the T
junction, and in Scott's time there was no exit 'excepting by a sort of
ladder composed by the branches and roots of trees'. Along the
gorge, a road (no cars) diverges S beside the Achray Water to arrive
at the sluices of the Strathclyde Water Department, on the far side
of which rises *Bealach nam Bo* (the 'pass of the cattle'), through
which the MacGregors drove their cattle plundered from the
Lowlands.

Loch Katrine, 9m long and 1m broad at its widest, derives its
name, according to Scott, from the 'caterans' (freebooters) who once
frequented its shores. Since as long ago as 1859 it has been one of
the chief sources of water for Glasgow, a function which involved

the raising of the water level by 17ft.

The W end of the Trossachs road reaches the loch at a huge car and coach park, from which however little can be seen of the water. So the best course is to enjoy a cruise on the steamer 'Sir Walter Scott' which, built in Dumbarton in 1900, dismantled, and then reassembled on the loch, survives as a much loved and much used piece of vintage nostalgia (Mid May–late Sept: Up to three sailings daily, some calling at Stronachlachar. Tel: 041-3365333. Fee). An alternative is to follow the road on the N bank (no cars) for 1m to the *Silver Strand*, with a view described in 'The Lady of the Lake', the lady being the fair Ellen Douglas after whom the island here, Ellen's Isle, is named. Less romantically, this island was used as the cattle-pen and larder of the MacGregors who here hid their rustled herds.

A821, now heading E beside Loch Venacher towards Callander, has various Scott associations ('Rob Roy', 'The Lady of the Lake', and the ballad 'Glenfinlas, or Lord Ronald's Coronach'). This last was set in *Glen Finglas* which ascends N from Brig o' Turk at the W end of the loch. This glen was visited in 1853 by Ruskin and Millais, the visit recalled by a celebrated portrait of the former. About 1m up the glen the public road ends at the reservoir dam (1965), but a path continues along the E side of the water.

22   Glasgow to Stirling via Kilsyth

A803 to Kirkintilloch. B8023 to Kilsyth. A803 and M80 to Stirling.—After breaking clear of Glasgow and Kirkintilloch, and as far as Banknock (Bonnybridge), the road runs below the Kilsyth Hills (up to 1870ft) on the N and, to the S, the partly bare and partly wooded ridge which carries the Antonine Wall.

SOME HOTELS. **Bonnybridge**. *Norwood House*, Larbert Road. Tel: (032481) 812929. See also Rte 9, **Falkirk**.

Total distance 24m.—*8m* **Kirkintilloch**.—*3m* **Kilsyth**.—*4m* **Banknock**.—*9m* **Stirling**.

Glasgow (see Rte 19) is left by way of the cathedral, followed by Castle Street and Springburn Road.—*8m* **Kirkintilloch** in part stands on the site of a Roman fort, though nothing can now be seen. However *Barony Chambers Museum* (Tues., Thurs., Fri., 14.00 to 17.00. Sat., 10.00 to 13.00. 14.00 to 17.00. Tel: 041-7751185. Free), at the Cross, tells the more modern local story of weaving, mining, iron founding and other industrial activities. Beyond Kirkintilloch A803 provides the fast onward road, but B8023 touches the Antonine Wall and the now quiet Forth-Clyde canal.—*2m* (from the junction of A803 and B8023), *Bar Hill*, with a fort, rampart and ditch, rises immediately to the S. The hill marks the S end of the best surviving continuous stretch of the wall, the N end being at Castlecary (see below).—Now running with the Forth-Clyde canal, B8023 in *1m* joins B802, immediately SE of the junction being the *Croy Hill* Antonine site with traces of a fort, a ditch and two beacon platforms.

It was around the loch to the E of **Kilsyth**, just N of Croy Hill, that in 1645 Montrose defeated the Covenanters, losing only ten of his own men but killing some 6000 of the enemy. *Colzium Country House and Park* (Daily, dawn to dusk. House closed when booked for functions. Free) is a 19C residence, now serving as a local museum and art gallery, with a park containing the remains of a castle razed by Cromwell.—*4m* **Banknock**, where A803 crosses A80 at the start of M80. *Castlecary*, just S of this point and beyond the canal, is another site of an Antonine Wall fort, but the site is crossed by the railway and little is now convincingly visible above ground. B816, followed E from here, reaches Bonnybridge and the Antonine sites of Seabegs Wood and Rough Castle, for both of which see Rte 9. **Cumbernauld**, 2m farther S by A80, although today a satellite spread, has its name in history through the signing in 1640 of the Bond of Cumbernauld by which Montrose, protesting against 'the particular and direct practising of a few', signalled his first move in his quarrel with the ambitious Argyll and the extremist Covenanters. *Palacerigg Country Park*, rather over 1m E of the town, offers a nature centre and a variety of wildlife in paddocks (Park: Dawn to dusk. Nature Centre: Summer, daily, 10.00 to 20.00. Winter, daily, 10.00 to 16.30. Tel: 02367-20047. Donation).

From Banknock M80 heads first E and then N, in *3m* passing *Dunipace*, reputedly a boyhood home of Wallace, and then (*3m*) reaching Junction 9 where the motorway should be left for (*1m*) the *Bannockburn Heritage Centre* and (*2m*) **Stirling** , for both of which see Rte 23.

23   Stirling and Environs

With a name prominent in the martial and political annals of Scotland, the royal burgh of Stirling stands proud and conspicuous on rising ground above the river Forth, with its famous castle higher still on a precipitous volcanic plug (250ft).

> **Tourist Information**. Albert Place, Dumbarton Road.—30,000 inhab. *ECl.* Wed.
>
> SOME HOTELS. *Kings Gate*, 5 King Street. Tel: (0786) 73944. *Park Lodge*, 32 Park Terrace. Tel: (0786) 74862. *Stakis*, Murray Place. Tel: (0786) 72017.—At Bannockburn Heritage Centre: *King Robert*, FK7 OLJ. Tel: (0786) 811666.

History. Stirling's history is substantially that of its castle. The early inhabitants may have been ancient Britons (Welsh) for the name appears to be a corruption from the Welsh for 'Place of Striving'. Another ancient name, probably poetical, was 'Snowdoun'. The Romans may have occupied the rock, and legend credits King Arthur with having later taken it from the Saxons, but it is definite that Alexander I died in the castle in 1124 and William the Lion in 1214. Stirling surrendered to the English in 1296 but was retaken the next year by Wallace after winning the Battle of Stirling Bridge and then became the last place in Scotland to hold out against Edward I. He laid furious siege to the castle in 1304, stripping lead from church roofs as far away as Perth and St. Andrews with which to feed his catapults bombarding from nearby Gowan Hill. When eventually the garrison capitulated, they numbered only 150 men. Ten years later the Scots under Edward Bruce besieged the castle and made a bargain with the governor, Sir Phillip Mowbray, whereby it would be yielded if not relieved by mid-summer 1314. Edward II marched to raise the siege, only to be routed at Bannockburn. The castle then surrendered and was dismantled in accordance with Bruce's normal policy. Under the Stuarts Stirling became a favoured royal residence. James III was born here in 1451. In 1488, after being defeated by rebel lords at Sauchieburn to the S, he was treacherously murdered and then buried at Cambuskenneth Abbey. After Flodden in 1513 James V was brought to Stirling for safety; later he spent much time here, making a practice of moving in disguise among his subjects, the better to understand them. His daughter, Mary, Queen of Scots, was crowned here at the age of nine months and stayed here until she left for France. Her son, James VI, also spent his childhood at Stirling, with George Buchanan as his tutor. In 1651 the castle was taken by General Monk, and in 1746 it was unsuccessfully besieged by the Young Pretender.—The office of the Keeper of Stirling Castle, hereditary in the Erskine family from 1370 (with one short break), was forfeited by the Earl of Mar in 1715 after the battle of Sheriffmuir, but was restored to the Earl of Mar and Kellie in 1923.

Stirling Festival Fortnight of Music, Drama and the Arts, with exhibits and performances of international standard, is held annually in August.

Stirling Town.

The town centre may be taken to be the *Old Burgh Building*, bearing a steeple and a figure of Wallace. From here Corn Exchange Road runs SW, along its short length being the Public Library and, opposite, the *Municipal Buildings* in which the town's history is told in stained glass. Just beyond there is a picturesque length of old town wall. Corn Exchange Road soon merges with Albert Place, with on the left another section of wall and on the right the **Smith Art Gallery and Museum** (Wed.–Fri., Sun., 14.00 to 17.00. Sat., 10.30 to 17.00. Tel: 0786-71917. Free), offering temporary exhibitions and some permanent material on Stirling's past. A short way beyond, across Queen's Road, are (N) the grassy terraces of *King's Gardens*, with the mound known as the King's Knot, showing the layout of a formal garden, perhaps of James V or earlier.

In the N of the town, about ¾m from Old Burgh Buildings and reached by Barnton and continuation streets, the Forth is crossed by three bridges: the railway bridge in the S; the main A9 road bridge in the centre, carrying Rtes 25A and 25B to Perth; and then the *Old Bridge*. This last, built in c 1400, still a footbridge and used it is said by every Scottish sovereign between Robert III and Charles II, was long of key strategic importance as the most southerly crossing of the river. But the Stirling Bridge which gave its name to the battle won by Wallace in September 1297 would have been a wooden affair. Wallace was encamped around Abbey Craig, the rock now crowned with his monument. Refusing to accept terms, he waited until the bulk of the English army had foolishly crossed the bridge and then fell on them, killing most and driving the survivors into the river to drown.

Spittal Street climbs away NW from Old Burgh Building towards the castle, soon merging into St. John Street which comes in from the left. Here No. 23 (restored), bearing a pair of scissors in relief, was a hospice founded 'for the support of the puir be Robert Spittal taillyour to King James the 4 anno 1530'. This Robert Spittal was clearly both a prosperous and charitable tailor and a man of varied talent for he also built the bridge over the Teith at Doune. Farther up, set back on the left, is the attractive **Cowane's Hospital** or **Guildhall** (Mon.–Fri., 09.30 to 17.30 or 16.30 in Oct–April. Tel: 0786-75019. Free), built between 1634–49 by John Cowane 'for the entertainment of decayed breithers', or, in other words, unsuccessful members of the Guild of Merchants. The outside of the building bears appropriately pious inscriptions, while inside (much altered in 1852) hang portraits of deans of the guild.

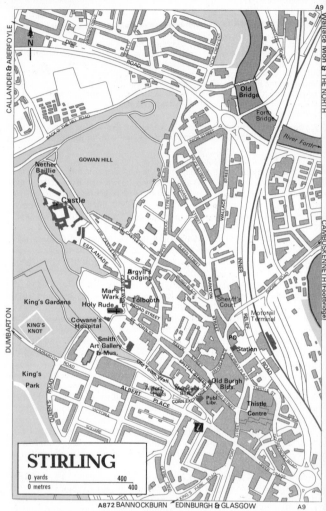

Just above is the **Church of the Holy Rude**, in which in 1544 Mary
of Guise was appointed regent and in which also, in 1567, her
grandson, then one year old, was crowned James VI, John Knox
preaching the sermon. This is a fine Gothic edifice, built up a slope
and thus with a choir noticeably higher than the nave. At the W end
there is a plain, square, battlemented tower (90ft), still visibly bearing
marks inflicted by Monk's siege guns in 1651. Inside, the nave of
five bays with massive rounded piers was begun in c 1415, from
which period survive an oak roof and vaulted arches, while the choir,
in which the infant James VI was crowned, dates from a century later

(1520–23) and is notable for its high-pitched ceiling. In the vaulted N chapel there is a font which once served as a piscina in Cambuskenneth Abbey.

Alongside the church, and looking down Broad Street, sits the rather forlorn ruin known as **Mar's Wark**, all that survives of a palace started by the Earl of Mar in 1570–72 but never really completed. The fast eroding heraldry, sculpture and rhyming inscriptions, as also, above the entrance, the royal arms flanked by those of Mar and his countess, combine as a reminder of Renaissance taste and of the wealth to indulge it, while interest is added by reflecting that much of the stone was looted from Cambuskenneth. James VI and his queen lived here for a while, and the building remained a fine residence of the earls of Mar until 1715 when the misguided 6th Earl, leader of the '15, had to flee the country. Ironically the place was largely destroyed by Jacobite forces during the '45.

Opposite, and in some contrast, stands *Argyll's Lodging*, a handsome and complete example of a 17C town house, built in 1632 by Sir William Alexander of Menstrie (later Earl of Stirling). He soon died insolvent and his house passed (1655) to the Argyll family who enlarged it in 1674. In 1799 the Lodging served as a military hospital and in 1964 it became a youth hostel.

Beyond, the road reaches the **Castle Esplanade**, largely serving as a car park. Here are a modern statue of Bruce in the act of sheathing his sword after Bannockburn and also a *Visitor Centre* (NTS. April–Sept: Mon.–Sat., 09.30 to 18.00. Sun., 10.30 to 17.30. Oct–March: Mon.–Sat., 09.30 to 17.05. Sun., 12.30 to 16.20. Closed throughout Jan. Fee for audio-visual), providing an audio-visual introduction to the castle. From here a scenic walk rounds the castle, while another path, from the farther side of the Esplanade, descends in steps into the dip between the castle and the church of the Holy Rude. Once a tilting ground, with the lady onlookers arrayed along the western ridge, this is now part public garden and part cemetery, the latter a sombre and even eerie place with gaunt tombs inviting graffiti, a solid Covenanter memorial pyramid, and a desolate representation of the Wigtown Martyrs who, one of them headless (though there is talk of restoration), languish in Victorian bathos under a glass dome.

The return to the lower town may be made down Broad, Bow and Baker streets, in the first of which the *Cross*, flanked by cannon, marks the spot where in 1571 Archbishop John Hamilton (see also Rte 20, Dumbarton) was tried and hanged on the same day; as a member of Mary's faction he was automatically judged guilty of complicity in the murder of Darnley. The adjacent Tolbooth of 1701 was the design of Sir William Bruce.

**Stirling Castle.

Stirling Castle (AM) is open April–Sept: Mon.–Sat., 09.30 to 17.15. Sun., 10.30 to 16.45. Oct–March: Mon.–Sat., 09.30 to 16.20. Sun., 12.30 to 15.35. Castle closes 45 minutes after the above last-ticket times. Fee. With most of the principal buildings dating from the 15 and 16C, the castle is a truly magnificent example of military and domestic architecture on a royal scale. The audio-visual presentation in the NTS Visitor Centre on the Esplanade provides an admirable introduction.

The outworks of the first moat date from the time of Queen Anne, and *Queen Anne's Garden* lies to the left. The drum-towers of the gatehouse were erected by James IV who also built the square *Princes' Tower* (left) in which James VI was educated by George ·Buchanan.

The **Lower Square** has on its left the Palace and, ahead, the Great Hall, both also forming sides of the Upper Square. To the right in the Lower Square, near the castle well, are some vaults that served as the palace kitchens, and farther on is the vaulted entrance (perhaps 14C) to the Nether Baillie.

Around **Upper Square** are grouped the Palace, the Great Hall, the Chapel Royal and the King's Old Buildings.

The *Palace* (c 1540) is notable for its curious pillars and emblematic figures, among these being types of Scottish soldiers of the 16C and grotesque representations of a king, a queen, a chamberlain, a cook, lust, Venus and others. The apartments surround the 'Lion's Den', traditionally the place where the royal beasts were caged (it is known that James III and IV both kept lions).—The *Great Hall* was built for James IV in about 1500.

The *Chapel Royal*, begun in 1501 by James IV as a collegiate church, was rebuilt in 1594 by James VI, who had been baptised in it. Today the line of the original chapel (in which Mary, Queen of Scots, was crowned at the age of nine months) can be traced by differently shaded stones outside, while James VI's chapel, with 17C frescoes, now serves as a Memorial Hall for the regiment, the Argyll and Sutherland Highlanders.

The *King's Old Buildings* (so called because the present buildings are probably on the site of an older palace) bear a tablet in memory of Sir William Oliphant, the heroic commander who in 1304 held out so long when besieged by Edward I. Here the *Museum of the Argyll and Sutherland Highlanders* (Easter–Oct: Mon.–Fri., 10.00 to 17.30 or 16.00 in Oct. Free) displays a notable collection of medals.

A passage from the NW corner of Upper Square admits to the *Douglas Garden* in a room near which the 8th Earl of Douglas, a distrusted nobleman who had been invited to confer, was in 1452 stabbed by James II and then thrown out of the window (just above the end of the passage). A skeleton found in the garden in 1797 may have been his.

Beyond, at the NW corner of the ramparts, *Queen Victoria's Look-Out* has a balustrade bearing the initials of royal visitors, while a small round hole in the wall is said to have been made especially for the child Mary, Queen of Scots. The view embraces Campsie Fells to the SW; then, to the NW, Ben Lomond and Ben Vorlich above Loch Lomond, Ben Venue above The Trossachs and Loch Katrine, and Ben Ledi between Loch Venacher and the Pass of Leny. To the NE are the Ochil Hills while, closer, the twisting Links of Forth, the Wallace Monument and Cambuskenneth Abbey can be seen. Just below the castle is *Gowan Hill*, whence Edward I bombarded Stirling in 1304 and on which in 1746 the Young Pretender planted his batteries so as 'to oblige the citizens and spare the town', only to have them speedily silenced by the castle's guns. Near the hill's N angle is the Heading Hill, the place of execution.

Below the rampart, farther on, an ancient sally-port can be seen, very probably the exit used by James V when he went out in disguise to mix with the people.

Environs of Stirling.

Of the places mentioned below, Bridge of Allan, the Wallace Monument and Cambuskenneth Abbey are all N and E of Stirling and
conveniently visited as a group. The Bannockburn Heritage Centre,
however, is 2m S.

Bridge of Allan, 2m N, now a quiet and delightfully situated
residential small town, was in Victorian times a popular and elegant
spa, famed for its saline waters as also, since Burns wrote his 'Banks
of Allan Water', for its river. To the SE of the town are the modern
buildings of the *University of Stirling* (1967), blending surprisingly
well into the parkland of the Airthrey estate, the castle of which
(Robert Adam, with considerable 19C addition) is now a university
department. The public are admitted to the grounds, in which a stone
beside a road interestingly records 'Pathfoot village was built around
this standing stone. Beside it was held an annual tryst (fair) in the
18C'. The university's MacRobert Arts Centre provides theatre, opera,
ballet, films, concerts and exhibitions (Box Office. 0786-61081).

Immediately S of the university the ugly and over-conspicuous
Wallace Monument (Daily, 10.00 to 20.00 in May–July; to 19.00 in
April and Aug; to 18.00 in March and Sept; to 17.00 in Feb and Oct.
Tel: 0786-75019. Fee) perches high on the rock of Abbey Craig,
around which Wallace camped in 1297, watching for the English to
attempt the crossing of the Forth. Built in 1870 and bearing a statue
of Wallace, the monument today houses an exhibition of armour,
including Wallace's two-handed sword, while audio-visual displays
tell the story of the district and its heroes.

The ruins of **Cambuskenneth Abbey** (AM. April–Sept: Mon.–Sat.,
09.30 to 19.00. Sun., 14.00 to 19.00. Fee) are enclosed within a crooked
loop of the Forth, 1m S of the Wallace Monument (the only road
approach) and the same distance E of Stirling (footbridge). The name,
Field of Kenneth, may reach back to a King Kenneth, traditionally
supposed to have defeated the Picts here in the 9C, but three centuries
would pass before this abbey was founded, in c 1140 by David I for
Austin Canons. Because of its closeness to Stirling Castle the abbey
was from time to time used for meetings of the Scottish parliament
and other bodies, a notable occasion being Bruce's parliament of
1326. In 1604, by now a victim of the Reformation, the abbey was
given to the Earl of Mar who reduced it to ruins in order to use the
stone in the building of his palace in Stirling (Mar's Wark).

James III, murdered after Sauchieburn (see below), and his queen,
Margaret of Denmark, were buried here, and two coffins, containing
skeletons believed to be theirs, were found during excavations in
1864; on the instructions of Queen Victoria these were reburied
beneath a memorial at the site of the high altar. The ruins include a
14C detached tower, the W doorway of the church, and another
building thought to be part of the infirmary. The tower contains two
rooms showing various sculpted stones and an ancient dug-out canoe,
found in the Forth, while stone nesting boxes suggest that the
infirmary was later converted into a dovecot.

The *Bannockburn Heritage Centre** (NTS and STB. Site always
open. Visitor Centre open March–Oct: Daily, 10.00 to 18.00. Fee for
audio-visual presentation) is off M80/M9 at Junction 9, 2m S of
central Stirling, from where the approach is by A872. The exact site
of the battle, fought in June 1314, is disputed, but most visitors will
readily enough accept that it was around here, and that the Borestone

rotunda could well have been Bruce's command post.

Stirling Castle, held by the English, was being besieged by Bruce's brother, Edward. Impatient, Edward made a bargain with the English governor, Sir Philip Mowbray, that if by midsummer (1314) no English army had come within three miles of Stirling, then the castle would surrender. The English army, hastening to raise the siege, was led by Edward II in person and was greatly superior in numbers. But Robert Bruce, with a force almost entirely composed of pikemen, strengthened his carefully chosen position by strewing his front with caltrops (spiked iron balls) and planting sharp stakes in concealed pits, so as to break the attack of the English cavalry. Although thus defeated, the English stood their ground until the Scottish camp-followers, like a fresh army, suddenly appeared from over Gillies Hill (1m NW of today's memorial site). The subsequent English rout was complete and their losses immense. Stirling surrendered, Edward II fled to Dunbar, and the independence of Scotland was assured.

The memorial proper takes the form of a heroic, bronze equestrian statue of Bruce (Pilkington Jackson, 1964), while the rotunda alongside encloses the Borestone site, traditionally Bruce's command post. Fragments of the borestone, in which Bruce's standard is said to have been planted, can be seen in the visitor centre where an audio-visual presentation explains the events leading up to the battle and the battle itself. Facilities here include tourist information, food and a shop.

Bannockburn House, just E of Junction 9, served as the Young Pretender's headquarters in January 1746, and it was here that he first met Clementina Walkinshaw, later his mistress and mother of his natural daughter.—The name Sauchie appears frequently in the area a mile or so to the W of the motorway, a reminder of the battle of *Sauchieburn* in 1488. Here James III was defeated by the rebel lords, with his son more or less captive in their midst. As the king fled he was thrown from his horse and carried unconscious to a nearby mill, there being stabbed to death by a man disguised as a priest bringing the Last Sacrament. He was buried at Cambuskenneth Abbey, and tradition holds that his son, James IV, overcome with remorse, for the rest of his life wore an iron belt around his body.

For Stirling to **Edinburgh** via Falkirk and Linlithgow, see Rte 9; to **Edinburgh** via Culross and Dunfermline, see Rte 31; To **Glasgow**, see Rte 22; to **Pitlochry**, see Rte 24; to **Perth**, see Rte 25.

24   Stirling to Pitlochry via Killin and Aberfeldy

A84 to Lochearnhead. A85 and A827 to Killin, Aberfeldy (alternative through Glen Lyon) and Ballinluig. A9 to Pitlochry.—After Callander the scenery quickly becomes more grandly Highland, reaching its best along Loch Tay or the suggested alternative of Glen Lyon.

SOME HOTELS. **Doune**. *Creity Hall*, FK16 6AE. Tel: (0786) 841215. **Callander**. *Bridgend House*, Bridge Street. Tel: (0877) 30130. *Lubnaig*, Leny Feus. Tel: (0877) 30376. *Roman Camp*, Main Street. Tel: (0877) 30003. **Lochearnhead**. *Mansewood Country House*, FK19 8NS. Tel: (05673) 213. **Killin**. *Bridge of Lochay*, FK21 8TS.

Tel: (05672) 272. *Killin*, FK21 8TP. Tel: (05672) 296. **Kenmore**.
Kenmore, The Square. Tel: (08873) 205. **Fortingall**. *Fortingall*, PH15
2NQ. Tel: (08873) 367. **Coshieville**. *Coshieville*, PH15 2NE. Tel:
(08873) 319. **Aberfeldy**. *Cruachan House*, Kenmore Road. Tel:
(0887) 20545.

Total distance 73 or 81m.—*8m* **Doune**.—*7m* **Callander**.—*16m*
Lochearnhead.—*7m* **Killin**.—*22* or *30m* **Aberfeldy**.—*13m* **Pitlochry**.

Leaving **Stirling** (see Rte 23) by its NW corner, A84 at once crosses
the motorway and in *5m* reaches **Scotland's (Blair Drummond) Safari
Park** (Approx. April–Oct: Daily, 10.00 to 16.30. Tel: 0786-841456.
Fee). The wild animal reserves—with lions, tigers, giraffes, a monkey
jungle and many other species—are toured either in the visitor's own
car or by safari bus, and other attractions include a boat around
Chimp Island, aquatic mammal shows, a hippo pool, pets' corner and
an adventure playground.—The nearby church of *Kincardine-in-
Menteith*, by the junction of A84 and A873, was built by Richard
Crichton in 1816 and will be of interest to Drummonds for the several
17 to 18C family monuments, including a notable brass commemorating George Drummond who died in 1717.

3m **Doune** (4000 inhab. *ECl*. Wed.), once noted as a drover centre
and for its sheep and cattle fairs, and during the 17C for the
manufacture of pistols (crossed pistols still feature in the town's arms),
is today visited for its castle, to the S., and its motor museum, to the
N. The bridge here over the rapid river Teith was built in 1535 by
Robert Spittal, formerly tailor to James IV (see also Stirling, Rte 23),
reputedly to spite the ferryman who had refused him passage because
he had no money on him.

Doune Castle (AM. Standard, but closed Oct–March. Fee). One
of the largest, best-preserved and best-restored examples of late 14C
military-domestic architecture in Scotland, and (to quote the
authority, W.D. Simpson) 'the highest achievement of perfected
castellar construction', Doune is outstanding, if not unique for the
way in which it helps the visitor to assemble a picture of medieval
life in such a place.

History. At the time of the castle's building the lands known as Albany
comprised roughly modern Perthshire, Stirling and Fife. Strategically the two
routes from Edinburgh to Inverlochy, and from Glasgow to Perth and Inverness,
intersected at Doune and this, coupled with the feud between Albany and the
Lord of the Isles over the claim to the earldom of Ross, probably prompted the
building of this castle by Robert, Duke of Albany (died 1419) and his son,
Murdoch. But when Murdoch was executed in 1425 Doune was forfeited to the
crown, later to be settled by James IV on his queen Margaret. Margaret's third
husband was Lord Methven, a descendant of the dukes of Albany, and the
office of constable of the castle became hereditary in his family, the earls of
Moray, who today enjoy the title of Lord Doune. In 1745–46 the castle was held
for the Young Pretender by MacGregor of Glengyle and into it were herded
the prisoners taken at Falkirk. By the end of the 18C Doune was a roofless ruin,
so remaining until 1883 when the 14th Earl began a careful restoration.

Occupying a well-chosen triangular site, protected on two sides by
the Teith and Ardoch and on the third by a deep moat, the castle
encloses a large court with a square gatehouse tower, 95ft high, at
the NE corner and another tower on the W side. The main block is
of four storeys and an attic, while the round tower which flanks the
portal rises to five storeys.

For the modern visitor the essence of the castle is the Gatehouse complex which, complete with its own water supply, formed a self-contained defensive residence. Here is still the entrance, from which a vaulted passage slopes up towards the court. Along this passage can be seen the slots for the portcullis, the great iron gate, and vaulted rooms on either side, the northernmost on the right-hand side being the prison. Standing in the court and racing N, the Retainers' Hall is to the left and the Lord's Hall to the right, both on the first floor, the former raised above vaulted cellars with service stairs. The magnificent Lord's Hall has been somewhat modernised, but some original features can still be noted; for instance, the fireplace in two compartments, and the passage through the thickness of the S wall leading to the steward's chamber, with a window opening on to the hall so that he could keep an eye on things.

A stair climbs to the Lord's Private Room in the corner round tower, complete with privy and, in the floor, a hatch through which water was drawn up direct from the well below. Another stair out of the Lord's Hall ascends to the hall above, this being the Solar or general living room of the lord and his household; it is provided with an oratory, complete with octagonal piscina and sacrament house. The Retainers' Hall is covered by an open timber roof which, though modern, follows the pattern of the original. The octagonal hearth is in the middle of the floor, and on the floor too can be seen the bases of the screens which defined the enclosure in which food brought up from the kitchens was cut up. These Kitchens, with an immense fireplace, are on the E of the court and linked to the Retainers' Hall by a service room, provided with a chute for rubbish.

Doune Motor Museum (April–Oct: Daily, 10.00 to 17.00. Tel: 0786-841203. Fee) houses Lord Moray's collection of some 40 vintage and later thoroughbred cars, these including examples of, amongst many others, Hispano Suiza, Bentley, Jaguar, Lagonda, BMW and Aston Martin, as also the world's second oldest Rolls Royce. Nearly all the cars are maintained in running order and some even compete in Doune Hill Climb events held in April, June and Sept.

7m **Callander** (2000 inhab. *ECl.* Wed. *Inf.* Leny Road. Easter–Sept.), at the very foot of the Highlands and under 9m from the Trossachs (see Rte 21; reached by A821 along the shore of Loch Venacher), can at times be a somewhat over-popular resort. Nevertheless this beautifully sited place, with its several hotels, restaurants and other amenities, including shops which remain open until late, is an excellent touring base. In the E part of the town a small road leads N to a car park beyond which a path continues to the *Bracklinn Falls*; and, roughly opposite, a path off the S side of the main road reaches a strange, long, curving embankment, known as Roman Walk and once thought to be the Roman camp known to have been established here. However the site of the camp, built by Agricola in the 1C, has now been officially located as having been near the farm of Bochastle, between the rivers 1m W of the town centre.

The **Pass of Leny**, *2m* W of Callander, is a fitting gateway to the Highlands; a narrow glen into which are squeezed the road, the old railway and the river tumbling down as rapids and falls. Emerging, the road skirts the narrow length of Loch Lubnaig as the scenery becomes increasingly broken and wooded with bare moor and mountain looming above.—At (*6m*) **Strathyre**, in the heart of Strathyre Forest, a Forestry Commission *Information Centre* (May–Sept: Daily, 09.00 to 19.00. Free) and picnic area mark the starting points of trails on both sides of the river Balvag, those on the W being exacting and giving access to Beinn an Sithein (1800ft). It was at the farm of *Ardvoch*, just across the river, that the Gaelic poet and evangelist Dugald Buchanan (1716–88) was born.

4m **Balquidder**, 2m W of the main road, should not be bypassed, least of all by anyone bearing the name of MacGregor, for here, beside the intermixed ruins of two ancient churches, are what are said to be the tombs of Rob Roy and close members of his family. It seems certain that he, his wife and his two sons lie somewhere here, so one might as well accept that the tombs are indeed those under the three unidentified stones within an iron railing, even though these stones would seem to date from long before Rob Roy's time. The central stone, claimed to be Rob Roy's, is a rough slab of slate, carved with a cross, with a sword on one side and a kilted figure with a dog or other animal at his feet on the other. A second stone, bearing the MacGregor arms (a pine torn up by the roots and crossed by a sword piercing a crown, an allusion to the claim to be of royal blood made by the chiefs of the clan) is supposed to commemorate Rob Roy's sons, Coll (died 1735) and Robert or Robin Oig (executed 1754). The last stone may be that of Rob Roy's widow Helen.

The adjacent ruins are those of two churches, the first dating back to the 13C or earlier, the other a church of 1631 which was built partly on top of the first. It was in the earlier church that in 1589 the Clan MacGregor gathered around the head of the king's forester and vowed to protect those who had cut it off (see Ardvorlich House under Lochearnhead below). Within the present 19C church can be seen the bell of the second church; a 17C chest, said to have belonged to Campbell of Glenorchy (died 1631); a Gaelic bible of c 1688; quaint long offerings ladles, dating from the 18C and still in use; and the St. Angus stone of the 8C together with an effigy of this shadowy local saint.

4m **Lochearnhead**, a popular centre for water sports and walking, marks the W extremity of *Loch Earn*, a lovely Highland loch overlooked by mountains rising to over 2000ft. Slicing seven miles eastwards to St. Fillans (see Rte 25B) the loch carries the main A85 along its N shore and a minor road beside the other. Along the latter *Ardvorlich House* (3m. No adm.) witnessed that bloody and grisly occasion of 1589 when the MacGregors, having murdered the king's forester in revenge for a real or supposed grievance, placed his severed head on a dish, with a crust between the teeth, and presented it to his sister. Nearby, beside the road, stands the tombstone of seven Macdonalds of Glen Coe, killed in a marauding attack on the house.

A85 now steadily climbs wild and rocky Glen Ogle to reach the watershed in *4m* at 948ft beside Lochan Larig Cheile, beyond which a steeper descent in rather over *1m* makes the junction with A827, the road now followed by this Rte. A85, heading W along Glen Dochart, in 10m meets A82 at Crianlarich on Rte 20.

2m **Killin** (600 inhab. *ECl.* Wed. *Inf.* Main Street. Easter–Sept) is approached beside the river Dochart, here tumbling as falls and rapids in its haste to swell Loch Tay, a short mile below the village. With a sharp bend A827 crosses the rapids by an old bridge at a point where the river is divided by two islets, the lower of which, *Inch Buie*, long served as the burial place of Clan MacNab, the most powerful family in this district until the MacNab emigration to

Canada in 1833 (Access through gate on bridge; key from Tourist Information).

For all its small permanent population, Killin prospers as a year-round resort, in summer as popular with motorists and walkers as it can be busy with skiers in winter. Within the village *Killin Church*, dating from 1744 but on a very early Christian site, merits a visit for its seven-sided 9C font. The monument in front of the church is to the Rev. James Stewart, the first to translate the New Testament into Scottish Gaelic (1797). *Finlarig Castle* (Reasonable hours. Free), ½m N, is reached by crossing the iron bridge over the Lochay opposite Queen's Court Hotel. A sombre and now dangerous ruin half-hidden on a tree-covered mound, this was once Clan Campbell's centre; the lair too of Black Duncan of the Cowal, a notorious chief of that clan. The gruesome beheading pit, immediately adjacent and thought to be the only surviving example in Scotland, does not seem out of place in these gloomy surrounds.

Loch Tay (at a height of 335ft; 14m long and averaging ¾m in breadth; in places over 500ft deep) is grandly set below mountains and famous for its salmon. The loch's chief feeders are the Dochart and Lochay at the W end, while from its E issues the river Tay. Roads skirt both shores, that along the N being the main road and the shorter. The small S shore road keeps closer to the water and commands the finer views, especially across to Ben Lawers.

Between Killin and Aberfeldy, and keeping to the N of Loch Tay, there is a choice of two roads. The direct and fast road (22m) is A827 running beside and above the loch. The alternative (30m) is the much more scenic and interesting, but slower, more northerly road through Glen Lyon, the wild setting for a brew of ancient settlement, early Christian legend, murderous clan feuding and, for good measure, modern engineering.

Killin to Aberfeldy beside Loch Tay.

Leaving Killin A827 crosses the Lochay and then bears E, in *4m* reaching the unclassified road which climbs to the *Ben Lawers Visitor Centre* (just over 1m; see alternative road below) and then drops into Glen Lyon.—*8m* **Fearnan**, from where a road crosses (2m) into Glen Lyon. Now at loch level the road fringes the wood of *Drummond Hill*, with, just short of Kenmore, a Forestry Commission picnic site at the start of a network of walks.—*4m* **Kenmore** is a 'model' village at the outflow of the Tay, crossed here by a bridge of 1774. *Taymouth Castle* (no adm.), with its imposing turreted entrance in the village, is the early 19C successor of a mansion built in c 1573 by Colin Campbell of Glenorchy. In 1837 the Earl of Breadalbane reintroduced here from Sweden the capercailzie wood-grouse, which had become extinct in Scotland, and in 1940–46 the castle served as a hospital for Polish officers.

Climbing, and edging the SE flank of the Taymouth estate, with occasional views down to the baronial pile, the road in *2m* reaches *Croftmoraig*, with, near the S side of the road, a double stone circle and a cup-marked stone.—*4m* **Aberfeldy**, see below.

Killin to Aberfeldy via Glen Lyon.

The lochside road is followed for *4m*, at which point an unclassified road climbs up to (*1m*) the *Ben Lawers Visitor Centre* (NTS. Easter–May, and Sept: Daily, 11.00 to 16.00. June–Aug: Daily, 10.00

to 17.00. Fee). Ben Lawers (3984ft), declared a national nature reserve in 1975 and managed jointly by the National Trust for Scotland and the Nature Conservancy Council, combines fine scenery and views with much of outstanding natural history and geological interest. Geologically the mountain represents an overfold in which the oldest rocks, perhaps 600 million years old and then a deposit on the sea floor, are now those on the surface. Botanically the area is known for its alpine plants, while buzzard, kestrel, grouse, golden plover and curlew are among the birds that may be spotted from the nature trail (booklet). The Visitor Centre provides imaginative displays and an audio-visual presentation explaining the mountains's geology and natural history, advice on walks, ranger service, and leaflets and booklets as attractive as they are instructive.

The minor, unfenced road continues N across bare mountain to Lochan na Lairige, in scenery of dark grandeur, thence dropping to (7m) **Bridge of Balgie** in Glen Lyon. Here, although this Rte turns E, it is well worth considering driving westward along the little road which, never straying far from the rock-strewn river, twists and switchbacks across open turf and moorland below broad-shouldered mountains to end at the foot of the great wall of Loch Lyon's dam. Here, and during the preceding mile or two, humps of turf or ribbles of stone, marked on the map as 'homesteads' or simply as tiny circles, represent what may once have been brochs or perhaps hut settlements.

St. Adamnan, 9th Abbot of Iona and best known for his 'Life of St. Columba', may well have spent his later years evangelising in this glen, living and building a meal-mill at what is now Milton Eonan (or Mill of Adamnan) just S of the bridge of Balgie, while the church at nearby *Innerwick*, claiming to stand on the site of one founded by Adamnan, proudly guards the saint's handbell.

As the glen descends eastwards the scenery changes, the open moor giving way sometimes to defiles below hidden heights, sometimes to lengths and patches of woodland.—*6m* (from Bridge of Balgie) *Carnbane Castle*, now mere fragments high on a knoll above where the road kinks across a burn, recalls the bitter feud fought out in this glen between the Campbells of Glen Lyon, later to become notorious for the massacre in Glen Coe, and the MacGregors, the latter landless and thus, it must be admitted, little better than bandits. Here at Carnbane, and in easier days, the clan chief Gregor MacGregor had loved and married Marion Campbell. Now, in 1565 and on the run, he sought refuge here, only to be trapped by the Campbells and soon executed in the presence of his pregnant wife.

Just over *1m* farther the mansion called *Chesthill*, once the home of Campbell of Glen Lyon, appears on the left, opposite being perhaps the most charming combination of natural and man-made features to be found in the glen—a cascade dropping through the neat arch of a bridge which, Roman or not (for it is called *Roman Bridge*), is nevertheless perfection in this setting.—*2m MacGregor's Leap*, marked by a stand of larches, is the spot where Gregor MacGregor hurled himself across a river chasm in order to escape the Campbell hounds.

Almost immediately beyond, the tight and wooded glen opens abruptly before (*1m*) **Fortingall**, a place with a strange tale, for here, it has long been believed, was born Pontius Pilate, child of the union of a Roman envoy to the local chief and of a woman of his tribe. And if the ancient yew still clinging to life in the churchyard is really, as claimed, 3000 years old, then it would have already known 1000 years by the date of Pilate's birth. Older still, though, are the standing stones between the village and the river, tantalisingly mute evidence of even remoter people who once lived and held their rites in this valley.—*3m* **Coshieville** marks the junction with B846, originally one of Wade's military roads. Here *Comrie Castle*, a small ruined keep beyond the river, was an early stronghold of the Menzies, while grim *Garth Castle*, 1m N along B846 and across the Keltney Burn, was built by the Wolf of Badenoch. And a mile or so beyond Garth will be found *Glengoulandie Deer Park* (Easter–Sept: Daily, 09.00. Last adm. two hours before dusk. Tel: 08873-509. Fee), a scenic park showing red deer, highland cattle, rare breeds of sheep and much else of natural interest.

From Coshieville this Rte continues E along B846 and in *2m*, near standing stones, passes below the hamlet of **Dull** in which an ancient one-armed cross, probably marking a limit of sanctuary, is all that survives of a distinguished monastic centre of learning. The place's origins are lost in a confusion of legend, but of several stories the most insistent goes back to St. Adamnan. On his deathbed higher up Glen Lyon he instructed that his body be carried down the glen to a point where a cord securing the body to the bier would snap. Here he was to be buried, a church was to be built and a teaching monastery was to be founded. All this duly happened at a place called Tulli, which by a neat if elastic interpretation of philological law readily becomes Dull. Be this as it may, this district is known as Appin of Dull (Appin meaning Abbey lands), and there can be no doubt that, from very early times, Dull was known as a seat of Culdee and, later, Catholic theology.

2m **Castle Menzies** (April–Sept: Mon.–Sat., 10.30 to 17.00. Sun., 14.00 to 17.00. Tel: 0887-20982. Fee), now housing the Menzies clan museum, is a particularly fine example of a 16C Z-plan tower-house of the period marking the transition from fortification to residence—*1m* **Aberfeldy** (see below).

Aberfeldy (1500 inhab. *ECl*. Wed. *Inf*. 8 Dunkeld Street. Easter–mid Sept.) stands on both sides of the Urlar Burn near where it meets the Tay, here crossed by *Wade's Bridge* of 1733–35, generally accepted as the most distinguished of the many he built, although the credit for the bridge's architectural elegance must of course go to its designer, William Adam. Optimistically Wade incorporated a plaque announcing that he laid the first stone on 23 April 1733 'and finished the work in the same year', whereas in fact he ran into problems—in his own words 'so much plague, vexation and disappointments that staggers my philosophy'—and it was not until 8 August 1735 that the bridge was formally opened. Beside the bridge a large cairn carrying a kilted figure (1887) commemorates Wade's raising of the Black Watch in 1739. The *Birks of Aberfeldy* (birk meaning silver birch), their immortality assured by Burns despite the suggestion that he really meant Abergeldie, line the Urlar Burn, about 1m up which are the *Falls of Moness*.

Twisting with the course of the Tay, A827 in *3m* reaches Grandtully Castle (pron. Grantly; no adm.), built in 1560 but since twice enlarged, ½m SW of which is 16C *St. Mary's Church*, with a contemporary wooden painted ceiling, lively with heraldry and all manner of symbolism.—*3m* The road crosses the Tay near standing stones and in another *3m* reaches *Logierait*, today no more than a village at the confluence of the Tay and Tummel but once the site of a court notorious for the despotic power wielded by the lords of Atholl. There was a prison here, too, from which Rob Roy escaped in 1717 and into which later the Young Pretender threw prisoners taken at Prestonpans.

A9 is met at *Ballinluig*, immediately across the Tummel, **Pitlochry** (see Rte 27) being *4m* to the N.

25   Stirling to Perth

There is a choice of three roads. A., via Auchterarder (33m), is the central and most direct. B., via Crieff (38m), the best scenically, also enables diversions to be made to the E end of Loch Earn or northward up the Sma' Glen. C., via Dollar (37m), represents a southerly loop. All three roads traverse generally pastoral country mixed with hills and woodland.

For **Stirling**, see Rte 23. For **Perth**, see Rte 26.

A. Via Auchterarder

A9 (with bypasses) to Auchterarder. B8062 to Dunning. B934 to Forteviot. B9112 to Perth.

SOME HOTELS. **Dunblane**. *Red Comyn Inn*, Perth Road. Tel: (0786) 824343. *Stakis Hydro*, FK15 OHG. Tel: (0786) 822551. **Auchterarder**. *Coll Earn House*, High Street. Tel: (07646) 3553.

Total distance 33m.—*6m* **Dunblane**.—*5m* **Greenloaning**.—*9m* **Auchterarder**.—*13m* **Perth**.

Both M9 and A9, the latter passing the Wallace Monument and running through Bridge of Allan (see Rte 23), provide easy approaches to (*6m*) **Dunblane** (4500 inhab. *ECl.* Wed. *Inf.* Stirling Road. Easter–Sept.), an ancient and incidental small town sprawled over hills and with some quaint narrow streets above the Allan Water, here crossed by a bridge in origin of 1409. The essence of the town, though, is its cathedral, standing within a gracious close of 17–19C houses.

*Dunblane Cathedral (AM. Standard. Free) is a noble 13C Gothic edifice incorporating a part-12C Norman tower.

History. Dunblane was made a bishopric by David I who founded this cathedral in c 1150 on, it is believed, the site of a primitive church built in the 6C by St. Blane. But of David's work all that survives are the two lower storeys of the tower, and the existing church, including the tower's upper levels, must, apart from some alterations and additions of the 15C, be credited to Bishop Clement (1233–58). Neglected after the Reformation, the roof of the nave caved in during the late 16C, although the choir continued in use for 300 years as parish church. A thorough and admirable restoration of the nave was completed by Rowand Anderson in 1893, followed by that of the choir by Robert Lorimer in 1914.—The saintly Robert Leighton (1611–84) was bishop here from 1662 until his translation in 1670 to the archbishopric of Glasgow.

The West Front is the most noteworthy external feature, a good example of pure EE comprising a deeply recessed portal surmounted by three tall lancets. Above, and seen only from the outside, is the so-called 'Ruskin Window', a pointed oval adorned with carved foliage, owing its name to the enthusiastic praise given to this West Front by John Ruskin.

Inside the cathedral the aisled Nave of eight bays has a fine clerestory with double arches towards the W and single towards the E. The stained glass and the roof are modern. At the W end are six carved stalls, known as the Bishop's Stalls because they were provided by Bishop Chisholm in 1486; and to the S is the entrance to 'Katie Ogie's Hole', a strange small vaulted chamber in the W wall, of unexplained name and unknown origin though more than likely to have been a hermit's cell. At the W end of the North Aisle is a stone of c 900 bearing a Celtic cross and allegorical carvings, while farther E lie effigies (1271) which may represent Malise, 5th Earl of Strathearn, and his countess. At the E end of the South Aisle, sometimes behind a curtain, will be found the effigy of Bishop Ochiltree who crowned James II in 1437.

In the Choir of six bays three slabs in the centre recall a mass murder of 1502, for they commemorate Margaret Drummond, mistress of James IV, and her two sisters, all poisoned at Drummond Castle by a group of nobles determined that the king should marry (as he did) Princess Margaret of England. An effigy on the N wall may be that of Bishop Clement, builder of the cathedral, or, some say, of Bishop Finlay Dermoch, responsible for the still surviving bridge over the Allan Water. The misericord stalls are attributed to Bishop Ochiltree and would thus be of the 15C, while the reredos and organ-case are by the Clow brothers working to Lorimer's design of 1914. The low-vaulted Lady Chapel, adjoining the choir on the N, serves as the war memorial (by Robert Lorimer; windows by Douglas Strachan).

In the close the 17C *Dean's House* (June–Sept: Mon.–Sat., 10.30 to 12.30. 14.30 to 16.30. Tel: 0786-823179. Donation) houses the small cathedral museum and library (enquire about Bishop Leighton's Library, in another 17C building opposite the Dean's House).

Sheriffmuir, 2½m E of Dunblane, was the setting of the battle of November 1715 which, although in itself indecisive, nevertheless marked the end of the '15 Jacobite rebellion. The moor is crossed by two unclassified roads, one running NE out of the SE outskirts of Dunblane, the other heading N out of Bridge of Allan, and the battle was fought within the angle of the junction of these roads. The forces of the Old Pretender, 12,000 strong, were led by the Earl of Mar; those of George I, 4000 strong, by the Duke of Argyll, whose object it was to prevent Mar from crossing the Forth to join his friends in the south. The right wing of each side was victorious, and the left of each routed, but it was Mar who judged it prudent to withdraw.

5m **Greenloaning**, where Rte 25B diverges N, soon passing Ardoch Roman Camp.—*7m* **Gleneagles**, a name often associated mainly with the famous golf hotel here, is in fact a southward-running wooded and moorland glen (whose name means 'churches' and, disappointingly perhaps, has nothing to do with eagles) through which A823 climbs across the Ochil Hills, from the watershed dropping down Glen Devon to meet Rte 25C at Yetts o' Muckhart. Near A9, at the N end of Glen Eagles, is *Gleneagles House* (no adm.), built in 1624 with stones from the former castle and over many centuries the seat of the Haldanes; the chapel (adm. by written request) dates from 1149 and shelters both ancient and modern Haldane memorials.

2m **Auchterarder** (bypass) is a narrow, stretched kind of village which was spitefully burnt by the Earl of Mar after the fiasco on Sheriffmuir, and later, in 1834, figured in Scottish Church history as the scene of the first of the patronage disputes that culminated in 1843 in the Disruption and the founding of the Free Church of Scotland. The *Glenruthven Weaving Mill* (Tel: 07646-2079), in Abbey Road, boasts the only working steam textile engine in Scotland. Here, too, weaving is demonstrated while exhibits illustrate the history of steam and weaving and a shop sells local and other products. Just S of Auchterarder is 19C *Kincardine Castle* (no adm., but pony trekking. Tel: 07646-2261), near which is a fragment of its medieval predecessor, a seat of the Grahams, dismantled in 1646 by Argyll during his struggle with Montrose (James Graham).

There are also two places of contrasting interest to the N of Auchterarder, one ancient and one modern. The latter is the *Strathallan Aircraft Museum* (April–Oct: Daily, 10.00 to 17.00. Tel: 07646-2545. Fee), 2m N by B8062, with a collection of aircraft and equipment dating back to 1930 although the emphasis is on the last war. In summer there are flying displays. The ancient site is *Tullibardine Chapel* (AM. Reasonable hours. Free), 3m NW by A823. Founded in 1446 this is a rare—because it is so complete and unaltered—survival of a rural collegiate chapel, the roof and heraldic detail being especially noteworthy. Formerly a mausoleum of the dukes of Atholl, the chapel is now that of the earls of Perth, and it

The church of Dunning with its fine 13C tower.

may be noted that Tullibardine gives the courtesy title of marquis to the eldest sons of the dukes of Atholl, who were earls of Tullibardine before elevation to dukedom.

From Auchterarder A9 provides the fast approach to Perth, but this Rte visits some places of minor interest along B8062, B934 and B9112 a mile or so to the S of the main road.

5m **Dunning** where the church has a fine square tower of c 1210, not dissimilar to that at Muthill (Rte 25B). An outside stair beside the tower ascends past a blocked Norman archway, and at the top of the tower Norman arches with inset pillars are an unusual feature.—*3m Forteviot*, today a mere hamlet, bears no trace of its ancient importance as the capital of the Picts after the Roman departure; nor as the place in which Kenneth I, first king of the united Picts and Scots, died in 860; even less in support of the tradition that the mother of Malcolm Canmore was a daughter of a miller of Forteviot. At *Forgandenny*, 2m E by B935, the church shows some Norman fragments, has a belfry of c 1600 and an unusually elaborate font and bracket of 1744.—At Forteviot B934 crosses first the railway and then the river Earn, this Rte then turning sharply E along B9112 to pass just S of the site of the battle of Dupplin of 1332. Here Edward Balliol and the 'disinherited barons' (i.e. the faction that had opposed Bruce and been disinherited by him) defeated the regent Mar, who was slain.—*5m* **Perth**, see Rte 26.

B. Via Crieff

A9 to Greenloaning. A822 to Crieff. A85 to Perth.

SOME HOTELS. **Dunblane**. See Rte 25A. **Muthill**. *Drummond Arms*, Willoughby Street. Tel: (076481) 233. **Crieff**. *Hydro*, PH7 3LQ. Tel: (0764) 2401. *Crown Inn*, 33 East High Street. Tel: (0764) 3283. *Gwydyr House*, Comrie Road. Tel: (0764) 3277. **Comrie**. *Royal*, Melville Square. Tel: (0764) 70200. **St. Fillans**. *Four Seasons*, PH6 2NF. Tel: (076485) 333. **Huntingtower**. *Huntingtower*, PH1 3JT. Tel: (073883) 241.

Total distance 38m.—*6m* **Dunblane**.—*5m* **Greenloaning**.—*10m* **Crieff**.—*11m* **Methven**.—*6m* **Perth**.

For **Stirling** to (*11m*) **Greenloaning**, see Rte 25A.—*2m Braco* is a village adjacent to **Ardoch Roman Camp**, today a complex of earthworks representing one of the largest Roman stations in Britain. Most active during the 2C, it seems, however, probable that the station continued in use as an outpost even after the completion of the Antonine Wall well to the S. At the N end of Braco the road crosses the little river Knaik, here, beside the modern bridge, being the overgrown arch of an ancient predecessor, in origin surely Roman. The main Roman complex is immediately E of the road just beyond the bridge. The central area (420ft × 375ft) is on the customary Roman rectangular plan, with sides roughly facing the cardinal points, but on the N and E, instead of the usual rampart and ditch, there are five trenches with strong earthen ramparts between them. The W and S sides are less well preserved. The camp buildings would have been of wood, and the stone foundations traceable in the middle of the area are those of a medieval chapel and its churchyard walls.

Continuing N, A822 soon cuts across more, but only vaguely visible Roman works to reach (*5m*) the small town of **Muthill**, known for its ruined 15C Church (AM. Reasonable hours. Free). Here, embedded in the end of the nave, is a square 12C tower of a tall type special to central Scotland and in which the height and heavy stonework recall Saxon and even Celtic tradition. Inside are effigies of Sir Muriel Drummond (died 1362) and of his wife.

1m **Drummond Castle Gardens** (April. Sept: Wed., Sun., 14.00 to 18.00. May–Aug: Daily, 14.00 to 18.00. Tel: 076481-257. Fee) form part of the park extending to the W of the road. The main feature is the Italian-style garden, laid out formally on a series of natural terraces and showing an extraordinary multiple sundial of 1630, the design of John Mylne. The castle (no adm.) was founded in 1491 by John, Lord Drummond, and it was here, only a few years later in 1502, that Margaret Drummond and her sisters were poisoned (see Rte 25A, Dunblane Cathedral). Later the Drummonds became earls of Perth and staunch Jacobites, their castle being badly damaged by bombardment by Cromwell and later, in 1745, deliberately part demolished to prevent its occupation by Hanoverian soldiery. Today only the square tower is original, the remainder representing rebuilding in the old style. So strong here was the contempt for the Hanoverians that, it is said, the Pond of Drummond, to the N of the long drive, was dug in order to flood ground 'desecrated' by being allotted to Hanoverian supporters.

2m **Crieff** (5500 inhab. *ECl.* Wed. *Inf.* James Square) was, until superseded by Stenhousemuir in 1770, long the site of one of Scotland's great 'trysts', or cattle markets, thronged with drovers from the Highlands and buyers from the south. Today, attractively situated above the river Earn, within easy reach of Loch Earn, the Sma' Glen and similar scenic districts, and with many hotels, the town is not only a popular touring centre but also a place with modest attractions of its own.

From James Square, the town centre, East High Street passes the *Town Hall*, at the entrance to which can be seen the old stocks and also the slender octagonal Cross (1688) of the 'Burgh of Regality of Drummond' which was for long the town's resounding name. Farther on, and on the left, is the much older *Mercat Cross*, dating to the 10C, bearing Celtic design and originally associated with an ancient church site. *Crieff Visitor Centre* (Mon.–Fri., 09.00 to 17.00. Shop and restaurant also open Sat. and Sun. Tel: 0764-2578. Free), just S of the river on A822, offers tours around Scotland's oldest pottery (*Thistle Pottery*. Tel: 0764-3515), adjacent being *Perthshire Paperweights* (Tel: 0764-2141), where the manufacture of paperweights based on 19C French designs can be watched. Opposite, at *Stuart Strathearn Crystal* (Tel: 0764-2942. Free) visitors can watch the manufacture of hand-made crystal (Mon.–Fri. only) and also see a video on the subject and buy from the shop. *Glenturret Distillery*, beside the river Turret about 1m N of Crieff, was established in 1775 and is thus one of Scotland's oldest. Today the visitor is offered a tour, a free dram and an audio-visual presentation and museum (Jan. and Feb: Shop only. 14.00 to 16.00. March–June and Sept–Oct: Mon.–Fri., 10.00 to 12.00. 13.30 to 15.30. July and Aug: Mon.–Sat., 09.45 to 16.00. Nov and Dec: Mon.–Fri., 14.00 to 15.30. Tel: 0764-2424. Free tour but fee for audio-visual and museum).

In the grounds of 17–18C *Ochertyre House* (2m NW) a mausoleum stands on the site of a church where in 1491 many of the Murrays, with their wives and children, were burned by the Drummonds.—*The Knock* (911ft) is a wooded hill and public park immediately N of the town (view indicator).

Bibliophiles will surely drive 4m SE to visit *Innerpeffray Library* (Mon.–Sat. except Thurs., 10.00 to 12.45. 14.00 to 16.45. Sun., 14.00 to 16.00. Tel: 0764-2819. Fee), Scotland's oldest library, founded in 1691 by David Drummond. Originally housed in the attic of the adjacent chapel, the collection was moved between 1750–58 to its present building, erected by Archbishop Hay Drummond who at the same time added his own library. The borrowers' ledger dates from 1747, and among the thousands of books, largely theological and classical, the oldest printing is of 1508 which historical interest is provided by the pocket bible Montrose carried at his last battle at Carbisdale.—Adjoining the library are the burial chapel of the Drummonds, founded in 1508 as a collegiate church on the site of an older chapel, and also a ruined tower-house of 1610. But long before this there was an important Roman ford and road junction here, both guarded by a fort at Strageath on the S bank.

CRIEFF TO LOCH EARN (A85 W. 12m). **Comrie**, a scenically situated summer resort half-way to Loch Earn, straddles the fault which, in geological terms, separates the Highlands from the Lowlands and is thus subject to occasional tremors which, however, rarely do more than perhaps rattle the crockery. In Drummond Street will be found the *Museum of Scottish Tartans* (April–Sept: Mon.–Sat., 09.00 to 17.00. Sun., 14.00 to 16.00. Oct–March: Mon.–Fri., 10.00 to 16.00. Sat., 10.00 to 13.00. Tel: 0764-70779. Fee), where the Scottish Tartans Society holds its collection of over 1300 tartans and much else of associated interest, including a reference library, prints, maps, documents and a system recording the details of every known tartan. Wool plucking, combing, dyeing and weaving—all as done before 1745—are demonstrated in an 18C weaving shed. The hill of Dunmore (837ft) rises 1m N of Comrie, the access path being linked with the scenic *Glen Lednock Circular Walk* (4m) which passes the Devil's Cauldron, a rock chasm through which falls force their way. The *Melville Monument*, crowning Dunmore, commemorates the statesman Henry Dundas, 1st Viscount Melville (1742–1811). He was also Baron Dunira, the name of an estate to the W of Comrie, and he retired to this district after impeachment (and acquittal) regarding his handling of Admiralty funds.

West of Comrie the mountains close in as the road follows the Earn to its outflow from Loch Earn at the village of *St. Fillans*. To the SE of the village, S of the river and beyond the golf course, there is a ruined chapel, dating from c 1500, since 1586 the burial place of the Stewarts of Ardvorlich (on the S shore of the loch near its W end; see Rte 24), and believed to mark the site of St. Fillan's 8C cell. Roads either side of Loch Earn in 7m reach *Lochearnhead* on Rte 24.

On the NE edge of Crieff A85 passes the Golf Course, on which there are three large standing stones bearing cup-and-ring markings, and in rather under *2m* reaches *Gilmerton*. Here A822 heads N to enter in 4m the **Sma' Glen**, a stony moorland valley and historic Highland gateway through which the Young Pretender retreated and along which, soon afterwards, General Wade drove one of his military roads. The junction with B8063, 3½m N of Gilmerton, marks the site of a Roman signal station, while, c 1½m farther N, *Ossian's Stone*, between the road and the Almond stream, marks, to quote Wordsworth, the 'still place' where 'remote from men, sleeps Ossian in the narrow glen'.

3m **Fowlis Wester**, just N of A85, comes as a quaint hamlet with both ancient and very modern associations. The Cross, dating from the 8C, still carries a few links of the jougs, sufficient at any rate to conjure a picture of what it must have been like to be secured here by an iron collar. The *Church of St. Bean*, although built in the 13C (restored 1927), certainly occupies the site of a much older church, possibly founded by St. Bean who died in 720, and a Pictish stone, near the vestry and found embedded in the wall, is probably from St. Bean's time. Also near the vestry is an ancient headstone, a later copy of which surmounts the lych-gate, and in the churchyard there is a leper-squint. The modern association is provided by a piece of MacBean tartan, taken to the moon by the astronaut Alan Bean, and in the modern Ascension window the colouring of Earth was chosen from that of Earth as seen from the moon.—The very scanty ruins beside a minor road 2m SE of Fowlis Wester are those of *Inchaffray Abbey*, founded here in 1200 on the site of a Celtic church by Gilbert, Earl of Strathearn, and long famed for its silver reliquary of the arm of St. Fillan, taken by the abbot to Bannockburn and used to bless Bruce's army assembled before the battle.

At (*6m*) **Methven**, a name said to be a corruption of Vale of Bean, a fragment of a collegiate church of 1433 serves as a burial place for the Methven family. It was to the N of the village that Bruce was defeated in 1306 by the English under the Earl of Pembroke, and it was at Methven Castle (no adm.), to the E and well seen above the road, that Margaret Tudor, widow of James IV, died in 1541, 28 years after the loss of her husband at Flodden. *Tibbermore*, 2m SE, was the scene in 1644 of the first battle between Montrose and the Covenanters, when Montrose, leading a motley force of about 1100 ill-clad Irish and 1300 better clad but ill-armed Highlanders, defeated a mob of 6000 Covenanters, citizens of Perth and others hastily gathered together under Lord Elcho. Montrose then entered Perth.

4m **Huntingtower Castle** (AM. Standard. Fee), a compact and intimate tower-house, part well-preserved and part restored, was until 1600 known as Ruthven Castle, the home of the Ruthvens, earls of Gowrie, notorious even by the standards of the day for their involvement in conspiracy. The construction here is most unusual, the castle comprising two 15C towers, only 9½ft apart and united by a late 17C building. The space between the towers is romantically known as the Maiden's Leap, from the tradition that the daughter of the 1st Earl (who, with his father, had plotted the murder of Rizzio) sprang across to avoid detection in an illicit love affair. Wall and ceiling paintings of c 1540 decorate the hall on the first floor.

Huntingtower, or Ruthven as it then was, was the scene of the so-called 'Raid of Ruthven' of 1582. James VI, then an insecure adolescent of 14, accepted an invitation to this hunting lodge of the 1st Earl, but, on arriving, found himself in the hands of a band of jealous nobles whose demands included the dismissal of two royal favourites, the Earl of Arran and Esmé Stuart, the latter a French cousin, possibly James's first homosexual partner and soon created Earl of Lennox. When James attempted to leave, another conspirator, the Master of Glamis, planted his back against the door, at which outrage James burst into tears. James was held for some ten months and the 'raid' (not to be confused with the Gowrie Conspiracy, Rte 26) gave the control of Scotland to the Gowrie faction, at least until the earl was beheaded two years later.

2m **Perth**, see Rte 26.

C. Via Dollar

A91 to Milnathort, where Rte 32 is joined to reach Perth by M90.
As far as Milnathort the road runs below the often steep slopes of
the Ochil Hills, cut by frequent small glens.

SOME HOTELS. **Yetts o' Muckhart** (Powmill, 2m S). *Gartwhinzean*,
FK14 7LW. Tel: (05774) 595. **Milnathort**. *Thistle*, New Road. Tel:
(0577) 63222. See also Rte 32 for hotels at **Kinross**.

Total distance 37m.—*9m* Tillicoultry.—*2m* Dollar.—*4m* Yetts o'
Muckhart.—*7m* Milnathort.—*15m* Perth.

5m **Menstrie Castle** (NTS. Nova Scotia Exhibition: May–Sept: Wed.,
Sat., Sun., 14.30 to 17.00. Free), built in the 16C, was the birthplace
and home of Sir William Alexander, 1st Earl of Stirling (c 1567–1640),
a man who, if without great distinction, combined the roles of minor
man of letters, courtier, and founder in 1621 of the colony of Nova
Scotia, thanks to James VI/I's grant to him of huge tracts of land in
what is now Canada. During the reign of Charles I Nova Scotia
baronetcies were created, and today an exhibition shows their
coats-of-arms.—*2m* **Alva** and *2m* **Tillicoultry** are both places born of
the 19C textiles industry, though the name Silver Glen, cutting in
from the N between the two, recalls that silver mining was once
important here. For *Gartmore Dam Country Park*, to the S on the way
to Alloa, see Rte 31.—*2m* **Dollar** is known for Castle Campbell and
for Dollar Academy, a distinguished school founded by John McNabb
(died 1802), a poor local lad who became a wealthy sea-captain.

Castle Campbell (AM and NTS. Standard, but closed Thurs.
afternoon and Fri. in Oct–March. Fee), perched on the steep slopes
of the Ochils and guarded by deep clefts which meet 300 yards
below, presides high and prominent above the town. The castle can
be reached either by car to within ½m or by a choice of taxing paths
climbing through the woodland of Dollar Glen (NTS).

At one time called Castle Gloom—situated in the parish of Dolour
(Dollar), beside the waters of the Bùrn of Sorrow, and with Gloom
Hill just to the E—the castle came to the Campbells by marriage in
the 15C, the present building being begun after 1481 by the Earl of
Argyll who changed the name in 1489. John Knox preached here in
1556 and, though Montrose failed to take the castle in 1645, it was
burned by Cromwell's troops nine years later. A vaulted pend of c
1600 admits to a court, where the 15C square NE tower, the castle's
main feature, is joined to the 16C S wing by a 16 or 17C range with
an open loggia. The great hall was on the first floor of the tower,
with the entrance to a pit prison to the right of the fireplace, and the
third floor is covered by a great ribbed barrel-vault, and early 17C
addition.

4m **Yetts o' Muckhart**, from where two roads head NW and N to
cross the Ochils and meet Rte 25A at Gleneagles and Dunning. To
the S, at *Rumbling Bridge*, the river Devon, tumbling down a ravine,
is spanned by three bridges—the present road bridge; a narrow arch

of 1713 put up by a local mason; and a footbridge, access to which and to the riverside path is through the grounds of the hotel. A mile or so E of Rumbling Bridge, approaching Crook o' Devon, will be found *Monarch Deer Farm* (Daily, daylight hours. Tel: 05774-310. Fee if no venison bought), with red deer, a shop and a picnic area by the river and its waterfall.—*7m* **Milnathort**, where Rte 32 is joined for (*15m*) **Perth**, see Rte 26.

26 Perth

A royal burgh of great antiquity and for a time capital of Scotland, and thus with a wealth of historical associations, Perth, with some 42,000 inhabitants, is today a mature and confident town spread comfortably along the W bank of the river Tay. The main town lies between the two large open park areas, about 1000 yards apart, known as North and South Inch.

Tourist Information. The *Round House*, Marshall Place; by the river at the NE corner of South Inch. Tourist Information is in itself interesting for occupying the former waterworks (1832), and here, today, the visitor can enjoy a stereophonic audio-visual programme on the attractions of the town and its environs. Open June–Sept: Mon.–Fri., 09.00 to 19.00. Sat., 09.00 to 18.00. Sun., 12.00 to 18.00. Oct–May: Mon.–Fri., 09.00 to 12.45. 14.00 to 17.00. Sat., 09.00 to 12.45. Tel: (0738) 22900 or 27108.

SOME HOTELS. *Royal George*, Tay Street. Tel: (0738) 24455. *Salutation*, 34 South Street. Tel: (0738) 22166. *Stakis City Mills*, West Mill Street. Tel: (0738) 28281. *County*, 26 County Place. Tel: (0738) 23618. *Station*, Leonard Street. Tel: (0738) 24141.

History. Whether or not Perth was once a Roman camp is disputed, though the city's rectangular street pattern suggests that it may well have been. Certainly, though, this district was known to the Romans, and when in c 80 Agricola's soldiers came into sight of the Tay and South Inch they are said to have shouted 'Ecce Tiberis. Ecce Campus Martius'. Later, in 846, Kenneth Macalpine established at nearby Scone the first capital of the joint kingdom of the Scots and Picts (Alba, later Scotia), and from this doubtless sprang the first township, its name then the Celtic Abertha, the place at the mouth of the Tay. This township was swept away by a flood in 1210, and in that same year William the Lion founded a royal burgh where modern Perth now stands. As capital of Scotland until c 1452 Perth was a civil and religious centre of importance, home to the large monasteries of the Black Friars, the Grey Friars, the White Friars and the Carthusians—all of which, thanks to John Knox's iconoclastic sermons preached from St. John's church in 1559, have now vanished.

Fortified by Edward I, Perth nevertheless fell to Bruce in 1311; but after the battle of Dupplin in 1332 it was occupied by Edward Balliol until again taken and held by the English between 1335–39. It was from the garden of the Blackfriars' monastery that Robert III and his queen witnessed the extraordinary clan combat (see below) on North Inch, and it was in this same monastery that James I was assassinated in 1437. In 1559, as noted above, Knox here preached his momentous sermons, and in 1600 Perth was the scene of the Gowrie Conspiracy (see below). During the fighting in the 17 and 18C Perth again many times changed hands. Montrose marched in after his defeat of Lord Elcho's Covenanters at Tibbermore in 1644; Cromwell followed, after a day's siege, in 1651; Claverhouse seized Perth in 1689 and, finally, the Jacobites occupied the town in both 1715 and 1745, rallying on North Inch and on the former occasion proclaiming the Old Pretender as king.

The art critic John Ruskin (1819–1900) spent much of his boyhood at 10 Rose Terrace, on the SW edge of North Inch. John Buchan, 1st Lord Tweedsmuir, born in Perth, for a while lived in York Place at the town centre.

North Inch is a large, open riverside park offering a variety of sports activities including golf, putting, bowls and the many indoor facilities provided by *Bell's Sports Centre* (Daily, 09.00 to 23.00 or 22.00 on Sat. and Sun. Tel: 0738-22301. Fees) on the W side of the park. But there was contest here of a more lethal kind in 1396 when North Inch served as the arena for a chivalric judicial fight between Clan Chattan and Clan Quhele (Kay), the point at issue being one of precedence—which clan should be entitled to the place of honour on a leader's right in battle. Thirty champions fought on each side, and as Clan Chattan was one man short they were joined by Hal o' the Wynd, a bandy-legged blacksmith who, though declaring himself an independent, not only contributed nobly to his side's victory but was also one of the few survivors. The affair is graphically described in Sir Walter Scott's 'The Fair Maid of Perth'.

Off the W of the park, and just N of Bell's Sports Centre, stands **Balhousie Castle** or, more grandly, the Tower-House of the Barony of Balhousie. First recorded in 1422, and probably built at about the same time, the castle was in more recent times rebuilt in Scottish Baronial style and now houses the *Museum of the Black Watch*, a regiment which has had close connections with Perth ever since its raising at Aberfeldy in 1739 (Mon.–Fri., 10.00 to 16.30 or 15.30 in Oct–April. Tel: 0738-21281, Ext. 30. Donation). Farther N, on Inveralmond Industrial Estate, glass-making may be seen, and the products bought, at *Caithness Glass* (Glass-making: Mon.–Fri., 09.00 to 16.30. Shop: Mon.–Sat., 09.00 to 17.00. Sun., 13.00 to 17.00. Tel: 0738-37373. Free).

Beyond the SW corner of North Inch, at the junction of Atholl Street and North Methven Street, stands *St. Ninian's Cathedral*, Perth's handsome episcopal cathedral, begun in 1850 for the diocese of St. Andrews, Dunkeld and Dunblane and completed in 1900.

A plaque on the corner of Charlotte and Blackfriars streets, off the S of North Inch, reminds that this is a corner of Perth which has witnessed dramatic and violent occasions. For here stood *Blackfriars Monastery*, founded in 1231 by Alexander II and destroyed as the result of Knox's preaching in 1559. Here homage was paid to England's Edward I in 1291; from the monastery's garden in 1396 Robert III and his queen presided at that murderous clan combat; and here in 1437 James I was assassinated by Sir Robert Graham, in spite of the devotion of one of the queen's ladies, Catherine Douglas, who thrust her arm through the rings of the door to serve as the missing iron bolt. She survived, and later married one Richard Lovell of Ballumbie.

The **Fair Maid's House**, in North Port (the site of Perth's castle) just S of Charlotte Street, was the old Glovers' Hall, chosen by Scott as the home of Catherine Glover, the heroine of his 'The Fair Maid of Perth'. The niche on the exterior corner once held a figure of St. Bartholomew, patron saint of the glovers, and inside there is a medieval wall, one of the oldest in Perth. The house now serves as a gallery, with changing exhibitions by Scottish artists (painting, sculpture, embroidery and other art forms), and also as a shop offering high quality Scottish craftwork and knitwear (Shop: Mon.–Sat., 10.00 to 17.00. Gallery: Mon.–Sat., 11.00 to 16.00. Sun., 11.00 to 17.00. Tel: 0738-25976. Free).

The city **Art Gallery and Museum** (Mon.–Sat., 10.00 to 13.00. 14.00 to 17.00. Tel: 0738-32488. Free), just E of the Fair Maid's House, is in George Street close to Perth Bridge, Smeaton's nine-arch work of 1723 (later widened). The building of 1935 incorporates the Classical facade of the old museum as also a statue of Provost Hay Marshall (1824). Among the varied permanent collections—fine and applied art, local history, archaeology, costume and suchlike—special mention may be made of the displays illustrating the whisky industry and local natural history.

From Perth Bridge, the wide tree-shaded Tay Street runs with the river, soon reaching the E end of High Street which, with Scott and South streets to the W and S, defines the compact heart of Perth. In High Street, near this corner with Tay Street, a plaque presented by 1st Polish Army reminds that Perth was the 'rallying place' for the Polish army in 1940–42. A short way farther along High Street, off the N side and opposite King Edward Street, the narrow *Guard Vennel* claims attention for having once housed the town guard and the mint, as also Wolfe who lived here for a while as a young officer. Opposite, a shield on a house marks the site of the guildhall of 1722 (rebuilt 1907). Beyond, the intimate Victorian *Perth Theatre* (1900) stands on the N side of High Street near the junction with Kinnoull Street, while to the S, between High Street and South Street, is the contrastingly modern *St. John's Centre* (1961).

Kinnoull Street is extended southward by Scott Street, which soon meets South Street, parallel to which on the S the name Charterhouse Lane recalls that near here stood the Charterhouse, an important Carthusian monastery founded in 1429 by James I and in which he and his queen, as also Margaret Tudor, widow of James IV, were all buried. Like all its fellows, the monastery was destroyed in 1559, and James I's tombstone was later removed to the church of St. John.

South Street, followed E, passes the *Post Office*, then reaching, set back in St. John Street, the **Church of St. John**, a church which has known much change and seen, too, something of history.

Founded in 1126 by David I, very possibly on the site of a Culdee church, and at the same time granted to Dunfermline Abbey, the church was first restored in 1328 by Robert Bruce, though work was soon halted by Bruce's death in the following year. There followed major restoration, amounting almost to rebuilding, during the 15 and 16C, the interior being divided in 1598 into two churches between which, in c 1773, a mid-church was inserted. The 19C brought further changes, some drastic, until finally, in 1926, yet more modification (by Robert Lorimer) enabled the church to house the County War Memorial. As to history, it was here, in David I's church in 1296, that the conquering Edward I kept the feast of the nativity of St. John the Baptist; and here, too, in 1335—though there seems no evidence for this tradition—Edward III slew his brother, the Earl of Cornwall. Then came 1559 and John Knox, preaching his inflammatory sermon urging the 'purging of the churches from idolatry' and sending an iconoclastic storm over Scotland, drastic and destructive far beyond the preacher's intentions if Knox's subsequent acid condemnation of the 'rascal multitude' was sincere. In 1644, after Tibbermore, Montrose confined 800 Covenanter prisoners here, and among the monarchs or would-be monarchs who worshipped here were Charles I in 1633, Charles II in 1650 and the Young Pretender in 1745.

As seen today the church is a cruciform edifice with a sturdy central tower surmounted by a 15C steeple. The N porch, with 15C vaulting, represents the lowest storey of a tower of David I's original church of c 1126, otherwise demolished in 1823; the choir dates from c 1440, the surprisingly low nave from about 50 years later, and the N transept stands as a rebuilding of 1828. The interior is said once to have boasted no fewer than 40 altars dedicated to as many saints, but these disappeared after Knox's sermon and today it is the choir, with its early roof and modern great E window (by Douglas Strachan), which is perhaps the most interesting area of the church. In part the choir is used to display the church's treasures, these including a call of early bells; the Hammermen's collecting box, once on their guild altar; the Nuremberg Cup (German, late 16 or early 17C); two steeple cups (London, early 17C); a baptismal basin (Edinburgh, 1593); pewter and various other items of interest.

The corner of South Street and St. John Street was once filled by the residence of the bishops of Dunkeld, built earlier than 1461 but demolished in 1861, and it is worth walking into Fountain Close,

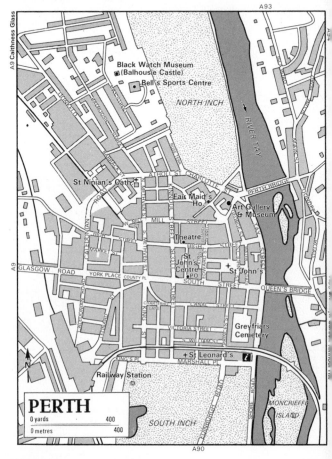

immediately E of St. John Street, where many snippets of information have been recorded on the whitewashed walls and at the end of which there is a pictorial impression of the bishops' house. Across the road, the *Salutation Hotel* (1695), with a distinctive frontage, is one of the oldest established hotels in Scotland, the place, too, chosen by the Young Pretender for his lodging in 1745, in Room 20 which is still in use.

South Street now meets Tay Street at Queen's Bridge, the building on the SW corner of the crossroads, the *Sheriff Court* (R. Smírke, 1820), occupying the site of Gowrie House, scene of the still mysterious Gowrie Conspiracy of 1600. Today a bronze tablet in one of the blind windows gives the modern visitor a hint of the picturesque

Perth. The Waterworks of 1832 now house Tourist Information.

old mansion (1520) which in its day was one of the chief ornaments of the city.

There are at least two versions of the *Gowrie Conspiracy*, one portraying the 3rd Earl of Gowrie as the villain, the other ascribing the initiative to James VI. Under the first version Gowrie and his brother Alexander Ruthven, keen to repeat the success of the 'Raid of Ruthven' (see Rte 25B, Huntingtower Castle), lured the king to Gowrie House with a tale of foreign treasure, there leading him to an upper room where Ruthven, after some heated words, attempted to bind the king. James, however, succeeded in giving the alarm through an open window, whereupon his attendants forced their way to his rescue, both Gowrie and Ruthven being killed in the fracas. The alternative version suggests that the whole affair was stage-managed by James, still smarting from his experience at Huntingtower and determined to wipe out Gowrie and his family. Certainly James hunted down Gowrie's two younger brothers, forcing one to flee abroad and imprisoning the other (Patrick) until 1622. A curious footnote is that Patrick's daughter, Lady Mary Ruthven, became the wife of the painter, Van Dyck.

Either way, at this spot, approaching 400 years ago, James VI not only rid himself of the unpleasant Gowries but also proscribed the very name of Ruthven. By a strange quirk of history, though, Lady Mary Ruthven survives in several portraits by her husband.

A short way S, beside Tay Street, *Greyfriars Cemetery* spreads over the site of the Franciscan monastery founded by Lord Oliphant in 1468 and, with all the others, destroyed in 1559. Beyond, and below the railway and footbridge, Tay Street reaches *Tourist Information* in its distinctive converted 19C waterworks building, this standing on part of the site of a massive fort planted here by Cromwell in 1652.

The large, green open expanse of **South Inch**, though in part given over to boating, putting, minigolf and children's paddling and play areas, must surely be a more disciplined place now than it was in the days when used for uncontrolled archery, competitive hucksters, and the burning of witches. On the N side the church of *St. Leonard's in the Fields*, with its crown steeple, was built by J.J. Stevenson in 1884, while the large building on the S side is the former *General Prison*, erected in 1812 for French war prisoners and enlarged in the 1840s.

The railway bridge, with a footpath, crosses above the N end of the long *Friarton* or *Moncrieffe Island* in the Tay, on which James VI's golf course still flourishes. Beyond the bridge is **Branklyn Garden** (NTS. March–Oct: Daily, 10.00 to sunset. Fee), begun by Mr and Mrs John Renton in 1922 on the site of an orchard. Within the garden's two acres are rhododendrons, herbaceous and peat garden plants, and, above all, alpines.—Beyond, *Kinnoull Hill* (729ft), rising abruptly above the Tay, is a noted local view point (indicator), with also a nature trail and woodland paths.

Elcho Castle (AM. Standard. Fee), on the right bank of the Tay 4m SE of Perth, was the home of that Lord Elcho who so unsuccessfully confronted Montrose at Tibbermore. Standing on or close to the site of a predecessor, said to have been one of Wallace's favourite retreats, the present castle is a well-preserved example of a 14–16C fortified mansion. The wrought-iron grills protecting the windows are especially noteworthy.

For **Scone Palace**, see Rte 28.—For Perth to **Stirling**, see Rte 25; to **Pitlochry**, see Rte 27; to **Braemar**, see Rte 28; to **Aberdeen**, see Rte 29; to **Dundee**, see Rtes 30 and 33D; to **Edinburgh**, see Rte 32.

27   Perth to Pitlochry and Newtonmore

A9 (old road between Pitlochry and Clan Donnachaidh museum).—Pastoral at first, becoming increasingly hilly and wooded after Dunkeld and, beyond Blair Atholl, ascending Glen Garry to break out on to high open moor bounded by bare mountains lifting to over 3000ft. The watershed is the Pass of Drumochter (1484ft), beyond which the road follows Glen Truim down to the gentler and more cultivated but still scenic valley of the Spey.

Note: This road was first laid out by General Wade in 1726–33, improved in 1830 by Telford, reconstructed in 1925–28, and, since then, has been under almost constant attention as Scotland's main N–S artery. Today a dual carriageway trunk road, the modern A9 bypasses virtually all the places mentioned along the Rte below and, although signing is good, care must be taken not to get swept beyond the objective.

The railway follows much the same course as the road, at Drumochter reaching the highest level of any extant railway in Britain.

SOME HOTELS. **Dunkeld**. Atholl Arms, Bridge Street. Tel: (03502) 219. **Pitlochry**. Atholl Palace, Atholl Road. Tel: (0796) 2400. Fishers, 75–79 Atholl Road. Tel: (0796) 2000. **Kinloch Rannoch**. Loch Rannoch, PH16 5PS. Tel: (08822) 201. Dunalastair, PH16 5PW. Tel: (08822) 323. **Blair Atholl**. Glen Tilt, PH18 5SU. Tel: (079681) 333. **Dalwhinnie**. Grampian, PH19 1AB. Tel: (05282) 210.

Total distance 63m.—13m **Dunkeld**.—12m **Pitlochry**.—7m **Blair Atholl**.—16m **Pass of Drumochter**.—15m **Newtonmore**.

Perth (see Rte 26) is left by Dunkeld Road out of the city's NW corner, A9 soon being joined to cross, though scarcely noticeably, the small river Almond which flows into the Tay to the E of the road beyond the railway and close against the W bounds of Scone Palace park. Here at the confluence once stood the Roman station which later received the Celtic name of Åbertha, forerunner of Kenneth Macalpine's capital.—3m **Luncarty**, to the E, was in 990 the site of a great battle in which Kenneth II crushed the Norsemen; a battle, too, which should interest anyone bearing the name of Hay since, or so the tale goes, the Scots were rallied at a critical moment by a peasant called Hay, armed with no more than a plough yoke. After the battle Hay was rewarded with land, and it is he who is the legendary ancestor of the Hays of Tweeddale; but, it must be said, several families of the name of Hay show a peasant with a yoke as part of their coats-of-arms. Another incident during the battle is said to have led to the adoption of the Thistle as the emblem of Scotland (see Aspects of Scotland, Thistle). Precisely where this battle was fought is disputed, but the hamlet of Battleby, ½m SW of Luncarty, is a tempting choice.

The road crosses the railway before curving W into the wooded Pass of Birnam, cutting between Birnam Hill (1324ft. W) and the Tay (E) and once known as the 'Mouth of the Highlands' out of which swarmed the Highlander bands of Montrose and the Young Pretender. The S slopes of the hill, with a hill fort known as Duncan's Castle, are clothed by Birnam Wood, that same wood which, in Shakespeare's 'Macbeth', by moving to Dunsinane (see Rte 29), spelt the end for Macbeth. On Terrace Walk, which follows the right bank of the Tay

for a mile below the village-resort of *Birnam*, some venerable trees
are claimed to be survivors of the original forest. In the churchyard
of *Little Dunkeld*, virtually joined with Birnam, lies Niel Gow
(1727–1807), a fiddler of humble origins but great musical distinction,
who, together with his four sons, did much both to preserve and add
to traditional Scottish melodies and reels. Together the family edited
the several volumes of airs preserved in the 'Gow Collection'.

This Rte now breaks away from A9 to cross a sylvan reach of the
Tay by Telford's bridge of 1809 and enter (*10m* from Luncarty)
Dunkeld (500 inhab. *ECl.* Thurs. *Inf.* The Cross. Easter–Oct), a small
and very ancient cathedral township in a tranquil riverside setting
below wooded mountains. The setting apart, the main attractions for
the visitor are the partially ruined cathedral and the early 18C Little
Houses.

History. First important as a residence of Pictish kings and soon afterwards a
Celtic centre (hence its name meaning Fort of the Celts), Dunkeld is traditionally
supposed to have been the site of a monastery founded in the 6C by St. Columba
and St. Mungo, or perhaps a century later by St. Adamnan. Certainly, though,
an abbey was established here by 729 by Celtic monks, who, driven out of Iona
by the Norsemen, brought with them the relics of St. Columba for which they
consecrated a shrine. Not long afterwards Kenneth Macalpine is said to have
treated Dunkeld as joint capital with Scone, while a bishopric, founded here
by either Alexander I or David I, flourished until the Reformation. This
bishopric's perhaps most distinguished incumbent was Gavin Douglas
(1474–1522), even if his life was devoted more to his literary pursuits (he is best
known for a scholarly translation of the 'Aeneid') and to his political scheming
than to the spiritual needs of his see.

In 1689, on 26 Aug, Dunkeld was the stage for the savage battle that was
the aftermath of Killiecrankie. The town, including the cathedral, was held by
1200 Cameronians, the newly raised Lowland regiment of extremist
Covenanters, against 500 Highlanders, victorious at Killiecrankie. Initially
successful, the Highlanders penetrated the town, whereupon the Cameronian
commander (Captain Munro, who had taken over from Colonel Cleland, already
killed) resorted to fire and Dunkeld was virtually gutted. The Highlanders then
withdrew, the cause of James VII/II was lost and the security of William and
Mary assured.

Rising both elegant and ruined from tree-shaded lawns beside the
Tay, it is not surprising that *Dunkeld Cathedral* (AM. Standard.
Free) appealed to the romantic yearnings of the Victorians. Parts of
the fabric date from the 12C—the nave piers may well be contemporary with the original foundation of the see—but in general the
remains are of the 14–15C. The nave and aisles have remained
roofless since the savage Reformation desecration of 1560, but the
choir, roughly repaired in 1600, was later thoroughly restored after
1815 and again in 1908.

Begun by Bishop Cardney in 1406 and consecrated by Bishop
Lauder in 1464, the Nave is remarkable for the Flamboyant tracery
of the aisle windows as also for the great W window which, curiously,
is not truly centred in its gable. The massive tower at the end of the
N aisle was started five years after the cathedral's consecration and
took some 32 years to build, being completed in c 1501; it contains
15C murals and a hog-backed tomb. Buried in the nave are, near the
W door, Colonel Cleland, the Covenanter commander (see above)
and minor poet; Bishop Cardney, in the S aisle; and, at the W end,
Charles Edward Stewart, self-styled Count Roehenstart (?1781–1854).
A teasing question mark hangs over this grave. In fact Stewart

appears to have been one of two well-born, exceptionally charming but eccentric brothers called Allan, both of whom claimed to be descendants of the Young Pretender, this one on the imaginative grounds that he was natural son of Charlotte (herself natural daughter of the Young Pretender and Clementina Walkinshaw) and the Swedish Count Roehenstart. The brothers' claim must have had some credibility—there was certainly rumour that Charlotte had some form of association with Roehenstart—for it seems to have been accepted in aristocratic circles, if only with amused tolerance. In 1854 Charles Stewart was killed in Dunkeld in a coach accident, and in resting here he may be said to have achieved a form of recognition.

The aisleless Choir, now serving as parish church, was started by Bishop William Sinclair in 1318 but not completed until 1400. It has an attractive blind arcade (N) and good plain sedilia (S), while at the E end survive the remains of a statue of its founder who died in 1338. Nearby, a recumbent armoured effigy is believed to be that of Robert II's natural son, the arrogant and vicious Alexander Stewart, Earl of Buchan, more notoriously known as the 'Wolf of Badenoch'. Among memorials are those to the Black Watch and Colonel Cleland, both against the E wall; and to the Scottish Horse regiment (see museum in the town) and their founder, the 8th Duke of Atholl (died 1942), both on the N wall. Also to be seen in the choir are two sobering reminders of the cruel hazards of medieval life—the Lepers' Squint, now partially filled in (N wall, near the pulpit), and the Whipping Pillar, by the stair to the organ loft. The E window, with St. Columba as the central figure, was gifted by Sir Donald Currie, the benefactor responsible for much of the restoration of 1908.

Behind the cathedral the so-called 'parent larch' reputedly represents the first larch to be planted in Scotland, by the Duke of Atholl in 1737.

The *Little Houses* (no adm.), which line Cathedral Street, delight both in themselves and as an inspiring example of imaginative conservation. Dating mainly from the rebuilding which followed the devastation caused by the battle of 1689, the houses, by 1950 in serious disrepair and in danger of demolition, then became the subject of an appeal by the National Trust for Scotland. So successful was this that the houses were restored, and, now let to tenants, provide a surely unique cathedral approach. One house, the *Ell House*, serves as the Trust shop (April–May. Sept–Christmas: Mon.–Sat., 10.00 to 13.00. 14.00 to 16.30. June–Aug: Mon.–Sat., 10.00 to 18.00).

In Dunkeld's delightful 18C square are *Tourist Information*, with a NTS photographic display and short audio-visual presentation, and also the *Museum of the Scottish Horse* (Easter–mid Oct: Daily, 10.30 to 12.30. 14.00 to 17.00. Fee), telling the story of this yeomanry regiment raised by the 8th Duke of Atholl, who died in 1942. *Stanley Hill*, behind the 'Little Houses', is a mound artificially landscaped in 1730 as a fortification by the Duke of Atholl and his brother, Lord George Murray, the Jacobite general; the suggestion that the mound may include the original dun of Dunkeld can be left to the visitor's individual wishful thinking.

ENVIRONS OF DUNKELD. Undoubtedly the most popular local objective is the Scottish Wildlife Trust's *Loch of Lowes* nature reserve, beside the loch of the same name under 2m NE of Dunkeld by A923. The reserve shelters a variety of birds, plants and animals—the highlight being a hide from which ospreys may be watched if the visitor is lucky in his timing—and a centre explains the local natural history (April, May, Sept: Daily, 10.00 to 19.00, June–Aug: Daily, 10.00 to 20.30. Tel: 031-2264602. Donation).

Just N out of Dunkeld a minor road leading W off A923 rounds below the hill of *Craigie Barns* (1106ft), curious for the fact that much of the growth covering its steep slopes has resulted from an ingenious plan by which canisters of seeds were fired at the then bare crags out of small cannon.

On the W side of the Tay there is the *Hermitage Woodland Walk* (NTS. 1m in length. Booklet) threading through the woods beside the Braan, the legacy of the interest in forestry, including the introduction of new species, shown by successive dukes of Atholl. Apart from offering much of natural beauty and interest, the walk passes a charming 18C bridge over a narrow gorge, a waterfall and two follies. The first folly is the Hermitage, or Ossian's Hall, built in 1758, converted to a romantic, mirrored waterfall room in 1783, largely destroyed by vandals in 1869 and now restored and refurbished. Beyond is Ossian's Cave, another 18C folly, neatly using a group of boulders and claiming to represent the kind of place in which such a bard would have lived.

This Rte now continues N along A9 which crosses the Tay 2m out of Dunkeld and in under 3m reached *Dowally*, beyond which a wide view opens out up the Tay, with the shapely Schiehallion (see below) and round-topped Farragon rising beyond the valley as the road approaches (3m) *Ballinluig* where Rte 24 comes in from the W. Here, at Ballinluig, the connoisseur of stone circles will enter the village and follow the old A9 northward for a few hundred yards, to the road's end where, on the E side, a modest circle awaits. Beyond Ballinluig, if Pitlochry, Bridge of Garry and Loch Tummel, Killiecrankie and Blair Atholl are the objectives, care should be taken to choose the town road rather than the bypass.

4m **Pitlochry** (2500 inhab. *ECl*. Thurs. *Inf*. 22 Atholl Road), at the geographic centre of Scotland and at the heart too of a far-flung district of immensely varied natural beauty, is one of the most visited inland resorts in the country. With a touch of old-world elegance and with plenty of local attractions, these including a distinguished theatre and the famous fish-pass, and generously provided too with hotels, Pitlochry is well sited as a base for day touring, whether perhaps to Aberfeldy and Loch Tay; or to the famous Queen's View, followed by an exploration along Loch Tummel and the remote country around Loch Rannoch; or past the battlefield of Killiecrankie and then up to the high, wide mountain and moorland to the N with the pastoral Spey valley beyond and below.

Pitlochry Festival Theatre, which started as a marquee in 1951, now occupies a purpose-built riverside (S bank) building opened by the Prince of Wales in 1981. The season of plays, concerts and other entertainment extends from May to October.—In summer *Highland Nights* are held twice weekly, with demonstrations of Highland and country dancing.—*Pitlochry Highland Games* are held annually on the second Saturday in September.

Immediately to the W of the town *Loch Faskally* curves away westward and northward, a lovely stretch of tree-surrounded water, 2½m long and created out of the Tummel river for hydro-electric purposes in 1950. Rowing and powered boats can be hired to enable the best of this loch to be enjoyed. At the S end of the loch, beside the large dam and power station, will be found the *Fish-Pass or Salmon Ladder* (Short walk from town centre. Motorists will find car parks on the N side of the river, whence they can walk across the dam. Alternatively the river can be crossed by Bridge Road at the SE of the town and signs then followed past the Festival Theatre. This latter approach is recommended to motorists planning to enjoy the drive along the S shore of Loch Tummel, described below). Yearly, between April and October, the salmon (electronically counted), spawned years earlier on the shingle beds of Scotland's northern streams and then finding their home in the Atlantic, make their way back to repeat the cycle. Provided with an observation room for the benefit of visitors, and with steps to the open top surface of the pools, the system is 900ft in length and comprises 34 pools connected by pipes.

Adjacent is the *Hydro-Electric Visitor Centre* (Easter or April–Oct: Daily, 09.40 to 17.30. Tel: 0796-3152 or 031-2251361. Fee) where video films, a scale model, easily understood diagrams and photographs combine to illustrate not only the Tummel Valley hydro-electric scheme but also how salmon and man share Scotland's northern lochs and rivers.

The **Tummel Valley Hydro-Electric Scheme** covers a large area of wild and lonely countryside and makes use of many lochs and streams. Essentially the scheme operates as two sections, Rannoch and Tummel. *Rannoch* itself divides into two. In the far W the water flowing off the desolate Moor of Rannoch is collected in Loch Eigheach, with Gaur dam and power station (1953 and the first in the scheme to operate under remote control) at its E end. Well to the N, to the E of Dalwhinnie on A9 farther along this Rte, are lochs An-t-Seilich and Cuaich, connected by tunnel and with a power station (1959) at the S end of the latter. From here water is discharged through an aqueduct across A9 and into Loch Ericht, which, dropping southward from Dalwhinnie, slices some 15 narrow miles through the mountains. Ericht also takes water from Loch Garry (5m to its E), the water arriving by tunnel at Loch Ericht power station (1962). From Loch Ericht, which represents the main Rannoch section storage reservoir, the water is tunnelled to Loch Rannoch power station (1930).

In the *Tummel* section there is a series of lochs, dams and power stations, some of these last (Errochty, Clunie and Pitlochry) constructed as part of the post-war Tummel-Garry scheme. Loch Rannoch and, high above to the N, Loch Errochty, are the main storage reservoirs. Travelling E and then S the lochs and power stations are Loch Dunalastair, channelling water by open aqueduct to the power station (1933) at the W end of Loch Tummel; Errochty power station, fed by tunnel from its loch; beyond the E end of Loch Tummel, Clunie dam, whence a tunnel carries water to Clunie power station at the N end of Loch Faskally; and, finally, at Loch Faskally's S end, Pitlochry dam and power station.

All the southern lochs lie along the roads from Pitlochry to Rannoch Station (see below).

From Pitlochry dam pedestrians may return to the town by crossing the dam; by the Port-na-Craig suspension footbridge a short way downstream; or, if more energetic, by skirting the wooded W shore of the loch, crossing to the E bank by a footbridge where the loch narrows by the boating station.

ENVIRONS OF PITLOCHRY. The *Black Spout*, a waterfall deep in woods 1½m SE of Pitlochry, is best reached by Knockfarrie Road (alongside the entrance to the Atholl Palace Hotel) and then through the woods.

Craigower (1300ft. NTS. Booklet), an 11-acre beacon hill rising immediately N of Pitlochry beyond the golf course and offering splendid views (indicator), can comfortably be climbed by following the signed Dunmore Trail. This varied circular walk of 3½m is named in honour of John, Earl of Dunmore (1939–80), member of the NTS Council, and of his father, Viscount Fincastle, killed in action in 1940.

From *Moulin*, just N of Pitlochry, a path ascends *Ben Vrackie* (2757ft) with a view indicator at the summit.—To the SE of Moulin, and reached by a short path, are the ruins of *Castle Dubh* (probably 13–14C), once a stronghold of Sir John Campbell of Lochow, a nephew of Bruce. Local tradition tells that when, in 1500, the garrison was stricken by plague, the castle was battered down by cannon to form a cairn over the dead.

To the S (2m) of Pitlochry the 8C *Dunfallandy Stone* should not be missed by anyone with an appreciation of Pictish art. The stone is reached by crossing the river by Bridge Road to follow the little Logierait road southward close to the Tummel; this road runs below A9, passes the entrance to Dunfallandy House Hotel and immediately reaches another turn to the right across a cattle grid. The stone is atop a mound a short distance up this driveway. Originally near Killiecrankie, this stone, now well protected behind glass, bears on one side a decorated cross, together with figures of Jonah, beasts and angels; and, on the other, two figures apparently in earnest conversation (said to be Saints Paul and Anthony), a horseman and various symbols, all within a frame of two serpents.

PITLOCHRY TO RANNOCH STATION (B8019 and B846, W. 35m). One of a number of Scottish roads claiming the title of 'Road to the Isles', though this one stops abruptly at the railway well short of the western sea, this is a scenically highly rewarding drive into a remote and sometimes desolate countryside of loch, forest and mountain; in places, though, and especially of course in summer, trees can interfere with the views. There is no road escape at the far end, so the return, if to Pitlochry, must be by more or less the same route. However there are lonely Highland roads linking Tummel Bridge and Dunalastair to either Calvine or Dalnacardoch on A9 to the N; another, southwards, links Tummel Bridge with Rte 24 at Coshieville; and from Kinloch Rannoch a minor road rounds the northern slopes of Schiehallion to meet the Coshieville road. Various hydro-electric installations are passed—power stations, dams, pipes and reservoirs—and interest can be added by first calling at the Pitlochry hydro-electric visitor centre (see also above for an outline of the Loch Tummel Scheme). There are hotels at Kinloch Rannoch.

The S shore of Loch Tummel is reached from Pitlochry along the W shore of Loch Faskally, the approach being past the Festival Theatre and then negotiating the obstacle of A9 by following the signs to Foss, a village towards the W end of Loch Tummel. Narrow, and dipping and rising through woods, this pleasant and little-used small road first reaches, some 1½m beyond A9 and on the left atop a bank, an ancient (?6C) stone known as the *Priest's Stone* and bearing the outline of a cross. The *Clunie Memorial Arch*, immediately beyond, in the shape of a tunnel and marking the entrance to Clunie power station, honours five workers killed during the construction of the tunnel (2m long. 1946–50) through which the waters of Loch Tummel are brought from Clunie dam. Just beyond, again, a sign indicates *Linn of Tummel View Point* (see below). The road continues along the loch's S side to join B846 which, taken southwards, travels through Strath Appin to pass Glengoulandie Deer Park and Garth Castle shortly before meeting Rte 24 at Coshieville; or, taken northwards, reaches Tummel Bridge where the modern bridge crosses the river beside its attractive stone predecessor of 1733. For W, N and E of Tummel Bridge see below.

The more important and more popular B8019 bears W across *Bridge of Garry* (about 3m N of Pitlochry). For Linn of Tummel, visited from here, see below) and in 4m arrives at the rocky spur known as ***Queen's View**, a justly renowned beauty spot with a superb vista up the length of Loch Tummel with the mass of Schiehallion as background. It is of interest that this spot apparently won its name long before Queen Victoria came here in 1886, and it may well be that the name reaches back to a visit by Mary, Queen of Scots, in 1564, the tradition being that she was so taken with this district that she ordered her harpist to extol it in music. *Schiehallion* (3547ft), which will dominate the southward view along most of this diversion, is an isolated and graceful conical peak of snowy quartzite which in 1774–76, and again in 1811, played a part in scientific history. On the first occasion the mountain was used by Nevil Maskelyne, the Astronomer Royal, in his experiments, through deviations of the plumb line, into determining the attraction of the mass of mountains, and from this the mathematician Charles Hutton deduced the mean density of Earth. On the second occasion similar use was made of the mountain by the Scottish mathematician John Playfair.

The Forestry Commission's *Visitor Centre* (April–Sept: Daily, 09.30 or 10.00 on Sun. to 17.30. Donation), with admirable displays including a slide show, interprets the natural history, forestry and other aspects of this district. Advice is also given on a choice of forest walks which, starting from the nearby Allean picnic site and in part rough and steep, visit an Iron Age fort and a reconstructed clachan (homestead).

Close beside the water, and sometimes frustratingly deep in trees, B8019 passes the Errochty power station and arrives at the loch's W end to join B846 at *Tummel Bridge*, which bridge, flanked by its pleasing stone predecessor of 1733, carries the latter road southward (see small print above). Another road (at Trinafour becoming B847), wild and remote as it travels northward, provides an opportunity, soon repeated at Dunalastair, to join A9 in some 9m at Calvine or Dalnacardoch, the former between Blair Atholl and the foot of Glen Garry and the latter well up the glen. If Dalnacardoch is chosen, then on the way a fine glimpse can be enjoyed of Loch Errochty and its dam.

The power station at Tummel Bridge is fed by aqueduct from the dam at *Dunalastair*, rather over 3m farther on and at the E end of its reservoir. Beyond the other end of the reservoir the neat village of **Kinloch Rannoch** stands, despite its name, at the foot rather than the head of Loch Rannoch, a beautiful sheet of water some 10m long and 1m broad. In the centre of the village an obelisk remembers Dugald Buchanán 'the Rannoch Schoolmaster, Evangelist, and Sacred Poet' (see also Rte 24, Strathyre). Roads fringe both sides of the loch, that on the N affording the better distant views. The unclassified S shore road soon enters *Rannoch Forest* to cross (3m from Kinloch Rannoch) the Carie Burn, by which the Forestry Commission's Carie Picnic Site is the start for a choice of forest walks ranging from 1m to 5m in scope and climbing to high ground overlooking the loch. *Dall*, 1½m farther on and now part of a school, is a mansion built in 1855 as a 'clan-seat' of the Robertsons, and, just beyond, the *Black Wood of Rannoch* shelters ancient trees officially accepted as survivors of the Caledonian Forest. At the W end of the loch the roads join, just W of the bridge over the Gaur being a house called Rannoch Barracks, a reminder that it was built to accommodate Hanoverian troops stationed here after the '45.

The river Gaur, barely 3m long and tumbling its way across desolate country, links lochs Rannoch and the wilder and much smaller Eigheach, beyond the latter being the road's end at Rannoch Station on the West Highland Railway (Glasgow to Fort William; see the introduction to Rte 44A).

At *Bridge of Garry*, *3m* N of Pitlochry and the start of the lochs Tummel and Rannoch diversion just described, there is a car park for the use of visitors to **Linn of Tummel** (waymarked walk of 2m; booklet from Killiecrankie), a popular NTS property of 47 acres of mixed woodland along the banks of the rivers Garry and Tummel and a place greatly admired by Queen Victoria whose visit here in 1844 is recorded by an obelisk. At the time of this visit the Tummel dropped as a sheer waterfall into the Garry, but much of this fall became a pool (Linn) in 1950 when the level of both rivers was raised by the creation of Loch Faskally. Today a wooden bridge crosses an early fish-pass, needed when the salmon were confronted by the then formidable Falls of Tummel, in their present more modest form still cascading a short way upstream.

Just N of Bridge of Garry, and now somewhat slashed by a ruthless A9, starts the ***Pass of Killiecrankie**, the wooded gorge through which the river Garry forces its way to join the Tummel and the site of the latter part of the battle of 27 July 1689 when the English troops of King William were defeated by insurgent Jacobite Highlanders under Claverhouse (Bonnie Dundee of ballad).

Battle of Killiecrankie. The English, commanded by General Mackay, had emerged at the upper end of the pass and had formed up facing N on the plateau above the Haugh of Urrard when the Highlanders received the signal to charge. 'It was past seven o'clock. Dundee gave the word. The Highlanders dropped their plaids. The few who were so luxurious as to wear rude socks of untanned hide spurned them away. It was long remembered in Lochaber that Lochiel took off what possibly was the only pair of shoes in his clan, and charged barefoot at the head of his men. In two minutes the battle was lost and won... and the mingled torrent of red coats and tartans went raving down the valley to the gorge of Killiecrankie' (Macaulay). But for the Highlanders victory was soured by the death of their leader, Dundee. Fatally wounded, he is said to have been carried to Urrard House, in the woods near the old A9 N of the NTS Visitor Centre, and a stone in the grounds, visible from this road, marks the spot where he fell. Although the Highlanders won this battle, they were unable to survive this loss and were decisively defeated three weeks later at Dunkeld.—This Pass of Killiecrankie long continued to have a baneful effect, and in 1746 German troops employed in subduing the Young Pretender's supporters refused to enter the pass, insisting that they had reached the last outpost of civilisation.

An excellent *Visitor Centre* (NTS. April–June and Sept–mid Oct: Daily, 10.00 to 18.00. July and Aug: Daily, 09.30 to 18.00. Fee) not only explains the battle and its historical background but also illustrates the local topography and natural history. At a corner of the car park, at the opposite end from the Centre, a small and rather unconvincing section of Wade's original road construction is indicated. From the Centre a path drops down the wooded hillside to the river far below, where the narrowest part of the gorge is known as the Soldier's Leap, a spot where a fleeing English soldier made a spectacular jump to escape the Highland pack hot on his heels. From here paths descend the gorge to Bridge of Garry and Linn of Tummel, for both of which see above.

Northward from the Visitor Centre the old A9 passes, to the right, the site of the battle proper, with the Claverhouse Stone marking the spot where the Jacobite commander fell, before reaching (*4m* from Bridge of Garry) **Blair Atholl**, the last place of any size before the ascent of Glen Garry. Here, although Blair Castle is likely to be the main objective, two more modest places propose themselves. One is the *Atholl Country Collection* (Late May–mid Oct: Daily, 13.30 to 17.30. Also from 09.30 in July and Aug. Tel: 079681-232. Fee), housed in the Old School (adjacent to a Craft Centre) and telling the story of village and glen life of the past. Among the features are a smithy, a crofter's byre and living room, and material on flax, on road, rail and postal services, and on the school, the church, the vet and the gamekeeper. At the other end of the village is the *Corn Mill* (April–Oct: Mon.–Sat., 10.00 to 18.00. Sun., 12.00 to 18.00. Fee), a water-powered mill dating back to 1613, still working and offering for sale oatmeal, flour and home baking.

*Blair Castle (Easter week. April: Sun and Mon. Late April–mid Oct: Daily. Mon.–Sat., 10.00 to 18.00. Sun., 14.00 to 18.00, but open 12.00 on Sun. in July and Aug. Last adm. 17.00. Tel: 079681-207. Fee). In wooded parkland at the end of a long avenue of limes, the castle is a straggling but elegant white Scottish Baronial mansion of various dates, as worth visiting for its historical associations as for its art and other contents.

The *Line of Atholl*. The last Celtic Earl of Atholl had died before 1211, the earldom then passing through the female line to David of Strathbogie (see also Rte 40, Huntly Castle) who however opposed Bruce and thus had his line forfeited. Later, in 1457, the earldom was conferred on Sir John Stewart of Balvenie (see Rte 39, Balvenie Castle), half-brother of James II and ancestor of the present family, and it was he who in 1475, when sent by James III to quell the uprising by the Lord of the Isles, received the uncompromising injunction, which later became the family motto, 'Furth Fortune and Fill the Fetters'. The direct succession ended in 1595, and until 1625 the earldom was held by the male heirs of the 1st Earl's brother, but in 1629 the title passed to John Murray, Master of Tullibardine. In 1703 the dukedom was created by Queen Anne.

Some **History**. Edward III visited here in 1336, and Mary, Queen of Scots, in 1564, on which occasion it is recorded that a hunt in Atholl Forest killed 360 red deer and five wolves. Garrisoned in 1644 by Montrose, held by Cromwell between 1652–60, and occupied by Claverhouse immediately before Killiecrankie, the castle was partly dismantled in 1690 to prevent its further occupation by the Highlander rebels. In 1746, just before Culloden and held by Cumberland, Blair was unsuccessfully besieged by the Jacobite Lord George Murray, brother of the Duke of Atholl, the castle thus achieving the distinction of being the last castle in Britain to come under siege. Queen Victoria visited here in 1844, afterwards granting the dukes the unique privilege of being allowed to retain a private army (the Atholl Highlanders).

The oldest part of the castle, Cumming's (or Comyn's) Tower on the NE, was built in c 1269 by John Comyn of Badenoch, and various alterations and additions have been made over the seven centuries that followed. By the mid 16C the castle had been extended southward, and the range of the great hall, between the two towers, had been built; there was major change in the 18C when the 2nd Duke remodelled Blair into a Georgian mansion, removing castella- tion and turrets to make way for low-pitched roofs and chimneys;

and finally, in the later 19C, the 7th Duke recastellated, at the same time adding the present entrance and ballroom.

The numerous rooms on view, 32 in all, present a remarkable picture of Scottish aristocratic life from the 16C to the present day. The collection of arms is one of the best in Scotland and includes the armour worn by Lord Glenlyon at the strange Eglinton Tournament (see Rte 16). Family portraits range over 300 years and include works by Lely, Ramsay, Zoffany, Landseer and Raeburn. Also on show are many Jacobite relics; a superb collection of china, especially Sèvres, Meissen and Dresden; Brussels tapestries made for Charles I, sold by Cromwell and later bought by the 1st Duke; and Georgian and Victorian toys. Additionally there is a Natural History Museum covering birds and animals native to the Highlands, and especially to Atholl.

Beinn a' Ghlo (3671ft; Mountain of the Mist) is a mountain group NE of Blair Atholl with three principal summits: *Carn nan Gabhar* (3671ft), *Carn Liath* (3193ft), and *Airgiod Bheinn* (3505ft). Carn Liath, 5m in a straight line from Blair Atholl, is the most easily reached, by way of the road from Blair Atholl up Glen Fender to Kirkton. The climb of c 2000ft is over rising moor to final steep slopes.

The old A9 in *3m* reaches the car park for the **Falls of Bruar**, the upper falls being found along a path which ascends through woods to a point where the Bruar cascades as rapids through a steep and narrow rocky cut. But there were not always woods here, and when Burns visited in 1787 he was so disappointed to find the stream tumbling through treeless moorland that he wrote 'The Humble Petition of Bruar Water', a plea which so touched the 4th Duke of Atholl that he planted this place with firs. The adjacent *Clan Donnachaidh Museum* (April–mid Oct: Mon.–Sat., 10.00 to 13.00. 14.00 to 17.30. Sun., 14.00 to 17.30. Tel: 079683-264. Free)—the name is the Gaelic for the clan group, Donnachy—is the place for Robertsons, Duncans, Reids, MacRoberts, Duncansons, Colliers, MacIvers, Inches, Maclagans, MacConachies, Roys, MacInroys, Donachies, Starks, MacRobies, Roberts, Dunnachies, MacDonachies, Tonnochys and Skenes. Exhibits ancient and modern, including material on the '15 and '45, cover the story of these intricately related families.

The museum is beside A9, opposite being Glen Errochty along which B847 traverses open and empty country before dropping down into the Rannoch and Tummel valleys. A9, now rejoined by this Rte, gradually ascends Glen Garry, achieving a mere 800ft in some 13m and passing (*6m*) *Dalnacardoch Lodge*, once well known as a coaching inn and standing on the site of the hut which was Wade's headquarters when he was building this stretch of the road in 1729. From here another small road makes its lonely way S through the hills towards the Rannoch and Tummel valleys, at a viewpoint on the way affording a striking glimpse of Loch Errochty. It was between Dalnacardoch and (*5m*) *Dalnaspidal Lodge* (1422ft) that Wade's troops working S from Inverness met those who had built up from Dunkeld, an occasion commemorated by a stone which over the years has suffered several moves as the road has been realigned and improved and which at present is seen only from the southbound carriageway. As the name suggests, Dalnaspidal was the site of a field hospital. Next, in *2m* and in increasingly desolate surroundings, the road arrives at the watershed **Pass of Drumochter** (1484ft) where the railway alongside breasts the highest railway summit in Britain. To the left the two prominent hog-backed hills are known as the *Sow of Atholl* (S) and the *Boar of Badenoch* (N).

6m **Dalwhinnie** (1180ft) is a bleak and frequently windswept village at the head of Glen Truim (N) as also of *Loch Ericht* which, today playing its part in the hydro-electric scheme, angles a narrow and lonely 15m southwards before discharging along the short river Ericht into Loch Rannoch. Here, below Ben Alder above the W shore towards the S end of the loch, Cluny's Cave, or Prince Charlie's Cave, is where the Young Pretender and Cluny Macpherson hid after Culloden (no road access).

This wild and forbidding country around Dalwhinnie was long a favourite gathering place of the Highlanders, who here often successfully held their own against a far larger force of disciplined troops. Here Cromwell's Ironsides were checked by the men of Atholl, and here also in 1745 General Cope declined to encounter, in this their native stronghold, the Young Pretender's Highlanders descending from the Pass of Corrieyarrick. Cope retired to Inverness, leaving open the road to Edinburgh and the Lowlands, and thus assuring his own defeat at Prestonpans.

Descending Glen Truim into more fertile country, with opening views of mountains ahead, A9 enters the Spey valley close to the confluence of Truim and Spey, a spot to be noted by Camerons and Mackintoshes, for here in 1386 these two clans met in battle.—*9m* (from Dalwhinnie) **Newtonmore** (see Rte 50), bypassed by A9, lies just to the N beyond the Spey.

28   Perth to Braemar

A93.—Beyond Blairgowrie, and more steeply after Spittal of Glenshee, the road climbs into the mountains to the watershed of Cairnwell Pass (2199ft), the highest main road pass in Britain. Thence a scenic descent beside Clunie Water with views of the Grampian ranges ahead.

SOME HOTELS. **Blairgowrie**. *Altamount House*, Coupar Angus Road. Tel: (0250) 3512. *Kinloch House*, Kinloch, PH10 6SG. Tel: (025084) 237. **Bridge of Cally**. *Bridge of Cally*, PH10 7JJ. Tel: (025086) 231. **Kirkmichael**. *Log Cabin*, PH10 7NB. Tel: (025081) 288. **Spittal of Glenshee**. *Dalmunzie House*, PH10 7QG. Tel: (025085) 224.

Total distance 51m.—*10m* **Bridge of Isla**.—*4m* **Blairgowrie**.—*6m* **Bridge of Cally**.—*15m* **Spittal of Glenshee**.—*7m* **Cairnwell Pass**.—*9m* **Braemar**.

Perth, see Rte 26, is left by way of Perth Bridge and Main Street, followed by a left fork on to Isla Road.

2m **Scone Palace** (pron. Scoon. Easter–mid Oct: Mon.–Sat., 10.00 to 17.30. Sun., 14.00 to 17.30, but open at 11.00 in July and Aug. Tel: 0738-52300. Fee). The present castellated mansion (1803–08), seat of the Earl of Mansfield, is the successor of a 16C house which itself succeeded the abbey and palace destroyed in 1559 by the Reformation mob after John Knox's sermon in Perth. However, the early gateway still stands and a part of the 16C house survives incorporated into today's building. But Scone's story starts many centuries earlier than any of these dates, and, though relatively modern in itself, today's palace offers the visitor not only ancient historical associations but also, in the more recent context, exquisite furniture, china, ivories and needlework.

History. For most people Scone is first and foremost associated with the *Stone of Scone*, traditionally and obscurely linked with both Jacob's Pillow at Tara in Ireland and with Columba's Pillow on Iona. Said to have served as the throne on which Columba crowned Aidan at Dunadd in 574, and later to have been moved to Dunstaffnage, the stone, by now the sacred symbol of sovereignty, is supposed to have been brought to Scone in the 9C by Kenneth Macalpine, Scone thus becoming, perhaps in partnership with Dunkeld, the seat of government in those Pictish-Celtic times. Edward I removed the stone to London's Westminster Abbey in 1297, but, despite this, all the Scottish kings, including Bruce, were crowned here until James I. Later James IV upheld the tradition in 1488, and in 1651 Charles II did the same. Scottish romantics claim that the stone carried off by Edward I was a planted replica and that the real stone was hidden in a cave, where it still awaits discovery.

The Moot Hill, still in front of the palace, was a solemn meeting-place even before Kenneth Macalpine's time. Later, in c 1120, a priory was founded here by Alexander I, this being raised to abbey status in 1164, and it was here that the parliament was held which decided that the Stewart line should succeed that of Bruce. Robert II, the first of these Stewarts, was buried here in 1390. Many centuries later, in 1716, the Old Pretender kept regal state here, and the Young Pretender slept here in 1745.

The ancient *Moot Hill* carries the family chapel, rebuilt at the same time as the palace but incorporating an aisle of a parish church of 1624, built by Viscount Stormont whose marble and alabaster tomb and effigy are here. The tour of the *Palace* embraces the main rooms, including the elegant Long Gallery. Among the things to be seen are a notable collection of 17 and 18C ivories; superb French furniture, including a writing table made for Marie Antoinette; embroidered bed hangings worked by Mary, Queen of Scots; and, on the Drawing Room walls, Lyons silk of 1804. The *Woodland Garden and Pinetum* (with, for the children, an adventure playground) include one of the finest collections of rare conifers in Britain, some of the trees being over 130 years old and 140ft high. David Douglas (1798–1834), the botanist after whom the Douglas Fir was named, was born on the estate and worked here as an under-gardener.

8m **Bridge of Isla** spans the Isla a little above its junction with the Tay, across the bridge being Meikleour House, the grounds of which are marked by a famous *Beech Hedge*. Planted in 1746 and now some 85ft high, the hedge borders the road for 580 yards. From here anyone interested in the Romans will divert W along A984 which crosses Cleaven Dyke, possibly Roman in origin, and after 3m, opposite the junction with B947, reaches a track which leads S to *Inchtuthill Roman Camp* in a bend of the Tay. Built in c 83, this camp was early abandoned. But ramparts, ditches and various other earthworks survive, and in 1961 Inchtuthill gained fame through the discovery here of no less than seven tons of unused Roman nails, an intriguing glimpse of a provisioning blunder of the past.

4m **Blairgowrie** (6000 inhab. *ECl.* Thurs. *Inf.* Wellmeadow. Easter–mid Oct), known for its surrounding acres of raspberries, can be a useful stop before the mountains and even offers, in the Episcopal church, a painting by Mattia Preti (1613–99), also known as 'Il Calabrese'. *Ardblair Castle* (By appointment. Tel: 0250-3155), 1m W by A923, although on 12C foundations, dates mainly from the 16C.

The home of the Oliphants, who were staunch Jacobites, the castle houses Jacobite relics and also material on Lady Carolina Nairne (1766–1845, née Oliphant). Christened Carolina, in obstinate if belated honour of the Young Pretender, she achieved modest fame by writing a number of popular songs, amongst these being 'Charlie is my Darling' and 'Caller Herrin'. This road (A923) continues W to Dunkeld, soon passing a series of small lochs, in one of which (Loch Clunie) there is an island with the ruins of a castle built c 1500 by Bishop Brown of Dunkeld.

6m **Bridge of Cally** marks the junction with A924 running with Strathardle, a road providing a good connection across to (6m) Kirkmichael and (a further 11m) Pitlochry. *Kindrogan Field Centre* (2½m beyond Kirkmichael) runs courses for professional and amateur naturalists and also provides a nature trail (1m. Booklet. Tel: 025081-286) telling the local story from the early 18C to the present day.

A93 now starts to climb beside the Black Water, soon entering Glenshee, with the castle of Dalnaglar prominent across the valley to the E, and in *15m* reaching **Spittal of Glenshee** (1125ft), a village at the junction of Glen Beg and Glen Lochy whose streams here unite to form the Shee or Black Water. From its name perhaps once a travellers' hospice, Spittal of Glenshee is today popular in summer as a centre for walking and in winter as a base for skiing at Cairnwell. Diarmid's Tomb, ½m E on the left bank of the Shee, is a tumulus.—Climbing more purposefully now the road makes for (*7m*) **Cairnwell Pass** (2199ft). Below Cairnwell (W. 3059ft) and Meall Odhar (E. 3019ft), the latter a spur of the mighty Glas Maol (3504ft), this bare and lofty ridge, the highest main road pass in Britain, is, with its Cairnwell chairlift, ski-tows, hang-gliding and ever expanding facilities, as popular in winter as it is in summer. For ski information, apply Glenshee Information Officer, Newton Terrace, Blairgowrie, Perth, Tayside. Tel: (0250) 2785. For Chairlift, Tel: (03383) 343.

From Cairnwell the Clunie Water accompanies the northward descent of *9m* and 1100ft to **Braemar** (see Rte 37), sheltered beside the Dee below the Grampians rising beyond.

29   Perth to Aberdeen via Forfar and Stonehaven

A94 to Glamis. Choice to Brechin of A94 and B9134 via Forfar and Aberlemno, or A928, B957 and A94 via Kirriemuir and Finavon. B966 and A94 to Stonehaven. A92 to Aberdeen.—For the most part farmland, but with several outstandingly scenic glens meandering deep into the wooded foothills and mountains.

SOME HOTELS. **Meigle.** *Kings of Kinloch*, Coupar Angus Road. Tel: (08284) 273. **Forfar.** *Royal*, 31 Castle Street. Tel: (0307) 62691. **Glen Clova (Rottal).** *Rottal Lodge*, DD8 4QT. Tel: (05755) 224. **Brechin.** *Northern*, Clerk Street. Tel: (03562) 2156. **Edzell.** *Glenesk*, High Street. Tel: (03564) 319. **Fettercairn.** *Ramsay Arms*, AB3 1XX. Tel: (05614) 334. **Stonehaven.** *Commodore*, Cowie Park. Tel: (0569) 62936. *Heugh*, Westfield Road. Tel: (0569) 62379.

Total distance 83m via Forfar. Via Kirriemuir is 3m longer.—*13m*
Coupar Angus.—*12m* **Glamis.**—*5m* **Forfar.**—*11m* **Brechin.**—*5m*
Edzell.—*5m* **Fettercairn.**—*17m* **Stonehaven.**—*15m* **Aberdeen**.

Perth, see Rte 26, is left by Perth Bridge and Main Street, followed
by a right fork along Strathmore Street. After (*6m*) **Balbeggie** the
Sidlaw Hills rise to the E, at their southern end, just N of B953 and
about 4m out of Balbeggie, being *Dunsinane Hill*, bearing the remains
of an ancient fort generally identified as the Dunsinane of
Shakespeare's 'Macbeth'.

In the play the apparition foretold that Macbeth would never be vanquished
until 'great Birnam Wood to high Dunsinane Hill shall come'. Later, while
Macbeth held out in this fort of Dunsinane, his enemies met at Birnam (Rte 27)
where their leader, Malcolm, ordered 'Let every soldier hew him down a bough
and bear't before him'. Thus Birnam came to Dunsinane and Macbeth met his
end. Although Shakespeare places the death of Macbeth at Dunsinane, it seems
more probable that this occured farther N at Lumphanan (see Rte 37).

7m **Coupar Angus** is so called to distinguish it from Cupar on the
Fife peninsula. The tolbooth dates from 1762, and, beside the Dundee
road (A923), there survives a fragment which is all that remains of a
once wealthy abbey, founded in 1164 for Cistercians by Malcolm IV
and destroyed in 1559. At Pitcur, 2m farther along this road, there is
a square keep, once a seat of the Hallyburtons. Here an ancient holly
tree is said to mark where Claverhouse (Dundee) and Hallyburton
breakfasted on 27 July 1689; in the evening both met their deaths at
Killiecrankie.—*5m* **Meigle** is famed for its *Museum* (AM. Standard,
but closed Sun. Fee) housing a notable collection of some 30 Early
Christian inscribed stones of the 7–10C, all found at or near the
old churchyard. The carvings are of great variety, curiosity and interest
and it is rewarding to use the official leaflet which details each stone.
Belmont Castle, ½m S, was for many years .the home of Sir H.
Campbell-Bannerman (1836–1908), the prime minister; he is buried
in Meigle churchyard.

From Meigle a pleasant diversion can be made northward to Alyth (4m) and
thence up Glen Isla. *Alyth*, with the burn of the same name rippling along the
main street, offers an arcade of a 13C church, a small Folk Museum (May–Sept:
Tues.–Sat., 13.00 to 17.00. Free), and, on top of Barry Hill just NE, an Iron Age
fort. *Glen Isla* winds up into hilly country to reach Glen Shee (Rte 28) in some
15m.

5m Eassie, where there is an elaborately carved Early Christian stone
in the churchyard.—*2m* **Glamis** (pron. Glahms) is a neat village, most
famed of course for its castle but also providing two more modest but
nonetheless rewarding attractions. One of these, in the Manse garden,
is the so-called *Malcolm Stone*, traditionally held to be the grave-slab
of Malcolm II, said to have died or been murdered in or near the
castle in 1034. In fact this stone, nearly 9ft in height, is probably
rather earlier in date, but may nevertheless have marked the burial
place of some chieftain or leading churchman. Features of the stone
are, on one side, serpent, fish and mirror symbols; and, on the other,
a particularly fine cross with a variety of symbols in the quarters. The
village's other attraction is the *Angus Folk Museum* (NTS. Easter.
May–Sept: Daily, 12.00 to 17.00. Fee), housed in an attractive terrace
of restored early 19C cottages and illustrating local domestic and
agricultural life in the 19C and earlier.

*Glamis Castle (Easter. May–Sept: Daily except Sat., 13.00 to 17.00. Tel: 030784-242. Fee) is the imposing and historic home of the earls of Strathmore and Kinghorne. The castle owes its present aspect (1675–87), with its almost theatrical clusters of turrets and battlemented parapets, to the 1st Earl of Strathmore, but portions of the high square tower, with walls 15ft thick, are considerably older.

History. There has been a building here from very early times, and, as noted above, Malcolm II may have died or been murdered in or near the castle in 1034. On the burning (in 1540) of Lady Glamis for witchcraft and conspiring to murder James V, the castle was forfeited to the crown, but when later her innocence had been established it was restored to her son, whose descendant, Patrick Lyon, became Earl of Strathmore in 1677. In 1715 the Old Pretender stayed here for some time and held his court, while in modern times this was the childhood home of Queen Elizabeth, the Queen Mother, and birthplace in 1930 of Princess Margaret.

The *Dining Room*, in a wing burnt down in 1800 and with decoration of immediately after that date, contains family portraits. The *Crypt*, originally the hall, shows armour and weapons. The trap into the dungeon below, now a wine cellar, can be seen from the latter, and on this level too is the old *Kitchen*, used until the 17C. In the *Drawing Room* are an Italian plasterwork ceiling of 1621 and a fine fireplace, the latter possibly by the Dutch sculptor Jan Santvoort (c 1684). Portraits here include one of the 1st Earl and his sons, and one by Kneller of Claverhouse; here too is a suit of jester's motley, the family enjoying the curious distinction of being the last in Scotland to offer such employment. In the *Chapel* there are panels of c 1686 by the Dutch artist Jacob de Wet (see also Rte 18, Holyrood), and in the 17C *Billiard Room* Mortlake tapestries. The *King Malcolm Room* is so named because, traditionally anyway, this was where Malcolm II died. Today the room is distinguished by blue linen wall hangings by Helen (died 1708), wife of the 3rd Earl, and by a strange fireplace, the central panel of which is of repoussé leather polished to resemble wood.

The *Royal Apartments* were arranged for the Queen Mother, when Duchess of York, but the room in which Princess Margaret was born, in the private wing, is not shown. *Duncan's Hall*, showing portraits of James V and Mary of Guise, is of particular interest both as the oldest part of the castle, when it may have served as guardroom to the crypt or hall, and also as the setting of Shakespeare's 'Macbeth'. The *Family Exhibition* includes clothing (Royal Stuart tartan), sword and watch belonging to the Old Pretender and Claverhouse's bullet-proof coat.

The *Grounds* include a late 19C formal garden and an Italian garden. On the lawn stands a Baroque sundial, with facets for each month, placed in this position by the 1st Earl. There was a time when Glamis could boast seven gateways, but these were demolished in 1770 by 'Capability' Brown, and today only two turrets survive. On the exterior of the castle some of the sculpture (bust of the 1st Earl over the front door; coats-or-arms either side of the round tower) is probably the work of Jan Santvoort.

From Glamis there are alternative roads to Brechin; a southerly one through Forfar and Aberlemno, and a slightly longer (3m) northerly one through Kirriemúir and Finavon. The former passes the ancient priory of Restenneth and then the notable group of Pictish stones at Aberlemno; the latter will be chosen by lovers of the works of J.M. Barrie as also by those with the time to divert up the beautiful glens of Prosen and Clova.

Glamis to Brechin via Forfar and Aberlemno.

5m **Forfar** (10,500 inhab. *ECl.* Thurs.) lies at the E end of the small loch on the shores of which was fought one of the last battles between the Picts and Scots before the combining of the two kingdoms in c 845. Today a lively place of some character with its often narrow and in part cobbled streets, Forfar was in ancient times the place where Malcolm Canmore is said to have first conferred surnames and titles on the Scottish nobility, and, in a more recent context, a wartime base for Polish troops. Both occasions are remembered; the latter by a plaque on the District Council building in the town centre, and the former by an octagonal turret, formerly the cross of c 1640, which, reached by steps out of Canmore Street, marks the site of Canmore's castle. Forfar *Museum and Art Gallery* (Mon., Tues., Wed., Fri., 09.30 to 19.00. Thurs. and Sat., 09.30 to 17.00. Tel: 0674-3232. Free) is housed in the public library, Meffan Institute. Largely devoted to local history and activities, the exhibits include the burgh regalia, material on local archaeology and the flax industry, the 'Forfar bridle', used as a gag for witches who were mercilessly hounded here, and paintings largely of regional interest.

Restenneth Priory, 1½m E of Forfar off B9113, is supposed to have been founded in c 710 by the Pictish King Nechtan for St. Boniface, then refounded in c 1153 by Malcolm IV for Augustinians from Jedburgh. The tall tower, primitive both in its stonework and detail, is certainly pre-Norman (spire 15C), and what is particularly interesting is that the lower part is considerably older than the upper, this leading to the suggestion that this may in fact have been a W porch of Nechtan's ancient church. The rest of the church is of the 12C. *Dunnichen Hill*, 3m E of Forfar to the S of A932, was the site of the battle of Nectansmere (685), in which Egfrith of Northumbria was killed by the Pictish King Brude, this ending Anglian penetration into this part of Scotland.

B9134 is now followed out of Forfar to reach in *5m* the village of **Aberlemno**, famed for its *Pictish Stones, four of which are to be seen, one in the churchyard and three others beside the road in the village. The stone in the churchyard, dating from the 8C, bears on one side a Celtic cross, with entwined beasts, and on the other a vivid battle scene. The largest stone beside the road also shows a Celtic cross, this time flanked by two sorrowing angels holding books, while on the reverse there is a hunting scene above two typically Pictish symbols. More symbols decorate the remaining two simpler stones.—*2m Melgund Castle*, on the right down a side road and now a ruin, is said to have been built by Cardinal Beaton.

4m **Brechin** (7500 inhab. *ECl.* Wed.), perched on a steep slope above the South Esk, is most noted for its Cathedral and associated Round Tower. The squat little *Cathedral*, founded by David I in 1150 and now the parish church, is successor to an early Celtic abbey, but of David I's work nothing visible survives. As seen today the oldest parts of the building, the nave piers, date from the 13C, while the broad, projecting tower, with a low spire, though begun in the early 13C took some two centuries to complete. The choir was ruined at the Reformation, and in 1807 the transepts were demolished, but, later, more sensitive influences prevailed and in 1900–02 the choir

Brechin Round Tower. Built by Irish masons between 990 and 1012 and probably associated with the predecessor of the adjacent 13C cathedral.

was roofed and reglazed and the transepts at the same time rebuilt. For most visitors entering the cathedral the SW corner, beside an arc of the base of the Round Tower, will prove the most interesting, here being a number of ancient grave-slabs (10–13C), some showing good strapwork, a carved cross of the same period, and the cathedral's silver and pewter.

The *Round Tower* (87ft) was built by Irish masons between 990 and 1012 and is the older of the only two Scottish mainland round towers of this kind, the other being at Abernethy (Rte 33D). In Ireland some 80 of these towers survive and, as in Ireland, the probability is that there was once an associated detached church, the predecessor until the 13C of the cathedral then started. On the W side there is a narrow doorway, 6ft above ground level, with typically Irish inward inclining jambs, the whole surrounded by a beaded moulding and surmounted by a Crucifixion, this last being rare in Pictland where the figure of Christ never appears on the crosses to be seen on so many sculpted stones. At the sides are two Culdee ecclesiastics.

In the small town the steep High Street was until the late 18C a main route for traffic crossing Brechin bridge, until then the only one over the South Esk. Here in High Street today a circle of stones set into the road marks the site of the mercat cross, demolished in 1767, while in various corners of the town neat plaques draw attention to the past. To the N, across the main through road, can be seen parts of the walls of the chapel of the *Maison Dieu* hospice founded in 1267. The local *Museum* (Mon.–Fri., 09.30 to 18.00 or 19.00 on Wed. Sat., 09.30 to 17.00. Tel: 03562-2687. Free) is in the public library in St. Ninian's Square in the E part of the town, and in this square too the Brechin Railway Preservation Society occupies the former station of the old Caledonian Railway. The plan is to run the line as far as Bridge of Dun (4m E), but, meanwhile, various steam units, rolling stock and suchlike can be seen (open most weekends; steam days in summer).

Glamis to Brechin via Kirriemuir.

Glamis is left by A928 for (*4m*) **Kirriemuir** (5000 inhab. *ECl.* Thurs.), visited as the birthplace of J.M. Barrie (1860–1937) and as the 'Thrums' of his stories. *Barrie's Birthplace* (NTS. May–Sept: Mon.–Sat., 10.00 to 12.30. 14.00 to 18.00. Sun., 14.00 to 18.00. Fee) is at 9 Brechin Road, and here today a museum recalls Barrie's achievements in the world of letters, at the same time indicating the various local places which feature in the novels. The outside wash-house, said to have served as his first theatre, now houses a Peter Pan display. Also of interest in the town are the quaint old Town Hall, a shield on the new Town Hall recording gratitude for hospitality given to Polish army units in 1940–41, and, at the top of the town in a pavilion behind the cemetery in which Barrie is buried, a *Camera Obscura* (summer only) providing a wide panoramic view.

Two of Scotland's loveliest glens, Prosen and Clova, can conveniently be toured from Kirriemuir. **Glen Prosen**, the western and more modest of the two and penetrating the mountains for some 12 wooded miles, has, for much of its length, roads along both sides, that on the S being the more scenic and incidental. A good circuit can be made from Kirriemuir by heading N for Pearsie and then *Glenprosen* village which is where the two roads meet. From here *Runtaleave*, the head of the glen so far as the road is concerned, is

3m farther. The return can be made down the N side, below the hilltop Airlie Monument commemorating the 8th Earl (1856–1900), killed in the South African War, and passing a roadside memorial to Captain Scott and Doctor Wilson, the Antarctic explorers who here planned their ill-fated expedition of 1910–11.—**Glen Clova** (B955) penetrates some 14m from its foot at *Dykehead*, soon offering a road choice either side of the broad valley as far as *Clova*, from where a small road, now close-hemmed by mountains, continues another scenic 3m to the Forestry Commission's *Glen Doll* picnic site, in fine surroundings beside the South Esk.

Glen Clova enjoys a historical association as the scene of the so-called Start, an abortive attempt by the young Charles II in 1650 to shake himself free of his fanatical Presbyterian supporters. After resting at Cortachy (a castle amid fine trees beside the road near Dykehead) he rode up the glen to Clova, where, however, his Highlander partisans failed to keep the promised rendezvous and Charles was forced to return more or less captive to the sermons and suffocating austerities of Presbyterian Perth.

The main axis of this Rte continues (below) from Kirriemuir. But if the next objective is Edzell, then the choice should be the pleasant ridge-road which, starting from Dykehead and travelling by way of Fern and Kirkton of Menmuir, affords splendid views over the coastal levels. Rather over half-way along this road, 2m beyond Kirkton, a sign at a crossroads points N to the White and Brown Caterthuns, two notable examples of hill forts which enjoy the bonus of being easily accessible from a parking area, itself worth a visit for the views both inland and towards the coast. The *White Caterthun* (976ft), only a few hundred yards away to the W and owing its name to its stonework, dates from about the 1C and preserves one of the most impressive stone and earthwork defensive complexes in Britain, comprising a rampart, perhaps once as much as 40ft thick, a ditch and outer earthworks. The *Brown Caterthun* (943ft), generally probably of earlier date but spanning several structural periods, shows at least four and probably as many as six concentric defences, each provided with several entrances.

Assuming the main Rte is followed, Kirriemuir is left by B957 for (*8m*) **Finavon** where A94 is joined. *Finavon Doocot* (generally open daily in May–Sept. Doocot exhibition), beside A94 and the largest in Scotland, is a twin-chambered sloping-roof type with some 2100 boxes, many of which are still in use. Nearby *Finavon Castle*, now a crumbling ruin but once a sturdy keep of the earls of Crawford, although built in the late 16C stands on foundations of c 1300; it collapsed in 1712 through undermining by a stream.—*7m* **Brechin**, see above.

A94 is the fast road to Stonehaven, but this Rte makes a more interesting northerly loop, following B966 through Edzell and Fettercairn to rejoin A94 near Fordoun.—*3m* The village of *Inchbare* stands at a crossroads, a short way to the E being *Stracathro Church*, in the churchyard of which, on 10 July 1296, John Balliol renounced his crown in favour of England's Edward I, formally handing over the realm of Scotland to Edward's representative, the Bishop of Durham. Near here, too, in 1452, was fought the battle in which the Earl of Crawford, a partisan of the Douglases in their struggle against James II, was defeated by the king's supporters under Huntly.—*2m* *Edzell* is a neat modern village, best known for its castle.

*Edzell Castle. The Summer House at a corner of the early 17C
Pleasance.*

*Edzell Castle (AM. Standard, but closed Tues., and Thurs.
mornings. Fee) is 1m **W** of the village, and as it is approached the
earthworks can be seen of the earlier Norman stronghold. Adjoining
this was the parish church, transferred in 1818 to its present site, and
in its graveyard are a Celtic stone and the burial aisle of the Lindsays
of Glenesk.

History. The original castle was the stronghold of the Stirlings of Glenesk. In
the mid 14C the Stirlings were replaced by the Crawford Lindsays, who in the
16C, with an eye more to shelter and comfort than to defence, indulged
themselves with the elegant new castle seen today. This comprises the tower-
house (early 16C), to which was added (1580) the mansion around the courtyard,
followed in 1604 by the Pleasance, the achievement of Sir David Lindsay, Lord
Edzell. In 1562 Mary, Queen of Scots, while making her northern progress,
stayed here and held council. Later the castle was twice visited by James VI,
and in the 18C it suffered from occupation by Hanoverian troops.

Entrance is by way of a breach in the courtyard E wall, the tower-house
then being ahead left, joined by the shell of a range of buildings to
the lower and much damaged Round or North Tower. The Great Hall
is inside the tower-house on the first floor.

But Edzell's unique feature is its ***Pleasance**, or walled garden,
created, as noted above, by Sir David Lindsay in 1604 and especially
remarkable for its symbolic sculpture. It is contained within a square
enclosure, with the arms of its creator and its date appearing over a

doorway in the NE corner. The walls are decorated with bas-reliefs (copies of German originals after Dürer) of the Cardinal Virtues (W), the Liberal Arts (S), and the Planetary Deities (E), these last being executed with particular strength. The walls are also indented with large square holes (flower-filled in summer) which, seen from a distance, form, in combination with their surrounds, the Lindsay arms. The box hedge (1932) in the centre spells the family motto, 'Dum spiro spero'—'While I breathe I hope'. In the S corner once stood the Bath House, an unusual luxury by early 17C standards; it was pulled down at an unknown date, but the foundations were exposed in 1855 and show that the building was a comfortable and elegant affair with bath, dressing and sitting room, this last with a fireplace. The Summer House, at the E corner, is provided with a stone bench round the wall, a small stair-turret and a closet with twin privies.

Edzell stands at the mouth of wooded **Glen Esk** which curves some 14 northward and westward miles into the mountains, along its course offering both scenery and a touch of history; history because it was probably up this valley that Macbeth fled before crossing the mountains by the Fir Mounth to meet his end at Lumphanan, north beyond Deeside. There is prehistory, too, in the form of *Colmealie Stone Circle*, a rough, unpretentious, almost miniature affair found some 6m out of Edzell beside some farm buildings a few yards up a track from where the road touches the river. Not far beyond comes the *Glenesk Folk Museum* (Easter, and then Sun. until June–Sept when daily, 14.00 to 18.00. Tel: 03567-236. Fee) where the exhibits tell the story of everyday life in the glen between 1800 and modern times. The road ends at *Invermark Castle*, the shell of the tall tower-house—typical with its high, barred entrance and windows—which once deterred raiders descending out of the mountains to pillage the rich glen and the open lowlands at its foot. Beyond Invermark, a track leads in about a mile to *Loch Lee*, set below high brown mountains and once home to a village community, as evidenced by a ruined church (on, it is said, an ancient Culdee site) and its forlorn graveyard.

From Edzell village this Rte continues E, still on B966, to (5m) **Fettercairn**, a trim small place which welcomes the visitor through a turreted arch, built to commemorate a visit by Queen Victoria and Prince Albert in 1861. Of more interest, in the pleasing square, stands the shaft of a *Mercat Cross*, bearing marks indicating the length of the Scots ell and also an iron hasp to which the jougs were attached. In fact this was not properly Fettercairn's cross, but that of the township of Kincardine (see below). *Fasque* (May–Sept: Daily except Fri., 13.30 to 17.30. Tel: 05614-201. Fee), rather over 1m N of Fettercairn on B974, is a mansion of 1809, acquired soon after that date by the father of the statesman W.E. Gladstone. The latter spent his honeymoon here but made his home at his wife's Hawarden Castle (see 'Blue Guide Wales'). Life in Victorian times is the theme here.

B974, the lonely Cairn o' Mounth road, passes Fasque on the left and then, on the right before reaching Clattering Bridge, an earthwork known as *Green Castle*, believed to have been the stronghold of Finella, daughter of the lord of Angus reputed to have murdered Kenneth II while on a pilgrimage from Kincardine to the shrine of St. Palladius at Auchenblae. The lady's name survives as Strath Finella which runs NE from Clattering Bridge. Beyond the Cairn o' Mounth watershed at 1488ft, the road descends to reach Deeside at

Banchory some 15m from Fettercairn.

Laurencekirk, 4m SE of Fettercairn by B9120, is the chief town of a fertile district known as the Howe of Mearns, lands which once belonged to Mernas, brother of Kenneth II. The small town, founded by Lord Gardenstone in 1779 as a centre for linen weaving, also became famed for its snuff boxes of exceptional design (by Charles Stiven) with a concealed hinge and pin.

Still travelling NE on B966 this Rte in under 2m passes (N) earthworks and foundations on a mound, these marking the site of *Kincardine Castle*, the sole vestige, apart from the shaft of its cross in Fettercairn, of the royal residence and associated township which once flourished here. Here, it is said, Kenneth II was murdered in 994 by a lord of Angus, and from here, too, in 1296, John Balliol wrote to Edward I offering to abdicate.—*4m* **Auchenblae**, where the ruined *Chapel of St. Palladius* (1243) recalls in its dedication an early Irish churchman said to have brought Christianity to the Mearns and to have been buried here by his disciple Ternan who erected a shrine over his master's tomb.—Rejoining A94 this Rte soon reaches (*4m*) *Bridge of Mondynes*, just NW of which is *Glenbervie*, home of Burns's ancestors whose graves, including that of his great-grandfather, James Burnes (sic), will be found in the churchyard. Nearby there is a Burns memorial cairn.

7m **Stonehaven** (8500 inhab. *ECl.* Wed. *Inf.* Market Square. Easter and May–Sept) can almost be said to be two towns, with Old Stonehaven around the harbour and 19C New Stonehaven above. For the visitor the old town is the more picturesque and interesting, here being the late 16C *Tolbooth*, built to serve as a storehouse and later, in 1748–49, used as a prison for the local Episcopal clergy, who nevertheless managed, through a barred window, to baptise children held up to them. Today the building houses a small museum of local history and fishing (June–Sept: Mon., Thurs., Fri., Sat., 10.00 to 12.00. 14.00 to 17.00. Wed. and Sun., 14.00 to 17.00. Tel: 0779-77778. Fee).

For *Dunnottar Castle*, immediately S of Stonehaven, see Rte 35.

The road known as the **Slug Road** (A957), linking Stonehaven with Crathes on Deeside, was completed in 1800. The *Aäquhollie Stone*, interesting because of its clear Ogham inscription, stands N of the road a short way out of Stonehaven (turn right opposite the entrance to Ricarton House, then left; the stone is on the right just beyond the first farm).

The **Elsick Mounth Road** (B979), farther NE, also links Stonehaven with Deeside, near Peterculter. This is a much older road, said indeed to have been used by the Romans whose camp of *Raedykes*, one of their northernmost main marching camps, lies along the ridge between B979 and A957. The camp was probably never fully finished and may be the site of the battle of Mons Grampius (84) in which the northern tribes were defeated by Agricola.

Now following A92 this Rte passes (*5m*) **Muchalls Castle** (May–Sept: Tues. and Sun., 15.00 to 17.00. Tel: 0569-30217. Fee) which, though comparatively small, is a complete and typical example of a 17C laird's house, still in private occupation today. Built in 1619–27, the house is noted for its moulded ceilings and a secret stairway. Along the coast between Muchalls and Aberdeen there is a chain of what were once busy fishing villages—Muchalls, Newtonhill, Portlethen and Findon, this last giving its name (Finnan) to smoked haddock—which today, though, are increasingly developing as Aberdeen dormitories.—*10m* central **Aberdeen**, see Rte 36.

30 Perth to Dundee (Direct)

A85.—This road traverses the level tract between the Sidlaw Hills and the Tay, here temporarily opening as a wide estuary before narrowing to pass between Dundee and the NE tip of the Fife peninsula. Known as the Carse of Gowrie, this tract has long been famed for its fertility, though less perhaps for its tourist interest and Rte 33D (only 6m longer) offers a more interesting alternative S of the Tay and through northern Fife.

SOME HOTELS. See **Perth** (Rte 26) and **Dundee** (Rte 34).

Total distance 22m.

Perth, see Rte 26, is left by either Perth or Queen's Bridge, and then Gowrie Street followed by Dundee Road. A85 runs below the steep slope of Kinnoull Hill, skirting a pleasant stretch of the Tay, across which stands ruined Elcho Castle, described under Rte 26.—*10m Megginch Castle Gardens* (April–June, Sept: Wed., 14.00 to 17.00. July and Aug: Mon.–Fri., 14.00 to 17.00. Tel: 08212-222. Fee) include ancient yews, for which an age of 1000 years is claimed, a 16C rose garden, a 19C flower parterre and a dovecot. The castle (no adm.) is an enlargement of a 15C original. To the N of A85, along the more or less parallel minor roads, there are two other castles (both no adm.) of minor historical and some architectural interest. *Fingask*, with a tower of 1594 and additions of 1675, twice provided refuge for the Old Pretender, while *Kinnaird Castle*, 2m NE of Fingask and high above its village, is a tall (restored) 15C tower.

Back on A85, between *4m Inchture* and *2m Longforgan*, will be seen the stately *Castle Huntly* (no adm.), the tower of which, much altered in the 17–18C and now incorporated into a college, was first raised in 1452 by Lord Gray of Fowlis, Master of the Household to James II. This same Lord Gray also built, in 1453, the *Church of St. Marnan* at Fowlis Easter, 2m N of Longforgan, where some curiosities will be found both within the church and in its churchyard. In fact Lord Gray's church was successor to a chapel of c 1150, built when these lands were given by David I to William Maule as a reward for military service; later, in 1377, the estate passed by marriage to the Grays who in 1242 dedicated the chapel to St. Marnan, an Iona contemporary of Columba. Today, a harsh note in an otherwise tranquil spot, jougs still hang by the W door, while in the churchyard an ancient cross and tomb invite speculation. In fact the former probably has nothing to do with the latter, if only because it stands at the tomb's foot rather than at its head. It has been suggested that the cross may mark, or have marked, an early church meeting-place, and that the grave-slab, ornamented with a hunting horn, may cover a 16C forester. Inside the church are a bronze alms dish (German, 1487), embossed with a scene of the Garden of Eden; 15C oak doors which were once part of the rood screen; and, of particular interest, pre-Reformation paintings on oak, quaintly representing the Crucifixion, the Virgin, St. John the Baptist and St. Catherine, with an entombment below.

From Fowlis Easter Dundee can be reached by minor roads passing close to *Camperdown Park* (see Rte 34). Along A85 (*2m*) **Invergowrie**, now a suburb of Dundee, is said once to have been a favourite residence of Alexander I.—*4m* central **Dundee**, see Rte 34.

31   Edinburgh to Stirling via Dunfermline, Culross and Alloa

A90 across the Forth Bridge. A823 to Dunfermline. A994 and B9057 to Culross and Kincardine. A977 and A907 to Alloa and Stirling.—Of no particular scenic merit, this Rte runs through the SW corner of Fife (see Rte 33).

SOME HOTELS. **Dunfermline**. *Keavil House*, Crossford. Tel: (0383) 736258. *King Malcolm*, West Pitcothrie. Tel: (0383) 722611. **Culross**. *Red Lion*, Main Street. Tel: (0383) 880225. **Airth**. *Airth Castle*, FK2 8JF. Tel: (032483) 411.

Total distance 36m.—*13m* **Dunfermline**.—*7m* **Culross**.—*4m* **Kincardine**.—*5m* **Alloa**.—*7m* **Stirling**.

From central **Edinburgh** (see Rte 18) Queensferry Road (A90) in *10m* reaches and crosses the *Forth Road Bridge*, for which, as also for the adjacent railway bridge and the approach from Edinburgh, see Rte 9. Here, by the bridge's N end, Rte 32 continues N, while Rtes 33A and 33C head E across Fife. This Rte takes A823 which cuts off NW for Rosyth and Dunfermline. *Rosyth* lies around the anchorage of St. Margaret's Hope, much of the land here having been acquired by the government in 1903 to house the naval base and dockyard. The castle (no adm.) is a 15C tower with additions, and to the W of the town towards Charlestown can be seen old limekilns built out of the rock at the foot of the cliff. It was between Rosyth and Dunfermline in 1651 that a battle was fought between Cromwell's troops and supporters of Charles II, the latter mostly Macdonalds. Decisively defeated, the clan suffered heavy losses and their chief, Hector Macdonald of Duart, was taken prisoner.

3m **Dunfermline** (50,000 inhab. *ECl.* Wed. *Inf.* Glen Bridge Car Park. May–Sept), most royal of royal burghs, and since at least Malcolm Canmore's time (11C) intimately associated with the births, lives and burials of Scotland's royalty, is visited today for the abbey, monastery and palace ruins which reflect that past, as also, in a more modern context, as the birthplace of the munificent philanthropist Andrew Carnegie.

History. The name Dunfermline means Fort of the Crooked Linn, this probably referring to the primitive castle which Malcolm Canmore held here beside a bend in the burn running through Pittencrieff Glen, where what may well be the remains of this fort can still be seen as a mound called Malcolm's Tower. The Saxon princess Margaret, sister of Edgar Atheling and fleeing from the Normans, was shipwrecked in the Forth and brought to Dunfermline where Malcolm married her in 1067. Malcolm and Margaret then built their palace and, a little later, founded a priory. This palace was to remain a favourite with successor kings, and the priory, promoted to abbey by David I, superseded Iona as their place of burial. Edward I held court here during his second invasion of Scotland (1303). And Charles II stayed here in 1651 before his march to defeat at Worcester, and it was while here that he was forced to accept the Covenants.

The *Andrew Carnegie Birthplace Museum* (April–Oct: Mon.–Sat., 11.00 to 17.00. Sun., 14.00 to 17.00. Nov–March: Daily, 14.00 to 16.00. Tel: 0383-724302. Free) is an urban cottage at the corner of Moodie Street and Priory Lane in the lower, S part of the town. In brief, the museum and the associated memorial hall tell the story of Carnegie's youth, of the fortune he made, and of his munificent benefactions.

Born here in poor circumstances, Andrew Carnegie (1835–1919) emigrated with his family to Pennsylvania, there rising to enormous wealth and power through his flair in the iron and steel industries. He became renowned as a philanthropist, his gifts amounting to millions of dollars in both America and Britain. Nor did he forget his native town, which has benefited much from the Carnegie Dunfermline Trust (1904), Pittencrieff Glen, baths, library, etc., as well as an annual festival of music and drama, being among the causes supported. Dunfermline is the headquarters of this local trust, of the Carnegie Hero Fund, and of the United Kingdom Trust.

The abbey and the monastery and palace ruins, forming a compact group a short way up the hill, can be approached along either side, by Monastery Road on the W or St. Margaret Street (with a car park) on the E.

The *Abbey Church* (AM. Standard, but closed during services. Free) is in two parts; a Norman nave of 1150 and a spacious Gothic choir, built by William Burn in 1817–22 and serving as parish church.

The nave, standing in part on the foundations of the earlier church, is a substantial relic of the church begun by David I in 1128 when he raised Malcolm Canmore's and Margaret's priory to the rank of abbey. An elegant choir and transepts, added in 1250, were wrecked by Reformers in 1560 and finally swept away in 1817 to make way for Burn's choir-church. Malcolm and Margaret, who both died in 1093, were buried in a special chapel (now only foundations) outside the church. Their sons (Edgar, Alexander I and David I) and their descendants (Malcolm IV, Alexander III and Robert Bruce) all lie in the church.

Seen from the outside the *Nave is somewhat marred by the great size of the buttresses added in the 16C. The imposing W doorway is flanked by towers, the one on the N rebuilt with its spire in c 1590, the other surviving longer until rebuilt in 1887 after being damaged by lightning. The interior is of six bays, with tall round piers and round arches, the SW arch, however, built by James VI in Gothic style. The E piers are typically grooved with zigzags and spirals, and the elaborate zigzag Norman mouldings on the inner arch of the N porch contrast with the later groined roof. The aisles have original quadripartite vaults and blind arcading; the triforium and clerestory are plain. In the N aisle there is a memorial to George Durie, the last abbot (1560), and the glass of the large, 'historical' W window was designed by Noel Paton.

The Choir (parish church) carries a heavy square tower, the balustrade of which incongruously flaunts in large stone letters the words 'King Robert the Bruce'. Beneath the pulpit is the grave of Robert Bruce (1274–1329), marked by a memorial brass. During the excavations in 1818 Bruce's body was revealed wrapped in a shroud interwoven with threads of gold and encased in two lead coverings; it was placed in a new coffin and reburied. Outside the choir, at the E end of the church, are the foundations of the Shrine of St. Margaret, the burial place of herself and her husband. Nearby (NE) is the sarcophagus tomb (1875) of Robert Erskine (1685–1752), minister of the abbey and one of the leaders of the Seccession movement.

The *Monastery* domestic buildings were ranged S of and below the church, the chief remains today—its stones, as also those of the palace, were pillaged in 1610 for the building of Pittencrieff House (see below)—being those of the refectory, which must have been a fine hall indeed judging from its elegant window of seven lights, the upper parts filled with quatrefoils. An arch crosses the road to what is left of the *Palace*, at times also doubling as guest house for the abbey. Destroyed by fire in 1304, when Edward I left, the palace was rebuilt by James IV in 1500 and it was occupied by Mary, Queen of Scots, in 1561. But today a kitchen is about all that identifiably remains of this favourite royal residence and, indeed, nursery, for here were born (to Margaret) Maud, wife of Henry I of England, and her brothers, later kings Edgar, Alexander I and David I; David II (1324) and James I (1394); and the children of James VI/I, Elizabeth (1596), afterwards Queen of Bohemia, and, in 1600, Charles I.

Opposite the W door of the Abbey Church is an entrance to *Pittencrieff Glen*, once Malcolm Canmore's park, today a large ornamental estate with superb gardens, presented to the town by Andrew Carnegie in 1903. Here Canmore's memory lives on in the ruin of *Malcolm's Tower* beside the burn, while *Pittencrieff House* (May–Sept: Daily except Tues., 11.00 to 17.00. Tel: 0383-722935. Free) houses a museum of local history and a distinguished costume collection. The house, built in 1610, in part with stones pillaged from the monastery and palace, has known many owners, the last individual being Andrew Carnegie who was laird for a brief year before in 1903 handing over the property to the town.

Dunfermline's *Public Library* (Tel: 0383-723661), just E of the abbey, owes its origin (1883) and much of its later prestige to Carnegie and the Dunfermline Trust. It houses the distinguished Murison Burns Collection of Burns material, this including books, pamphlets, prints and even commemorative pottery. Just N of here, in High Street by the 19C guildhall, stands the cross of (in part) 1626, while the site of its predecessor of 1396 is marked out on the ground. High Street, followed E, becomes East Port, off which Viewfield Road drops S to a car park conveniently placed beside *Dunfermline Museum* (Mon.–Sat., 11.00 to 17.00. Tel: 0383-721814. Free). Here the local story is attractively told, some emphasis being placed on the damask linen industry, illustrated by examples of this craft together with a handloom of 1835, complete with Jacquard harness and pattern cards.

A994 and B9057 are now followed W for (7m) *Culross*, but noting, beside the road just E of the town, the remains of *St. Mungo's Chapel* (NTS), built in 1503 by Glasgow's Bishop Blacader.

Culross is the traditional site of a 5 or 6C religious house, presided over by St. Serf or Servan. St. Mungo, or Kentigern, founder of Glasgow cathedral and patron saint of that city, is said to have been born here. The story goes that his mother, Thenew, of a pagan family, secretly married the Christian King Owen of Strathclyde. Disowned then by her father she was forced to flee from her home in Lothian, crossing the Forth alone in a small boat which was driven ashore at the spot now marked by this chapel. And here she gave birth.

During the 16–17C Culross was a busy community, thriving through its trade in coal and salt, its salt-pans being visited by James VI who made the town a royal burgh in 1588. The coal and salt trades were much expanded by the energetic and businesslike Sir George Bruce (died 1625).

Culross survives as perhaps the most perfect example of a small Scots town of the 16–18C. That this is so is in large part due to the care and imagination of the National Trust for Scotland which, over the last 50 years, has acquired and restored many buildings. The lower town, beside the Forth, is connected with the upper and the abbey by steep, narrow flagstone streets.

The *Palace* (AM. Standard. Fee) was built in 1597, and extended by a N wing in 1611, for Sir George Bruce, and, with its stepped gables and pantiled roofs set about an open court with terraced gardens behind, is a charming example of the smaller type of Scottish town mansion. Many of the panelled rooms are, in typical Scottish style, painted all over with scenes from the scriptures etc. The *Town House* (NTS. May–Sept: Daily except Fri., 09.30 to 12.30. 14.00 to 17.00. Fee), or tolbooth, dates from 1626 except for its tower which is of 1783. Handed over to the National Trust by the local council in 1975, the building now houses a Visitor Centre with an audio-visual presentation.

Behind the palace stands the Cross, supported by a modern shaft, and here too is the curious, corbelled-out turret known as the *Study of Bishop Leighton* (NTS. April and Oct: Sat. and Sun., 09.30 to 12.30. 14.00 to 16.00. Otherwise by appointment. Tel: 0383-880359).

The *Abbey*, at the top of the town, was founded for Cistercians by Malcolm, Earl of Fife, in 1215. The church, dating in large part from c 1300 but rebuilt under James IV, preserves intact its choir and splendid central tower, these parts now serving as parish church. The nave however, of which the S wall is probably original to 1215, is in ruins. In a chamber on the N side are the alabaster effigies of Sir George Bruce (died 1625) and his numerous family. Of the monastic buildings little survives, much of their stone having been used in the building of Abbey House (no adm.) just above; begun in 1608 and altered in 1670, the house was remodelled in 1952.

Continuing W, B9057 soon passes *Dunimarle Castle Museum* (April–Oct: Daily, 14.00 to 18.00. Tel: 0383-229. Fee), showing furniture, paintings, silver, glass and suchlike, to reach (*4m*) **Kincardine**, a small river port at the N end of a fine bridge of 1936. Connoisseurs of follies will cross the bridge to see the bizarre *Pineapple* (NTS. Picnic area; off B9124 to the N of Airth), built in 1761 by an unknown architect as a garden retreat. Sir John Dewar (1842–1922), inventor of the vacuum flask, was born in Kincardine, and *Tulliallan Castle* (1824), at the N end of the town, was occupied by the Polish General Sikorsky as his headquarters during the 1939–45 war; beyond extends an important Forestry Commission tree nursery.

3m **Clackmannan**, reached by A977 and A907, stands just to the S of the latter road and rewards the short diversion with a stepped 17C *Cross*, the tower of the old *Tolbooth* (1592), which, with its courtroom, prison and jailor's dwelling once extended some 40ft to the E, and the mysterious *Stone (Clach) of Mannan*, all these grouped in the village square. The stone, then recumbent, was placed on its present shaft in 1833 and is sometimes said to be sacred to the pagan god, Mannan. *Clackmannan Tower* (no adm. but well seen from outside), on a hill to the W appropriately known as King's Seat, is a tall and ancient tower said to have been a residence of Malcolm IV. *Gartmorn Dam Country Park* (Tel: 0259-214319), a short way N of Clackmannan, offers a nature reserve, a reservoir, the oldest dam in Scotland and a visitor centre.

2m **Alloa** (26,000 inhab. *ECl.* Wed.) is a bustling industrial town, with spinning, glassmaking and brewing among its main pursuits, while *Alloa Tower*, in the lower E part of the town, provides a reminder of medieval times. Dating from the 15C the tower was built by the Erskine family (later earls of Mar) and was at times in turn the childhood home of James V, Mary, Queen of Scots, James VI and his sons Henry and Charles. Alloa stands at the SE end of the *Links*

The Pineapple, Kincardine. An 18C Garden Folly.

of the Forth, the tortuous stretch of the river between here and Stirling, so famed for its fertility that a saying runs 'A crook o' the Forth is worth an earldom o' the North'.—*2m Tullibody*, in which there is a small pre-Reformation church, of which John Knox recorded that the French troops sent to help Mary of Guise, 'expert enough in such feats, tuke down the roof to make ane brig over the Devon', and so escaped to Stirling. Robert Dick (1811–66), the geologist, was born here.—*5m* **Stirling**, see Rte 23.

32   Edinburgh to Perth

A90 across the Forth Bridge. M90 to Exit 5. B9097, B920, A911 and A922 around Loch Leven to Kinross. M90 to Perth.—Farmland, with hills.

SOME HOTELS. **Kinross**. *Green*, 2 The Muirs. Tel: (0577) 63467. *Windlestrae*, The Muirs. Tel: (0577) 63217.

Total distance 45m.—*10m* **Forth Bridge (N)**.—*10m* **M90 Exit 5**.—*6m* **Scotlandwell**.—*4m* **Kinross**.—*15m* **Perth**.

From central **Edinburgh** (see Rte 18) Queensferry Road (A90) in *10m* reaches and crosses the Forth Road Bridge, for which, as also for the adjacent railway bridge and the approach from Edinburgh, see Rte 9. Here, at the N end of the Forth Bridge, Rte 31 bears W while Rtes 33A and 33C lead off E.—M90 now crosses a western part of Fife (see Rte 33), to the W, between Exits 4 and 5, being *Blairadam Forest*, an estate bought by William Adam in 1731.

10m **M90 Exit 5** where the motorway is left for an anticlockwise circuit of Loch Leven. However, at Gairney Bank, immediately N up B996, visitors with an interest in Scottish Church history will find a roadside monument commemorating the foundation here in 1733 of the first Secession presbytery.

Loch Leven, celebrated as much for its pink trout as for the imprisonment and romantic escape of Mary, Queen of Scots, is 3½m long by 2m broad and a *National Nature Reserve*, the most important freshwater area in Britain for migratory and breeding wildfowl, notably pink-footed and greylag geese and many varieties of duck (Restricted access. Tel: 031-4474784). There are two principal islands, on one of which, near Kinross, stands Loch Leven Castle (see below); on the other, *St. Serf's Island* at the SE, are the ruins of a priory, founded on the site of an earlier Culdee settlement. Andrew Wyntoun (died c 1420), one of the earliest of the Scots chroniclers, was prior here.

B9097 in under *2m* reaches *Vane Farm Nature Centre* (RSPB. Jan–March: Sat., Sun., 10.00 to 16.00. April–Dec: Daily except Fri., 10.00 to 17.00. Tel: 0577-62355. Fee), the first nature centre to be established in Britain. In a converted farm building, the Centre has arranged displays explaining the local geography, geology, wildlife, botany etc., while, additionally, there are a picnic area, a nature trail, and a hide from which between late September and April feeding wild geese and duck can be observed.—*2m New Gullet Bridge* whence B920 is followed N for (*2m*) *Scotlandwell* with, in the village, an ancient well from which Agricola's soldiers are said to have drunk

in 84 and where also, it is claimed, Bruce was cured of leprosy by
the local Red Friars who had established a hospice here in 1250 (he
is nonetheless generally believed to have died of leprosy in 1329).
By way of contrast, nearby Portmoak airfield is a gliding centre, good
use being made of the thermals produced by Bishop Hill to the
N.—*1m* Kinnesswood, for *Michael Bruce's Cottage* (April–Sept: 10.00
to 18.00. For keys, apply the Garage. Tel: 059284-255. Donation),
birthplace of Michael Bruce (1746–67), known as the Gentle poet of
Loch Leven and author of the 'Ode to the Cuckoo'. Beyond, A911
curves W to pass the ruin of *Burleigh Castle*, an early 16C tower with
a rather later courtyard wall, once a stronghold of the Balfours and
several times visited by James VI.—*1m Milnathort*, where Rte 25C
comes in from Stirling.

Kinross (2500 inhab. *ECl.* Thurs. *Inf.* Turfhills. Easter–Oct) is under
2m S of Milnathort by A922. The 17C *Tolbooth* was repaired and
decorated in 1771 by Robert Adam, adjacent being *Kinross Museum*
(Tues.–Sat., 13.00 to 17.00. Tel: 0738-32488. Free) bearing a plaque
recording the gratitude of the Polish Tank Training Centre, here
between 1942–48. But the main tourist objective here is *Loch Leven
Castle* (AM. Standard, but closed in winter. Fee includes ferry with
frequent service), the island-prison of Mary, Queen of Scots. A
compact square tower standing in a court surrounded by a curtain
wall, the castle dates in part from the early 14C when, in 1335, it
was unsuccessfully besieged by the English who attempted to drown
the place by damming the river Leven and thus raising the loch level.
The round tower, at an angle of the wall, is an early 16C addition,
as are also probably the remains of a hall and kitchen.

Here Mary was brought on 16 June 1567 after her surrender at Carberry Hill,
and here she remained for nearly 11 months in the custody of the local laird,
Sir William Douglas. Her treatment was unsympathetic, she was much of the
time in poor health and she suffered a miscarriage, thought to have been of
twins. In Mary's time the surrounds of the castle were very different to what
the visitor sees today; the island was even smaller and the loch nearly four
times larger. The tower, at this time entered through a low round-headed door
on the first floor, comprised two vaulted chambers below (a store and a kitchen)
and three storeys above, the wooden floors of which have long disappeared.
Here dwelt Douglas and his wife. Their prisoner was probably held in the round
tower (described by Scott as 'rude and inconvenient'), and here, on 23 July
1567, threatened by Lord Lindsay, 'the rudest, most bigoted and fiercest of the
confederated lords' who was 'so unmanly as to pinch with his iron glove the
arm of the poor queen' (Scott), Mary signed a deed of abdication in favour of
her son, and another appointing her half-brother, Moray, regent.
    Many attempts to rescue the queen were made, but eventually through her
personal charm she succeeded in touching the heart of George Douglas,
youngest brother of Sir William. His undisguised devotion led to his expulsion
from the island, but he left behind him a like-minded kinsman, William Douglas,
a lad of 16 who, on the night of 2 May 1568, while everybody was at supper,
got hold of the keys, placed the queen in a boat, and, having locked the gates
behind him, threw the keys into the water. On reaching the shore, Mary was
received by Lord Seton, George Douglas and Sir James Hamilton and escorted
to Niddry Castle (see Rte 8). Thirteen days later she was defeated at Langside.

M90 is now rejoined for (*11m*) *Exit 9* for Rte 33D.—*4m* central **Perth**,
see Rte 26.

33 Fife Peninsula

Fife, now one of the local government regions of Scotland, has since long ago been known as the Kingdom of Fife, perhaps because the region includes Abernethy, an ancient Pictish capital, or perhaps simply because it has long been one of the richest and most self-contained parts of Scotland. One of its latest assertions of independence was its successful opposition to official plans to merge Fife with Tayside under the 1975 local government reorganisation. Properly Fife embraces also the district extending SW from Loch Leven as far as Kincardine and including Dunfermline. This area is described under Rte 31.

The Fife peninsula, bounded on the N by the Firth of Tay and on the S by the Firth of Forth, is some 30–35m long by 20m broad. Until a few years ago the peninsula was something of a pocket and for this reason often bypassed, but since the building of the Tay road bridge in 1966 there has been an outlet at the NE corner to Dundee. Scenically the outstanding feature is the string of quaint and picturesque ancient little fishing ports lining the E part of the S coast (roughly Elie to Crail, known as the East Neuk); otherwise Fife is generally farming land, with some high moorland patches. Of many interesting and historical sites, special mention may be made of Falkland Palace, the round tower at Abernethy and the town of St. Andrews.

Fife is described in four sections: A. Edinburgh to St. Andrews round the coast. B. St. Andrews. C. Edinburgh to Dundee via Falkland and Cupar. D. The North (Perth to Dundee).

A. Edinburgh to St. Andrews round the Coast

A90 across the Forth Bridge. A92 from the N side of the Forth Bridge to Kirkcaldy. A955 to Leven. A915 to Kirkton of Largo. A917 to Crail and St. Andrews.

SOME HOTELS. **Kirkcaldy.** *Parkway*, Abbotshall Road. Tel: (0592) 262143. **Leven.** *Old Manor*, Leven Road. Tel: (0333) 320368. *Lundin Links*, Leven Road. Tel: (0333) 320207. **Anstruther.** *Craw's Nest*, Bankwell Road. Tel: (0333) 310691, *Smugglers Inn*, High Street. Tel: (0333) 310506. **Crail.** *Balcomie Links*, Balcomie Road. Tel: (0333) 50237.

Total distance 55m.—*10m* **Forth Bridge (N)**.—*4m* **Aberdour**.—*2m* **Burntisland**.—*5m* **Kirkcaldy**.—*10m* **Largo**.—*5m* **Elie**.—*5m* **Anstruther**.—*4m* **Crail**.—*10m* **St. Andrews**.

From central **Edinburgh** (see Rte 18) Queensferry Road (A90) in *10m* reaches and crosses the *Forth Road Bridge*, for which, as also for the adjacent railway bridge and the approach from Edinburgh, see Rte 9. Here, at the N end of the Forth Bridge, Rte 31 bears W while Rte 32 continues N and Rte 33C aims NE. This Rte drops into the small town of **Inverkeithing**, granted a charter by William the Lion in 1165 and the birthplace of Sir Samuel Greig (1735–88), the admiral who created a Russian navy for Catherine the Great (plaque in High Street). More about this admiral can be learnt at the *Inverkeithing Museum* of local history (Wed.–Sat., 10.00 to 12.30. 14.30 to 17.00.

Sun., 12.00 to 17.00. Tel: 0383-413344. Free), at the W end of the town and housed in what was once the 14C friary and hospice of the Grey Friars. At the E end of the town stands the *Cross* (1399; with unicorn of 1688), near here also being the *Town House* of 1755; the attractive, turreted 17C *Church Hall* or *Fordell's Lodging*; and the *Church* (1826 but with a medieval tower) in which there is a late 14C font.

2m A92 skirts the industrial area and new town of *Dalgety* which has grown near where once stood the seat of the Earl of Moray, granted lands along this coast by Bruce. *St. Bridget's Church*, dating from 1244 and now roofless, is by Dalgety Bay to the SE of the town. The E part represents the old church, the structure to the W being a later two-storey building with a laird's loft and a burial vault.

2m **Aberdour** is a small summer resort whose castle, ancient church and dovecot form an exceptionally attractive medieval group. The *Castle* (AM. Standard, but closed Thurs. afternoon and Fri. Fee), standing on 14C foundations, has as its core a 14C tower on to which other buildings were grafted during the 16 and 17C. Originally a stronghold of the Morays, the castle later passed to the Douglas earls of Morton, and today preserves some murals. *St. Fillan's Church* is part Norman and part 16C, the Norman parts being the chancel, the chancel arch, the N wall of the nave and the windows of both chancel and nave. There is a leper-squint in the W wall, and the exterior S wall bears a tablet to Robert Blair (died 1666) who was at one time tutor to Charles I.

Aberdour is also a place from which to reach **Inchcolm Island**, with the ruin of *St. Colm's Abbey* (AM. Standard, but closed Wed. afternoon, and Thurs. in winter. Fee. Tel: 0383-860335 for boat. See also Rte 18, Edinburgh, F.). First this was a priory, founded for Augustinians in 1123 by Alexander I in gratitude for the help given by the island's hermit when he was shipwrecked here, and it is just possible that a primitive cell on the NW may have been that of this hermit. Alexander's priory was raised to abbey in 1235, the remains of which include a small 13 or 15C church; an octagonal chapter house with a stone roof (c 1283); and a 14C cloister, with vaulted dorter, frater and guesthouse above. In Shakespeare's 'Macbeth', St. Colme's Inch is mentioned as the burial place of the defeated Sweno of Norway, and a hog-backed gravestone W of the church may date from this time.

2m **Burntisland** (6500 inhab. *Inf.* 96 High Street), a cheerful place with sands, and backed by Links, in summer the scene of a programme of enterprising events, happily enough accepts the accolade of Playground of Fife. Staider visitors, and especially those with a feel for unusual church architecture, may well prefer to make for the most interesting church, while romantics may pause outside Rossend Castle and ponder the fate of Pierre Chastelard.

Tradition is that the harbour was used by Agricola in 83 and that his troops also built a fortified camp on Dunearn Hill. Mary, Queen of Scots, visited here in 1563 (the occasion of the Chastelard affair), and James VI in 1601 when, at a General Assembly in the church, he suggested the need for a new translation of the Bible, this suggestion eventually leading to the Authorised Version of 1611. In 1651 the town is said to have surrendered to Cromwell, on the pragmatic condition that he repaired its harbour and streets.

The *Church* (inquire at Tourist Information regarding opening) is one of the most original and most remarkable post-Reformation churches in Scotland. As long ago as 1120 David I granted land for a church on this site, but the first was not built until 1234. The present building (1592) is octagonal in plan, with an external stair to a Sailors' Loft and a tower of 1749. Particularly noteworthy are the superb canopied central pew (1606) and the elaborately carved and painted Trades' Lofts (17 and 18C).

It was to *Rossend Castle* (no adm; restored as offices), then a 15C tower, that Mary, Queen of Scots, came in 1563, pursued by her over-romantic admirer, the French poet Pierre Chastelard. Found hiding under Mary's bed, he was pardoned, but soon again, and equally unsuccessfully, hid in her room. This time there could be no pardon and he was beheaded in St. Andrews the following day. Romantic to the end he went to the scaffold reading his friend Ronsard's 'Hymne de la Mort' and as his last words declaimed 'Adieu, toi si belle et si cruelle, qui me tues et que je ne puis cesser d'aimer'. In the following century a house was grafted on to the original tower, and a painted ceiling (c 1610) from this, 'discovered by accident in 1957, is now in the Royal Museum of Scotland in Edinburgh. *Burntisland Museum* (Mon.–Sat., 10.00 to 12.30. 13.30 to 17.00. Tel: 0592-260732. Free), in the library in High Street, modestly tells the local story, especially as regards shipbuilding and Forth ferries.

Approaching (*2m*) **Kinghorn** the coastal road is successor to the track along which Alexander III rode in 1286—as far, that is, as the spot where a roadside monument (of 1883) now records his death. The king was returning in the dark to the royal residence at nearby Pettycur when, it is said, his horse stumbled and he fell. Some such violent death had been predicted by an apparition at his wedding feast in Jedburgh Castle the previous year; and, the previous day, Thomas the Rhymer, challenged by the Earl of Dunbar to predict the morrow, had replied that it would be a day of calamity.

The fortified island of **Inchkeith**, 3m SE, was the scene of a bizarre linguistic experiment reputedly set up by James IV, who, wishing to study primitive speech, interned there two infants under the care of a dumb woman. The eventual finding, apparently, was that they both 'spak guid Ebrew'. In 1547, after the battle of Pinkie, the English planted a fort on the island, but from 1549 to 1567 it was garrisoned by the French supporting Mary of Guise.

3m **Kirkcaldy** (50,000 inhab. *ECl.* Wed. *Inf.* Esplanade. Easter–Oct), chartered since 1363 and a royal burgh since 1644, is a busy place which successfully combines industry with the amenities of a coastal resort, and which also has two notable museums. Once little more than one long street—and it still stretches along over 4m of waterfront—it was, and sometimes still is, known as the 'Lang toun of Fife'.

Michael Scot, the Wizard, was born near here (at Balwearie, 1½m SW) in c 1175. Adam Smith also was born here in 1723 (plaque in High Street) and returned to write his 'Wealth of Nations', and Robert Adam, born in 1728, was another distinguished native. Thomas Carlyle was a teacher at the burgh school (plaque in Kirk Wynd).

In the town centre stands the imposing *Town House* (by Carr and Howard, 1939–56) with, on top, Kirkcaldy's patron, St. Bryce, fashioned in wrought-iron and blessing the people. The Museum and Art Gallery and the adjacent Industrial Museum will be found above the War Memorial Gardens near the station.

Museum and Art Gallery (Mon.–Sat., 11.00 to 17.00. Sun., 14.00
to 17.00. Tel: 0592-260732. Free). While the museum part offers much
of interest—local archaeology, history, geology and natural history,
as also material on Smith and Carlyle—it is the *Art Gallery that
achieves distinction, with a small but brilliant collection in which
many of the works are by Scottish artists. Names represented here
include Andrew Geddes, S.J. Peploe, Henry Raeburn, W.Q. Orch-
ardson, William McTaggart (a whole room, including his touching
'Helping Granny'), W.R. Sickert, L.S. Lowry and L.E. Boudin.

The admirable *Industrial Museum* (May–Aug: Mon.–Sat., 14.00
to 17.00. Tel: 0592-260732. Free) covers many aspects of local
industry, with some emphasis on linoleum, for which the first factory
was established here in 1847. Also to be seen are a blacksmith's
forge and a collection of horse-drawn vehicles.

In front of the Museum and Art Gallery a plaque commemorates
Sir Sandford Fleming (1827–1915), native of Kirkcaldy, chief engineer
of the Canadian Pacific Railway and author of Standard Time, while,
across from the War Memorial Gardens, Adam Smith is remembered
by the *Adam Smith Centre*, with a theatre and other facilities.

In the lower town, skirting the Forth, the Esplanade is the scene
in spring each year of the Links Market, with origins reaching back
to 1304 and believed to be the largest street fair in Britain. To the E,
in High Street, near the docks, *Sailor's Walk* is a group of 17C houses
restored by the National Trust for Scotland. Among Kirkcaldy's
several attractive parks, *Ravenscraig*, to the E beside the shore and
with a nature trail, is perhaps the most worth a visit, if only to see
the ruin of Ravenscraig Castle. Dating from 1460, the castle was
begun by James II as a dower-house for his wife Mary of Gueldres,
but the work stopped three years later when the lady died. James III
handed the place over to William Sinclair, Earl of Orkney, and it was
finally demolished by Monk in 1651.

Dysart, once a royal burgh in its own right but since 1930 integrated
as an eastern suburb of Kirkcaldy, is an old port and still a place of
character, with some quaint streets and houses with stepped gables.
The *John McDouall Stuart Museum* (June–Aug: Daily, 14.00 to 17.00.
Tel: 0592-260732. Free), in Rectory Lane, should be of particular
interest to Australians. Here, in the restored 17C house in which the
explorer was born in 1815, is shown material on his journeys between
1858–62 and, in particular, on his S to N crossing through Australia's
central desert.

Beyond Dysart, West Wemyss, Coaltown of Wemyss and East
Wemyss follow one another in quick succession, the name deriving
from 'weems', or caves, of which there are several along this coast,
although most are in poor condition and difficult of access. *Wemyss
Castle* (no adm.), on a rocky height overlooking the sea just N of
West Wemyss, dates from the 15–17C (restored) and is said to have
been the place where Mary first met Darnley five months before their
marriage, while ruined *Macduff's Castle*, to the E of East Wemyss,
was in all probability a stronghold of the ancient earls of Fife.

5m (from Kirkcaldy) *Buckhaven*, now industrial, recalls its fishing
past at the Buckhaven Museum (Mon.–Fri., except Wed., 14.00 to
17.00. Tel: 0592-260732. Free) above the library in College Street.
Methil, just beyond, is also industrial, while sandy *Leven* caters for
the beach visitor.—At (*4m* from Buckhaven) *Lundin Links* three large
standing stones can be seen on the golf links.

1m **Largo** comprises Upper and Lower Largo, the former also known as *Kirkton of Largo*, with a parish church first consecrated in 1243 although the chancel is the only pre-Reformation survival. More interesting perhaps are a Pictish cross-slab in the churchyard and a tablet on the churchyard wall recording that it was built in 1657 by one John Wood (possibly a descendant of Sir Andrew Wood, see below, buried here) 'after 55 years absence returning from his travels'. *Lower Largo* was the birthplace in 1676 of Alexander Selkirk, better known as Robinson Crusoe; he was the son of a cobbler and his statue, nicely traditional in pose and clothing, stands at the cottage. Another Largo seaman was Sir Andrew Wood (died 1515), captain of the famous Scottish warship 'Yellow Carvel' and victor of a naval engagement in the Forth in 1498 when he both defeated and captured the English admiral, Stephen Bull.

A915 now heads N for St. Andrews while this Rte takes A917 to keep along the coast, though perhaps briefly diverting along B942 to *Colinsburgh*, a village founded in the 18C by Colin, Earl of Balcarres, a staunch Jacobite, as a home for his soldiers when it seemed clear that the Stuart cause was finally lost.—*5m* **Elie**, and its westerly continuation *Earlsferry*, are both summer resorts with good sands on which rock-hounds may sometimes find garnets. Earlsferry owes its name to a tradition that it was from here that Macduff, fleeing from Macbeth, was ferried across the Forth, while Elie preserves the more modern story that Lady's Tower, to the E of the harbour, was the beach house from which a noted local beauty, Lady Janet Anstruther, was wont to bathe—but not before she had sent a servant through the streets ringing a bell to warn people to keep away.

For the next ten or so miles A917 runs with the East Neuk, the stretch of coast along which are strung Fife's several quaint little ports. Not that these are the only attractions here, for within the ports, and between them, will be found ruined castles, ancient and interesting churches, a notable fisheries museum and even a visitable lightship. Ruined *Ardross Castle* (14C) appears first, closely followed by *Newark Castle* on its headland, once the home of the Abercrombies but in c 1649 bought by General David Leslie, the Covenanter commander, who became Lord Newark. Then in (*2m* from Elie) **St. Monance** there is the ancient *Church of St. Monan*, built by David II in c 1362 in gratitude for his recovery at the saint's shrine from a wound. Today the church comprises transepts and choir, with a squat square tower surmounted by an octagonal steeple, while a groined roof and ogee-headed sedilia are features of the interior.

2m **Pittenweem**, the principal fishing base along this coast and with medieval and even earlier religious roots, was the place where Robertson and Wilson in 1736 robbed the customs collector, a crime which led to Wilson's being hanged in Edinburgh (Robertson escaped) and the subsequent riot and lynching of the guard commander, Captain Porteous (see Rte 18, Edinburgh, Grassmarket). Today a plaque on a house in Routine Row, near the parish church in the E part of the town, recalls the crime. This *Parish Church* preserves its tower of 1588, with a balustrade on top and the old prison, where doubtless Robertson and Wilson were held, at the foot, here also being the Cross of 1711. Immediately E, in the ground of the Episcopal church, are the remains of a priory founded in 1114 and later (1318) associated with that on the Isle of May (see below); that this was a

sizeable place with land extending some way farther is evident from
the length of old wall which bounds the seaward end of Abbey Walk
Road.

A yet older religious link is provided by *St. Fillan's Cave* (Daily,
10.00 to 13.00. 14.30 to 17.30. Tel: 0334-73344. Fee), said to have
been the retreat of the 9C hermit whose relic, cherished by Inchaffray
Abbey, was so effectively used to bless Bruce's army before
Bannockburn. Since long ago treated as a shrine, and later physically
connected to the priory above, the cave was at one period used as a
store for fishing gear until rededicated in 1935. At the E end of the
harbour *The Gyles*, restored by the National Trust for Scotland, form
a pleasing group of 16C houses.

Two very opposed themes—domestic architecture of the 16–17C
and a steam railway—may prompt short diversions northward. *Kellie
Castle* (NTS. April and Oct: Sat. and Sun., 14.00 to 18.00. May–Sept:
Daily except Fri., 14.00 to 18.00. Garden and grounds open all year,
daily, 10.00 to dusk. Fee) is on B9171 3m NW of Pittenweem. Although
its oldest part is traced to c 1360, this castle is essentially a good
example of 16–17C domestic architecture, consisting of two 16C
towers united by a 17C range with some notable plasterwork and
panelling with painted landscapes. Kellie was built by the Oliphants,
but sold in 1613 to Thomas Erskine, 1st Earl of Kellie, the man who
killed Ruthven in the Perth Gowrie Conspiracy. Abandoned in 1830,
the castle was restored from 1878 by Professor James Lorimer, and
a room contains a display on the work of the architect Robert Lorimer.
The layout of the walled garden is late Victorian.—*Lochty Private
Railway* (Roughly early June/early Sept: Sun., 14.00 to 16.45. Tel:
0592-264587. Fee) is on B940, less than 2m N of Kellie Castle. Opened
in 1967 as the first preserved steam passenger line in Scotland, the
railway represents a section of the former East Fife Central Railway.
At present there are four steam engines, two diesels and a collection
of carriages and wagons, and trains run over a short stretch.

1m (from Pittenweem) **Anstruther** (3000 inhab. *ECl.* Wed. *Inf.*
Scottish Fisheries Museum. May–Sept) is more grandly and more
properly the 'United Burgh of Kilrenny, Cellardyke, Anstruther Easter
and Anstruther Wester', which locally abbreviates to 'Anster'. Until
the departure of the herring in the 1940s Anstruther was a main
centre of Scotland's herring fishing, and it is thus appropriate that
the town should now be the home of the *Scottish Fisheries Museum*
(April–Oct: Daily, 10.00 to 17.30. Sun., 14.00 to 17.30. Nov–March:
Daily except Tues., 14.00 to 17.30. Tel: 0333-310628. Fee), housed
mainly in a group of buildings known as St. Ayles, but also in two
adjoining houses and at the harbour. In addition to the range of
exhibits there is a lecture hall for special exhibitions and an aquarium
with wall tanks and a floor pool.

During the 15C St. Ayles Chapel stood here, on the site of the N building, and
a relic survives in the double-pointed arch window-head rebuilt into the present
structure and overlooking the courtyard. The building known as Abbot's
Lodging, on the E side of the courtyard, is of the early 16C and served as
quarters for the Abbot of Balmerino when he visited Anstruther, presumably to
check on the operation of the charter of 1318 which gave to his abbey the right
to lease booths to the local fishermen.

The museum illustrates many aspects both of sea fishing and of the
life in fisher communities, all imaginatively interpreted by means of

model and actual boats, tableaux in authentic costume and several striking paintings. The West Room and West Gallery are devoted to the days of sail, a period evoked by beautifully made boats, fishing nets and gear, a diorama of fishing methods, nostalgic photographs as also paintings by John McGhie, Sam Bough and ordinary fishermen. The Courtyard Gallery, by contrast, displays marine engines, while the Long Gallery (with a whaling exhibition in an adjacent corridor) shows a map of fishing communities and a tableau of ancillary trades such as gutting, packing and coopering. The Ship Loft, with a huge mural of a harbour scene, is devoted to steam; in the Courtyard are the wheelhouse from a modern trawler, as also various small boats and gear; and the Abbot's Lodging shows a typical fisher family room of c 1900, net loft above. In the Harbour there are actual veteran vessels.

The two adjoining houses serve as both storage area and galleries, among the themes being sea salmon fishing and 'This Modern Age'.

The *North Carr Lightship* (Mid May–mid Sept: Daily, 10.00 to 17.30. Tel: 0334-53722, Ext. 435. Fee), now calm in Anstruther harbour but from 1933–75 stationed at the treacherous Carr Rocks off Fife Ness, is a maritime museum of a different kind in which the visitor can see at first hand the cramped conditions under which a lightship crew worked and lived.—In the town, *Buckie House*, in High Street, a merchant's house mainly of the 18C but in origin of 1692, was restored by the National Trust for Scotland and in part serves as an art gallery. *Cellardyke*, the eastern part of Anstruther and the old fishing centre, owes its curious name to the cellars and dykes, built respectively below and above the hill, to protect fishing gear; and the name Cardinal Steps Bathing Pool recalls that the pool occupies the site of the landing steps below a palace which Cardinal Beaton once owned here.

In May–Sept there are boat excursions to the **Isle of May**, c 6m to the SE in the mouth of the Firth of Forth (Tel: 0333-310215). The small battlemented Beacon is a relic of a lighthouse of 1636. Long before this, though, there was a Benedictine priory here, founded by David I in c 1153 but abandoned in c 1312 when its inmates moved to the doubtless greater comfort of Pittenweem. And strange things are said to have happened here. When, for instance, St. Adrian was murdered here by Norsemen in c 870, his stone coffin miraculously floated across to Anstruther where it is still identified in Anstruther Wester churchyard. And when once the Devil visited here, he became so enraged about something that he hurled a huge stone at the church at Crail, the stone landing against the churchyard wall where it can still be seen.

Just NE out of Anstruther the road passes *Kilrenny*, where the church, with a 15C tower, traces its origin to a foundation of c 865, before reaching (*4m*) **Crail**, a royal burgh since 1310 under a charter granted by Bruce. This is a picturesque small place, especially around the harbour area, with partly cobbled and tree-lined streets, restored crow-stepped and red-tiled 17–18C houses, a mercat cross topped by a unicorn and a *Tolbooth* (or Town House) dating in part from the 16C. And there are glimpses here of a remoter past, in three ancient stones to be found at the interesting *Collegiate Church of St. Mary*, in part reaching back to the 12 or 13C. Here the 8C Pictish cross-slab in the entrance lobby is just that, but there is another stone, near the door, showing an indentation said to be the result of generations of local bowmen sharpening their arrow tips, while, outside the churchyard gate, there is a third stone, the very one which the Devil hurled at the church from the Isle of May. And in the churchyard a ghoulish touch is provided by a solid, square building of 1826 bearing the inscription 'Erected for securing the dead', a visible reminder of body-snatching days. The town's *Museum and Heritage Centre* (June–mid Sept: Mon.–Sat., 10.00 to 12.30. 14.00 to 17.00. Sun., 14.00 to 17.00. Tel: 0333-50869. Fee), at 62 Marketgate, well illustrates most aspects of Crail's varied past, including even material on the wartime Royal Naval Air Station.

Fife Ness, beyond Crail, is the eastern promontory of the Fife peninsula. It was at *Balcomie* tower, to the N of the minor road out to the Ness, that Mary of Guise, just landed in Scotland as the bride of James V, was received and entertained in 1538, while opposite, running S from the road, a ridge and earthwork known as *Danes Dyke* is said to have been thrown up either by, or as a protection against, the Norsemen.

10m **St. Andrews** , see Rte 33B, immediately below.

B. St. Andrews

One of the historic towns of Scotland—secular, spiritual and academic—and hallowed in the world of golf, St. Andrews, or at any rate that part of it likely to interest the touring visitor, stretches along a broad generally E to W axis, with the sea on the N and South Street defining the S. At the E end are the harbour and the venerable ruined cathedral, at the W the Royal and Ancient Golf Club, while, between, three streets fan out westward from the vicinity of the cathedral. These are North Street, Market Street and South Street, this last being the main street. All three are flanked by gracious and dignified buildings and, with their narrow connecting streets, make up a legacy of thoughtful planning and good taste.

Tourist Information. South Street.—11,500 inhab. *ECl.* Thurs.

SOME HOTELS. *Old Course and Country Club*, Old Station Road. Tel: (0334) 74371. *Rufflets*, Strathkinness Low Road. Tel: (0334) 72594. *Scores*, The Scores. Tel: (0334) 72451. *Ardgowan*, 2 Playfair Terrace. Tel: (0334) 72970.

History. That St. Regulus, or Rule, bearing the relics of St. Andrew, was shipwrecked here in the 4C is one of the many convenient legends of Scottish history. It seems more likely that these relics were brought here in the mid 8C, at about which time a Culdee settlement was founded, its chapel first being on a rock by the shore, this soon followed by a church on Kirk Hill, traces of a successor of which (St. Mary of the Rock) can still be seen. In due course this Culdee settlement became a priory and bishopric which, by the beginning of the 10C, had superseded Abernethy in the primacy of Scotland.

Much happened during the 12C, starting with the appointment as bishop in 1124 of Robert, prior of the Augustinian house at Scone, a move which soon led to an influx of Canons Regular, the founding of the cathedral in 1160, and, forty years later in 1200, the start of the construction of the castle as an episcopal residence. Promotion to archbishopric came in 1472, one of the first to hold this rank being William Schevez or Schivas (died 1497), counsellor of James IV.

The 15C saw the start of some 150 years darkened by religious burnings and murder. John Risby was one of the first to suffer, burnt here in 1407 for heresy, followed a few years later (1433) and for the same offence by the Bohemian Paul Crawar. Patrick Hamilton went to the stake in 1528, and the burning by the Catholic Cardinal Beaton of the Protestant George Wishart in 1546 was almost immediately avenged by the former's murder. Another victim

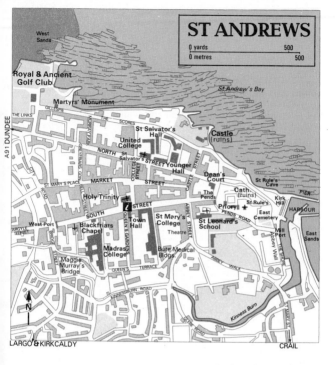

(1558) was Walter Myln, the last Reformation martyr (Reformation martyrs are commemorated by the *Martyrs' Monument* on the green near the sea at the NW of the town a short distance E of the Royal and Ancient club house). But the 16C was also something of a royal century, starting in 1538 with the ceremonial welcome of Mary of Guise before her marriage to James V and followed in 1563 and 1564 by visits by her daughter Mary, Queen of Scots. And in 1583 the young James VI found shelter here after his experience at Huntingtower.

The **University** of St. Andrews, the oldest in Scotland, was founded in 1412 by Bishop Henry Wardlaw and confirmed the following year by a bill of Pope Benedict XIII. In 1450 the college of St. Salvator was founded and in 1512 that of St. Leonard, the two being merged in 1747, though St. Leonard's has now been revived as a postgraduate college. St. Mary's College, founded in 1538, houses the theological faculty. The traditional red-gowned undergraduate promenade on Sundays from the university chapel to the pier is a colourful spectacle.

Golf. The Royal and Ancient Golf Club, now the world's premier club and the ruling arbiter on the game, was founded in 1754, as the Society of St. Andrews Golfers, by 22 'noblemen and gentlemen being admirers of the ancient and healthful exercise of golf'. The autumn meeting, when the captain for the ensuing year plays himself into office, is the principal event of the year.

There are four (Links Trust) courses, all of 18 holes and all to the NW of the town. The *Old Course* (4m), always the favourite, starts from the Royal and Ancient Golf Club House. The others are the *New Course* (3¾m), the *Jubilee Course* (2¾m) and the *Eden Course* (3½m). All the above are the property of a Links Trust and, on payment of a green fee, are open without introduction o the need to belong to a club. However, advance reservation (at least eight weeks) is advisable (Links Management Committee, Golf Place, St. Andrews, Fife. Tel: 0334-75757) and for the Old Course there is also a ballot system (Tel: 0334-73393). *Balgove Links* provides a fifth course.

The description below starts from West Port, at the W end of South Street, continues through the town to the cathedral, then returns westward past the castle and through the university fronting North Street. The total distance on foot is about 1½m.

West Port, one of the few surviving Scottish city gates, was rebuilt in 1589, but the side arches are 19C additions as is the figure of David I. Beyond, in South Street and the turnings off it, there are many pleasing 18C houses, as also older buildings. On the S the first place of interest is *Blackfriars Chapel*, a fragment (1525) of the church of the Dominican friary founded in 1274 by Bishop Wishart but destroyed by a Reformation mob in 1559. The chapel now stands within the grounds of Madras College, a school founded in 1832 from a bequest of Andrew Bell, a native of St. Andrews who made his fortune in India. The *Town Hall* (Tourist Information), beyond on the right on the corner of Queen's Gardens, shows portraits and articles of municipal historical interest, these including the headsman's axe.

Holy Trinity Church, opposite the Town Hall, was founded in 1410 but has since been many times altered, the two most notable architectural events being an indifferent rebuilding of 1799 followed in 1906–09 by rescue by MacGregor Chalmers who in his redesign followed the old lines and retained as much as possible of the original work, including the fine tower which is pre-Reformation. It was in this church in 1547 that John Knox preached his first public sermon, but, despite this, and certainly unexpected in a Presbyterian church, the most striking feature of the interior (S transept) is the elaborate marble monument to the Catholic Archbishop Sharp, carved in Holland and erected by his son, with a fulsome inscription and a representation of the archbishop's particularly brutal murder (see Rte 33C, Magus Muir). To the SE is the Memorial Aisle, with two surviving choir stalls (c 1505) and the silver Book of Remembrance (in a shrine recess), made after the last war, while on the N side the Playfair Aisle commemorates Sir Nigel Playfair (1874–1934) and members of the family. The E and W windows, and 11 others in the church (1910–50) are the work of Douglas Strachan.

The pulpit, lectern and font commemorate 'A.K.H.B.' (Dr Boyd), minister of this church in 1865–99; he was appointed Moderator of the General Assembly, and, as A.K.H.B., became known as the author of 'The Recreations of a Country Parson' and 'Graver Thoughts of a Country Parson'.

St. Mary's College, on the S side of South Street roughly opposite Holy Trinity, is readily identified by the coats-of-arms of past chancellors on the street facade. Founded in 1538 by Archbishop Beaton, the college has since 1579 been the theological faculty of the university. The older buildings form two sides of an attractive quadrangle in which a thorn tree planted by Mary, Queen of Scots, still flourishes.

Beyond Abbey Street, and again on the S, *St. Leonard's School*, a girls' residential school since 1877, occupies the site and some of the old buildings of St. Leonard's College which was founded in 1512, on the site of an older hospice, by Prior John Hepburn and Archbishop Alex Stewart; the latter was natural son of James IV, with whom he died at Flodden (1513). Until 1747, when the college was united with St. Salvator and the domestic buildings were sold, this college enjoyed great distinction. George Buchanan was principal in 1566–70, John Knox resided here, and it was here that so many of the youthful Reformers studied that the phrase to have 'drunk at St. Leonard's Well' became accepted as meaning having imbibed Protestant doctrine. The school's library is in *Queen Mary's House*, on South Street, a 16C house once belonging to a merchant, Hugh Scrimgeour, in which Mary, Queen of Scots, probably stayed (1563–64) and Charles II certainly did in 1650.

South Street ends almost opposite the cathedral entrance (see below), on the right here being *The Pends*, two fine 14C arches, once the chief entrance to the precinct of the priory which is surrounded by a daunting defensive wall (16C but on earlier foundations) 25ft high, c 1m in circumference and distinguished at intervals by towers, gunloops and carved heraldic panels. On the right, beyond The Pends, is the entrance to *St. Leonard's Chapel* (Mon.–Fri., 10.00 to 16.00. Free), founded in 1512 as the chapel of St. Leonard's College. After a period as a parish church (1578–1671), the chapel stood neglected until 1910 when the university began a long programme of restoration successfully completed in 1952. Pends Road drops down to the harbour (the main pier of which was rebuilt in the 17C with stones from the cathedral and castle ruins), passing on the right the gateway of the *Hospitium Novum* of the priory, once a residence of Archbishop Sharp, and ending at the *Mill Port* where there is another gate in the precinct wall.

Facing the cathedral entrance, a group of 16–17C houses known as *Dean's Court* stand on the site of the former Archdeacon's Lodging. Here the arms over the old gateway are those of George Douglas, the young man who engineered the escape of Mary, Queen of Scots, from Loch Leven.

For all that it is in ruins, the *Cathedral (AM. Standard. Fee for St. Rule's Tower and the museum), with its lofty, near perfect E end wall, still impresses both visually and as an example of 12C and later achievement. The Church of St. Rule, of earlier date than the cathedral, is also within this precinct.

History. Although founded in 1160 by Bishop Arnold, the cathedral was finished and consecrated only in 1318, in the presence of King Robert the Bruce. Later these walls saw both pomp and despair, the former exemplified by the marriage of James V and Mary of Guise, the latter by the trial and condemnation for heresy of such as Patrick Hamilton, George Wishart and Walter Myln. John Knox can probably be blamed for the cathedral's loss of its images and 'popish' ornaments, but there is no evidence that the Reformation brought structural damage, and it was probably a combination of neglect and the elements that led to the ruinous state recorded as early as 1649, by which time the place was being freely pillaged for stones for the town's defences and the harbour, not to mention the citizens' houses which continued to benefit until as recently as about 1826.

When perfect the cathedral was 355ft long and about 160ft wide across the transepts, the largest in fact in Scotland. Today the only significant remains standing are parts of the E and W ends (from the visitor's point of view the two essentials here, entirely isolated from one another, and a part too of the S wall of the nave. The remainder of what must have been a truly beautiful edifice survives as no more than a ground plan defined by lines filled with granite chips.

St. Andrews Cathedral. The 12C E front, with its original triple lancets but 15C main window.

The 12C *•E Front* stands balanced and perfect, with flanking turrets, three narrow round-headed lancets at the bottom, and above (a 15C insertion), a large pointed window. The *W Wall* (1273–79; not the original front which was two bays farther W) has a deeply recessed central doorway, surmounted by a blind EE arcade and flanked by a turret still propped by a flying buttress. From here the S wall of the nave of 11 bays runs westward, the W bays having late 13C windows, while those to the E are of a century earlier.

On the E side of the cloister is the triple entrance to the chapter house of c 1250, extended E by Bishop Lamberton in 1313–21. Between this and the S transept is a slype, once vaulted, while to the

S is what was the warming house (now museum, see below) above which was the dorter. The undercroft of the refectory, on the S side of the cloister, was reconstructed in c 1899.

Close to the SE angle of the cathedral is the **Church of St. Rule**, built in 1127–44 by Yorkshire masons for Bishop Robert (see town history). The nave has vanished, but the oddly narrow choir survives as does also the slender *Tower* (108ft. Fee for ascent of 158 steps). The same ticket admits to the *Museum*, in the former warming house in the cloister, showing Early Christian carved stones, medieval monuments, and various local relics.

Kirk Hill, between the precinct and the foot of the pier, is probably the site of the earliest Culdee settlement, here today being traces of the church of St. Mary of the Rock (c 1250). In the cliff below is *St. Rule's Cave*, perhaps better known as Lady Buchan's Cave after an 18C lady who fitted it up as a summer house.

The **Castle** (AM. Standard. Fee), long the august palace of the bishops, the scene too—at any rate as seen through modern eyes—of much barbarity, survives as no more than a shattered ruin on a rock beside the sea some 300 yards NW of the cathedral.

History. Started by Bishop Rogers in 1200 as the bishop's palace, the castle was rebuilt after Bannockburn by Bishop Lamberton and has since several times been modified. Later, it was the prison of Gavin Douglas, Bishop of Dunkeld, and of many early Reformers, and in 1546 the scene of two barbarous deaths. The first, in March, was that of George Wishart, burnt at the stake in front of the castle by Cardinal Beaton who showed no mercy to Reformation leaders and watched the burning in comfort from the castle walls. But next, two months later, it was Beaton's own turn, when several friends of Wishart, headed by Norman Leslie, son of the Earl of Rothes, seized the castle, butchered Beaton and hung his corpse over the battlements. Joined by many Reformer adherents, including John Knox, they held out until the castle was taken by a French fleet in July 1547, when Knox and many of the garrison were sent to the galleys at Nantes. The castle passed into the possession of the town in the 17C and was from then on neglected.

A modern bridge crosses the moat to the entrance, flanked by guardrooms, beyond being the courtyard, with the castle well. In the so-called Sea Tower, at the NW angle, there is a strange bottle-shaped dungeon, some 25ft deep, in which several Reformers are said to have been held, and into which also the body of their persecutor Beaton was thrown and covered with salt—'to await', said Knox, 'what exsequies his brethren the bishops would prepare for him'. At the NE angle is the Kitchen Tower, while the strong tower at the SW angle is supposed to have contained Beaton's apartments.

Castle Street, followed S, crosses North Street, near the intersection, at 12 North Street, being the **Preservation Trust Museum** (March–June and Sept–Nov: Tues.–Fri., 14.00 to 17.00. July and Aug: Tues.–Sun., 14.00 to 17.00. Tel: 0334-73812. Fee). Here, in a reconstructed 17C house, can be seen a 19C grocer's shop, a chemist of the same period, and, on the upper floor, a nostalgic collection of scrapbooks, postcards, photographs and much else to carry the visitor back to the St. Andrews of a century or so ago.

Many of the main university buildings fill the NW angle between Castle Street and North Street, first along North Street being *Younger Hall* (1929), beyond which is **St. Salvator's College**, founded on this site in 1450 by Bishop James Kennedy (grandson of Robert III and Chancellor of Scotland) and still the main focus of university life.

However, of Kennedy's original building the only survivor is the church, now the university chapel, with a lofty tower. Inside are Bishop Kennedy's elaborately decorated tomb and, in the vestry, a mace of Kennedy's time (made in Paris in 1461) still borne on ceremonial occasions. The *Crawford Centre for the Arts* (Mon.–Sat., 10.00 to 17.00. Sun., 14.00 to 17.00. Tel: 0334-76161, Ext. 591. Free), at 93 North Street and a part of the university, presents exhibitions of Scottish and other art as well as theatre and music.

Mellow and dignified though the streets are today, this tour of St. Andrews ends on a sombre note. It was before the gate of St. Salvator's that Patrick Hamilton, the first martyr of the Scottish Reformation (see also Rte 57, Fearn), was burnt in 1528, his courageous death achieving the opposite of what his persecutors hoped, for, it was said, 'the reek of Patrick Hamilton infected all it blew on'. College Street, opposite St. Salvator's, links North Street to Market Street, a St. Andrew's cross on the ground marking the site of the old market cross, beside which the Bohemian Paul Crawer was burnt for heresy in 1433 and the compulsively romantic Pierre Chastelard met his end in 1563 (see Rte 33A, Burntisland).

C. Edinburgh to Dundee via Falkland and Cupar

A90 across the Forth Bridge. B981 and A910 to Auchterderran. B921 to Glenrothes. A92 and A912 to Falkland. Minor roads followed by A92 to Cupar. A916, B939 and unclassified S around Cupar through Ceres to Dairsie. A91, A919 and A92 to Leuchars and Dundee.

SOME HOTELS. **Glenrothes**. Stakis *Albany*, North Street. Tel: (0592) 752292. **Cupar**. *Eden House*, 2 Pitscottie Road. Tel: (0334) 52510. **Newport-on-Tay**. *Sandford Hill* (at Wormit), DD6 8RG. Tel: (0382) 541802.

Total distance 60m.—*10m* **Forth Road Bridge (N)**.—*8m* **Lochgelly**.—*7m* **Glenrothes**.—*5m* **Falkland**.—*10m* **Cupar**.—*4m* **Ceres**.—*2m* **Pitscottie**.—*3m* **Dairsie**.—*4m* **Leuchars**.—*5m* **Newport-on-Tay**.—*2m* **Dundee**.

From central **Edinburgh** (see Rte 18) Queensferry Road (A90) in *10m* reaches and crosses the *Forth Road Bridge*, for which, as also for the adjacent railway bridge and the approach from Edinburgh, see Rte 9. Here, at the N end of the Forth Bridge, Rte 31 bears W while Rte 32 continues N and Rte 33A follows the coast eastward. For *Inverkeithing*, just below and E of the N end of the bridge complex, see Rte 33A.

This Rte follows B981 N, parallel to the motorway, to reach (*4m*) *Crossgates*, whence A910 is followed through industrial *Cowdenbeath* to (*4m*) also industrial *Lochgelly*, both of these places once centres of a coal mining district. *Lochore Meadows Country Park*, 2m N of Lochgelly off B920, is the outcome of an internationally acclaimed reclamation project under which a drab and desolate mining wasteland has been transformed (Park open dawn to dusk. Visitor Centre open daily 09.00 to 20.00 in summer or 17.00 in winter. Tel: 0592-860086. Free, but fees for sports).

A910, followed by B921, in *5m* reaches *Glenrothes Airfield* at a crossroads. Here enthusiasts for ancient early Christian stones will divert 1m S along B922 to see the *Dogton Stone*, off the road to the W near Dogton Farm where permission may be asked to park the car and advice sought on the path (200 yards) to follow to avoid damage to crops. Dating from the 10C and, though the top and arms are now missing, once a cross, it is still possible to make out a horse on the E face and a serpentine design on the S.

2m **Glenrothes** (27,000 inhab. *ECl*. Tues.), designed for the needs of the local collieries but, now that these are exhausted, devoted to light industry, is an interesting 'new town' development which has benefited from being individual rather than a satellite to some city. Some of the buildings (generally 1960 on) merit attention, as do also many examples of contemporary sculpture. Among the buildings are *St. Columba's Church* (1960), by Wheeler and Sproson, with a lofty, detached steel and glass tower and a mural by Alberto Morocco; *St. Paul's Church* with an altarpiece by Benno Schotz, who also devised the statue at the town centre; and the imposing *High School* (1966) with a remarkable patterned glass facade. As to the sculpture, Glenrothes boasts what must surely be an almost unique assemblage, largely because in 1968 the Development Corporation appointed an artist, David Harding, 'to contribute creatively to the external built environment of the town'.

Glenrothes offers all the many facilities to be expected of such a development, including the *Kingdom Centre*, one of Europe's largest shopping malls, and also *Balbirnie Park*, with a fine craft centre and a stone circle, the latter interesting both as such and for having been moved 100 yards when threatened by road construction. At **Markinch**, now effectively an E suburb but claiming once to have been the Pictish capital of Fife, are the ruins of *Balgonie Castle* (no adm., but well seen between A911 and B921), with a 15C tower and a later courtyard, once the home of Leslie, Lord Leven (died 1661), commander of the Scots at Marston Moor.

Falkland, *5m* N by A92 and A912, could scarcely provide a greater contrast to Glenrothes, the latter uncompromisingly of today, Falkland a dignified little royal burgh of 1458, particularly rich in restored 17 to 19C small houses and its name synonymous with that of the elegant palace built and loved by James IV and V. But humbler people lived here too, one such being Richard Cameron, the Covenanter leader (see Rte 11, Sanquhar), who was born here and became the village schoolmaster.

Falkland Palace (NTS. April–Sept: Mon.–Sat., 10.00 to 18.00. Sun., 14.00 to 18.00. Oct: Sat., 10.00 to 18.00. Sun., 14.00 to 18.00. Fee). Visits are by guided tour only, lasting 40 minutes. Visitor Centre, shop, etc.

History. An earlier castle here, mentioned in a charter of 1160, belonged to the Macduffs, the powerful earls of Fife, and in 1371 passed to Robert III's ambitious brother, the Duke of Albany, who in 1402 reputedly here starved to death his nephew David, Duke of Rothesay and heir to the throne. The dry, official announcement, however, was that that 'dissolute prince' had 'died by the visitation of providence and not otherwise' (be this as it may, Albany seemingly deemed it prudent to expiate by founding the Albany Aisle in Edinburgh's St. Giles Cathedral). In 1425 Albany's son and grandsons were all executed by James I and the castle became royal property.

The Palace, begun by James IV before 1500, became a favourite seat of the Scottish court, and the phrase 'Falkland bred' implied courtly manners. It was James V though who completed and embellished Falkland (1525–42), and it

Falkland Palace. The creation of James IV and V and long a favourite seat of the Scottish court.

was here that he died in 1542, broken-hearted after his defeat at Solway Moss. A few days before his death, he learnt of the birth of his daughter, Mary, and commented: 'God's will be done; it cam wi' a lass and it'll gang wi' a lass'—a reference to the fact that the Stuarts had obtained the throne by marriage to Bruce's daughter. Later, Mary and her son, James VI, both highly appreciated the fine hunting in this neighbourhood, and it was from Falkland that James rode to Perth and the drama of the Gowrie Conspiracy. Charles I in 1633 and Charles II in 1650 visited Falkland, but in 1654 it was occupied and part burned by Cromwell's troops; in 1715, after Sheriffmuir, Rob Roy occupied the palace and levied contributions from the town. In 1887 the Falkland estates were purchased by the 3rd Marquis of Bute, Hereditary Constable, Captain and Keeper, who restored the S range, and in 1952 the National Trust for Scotland was appointed Deputy Keeper.

The S wing, the one restored by the Marquis of Bute and the only one in tolerable preservation, presents to the street an elegant ornamental facade with narrow mullioned and grated windows, and has an imposing gatehouse of c 1537 flanked by loop-holed round towers.

The inner court was originally enclosed on three sides. Here the facade of the S wing is somewhat French in character, perhaps reflecting the taste and influence of James V's two French wives; it is divided by buttresses, faced with Renaissance columns and entablatures, the upper windows being flanked with medallion heads of kings, queens and dignitaries. The E wing has a similar but less elaborate facade, while on the N side of the court can be seen the foundations of the great hall begun by James IV.

In the restored interior of the S wing, a corridor with 17C Flemish tapestries, a 19C oak ceiling, and stained glass showing the escutcheons of Scottish monarchs and their consorts, leads to the chapel which retains its original walls and ceiling. The royal apartments were in the damaged E wing and here may be pointed out the door by which the youthful and adventurous James V was wont to sneak out in disguise, what is probably the room in which he died (restored and furnished), and a dungeon dubbed 'Rothesay's' by Scott in his 'Fair Maid of Perth'.

In the Garden, which contains the royal tennis court of 1539, are indicated the sites of the keep and curtain wall of the early castle of the Macduffs.

Minor roads lead E through Newton of Falkland and *Freuchie* to reach A92, Freuchie having once been the place to which Falkland courtiers who had in some way offended were banished. Hence the Fife expression of derision, 'Awa tae Freuchie and eat mice'.—*6m Pitlessie* provided the scene for the painter David Wilkie's first and possibly most famous work, 'Pitlessie Fair', now to be seen in Edinburgh's National Gallery. The artist was born in 1785 in the manse of Cults, just SE of Pitlessie.—*4m* **Cupar** (6000 inhab. *ECl.* Thurs. *Inf.* Fluthers Car Park. May–Sept) has a charter of 1381. The town claims, though, to have been a royal burgh some 200 years before this, and it does seem to be fact that Alexander III held an assembly here in 1276. And the earls of Fife had a stronghold here, too, on the NE hill (Castlehill). Although today a busy shopping and administrative centre, Cupar manages to retain something of the air of an old burgh, with quite dignified main streets, narrow wynds, several 18 and 19C houses, and, at the head of Crossgate, a *Cross* of 1683, scarcely improved by a Victorian unicorn. The *Old Parish Church*, on the SW hill, although effectively of 1785, nevertheless retains three bays and a tower of 1415, the spire being an addition of 1620; in the churchyard are buried the hands of Hackston of Rathillet (see Magus Muir, below) and also the heads of two other Covenanters dismembered in Edinburgh.

A91 provides the direct road to St. Andrews, or, using A92, to Dundee. However, there are several places of varied interest to the S and E of Cupar, so this Rte makes a loop using A916, B939 and a minor road to regain A91 at Dairsie.

A916, followed S out of Cupar, in under *2m* passes between the mansion of Hill of Tarvit (E) and Scotstarvit Tower (W). *Hill of Tarvit* (NTS. April and Oct: Sat., Sun., 14.00 to 18.00. May–Sept: Daily except Fri., 14.00 to 18.00. Garden and grounds open all year 10.00 to dusk. Fee) architecturally provides a good example of the work of Robert Lorimer who in 1906 remodelled this mansion of 1696. Here too are to be seen antique furniture, Flemish tapestries, Chinese porcelain and bronzes, Dutch paintings and also paintings by Raeburn and Ramsay. The keys of *Scotstarvit Tower* are held at Hill of Tarvit. Dating from c 1579, this L-shaped building of five storeys was the home of Sir John Scot (1585–1670), a noted scholar, geographer and cartographer.

2m **Ceres** (on B939), little more than a village, is the home of the *Fife Folk Museum* (April–Oct: Mon.–Sat. except Tues., 14.00 to 17.00. Sun., 14.30 to 17.30. Tel: 0334-82543 or 0337-30410. Fee), housed in the 17C weighhouse near the medieval bridge, as also of the *Provost*, a strange 17C stone figure at the village crossroads, said to represent a former provost and to have been carved by a local man. This jovial fellow, long lost until found in the undergrowth of a nearby garden, was set up in his present position in 1939.—*2m* *Pitscottie* crossroads. Here, although this Rte now takes to a minor road heading due N, connoisseurs of 17C Covenanting murders will first continue 3½m along B939 to the crossroads immediately S of Strathkinness. *Magus*

Muir (sign 350 yards S of the crossroads) is where on the night of 3 May 1679 a party of Covenanters, headed by Balfour of Kinloch and Hackston of Rathillet, waylaid and butchered Archbishop Sharp (the Episcopalian Archbishop of St. Andrews) in the arms of his daughter, herself wounded in her vain efforts to protect her father. Later Hackston was caught and dismembered in Edinburgh, his hands being buried in Cupar old churchyard. Today a path (about ½m) leads to two monuments, one to five Covenanters executed in connection with the murder but in fact innocent, the other (100 yards away) marking the site of the murder.

Murder of Archbishop Sharp on Magus Muir. His gallant daughter Isabella was wounded as she threw herself between her father and the assassins.

From Pitscottie a minor road runs N through *Dura Den*, a narrow sandstone cleft noted for important discoveries of fossil fish, to (*1m*) *Kemback*, with, in the ruin of the earlier church, the effigy of the wife of Miles Graham, one of the murderers of James I in 1437. Reputedly she betrayed her husband, albeit under torture, and her ghost now haunts the neighbourhood. A short way beyond, the road crosses *Dairsie Bridge*, a bridge of three arches built in c 1522 by Archbishop Beaton across the Eden. The ruin above the river is *Dairsie Castle*, on the site of a predecessor in which David II may have spent a part of his youth, while the nearby *Kirk of Dairsie* was built in 1621 by Archbishop Spottiswood as part of his vain endeavour to bring Scotland into conformity with England. A21 is joined at *Dairsie*, rather under *2m* N of Kemback, this road in *2m* reaching *Guardbridge* from where A919 is followed N.

2m **Leuchars**, a village justly celebrated for its 12C ***Church**, the E end of which is perhaps the most beautiful fragment of Norman work in Britain. Here the exterior of the apse is arcaded, with superb blind arches and pilasters showing axe marking, while, inside, the mouldings of the arches at the entrances to the choir and apse are of great richness.—The nearby RAF station was the base of a Norwegian squadron during the last war and a memorial stands by the entrance. *Earlshall Castle* (Easter Sat., Sun., Mon. Then, until last Sun. in Sept: Thurs.–Sun., 14.00 to 18.00. Tel: 033483-205. Fee), 1m

E of Leuchars, dates from the 16C. Inside the castle the main features are the painted ceiling in the long gallery and a collection of Scottish weapons, while the grounds (nature trail etc.) are known for their topiary.

Tentsmuir Forest, to the N of Leuchars and occupying the NE corner of Fife between the Tay and Eden estuaries, spreads over an area of some 5m from N to S and 3m from E to W. Here will be found a Forestry Commission picnic area, and woodland and shore trails along which may be seen deer as well as many bird species, these perhaps including capercaillies, terns, eider and waders, while seals are common on the Eden sandbanks. There are also two nature reserves. *Tentsmuir Point* (open access), at the NE corner, comprises foreshore (Abertay Sands, a winter roost for wildfowl), an area of dunes and some patches of marsh. The other reserve is *Morton Lochs* (restricted access. Tel: 031-4474784) which are artificial lochs lying between B945 (at Kirktonbarns) and the forest. On the main migration path of wildfowl and waders, the lochs, then badly silted, were in 1976 deepened and given islands and promontories.—It is of interest that Tentsmuir has yielded some of the earliest evidence of man's presence in Scotland, c 8000 years ago.

5m **Newport-on-Tay** is a summer resort at the S end of the Tay Road Bridge, beside which there is a large car park with a splendid view across to Dundee; but with, also, a memorial to five men who lost their lives during the bridge's construction.

The *Tay Road Bridge* (toll) was built in 1963–66. Over a mile in length and with a height of 120ft above the water, the bridge has 42 spans, these including four wider ones of 250ft for navigation.

The *Tay Rail Bridge*, 2m W of the road bridge, was built in 1883–88 about 20 yards W of the site of its predecessor (1871–78), the central spans of which collapsed in a gale during the night of 28 December 1879 when a train was crossing, around 100 people losing their lives as the train plunged into the water. The graceful curve of the present bridge is 2m long, has 73 pairs of piers, and the rails are 92ft above the water.—Prior to the construction of the bridge, the train brought its passengers to Tayport, whence they crossed the river by ferry. One of the oldest in Scotland, this ferry is mentioned in records of as long ago as 1474.

2m **Dundee**, see Rte 34.

D. Northern Fife (Perth to Dundee via Newburgh)

A912 and A913 to Newburgh. Unclassified to Balmerino and Newport-on-Tay. A92 to Dundee.—This Rte provides an alternative to Rte 30.

SOME HOTELS. As the distance of this Rte is only 28m, see **Perth** (Rte 26) or **Dundee** (Rte 34). See also **Cupar** and **Newport-on-Tay** (Wormit), both on Rte 33C.

Total distance 28m.—*4m* **M90, Exit 9**.—*4m* **Abernethy**.—*3m* **Newburgh**.—*10m* **Balmerino Abbey**.—*5m* **Newport-on-Tay**.—*2m* **Dundee**.

Perth (see Rte 26) is left by crossing the South Inch by Edinburgh Road, A912 then running through Bridge of Earn to cross M90 and reach (*6m*) *Aberargie* where A913 forks E.—*2m* **Abernethy**, now no more than a large village and not officially in Fife, was once a Pictish capital, an important Church centre in 862–87, and also, or so it is said, the place where in 1072 Malcolm Canmore did homage to William the Conqueror. Today, though, Abernethy's fame is through its *Round Tower*, one of only three such in Scotland, the others being at Brechin and on the Orkney island of Egilshay. With a lower part ascribed to the 9C and the upper, presumably replacement, to the 11 or 12C, Abernethy's tower is 74ft high and tapers in circumference from 48 to 32ft. At the tower's foot there is a Pictish stone incised with ritual designs, while from the tower itself hang joug, complete with heavy padlock.

3m **Newburgh** is of more interest for two sites nearby than for itself. *Macduff's Cross*, a curiosity 1½m S off the minor road to Lochmill, is now a pedestal within a circle of stones, the original cross having been badly damaged by Reformers in 1559. Traditionally this spot was sanctuary for any member of Clan Macduff guilty of murder in hot blood; however, to achieve full atonement, the offender had to touch the cross, wash nine times, and pay a fine of nine cows, each tied to the cross. The other site is *Lindores Abbey*, once one of the great religious communities of Fife but now scanty ruins—the arch of the main entrance and a part of the W tower are about the only features standing—spread over a wide area about 1m E of Newburgh. The abbey was founded in 1191 for Tironensians by David, Earl of Huntingdon, on his return from a crusade. Later the unhappy Duke of Rothesay (see Rte 33C, Falkland) was buried here, and, later still, the abbey was still of sufficient importance to attract a visit by John Knox who records the burning of the monks' mass books.

To the S, off the SW of Lindores Loch, is the ruined church of *Abdie*, in the graveyard of which is buried Rear Admiral Maitland, commander of the 'Bellerophon' which carried Napoleon from Rochefort to Plymouth after Waterloo.

The minor coastal road is now followed for *10m* to **Balmerino Abbey** (NTS. View only from outside during restoration), unusual if not unique for having been jointly founded in 1229 by both a king, Alexander II, and his mother Ermengarde, the latter buried here in 1234. As at Lindores the remains are scanty, if more compact, and it is not easy to picture this as a once flourishing Cistercian colony from Melrose; the abbey, in fact, which controlled the fishing at Anstruther where its abbot's house survives as a part of the Scottish Fisheries Museum. Balmerino was largely destroyed by the English in 1547, attempts to rebuild being cut off by the Reformation.

For the **Tay Bridges** and (*5m*) **Newport-on-Tay**, see Rte 33C which is joined at the latter.—*2m* **Dundee**, see Rte 34.

34   Dundee

Lying along the N shore of the Firth of Tay, here 2m wide and crossed by road and rail bridges (for both of which see Rte 33C), Dundee is a busy commercial and industrial city and port which, despite the demolition of much of the heart of the old town—a 19C insensitivity unusual in Scottish cities—nevertheless achieves an acceptable if unexciting blend of the modern style and of some solid, handsome older buildings.

Tourist Information. Nethergate Centre, opposite City
Churches.—182,000 inhab. *ECl*. Wed.

SOME HOTELS. *Angus Thistle*, 101 Margetgait. Tel: (0382) 26874.
Queen's, 160 Nethergate. Tel: (0382) 22515. *Invercarse*, 371 Perth
Road. Tel: (0382) 69231.

History. Dundee seems to have been made a royal burgh by William the Lion
in about 1190, thereafter quickly developing to become one of the chief towns
of Scotland and one known also to Wallace who received some schooling here.
Later it was the first town in Scotland wholeheartedly to accept the Reformed
religion, George Wishart, burned at St. Andrews in 1546, being a leading figure.
It was also a town which knew all too much of war—in 1547 the forces of
England's Henry VIII held, plundered and burned the town for a week; in 1645
it was stormed by Montrose; and in 1651 it was taken and treated with the
utmost severity by Cromwell's General Monk.

Graham of Claverhouse ('Bonnie Dundee' of ballad), born here in 1649, is
perhaps the best known historical name associated with the city; he became
hereditary constable of Dundee in 1683 but enjoyed the title of Viscount Dundee
for less than a year before his death at Killiecrankie. The Old Pretender spent
a night here in 1716, and the Jacobites held the town from September 1745
until after Culloden.

Dundee ships have explored the Arctic (in search of Franklin) and the
Antarctic (Scott's 'Discovery' in 1901), and whaling was important during the
latter half of the 18C.

The description below takes **City Square**, with Nethergate the
modern city centre, as its starting point, in turn looking at three
districts—to the S and SE towards the river and harbour; to the E
towards Seagate and the old city centre; and to the W and N for
several other points of interest. Finally three short sections describe
some of Dundee's parks; Broughty Ferry and Claypotts Castle; and
also Tealing Dovecot and Earth-house, some 5m N off A929.

To the S and SE of City Square the complex of roads forming the
approach to the Tay road bridge has taken the place of the older
docks, while the waterfront between the rail and road bridges is
being extensively redeveloped, a main attraction here being a special
dock for Scott's '*Dicovery*' (Tel: 0382–27723), a triple-masted, square-
rigger purpose-built in Dundee in 1901. At the harbour, in Victoria
Dock, sits the '**Unicorn**' (Easter–Sept: Mon.–Sat. except Tues., 11.00
to 13.00. 14.00 to 17.00. Sun., 14.00 to 17.00. Tel: 0382-22263. Fee),
a frigate of 46 guns, launched in 1824 and the oldest British warship
still afloat.

In City Square, to which it presents an effective N facade of ten
Doric columns, stands *Caird Hall*, a handsome building covering two
acres, built in 1914–23 chiefly with a bequest from Sir James Caird
(died 1916), a prominent Dundee industrialist. To the E, within the
angle of High Street and Commercial Street, *St. Paul's Episcopal
Cathedral* (by George Gilbert Scott) occupies the site of the old castle
(plaque), destroyed in c 1314. A plaque also marks the site of the
birthplace of Admiral Duncan (1731), victor of Camperdown against
the Dutch in 1797, and an adjoining house was where the Old
Pretender stayed. No. 8 Castle Street, beside the cathedral, may
interest philatelists as the place where stood the shop and printing
works of James Chalmers, inventor in c 1834 of the adhesive postage
stamp. Seagate leads N off Commercial Street, a plaque on the S
side recalling the old town centre where stood the cross and tolbooth,
while in Cowgate, the parallel street to the N of Seagate, are *St.
Andrew's Church* (1774), a typical example of the work of Samuel

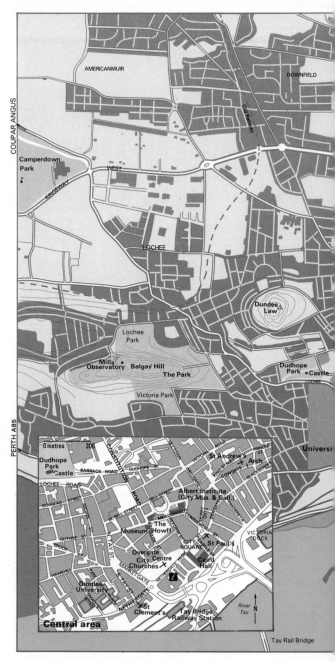

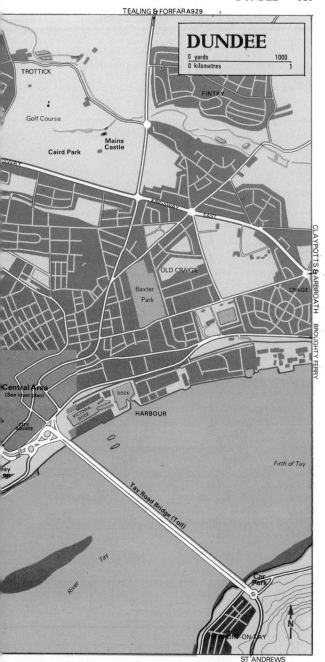

TEALING & FORFAR A929

DUNDEE

0 yards   1000
0 kilometres   1

TROTTICK

FINTRY

Golf Course

Mains
Castle

Caird Park

KINGSWAY

KINGSWAY EAST

CLAYPOTTS & ARBROATH

OLD CRAIGIE

Baxter
Park

CRAIGIE

BROUGHTY FERRY

Central Area
(See inset plan)

DOCK

VICTORIA
DOCK

HARBOUR

CITY
SQUARE

way

Firth of Tay

Tay Road Bridge (Toll)

Tay

River

Car
Park

Firth of Tay

NEWPORT-ON-TAY

N

ST ANDREWS

Bell, and, just NE, the *Wishart Arch* (or East Port, or Cowgate Port), dating from 1591 and the only surviving city gate. The arch's name honours George Wishart, the Reformer burnt at St. Andrews in 1546, who, in 1544 from this gate's predecessor, at a time when Dundee was stricken by plague, preached in two directions, to the plague-stricken outside and to the still unaffected within.

Nethergate leads W from City Square, with, on its N side, the so-called **City Churches**, a large cruciform pile comprising three churches under one roof, now surrounded on three sides by a pedestrian shopping precinct. The dominant feature here is the fine 15C tower of *Old Steeple* (or *St. Mary's Tower*), the only surviving part of the pre-Reformation church of St. Mary.

The story here is one of remarkably determined survival against the English and other disasters. It all started in c 1195 when David, Earl of Huntingdon, survived a storm at sea and, in obedience to a vow made during the storm, founded a chapel here. This was destroyed by the English in 1296 and again in 1385, but, such was the sanctity of this site, a church was rebuilt before 1480. The nave was battered down by an English fleet in 1547, and in 1651, when Monk assaulted Dundee, the garrison took to the Old Steeple and gallantly held out until burning straw was heaped against its base. Despite all this the building was gradually extended until by 1783 it embraced the four churches of St. Mary, St. Paul, St. Clement and St. John. Then in 1841 disaster struck again, this time as a fire which caused almost complete destruction. But, as always, the churches were rebuilt, although after this the congregation of St. Paul was accommodated elsewhere.

Beside Nethergate, below the Old Steeple, stands the *Cross*, a replica of the one that stood in Seagate but incorporating the original shaft. And in the pedestrian precinct a plaque with a biographical summary commemorates William Lion Mackenzie (1795–1861), born in Dundee and in 1834 first mayor of Toronto, Canada.

Nethergate continues W, with on its S side, *St. Andrew's RC Cathedral* containing a mosaic reredos of 1963 by Walter Pritchard, depicting Christ the King and Saints Peter and Clement. Opposite and beyond are the buildings of the **University** (1967).

The original University College was endowed by John Boyd Baxter and Miss Baxter of Balgavies, and opened in 1883 in some old houses on this site. It was incorporated with the University of St. Andrews in 1890–95 and again, after a brief separation, in 1897. In 1954 the college combined with others to form Queen's College, and independence from St. Andrews and individual university status were finally achieved in 1967.

To the N of the City Churches and the pedestrian precinct is **The Howff**, for three centuries, until 1857, the city's chief burial ground, a sombre, eerie place yet a treasure-house for the connoisseur of quaint tombstones and the backward glimpses afforded by their inscriptions. And there are touches of history here too, for once this was the orchard of a Franciscan monastery, founded by Devorguilla Balliol in c 1270 and destroyed in 1548. Then in 1564 Mary, Queen of Scots, gave the ground to the town, and from then on it was used not only as a burying ground but also as a meeting-place (howff) of the Incorporated Trades, a practice which continued until the opening of a Trades Hall in 1778.

Near the NW corner of The Howff, on the corner of Barrack Street and Meadowside, is the **Barrack Street Museum** (Mon.–Sat., 10.00 to 17.30. Tel: 0382-23141, Ext. 136. Free) illustrating local history and natural history.

The city's **Central Museum and Art Gallery** (Mon.–Sat., 10.00 to 17.30. Tel: 0382-23141, Ext. 136. Free), in Albert Square, just NE of The Howff, is housed in the former Albert Institute, a substantial Victorian Gothic building of 1867, enlarged in 1887 and with, in front, a statue of Burns (by John Steell). Museum exhibits concentrate on regional collections of archaeological and general historical material, the latter including an instructive gallery on Trade and Industry, while the Art Gallery shows works by Flemish, Dutch, French, British and, in particular, Scottish artists with some emphasis on the Victorian years.

PARKS. Four Dundee parks may be mentioned. **Dudhope Park**, the nearest to the city centre, less than 1m to the NW of City Square, includes *Dudhope Castle* (no adm.), of some interest as being, at least in its early form, the 14C successor of Dundee's original castle, the site of which is now occupied by St. Paul's Cathedral. At one time a seat of the Scrimgeours, whom Wallace had appointed hereditary constables of Dundee, both the castle and its accompanying title passed through several hands until acquired by Claverhouse in 1683. In turn wool mill, barracks and part of a college of technology, the structure has undergone constant alteration. Behind rises *Dundee Law* (571ft; view indicator), crowned by Dundee War Memorial.

On **Balgay Hill**, roughly 1m W of Dudhope Park, stands the *Mills Observatory* (Oct–March: Mon.–Fri., 15.00 to 22.00. Sat., 14.00 to 17.00. Tel: 0382-23141, Ext. 136. Free) with a ten-inch refracting telescope and other instruments, as also a planetarium and displays on astronomy and space exploration.—In **Caird Park** (N, beyond the ring road) are the remains of 16C *Mains Castle* (or *Fintry Castle*), built in c 1550 by Sir David Graham, beheaded in 1593.

Camperdown Park (Tel: 0382-23141, Ext. 243), 3m NW of central Dundee off A923, is a large park offering a nature trail, a golf course, riding, play areas, a *Wildlife Centre* (Daily, 10.30 to 16.00 or later in summer) and much else. *Camperdown House*, at the park's centre and with a restaurant, is an imposing mansion built by William Burn in 1824 for Robert Duncan, son of Admiral Duncan, the victor of Camperdown.

BROUGHTY FERRY is a coastal E suburb of Dundee, popular for the sandy beaches between here and Monifieth a couple of miles NE. **Broughty Castle** (Mon.–Thurs. and Sat., 10.00 to 13.00. 14.00 to 17.30. Tel: 0382-23141, Ext. 136. Free), conspicuous by the sea, was first built in the 15C, occupied by the English in 1547 after their victory at Pinkie, and stormed in 1550 by French auxiliaries in Scots service. Today the castle houses a museum devoted largely to the ecology of the Tay and to the maritime aspects of Dundee's past, with some emphasis on whaling. **Claypotts Castle** (A.M. Standard, but closed in winter. Fee), just N of Broughty Ferry at the intersection of A92 and B978, is one of Scotland's most complete Z-plan tower-houses, with two round towers, stepped gables and intact roof. Although the castle dates from 1569–88, the lands of Claypotts are of far earlier identification, being mentioned in a document of 1365 in connection with the abbey of Lindores (Rte 33D) which at that time was the superior of Dundee's St. Mary's church. When the castle was built the lands were owned by the Grahams of Claverhouse, but were forfeited to the Douglases in 1689 after Dundee's death at Killiecrankie.

TEALING DOVECOT AND EARTH-HOUSE. 5m N off A929. This is a worthwhile diversion if only for the most unusual and attractive design of the *Dovecot* which is built in the shape of a small house; dated 1595, it bears on a gable the initials of Sir David Maxwell. The *Earth-house*, well seen because it is now roofless, has an exceptionally long curving passage. Immediately on the right inside, at ground level, there is a cup-and-ring stone, much older of course than the earth-house and certainly once set up as a ritual stone elsewhere.

For Dundee to **Perth** (direct), see Rte 30; to **Perth** via Balmerino and Newburgh, see Rte 33D; to **Edinburgh** via Cupar and Falkland, see Rte 33C; to **Montrose** and **Stonehaven**, see Rte 35.

35   Dundee to Stonehaven via Montrose

A92.—Generally cultivated land, with coastal towns and coastal views, rocky in the northern part.

SOME HOTELS. **Carnoustie**. *Carlogie House*, Carlogie Road. Tel: (0241) 53185. *Glencoe*, 8 Links Parade. Tel: (0241) 53273. **Arbroath**. *Rosely*, Forfar Road. Tel: (0241) 76828. *Park*, John Street. Tel: (0674) 73415. *Links*, Mid Links. Tel: (0674) 72288.

Total distance 48m.—*10m* **Carnoustie**.—*6m* **Arbroath**.—*12m* **Montrose**.—*12m* **Inverbervie**.—*7m* **Dunnottar Castle**.—*1m* **Stonehaven**.

Dundee (see Rte 34) is left by A92, passing *Claypotts Castle* (see also Rte 34) and in *6m* reaching the intersection with B962. Here *Ardestie Earth-house*, within the NW angle of the intersection, is roofless and thus offers a painless opportunity to study the layout of one of these curious and unexplained excavations; and this site is of added interest for its association with an Iron Age settlement, the foundations of the houses being clearly seen, as also the line of an internal drain and what seems to have been a shallow tank, possibly used for keeping shellfish fresh. Nearby *Carlungie Earth-house* is also roofless and shows a long, twisting passage off which branch three short secondary passages; it is reached by driving another mile E along A92 and then following a minor road N for half a mile.

Two country parks, both to the N, are within easy reach of the Ardestie intersection. *Monikie Country Park* (Tel: 082623-202) is 2m N off B961 and *Crombie Country Park* (Tel: 02416-360) a further 2m NE off the same road. Both parks offer wildlife, guided walks, ranger services, angling and children's picnic and play areas.

At (*4m*) *Muirdrum* A92 intersects B9128 (N) and A930 (S), a short way down the latter being **Carnoustie** (9000 inhab. *ECl.* Tues. *Inf.* 24 High Street), known for its sands and several golf courses. About 2m NW of Muirdrum, on the left off B9128, once stood Panmure House, built in the later 17C and demolished in 1955; but the gates survive, not opened since the 4th Earl fled to France after the collapse of the '15.

6m **Arbroath** (24,000 inhab. *ECl.* Wed. *Inf.* Market Place), royal burgh of 1599 and popular holiday resort, is best known for its ruined and historic abbey and also for St. Vigean's Museum. But there are other places of interest too. For instance the *Art Gallery* (Mon.–Fri.,

09.30 to 18.00. Sat., 09.30 to 17.00. Tel: 0241-72248. Free), in the
Library, Hill Terrace, the place for paintings by local artists or by
other Scottish artists who have painted this district. Or the *Signal
Tower Museum* (April–Sept: Mon.–Sat., 10.30 to 13.00. 14.00 to 17.00.
Sun. in July and Aug, 14.00 to 17.00. Oct–March: Mon.–Fri., 14.00
to 17.00. Sat., 10.30 to 13.00. 14.00 to 17.00. Tel: 0241-75598. Free),
in Ladyloan W of the harbour, which is housed in what was once the
shore base of the Bell Rock lighthouse and illustrates the history of
Arbroath, with particular reference to fishing, flax and the Bell Rock
(see below). And there is also the *Cliffs Nature Trail*, 3m in length
and for the most part using reasonable paths (booklet from Tourist
Information).

   Arbroath Abbey (AM. Standard. Fee), in the town centre, is an
outstandingly beautiful ruin of red sandstone, essentially EE in period
though also with many traces of Norman.

History. The story behind the foundation of this abbey is interesting both in
itself and as being perhaps typical of the kind of incident which could lead to
a foundation. The murder at Canterbury of Thomas à Becket led to a rebellion
by the English barons and Scotland's King, William the Lion, himself an English
landowner, joined in. He was defeated and captured at Alnwick (1174) on the
very day that Henry II suffered penance by being scourged by the Canterbury
monks. So impressed was William by this coincidence that on his release and
return to Scotland he founded Arbroath (1178) as a Cluniac priory dedicated to
Becket. There were two fires during the construction, and the building was not
finished until 1233, 19 years after its founder's death. The priory was promoted
to abbey in 1285.
   Undoubtedly the abbey's most historic moment was in 1320 when the Estates
of Scotland met here and formally asserted Scotland's independence of the
English crown (Declaration of Arbroath), sending a letter to Pope John XXII
acknowledging Robert Bruce as king. However it was not until 1324 that Rome
addressed Bruce as king and not until 1328 that England's Edward III fell in
line.
   The abbey was sacked by Ochterlony of Kelly (Kelly Castle is 2m W of
Arbroath) in c 1600, but its ultimate ruin was due to post-Reformation neglect
and the town's habit of removing and then either selling or using the stones.
Among famous abbots were Bernard de Linton, the probable author of the
declaration of independence; the three Beatons (Cardinal David, and two
Archbishops James, uncle and nephew of the cardinal); and Gavin Douglas,
Bishop of Dunkeld.

Above the fine semicircular W doorway, with its deep EE mouldings,
is an arcade of six pointed arches, but of the rose-window only the
lower arc remains. Much of the NW tower and part of the SW
survives. The S wall and S transept remain, showing some pier bases,
this S transept, with arcades and triforium intact, having a magnificent
circular window, known as the 'Round O of Arbroath', once always
kept lighted as a beacon for navigation. Next to this transept there
is a vaulted structure with remarkable acoustics, probably formerly
the sacristy, surrounded within by sedilia.
   At the E end were once three rows of lancets, emphasising the
length of the church, but of these only the lowest now survives.
   The massive gatehouse tower flanks an arch, or pend, above which
was the chamber in which the Declaration was signed. The *Abbot's
House, to the S, shows a fine vaulted kitchen, while the hall above,
still with some 13C tiles, has been restored and fitted up as a Museum
showing documents, relics and sculpture, among this last being a
headless effigy with the feet resting on a lion which is supposed,

though really on no more evidence than this lion, to represent the abbey's founder, known to have been buried before the high altar.

St Vigean's Museum (For opening ask Information, Tel: 0241-72609), in a converted cottage in Arbroath's NW suburbs (sign off A92), shows an important collection of Pictish and Celtic Early Christian sculptured stones. The stones are admirably arranged and displayed, and the lively detail on many of them repays study.

Inchcape (Bell) Rock. This rock, covered by water at high tide, is 11m out to sea SE of Arbroath and is said to have taken the name of Bell Rock from a bell placed there by an abbot of Arbroath; later, tradition continues, the bell was removed by a pirate, Sir Ralph the Rover, hoping to trap ships but in fact himself being wrecked here ('Sir Ralph the Rover tore his hair, He curst himself in his despair'—as Southey put it in his ballad).

7m **Red Castle,** a stark red sandstone ruin overlooking Lunan Bay, can be well seen below A92 and is easily reached by a minor road. Although dating from the 15C the castle replaced an earlier stronghold built for William the Lion by Walter de Berkeley, probably as a defence against the Danish pirates who even in William the Lion's time constantly raided this coast. William may well have stayed here from time to time during the building of his priory at Arbroath, and later, in 1328, Bruce gave the castle to his son-in-law Hugh, 6th Earl of Ross. Eventually, in 1579, the place seems to have met an undignified end, being largely destroyed during a marital feud between Lady Invermeith, the then occupant, and her divorced husband, James Gray.

5m **Montrose** (10,000 inhab. *ECl.* Wed. *Inf.* 212 High Street) fills a broad tongue of land projecting southward between the sea and *Montrose Basin*, a tidal lagoon about 2m square through which the South Esk reaches the sea. An effort made to drain the basin in 1670 was foiled by a storm, and it survived to become today a nature reserve which is a rich habitat for migrating waders and wildfowl as· also huge flocks of geese.

The town's connection with James Graham, the great Marquis of Montrose, is small; merely that he was born in 1612 at Old Montrose, on the SW side of the Basin.

History. Montrose has many times been touched by history; military, political and even educational. The castle here was taken by Edward I in 1296, and it was here that John Balliol personally made his submission after his formal abdication at Stracathro near Brechin. Then, in the following year,· Wallace destroyed the castle, while in 1330, according to Froissart, it was from Montrose that Sir James Douglas sailed for the Holy Land, carrying with him the heart of Bruce. The year 1554 brought· a more erudite note when John Erskine of Dun established here Scotland's first school for the teaching of Greek, the first teacher being a Frenchman, Pierre de Marsiliers, and his pupils including the Reformers George Wishart and Andrew Melville. Later, the '15 ended here with the secret embarkation on 4 February 1716 of the Old Pretender and the Earl of Mar.

Well planned, with a spacious wide High Street and several dignified if modest buildings, this is a town of quiet distinction. The *Old Church*, in High Street, with its pinnacled square tower carrying a graceful steeple of 1834 by Gillespie Graham sets the tone, near it being the *Old Town Hall* of 1763, though with additions of 1813. Behind, in Panmure Place, is the *Museum and Art Gallery* (April–Sept: Mon.–Sat., 10.30 to 13.00. 14.00 to 17.00. Also Sun. in July and Aug,

14.00 to 17.00. Oct–March: Mon.–Fri., 14.00 to 17.00. Sat., 10.30 to
13.00. 14.00 to 17.00. Tel: 0674-73232. Free), with good displays
illustrating local history—the Pictish stones, material on whaling, and
the geology collections being of some note; also, in the garden beside
Museum Street, can be seen a length of the stone balustrade of the
old Montrose suspension bridge (1828–1928). To the E stands the
New Town Hall (1963) interestingly constructed in the body of a 19C
church, and, beyond, links extend to a sandy shore. Visitors with an
interest in sculpture will probably wish to take in the *William Lamb
Memorial Studio* (June–Sept: Sun., 14.00 to 17.00. Also Wed. in July
and Aug at the same times. Tel: 0674-73232. Free) at 24 Market
Place, where a selection of the works of this Montrose sculptor and
etcher (1893–1951) is shown in his studio.

Two places near Montrose also perhaps merit a visit. *House of
Dun* (NTS. For opening ask Tourist Information), 4m W of Montrose
on A935, was rebuilt in 1730 by William Adam from the earlier house
in which John Erskine (see History) was born, and, if only for its
plasterwork, is likely to be of general interest. Very different, and of
specialised appeal, is the *Sunnyside Museum* (Feb–Nov: Wed., 14.00
to 16.00. Tel: 067483-361. Free) in Sunnyside Royal Hospital at
Hillside, 3m N of Montrose on A937. This hospital of 1781 was
Scotland's first mental hospital and its museum tells its story and that
of psychiatry in Scotland.

12m **Inverbervie** lies on the S bank of Bervie Water, while on the
N side is Bervie Brow (450ft) and its promontory *Craig David*, the
place where David II and his queen landed in May 1341 after nine
years of exile in France during the ascendancy of the Balliols; his
ship was driven ashore by a storm and the rock known as the King's
Step is said to be the spot where he actually set foot in Scotland. The
town was made a royal burgh the following year. From Inverbervie
a short diversion (2m) can be made along.B967 to *Arbuthnott Church*,
mainly of the 16C but with a chancel dating from 1242. The Arbuthnott
Aisle here, with a priest's chamber above, was the burial place of
the Arbuthnott family, lairds of nearby Arbuthnott House since 1206.

At (*2m*) *Roadside of Kinneff* a minor road leads 1m SE to **Kinneff
Church** where (in association with Dunnottar Castle, see below) this
Rte touches one of the several adventures of the regalia of Scotland
(see also Rte 18, Edinburgh, Edinburgh Castle). During the
Cromwellian wars the Scottish regalia were brought to Dunnottar for
safety, and when the castle was besieged in 1652, Ogilvy, the
governor, determined to hold out until the regalia were secreted
away. This was achieved through the ingenuity and courage of Mrs
Grainger, wife of the minister of Kinneff, who obtained permission
to enter the castle ostensibly to visit Ogilvy's wife. When she left, it
was with the crown in her apron, while her serving woman carried
the sword and sceptre in a bundle of flax. The story further insists
that the English commander courteously helped Mrs Grainger into
the saddle. Back at Kinneff Mrs Grainger handed the regalia to her
husband who hid them beneath the pulpit where they rested in safety
until the Restoration eight years later.

But the church as seen today dates largely from 1738 and only a
part survives—with monuments to the Rev. Grainger and Ogilvy—of
the original church which sheltered the 'Honours of Scotland'.
Romantically though the story may read at a distance of over 300
years, it was scarcely so for some of those concerned, though

all—Ogilvy and his lady, the minister and his—emerged with credit, refusing, even under torture, to reveal anything. Their rewards came with the Restoration when Ogilvy received a baronetcy and the Graingers a pension.

5m **˚Dunnottar Castle** (Mon.–Sat., 09.00 to 18.00, but closed Sat. in Nov–March. Sun., 14.00 to 17.00. Tel: 0569-62173. Fee), an isolated and extensive ruin, sprawls over a great crag, surrounded on three sides by sea and rocks and on the fourth by a deep cleft left when the crag split from the main cliff. Among the most theatrically sited in Scotland, the ruins are more akin to those of a fortified township than of just a castle.

History. During the Dark Ages this rock was the site both of a Pictish fort and of an Early Christian chapel, the former recalled by the 'Dun' in this place's name, the latter by the fact that the ravine down which the castle is approached is known as St. Ninian's Den. Records indicate that there was a castle here in the early 13C, and also that a church (of St. Ninian) was consecrated here in 1276. In 1297, when the English held the castle, Wallace stormed it, burning many of the garrison who had taken refuge in the church. However, despite this, Dunnottar remained in English hands.

The oldest surviving buildings today are the great square tower and chapel, said to have been built by Sir William Keith, great Marischal of Scotland, in c 1392. The gatehouse (c 1575) was the strongest in Scotland and, like the 'lodging' in the courtyard, was built by the 5th Earl Marischal. In 1645, the 7th Earl Marischal, a stubborn Covenanter, withstood a siege by Montrose, who in revenge wasted the country for miles around and burned the town of Stonehaven. As the Chronicler vividly puts it, the country was 'uterlie spoilzeit, plunderit and undone'. There followed the Cromwellian siege and the incident of the regalia as described above (Kinneff Church). In 1687 Dunnottar was the prison of 167 Covenanters, held under brutal circumstances in a dungeon (the 'Whigs' Vault') open to the sea. Finally, the staunchly Jacobite 10th Earl Marischal had to forfeit the estate in 1716, and thereafter the castle was gradually dismantled.

Signs identify the various buildings which make up these complex and sprawling ruins, and the local booklet explains their detail. The outstanding features are the once formidable *Gatehouse* (1575); the huge *Well*, 30ft across and 25ft deep; the *Drawing Room*, with its modern (1927) painted and carved ceiling; and the breathtaking view from the *Marischal's Suite*, perched high above the rocks. Also the exceptionally interesting great range of *Domestic Buildings*—immense kitchen, with sink, sluice and ovens; the bakery and its capacious oven; wine vault and brewery. Finally there is the grim *Whigs' Vault* (the name Whig was bestowed on 17C Scottish Presbyterians), the prison for over two summer months in 1684 of 122 men and 45 women. Many died, and in desperation 25 attempted an escape along the rock face. Only ten got away, some were killed and the others were cruelly punished. The *Covenanters' Stone*, in Dunnottar churchyard, commemorates those who died as prisoners or in attempting to escape.

1m **Stonehaven**, see Rte 29.

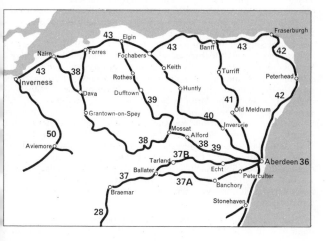

North East Scotland is made up of a wooded and undulating agricultural and pastoral centre, bordered by the sea to the N and E; by Deeside, famed for its forest and mountain beauty and its royal associations to the S; and, to the W, by high bare moor and mountain. Round the coasts, especially in the NE, there are stretches of steep cliff and rock (notably *Bullers of Buchan*, S of Peterhead), but for the most part the through-roads run inland and short diversions must be made to see the coast's scenery and small ports.

That the fertile lowland districts were widely inhabited in prehistoric times is clear from the many stone circles, those in the SE corner even being of a distinctive local style (Recumbent Stone). The North East moves into history in the 9C with the union of Dalriada and Pictland by Kenneth Macalpine, among the best known (thanks to Shakespeare) of his shadowy early successors being Duncan and Macbeth. The former may have been murdered at *Forres*, as were others before him, and Macbeth probably met his end at *Lumphanan*, near Deeside, where the great motte on which stood his primitive stronghold can still be seen. By the 13C power was largely in the hands of the Norman Comyns, earls of Buchan, the first Comyn having married a daughter of a local chief. (It was this Comyn who in 1219 founded *Deer Abbey*.) But Bruce's struggle against the English was equally a struggle against the Comyns, and in 1307 he twice defeated them (at *Slioch*, near Huntly, and at *Barra Hill*, near Inverurie), thereafter laying waste the land and installing his own supporters in the former Comyn strongholds. To Sir Adam Gordon went Strathbogie, later *Huntly Castle*, and there followed some 250 years during which the Gordons (later, earls of Huntly) ruled the

North East like kings. Their sway ended with the bizarre events of 1562.

The 4th Earl was as powerful and arrogant as any of his forerunners, and his third son, Sir John Gordon, a swashbuckling character who had let it be known that he was a candidate for the hand of the queen, Mary. Mary marched N, intending to combine a formal royal progress with curbing the Gordons. Her progress, however. became a running skirmish with Sir John, whose intention it was to abduct her. She wisely avoided the Gordon stronghold of Huntly and made for the royal castle at Inverness, where she interpreted the refusal of the governor, another Huntly son, to admit her as evidence of open rebellion. She gained admittance, however, and hanged the governor from the battlements. Back in Aberdeen, Mary outlawed both the Earl and Sir John. The former's redoubtable countess then came on the scene, urging her husband to fight because she had been advised by her witches that that evening he would lie unscratched in Aberdeen's tolbooth. The rival forces met at *Corrichie* (15m W of the city; memorial) and both the Earl and Sir John were captured. The former promptly died of heart failure, and his unwounded body was dumped in the tolbooth, thus at least satisfying the promise of the witches. Later the body was embalmed, brought to Edinburgh, and formally tried for treason. Sir John was executed, with Mary an unwilling spectator.

Thus ended the era of absolute Gordon power, for centuries the main feature of life throughout the North East, and although there was a half-hearted rebellion by Errol, Huntly and others against James VI in 1594 (this resulting in the destruction of Errol's *Slains Castle* on the E coast, as also much of the Gordon *Huntly Castle*), and although Montrose was active here, generally the North East remained loyal to the crown. Little enthusiasm was shown for the Jacobite cause, although George Keith, the 10th Earl Marischal, was exiled for permitting the Old Pretender to land at Peterhead, and although the Earl of Mar raised the latter's standard at Braemar.

To a majority of visitors the North East will mean upper Deeside, which many will reach from the S, by crossing the Cairnwell Pass (Rte 28) to *Braemar*, from where the North West rather than the North East may well be the next objective. This can best be achieved by taking the old (Hanoverian) military road N from *Balmoral*, this becoming the *Lecht Road* where it crosses the high moor (2100ft) before descending to *Grantown-on-Spey*, whence roads radiate in all directions. Twenty miles NW of here, near Inverness, are two of the most important sites in this part of Scotland. These are the battlefield of *Culloden*, the last battle to be fought on British soil and one which not only ended all the hopes of the House of Stuart but also signalled the end of a centuries old Highland way of life; and, nearby, *Clava Cairns*, an outstanding group of prehistoric tombs and stones.

But not everybody will head NW and for those who travel down Deeside there are several places meriting a stop. These are described under Rtes 37A and 37B, the former being the main road and the latter the smaller B9119 a short way to the north. This latter road is less crowded, and passes some unusual sites, such as *Culsh Earth-house*, near Tarland; the great walled motte at *Lumphanan*, associated with Macbeth; and *Craigievar Castle*, perhaps Scotland's most perfect tower-house, virtually untouched since its building in the 17C.

The remainder of the North East is described under Rte 36 (Aberdeen); five Rtes radiating from the city; and Rte 43, which travels the length of the N coast.

Aberdeen, the 'Granite City', with its striking yet dignified inner city buildings, granite and sandstone 14–15C cathedral, and its large harbour area around which anyone can wander more or less at will, deserves at least a day. The radiating Rtes all end at places along the N coast and the one chosen will depend on individual taste and plans. Rtes 39 and 40, though, follow roughly parallel courses through the heart of the North East and most principal sites are close to them, e.g. the sculptured stones, stone circle and other sites between *Inverurie* and *Insch*; the great castles of *Kildrummy*, *Huntly* and *Balvenie*, each with its story of past bloodshed and all notable as ruins; and the whisky distilleries strung along the '*Whisky Trail*'.

Along the N coast there are many little-visited corners, but **Elgin** stands out as the principal centre. Within the town is the cathedral, one of the loveliest ruins in Scotland, while, as a change from ruins, *Pluscarden Abbey* to the SW shows how a flourishing modern religious community can be grafted on to what was left by the old. Near Elgin also are 12C *Birnie Church*, with its surrounding ancient standing stones certainly one of Scotland's oldest sites continously used for ritual, first pagan then Christian; *Spynie Palace*, fortified home of Elgin's bishops; and *Duffus Castle*, where a medieval stone keep balances uneasily on an older motte. To the W is *Forres*, associated with Macbeth and having, on the town's E edge, the famed *Sueno Stone* with its vivid battle scenes. A few miles before Inverness, *Culloden* and *Clava Cairns* lie just to the south.

36 Aberdeen

Granite, solid and confident, Aberdeen's foundations are its distinguished university and its port at the mouth of the Dee, the latter, still active with fishing, in recent years also bringing a new prosperity as a service and supply base for companies exploiting North Sea oil and gas. Within and around the city there is much of historic and artistic interest—a good two days here would not be wasted—while for the visitor with other tastes there are the attractions of superb sands, a long esplanade, golf links and all the best in family entertainment.

Tourist Information. St. Nicholas House, Broad Street. Tel: (0224) 632727, or, for accommodation, 637353. Additionally there is an information kiosk at the railway station; and, from mid May–end Sept, there is an information caravan by the A92 southern approach to the city.—214,000 inhab. *ECl*. Wed.

Public Transport. Bus route maps and timetables from Tourist Information. Or telephone Grampian Transport on (0224) 637047.

Railway and Bus Stations. Guild Street.

Airport. Dyce, 6m NW. Town terminal, Guild Street.

Steamers. P. and O. Ferries scheduled sailings to Shetland (Lerwick).

ABERDEEN

0 yards   1000
0 kilometres   1

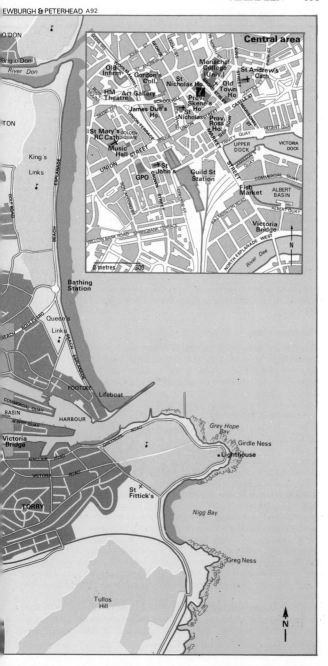

EWBURGH & PETERHEAD A92

O'DON

Brig o' Don
River Don

TON

King's
Links

GOLF ROAD

ESPLANADE

BEACH

Bathing
Station

Queen's
Links

BEACH BOULEVARD

BEACH ESPLANADE

FOOTDEE

Lifeboat

COMMERCIAL QUAY

BASIN
ALBERT QUAY

HARBOUR

Victoria
Bridge

SINCLAIR ROAD

VICTORIA ROAD

TORRY

Tullos
Hill

Grey Hope
Bay

GREYHOPE ROAD

Girdle Ness

Lighthouse

St
Fittick's

Nigg Bay

Greg Ness

N

Central area

SKENE SQ.

JOHN ST.

ST. ANDREW ST.

WOOLMANHILL

GORDON ST.

LOCH ST.

BLACKFRIARS ST.

SPRING GARDEN

N. NORTH ST.

KING ST.

PARK ST.

Old
Infirm.

Gordon's
Coll.

Marischal
College
(Univ.)

St Andrew's
Cath

HM Art Gallery
Theatre

St
Nicholas Ho.

Old
Town
Ho.

ROSEMOUNT VIADUCT

SCHOOLHILL

BROAD STREET

GALLOWGATE

CASTLE ST.

KING STREET

James Dun's
Ho.

 ST.
NICHOLAS ST.

Prov.
Skene's
Ho.

St
Nicholas

UNION ST.

Prov.
Ross
Ho.

SHIPROW

REGENT QUAY

St Mary's
RC Cath

ROSEMOUNT VIADUCT

GOLDEN
SQUARE

UNION TERRACE

BRIDGE ST.

MARKET STREET

TRINITY QUAY

UPPER
DOCK

VICTORIA
DOCK

Music
Hall

UNION STREET

BON ACCORD ST.

CROWN ST.

St
John's

GPO

Guild St
Station

COLLEGE ST.

COMMERCIAL QUAY

Fish
Market

ALBERT BASIN

ALBERT QUAY

YELLOWBANK ROAD

SPRINGBANK TERRACE

PALMERSTON ROAD

NORTH ESPLANADE WEST

Victoria
Bridge

River Dee

N

0 metres   300

SOME HOTELS. All the following have parking. **Main City**.
Station, 78 Guild Street. Tel: (0224) 587214. *Caledonian Thistle*,
10–14 Union Terrace. Tel: (0224) 640233. *Royal*, 1–3 Bath Street.
Tel: (0224) 585152.—For **Old Aberdeen**. *Northern*, 1 Great
Northern Road. Tel: (0224) 483342.—**Airport**. *Skean Dhu*, Argyll
Road. Tel: (0224) 725252.

History. Undoubtedly there were prehistoric settlements along this estuary of
the Dee, and undoubtedly, too, Romans, Picts and Scots were here. Later, in
1136, David I allowed a tithe to be levied on all craft in and out of the Dee. But
the earliest existing charter as a royal burgh is that of William the Lion of 1179.
In 1306 Bruce sought and received refuge here, later showing his gratitude by
giving the so-called 'Freedom Lands' to the town, lands which still even today
provide a good income, and a gift remembered by a memorial in Hazlehead
Park. The year 1337 was another important date, for after the destruction of the
castle and the burning of the town by Edward III Aberdeen was rebuilt on a
more generous scale. During the 17C Montrose three times occupied the city,
twice as a leader of the Covenanters and once as a royalist, then Commonwealth
military occupation followed for some years after 1651. Although Jacobite
declarations were made in 1715 and 1745, Aberdeen was never really in
sympathy; the contrary, indeed, since it was from here that Cope embarked for
Dunbar and his defeat at Prestonpans, and in the following year Cumberland
stayed six weeks here prior to Culloden.—The *University* includes Marischal
College in the city centre and King's College in Old Aberdeen. Although in
1641 Charles I chartered the two as a single university, they separated at the
Restoration and their present union dates from 1860.

Aberdeen is both conveniently visited and conveniently described as
three districts: the Main City, the Harbour and beyond, and Old
Aberdeen.

The Main City

The central area is quite compact and most places of interest can
comfortably be visited on foot. Union'Street (begun in 1800, its name
commemorating the union of the parliaments of Great Britain and
Ireland) is the city's long and main E–W axis, the description below
starting beyond the E end, at the Mercat Cross, and then travelling
westward along Union Street and its northern parallels, Upper
Kirkgate and Schoolhill.

In the middle of Castle Street—less a street than an open rectangle
off the E end of Union Street—stands the *Mercat Cross of 1686,
perhaps the most notable such in Scotland with its unicorn and
hexagonal base on which are panels with medallion heads of
monarchs from James I to VII/II, together with heraldic coats-of-arms.
This Mercat Cross was of course the focus of commercial activity,
while the **Town House** (contact Town Sergeant's Office here for tour,
Mon.–Fri., 09.00 to 17.00. Tel: 0224-642121), forming the corner with
Broad Street, provided the administration, today's striking building
of 1868 incorporating the tower and spire of the tolbooth (1616 and
1704; entrance to Lodge Walk), long the prison and the place outside
which public executions took place until as recently as 1867. Within
the Town House is the *Charter Room* (apply City Archivist. Tel: 0224
642121), showing the charter granted by William the Lion as also the
burgh records, complete but for one volume, from 1398 to the present
day.

There is much of both historical and current interest to be found
in the close surrounds of this Castle Street rectangle, starting with
the fact that this was indeed the approach to Aberdeen's castle,

destroyed in 1337 by Edward III and now represented by a cluster of high-rise buildings immediately to the E behind the Salvation Army Citadel. A more modern, and transatlantic interest awaits in King Street (N), for here **St. Andrew's Cathedral** is the Mother Church of the Episcopal Communion in America, with a memorial commemorating Samuel Seabury, first bishop in the United States, consecrated in Aberdeen in 1784. The interior here is most striking with its contrast between the white of the walls and pillars, the blue E window and the sharp bright colouring of the ceiling coats-of-arms, those above the N aisle being of all the American States, those above the S aisle of all those Aberdeenshire families who held loyal to the Jacobite cause.

Alongside (at 21 Castle Street) are *Peacock Printmakers* (Tues.–Sat., 09.30 to 17.00. Tel: 0224–639539. Free), an association founded in 1974 to encourage printmaking (etchings, screenprints, lithographs, relief prints) in the NE of Scotland. For the visitor there is a viewing gallery, a museum and explanatory display, and the opportunity to buy members' work. The adjacent *Artspace Galleries* (Mon.–Sat., 10.00 to 17.30. Tel: 0224-642858. Free) mount exhibitions by local, national and international artists.

From the E end of Castle Street, Justice Street and Beach Boulevard lead across Queen's Links to reach Beach Esplanade, over 2m in length from the Don in the N to the harbour entrance at the S. Here, in the area around the seaward end of Beach Boulevard, are such resort attractions as a beach ballroom, a children's village and adventure playground, and an amusement centre and park. At its S end Beach Esplanade ends at *Footdee* (or, locally, Fittie), a planned fishing village built in 1809 to replace an older settlement.

In Marischal Street, leading S out of Castle Street, there can be dark echoes, for here the offices of the Bank of Scotland occupy the site of the town mansion of the Earl Marischal, from a window of which in 1562 Mary, Queen of Scots, was forced to watch the execution of Sir John Gordon, her swashbuckling but little encouraged admirer who, openly expressing intentions of abduction and marriage, had harried her state progress into the North. At this same time the body of Sir John's father, the Earl of Huntly, who had rebelled, been defeated at Corrichie on Deeside, then wisely died of heart failure, lay across the way in the tolbooth prior to being embalmed and taken to Edinburgh for a ghoulish trial for treason (see North East introduction, above).

The **Aberdeen Maritime Museum** (Mon.–Sat., 10.00 to 17.00. Tel: 0224-585788. Free) can be found in Shiprow, leading SW out of Castle Street and, until as late as the mid 18C, the city's only connection with its upper harbour. The museum is housed in Provost Ross's House (1593), once the home of a late 16C merchant and in the 18C that of Provost Ross, another merchant with substantial maritime interests.

The museum is arranged on three levels, of which the ground floor is partly administrative with museum and NTS shops and partly allotted to temporary exhibitions and an introductory room. On the first floor the central feature is the Picture Gallery, the museum themes on one side being Fishing and Aberdeen Harbour and, on the other, Wrecks and Rescues, the North Boats (vessels to Orkney and Shetland), and the Duthie Room, the 1884 office of a shipowner. Above, on the second floor, the themes are Local Shipbuilding and

Shipowning, the London Boats (the Aberdeen Steam Navigation Company operated from 1835 until the early 1960s), a Viewing Platform (hand-rivetting) and North Sea Oil and Gas.—The building, owned by the National Trust for Scotland, is leased to the city. In addition to a NTS shop there is an admirable audio-visual presentation on NTS Grampian properties (May–Sept: Mon.–Sat., 10.00 to 17.00. Free).

From the W end of Castle Street there is a westward choice between Union Street, stretching away for a somewhat daunting straight mile, or a more broken northerly arc following Broad Street, Upperkirkgate, Schoolhill and Union Terrace, this last rejoining Union Street well along its length. This northerly arc, by far the more interesting, is the course now followed.

The short length of Broad Street is dominated by two conspicuous and wildly contrasting buildings—on the W side the towering modern slab of **St. Nicholas House** (Municipal offices. *Tourist Information*) and, opposite, the pinnacled splendour of *Marischal College, since 1860, with King's College in Old Aberdeen, forming Aberdeen University but founded here three centuries earlier than this, in 1593, by George Keith, the cultured 5th Earl Marischal. Keith's early college occupied the buildings of the Greyfriars' monastery, defunct since the Reformation, these remaining in use until c 1844 by which date they had been replaced by the first buildings of the present quadrangle; today the monastery lives on as no more than a seven-light gable from its church, preserved and incorporated in the present Greyfriars Church, a rebuilding of 1903 at the college's S front. The college, flaunting that breathtaking pinnacled facade of 1906, is considered to be one of the world's most extravagant granite achievements, and the *Mitchell Hall*, with a window illustrating the history of the college, and the *Portrait Gallery* are open·at reasonable times when not in use for functions (please contact the sacrist). The *University of Aberdeen Anthropological Museum* (Mon.–Fri., 10.00 to 17.00. Sun., 14.00 to 17.00. Tel: 0224-480241. Free) illustrates the arts, crafts and customs of peoples worldwide from ancient to modern times, a section being devoted to Scotland's, and especially Grampian's, prehistoric inhabitants.

Opposite—almost hiding beside St. Nicholas House, dwarfed by it and providing yet another contrast in this corner of Aberdeen—is *Provost Skene's House (Mon.–Sat., 10.00 to 17.00. Tel: 0224-641086. Free). Built in c 1545, and now Aberdeen's oldest surviving example of a private house, this pleasant turreted place came to the Skene family in 1654 and is named after Sir George Skene, provost of Aberdeen (1676–85), and known to have carried out extensive repairs and restoration. Of more historic interest, and indicative of the status at the time of a house such as this, is that the Duke of Cumberland chose this as his residence for some six weeks before Culloden, the house at this period (1732–1832) being split into two. Acquired by the city in 1926, the house is now the perfect frame for several exquisitely period-furnished rooms (Georgian, Regency, Victorian), while there is also a small but most instructive area devoted to the story of local civic and domestic life.

Upperkirkgate, leading W, crosses the N end of St. Nicholas Street, now the long *St. Nicholas Centre*, offering a break for shopping, immediately beyond on the left, set back in green surrounds, being the **Church of St. Nicholas** (access also from Union Street. Mon.,

Thurs., Fri., 12.00 to 16.00. Sat., 10.00 to 12.00). In origin a 12–15C structure, first mentioned in 1157, this is no ordinary church. Long the largest parish church in Scotland, it was divided into two at the Reformation, but, with what is known as the Transept—a kind of common vestibule between the West and East churches—in effect the building is in three parts. Some ancient effigies and memorials, interesting in their local context, and some curiosities reward the visitor. The *West Church*, a rebuilding of 1755, shows some good contemporary woodwork, but is better known for four large embroidered panels (Finding of Moses. Finding of Jephthah. Esther. Susanna and the Elders), attributed to Mary Jamesone, daughter of the painter George Jamesone (?1587–1644). The *East Church*, although a rebuilding of 1877, preserves its 15C crypt (St. Mary's chapel), a simple little stone-vaulted place, founded in 1420 and in part restored in 1898, which over the years has also served some surprising secular purposes. During the 17C, for instance, witches were imprisoned here, and iron rings to which these much-feared wretches may have been secured are shown; in the following century a plumber took over, using this crypt as his workshop; and in the early 19C the poor shuffled through here to receive their portion from a soup kitchen. But, bar possibly those iron rings, no secular physical reminders survive, though from the crypt's spiritual years there are fragments of 16C stalls and some 17C panels and seats.

The so-called *Transept*, above an older structure discovered below the floor and now covered, has a spire replacing one lost by fire in 1874 and also a carillon of 48 bells dating from 1932. Here, in Collison's Aisle (N), an effigy may be that of Alderman Davidson, killed at Harlaw in 1411 and leader of the Aberdonians in the battle (see Rte 40), while a tablet to the wife (died 1568) of Canon Heriot recalls the name of the first Protestant minister of Aberdeen. In Drum's Aisle (S) there are reminders of the lands of Drum (Rte 37A) in the forms of the 15C effigies of Forbes of Drum and his wife, and also of a rare medieval brass, an unfinished inscription to Sir A. de Irwyn, known to have died in 1457 and thus a close descendant of Bruce's standard bearer. Here, too, are an interesting Mortification List, spanning 1616 to 1792, and a tablet to Robert Gordon, founder of Gordon's College (see immediately below).

Schoolhill is now ascended to pass, on the right at the top of the rise and marked by an archway, what is now called *Robert Gordon's Institute of Technology*, founded in 1739 as Robert Gordon's College for-the board and education of the sons of burgesses. The central block (1746) is by William Adam, and the statue by the arch is of General Gordon of Khartoum, no relation, though, to the college's founder. Roughly opposite, at 61 Schoolhill, is *James Dun's House* (Mon.–Sat., 10.00 to 17.00. Tel: 0224 646333. Free), the 18C town house of a former master and rector of Aberdeen Grammar School, now restored as a museum mounting varied exhibitions and audio-visual presentations.

The city **Art Gallery** (Mon.–Sat., 10.00 to 17.00, but to 20.00 on Thurs. Sun., 14.00 to 17.00. Tel: 0224 646333. Free), on the corner of Schoolhill and Blackfriars Street, shows good permanent collections of 18–20C art, the emphasis however being on contemporary work. The ground floor is devoted largely to the decorative arts, the collection of silver, and in particular of Aberdeen work, being especially notable. The fine art gallery, on the upper floor, includes the unique *Macdonald Collection of 92 portraits of British artists, nearly all painted by themselves, while names such as Raeburn, MacEvoy, Zoffany, Reynolds, Romney, Augustus John, Toulouse Lautrec and Orpen give a measure of the gallery's quality and scope. Additionally the gallery mounts a full programme of temporary exhibitions, music recitals, dance, poetry readings and lectures.—The austere *War Memorial Hall of Memory* opens out as a part of the ground floor.

Woolmanhill, running NW off Blackfriars Street, recalls that this was once the site of the wool market.

Schoolhill now becomes Rosemount Viaduct, with, on the right, *His Majesty's Theatre* (1906) and, opposite, an open space with a defiant statue of Wallace and a seated one of Prince Albert. Here Union Terrace bears S beside gardens above the railway to join Union Street, with a statue of Edward VII on the corner of Union Bridge, not immediately recognised as a bridge now that the S side is built over.

From this point many visitors may well return E, passing the Union Street entrance to the Church of St. Nicholas, marked by an Ionic colonnade of 1820 built in emulation of London's Hyde Park Corner. There remain, however, places of interest westward along Union Street, at least as far as (c ½m) the point where the street ends, forking right as Alford Place and left as Holburn Street. On the right, with classical columns, is the *Music Hall* of 1820, while just beyond in Huntly Street the spired RC *St. Mary's Cathedral* dates from 1859–69. Crown Street, opposite the Music Hall, leads by way of Crown Terrace (opposite the main *Post Office*), to *St. John's Church*, of interest to connoisseurs of fonts, the one here, early 16C and showing the Five Wounds of Christ, having originally been in the now ruined church at Kinkell (Rte 40). At the W end of Union Street can be seen the Tudor edifice of *Christ's College* (1851), academically linked with the university's Faculty of Divinity.

WEST BEYOND UNION STREET. Albyn Place, with distinguished 19C granite mansions, becomes Queen's Road off which, in just under 1m from the W end of Albyn Place, leads Viewfield Road, with the *Gordon Highlanders' Regimental HQ and Museum* (Wed. and Sun., 14.00 to 17.00. Tel: 0224-318174. Donation). *Hazlehead Park*, beyond, provides sports facilities, gardens, exotic trees and shrubs, woodland and nature walks, as also, for the children (summer only) such attractions as a maze, electric cars and trampolines.

SOUTH OF UNION STREET. From the W end of Union Street, Holburn Street in 1½m reaches the *Bridge of Dee*, on the road to Stonehaven. A structure of seven ribbed arches bearing inscriptions and coats-of-arms, this bridge was built by Bishop Dunbar in 1520–27, but widened in 1842 when its W face was replaced so as to preserve the medieval appearance. Nearby, off Riverside Drive, Ruthrieston Pack Horse Bridge is in origin of 1694. Central Aberdeen can pleasantly be regained by following Riverside Drive along the left bank of the Dee, this road passing *Duthie Park*, with gardens, exotic birds, an aquarium, winter gardens (daily, 10.00 to dusk) and, in summer, a boating pond and other amusements.

The Harbour and Beyond

Market Street, dropping S off Union Street opposite St. Nicholas Centre, and with on the right the older *Market Centre*, soon reaches the harbour at its NW corner. Nearby, in Shiprow, is the *Maritime Museum* (see above), a prior visit to which could greatly add to the interest of a tour of the harbour area.

History. It was in 1136 that the port received its first recorded formal recognition when David I allowed a shipping tithe to be levied. But despite impressive growth in both fishing and continental trade little was done over the long medieval centuries throughout which the harbour remained essentially an uncontrolled estuary of islands and shifting sands. Then in 1596 came the first awakening when, to raise money for improvement, James VI allowed Aberdeen to impose charges on ships using the harbour, the result being the construction in 1607 of a bulwark along the S shore of the estuary near the river mouth, the aim being to increase tidal scour and thus deepen the entrance.

But over another century and a half would elapse before it became accepted that the port could no longer cope with the accelerating trade resulting from the Act of Union and John Smeaton was called in to advise, his main recommendation being the construction of the North Pier (1780). Telford soon followed (1802) with several proposals, and, although these were not fully accepted, the mid 19C saw the extension of the North Pier, the construction of a southern breakwater, the development of Victoria Dock and the start of work on various quays. But the major undertaking of the 19C was the diversion (1869–73) of the Dee (which hitherto had run through what is now Albert Basin), this enabling sandbanks to be reclaimed and the harbour to begin to assume its present basic plan.

During the present century improvements have been constant and major, and since 1969, though the basic geography remains, the port has been virtually rebuilt to meet the needs of fishing, roll on/roll off, and oil-related activities.

Unlike many ports, Aberdeen allows virtually unrestricted motor and pedestrian access, but the Harbour Board do ask visitors to appreciate that this is a busy area, to drive slowly and generally to exercise caution.

Market Street reaches the harbour at its NW corner, near *Upper Dock* (the W extension of Victoria Dock), a corner which recalls the earliest quayhead which lay just to the rear of today's Trinity Quay, here running E. Here, too, in 1582, the first crane was erected, and from•here, also, the narrow, cobbled Shiprow provided the only access to the trading area around the Mercat Cross. Trinity, Regent and Waterloo quays mark the N side of *Victoria Dock*, developed in the 19C after Telford's proposals, honoured in 1848 by the entry of the royal yacht carrying Queen Victoria and her family, and in the 1970s drastically modified by the removal of the dock gates. The *P. and O. Ferries (Shetland) Terminal* now operates on Jamieson's Quay on the S side of the Upper Dock.

Market Street continues S to pass on the left (Commercial Quay West) the modern **Fish Market**, Scotland's largest, opened in 1982 by the Queen, accompanied by Princess Anne. The bustling auction (Mon.–Fri., 04.00, sales starting 07.30) is popular with early-rising visitors, who may care to reflect that they are witnessing an activity already well established as long ago as 1281 when an agent of Edward I came to Aberdeen charged with buying 100 barrels of sturgeons and 5000 salt fish. *Albert Basin*, beyond, with Commercial Quay along its N and Albert Quay along its S, in part representing the former channel of the Dee, was developed as a result of the river's diversion in 1869–73.

Market Street now reaches Victoria Bridge, crossing the modern course of the Dee. North Esplanade West, becoming Riverside Drive, passes *Duthie Park* before reaching *Bridge of Dee*, for both of which see above. Across the river, Sinclair Road, leading E, in about half a mile reaches a point offering a good view northwards across the harbour, beyond becoming Greyhope Road which, very roughly, marks the line of the bulwark built in 1607. With views across to

Footdee and the North Pier, Greyhope Road rounds a golf course and passes the foot of the southern breakwaters to reach the grassy headland of *Walker Park*, with *Girdleness Lighthouse* (after 14.00, if convenient to keepers. Prior arrangement by telephone to 0224 871142).

Old Aberdeen

Although incorporated with Aberdeen proper since 1891, Old Aberdeen, 1½m N of the main city, remains an aloof, academic and even venerable quarter offering a total contrast to the bustle of Union Street and its surrounds. By car, Old Aberdeen is best reached by way of King Street, then left a short distance up St. Machar Drive. On foot, the direct and pleasantest route is from Broad Street along Gallowgate, Mounthoolie, King's Crescent, Spital and College Bounds.

Old Aberdeen comprises two distinct parts, separated by the busy St. Machar Drive, a useful and necessary road but one on which Old Aberdeen's two sections prefer to turn their backs. To the S is High Street, with King's College; to the N the cathedral with, beyond, the ancient Brig o' Balgownie. Some of the streets impose car restrictions.

SOUTH OF ST. MACHAR DRIVE. The N end of High Street is straddled by the *Town House* of 1788, used as such until the incorporation with Aberdeen proper in 1891 and now a library.

Beyond are the gracious buildings of **King's College** (16C and later), founded by Bishop Elphinstone in 1495 during the reign of James IV and thus a century older than Marischal College, the other component of Aberdeen's university. The *Round Tower*, through the passage in the SE corner of the quadrangle, is a defensive work of 1525, while *Cromwell's Tower*, E of the chapel, dating from 1658 and originally a hall of residence, was in part paid for by contributions by some of Cromwell's officers, one of these being General Monk. But most visitors will aim for the *Chapel*, built in 1500– 05 with an elegant lantern tower, the crown of which was rebuilt after a storm in 1633 (Mon.–Fri., 09.00 to 17.00. Sat., 09.00 to 12.30. Also open for Sun. services during term. Tel: 0224 480241). First Catholic, then Protestant, the chapel is now interdenominational. The antechapel, arranged as a war memorial, is separated from the chapel proper by the former rood screen. The main features of the main chapel are a double row of canopied stalls, some with misericords; the pulpit (1540; brought from the cathedral and much restored) bearing the heads of Scottish kings from James I to VII; and, offering a more modern touch, the seven windows by Douglas Strachan. Bishop Elphinstone, founder of college and chapel, lies below the floor (though his elaborate cenotaph of 1931 is outside on the lawn) and another floor slab commemorates Hector Boece (died 1536), the Scottish historian and the college's first principal; while, against the E wall, an altar has been converted to serve as the tomb of Peter Udny, a sub-principal who died in 1601.

The curious and incongruous oriental gateway (c 1830) on the other side of High Street and marking the way to halls of residence was once the gate to nearby Powis House and reminds of that family's associations with the Middle East.

NORTH OF ST. MACHAR DRIVE. Opposite High Street the road called Chanonry passes *Cruickshank Botanic Gardens* (Mon.–Fri., 09.00 to

16.30. Sat. and Sun. in May–Sept, 14.00 to 17.00. Tel: 0224 480241. Free), the university's gardens with extensive collections, shrubs, Alpines, heather, succulents and rock and water gardens being among the features here.

*St. Machar's Cathedral (Daily, 09.00 to 17.00), part ruin but its nave intact, is a place of mellow antiquity, imposing yet simple, its granite touched by sandstone and the whole a monument to three bishops who, though spanning two centuries, seem to have shared a common sensitivity. In its name, the cathedral recalls a saint who may have been a follower of Columba and who, on a mission to convert the Picts, is said to have planted a chapel here during the 6C; the title of cathedral recalls a bishopric, reputedly founded at Mortlach (see Rte 39) by Malcolm II in 1010 and transferred to Aberdeen by David I in 1137.

Be the above as it may, the earliest stonework surviving is of the 14C, this—finely carved sandstone and the work of Bishop Kininmunde, 1356–62—comprising (E exterior) two of the external piers at the crossing, now partly buried in the modern gables, and a portion of the ruined transepts. The rest of the cathedral—except for the sandstone steeples added to the two W towers by Bishop Gavin Dunbar in c 1522—is largely granite, mainly of the 15C and the work of Bishop Leighton (Lichtoun) whose tomb recess is in the N transept which he founded in 1424. Bishop Dunbar's handsome canopied tomb is in the opposing transept.

Before entering the cathedral it may add interest to the view of the exterior to picture that it once had a central tower, completed in c 1512 but which collapsed in 1688, owing, it is said, to the removal of stones from the choir by Cromwell's soldiers building a fort over 30 years earlier on Aberdeen's Castle Hill.

The nave now serves as parish church. Here the principal feature is Bishop Dunbar's flat ceiling of panelled oak (c 1520; restored), with its 48 shields glittering with the blazonries of Pope Leo X, the Emperor Charles V, St. Margaret, the kings and princes of Christendom, and the bishops and nobles of Scotland. Also of interest, and all well explained by notices, are a small 15C wall effigy of Canon Dodds, near the E end of the S aisle; in the NW corner an effigy (reconstructed) of Bishop Leighton; the font, by Hew Lorimer in 1953, showing St. Machar baptising in the Don; the war memorial window by Douglas Strachan; and the Charter Room, showing documents, seals and other relics.

Beyond the cathedral, to the NW in Tillydrone Road, now stands the so-called *Wallace Tower* (no adm.), interesting as a Z-plan tower-house built in central Aberdeen's Nether Kirkgate in 1616 and rebuilt on this site in 1963.

*Brig o' Balgownie, or Auld Brig o' Don, spanning a deep pool of the Don and the oldest medieval bridge in Scotland, is roughly ¾m N of the cathedral. On foot the bridge can be reached through Seaton Park, but motorists should drive N along King Street, soon bearing left along Don Street at a sign opposite a group of high-rise flats. In bare architectural terms this is a late 13 to early 14C (restored 1607) bridge in the form of a pointed arch 62ft wide. But there is more to this beguiling corner. Bruce, for instance, is involved, seemingly personally ordering the completion of work begun in the 1280s but held up by the wars of the time, while an early bishop, Cheyne, is credited with carrying out his king's wishes and complet-

ing the bridge by perhaps 1320. And this despite Thomas the
Rhymer's gloomy prediction that the bridge would fall should it be
crossed by an only son riding a mare's only foal. Centuries later
Byron, in his 'Don Juan', named 'Balgounie Brig' as one of his Scottish
nostalgia, adding in a note—and doubtless well aware that the dark
pool below was the haunt of witches—'I still remember ... the awful
proverb which made me pause to cross it, yet lean over with a childish
delight, being an only son'.

For Aberdeen to **Stonehaven**, **Forfar** and **Perth**, see Rte 29; to **Banchory** and
Braemar, see Rte 37A; to **Echt** and **Tarland**, see Rte 37B; to **Grantown-on-Spey**,
Nairn and **Forres**, see Rte 38; to **Dufftown** and **Elgin**, see Rte 39; to **Huntly** and
Fochabers, see Rte 40; to **Macduff** and **Banff**, see Rte 41; to **Peterhead** and
Fraserburgh, see Rte 42.

37 Aberdeen to Braemar (Deeside)

Two roads are described below. The first, Rte 37A along the main
A93, closely follows the Dee; the second, Rte 37B, choosing roads
roughly parallel a few miles to the N, joins Rte 37A at the W end of
Muir of Dinnet, some two thirds of the distance to Braemar. There is
little difference in either mileage or in scenery—the best of the
scenery starts to the W of Muir of Dinnet—and the choice is therefore
likely to be made principally on grounds of what there is to be seen,
though bearing in mind that the several linking roads allow a
meandering flexibility between the alternatives. Stone circle and
earth-house enthusiasts will choose Rte 37B.
    Two points may be borne in mind. First, that Deeside is a popular
touring area and that A93 can be a busy road in summer. Second,
that, although Deeside offers a choice of moor and mountain walks,
this can be treacherous terrain and local advice should always be
sought before adventuring far.

A. Via Peterculter and Banchory

A93.—Pleasant, pastoral river valley scenery gradually becomes
increasingly wooded and Highland, especially after Ballater as the
Grampian mountains and their SE spur, The Mounth, close in. The
main road runs with the N side of the Dee, but for much of the way
good but less used roads, scenically no different, follow the S bank;
there are several bridges.

SOME HOTELS. **Banchory**. *Banchory Lodge*, Dee Street. Tel:
(03302) 2625. *Tor-Na-Coille*, Inchmarlo Road. Tel: (03302) 2242.
Aboyne. *Birse Lodge*, Charleston Road. Tel: (0339) 2253. **Ballater**.
Tullich Lodge, AB3 5SB. Tel: (0338) 55406. *Darroch Learg*, Braemar
Road. Tel: (0338) 55443. **Braemar**. *Invercauld Arms*, AB3 5YR. Tel:
(03383) 605.

Total distance 54m.—*8m* **Peterculter.**—*9m* **Banchory.**—*8m*
Kincardine O' Neil.—*4m* **Aboyne.**—*4m* **Dinnet.**—*6m* **Ballater.**—*7m*
Crathie (Balmoral).—*8m* **Braemar.**

Aberdeen (see Rte 36) is left by Union Street, Holburn Street and Great Western Road.—*8m* **Peterculter** recalls through its name that until early medieval times the lands here on both sides of the Dee made up the district of Culter, pronounced, then as now, Kooter. Then in the late 12C William the Lion granted the S bank to the Knights Templar who built a chapel to St. Mary. This S bank then became, and still is, Maryculter, while the N, already with a chapel to St. Peter, became Peterculter. The ruin of the Templars' chapel, later used by the Hospitallers and then parish church until 1787, is in Templars' Park by the river S bank. *Blairs College* (by appointment. Tel: 0224-867626), 1½m E of the B979 river bridge, a Roman Catholic foundation of 1827 (though the buildings are later: 1897–1908), owns many treasures, notably a famous portrait of Mary, Queen of Scots, found concealed at Douai after the French revolution, and all that remains of the library of the Scots College in Paris.

Leaving Peterculter A93 crosses the Leuchar Burn, from the bridge over which can be seen a statue of Rob Roy. Quite why this far from worthy character merits this honour is unclear; all that seems known is that he once crossed this burn on his way back from Aberdeen, and that this statue is the third in a long succession.

3m ***Drum Castle** (NTS. May–Sept: Daily, 14.00 to 18.00. Grounds open all year, daily, 09.30 to sunset. Fee) presents an astonishing but paradoxically balanced contrast between its massive, battlemented late 13C keep and the gracious Jacobean mansion grafted on to it in 1619. The keep seems to have been built in 1296 by Richard Cementarius, who somewhat improbably combined the post of provost of Aberdeen (the city's first) with that of royal mason. But soon afterwards, in 1324, Bruce conferred the lands of Drum on his standard and armour bearer, William de Irwin, whose descendants remained in possession until 1975 when the estate passed to the National Trust for Scotland. Within the castle are family portraits, antique furniture and suchlike, while the grounds of 400 acres offer woodland walks, an arboretum and an adventure playground.

4m ****Crathes Castle** (NTS. Easter. May–Sept: Mon.–Sat., 11.00 to 18.00. Sun., 14.00 to 18.00. Guided tours. Visitor Centre, garden and grounds open all year, daily, 09.30 to sunset. Fee) is at the heart of a district known as Leys, granted in 1323 by Bruce to Alexander Burnett (Burnard) whom he appointed Royal Forester of the Forest of Drum, the then huge forest here which Bruce designated a royal hunting reserve. These early Burnetts lived not here at Crathes, but in a wooden dwelling on a loch island, now represented by a marsh 2m NW and to the E of A980, and today's castle—a tower-house sprinkled with turrets, dormers and gables, its fairy quality enhanced by the many facets glimpsed from different corners of the grounds—though begun in 1553 was not completed and occupied until 1594. Extensions were grafted on during the 17 and 19C, much of this part now replaced by rebuilding after a fire in 1966.

In the main hall hangs the ancient jewelled and ivory Horn of Leys, said to have been presented by Bruce as a token of tenure. And at the top of the castle the Long Gallery, with a rare 17C oak ceiling, affords some original views over the grounds. In between—and the glory of Crathes—are the Room of the Nine Nobles, the Room of the Green Lady and the Room of the Muses, each with its crowded painted ceiling, the work of unknown artists but men of imagination and skill for, working awkwardly above their heads, they also had to adapt their work—a weird mixture of pictures, designs and lengthy written messages—to the constricting run of the panels and beams.

Inside, like any other tower-house, Crathes may seem cramped. Outside, though, it is generous with space, its 600 acres offering no less than eight gardens, separated either by borders or by yew hedges of 1702; several nature trails, including one for the disabled; an adventure playground, as also a NTS Visitor Centre, picnic area and suchlike.

2m **Banchory** (5300 inhab. *ECl.* Thurs. *Inf.* Dee Street car park. Easter and May–Sept), its name meaning Fair Hollow and certainly pleasantly enough sited between the hills and the Dee, has a story reaching back to St. Ternan, who came here in the 5C to convert the Picts and, it is thought, established himself and his small monastery at the spot now occupied by the churchyard, in which survive traces of a medieval church. In more recent times lavender has become a local industry. Today something of the past can be learnt at the *Museum* (June–Sept: Daily, except Thurs., 14.00 to 17.00. Tel: 0779-77778. Free), towards the W end of High Street, while the lavender business and its associated activities can be appreciated at *Ingasetter*, North Deeside Road (Mon.–Fri., 09.00 to 12.30. 13.30 to 17.00. Longer opening, including Sat. and Sun., in July and Aug. Tel: 03302-2600. Free).

Just S of the town the Dee is joined by the Feugh, crossed by the narrow *Bridge of Feugh* (1790), beside which there is a footbridge from which the visitor may be lucky enough to see salmon leaping up the ledges. For Banchory S to *Fettercairn* by B974 (Cairn o' Mounth) and to *Stonehaven* by A957 (Slug Road), see Rte 29.

A980, leading N out of Banchory, in just over 1m passes the W end of the marsh area where was once the loch on a crannog of which the early Burnetts of Crathes had their home. And here, too, many centuries earlier, St. Ternan may have found a reasonably safe refuge among the pagan Picts. Beyond, the road is joined by B977, 2m due N of the intersection, on the E slope of *Hill of Fare*, being the site of the battle (Corrichie) of 1562 at which the great Gordon Earl of Huntly was defeated by the adherents of Mary, Queen of Scots, under Moray, the Earl himself dying of a heart attack. A monument (1952), 3m NE beside B977, commemorates the occasion.

At (*8m*) **Kincardine O' Neil** the ruined *Church of St. Mary* not only has a story, but one also which, given a discerning eye, can in part be read in stone. Originally this church was attached to a hospice, both erected here in 1231 by Allan Durward to serve the needs of indigent travellers using the bridge which his father Thomas had built to link with the track making for the Cairn o' Mounth pass (today B974). Although that once so important bridge has long disappeared, the church remains, together with what are probably traces of the hospice in the form of foundations of an E extension to the church. The further evidence can be seen in the line of a floor which crossed the outside of the E gable, and also, on either side of the two inserted windows, the frames of two original windows which would have opened into the church. The hospice would have had an upper floor serving as a dormitory and the occupants would have been able to hear services through these inward opening windows. It also seems likely that the two inserted E gable lancets were originally those of the hospice, demolished it is thought in the early

17C.—A mile or so beyond the village, close to the Gibbet Stone, a minor road leads N for *Lumphanan* (see Rte 37B).

4m **Aboyne** is a village set around a large green, first laid out in 1676 and the scene today of the annual Aboyne Games, one of the main events of the Highland season. *Aboyne Castle* (no adm.), to the N of the village and dating from 1671–1869, replaced 13C Coull Castle the scattered remnants of which can be seen beside B9094 2m N (see Rte 37B).—The scenic **Glen Tanar** ascends SW from Aboyne to traverse the forest of the same name, its oak, shipped down the Dee until well into the 19C, once much in demand for shipbuilding. On the approach to the glen are the *Chapel of St. Lesmo* (1870) with a river boulder serving as altar, and *Braeloine Interpretive Centre* (April–Sept: Daily, 10.00 to 17.00. Tel: 0339-2072. Donation) for waymarked walks and material explaining the farming, forestry and wildlife of this estate. The Fir Mounth, a track climbing across the mountains to cross the watershed at 2364ft and reach Tarfside in Glen Esk in some 12m, may well be the route used by Macbeth when fleeing from Dunsinane to defeat and death at Lumphanan.

Continuing W, A93 reaches (*4m*) **Dinnet**, beyond the village running between Loch Kinord on the N and, on the S, *Muir of Dinnet*, the latter, together with a considerable area to the N of the road, forming a national nature reserve of heath, scrub and birch, broken by fen and open water and important for breeding and wintering wildfowl.—*2m* **Junction with A97**, where Rte 37B joins. For *Burn o' Vat*, *Loch Kinord*, *Loch Davan* (all within the area of the nature reserve) and the battle of 1335 fought below the hill of *Culblean*, see the end of Rte 37B.—Of (*3m*) **Tullich**, claiming once to have been a royal burgh, little now remains bar a ruined church of c 1400, built on the site of an early chapel and today worth visiting for its several Pictish stones with their strange and varied symbols. Just beyond the church, B972 branches away to bypass Ballater and cut through the steep and wooded Pass of Ballater. This Rte stays with A93 which almost at once crosses the old railway track, now a pleasant walkway where once ran Queen Victoria's royal train.

1m **Ballater** (1180 inhab. *ECl.* Thurs. *Inf.* Station Square. Easter and May–Sept) owes its existence to an old woman and a Jacobite. The former did no more than cure herself of scrofula by obeying a dream and bathing in water near the N foot of Pannanich Hill, 2m SE of Ballater. The Jacobite was Francis Farquharson of Monaltrie, captured at Culloden, sent to London, sentenced to be hanged and at the last minute reprieved, though his home, Monaltrie House to the N of today's town, was burnt down by government troops. Exiled for 20 years, he returned home and shrewdly exploited the old woman's lead, building Pannanich Lodge—today Pannanich Wells Hotel, 2m E on B976—as a spa. So successful was this venture that in 1800 Francis Farquharson's nephew, William, decided to continue the exploitation by starting to lay out what would become Ballater, soon in the 19C, as it is today, a spacious small planned town and summer centre in lovely surrounds of woodland and mountain.

The car and the holiday coach have now taken the place of the railway, which, running from Aberdeen, ended here, Queen Victoria having made clear that she would not tolerate its coming any closer to Balmoral. She made good use of it, however, and over many years Ballater's station enjoyed a royal cachet. It was Queen Victoria, too, who in 1885 opened the present *Royal Bridge* across the Dee, the latest in a series of four, two predecessors being wrecked by floods in 1799 and 1829, while the third was a wooden affair of 1834.

GLEN MUICK, ascending for some 8m southward into woods and mountains, is both scenic and of royal Victorian interest. Just outside Ballater, by the junction with the S Deeside road, a typical turn-of-the-century scene is recalled by a cairn commemorating an occasion in 1899 when Queen Victoria, out for a drive, by chance met, and then reviewed, a battalion of the Gordon Highlanders, shortly before their embarkation for South Africa. Farther S, 2m up the W bank of the Muick, is the mansion of *Birkhall*, built in 1715, later bought by Prince Albert, and in 1856 rented by Florence Nightingale who from here, encouraged by Queen Victoria ('Such a head! I wish we had her at the War Office' was the queen's opinion), started the pestering which persuaded the army authorities to form the Army Medical Service, later to become the Royal Army Medical Corps.

The longer road (the Capel Mounth), running with the Muick's E bank, passes the cascade of *Linn of Muick* to end just short of Loch Muick at *Spittal of Glenmuick*, with a mountain rescue post and a Scottish Wildlife Trust's visitor centre. Here, in this area, there are two more royal associations. *Allt-na-Giubhsaich*, a short mile away to the NW across the river, is a shooting lodge used by the queen and Prince Albert and known to them as The Hut (it has since been much enlarged). From here a track climbs to the, in part precipitous, eyrie of *Lochnagar* (3786ft), more than once ascended by the queen, although she did have the benefit of ponies. *Glas-allt-Shiel*, on the W shore of the loch towards its S end, was a less happy place, built by the queen as a retreat in 1868 and sometimes called her 'Widow's house'. From here another track climbs Lochnagar, while a second heads W for *Dubh Loch* at 2090ft.

˙From Spittal of Glenmuick the road continues as the *Capel Mounth* track, climbing to 2250ft before descending to Braedownie in Glen Clova (see Rte 29).

Leaving Ballater, A93 in *1m* is joined by B972 at *Bridge of Gairn* at the W end of the Pass of Ballater, here being the *McEwan Gallery* (June–Oct: normal hours. Tel: 0338-55678. Free) showing 18–20C watercolours and oils, many by Scottish artists and of Scottish landscapes.

Already forecast by Ballater's pass and surrounds of steep and wooded hills, the scenery now changes, becoming distinctly Highland as A93 accompanies the Dee's upper reaches. In some *4m* from Bridge of Gairn, soon after a picnic site, there is a Standing Stone to the right of the road, site of the spot where in the 9C St. Manire founded a chapel. Beyond, in *1m*, on the S bank of the river and reached by a private suspension bridge, stands *Abergeldie Castle* (c 1550; no adm.), home in turn of Queen Victoria's mother, of Eugenie, widow of Napoleon III, and of the future Edward VII and his princess, Alexandra.—*1m* **Crathie**, where the church, a neat little granite place of 1895 and housing many royal gifts, will for most people be associated with church attendances by the royal family when in residence at adjacent Balmoral. The church is successor to a simple predecessor of 1804 in which Queen Victoria worshipped for most of her reign, starting in 1848 when she first came to Deeside.

Balmoral Castle, a personal royal home as opposed to an official residence, is just across the river from Crathie. The grounds and an exhibition are open, except when the family are here, May–July: Daily except Sun., 10.00 to 17.00. Tel (Ballater Tourist Information): 0338-55306. A fee is charged which, however, is donated to charity.

Once a 16C tower of the Gordons (enlarged c 1835) stood here, on an estate first leased and then in 1852 bought by Prince Albert. Today's large, white granite Scottish Baronial mansion—beyond a sweep of lawn and framed by trees—can architecturally be credited to William Smith, city architect of Aberdeen, acting very closely, though, with the prince. In 1855 the family moved in, whereupon the adjacent Gordon tower was demolished, to be recalled only by a stone marking its site. Of interest around the grounds and estate, generously planted by Prince Albert with conifers and other trees, are Queen Victoria's garden cottage; the gardens originally planned by Queen Mary; and seemingly countless statues, memorials and cairns each telling of some royal person or event.

Beyond Crathie, A93 loops with the Dee, then, straightening, passes, just under 2m from Crathie, the *Cairn na Cuimhne*, a mound with a few trees beside the river below the road. A modest enough spot now, possibly only fleetingly glimpsed because traffic can be fast here, this was once the important rallying place of the Farquharsons; before each foray each man deposited a stone, removing it when and if he returned, the balance recording the clan's loss.—*3m Invercauld Bridge*, where the Dee is crossed, was built by Prince Albert when the old bridge of 1752, still to be seen and evocatively attractive a few yards downstream, became royal property and the S Deeside road through the estate was closed. *Invercauld House* (no adm.), soon seen to the N, a 15–16C core with additions and the seat of the Farquharsons, is the place from which in 1715 the Earl of Mar called out the clans in support of the Old Pretender.

3m **Braemar** (400 inhab. *ECl.* Thurs, but no closing in June–Sept. *Inf.* Balnellan Road. Easter and May–Oct), a scattered village at 1100ft near where the Cluny joins the Dee, may be small but is nonetheless, and on several counts, one of the best known of Highland names—for history, for scenery and walks, for two castles, for the most prestigious of all Highland Gatherings, and even for its festival and theatre.

Braemar Castle (May–early Oct: Daily, 10.00 to 18.00. Tel: 03383-219. Fee), a towered and turreted fortress-home beside A93, was built (though on ancient foundations) by the Earl of Mar in 1628; attacked and burnt by the Farquharsons in 1689; garrisoned by Hanoverian troops after the '15; and, after the '45, repaired and again garrisoned to protect the military road from Perth across Dee and Speyside to Fort George on Moray Firth. Later, it was acquired by the Farquharsons of Invercauld who converted the castle to residence. Among notable features are the round central tower, the iron gate, the barrel-vaulted ceilings, and the star-shaped curtain wall, loopholed for muskets, which represents the defensive work carried out after the '45.

Within the village, adjacent to Tourist Information, there survives, but only just, the far older and very different *Kindrochit Castle*, today no more than an ancient fragment. The name means Head of the Bridge, and this once formidable stronghold commanded all the glens converging on this point. A castle here is thought to have been occupied by Malcolm Canmore in the 11C, but today's stones date from a 14C fortified hunting lodge of Robert II. Rebuilt in about 1390, Kindrochit was, and has remained, derelict since about 1600 by which time the powerful Braemar Castle was taking shape.

It was on a mound now covered by the *Invercauld Arms* that the Earl of Mar raised his standard in 1715, an event commemorated by a stone (1952) on the roadway opposite, as also by a plaque inside the hotel where, furthermore, latter-day Jacobites may still drink a toast in the Earl of Mar's bar. At an angle across the road is the *Invercauld Festival Theatre*, used for a range of Scottish entertainments over the July–Sept period; formerly a church, converted in 1949, the theatre shows some striking murals. Finally, a cottage, on the left a short way along Glenshee Road (A93), is the place where R.L. Stevenson spent the summer of 1881 writing 'Treasure Island'.

The *Braemar Royal Highland Gathering* (first Sat. in Sept), under royal patronage and frequently attended by royalty, is Scotland's most prestigious Gathering. The site, now, and since 1905, is the Princess Royal and Duke of Fife Memorial Park in the W area of the village, but previous sites have included Braemar Castle, Balmoral and Invercauld House as, doubtless, many others over the centuries since that day when, it is claimed, Malcolm Canmore summoned the clans to the Brae of Mar for contests which would enable him to select the bravest and best as his soldiers. (Seats may be reserved, after about 20 March, by application to the Bookings Secretary, B.R.H.S. ·Society Office, Braemar, Aberdeenshire. Remittance and stamped addressed envelope must accompany applications. Accommodation queries should be addressed to the Area Tourist Office, 45 Station Road, Banchory, AB3 3XX.)

TO LINN OF DEE (W, 6m). This minor road in under 2m arrives at a point commanding a view of the opening of Glen Quoich, ascending NW towards the piled heights of the Cairngorms, 2m farther on being Victoria Bridge leading across to Mar Lodge Hotel, completed in 1898 but successor to other lodges occupying sites nearby. Next comes the hamlet of *Inverey*, with a monument of 1934 recalling the birth here of John Lamont (1805–79), son of a local forester who, after attending the Scots Benedictine College at Ratisbon, turned secular, studied in Munich and later became, as Johannes von Lamont, astronomer royal of Bavaria. A glen track ascends Glen Ey to reach, in a long mile, the site known as the *Colonel's Bed*, a small gorge in which Colonel John Farquharson successfully hid while fleeing after Killiecrankie.

The public road ends at **Linn of Dee** bridge, a scenic spot where the Dee forces itself through a narrow rock cleft.

Braemar, with nearby Inverey and Linn of Dee, are well known as starting places for walks and climbs. The choice extends from local walks of a mile or two, through mountain climbs (e.g. Lochnagar, 3786ft; Morrone, 2819ft) to ambitious undertakings such as down Glen Tilt to Blair Atholl, some 29m, or even into or across the Cairngorms. The favourite Cairngorm routes are either by Lairig Ghru, the pass below the W of Ben Macdui, or by Glen Derry and Glen Avon. Private estates, the importance of not disturbing deer or birds, and the height and remoteness of some of the treks all impose certain restrictions and it is most important to seek local advice before setting off. The 'Braemar Official Guide' suggests and describes a number of walks.

For Braemar over the *Cairnwell Pass* to **Perth**, see Rte 28.

B. Via Echt and Tarland

A944 out of Aberdeen, after 6m diverging on to B9119 as far as Ordie. A97 to junction with Rte 37A near W end of Muir of Dinnet. A93 to Braemar.—Pastoral and agricultural countryside gradually becoming more wooded and undulating. Highland scenery W of Muir of Dinnet. *Note*: A torch will be necessary for Culsh Earth-house.

SOME HOTELS. See Rte 37A.

Total distance 55m.—*13m* **Echt.**—*11m* **Intersection with A980** (for **Craigievar** and **Lumphanan**).—*6m* **Tarland.**—*2m* **Ordie.**—*4m* **Muir of Dinnet** (Rte 37A).—*19m* **Braemar.**

Aberdeen (see Rte 36) is left by Union Street, Albyn Place and Queen's Road, passing Hazlehead Park, A944 being exchanged in *6m* for B9119.—*4m* *Garlogie*, a village just to the S of which is *Cullerlie Stone Circle*, a ring of eight boulders within which are several small cairns, perhaps used for cremations. It has been suggested that this may have been the tomb of a chief, with the cairns representing dependants, perhaps ritually killed at the time of his burial.—*3m* **Echt**, just over 1m NW of which is the *Barmekin of Echt*, an isolated conical hill (900ft) crowned with five rings of Iron Age fortifications notable for their several entrances (reached by a farm road off B977 and then on foot).—*1m* *Sunhoney*, a farm behind which there is a circle of sizeable stones, pleasingly set in a ring of trees. This circle is of the Recumbent Stone type, the recumbent monolith here being exceptionally long (17ft).

A stop should surely be made at (*1m*) *Midmar* where, to the S of the road, can be seen an attractive turreted castle (1575; no adm.). More interesting, though, is the 17C church, less for itself, though the private door for the laird is unusual, than for the fact that there is a stone circle in the churchyard and that this site has therefore been used for ritual purposes, if with breaks, over a period of several millenia. The circle shows the usual local recumbent stone and flankers, and traces can also be seen of some structure that stood just inside of these three stones. For *Hill of Fare* (Battle of Corrichie), rising to the S of Midmar, see Rte 37A.

In *9m* B9119 is crossed by A980, with Craigievar Castle just to the N and Lumphanan and its Macbeth associations a short distance to the S.

The great thing about ***Craigievar Castle** (NTS. May–Sept: Daily except Fri., 14.00 to 18.00. Guided tour. Grounds open all year, daily, 09.30 to sunset. Fee) is that for all practical purposes no one has changed it. This slim tower-house, arguably Scotland's purest and loveliest—smooth below as a concession to defence, but crowned with a seemingly haphazard collage of turrets, stepped gables, cupolas and precipitous roofs—stands today virtually as it did in 1626 when it was completed for William Forbes, Baltic merchant (he was known as 'Danzig Willie') and brother of the Bishop of Aberdeen. Lighting has never been installed here so, it has to be said, a tour of the interior can sometimes be disappointing. Yet this very lack of light, coupled with other features, can sharply bring home the discomforts with which this place's owners, not to mention their servants, had to contend, while, even on a dull day, the splendid decorated plaster ceilings, and especially that in the hall, can still provide their own illumination. The tour around the rooms reveals

Romantic Craigievar. Unchanged since completed for 'Danzig Willie' in 1626.

some surprising domestic aspects, portraits by Raeburn, and, to the architecturally aware, that the builders' external ·lightheartedness was not as haphazard as might appear. The grounds offer a picnic area and walks.

A980, followed S from the crossroads, almost at once enters territory associated, in tradition if not in fact, with the last hours of Macbeth. On the left, under a mile before reaching Lumphanan, a small ring of trees up on the slope is known as *Macbeth's Cairn*, reputedly the actual spot at which he met his end. Beyond, just SW of **Lumphanan**, the *Peel Ring* is a huge and particularly good example of an early medieval motte, complete with wall, earthworks and ditches. The stone wall is probably of the 12 or 13C, but before this there would have been a wooden palisade, behind which, it could well be, Macbeth in 1057 made his last stand against Malcolm Canmore, dying either here or perhaps while struggling up that hill to the N.

Continuing W from the crossroads, B9119 almost at once passes *Corse Castle* (1581; no adm.), a small but satisfactory ruin in the grounds of Corse House. The castle belonged to William of Craigievar's brother, Patrick, later Bishop of Aberdeen, who had a unique constructional problem because of a visit by the Devil who, being worsted in an argument, flew off in a rage, carrying with him the whole of the front of the castle.

4m ***Culsh Earth-house**, beside the road, is one of the best and most accessible of these unexplained tunnel excavations, the particular features here being exceptionally massive roof slabs and a passage which is not only wider and higher than others but also ends in a broadening rather than a true chamber.—*2m* **Tarland**, just S of which, on a rocky knoll beside A9094, is what is left of *Tomnaverie Stone Circle*, an example of the Recumbent Stone type. *Coull Castle*, on the left a little farther along B9094, was the ancient predecessor to Aboyne Castle. Once a great stronghold of five towers, built in imitation of Kildrummy and belonging to the Durwards, it is said to have been destroyed in the early 14C in one violent night of fire, so that, today, it survives as no more than fragments on a rise.

2m Ordie crossroads where B9119 is exchanged for A97 southwards, a road which runs below *Culblean Hill* (2m W. 1983ft), scene of a historic battle of 1335, during the wars with England's Edward III, which may be said to have confirmed Bannockburn, fought 20 years earlier. The two lochs, *Davan* to the N and *Kinord* to the S, squeezed within the angle of A97 and B9119, also played their part in events which started with the siege by the pro-English Earl of Atholl of Kildrummy Castle (see Rte 38), held by the wife of David II's adherent, Sir Andrew de Moray (for Atholl's wife, see Rte 38, Loch-in-Dorb). Moray, approaching from the S, installed himself in the Hall of Ruthven, a small castle on an island in Loch Davan and, learning of this, Atholl marched S to challenge him, the result being the battle (commemorative stone beside A97) in which Atholl met both defeat and death. After the battle one of Atholl's adherents, Sir Robert Menzies, took refuge on a fortified crannog in Loch Kinord from where, wisely, he negotiated his return to the Scottish cause. Three hundred years later, in 1646, this crannog castle, held for Charles I, was surrendered to the Covenanter Leslie and then demolished, so effectively that it has disappeared.

A97 passes, on the right, *Burn o' the Vat*, a popular picnic area with a short path to a fissure in the Vat burn with a curious rounded cauldron and cascade behind which various people are supposed to have hidden, including 17C freebooters and a fugitive of the '45.

4m **Junction with A93**. For from this point to (*19m*) *Braemar*, see Rte 37A.

38   Aberdeen to Nairn and Forres via Grantown-on-Spey

A944 to Dunecht. Unclassified to Castle Fraser and Monymusk. B993 to Tillyfourie. A944 to Mossat. A97, B973 and A939 through

Tomintoul and Grantown-on-Spey to Dava fork. A939 to Nairn or
A940 to Forres.—After Alford, increasingly high and open moor,
beyond Corgarff Castle following the fine 18C military Lecht Road
rising to 2100ft with some steep gradients. Beyond Grantown, moor
followed by woods.

SOME HOTELS. **Monymusk**. *Grant Arms*, AB3 7HJ. Tel: (04677)
226. **Kildrummy**. *Kildrummy Castle*, AB3 8RA. Tel: (03365) 288.
Strathdon. *Colquhonnie*. Tel: (09752) 210. **Tomintoul**. *Gordon
Arms*, The Square. Tel: (08074) 206. *Richmond Arms*, The Square.
Tel: (08074) 209. **Grantown-on-Spey**. *Garth*, Castle Road. Tel:
(0479) 2836. *Ben Mhor*, High Street. Tel: (0479) 2056. *Coppice*,
Grant Road. Tel: (0479) 2688.

Total distance 95m to Nairn or 92m to Forres.—*15m* **Castle
Fraser**.—*11m* **Alford**.—*7m* **Mossat**.—*2m* **Kildrummy Castle**.—*15m*
Corgarff Castle.—*10m* **Tomintoul**.—*12m* **Grantown-on-Spey**.—*8m*
Dava.—*15m* **Nairn** or *12m* **Forres**.

Aberdeen (see Rte 36) is left by Union Street, Albyn Place and
Queen's Road, passing Hazlehead Park.—*12m Dunecht*, from where
a minor road heading NW in *3m* reaches **Castle Fraser** (NTS.
May–Sept: Daily, 14.00 to 18.00. Garden and grounds open all year,
daily, 09.30 to sunset. Fee). Here a Fraser father and son, working
between 1575 and 1636 with the local master masons Bel and Leiper,
achieved a castle and home which well holds its own with such as
Crathes and Craigievar. The great hall and an exhibition on the Mar
castles are main features of the interior, while the grounds provide
a walled garden and picnic area.

From Castle Fraser minor roads wander *3m* NW to the village of
Monymusk, today apart and quiet but, if local tradition is accepted,
resounding with martial activity one day in 1307 when Bruce and his
army camped on Camp Field to the E of Monymusk House before
moving out to defeat John Comyn at Barra Hill (see start of Rte 41).
The house (no adm.) traces its roots to an early priory, first Culdee
and then in the 13C Augustinian, which at the Reformation became
a part of a castle (of the Forbes), this in turn developing into today's
mansion; and the village church, too, dates well back, as a Norman
survival of c 1170, restored in 1929. *Pitfichie Castle*, a tower 1m N
along the W bank of the Don, well shows how a round tower attached
to the corner of a keep gave defensive command along two sides,
while the road up the other side of the Don in 4m reaches the more
peaceful objective of the Forestry Commission's *Don View Visitor
Centre* with exhibits about local forestry and walks.

From Monymusk B993 and A944, rejoined at Tillyfourie, in *8m*
reach **Alford**, scene in 1645 of a battle won by Montrose against the
Covenanters but today, with a museum and a narrow-gauge railway,
rather surprisingly associated with transport. The *Grampian Transport
Museum* (April–Sept: Daily, 11.00 to 17.00. Tel: 0336-2292. Fee)
shows material spanning from the horse to steam, while the *Alford
Valley Railway* (June–Aug, daily. April, May, Sept, Sat. and Sun.
only. 11.00 to 17.00. Tel: 0336-2107. Fee), using 2ft gauge, runs
roughly every half hour to Haughton Country Park. *Balfluig Castle*
(1556; restored), 1m SE, was a tower-house of the Forbes who now
occupy 19C *Castle Forbes* (no adm.), 3m NE. More worth a visit,
though, if only because of its poignant story, is *Terpersie Castle*, 4m
NW of Alford, a lost, neglected small ruin, from the date carved on
one of the window-sills probably built in 1561. Here George Gordon,
the last owner, who had fought at Culloden, was captured in his

castle, and later executed, after having been inadvertently given away by his own children.

Just outside Alford A944 turns sharply right, at about the point where Montrose won his battle, to cross the Don and then closely follow the river for most of the way to (7m) *Mossat* where Rte 39 to Dufftown and Elgin breaks away N. This Rte turns S and in *1m* reaches *Kildrummy*, beside whose church are the remains of a medieval predecessor, with a 14C tomb of Forbes of Brux and an Elphinstone vault of 1605. Beyond (*1m*) appears ruined *Kildrummy Castle* (AM. Standard. Fee), visually formidable and exciting, architecturally instructive, historically both important and the scene of treachery and intrigue.

History. First built in the early 13C on the orders of Alexander II, the castle later fell to England's Edward I who ordered alterations in 1296–1303. Soon after this the Scots gained the castle, Bruce sending his wife and children here for safety when he fled to Rathlin in 1306. But the Scots' tenure was as shortlived as its end was bloody. Besieged again by the English, Kildrummy fell, through, it is said, the treachery of its blacksmith who, having been promised as much gold as he could carry, fired the place, thus leaving the defenders no choice but to surrender. Bruce's wife and children escaped to Tain (Rte 57), but his brother Sir Nigel was executed; the garrison was all 'hangyt and drawyn'; and the promise made to the blacksmith was honoured by the pouring of molten gold down his throat. In 1335 the castle, since Bannockburn in Scots' hands and defended by Lady Moray, again came under siege, this time though being saved by Sir Andrew Moray's victory at Culblean (see end of Rte 37B). In 1404 Alexander Stewart, illegitimate son of the 'Wolf of Badenoch' (and later victor of Harlaw, see Rte 40), here kidnapped the widowed Countess of Mar (it was he who had had her husband killed), then forced her to marry him and bestow on him the title of Earl of Mar. Later, Kildrummy became the seat of the Erskines of Mar, and it was here that the final plans were laid for the '15. After this rebellion's failure the castle was forfeited and much dismantled.

Despite such a history the ruins survive as an extensive and solid example of two stages of late 13–early 14C defensive building. There is the original courtyard system of a broad ditch and curtain wall with several round towers·and, larger than the others and with its own well, a main keep, at the time of its building regarded as the last stand for defence. Then there is the twin-towered gatehouse, almost certainly an addition by Edward I and indicative of how defence thinking was shifting from the idea of a central keep to one forward on the perimeter. Within the complex, the layout of the domestic buildings—hall, solar, kitchen—can be traced below the inner side of the N wall, while, projecting from the E wall, the chapel gable (mid 13C) with its three elegant lancets provides a softer though almost incongruous note in this setting of brute strength.

Adjacent, and associated with a hotel, are *Kildrummy Castle Gardens* (April–Oct: Daily, 09.00 to 17.00. Tel: 03365-264. Fee), a main feature of which is a water garden spanned by a replica of Aberdeen's ancient and legendary Brig o' Balgownie.

Meeting the Don, A93 turns W with the river to pass (rather over *3m* from Kildrummy Castle) *Glenkindie House*, in the grounds of which there is an earth-house, distinctive for having only a short passage but also a second chamber reached from the main chamber through a restricted hole (ask permission at the house's westernmost lodge, from where the earth-house is a short way away in a clump of trees on the left of the drive. Torch needed for inner chamber).

This Rte (A97 followed by B973) now remains with the river Don for some 12m as far as, approaching Corgarff Castle, the junction of B973 with A939.

1m Bridge of Buchat, close to which is *Glenbuchat Castle* (no adm. but well seen from outside), a late 16C Gordon tower, of interest for later belonging to the tough and colourful John Gordon, popularly known as 'Old Glenbucket of the '45'. A staunch Jacobite, he fought at Culloden at the age of 68, escaped to Norway and in 1750 died impoverished in France. An apposite inscription over the door reads 'No thing on arth remanis bot fame'. *Glenbuchat Church*, 1m up the glen, will attract anyone with a feel for 17–18C Highland churches, of which this is a particularly attractive example. In origin of the 15C, and still preserving some stonework of that period, the church underwent reconstruction in 1629 and again towards the close of the 18C, noteworthy features now being the belfry and, inside the church, the laird's loft of 1828 and the box pews with their tables and moveable partitions.

A97 now turns S and in about *2m* is exchanged for B973 which accompanies the river W and in rather over *1m* passes *Colquhonnie Castle*, beside a hotel, a small ruin begun by Forbes of Towie in the 16C but never finished, because, it is said, three successive lairds fell off the top and were killed. A short *1m* beyond, at **Bellabeg**, the road crosses the Water of Nochty, on the far side being the *Doune of Invernochty*, a large grassy motte marking the site of the early (12C or before) stronghold of the Earl of Mar before the construction of Kildrummy. The Lonach Highland Gathering—so called from the name of a nearby hill and well known for its March of the Clansmen from Invererman, 2m SW—is held at Bellabeg, usually towards the end of August. Just beyond the Doune of Invernochty B973 passes but does not cross the graceful *Poldullie Bridge* (leading to the village of *Strathdon*). With a single arch of 70ft, the bridge was built in 1715 by Jack Forbes of Invererman, who, soon afterwards, was executed for his part in the '15.

In another *5m* (from Bellabeg), and still running with the Don, B973 joins A939, the latter representing the Hanoverian military road of 1752–54 from Perth via Braemar to Fort George on the Moray Firth. Nor is it long before the traveller is made uncompromisingly aware of this, for in *2m* appears **Corgarff Castle** (AM. Standard. Fee), the stark and ugly Hanoverian conversion into a fortified barracks of a mid 16C tower which, not much later in that same century, in 1571, was the scene of a particularly horrific example of clan history. It arose out of the feud between the Gordons and the Forbes, during which Corgarff, defended by the wife of the absent Alexander Forbes, was besieged by Adam Gordon of Auchindoun. The tower was set on fire and, rather than surrender, the gallant defender chose to perish in the flames together with her children and entire household. Later, and rebuilt, the tower sheltered Montrose in 1645 and in 1745 was used by the Jacobites. But it was in the following year that the Hanoverians began to give Corgarff its present barracks form, a conspicuous feature of which is the star-shaped loopholed wall of 1748. The castle remained in military occupation until 1830, in the later years playing a useful role in the suppression of smuggling, largely of whisky.

If Corgarff represents one aspect of the Hanoverian presence, the **Lecht Road**, which climbs steeply away northwards from 1330ft to 2100ft, represents a very different one, an achievement remarkable enough in the mid 18C and still admired and used today. From the shelter of a modern car the seemingly endless bleak moorland can be accepted and quickly traversed, but conditions were assuredly very different for the men of the five companies of the 33rd Regiment, credited, on a stone at *Well of the Lecht*, 2m N of the summit, with the building of the road from this point down into the valley of the Spey. Notorious for its snowfalls, the Lecht is today provided with skiers' tows (Lecht Ski Company, Corgarff AB3 8YP. Tel: 09754-240).

10m from Corgarff) **Tomintoul** (*Inf.* The Square. Easter. Mid May–Sept), in the midst of barren moorland and laid out by the Duke of Gordon in 1779, is the highest village in the Highlands (1160ft) though, curiously, not in Scotland (see Rte 10, Wanlockhead and Leadhills). The *Museum* (Easter. Mid May–Sept: Daily, 09.30 to 18.30. Tel: 0309-73701. Free) illustrates the local scene, touching aspects such as wildlife, geology, climate and local history with a reconstructed rural kitchen as an attractive feature.

Two whisky distilleries (successors of the 200 or so illicit ones which flourished in this part of Scotland before the Distilleries Act of 1824), both along B9008, can be visited from here, in a scenically pleasant round of some 20m. The first, 7m from Tomintoul, is *Tamnavoulin* (June–Sept: Mon.–Fri., 10.00 to 16.30. Tel: 08073-285. Free), with a visitor centre and also a picnic area beside the river Livet. *The Glenlivet*, 2m farther N (founded in 1824, using the present site since 1858, and the first to gain a licence and thus earn the right to 'The') offers tours and an exhibition (Easter–late Oct: Mon.–Fri., 10.00 to 16.00. Tel: 08073-427. Free). The nearby castle dates from 1586, and it was in this glen in 1594 that James VI in person defeated the rebel earls Huntly and Errol. From here A939 and Tomintoul can be regained in 10m by way of Strath Avon (B9136).

From Tomintoul A939 descends off the moors into the broad and wooded valley of the Spey which it reaches at (*12m*) **Grantown-on-Spey** (1600 inhab. *ECl.* Thurs. *Inf.* 54 High Street). Laid out in 1776 by Sir James Grant, and with a dignified length of wide, tree-lined main street, this is a spacious and sheltered place which, at the hub of several important touring roads, has become an established summer centre as also a base for winter sports.

This Rte here crosses, but does not continue with the Spey. For places to the SW such as *Castle Roy, Boat of Garten* (Strathspey Railway), *Loch Garten* (ospreys) and *Carrbridge*, see Rte 50. The scenically pleasant *Strathspey* extends some 20m NE to *Craigellachie* (on Rte 39), the main A95 running S and B9102 N of the river. The two places of specific interest, *Glenfarclas* and *Tamdhu* distilleries, are described under Craigellachie from which both are 6 or 7m distant.

Castle Grant (April–Oct: Daily, 10.00 to 17.30. Tel: 0479-3075. Fee), on the N outskirts of Grantown and the chief seat of the Grants for five centuries, is structurally a successful combination of a 15C keep and 18C extensions caried out by Robert and John Adam. Inside are Adam rooms, restored and given period furnishings, while the grounds, with views of the Cairngorms, provide a shop and tearoom, picnic area, archery, croquet, an adventure playground and a craft exhibition.

8m **Dava**, a road fork at which a decision must be made between A939 to Nairn or A940 to Forres. Each road passes close to a site of interest—Ardclach Bell Tower off A939; Randolph's Leap off A940—but a linking road (B9007) through Relugas enables both to be visited. But first a short diversion of 2m SW from Dava may be made to the bleakly sited moorland loch of *Loch-in-Dorb*, a lost place now but one which with its island castle, still surviving as a ruin, was of considerable importance during the 13–15C. First, in the 13C, the Comyns built the castle; in 1303 Edward I took it and greatly strengthened the defences; in 1336 the anglophile Countess of Atholl (for her husband, see Culblean, at the end of Rte 37B) held out here against David II until the siege could be raised by England's Edward III; and in 1372 the castle became a lair of the 'Wolf of Badenoch'. Finally, in 1456, Loch-in-Dorb's story ended with its dismantling by James II.

TO NAIRN (A939). *5m Ferness*, a village where B9007 is crossed, the northward stretch of which, beyond Relugas, passes close to Randolph's Leap (see below).—*1m Logie Bridge*, crossing the Findhorn, a river which drops off the high moor to cut a beautiful wooded and winding course through defiles and steep-sided hills. Just beyond, a minor road and lane in about 1m arrive at **Ardclach Bell Tower** (key at reasonable hours from cottage), a curious detached and fortified two-storeyed belfry of 1665, perched high above the Findhorn and combining the functions both of look-out and of summoning worshippers to the old church. Beside the approach lane stands a monument to Donald Mitchell (born 1782), Scotland's first missionary to India. From here some of the best of the Findhorn can be enjoyed by continuing along the minor road for about 3m to *Dulsie Bridge* where the river forces through a narrow cut below the valley coming in from the W.—*9m (from Logie Bridge)*, **Nairn**, see Rte 43.

TO FORRES (A940). In *7m* B9007 joins from the SW, providing a link across to Ardclach Bell Tower and the approach to (in 1m) *Randolph's Leap*, where amid beautiful woodland the Findhorn tumbles through a small gorge, in one spot with rocks only 10ft apart. A plaque tells the somewhat involved story behind the name, while a stone marks the astonishingly high level of the flood of 1829.—*5m* **Forres**, see Rte 43.

39   Aberdeen to Elgin via Dufftown

A944 to Dunecht. Unclassified to Castle Fraser and Monymusk. B993 to Tillyfourie. A944 to Mossat. A97, B9002 and A941 to Elgin.—Generally pastoral, but moor and upland between Alford and Dufftown, especially across the desolate Moor of Cabrach approaching the latter.

SOME HOTELS. **Monymusk**. *Grant Arms*, AB3 7HJ. Tel: (04677) 226. **Dufftown**. *Tannochbrae Guest House*, 22 Fife Street. Tel: (0340) 20541. **Craigellachie**. *Craigellachie*, Victoria Street. Tel: (03404) 204. **Rothes**. *Rothes Glen*, IU33 7AH. Tel: (03403) 254.

Total distance 67m.—*33m* **Mossat**.—*18m* **Dufftown**.—*4m* **Craigellachie**.—*12m* **Elgin**.

For Aberdeen to (*33m*) *Mossat*, see Rte 38.—*3m Auchindoir (St. Mary's) Church*, within the angle of A97 and B9002, though now a ruin, has features making a visit worthwhile. In origin a parish church of the 13C, the shell still shelters a 16C sacrament house, considered to be one of the best in Scotland, a Transitional door with a semicircular arch and dog-tooth moulding, and, in the N wall, a still graceful lancet. *Craig Castle* (Summer only and by appointment. Tel: 04648-202. Fee), just N and overlooking a wooded glen, has as its oldest feature a keep of 1528 or earlier, while the armorial decorative work and the gateway of 1720 are also notable.

B9002 in *4m* joins with A941 which heads across the *Moor of Cabrach*, a desolate tract below mountains of around 2000ft, to descend to bridge Glen Fiddich. Ahead—stark, forbidding yet inviting on its high moorland skyline—appears **Auchindoun Castle** (AM. View from outside only), reached by a track off A941 about 1½m short of Dufftown. The prehistoric earthworks scattered around tell that this lonely upland site was a defended one centuries before Auchindoun's central tower was built, probably in the 15C by James III's mason and favourite Robert Cochrane, later to become the stronghold of that Adam Gordon who in 1571 achieved notoriety through the burning of Corgarff and its household. A curiosity here is the absence of the normal tailored cornerstones, all removed to become parts of Balvenie Castle in Dufftown.

11m **Dufftown** (1600 inhab. *ECl* Wed. *Inf.* Clock Tower. Mid May–Sept) might be described as a place of four origins, all visibly surviving—Mortlach church with pre-Norman and earlier roots; Balvenie Castle representing the medieval centuries; the town itself, the creation in 1817 of James Duff, 4th Earl of Fife; and the whisky distilleries which since the late 19C have made their ever popular contribution.

The focus of this rather quaint small town is its pleasing central *Clock Tower* housing the local *Museum* (Mid May–Sept: Daily, 09.30 to 18.30. Tel: 0309-73701. Free) telling Dufftown's story from Mortlach to whisky. *Mórtlach Church*, ½m S, is basically 12C and something of this medieval building survives in the walls, while the lancets in the choir are 13C and the N aisle jumps into the 19C. But fact begins to mix with tradition as this church's earlier origins are sought, though it is not hard here to accept that this was where in c 1010 Malcolm II won a great victory over the Norsemen, as a result founding the bishopric which David I in 1137 transferred to Aberdeen where it is now represented by St. Machar's cathedral. Yet, shadowy though these events are, ancient stones here suggest an even remoter Christian presence.

Balvenie Castle (AM. Standard but closed in winter. Fee), on the N outskirts of Dufftown, survives as the substantial ruin of what was originally the 13C moated, courtyard stronghold of the Comyns. Some of the masonry undoubtedly belongs to this period, and on the SW and NW sides the ditch can still be seen, but there was major rebuilding during the 15 and 16C, the 4th Earl of Atholl (1542–79) being responsible for the tower-house which changed the castle's character from fortress to a nobleman's mansion. Balvenie was visited by Edward I in 1304, by Mary, Queen of Scots, in 1562, and in 1746 by Cumberland when the castle was occupied by his troops.

To the N of the castle, *Glenfiddich Distillery*, though dating from 1887, is briskly modern, with a visitor theatre (audio-visual presentation in six languages) and the latest in whisky technology. This is the only distillery in the Highlands in which malt whisky is actually bottled on the premises, this enabling the visitor to follow the whole process, 'from the barley to the bottle' with a free dram to close the tour (Mon.–Fri., 09.30 to 16.30. Also, early May–mid Oct: Sat., 09.30 to 16.30. Sun., 12.00 to 16.30. Closed for about three weeks over Christmas and New Year. Tel: 0340-20373. Free).

4m **Craigellachie** more or less marks the E end of Strathspey, the river crossed by a modern bridge (1973) just below Telford's graceful, iron single-span predecessor of 1815. From here a round of some 17m enables two distilleries to be taken in, the first, 6m SW along A95, being *Glenfarclas Distillery* (Mon.–Fri., 09.30 to 16.30. Also, mid July–Sept: Sat., 10.00 to 16.00. Tel: 08072-257. Free), founded in 1836. Just beyond, at Marypark, B9102 can be followed N for some 5m to reach *Tamdhu Distillery* (Easter–Sept: Mon.–Fri., 10.00 to 16.00. Tel: 03406-221, Free), built in 1896. Thence, B9102 joins A941 just N of Craigellachie bridge.—*3m* **Rothes**, with, at the S, the surviving wall of its castle, and, to the W, *Glen Grant Distillery* (Mid April–Sept: Mon.–Fri., 10.00 to 16.00. Children under eight not admitted to production areas. Tel: 03403-494. Free).—*9m* **Elgin**, see Rte 43.

40   Aberdeen to Fochabers via Huntly

A96 to Inverurie. B9001 and unclassified roads to Harlaw, Daviot (Loanhead Stone Circle), Pitcaple Castle, Chapel of Garioch and the Maiden Stone. B9002 and A97 to Huntly. A96 to Fochabers.—Pastoral and agricultural countryside, becoming higher and more wooded after Oyne.

SOME HOTELS. **Inverurie**. *Ardennan*. Tel: (0467) 21343, *Gordon Arms*, Market Place. Tel: (0467) 20314. **Pitcaple**. *Pittodlie House*, AB5 9HS. Tel: (04676) 202. **Insch**. *Rothney Arms*. Tel: (0464) 20604. **Huntly**. *Gordon Arms*, The Square. Tel:(0466) 2536. *Castle*, AB5 4SH. Tel: (0466) 2696. **Keith**. *Royal*, Church Road. Tel: (05422) 2528.

Total distance 61m.—*16m* **Inverurie**.—*15m* **Insch**.—*6m* **Leith Hall**.—*7m* **Huntly**.—*10m* **Keith**.—*7m* **Fochabers**.

From the roundabout beyond the E end of Castle Street, **Aberdeen** (see Rte 36) is left by way of West North Street, Causewayend and Great Northern Road. In the suburb of *Buckburn*, *4m* out of the city centre, A947 breaks away N for Dyce airport and Rte 41.—*8m* **Kintore** which, though small and quickly passed, nevertheless merits a few minutes pause, and not only because, surprisingly, this place has been a royal burgh since 1506. The *Town House* of 1737 is quaint with its external curving stairs, while the *Church* shows a pre-Reformation sacrament house, with a panel with angels displaying a monstrance, and, in the yard, a Pictish stone combining Christian and pagan symbols. *Balbithan House* (by appointment. Tel: 0467-32282. Fee), 2m NE across the Don, is a late 17C tower-house attractively combining with an old-world garden.

4m **Inverurie** (7000 inhab. *ECl.* Wed. *Inf.* Town Hall. Mid May–Sept), said to have been made a royal burgh by David I, though this status more probably dates from a charter given by Mary, Queen of Scots, is the largest centre within a district rich in prehistory and Pictish stones. Thus the *Museum* here, in the Public Library in the

Square, though small, is of particular interest for its local material (Mon.–Fri., 14.00 to 17.00. Sat., 10.00 to 12.00. Tel: 0779-77778. Free).

The Bass, on the SE of the town beside B993, and the stones in the adjacent churchyard, together remind of medieval and earlier times. The Pictish stones, one bearing a lively figure of a pony and another a clear 'spectacle' symbol, provide, as do all such, a tantalising glimpse into Dark Ages ritual. But The Bass requires no explanation; only imagination. Strictly military in purpose, this great mound, today green and bare, was thrown up in 1160 by David, Lord of Garioch and brother of Malcolm IV, to serve as the base, steep and surrounded by a formidable palisade of sharpened stakes, on which to place his wooden tower crowned with its defensive platform. From this would have grown the more sophisticated stone castle visited by Mary, Queen of Scots, in 1562. Just beyond The Bass a small road leads due S for 1m to ruined early 16C *Kinkell Church*, of interest because the parson here, Alexander Galloway, was well known as an artistic designer of sacrament houses and the one here bears his initials and the date 1524. Another curiosity is a tombstone of Gilbert de Greenlaw, killed at Harlaw (see below), economically re-used by a Forbes.

The *Brandsbutt Stone*, off A96 on the NW outskirts of Inverurie, stands as another reminder of this district's Pictish past, this one not only with typical symbols but also bearing an Ogham inscription.

There are several sites of interest either side of the next 6m of A96. This Rte therefore now chooses a meandering course along generally minor roads before first crossing, and then briefly rejoining A96 just before its fork with B9002 which is then followed.

Near the Brandsbutt Stone, B9001 forks N, in *1m* reaching a road to the left leading to *Harlaw House* in the grounds of which a monument of 1911 marks the site of the bloody Battle of Harlaw of 1411 and may also remind the visitor of some characters met elsewhere.

The Countess of Ross, niece of Donald, Lord of the Isles, renounced her title and entered a convent, Donald at once claiming the earldom, marching southward against James I, burning Dingwall and Inverness and threatening Aberdeen. Opposing him here was the self-made Earl of Mar, that same Alexander Stewart, illegitimate son of the 'Wolf of Badenoch', who, at Kildrummy, had forced the Countess of Mar, whom he had widowed, to marry him and give him the title. Mar won the battle, and Donald was forced both to renounce his claim and declare allegiance to the crown. But the cost was heavy, among the killed being Alderman Davidson of Aberdeen and Sir Alexander de Irwyn of Drum, both of whom, the former by an effigy and the latter by a brass, are remembered in Aberdeen's St. Nicholas church.

In *3m* farther along B9001 a side road, through Daviot, in *1m* reaches *Loanhead Stone Circle*, one of the leading examples of the Recumbent Stone type. A ring of rough erect stones surrounds a scatter of small stones, all that is left of what was once a large burial cairn, while pottery discovered here indicates that, perhaps 1000 years later, this place was inhabited, rather than used just for ritual and burial. There are other stone and earthworks adjacent. From here minor roads wander generally SW to *3m Pitcaple Castle* (if convenient. Tel: 04676-204) on A96, a 15–16C castle with two round towers and 19C additions, still in use as a family home. A tree in front of the house is the popular focus of interest here, for both Mary, Queen of Scots, and Charles II are said to have danced below it, the former in 1562,

Charles in 1650. But the latter year witnessed also a less happy occasion when Montrose arrived as a prisoner, preceded by a crier announcing him as James Graham, traitor.

A96 is crossed opposite Pitcaple, a small road being followed to (*1m*) *Chapel of Garioch*. The ruined tower (1530) of *Balquhain*, beside the road 1m E of here, was a seat of the Jacobite Leslies. In 1746 Cumberland ordered that it be burnt, but, so the story goes, a tenant of the Leslies bribed the soldiers to use damp straw. Beside the road, *1m* NW of Chapel of Garioch, stands the magnificent *Maiden Stone (9C), ranking among the most beautiful of Scotland's Early Christian monuments and taking its name from the comb and mirror carved at the foot. Of red granite and standing 10ft high, the stone bears a Celtic cross and Pictish symbols, including, on one side, a man between marine monsters, and, on the other, beasts, an 'elephant' and the mirror and comb.

The wooded ridge of *Bennachie* (1773ft), by some authorities held to be the site of Mons Graupius, rises immediately to the SW, with, on Mither Tap (1698ft), the E summit, the remains of a hill fort. Around Bennachie the Forestry Commission have laid out some of their finest forest walks, one car park being just W of the Maiden Stone and another at Puttingstone to the S of Oyne.

This Rte now briefly touches A96 before bearing left along B9002, beside which stands the pile of *Harthill Castle* (no adm.), probably begun by Patrick Leith of Barnis and completed by his son John in 1601. Less than a century later the last laird, hopelessly in debt, burnt the castle, rather than have it seized, and fled to London.—*2m* (from the Maiden Stone) *Oyne*, followed by (*3m*) **Insch**, 2m N of which (at Myreton, off the Largie road) there is another fine stone, the *Picardy Stone* (7 or 8C) showing a variety of symbols.

Just beyond Insch, the hill of *Dunnideer* rises emphatically above the railway to the N of B9002. Iron Age people built the first fort here, to be succeeded in 1260 by the stone stronghold of Sir Jocelin de Balliol, today a battered fragment but interesting for having been one of the first of the self-contained tower-house keeps which succeeded the courtyard style of castle represented by Kildrummy.

6m **Leith Hall** (NTS. May–Sept: Daily, 14.00 to 18.00. Garden and grounds open all year, daily, 09.30 to sunset. Fee), approached by way of a splendid avenue, offers a change from castles, for although the core here is a turreted tower-house of 1649, essentially Leith is now a large but unpretentious and attractive country mansion around a central courtyard. James Leith, the first to build here, seems to have come from a family which once lived in Leith, near Edinburgh, but moved to Aberdeen to become by the 14C prosperous shipowners, and in large part the exhibits in the house reflect the long tradition of military service later given by the Leiths and associated Hays. Prominent among these was Andrew Hay who achieved the distinction of being pardoned after Culloden, the document being among those shown here. Gardens, trails with a bird observation hide, Soay sheep, Highland cattle, a picnic area and even carved Pictish stones are among the attractions around the grounds.

In *2m* B9002 meets A97 below the high ground of *Clashindarroch Forest*, rising, 2m SW of this road junction, to *Tap o' Noth* (1851ft) crowned by a vitrified Iron Age fort. Much of this forest grows at between 1000 and 1500 ft and access roads, some only for walkers, climb the valleys which break these eastern slopes and meet Strath

Bogie which is now followed N as A97.

5m **Huntly** (4000 inhab. *ECl.* Thurs. *Inf.* 24 Gordon Street. Mid May–Sept), within the confluence of the rivers Deveron and Bogie, tends to be overshadowed, historically and touristwise though not physically, by its famed ruined Gordon castle. Yet this small town, though essentially a Gordon creation, has an identity of its own and, indeed, on the evidence of the two standing stones in the attractive Square, infinitely earlier origins than its castle. But in medieval times the town of course grew with the castle, being chartered in 1545 and then in the later 18 and 19C laid out and extended to settle to the plan it shows today. Material illustrating something of the town's development can be seen in the *Library Museum* in the Square (Tues.–Sat., 10.00 to 12.00. 14.00 to 16.00. Tel: 0466-2179. Free), while—an indication of the town's architectural merit—a leaflet obtainable from Tourist Information guides around an Architectural Trail.

The ***Castle** (AM. Standard. Fee), until 1544 known as Strathbogie Castle, is reached by Castle Street, running N from the Square to pass below an arch formed by buildings of Gordon Schools (founded in 1839 by the Duchess of Gordon), beyond being the fine approach avenue. Essentially what survives here are the Norman motte and bailey, the later tower-house palace, and the foundations of a court.

History. In both strategic and tactical terms the castle's site is an obvious choice, the former because it commands the roads from Strathdon and Aberdeen to Moray, the latter because of the defensive advantage provided by the two rivers.

Early history is of course that of the motte, 12–13C stronghold of the Scottish-Norman Duncan, Earl of Fife, and the place also in which in 1307, during his campaign against the Comyns, Bruce rested after an illness before

Huntly Castle, showing the 5th Earl's elegant oriel windows of 1602.

moving out to defeat the Comyns at Barra Hill. Just before Bannockburn, though, the then lord turned against Bruce, as a result losing his lands to the latter's loyal supporter, Sir Adam Gordon of Huntly (Gordon) in the Borders. In 1449 the Gordons were made earls of Huntly, but only three years later, during the civil disputes of 1452, their wooden castle was destroyed by the Douglas Earl of Moray. Replacement of the wooden structure by stone had probably already started before Moray's attack, which of course accelerated the process.

For the next century the Gordon earls of Huntly held autocratic sway over this part of Scotland, and it was here in 1496 that James IV, a frequent visitor, attended the marriage between Perkin Warbeck and Lady Catherine Gordon. Then in 1552 the colourful and energetic 4th Earl pulled down most of the 15C structure and built much of the basic palace fabric as seen today. But it was he, too, who, by rebelling against Mary, Queen of Scots, and being defeated at Corrichie, closed the era of Gordon power.

The 5th Earl also rebelled (against James VI) in 1594, his defeat in Glen Livet leading to the subsequent destruction of much of the castle. However, three years later he made his peace with the king, became 1st Marquis of Huntly and set about restoring his home. A man of refined taste, it is to his restoration that belong the building's most beautiful architectural features. The 2nd Marquis lost his head after supporting Charles I, first suffering the cruelty of being imprisoned in his own castle. After this, and with the move later of the family to what is now Gordon Castle at Fochabers, Huntly inevitably fell into disrepair.

The building is greatly complicated by the centuries of destruction, rebuilding and alteration. The main part, though, is the 4th and 5th earls' 16–17C *Palace*, using the older vaults as its foundations. Features are the elegant row of oriel windows (1602) with the stonework names of the 1st Marquis (5th Earl) and his wife; the elaborate heraldic ornamentation (which should be imagined as emblazoned in colour), particularly the *vertical panel above the main doorway, probably the finest heraldic doorway in Britain; and the fireplaces, again with heraldic and other ornamentation.

Below the palace is the 15C vaulted *Dungeon*, rather more roomy than in some castles but not much less grim. It is reached by a gloomy narrow passage, with outer and inner doors, the latter killing any lingering hopes of escape by opening into the dungeon several feet above its floor level. Along the basement passage walls can be seen graffiti, possibly the work of bored guards.

Outside the palace, on the N, the visitor stands within the outline of the *Court*, the remains on the W and E sides being respectively 16 and 17C but those on the N the foundations of what must have been a massive 15C tower. Within the court are the remains of a stable, possibly originally a chapel.

The *Motte* is self-evident; and across the grass on the E side of the castle runs the ancient cobbled entrance causeway.

10m **Keith** (4600 inhab. *ECl.* Wed. *Inf.* Church Road. Summer only) claims roots reaching back to before 700 when those living here beside the Isla were converted to Christianity by St. Maelrubha, and certainly existed as a community by the 12C when William the Lion chartered this place to Kinloss Abbey. Today Keith really represents an amalgam of three places. Old Keith, beside the river, dates from medieval times, a nice survival here (off Regent Street) being the *Auld Brig*, built in 1609 by Thomas Murray and Janet Lindsay whose names are cut into the S face; New Keith, above and to the E of the river, was laid out by the 2nd Earl of Seafield in 1750; and Fife Keith, on the opposite bank of the Isla, was founded by the Earl of Fife in 1817.

In addition to the Auld Brig, a church, an ancient tower and a distillery all merit a visit. *St. Thomas's Church*, in Chapel Street in the S part of New Keith, was built in 1830 with a facade copied from that of Santa Maria de Angelis in Rome. Inside are an 'Incredulity of St. Thomas', painted by François Dubois and presented by Charles X of France; a statue of St. John Ogilvie, Scotland's first post-Reformation saint, born near Keith in 1580, hanged in Glasgow in 1615 and canonised in 1976; and modern stained glass windows, by Father Ninian Sloane of Pluscarden Abbey. *Milton Tower*, in Station Road, survives as Keith's oldest building; part of a larger castle, built in 1480, this was long the seat of the Ogilvie family. *Strathisla Distillery*, in Seafield Avenue to the S of the station, was established in 1786 and is thus one of the oldest in Scotland (June–early Sept: Mon.–Fri., 09.00 to 16.30. Children under eight not admitted to production areas. Tel: 05422-7471. Free).—*Newmill*, just N of Keith, was the birthplace in c 1800 of James Gordon Bennett, founder of the 'New York Herald'.

7m **Fochabers** , see Rte 43.

41   Aberdeen to Macduff and Banff

A947 to Oldmeldrum. A920 to Pitmedden. B999 and B9170 to Methlick. B9005 to Fyvie. A947 to Macduff (Banff).—Generally pastoral and wooded.

SOME HOTELS. **Oldmeldrum**. *Meldrum House*, AB5 OAE. Tel: (06512) 229. **Methlick**, *Gight House*, Sunnybrae. Tel: (06514) 389. **Fyvie**. *Vale*. Tel: (06516) 376. **Turriff**. *Union*, Main Street. Tel: (0888) 62419.

Total distance 54m.—*16m* **Oldmeldrum**.—*18m* (via Pitmedden and Haddo) **Fyvie**.—*8m* **Turriff**.—*12m* **Macduff** and **Banff**.

From the roundabout beyond the E end of Castle Street, **Aberdeen** (see Rte 36) is left by West North Street, Causewayend and Great Northern Road.—*4m* **Buckburn**, whence Rte 40 follows A96.—*1m* **Dyce**, a name best known as Aberdeen's airport but a place notable also for two Pictish stones in the old church (St. Fergus), 1½m NW within the S side of a loop in the Don.—*11m* **Oldmeldrum**, 1m S of which, just E of B9170, rises *Barra Hill* (634ft) where in 1307, on Christmas Eve, Bruce decisively defeated John Comyn who may have camped within the hill's Iron Age fort.

From Oldmeldrum A947 provides the direct road to Fyvie. This Rte, however, takes an eastward loop, starting along A920, to include a clutch of outstanding National Trust and other sites.

5m ***Pitmedden Garden and Museum** (NTS. Garden and Grounds, daily, 09.30 to sunset. Museum and other facilities, May–Sept: Daily, 11.00 to 18.00. Fee). The *Garden* here is no ordinary garden, but the Great Garden laid out in 1675 by Sir Alexander Seton and recreated with all its elaborate floral designs by the National Trust. There are four formal parterres, three being taken from designs recorded as having been used in the gardens of Edinburgh's Holyrood House in 1647, while the fourth is a heraldic design based on Sir Alexander Seton's coat-of-arms (he was the first Baronet Pitmedden). Pitmedden also offers a *Museum of Farming Life*, with some both interesting and curious farming and domestic material, a visitor centre, picnic area, woodland and farmland walks (rare breeds of livestock) and an adventure playground.

Udny Castle (no adm. but well seen from the road) is a dramatic battlemented and turreted tower of the 15–17C, while the old churchyard in *Udny Green*, immediately S of the castle, contains a burial enclosure of the Setons of Pitmedden and also a mort-house for the prevention of body-snatching.

*Tolquhon Castle (AM. Standard. Fee) is just NW (*1m*) of Pitmedden off B999. The castle's situation beyond an unusually large, gently sloping forecourt, with an old yew tree pleasance along its W side, and the structurally and functionally abrupt contrast between a fortified exterior and a mainly residential inner court, combine to give Tolquhoun a distinction and interest all its own.

History. Unlike so many castles, Tolquhoun suffered little if at all from hostile attack. In the 14C it belonged to the Prestons, but in 1420, through the marriage of a Preston daughter, it passed to Sir John Forbes, the probable builder of the Auld Tower, sometimes still called Preston's Tower, the oldest part of the castle seen today. In 1584 the laird was the cultured William Forbes, who not only much enlarged Tolquhoun but took steps to ensure that posterity would know this; a precise inscription at the gatehouse reads 'Al this wark, excep the auld tour, was begun be William Forbes 15 Aprile, 1584, and endit be him, 20 October, 1589'. His master mason was Thomas Leiper, who was also responsible for his employer's elaborate tomb in the churchyard at Tarves (see below). For financial reasons, the estate had to be sold by the laird in 1716, though the castle remained occupied until the mid 19C.

The visitor's first impression is of a defensive stronghold, and even at the arched forecourt entrance there are gunloops, tactically constructed so that the central opening gives forward while the others are angled. Many such will also be seen in the castle itself. Two corner towers, one round and one square, provide the usual protection along all four of the castle's walls, while the main gatehouse, where the above inscription will be found, continues the defensive theme with its flanking drum towers, barred windows, two guard rooms and gunloops.

Beyond the gatehouse, in the inner court, there are still gunloops and heavily barred windows, while to the left is John Forbes's ruined Auld Tower, with a vaulted cellar. The well, too, is probably a survival from the older period. But the emphasis here is residential and domestic, the main rooms being along the S and W sides, with a wide stairway leading to the upper floor with the hall and laird's room, a practical feature of the latter being the private stair from the kitchen.

1m Tarves, where can be seen the elaborate tomb (by Thomas Leiper) of William Forbes and his wife, a Gothic structure with Renaissance detail and statuettes of the occupants.

1m **Haddo House**, at the heart of a splendid and much varied park, is approached from the S. The complex comprises the house, gardens and grounds, 177 acres of the last forming a Country Park controlled by Grampian Regional Council. (*House*. NTS. May–Sept: Daily, 14.00 to 18.00. Fee. *Garden*. NTS. All year, daily, 09.30 to 20.00 or sunset. Donation. *Country Park*. All year, daily, 09.30 to sunset).

Long the seat of the Gordon earls and marquises of Aberdeen, Haddo House was planned in 1731, for the 2nd Earl, by William Adam (father of Robert), to replace the old House of Kellie (burnt by

Covenanters in 1644) which for centuries had been the home of the Gordons of Methlick. The house is a masterpiece of symmetry, particularly pleasing being the high central section with its matching curving flights of stairs up to the first floor balcony, this being the normal entrance until 1880 when the 1st Marquis (7th Earl) inserted the present ground level door. Inside the house the elegant yet unpretentious rooms opening off the long curving passageway contain a notable collection of portraits, of which the most treasured is that by Lawrence of the 4th Earl, prime minister from 1852–55 and the man largely responsible for rescuing a neglected estate and making it what it is today. Here too are portraits of some of his friends and colleagues, such as William Pitt, Castlereagh, Wellington and Peel. The Chapel (1880), with stained glass by Burne-Jones, was the last work of the architect G.E. Street.—Features of the *Country Park* are a tree trail (booklet), bird hide, picnic area and interpretive centre.

The **Haddo House Choral and Operatic Society**, founded in 1945 by June, Marchioness of Aberdeen, and with its own theatre beside the house, has made its name as one of Scotland's leading musical bodies. Productions include opera and concerts in which internationally known artists often appear, and also performances of classic drama. For information contact the Choral'Secretary, Tel: 06515-666.

From *Methlick*, 2m NW of Haddo, B9005 heads NW, in a good 2m arriving at the hamlet of Stonehouse, from where a farm track and path in c ¾m reach *Gight Castle*, above the steep wooded bank of the Ythan. This is the sad and decaying ruin of the once formidable tower-house of the lawless Gordons of Gight, perhaps worth a visit as such and certainly worth one by anyone in search of Byronic associations. For this was the home of Lady Catherine Gordon, 13th laird in a succession reaching back to 1479 and mother of the poet Byron (1788), who was forced to sell Gight in 1787, in order to pay the gambling debts of her dissolute husband, 'Mad Jack' Byron. Thomas the Rhymer predicted 'when the herons leave the tree, the lairds of Gight shall landless be', and, sure enough, in 1787 the herons did exchange Gight for Haddo.

6m **Fyvie Castle** (NTS. For opening details ask nearest Tourist Information or Tel: 031-2265922), spanning from the 13C to Scottish Baronial and one of the stateliest castellated mansions in Scotland, is a place of five towers and of five families.

History. In the early 13C there was a keep here in the royal forest, but in 1338 the lands were granted to Sir James Lindsay, Earl of Crawford. This family, though, does not count among the five because the estate soon passed by marriage to Sir Henry Preston, builder of the SE and oldest surviving tower (*Preston Tower*). Later, and again by marriage, Fyvie went to the Meldrums who put up the *Meldrum Tower* (SW). However by 1596 the Meldrums, by then bankrupt, sold out to Sir Alexander Seton, and it was he who was responsible for the great central *Seton Tower*, with its twin drums, as also for the upper works and NW wing. In 1733 Fyvie was again sold, this time to the 2nd Earl of Aberdeen, the builder at the same time of Haddo House and remembered here by the *Gordon Tower* (NE). A third sale, in 1889, brought the estate to Alexander Forbes-Leith, an American industrialist and descendant of the Leith-Hays of Leith Hall (see Rte 40), who in 1890 raised the *Leith Tower* (NW) and, as Lord Leith, gave Fyvie its turn-of-the-century opulence. The above, of course, is a simplification; inevitably there was constructional overlapping, and it seems also virtually certain that the Preston Tower incorporates something of the earlier keep.

Acquired by the National Trust for Scotland in 1984, Fyvie was opened to the public in 1986.

Architecturally the two outstanding earlier features inside the castle are the great *wheel stairway, built by Sir Alexander Seton, bearing his crest and ascending through five floors; and, in the 17C morning room, the contemporary plaster ceiling and panelling. Otherwise the ambience here is the recreation of the lifestyle and taste of an immensely wealthy Edwardian, among the highlights being the many portraits, notably by Raeburn as also by Lely, Kneller, Romney, Opie and Hoppner; the 17C Brussels tapestries; the collection of armour in the entrance hall; and the billiard room which Lord Leith created out of the 18C kitchen.

From *Fyvie*, where the church merits a glance because of the Celtic stones built into its gable, this Rte heads N on A947.—*4m Towie (Tolly) Barclay Castle* (no adm.), a square and turreted 16C red tower with modern (1970s) upper floors which was once the home of the Barclays, the family to which belonged Prince Michael de Tolly, marshal in the Russian army during the Napoleonic wars.—*4m* **Turriff** enjoys the modest distinction of having been the scene of the first skirmish of the Civil War. In what has become known as the 'Trot of Turriff' (1639) a party of Royalist Gordons routed the Covenanters under the Master of Forbes. *Delgatie Castle* (written application), 1½m NE, a satisfying tower-house well seen from the minor road which passes it, dates from the 13C but has additions mainly of about 1570. Features of the interior are pictures and arms, painted ceilings of about 1590, and a portrait of Mary, Queen of Scots, hanging in the room which she used for three days in 1562. *Craigston Castle* (written application), on B9105 4m NE of Turriff, has been a seat of the Urquharts since the castle's building in 1604–07.

8m Eden Castle, 1m W of A947 down a side road, is today a mere tower remnant. Built in 1676 for the Nicholas family, the castle's downfall is ascribed to the curse of a mother who asked the laird to control her wayward son, which he effectively did by drowning the boy in the river.—*4m* **Macduff** and **Banff**, for both of which see Rte 43.

42 Aberdeen to Peterhead and Fraserburgh

A92, A975 and A952 to Peterhead. A952 and B9033 to Fraserburgh.—Scenically generally dull roads across open and sometimes bleak farming land, but plenty of rewarding coastal dunes and cliffs.

SOME HOTELS. **Ellon**. *Ladbroke Mercury*, AB4 9NP. Tel: (0358) 20666. **Peterhead**. *Waterside Inn*, 1 Fraserburgh Road. Tel: (0779) 71121. **St. Combs**. *Tufted Duck*, AB4 5YS. Tel: (03465) 2481.

Total distance 46m.—*12m* **Newburgh**.—*10m* **Cruden Bay**.—*6m* **Peterhead**.—*18m* **Fraserburgh**.

Aberdeen (see Rte 36) is left from Castle Street by King Street, the road soon crossing the Don into (*2m*) *Bridge of Don.*—*5m Balmedie Beach*, below sand dunes, offers a picnic area and other facilities. The junction with A975 is reached in another *3m*, this road being followed for *2m* to **Newburgh**, once an important port on the Ythan estuary.

Beyond the river bridge A975 runs with the NW boundary of the **Sands of Forvie Nature Reserve** (Warden Tel: 035887-330 or 352), an area of 1774 acres stretching with the shore for some 4m from the estuary of the Ythan to the village of Collieston. One of the largest and most untouched dunes systems in Britain, and embracing foreshore, dunes and estuary spit, with also some heath, rough pasture and even cliff, the reserve is not only of considerable botanical interest but is also known for flocks of wintering wildfowl as also for breeding eider and terns. But this tract was not always so desolate, and indeed was probably not swamped by the dunes until possibly the late 17C. The foundations of a Bronze Age village were excavated here in 1951; and the small, sad ruin of *Forvie Church* (close to the shore; 1m by path from E side of A975 bridge) is evidence of a medieval village, thought to have been swamped in a great gale of 1688 or, if a more colourful explanation is preferred, because of the curse pronounced by the three daughters of the local laird, smarting at being cheated of an inheritance.

Collieston, a village with its roots in fishing and smuggling, is 1½m SW of *Old Slains Castle*, given by Bruce to Sir Gilbert Hay (whose successors later became earls of Erroll) but now no more than a fragment, the result of being blown up by James VI in 1594 when the 9th Earl, together with the Earl of Huntly, unsuccessfully rebelled.

Ellon (4m NW of Newburgh by main road, or 5m W of Collieston by minor road. 6500 inhab. *ECl.* Wed. *Inf.* Market Street Car Park. Mid May–Sept), though today in large part a commuter town for Aberdeen, is a place of ancient origin, claiming in fact to have been a Pictish settlement before 400 BC. Later, Bruce's enemies, the (Comyn) earls of Buchan, ruled here, dispensing Norman justice from a site now marked by a monument beside the car park in Market Street. Today the river is crossed by a modern bridge, beside its picturesque predecessor of 1793, itself successor to what was long an important ford protected by Ellon's castle, a fragment of which can be glimpsed on the terrace above the N bank.—Another neglected medieval tower, that of *Esslemont*, stands 2m W beside A920.

10m (from Newburgh) **Cruden Bay** which, in modern terms, is the landfall of the oil pipeline from the Forties Field, over 100m away below the North Sea, and the start of the pipe section which continues S to Grangemouth. *New Slains Castle*, an extensive ruin overlooking the bay, recalls an earlier importance, for this was the great castle built in c 1597 by the 9th Earl of Erroll when, having been pardoned by James VI for his rebellion, he returned from exile and chose this site rather than that of the destroyed old castle near Collieston.—The *Bullers of Buchan*, rather over *1m* N of Cruden Bay and reached from A975, is a breathtaking natural feature where a cliff-edge path balances along the rim of a sheer 200ft-deep rock chasm, probably once an immense cave of which the roof has collapsed. Although particularly awesome in rough weather when the waves pound in through the natural archway—or boil, or bull; the name is a corruption from Norman French—this corner of the coast is in fact at any time worth a visit for its savage cliffs and rocks alive with seabirds.

5m **Peterhead** (17,000 inhab. *ECl.* Wed), solidly build in pink granite from local quarries, is, after Aberdeen, the largest town in Scotland's North East.

History. Peterhead was founded in 1593 by George Keith, 5th Earl Marischal, and for over a century the town's growth depended on this family; until, in fact, 1716 when the 10th (and last) Earl and his brother, James Keith, were exiled for having permitted the secret landing here of the Old Pretender. In the early 19C Peterhead was a busy whaling port, this being followed by the boom in herring fishing.

The town is best known for its immense harbour-bay, rounded by A952 approaching from the S. The N arm uses the island-promontory of Keith Inch, while the southern is a long breakwater constructed between 1886 and 1912 by convicts from the prison near its base. In the town, in front of the *Town House* of 1788, stands a statue of James Keith, of interest as much for its subject as for its provenance. In exile, James Keith became a close adviser of Frederick the Great of Prussia as also a field marshal in his army, in which capacity he was killed in battle in 1758; then in 1868 William I of Prussia presented this statue, which had long stood in Berlin, to Peterhead. The *Arbuthnot Museum* (Mon.–Fri., 10.00 to 12.00. 14.00 to 17.00. Sat., 14.00 to 17.00. Tel: 0779-77778. Free), in St. Peter Street, tells the local story, with emphasis on whaling and fishing.

A diversion may be made to **Deer Abbey** (AM. April–Sept: Thurs.–Sat., 09.30 to 19.00. Sun., 14.00 to 19.00. Fee), 10m W of Peterhead along A950. Although there is not a great deal left to be seen, these ruins are pleasantly sited and have some features of modest interest.

History. A Celtic monastery was founded by St. Drostan in the 7C at Old Deer, a village just SE of today's Deer Abbey. Of this Celtic monastery there is now no structural trace, although it has been suggested that the parish church stands on its site. There is, though, a priceless scholastic trace—the famed 'Book of Deer', now in the University Library at Cambridge. This, perhaps the most precious literary relic of the Celtic Church, is a 9C Latin manuscript of parts of the New Testament, annotated in Gaelic in the 11 or 12C by the monks of Deer, these Gaelic marginal notes being the earliest example known of written Scottish Gaelic.

Deer Abbey as seen today was founded—presumably with some link, however tenuous, to its Celtic predecessor—by William Comyn, Earl of Buchan, for Cistercian monks from Kinloss. It survived the overthrow of the Comyns by Bruce and thrived until the late 16C, after which it was abandoned and plundered as a source of building material. The site was bought in 1809 by the Ferguson family, their Admiral Ferguson in 1854 destroying virtually all that was left of the church in order to build a mausoleum on its site. This was removed in 1930, but two gravestones remain and the mausoleum's portico now forms the site's entrance.

The chief remains are to the S, though these were partly 'restored' in 1809. The buildings here, beyond the cloisters, were the kitchen and parlour, above which would have been the refectory and dormitory. Beyond is the abbot's house, between which and the infirmary to its N can be traced the main drain, carrying away from the reredorter at the NW angle of the abbot's house and then turning towards the river. Architectural fragments are preserved, these including two sedilia arches, a curious piscina with a basin on either side, and a part of an altar with a cavity for relics.

Aden Country Park, an estate of 300 acres just E off A950, provides woodland walks and an interpretive leisure area with an audio-visual presentation and an exhibition of farm machinery.

Leaving Peterhead A952 crosses the river Ugie, in *2m* reaching, in the village of the same name, late 16C *Inverugie Castle*, the birthplace in 1696 of that Marshal James Keith whose statue stands in Peterhead. Abandoned when the Keith brothers were exiled in 1716, their castle is now a sorry ruin, well reflecting Thomas the Rhymer's prediction, 'Inverugie by the sea, Lordless shall thy landis be'.—*2m St. Fergus*, with a North Sea Gas terminal, fed from the Frigg and Brent fields.

4m Crimond, just before which a minor road NE is worth exploring for a mile or so to the remains of ancient *St. Mary's Chapel* (perhaps founded in the 10C but structurally more likely 13C) from where there is a view across the often desolate but nevertheless interesting expanse of *Loch of Strathbeg*; interesting because, though now fresh water and a bird sanctuary, this was until as recently as 1720 a bay of the sea, and, it would seem, a lively enough place with a castle, a port and even the royal burgh of Rattray. In 1720, though, a storm blocked the channel with sand, and, today, Rattray and its castle, a few yards beyond the chapel, survive only as traces and names on some maps.

In well under *2m* beyond Crimond A952 meets the junction with B9033. *Mormond Hill* (768ft), rising 4m to the W, bears on its slopes a white horse and a white stag, both formed by exposing the quartzite. The horse is attributed to a Fraser who wished to commemorate his charger, killed on a battlefield; the stag, attributed to the laird of nearby Cortes, was cut in 1870.—From this road junction A952 provides the fast approach to Fraserburgh, as also the opportunity to visit (about halfway, and 1m W along B9032) *Memsie Cairn*, a Bronze Age heap, impressive for its size but without a visible entry.

This Rte now starts a short eastward loop along B9033 into a countryside of flat fields, dunes and long, open beaches, in *3m* reaching the former fishing but now mixed and residential shore village of *St. Combs*. West of the village, desolate on the flats beside the road, rears the stark fragment of *Inverallochy Castle*, surviving from the 13C as a reminder of the once powerful Norman Comyns. Beyond, *Inverallochy* and *Cairnbulg*, quaint with their rows of low granite 19C cottages, are astonishing twin one-time fishing villages, intimate either side of a now canalised stream yet, as will readily be seen, intensely individual.—*Cairnbulg Castle* (no adm.), seen to the S of B9033, is built around a core which, like Inverallochy, was Comyn but which—and in later centuries much changed—has since 1375, though with a break, been Fraser.

5m (from St. Combs) **Fraserburgh** (12,500 inhab. *ECl.* Wed. *Inf.* Saltoun Square. Mid May–Sept), a somewhat austere place but important with its port, fishing and industry, was founded in 1546 by Sir Alexander Fraser, laird of Philorth (Cairnbulg Castle). Two buildings of modest historical and architectural interest merit note. One, on Kinnaird's Head, is what is left of *Kinnaird Castle*, built in 1574 by the grandson of the town's founder, later much altered, and its top floor removed in 1787 to make place for the lighthouse lantern. The other, below, is the strange so-called *Wine Tower*, its purpose never satisfactorily explained but probably a 16C watch tower.—For Fraserburgh westward to *Inverness*, see Rte 43.

43   Fraserburgh to Inverness

B9031 to Macduff. A98 or B9139 to Portsoy. A98 to Fochabers. A96
to Elgin, Forres and Nairn but with N or S loops between Elgin and
Forres. B9090, B9091 and B9006 to Cawdor, Culloden and
Inverness.—In the E, an undulating road, a little back from high,
grassy cliffs and linking some picturesque fishing townships and
villages, on and close to pleasant bays and beaches. West of Banff,
a busier road, flatter and farther inland, but with many side roads
to the coast. Views across Moray Firth up the northern coast and
towards the Highlands.

SOME HOTELS. **Banff**. *Banff Springs*, Golden Knowes Road. Tel:
(02612) 2881. *County*, 32 High Street. Tel: (02612) 5353. **Cullen**.
Seafield Arms, Seafield Street. Tel: (0542) 40791. *Bay View*,
Seafield Street. Tel: (0542) 40260. **Buckie**. *Cluny*, 2 High Street.
Tel: (0542) 32922. **Fochabers**. *Gordon Arms*, 89 High Street. Tel:
(0343) 820508. **Elgin**. *Eight Acres*, Morriston Road, Sheriffmill. Tel:
(0343) 3077. **Nairn**. *Golf View*, Seabank Road. Tel: (0667) 52301.
Clifton, Viewfield Street. Tel: (0667) 53119.

Total distance 90m.—*20m* **Macduff**.—*12m* **Cullen**.—*10m*
Fochabers.—*8m* **Elgin**.—*12m* (direct by A96) **Forres**.—*11m*
Nairn.—*12m* **Clava Cairns** and **Culloden**.—*5m* **Inverness**.

From **Fraserburgh** (see Rte 42) the main road westward is A98,
looping far inland and with little of interest. This Rte chooses the
coastal B9031 which, with some steep hills, is slow but scenic and a
lot more interesting.

4m **Rosehearty**, founded in 1684 by Lord Forbes of Pitsligo and
long a thriving port, is now essentially a dormitory for Fraserburgh.
The Forbes' stronghold was *Pitsligo Castle*, a short way S, dating
from the 15–16C and now a ruin, beyond being the old (1634) and
new (1890) *Churches of Pitsligo*, the former a ruin but the latter
showing a Forbes loft and some rich Jacobean panels transferred
from the earlier church. The name Lord Pitsligo's Cave, on the shore
1½m SW of Rosehearty, recalls the staunchly Jacobite last Lord
Pitsligo, who, having fought in both the '15 and '45, spent the next
and last 16 years of his life as a hunted fugitive, returning home only
for burial in the family vault.

4m **New Aberdour**, from where a road drops down towards
Aberdour Bay, passing first the ruined medieval church with, beyond,
St. Drostan's Well, said—and it is easy enough to accept in this lost
corner—to have been the place where St. Drostan landed before
moving inland to convert the locals and found the Celtic monastery
at Old Deer (see Rte 42). Just above the beach a small road running
E soon reaches Dundarg House, beside which can be seen the stump
of *Dundarg Castle*, in turn Iron Age fort and Comyn stronghold before
being razed by Bruce.—In *6m* B9123 leads quickly into **Gardenstown**,
a terraced cliffside village, still picturesque despite its modern council
house screen and overlooked by the ruined *St. John's Church* (view),
placed here in 1004 in gratitude for the defeat of a Norse raid and
continuing to serve as parish church until 1830.

6m **Macduff** (4000 inhab. *ECl*. Wed. *Inf*. at Banff), until 1783 a
fishing village called Doune, was created by the 2nd Earl of Fife who
gave the new Doune his family name. The fishing harbour is the key
to the town, over which a fine view can be enjoyed from the high
War Memorial Tower on the Hill of Doune behind. *Tarlair*, just E,

was a spa during the 19C, but the medicinal well no longer flows and has been replaced by a more modern and more popular facility in the form of an open-air swimming pool, superbly sited within the rocky bay.—For Macduff to *Aberdeen*, see Rte 41.

Across the Deveron, and climbing in steeply linked terraces above the SW shore of its bay, **Banff** (3500 inhab. *ECl.* Wed. *Inf.* Collie Lodge of 1636) is a place of some style and character, reflecting, though, more of its 18–19C antecedence than that it was granted a charter by Malcolm IV in 1163 and further privileges by Bruce and Robert II. Of this ancient past there survives in fact only a fragment of the *Old Castle*—no more than a few walls and a ditch—once a royal residence and the birthplace in 1618 of the ill-starred Archbishop Sharp (the new castle, built on the same site by Lord Deskford in 1750, is now a municipal building). A similar contrast is provided by *St. Mary's Church*, with a pre-Reformation aisle remnant surviving in the old cemetery opposite the post office while its imposing successor (1790; steeple 1849) is one of a distinguished clutch of generally 19C buildings in the S part of the town.

Also to the S, beside the golf links, is *Duff House* (AM. Standard. Fee), designed by William Adam around 1725 for the 1st Earl of Fife and a notable example of Georgian Baroque. *Banff Museum* (June–Sept. Tel: 0779-77778. Free), in High Street, fills in on local history, while, for the children, there could be a short ride on the *West Buchan Railway*, a narrow gauge steam line (opened 1859) operating from the harbour (April, May, Sept: Sat., and Sun. June–Aug: Daily. Tel: 0779-812410).

7m **Portsoy** may be reached by either A98 or by B9139, the latter passing close to ruined *Boyne Castle* (1485), in the wooded glen of the Burn of the Boyne and long an Ogilvie stronghold. It was an Ogilvie Lord Boyne who in the early 18C developed Portsoy's harbour for the export of the famous local serpentine marble, with its subtle green and reddish colouring particularly popular in France where it was even incorporated into the Palace of Versailles. The stone is still to be found here along this incidental stretch of coast with its broken cliffs and rocky inlets, and souvenirs are offered at local workshops. From Portsoy the village of *Fordyce* is only 3m SW, a quaint spot clustered around a tower-house of 1592 and with a curious small church with a 17C belfry.

A98 runs below Sandend Bay, on the coast beyond the W end of which ruined *Findlater Castle* (path from Cullen) was once an Ogilvie and Gordon stronghold; a castle, too, whose Gordon governor of 1562 refused even to reply when Mary, Queen of Scots, requested entry.

5m **Cullen** (1500 inhab. *ECl.* Wed. *Inf.* 20 Seafield Street. June–Sept) is divided into an upper and a lower town by the long viaduct of the railway, closed since 1967 but surviving today as a monument as much to 19C engineering as to the power exercised by a laird of the time, the railway company having been forced to built this viaduct in 1886 when the Countess of Seafield refused to allow the line to cross the grounds of Cullen House, 1½m S. Today sections of the track serve as a pleasant coastal path, while *Cullen House* (built by the Ogilvies in about 1600 when they abandoned Findlater Castle but since much extended) has been converted into flats.

Beside the house's gates was the site of Old Cullen, established in about 1300 but in 1822–30 replaced (by the Earl of Seafield) by what is now the well planned upper town, still centred on its *Cross*

(1696, but with an older plaque of the Madonna) which the citizens brought with them. The *Auld Kirk*, though, survived unmolested. Essentially of the 14C, though incorporating 12C work, the church well merits a visit for the fine sacrament house in the N wall; for the imposing Seafield Loft of 1602; and for the huge Baroque tomb, with his armoured effigy beneath the canopy, of Alexander Ogilvy, who died in 1554, the year after he had made the church collegiate. This same Alexander Ogilvy can be met again in ruined *Deskford Church*, 4m S, where the finely carved sacrament house of 1551 bears a somewhat self-satisfied inscription recording that it was provided by him and his wife.

Descending to the lower town, A98 touches Cullen Bay, with its three distinctive red sandstone rocks known as the 'Three Kings of Cullen', to reach in *5m* **Buckie** (7500 inhab. *ECl.* Wed.), an important fishing port and, appropriately, home of the *Buckie Maritime Museum* (Mon.–Fri., 10.00 to 20.00. Sat., 10.00 to 12.00. Tel: 05422-32121. Free). Beyond, the road fringes *Speymouth Forest* (picnic area, walks) before reaching (*5m*) **Fochabers**, a regularly planned small town placed here in 1776 when transferred from its site close to *Gordon Castle* (no adm.) which, with old Fochabers' mercat cross by its entrance gates, is passed just beyond the town. Long belonging to the Gordons, and architecturally rarely left alone, the castle passed in 1836, on the death of the last Duke of Gordon, to the Duke of Richmond and Gordon.—For Fochabers to *Huntly* and *Aberdeen*, see Rte 40.

The river Spey is now crossed, offering roads descending either side. B9104, descending the E bank, in 4m reaches *Spey Bay*, where the *Tugnet Ice House Museum* (May–Sept: Daily, 10.00 to 16.00. Tel: 0343-45121. Free), set up in an ice house building of 1860, tells much about the Spey, with some emphasis on salmon and wildlife. The other bank is served by B9015 for *Garmouth* and *Kingston*, the former the place where Charles II landed in June 1650 after signing the Covenants. Kingston, at the estuary mouth, was so named in 1786 by two Yorkshiremen from Kingston-upon-Hull who came to buy timber from the Duke of Gordon and then stayed to establish a shipbuilding village; their yard closed in 1815, but wooden ships continued to be built here until 1890. The return to A98 may be made through the village of *Urquhart*, with a rough Stone Circle beside the road and once the site of a Benedictine priory founded by David I and in 1454 absorbed by Pluscarden (see below).

8m **Elgin** (16,500 inhab. *ECl.* Wed. *Inf.* 17 High Street), though most visited for its historic and still beautiful ruined cathedral, is a place with a past and a personality of its own even if much of what is to be seen along its pleasing long and broad High Street tends to be a replacement or token of that past.

History. Of ancient if shadowy origin, and first mentioned in 1190, Elgin was long a royal residence, and the occupation of its castle by Edward I in 1296 marked the northern limit of the English penetration. The 14 and 15C at least twice saw major destruction, in 1390 when a part of the town was burnt by the 'Wolf of Badenoch' (see also cathedral history) and in 1452 when the experience was repeated during the struggle between Huntly and Douglas. Attention in later centuries focused more on the cathedral, but the town as such was back in the news in 1746 when the Young Pretender spent 11 days here before Culloden.

The axis of the town is the High Street, long, broadening and aligned from W to E to end by the cathedral. *Lady Hill*, beside the W end and now with a lofty column commemorating the last Duke of Gordon (died 1836; see Gordon Castle above), was the site of the ancient castle, today only fragmentary traces but remembered also by its chapel of St. Mary from which this hill takes its name.

High Street still preserves a few of the old arcaded houses which once gave it elegant character, while a hotel off the S side occupies *Thunderton House*, the site (rather than the castle) of the royal residence, later the mansion of successive aristocratic families, and in 1746 the headquarters chosen by the Young Pretender. In the middle of the street stands *St. Giles Church* (a replacement of 1828), with on its W side a fountain marking the site of the tolbooth, and, at its E end, the *Muckle Cross*, originally erected in c 1650, destroyed in 1792 and rebuilt in 1888. The *Little Cross* (17C; restored), at the E end of High Street, marks the old boundary between the town and cathedral lands, while opposite is *Elgin Museum* (Mon.–Fri., 10.00 to 16.00. Sat., 10.00 to 12.00. Tel: 0343-3675. Fee), founded in 1842 by the Elgin Society and noted especially for its collection of fossils. To the S of Little Cross and entered from Abbey Street are the remains of a Franciscan friary, founded, though on another site, by Bishop John Innes in 1479 and now incorporated into a convent with the charming *Greyfriars Chapel*, well restored in 1896 by the 3rd Marquis of Bute.

Also worth a visit is *Old Mills* (July and Aug: Wed.–Sun., 10.30 to 17.30. Also at other times as advertised locally. Tel: 0343-45121. Fee), in Oldmills Road in the W part of the town, a restored 17C meal mill with roots in a royal charter of 1230 granting rights to the monks of Pluscarden.

**Elgin Cathedral (AM. Standard. Fee) was described by Bishop Barr in the 14C as 'the ornament of the district, the glory of the kingdom, and the admiration of foreigners'. Today, though long in ruins, Elgin's cathedral still merits similar praise.

History. The see of Moray was in existence before 1124, but for the following century the bishops' seat moved around between Birnie, Spynie and Kinneddar (for all of which, see below), settling only when this cathedral was founded in 1224. From then on, though, Elgin's story was to be punctuated by disasters. In 1270, probably before it was even completed, the structure was badly damaged by fire, and a century later, in 1390, the 'Wolf of Badenoch', having quarrelled with the bishop and been excommunicated, descended upon the town and cathedral with his 'wyld, wykked Helendmen'. The cathedral was then rebuilt with a central tower which, however, fell in 1506, was raised again in 1558, and collapsed once and for all in 1711. In 1555 the place was desecrated by what came to be called the 'Bloody Vespers', a murderous brawl between the Dunbar and Innes families, to be followed, only 12 years later in 1567, by (on the orders of the Privy Council) the removal of the lead from the roof in order to raise funds for paying the troops. In 1640 the beautiful rood screen, recorded as richly adorned and painted with biblical subjects, was torn down, and ten years later Cromwell's soldiery smashed the tracery of the W windows. The cathedral then gradually declined into ruin, despite the devoted attention early in the 19C of a poor shoemaker called John Shanks, whom the government appointed official Keeper in 1825.

The ruins now visited are those of a cathedral the length of which was c 260ft and the breadth across the transepts c 120ft. Two imposing W towers (before 1390) flank a handsome portal, deeply recessed with mouldings, now, like so much of the cathedral's carving, much defaced. The window above surmounts an interior arcade of four

bays. Of the *Nave* of six bays with double aisles about all that remains
are the stumps of some of the piers. The *Transepts* are known as the
Dunbar Aisle (N) and the Innes Aisle (S), the facade of the latter
including the oldest work in the cathedral, dating from 1224 and a
part which escaped, or at any rate survived, the attack by the 'Wolf
of Badenoch'; it is pierced by a doorway with toothed moulding
surmounted by a pointed oval, the round arch appearing in the upper
range of windows above the pointed.

The *Choir*, flanked by side chapels, has a graceful clerestory of
double and triple lancets of c 1270, while the raised chancel is lighted
from the E by two rows of five lancets, each framed in rectangular
mouldings, the whole surmounted by the perfect Omega window.
The S choir aisle, which has managed to keep its 15C vault, was
once a burial place of the Gordons. The tomb at the E end is that of
Bishop Winchester (died 1460); in the centre is the tomb of the
Gordon 1st Earl of Huntly (died 1470); and farther W there is an
armed effigy of Hay and Lochloy (died 1422).

On the N side of the central space will be found a cross-slab
(9–10C), carved on one side with a cross on the arms of which are
the symbols of four priests; on the other side are figures of a knight
carrying his hawk, a 'spectacle' symbol, a broken mace and a
half-moon.

Between the N aisle of the choir and the octagonal chapter house
is the small so-called *Lavatory* with a piscina which in the 18C played
its part in a remarkable story. In 1748, one Gilzean Anderson, the
half-crazed widow of a soldier, returned to her native Elgin and made
her home in this corner of the cathedral, using this piscina as a cradle
for her baby. The boy survived, enlisted in the Hon. East India
Company, rose to Lieutenant General and amassed a fortune, a part
of which he bequeathed to Elgin.

The interesting octagonal *Chapter House*, though originally of the
13C, is better preserved than most of the cathedral, partly because
it was well rebuilt after the 'Wolf of Badenoch's' raid and partly also
because it was used as a courthouse until 1731. The elegant central
pier and the groined roof are the features here.

Just NW of the cathedral stands the *Bishop's House*, dating from
1557 and bearing bishops' arms. Of the four gateways in the cathedral
precinct wall, the only survivor is the E gate, by the river and known
as *Pann's Port*.

For Elgin to *Dufftown* and *Aberdeen*, see Rte 39.

Leaving Elgin, A96 continues to provide the axis of this Rte. However,
as far as Forres (12m), this main road is of little interest, so northerly
(c 23m) and southerly (c 16m) loops are suggested as alternatives. Of
the two the northerly loop is by far the more incidental and varied,
though, to the S, little Birnie Church has deep prehistoric and Culdee
roots while, in sharp contrast, thriving Benedictine Pluscarden Abbey
is of both monastic and architectural importance. A generous network
of roads should allow a peripatetic course to be plotted to embrace
sites of individual choice.

Northerly Loop (Lossiemouth, Burghead, Kinloss)

A941, leading N out of Elgin, in rather over 1m passes (E) a turn to
the hamlet of *Spynie*, in the churchyard of which is buried Ramsay
MacDonald (died 1937; see below), just N being **Spynie Palace** (no

adm. but well seen from outside), the great ruined castellar palace of the bishops of Moray, serving as seat of the see until the consecration of Elgin in 1244 and thereafter as bishop's palace until 1686. Even in ruin the most splendid bishop's palace in Scotland, Spynie uncompromisingly illustrates that medieval bishops were—and indeed had to be—as feudal and military as their lay contemporaries. The early castle (14C) was a curtain-walled court, complete with angle towers and protected on the S and E by a moat, to which early in the 15C Bishop John Innes added his arms over the main entrance. But Spynie's most prominent feature is the massive David's Tower (c 1470–80), built by Bishop David Stewart—doubtless mindful of the murderous example set under similar circumstances by the 'Wolf of Badenoch' a century earlier—as defence against the Gordons, whose chief, the Earl of Huntly, he had rashly excommunicated. A century later, in 1562 and with the Gordons no quieter, Mary, Queen of Scots, stopped here during her combined royal progress and running campaign against that family.—A contrast is provided by *Kinneddar*, now little more than a churchyard beside B9135, 2m N, but also, before Elgin, a seat and castle of the see of Moray.

Lossiemouth (7000 inhab. *ECl.* Thurs. *Inf.* 17 High Street) is one with *Branderburgh*, the former representing the older town, founded as a port for Elgin after the Lossie silted up, the latter a 19C creation by the local laird, Colonel Brander, to meet the needs of the booming herring fishing industry. The sea is still the theme here, balanced now though by the air as represented by the adjacent RAF airfield. James Ramsay MacDonald, the first Labour prime minister, was born in 1866 at 1 Gregory Place (SE Lossiemouth), where the house, with a plaque, can be seen, though only from the outside. However, a reconstruction of his later study, complete with the original furnishings, is one of the features of the *Fishery and Community Museum* in Pitgaveny Street beside the harbour (March, April, Sept, Oct: Mon.–Sat., 14.00 to 17.00. June–Aug: Mon.–Fri., 10.00 to 13.00. 14.00 to 17.00. 18.30 to 20.30. Sat., 10.00 to 13.00. 14.00 to 17.00. Tel: 034381-3772. Fee).

B9040 fringes the N of the airfield and in 4 or so miles meets a turn S into the village of **Duffus**, for an ancient church and a spectacular castle. *St. Peter's Kirk*, a humble, lost little place just E of the present village, has roots and some stonework of at least 1226, the base of a 14C tower, the remains of a 16C porch, and, in the churchyard, the shaft of the 14C parish cross, this last reminding that this church stood at the heart of its village until planned 'new' Duffus arose in the early 19C. About *Duffus Castle, though, 1½m SE, there is certainly nothing humble. Although of no particular historical significance—the castle was a seat of the De Moravias, or Murrays, and in 1151 David I stayed here when founding Kinloss Abbey—this place is a theatrical complex rising out of the flat fields; a great circular ditch protects a large motte on which balance a battered tower and bailey wall, both of about 1300, the former split open, sliding, and dramatically illustrating the hazards of building massive stone keeps on earthen mottes never designed to support such. *Gordonstoun School* (no adm), 1m NE of Duffus village, educated the Duke of Edinburgh and the Prince of Wales.

Burghead, 4m W of Duffus, is a small fishing town laid out in the early 19C along a stubby headland that had already known successive

Iron Age and Norse forts. Today the attraction here is the intriguing *Burghead Well* (key from nearby house). Within the Iron Age defences, cut into the rock and fed by a spring, this is in fact something of an archaeological mystery in terms both of date and purpose, one of those sites which invite the visitor to speculate and reach what conclusion he will. Doubtless Iron Age defenders, and probably others before them, drank from this spring, the site later perhaps being converted to use as an early Christian baptistry, some evidence for this being the steps down into the water and, in the corners, a basin and a pedestal. Burghead also has its local *Museum*, at 16–18 Grant Street (Tues., 13.30 to 17.00. Thurs., 17.00 to 20.30. Sat., 10.00 to 12.00. Tel: 0309-73701. Free).

From Burghead B9089 in 7m reaches *Kinloss*, with, just S of the W part of the town, *Kinloss Abbey*, today a sorry, minor ruin, but once an important Cistercian foundation (1151) of David I who, lost in the forest, chose this site, then a clearing, after being guided to it by a white dove. After the Reformation the buildings served as a quarry, but there survive a round-headed archway, the vaulted E end of the church, and a part of the abbot's house. *Findhorn*, a fishing village and small resort 2m N at the narrow entrance to Findhorn Bay, is the third village of this name; its two predecessors, to the NW, were both swept away, the first in 1694 by storm-driven sand and the second by a flood in 1701.

Forres (see below) is reached in 3m, the road passing the famous Sueno's Stone (see under Forres).

Southerly Loop (Birnie and Pluscarden)

Birnie Church, 2½m S of Elgin on a minor road between A941 and B9010, secluded and modest though it is now, nevertheless represents a religious site, first pagan and then Christian, in use, if perhaps with breaks, from millenia ago until today. Several standing stones—one by the Minister's Gate, others incorporated in the churchyard wall—define a site of prehistoric ritual, followed in c 500 by a Celtic church dedicated to St. Brendan and followed again in 1140 by the present small Norman building, seat of the bishopric of Moray before Kinneddar, Spynie and Elgin and believed now to be Scotland's oldest parish church in unbroken use for worship. Architecturally an odd feature is that there is no E window, lighting coming through round-headed Norman windows; spiritually, the saying goes that to be thrice prayed for in Birnie Kirk will 'either mend ye or end ye'.

Pluscarden Abbey (Daily, 05.00 to 20.30. Tel: 034389-257. Donation), 5m SW of Birnie by minor roads, is a religious house on a far grander scale, ancient in origin but today occupied and being restored by Benedictine monks.

History. The abbey was founded in 1230 by Alexander II for the little known order of the Valliscaulians whose parent home in France was the priory of Val des Choux, the valley of the cabbages. Although damaged by Edward I in 1303, the abbey's worst experience came in 1390 when, as a dependency of the see of Moray, it was attacked and burnt by the 'Wolf of Badenoch', enraged at his excommunication by the bishop. In 1,454 Pluscarden absorbed the priory of Urquhart and became Benedictine, remaining such until suppression in 1560. There followed centuries of post-Reformation decay, with the abbey's buildings frequently serving as a quarry, until Pluscarden was bought by the Marquis of Bute. His son gave it to the Benedictines of Prinknash in England who since 1948 have followed a steady programme of restoration.

The main block of the abbey is made up of the E wing of the monastery, with the chancel, transepts and central tower of the church. Of the nave only foundations survive, but a part of the cloister has been restored. Inside the church, features of particular note are traces of murals (c 1500) showing St. John writing the Book of Revelations on Patmos; in the N transept, windows by Sadie McLellan (1960) portraying symbols showing the role of Mary in Christ's life; in the chancel (restored 1980) a 16C sacrament house from Flanders; and the Lady Chapel (opened on request), almost entirely of original masonry from the abbey's founding in 1230 but, by contrast, with modern windows made in the abbey workshops. The abbey's precinct wall, surrounding three sides, is, after that of St. Andrews, the longest in Scotland.

From Pluscarden, *Forres* (see immediately below) is reached in 8m by minor roads followed by B9010, passing close to *Blervie Castle*, a 16C tower, successor perhaps of the wooden castle in which Malcolm I may have been murdered in 954.

12m (from Elgin by A96) **Forres** (8500 inhab. *ECl.* Wed. *Inf.* Falconer Museum, Tolbooth Street. Easter and Mid May–Sept) is a pleasant small town, its name inseparable from Shakespeare's 'Macbeth' but otherwise far removed from its usually violent royal connection going back to the 10C and the shadowy kings of Scotia.

History. King Donald I was killed at Forres in c 900, and his son, Malcolm I, is said to have lived here, perhaps being murdered at Blervie Castle, 4m SE, in 954. Malcolm's son, Duff, was in turn slain by the governor of Forres in 967. In the early 11C Duncan I held his court here, and it was on their way to attend it that Macbeth and Banquo met on the 'blasted heath' (see below) the 'weird sisters', just three of the witches for which Forres was notorious. Whether Macbeth's subsequent murder of Duncan took place here, or at Cawdor, or, as placed by Shakespeare, at Inverness, will probably never be agreed. Forres continued to be a royal residence, but after the foundation of the powerful bishopric at Elgin in 1224 the castle's, and with it the town's, importance declined.

The castle has long disappeared, its site above the W end of High Street now marked by a memorial to a doctor hero of the Crimea, but something of the town's past can be experienced in the *Falconer Museum* (Easter. Mid May–Sept: Daily, 09.30 to 18.30. Other months: Mon.–Fri., 10.00 to 12.30. 13.30 to 16.00. Tel: 0309-73701. Free) in Tolbooth Street and named after Dr Hugh Falconer (1808–65), palaeontologist and botanist.

But it is *Sueno's Stone*, just NE of the town beside the Kinloss road, that provides the most exciting link with the local past, suggesting as it so vividly does that a great battle was fought here, though by whom against whom remains guesswork; that Sweyne of Denmark defeated Malcolm II in 1008 is one suggestion, but that this was the scene of a Norse defeat is also advanced. Whatever its story, here is a slim shaft, 23ft high, dated to the 9–11C, and bearing martial carving of mounted and foot soldiers, of headless bodies and bodiless heads (a number of skeletons were found here in 1813) and, particularly interestingly, of what may be a broch.

Forres lies beside some attractive and also unusual scenery provided by the river Findhorn, ascending S through its cuts towards Randolph's Leap and Ardclach Bell Tower (see Rte 38) and, close to Forres, entering the almost enclosed pocket of Findhorn Bay. This bay is flanked on the W by Culbin Forest, now covering a large area of dune formed largely by a storm of 1694. A panoramic impression of much of the district can be enjoyed from *Nelson's Tower*, erected in 1806 by admirers of the admiral on a hill at the SE of Forres.

For Forres to *Grantown-on-Spey* and *Aberdeen*, see Rte 38.

4m **Brodie Castle** (NTS. Easter. May–Sept: Mon.–Sat., 11.00 to 18.00. Sun., 14.00 to 18.00. Grounds open all year, daily, 09.30 to sunset. Fee) represents an unbroken family association since these lands were granted to the Brodies in 1160 by Malcolm IV. The early castle was burnt in 1645 during the Civil War, thereafter being largely rebuilt and extended in both the 17 and 19C. The interior shows an outstanding collection of paintings—embracing 17C Dutch, 18C English and French Impressionists and early English watercolours—and notable late 17C plasterwork (Dining Room and Blue Sitting Room), French furniture and porcelain of varied provenance. A woodland walk, wildlife hide, adventure playground, and a picnic area are all to be enjoyed in the park.—*Darnaway Estate Visitor Centre*, 1½m S of A96 roughly opposite Brodie Castle, offers an estate exhibition, woodland walks, picnic area and suchlike (June–Sept: Daily, 11.00 to 17.00. Tel: 03094-469. Fee).

Hardmuir, or, more popularly, *Macbeth's Hillock*, to the N of A96 about a mile after leaving Brodie Castle and now disappointingly cultivated and wooded, is supposed to be the 'blasted heath' on which Macbeth consulted the witches.—*4m* **Auldearn**, where 17C *Boath Doocot* (NTS. Donation) now stands on the motte which once supported the 12C royal castle of Eren. But, however peaceful the dovecot, the emphasis here is on battle, for here on 9 May 1645 Montrose raised his standard as a prelude to one of his most brilliant victories in which—and NTS provide an excellent plan and explanation—with 1500 foot and 200 horse he routed a force of Covenanters under General Urry.

3m **Nairn** (7500 inhab. *ECl.* Wed. *Inf.* 62 King Street. April–Sept), today essentially a family resort with long beaches backed by links, was long regarded as marking the boundary between the Lowlands and the Highlands, James VI remarking that the inhabitants of one end did not understand the language of the other. However it is now many years since Gaelic was spoken here, though the *Fishertown Museum*, in King Street, captures something of the past, with particular emphasis on herring fishing (May–Sept: Tues., Thurs., Sat., 14.30 to 16.30. Mon., Wed., Fri., 18.30 to 20.30. Tel: 0667-53331. Fee).—*Fort George* (AM. Standard. Fee), 8m W of Nairn and guarding the narrow neck of Moray Firth, ranks as the most outstanding example in Britain of Hanoverian military architecture; an irregular polygon with six bastions, the fort accommodated some 2500 men and today houses the regimental museum of the Queen's Own Highlanders (Seaforth and Camerons) (April–Sept: Mon.–Fri., 10.00 to 18.00. Sun., 14.00 to 18.00. Oct–March: Mon.–Fri., 10.00 to 16.00. Tel: 0667-62274. Fee).—For Nairn to *Grantown-on-Spey* and *Aberdeen*, see Rte 38.

At Nairn this Rte quits A96 to take a more southerly line along B9090 for Cawdor Castle, the prehistoric site of the Clava Cairns and the battlefield of Culloden.

5m **Cawdor Castle** (May–early Oct: Daily, 10.00 to 17.30. Tel: 06677-615. Fee) was promised to Macbeth by the witches and it just may have been here that he murdered Duncan. None of the present castle, however, dates from this remote period—the very early castle stood in any case about a mile NE—and what is seen today is the sturdy central tower of 1372 (fortified 1454) surrounded and softened by now mellow 16C buildings (remodelled in the 17C). Inside, seven or so centuries and 25 thanes, or at any rate the later years and later generations, have accumulated much 'of interest, whether 17C Flemish and English Mortlake tapestries; several portraits by artists such as Cotes, Romney, Lawrence and Reynolds; or curiosities ranging from the iron gate of Loch-in-Dorb Castle, through muskets captured from the French in 1797 when Lord Cawdor repulsed their farcical invasion of Wales (Fishguard), to some homely 18 and 19C domestic and kitchen equipment. Outside, gardens and several nature trails (booklet) ensure that the best of the beautifully wooded grounds is enjoyed.

Beyond Cawdor, and just after crossing the Nairn, B9090 is exchanged for B9091 which soon passes (2m from Cawdor) the entrance to *Kilravock Castle* (April–Sept: Wed. only. Tours at 14.00, 15.00 and 16.00, with, in July–Sept, an additional tour at 11.00. Tel: 06678-258. Fee), basically of the 15C and on lands which have been home of the chiefs of Clan Rose since the 13C. Here, on the eve of Culloden, the laird, although not a Jacobite, entertained the Young Pretender, while Cumberland, after celebrating his 25th birthday, slept in the laird's town house in Nairn.—*1m* Croy where B9091 merges to become B9006.

4m B9006 reaches a triangle of minor roads (enclosing the Cumberland Stone) just short of Culloden battlefield site (see below). *Clava Cairns (NTS and AM), with Camster's cairns on Rte 59 one of the two most exciting and archaeologically important cairn groups on Scotland's mainland, will be found less than a mile to the S across the river Nairn. Probably overlapping the Stone and Bronze ages (say 2000–1500 BC), here are three large burial mounds, each surrounded by standing stones, and also, at the NW of the site, a small stone circle on its own. Two of the cairns, those at the SW and NE, are passage-grave type, i.e. the burial chambers are approached by long narrow passages through the cairns. The central cairn is ring-type, and, though with no entrance, is unique in having unexplained stone pavements radiating from it. Many of the standing and other stones bear the mysterious ritual cup indentations and other markings, these best seen in some profusion on a kerb stone on the N side of the NE cairn. Within the small stone circle—modest compared to its neighbour cairns and possibly therefore representing a more modest burial—a depression suggests a grave, and one of the stones bears many cup markings.

*Culloden Battlefield (NTS. Site always open. Visitor Centre open April–May and Sept–mid Oct: Daily, 10.00 to 18.00 June–Aug: Daily, 09.30 to 20.00. Fee) lies either side of today's B9006 (there was no road here at the time of the battle), extending for about 1½m westward from the Cumberland Stone road triangle. Fought on 16 April 1746 between the Young Pretender and the Duke of Cumberland, Culloden, the last land battle of any significance to be fought in Britain, not only ended for ever any serious hopes that the Stuarts might regain the throne but also signalled the beginning of the end for a Highland way of life that had endured for centuries.

The Young Pretender's army, covering Inverness, consisted of some 5000

Highlanders, ill-armed, ill-fed and exhausted by an abortive attempt to surprise the enemy the night before. Against them the Duke of Cumberland advanced from Nairn at the head of 9000 men. The action began at 1 pm with an artillery duel, opened by the Jacobites but in which the Hanoverians quickly gained the upper hand, slaughtering the lines of Highlanders. The latter's only chance lay in the famed élan of a Highland charge, but for various reasons—the Young Pretender seems to have been willing to leave the initiative to Cumberland—the order came too late and, despite a fearless impetuosity which almost miraculously swept through the devastating grape-shot and even broke the Hanoverian first line, the attack faltered and the few survivors broke in retreat which quickly became a general Jacobite rout. Of the Hanoverian troops only 76 were killed, but 1200 Highlanders fell.

The carnage was enormously increased by Cumberland's brutal order to spare none of the wounded. For several days after the battle search parties massacred wounded clansmen who had dragged themselves into the neighbouring woods and farms, while Cumberland's cavalry even killed off spectators who had come out from Inverness. And when, after the capitulation of the town, the provost of Inverness ventured a protest against the inhumanity of the soldiery, it was only to be kicked down the stairs.

Now owned by the National Trust for Scotland and with its heart restored to something like its original topography, this site is something of a shrine, combining much of historical and military interest with a touch of Highland poignancy still insistent after two and a half centuries.

The natural boulder known as the *Cumberland Stone* is not, as sometimes supposed, the spot from which the Duke directed the battle—he was in fact well forward—though it is reasonable to accept that he was here beforehand, perhaps using this position as one from which to make his tactical plan. From here B9006 within 500 yards reaches the Hanoverian lines, near here being the NTS *Visitor Centre* which admirably explains the battle and its significance by means of a historical display and an audio-visual programme, backed up, for those in search of more detail, by a guide book and battle map folder. Here, too, a survivor of the battle, is *Old Leonach Cottage*, now given period furnishing.

The next 500 yards represent the heart of the site; initially the gap between the two armies but soon the field of battle. Here today, and within a clearing crossed by the road, are the *Well of the Dead*, a spring at which wounded Highlanders are said to have been killed while trying to drink, and the *Memorial Cairn* (1881) overlooking the scene of the fiercest of the fighting, while to either side of the road scattered stones mark the *Graves of the Clans*. Beyond, the road kinks to angle across the Jacobite lines, near here starting the Forestry Commission's *Culloden Battlefield Trail* past both sides' battle lines and various cairns. Beyond, again, beside the road, stands the *Irish Memorial* (1963), honouring the Irish who fought in the Jacobite cause.

From Culloden B9006 in *5m* reaches **Inverness**, see Rte 51.

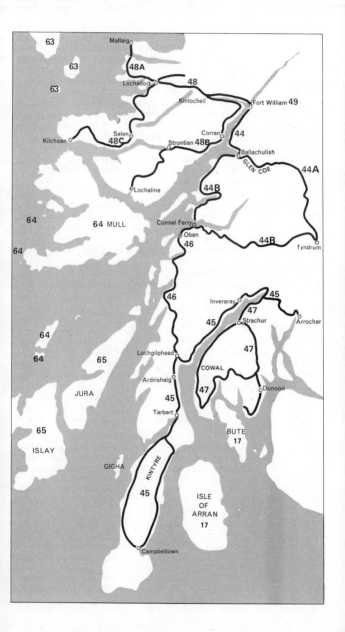

With minor variations the part of Scotland covered by Rtes 44 to 48 corresponds to the former county of Argyll (less its islands) which, under the local government reorganisation of 1975, officially lost its independent status and became absorbed into the Region of Strathclyde. The name has nevertheless been retained here, because for centuries this has been Argyll (the Coast of the Gaels) and because also, whatever new boundaries are drawn, the name will certainly live on.

Geographically Argyll comprises a mainland portion stretching from the head of Loch Long to Glen Coe and Fort William and, W of this, a coastline broken by sounds and long sea lochs into a fringe of peninsulas, large and small. The large peninsulas are the broad rectangle bounded by the sea, the Sound of Mull and Loch Linnhe; the long, thin finger of Oban and Kintyre; and, reaching into the Clyde, the many-pronged peninsula of Cowal. These peninsulas may be reached direct by road from their N; or alternatively from the S by car ferry. (Gourock to Dunoon; or via the islands of Bute or Arran to respectively Cowal and Kintyre.)

With scenery ranging from Highland and fretted coastal grandeur to forest and rich farming land; with a concentration of prehistoric sites unequalled elsewhere in Scotland, except perhaps in Orkney; historically the ancient cradle of Scotland, associated also with Columban Christianity; and having along its coast the embarkation ports for most of the Inner and Outer Hebrides, Argyll has long been a magnet for tourists.

The grandest scenery is in the N. Here, behind the lovely coasts of Moidart and Ardnamurchan, are the mountains of *Moidart*, *Sunart* and *Ardgour*, while across Loch Linnhe rises *Ben Nevis* (not actually in Argyll) with to its S the peaks that enclose *Glen Coe*. From here a wilderness of high mountain runs away S, across lonely Glen Etive towards the mass of *Ben Cruachan*, rising 3695ft above Loch Awe and with a power station built deep within its southern flank. The mountain mass ends with the heights of *Argyll Forest Park* filling the NE corner of Cowal, but even if, W and S from here, the mountain grandeur eases, Argyll still continues as a scenic country of hills, moor, woods and, above all, seascapes.

The historic interest of Argyll—and, however remote in time, the physical reminders are plentiful—is to be found mainly in the S; though two places of outstanding importance, Glen Coe and Glenfinnan, are in the N.

The extraordinary valley of burial cairns and ritual stones N of *Lochgilphead* evidences a sizeable and active population here in prehistoric times. In the early centuries of the Dark Ages Gaelic-speaking Celts (Scots), immigrants from Ireland, began to appear, people who by the end of the 5C had driven out or assimilated the native inhabitants and founded the small Kingdom of Dalriada, with its water and bog surrounded capital on the hill of *Dunadd*. With them these people are said to have brought from Ireland the sacred Stone of Destiny. By the mid 6C Christian missionaries were coming across, amongst them St Columba who by tradition landed at *Keil* at the foot of Kintyre, later moving on to establish himself on Iona. In 574 he is thought to have come to Dunadd and there officiated at the first Christian 'coronation', that of his kinsman Aidan. The Norse era followed, with raids and the establishment of coastal settlements which gradually became independent territories over which the Dalriadic kings lost power. (Kintyre remained under Norse influence until the 13C.) Meanwhile the capital of Dalriada is said to have moved (with the Stone of Destiny) to *Dunstaffnage*, N of Oban, and it could have been from here (c 850) that Kenneth Macalpine, partly by arms and partly by diplomacy, joined his kingdom to that of the central Picts and moved his court and the Stone of Destiny away from Argyll to Scone.

In Argyll there followed centuries during which the clans grew, spread and fought one another. During the early 12C a native ruler of Morvern, Somerled, a descendant of a branch of the Dalriadic royal house and married to the daughter of a Norse chief, rose to great power and through his three sons founded the various branches of Clan Macdonald. (It would be a Macdonald, John of Islay, who in 1386 would formally assume the title of Lord of the Isles, a lordship which claimed sway over plenty of mainland as well.) Later in the 12C Cailein Mor (Great Colin) of Loch Awe started the Campbell line, their chiefs later becoming earls, marquises and dukes of Argyll. These clans and others fought for power and land throughout Argyll, sometimes recognising, sometimes defying the Scottish kings. At the opening of the 14C Bruce was in Kintyre, occupying *Tarbert Castle*, but it was not until 1495 that royal authority was really asserted when James IV at *Mingary Castle* received the submission of the Macdonald Lord of the Isles. In the 17C Argyll had its share of the violence of the Civil War, and thereafter it was three times to achieve historical note. In 1685, after the Marquis of Argyll had tried to support Monmouth's rebellion, the Marquis of Atholl was ordered to punish the rebels, a task which the men of Atholl, eager to avenge Argyll's destruction of Atholl in 1653, discharged with brutal efficiency; secondly in 1692, with the infamous massacre of Glen Coe; and finally in 1745 when the Young Pretender raised his standard at Glenfinnan.

With its long, separated peninsulas Argyll is a scattered area for touring, but the route suggested below takes in most of what is best, both of history and scenery. The approach may be made either through Cowal or from Loch Lomond to *Inveraray*, long the headquarters of the Campbells (Argylls). South from here the unusual *Auchindrain Museum* is passed on the way to *Lochgilphead*, whence if time allows Kintyre may be toured. Otherwise the Oban road is taken, along or close to which are several important sites. These are the *Achnabreck Farm* cup and ring-marked rocks just outside Lochgilphead; *Castle Sween*, possibly the oldest stone castle in Scotland; *Dunadd*, Dalriada's first capital, where carvings possibly associated with early kingship ritual still survive; the concentration of prehistoric burial cairns and ritual stones between Dunadd and Kilmartin; and **Oban** itself, the principal town of Argyll and port for many excursions, notably to Mull and Iona. Just N is *Dunstaffnage Castle*, perhaps the site of Dalriada's second capital, then at *Connel* a diversion may be made c 14 miles E, to visit the 400 megawatt power station deep within the mountain of *Cruachan*. North from Connel the road leads to Loch Leven, down to which descends *Glen Coe*, as notorious for its massacre as it is renowned for its scenery.

A short way N of Loch Leven the *Corran* car ferry crosses Loch Linnhe to the western peninsula. Here there is a choice of roads: to *Lochaline* (car ferry to Mull); or W along Loch Sunart into *Ardnamurchan*, with *Mingary Castle* and, beyond, the lighthouse that stands on the most westerly point of mainland Britain; or, either N or through the centre, to the Fort William to Mallaig road, with *Glenfinnan* (monument and National Trust Visitor Centre) and other sites associated with the launching of the '45.

44   Tyndrum to Fort William

There is a choice of two beautiful Highland roads—A. Via Glen Coe
(46m) or B. Via Connel (68m)—the two joining at South Ballachulish,
on Loch Leven 13m short of Fort William. Both historically and
scenically the Glen Coe road is the better known, though in fact the
Connel alternative provides more varied and better loch scenery,
passes more places of interest and allows a short diversion to
Dunstaffnage Castle and Oban, both described under Rte 46. Separated by a wild mountain mass pierced by several long sea lochs,
the two roads offer no connecting links.

A. Via Glen Coe

A82.—High, bare moor and mountain, followed by a descent
through sombre and steep-sided Glen Coe and finishing at sea
level with views across the long narrow arm of Loch Linnhe to the
mountains of Ardgour.

SOME HOTELS. **Glen Coe**. *King's House*. Tel: (08556) 259.
Glencoe. Tel: (08552) 252. **Ballachulish**. *Ballachulish*, PA39 4JY.
Tel: (08552) 239. **Onich**. *Creag Dhu*, PH33 6RY. Tel: (08553) 238.
Onich, PH33 6RY. Tel: (08553) 214.

Total distance 46m.—*17m* **Glen Coe** (*White Corries—King's
House*).—*10m* **NTS Glen Coe Visitor Centre**.—*6m* **South
Ballachulish**.—*4m* **Corran Ferry**.—*9m* **Fort William**.

The **Railway** does not run through Glen Coe but leaves the road in
9m at Loch Tulla to traverse the desolate *Moor of Rannoch*—a
national nature reserve known for its variety of mire flora and
fauna—and reach lonely *Rannoch Station* (see Rte 27). Just N of the
station the watershed is crossed close to little *Loch Chlaidheimh*,
the name meaning 'sword' and deriving, it is said, from a meeting
between two chiefs who had agreed to parley unarmed. Both in
fact wore swords, so, having failed to outwit one another, they
hurled their weapons into the water. Just beyond *Courrour*, beside
Loch Sioliag, the line reaches its highest point (1354ft) before
descending along the E shore of *Loch Treig* so furrowed by burns
that the track requires some 150 bridges. For Hydro-Electric use of
Loch Treig, and the road from the N end of the loch to Fort
William, see Rte 50.

For **Tyndrum**, and the approach from Glasgow, see Rte 20. A82 leads
into increasingly lonely country, soon crossing the watershed at
1045ft and in *6m* reaching the hamlet of *Bridge of Orchy*, below (E)
Beinn Dorain (3524ft), the 'stormy mountain' of the poems of Duncan
Ban MacIntyre, the 'Burns of the Highlands', born beside nearby
Loch Tulla (see also Rte 44B). From here A8005 winds a brief 3m
NW before petering out as a hill track which, constructed for military
purposes in 1751, represents the old road and traverses the empty
tract of Black Mount before rejoining A82 in some 8m near White
Corries chairlift and King's House Hotel. Beyond Bridge of Orchy, in
3m, A82 touches the NE corner of Loch Tulla, a spot from which a
path leading NE in 1m reaches the ruin of *Achallader Castle*, a
stronghold originally of the Fletchers but later of the Glenlyon
Campbells, said here to have put the finishing touches to the plot for

the Glencoe massacre.

In *8m* a small crossroads is reached, the S arm of which (the old military road mentioned above) is the approach to *White Corries* ski centre, with tows and a chairlift, the latter riding to 2100ft and affording sweeping views (Chairlift. End May–early Sept: Daily, 10.00 to 17.00. In winter, normally weekends only and depending on snow conditions. Tel: 08556-226. Fee). The road opposite is for *King's House Hotel*, an inn once important as a military stage but now a grandly sited modernised hotel. Just beyond (1m) a small road descends SW down remote and scenic Glen Etive to pass rapids at Dalness and in 11m (from A82) reach Loch Etive (see also Rte 44B, Taynuilt).

King's House Hotel marks the upper entry to *Glen Coe, Scotland's most famous and most infamous glen, a great cleft of wild mountain grandeur down which, and surprisingly gently, the road descends for some 12m to sea level. With a name inescapably associated with the massacre of 1692, Glen Coe is equalled only by Culloden in its echoes of clan lament, but whereas Culloden stands for gallant sacrifice in honest battle, here the story is one of treachery and the murder of the harmless and defenceless. But however much the glen's savage and often dark slopes may be cited as reflecting that shameful February night, the prosaic fact is that in the main the massacre took place some ten miles below, where the glen is almost soft and green. Nevertheless the association is unavoidable, and since this valley surely witnessed both the approach of the Campbells and also the desperate flight of some of the Macdonald survivors, a summary of the story seems appropriate here.

The Highlanders had not willingly accepted William and Mary in place of James VII/II, and the London government fixed 31 December 1691 as the final date for submission. Macdonald of Glen Coe had delayed until the last moment, and when at length he went to Fort William he found no magistrate there competent to receive his oath and was forced to go to Inveraray, far to the S on Loch Fyne. When the papers arrived in Edinburgh, a few days late, they were suppressed by the Under Secretary of State, Sir John Dalrymple, Master of Stair, who was eager to use this opportunity of making an example and issued instructions which included the words 'To plunder their lands, or drive off their cattle, would be only to render them desperate; they must all be slaughtered, and the manner of execution must be sure, secret and effectual'. The task fell to Campbell of Glenlyon, who was instructed 'to fall upon the rebels and put all to the sword under seventy' and in particular to ensure that 'the old fox and his cubs do on no account escape your hands'.

Such were the orders received by Campbell of Glenlyon on 12 February 1692, by which date he and his 128 soldiers (feigning that they were on their way to Fort William where, however, their accommodation was not yet prepared) had already lived for two weeks on friendly terms with their Macdonald hosts. The massacre began at four the following morning, and of the 200 Macdonalds some 40 were slain, scant attention being paid to the age limit and the victims including the very aged, the bedridden and children. Others died from exposure, and even more would have perished had not storm and snow prevented Glenlyon's soldiers from blocking the passes as ordered.

Three years later, as the result of an official inquiry, the Scottish parliament voted that the killing had been murder. But King William's guilt was slurred over, and he, in his turn, sheltered the Master of Stair, who suffered only dismissal, while Glenlyon and his soldiers, by now serving in Flanders, escaped untouched.

If Glen Coe's infamy is perhaps largely for the historically sensitive, its scenery is for all, much of this (though not the site of the massacre)

now in the care of the National Trust for Scotland who own some
14,000 acres stretching from upper Glen Etive across the Coe to
include the great rock wall of Aonach Eagach. Outstanding walking
and climbing country rich in Highland flora and fauna, its detail,
together with the story of the massacre, is explained at the Trust's
Visitor Centre (see below).

Descending the glen from King's House the road in under *3m*
curves W below (N) the *Devil's Staircase*, a section of an old drover
and military road, now in disrepair, which climbs and crosses the
hills (1754ft) to reach Kinlochleven in 4m. Beyond, in another short
3m, comes *The Study* (studdie meaning anvil), a terrace above the
road and, at the head of the real pass, commanding perhaps the
finest view of the glen. To the N now hangs *Aonach Eagach*, while
opposite rise the *Three Sisters*, with, towards their W end and high
on the face of Aonach Dubh, a cleft known as *Ossian's Cave*,
traditionally if improbably the birthplace of the bard. *Loch Ach-
triochtan*, haunt of watersprites, is skirted to reach (*4m*) the *NTS
Visitor Centre* (April–May and Sept–mid Oct: Daily, 10.00 to 17.30.
June–Aug: Daily, 09.30 to 19.00. Fee). Just beyond, the road rounds
Signal Rock (across the river; footbridge), once a look-out and rallying
place of the Macdonalds, to enter the lower glen which, with (*3m*)
Glencoe village on sea Loch Leven, was the main scene of the
massacre. In the village the *Glencoe and North Lorne Folk Museum*
(Late May–Sept: Mon.–Sat., 10.00 to 17.30. Tel: Ballachulish Tourist
Information. Fee), housed in a restored croft, shows bygones, Jacobite
relics and some natural history material.

From Glencoe village the round of Loch Leven can be made,
which, though scenic, is slow and adds some 15m.

1m **Ballachulish** (1000 inhab. *ECl.* Wed. *Inf.* Tourist Office, with a
slate interpretive feature. May–Sept. Tel: 08052-296) was long known
for its slate quarries which flourished between 1693 to 1955. On the
island of St. Munda in the loch there are Macdonald graves.—*2m*
South Ballachulish, where Rte 44B joins from the S, combined Rte
44 here crossing the bridge spanning the narrow neck of Loch Leven.

From here northward the drive is more relaxed, for the most part
along a straight fast road beside the narrow inner arm of Loch Linnhe
with views across to the alternating valleys and high ground of
Ardgour (see Rte 48B).— *4m Corran Ferry* (Crossing 5 minutes. Daily,
frequent. Tel: 08555-243) provides a car ferry service to Ardgour and
a good road link across Morvern to Lochaline and the ferry to
Mull.—*9m* **Fort William**, see Rte 49.

B. Via Connel

A85 to Connel. A828 to South Ballachulish. A82 to Fort William.—
Highland and loch scenery, particularly fine at the Pass of Brander
where the road skirts Loch Awe below Ben Cruachan (3695ft).
From Connel northwards, sea lochs and islands.

SOME HOTELS. **Taynuilt**. *Polfearn*, PA35 1JQ. Tel: (08662) 251.
Connel. *Lochnell Arms*, North Connel. Tel: (063171) 408. *Ossian's*,
Bonawe Road. Tel: (063171) 322. *Falls of Lora*, Connel Ferry. Tel:
(063171) 483. **Port Appin**. *Airds*, PA38 4DF. Tel: (063173) 236.
Island of Lismore. *Isle of Lismore Guest House*, PA34 5UL. Tel:
(063176) 207. **Duror**. *Stewart*, Glen Duror. Tel: (063174) 268.

Total distance 68m.—*12m* **Dalmally.**—*6m* **Cruachan Power
Station.**—*5m* **Taynuilt.**—*6m* **Connel.**—*15m* **Port Appin
(Lismore).**—*11m* **South Ballachulish.**—*13m* **Fort William.**

For **Tyndrum**, and the approach from Glasgow, see Rte 20. A85 runs
with green Glen Lochy below (S) the heights of Ben Lui (3708ft) to
merge with Glen Orchy coming in from the NE and in *12m* reach
Dalmally. From here a short diversion SW along the old Inveraray
road in 1m reaches *Monument Hill*, providing a splendid view
towards Kilchurn Castle and across the islanded waters of northern
Loch Awe. The monument is to Duncan Ban MacIntyre (1724–1812),
the 'Burns of the Highlands', but more interesting perhaps, and
certainly more intriguing, is the flat stone beside it, seemingly of
unknown origin and bearing a neat incised cross.

Just beyond Dalmally A85 touches the NE arm of **Loch Awe**, a
huge long and narrow loch slicing some 23m SW, the southern and
main part of which is described under Rte 46. However,
Macnaughtons and Macarthurs may choose to divert 3m S along
A819 for a glimpse of two islands, *Innis Fraoch* with a ruined castle
of the former and *Innishail* with the remains of a 13C church and a
Macarthur burial ground. *Inistrynish*, beside A819 just SE of Innishail
and now no longer an island but a stubby promontory, has a name
(Isle of sculptors) inviting speculation, one suggestion being that this
was once perhaps the site of a colony of tomb carvers.

Ruined *Kilchurn Castle* (No adm., but well seen from outside),
occupying a spit jutting into Loch Awe's NE arm, is an oblong
structure with a square keep, the latter built in 1440 by Sir Colin
Campbell of Glenorchy, ancestor of the Breadalbane family. The
remainder represents addition of 1693 by Ian, Earl of Breadalbane,
whose arms, together with those of his wife, are over the gateway.
Until 1740 the castle was occupied by the family, but in 1746 it was
garrisoned by Hanoverian troops and in 1879 the top of one of the
towers fell in a gale.

A85 now hugs the NE and NW arms of Loch Awe to reach (*6m*
from Dalmally) **•Cruachan Power Station** (April–Oct: Daily, 09.00 to
17.00. Tel: 08662-673 or 031-2251361. Fee for underground tour.
Visitor Centre free), a 400 megawatt reversible pumped-storage
development which uses energy from thermal stations at times when
the load is low (night and weekends) to pump water from Loch Awe
to a reservoir filling a high corrie on Ben Cruachan (service road).
The water stored here is then used to generate electricity to meet
daytime peak loads, two inclined shafts supplying water to four
reversible pump/turbines in a power station deep within the mountain
and the water then being carried down to Loch Awe by a single
tailrace.

Opened by the Queen in 1965, Cruachan represents Scotland's
first large pumped-storage installation. For the visitor the attractions
are a picnic area beside the loch; a Visitor Centre with displays and
literature explaining the scheme; and a drive along the tunnel (about
¾m) to the power station in the heart of the mountain. This
last—whether for technical interest, or simply as an experience, or
even for botanical reasons for a special leaflet is provided describing
the plants growing here in totally artificial conditions—is very popular
and, since the number of visitors that can be accepted is limited, the
Electricity Board advise early arrival. The viewing gallery is reached

by a long flight of steps, which could prove difficult for the infirm or disabled.

Immediately beyond the power station, and still beside the water, A85 enters the **Pass of Brander**, scenically quickly narrowing as the loch becomes the river Awe, historically the scene of a battle (1308) between Bruce and Clan MacDougall of Lorne.

5m **Taynuilt**, now a pleasant village resort, was once Scotland's main iron-smelting centre, using charcoal from the oak and beech forests which in the 18 and 19C still covered this district. This period is well recalled by restored *Bonawe Iron Furnace* (AM. Standard, but closed in winter. Fee) which was opened in 1753 and operated until 1874. The furnace prided itself on the cannon and shot it provided for the navy, and the Nelson monument near the church was erected by the ironworkers in 1805 immediately after Trafalgar, even before, it is said, the admiral's remains had reached England. Here the river Awe flows into *Loch Etive*, curving here to run W to meet salt water at Connel or to pierce some 12m NE to the lonely reaches of Glen Etive which in turn ascends to the heights above Glen Coe. From the pier there is a good view up the loch on which there are twice-daily cruises (c 4 hours) between May and early Oct. Some cruises are combined with the mail service, which also runs (with passengers) three times a week in winter; calls may be made at Craig, Glen Noe, Inverliever, Dail and Lochetivehead (Tel: 08662-280).

Barguillean Gardens (April–Oct: Daily, daylight hours. Tel: 08662-254. Fee), 3m SW of Taynuilt on the Glen Lonan road, are pleasantly sited beside a loch.—A longer diversion (B845. 20m there and back) may be made southward up Glen Nant, the road almost at once entering forest, a survival of the ancient Forest of Lorne, with (3m from Taynuilt) the Glen Nant Forest Trail (interpretive panel. Trail 2½m). Beyond, the road reaches *Kilchrenan*, 3m E of which, are *Ardanaisaig Gardens* (April–Oct: Daily, 10.00 to dusk. Tel: 0631-63122. Fee) affording fine views across northern Loch Awe.

6m **Connel** which, though only a village, marks a water and road junction of some importance. Here a narrow channel links Loch Etive with the wide, islanded intersection of Loch Linnhe, the Firth of Lorne and, coming in from the W, the Sound of Mull, the resultant tides and currents forming, below Connel's bridge, the churning water known as the *Falls of Lora*. And here, too, Rte 46 joins from the S, Dunstaffnage Castle and Oban being respectively only 3 and 5m away.

This Rte now bears N on A828 to cross the bridge, just beyond which a minor road branches E for (4m) ruined *Ardchattan Priory* (always open), named after St. Cathan, a companion of St. Columba. A Valliscaulian house founded by the MacDougalls in 1231, this was later the site of a parliament convened by Bruce in 1308, notable for probably being the last at which Gaelic was officially spoken. *Ardchattan Gardens* (of the adjacent house) are open April–about Oct, daily. Tel: 063175-274. Fee).

Along the W side of **Benderloch**, a straggling village a short *3m* N of Connel, rises a small, rough ridge bearing traces of walls and vitrified fortification, insignificant and neglected now but nonetheless tempting with its tradition, however scorned by experts, that this was the Selma of Ossian's poems as also Beregonium, a name of somewhat dubious authenticity given by the 16C Scottish historian Boece to the ancient capital of the Fingalian kings.—*2m* **Barcaldine Sea Life**

Centre (April–Oct: Daily, 09.00 to 18.00 or 20.00 in July and Aug. Tel: 063172-386. Fee), perhaps the largest and most modern presentation in Britain of native marine life, includes a seal and tidal pools. *Barcaldine Castle* (written application only), 2m W, represents a restoration (1897–1911) of a tower-house built in 1579–1601 by Campbell of Glenorchy.

A828 rounds (5m) the head of Loch Creran, whence a minor road heads 3m NE for *Elleric*, starting point of a rugged forest walk (7m. 1500ft) across to Ballachulish, a challenge for the energetic able to arrange for the car to be driven to the other end.

Leaving Loch Creran the road runs with **Strath of Appin**, a name perhaps most associated (at any rate by readers of Stevenson's 'Kidnapped' and 'Catriona') with the 'Appin Murder' of 1752 when Colin Campbell of Glenure was shot by an unknown hand. Someone had to pay, so James Stewart ('James of the Glens') was accused, tried at Inveraray by a Campbell judge and a Campbell jury, and hanged near Ballachulish, presumably by a Campbell hangman (see also Keil, below).

At (5m) *Tynribbie*, a minor road bears W for **Port Appin** from where a ferry (no cars) crosses to the island of *Lismore* (Crossing 10 minutes. Roughly every 2 hours, but less frequent on Sun. Also by arrangement. Tel: 063173-217,. which number will also provide information on boats for viewing seals. Car ferry from Oban. Tel: 0631-62285). The island is perhaps more of ecclesiastical and scholastic than popular interest, having been the seat of the bishopric of Argyll (1200–1507), the bishops enjoying the title of 'Episcopi Lismorenses', and being also known for the 'Book of the Dean of Lismore', a manuscript collection of English and Gaelic poems, compiled in the 15C and of value to scholars for the light it throws on the works of Ossian. In more popular terms Lismore, the Great Garden, is some 10m long by 1m broad and served for most of its length by a road (B8045). Pleasant walking country, the island offers two ruined castles and a broch. *Coeffin Castle*, on the N coast in the N half of the island, dates from the 13C and was probably built by the MacDougalls of Lorne; *Tirefour Broch* is 1m SE by the other coast; *Achanduin Castle* (13C), by the N coast in the island's south, was that of the bishops.

1m Portnacruish, from where *Castle Stalker*, the restored 16C tower house built by the Stewarts of Appin, is well seen on its islet (By arrangement. Tel: 08832-2768, or 063173-234, Fee, including boat). The road now hugs Loch Linnhe to reach in 5m the hamlet of *Keil*, burial place of James Stewart, falsely hanged for the 'Appin Murder', and then in another 5m **South Ballachulish** where Rte 44A is joined. For South Ballachulish to (13m) **Fort William**, see Rte 44A.

45 Arrochar to Lochgilphead and Kintyre Peninsula

A83 (with B8024) to Campbeltown, following the W coast of Kintyre. B842, B8001 and A83 from Campbeltown to Tarbert along the E Kintyre coast.–Initially splendid Highland scenery across Argyll Forest Park and as far as Loch Fyne. Beyond, an always

scenic mixture of cultivated land, wood, hills and moorland, most of
the way beside wide sea lochs or open water with views across to
Cowal and the islands of (E) Arran and (W) Gigha, the latter
distantly backed by Islay and Jura.

SOME HOTELS. **Inveraray**. *Argyll Arms*. Tel: (0499) 2466. *Fern
Point*. Tel: (0499) 2170. **Lochgair**. *Lochgair*, PA31 8SA. Tel:
(054682) 233. **Lochgilphead**. *Stag*, Argyll Street. Tel: (0546) 2496.
Tarbert. *Bruce*, Harbour Street. Tel: (08802) 577. *Stonefield Castle*.
Tel: (08802) 207. **Isle of Gigha**. *Gigha*, PA41 7AD. Tel: (05835) 254.
Bellochantuy. *Putechan Lodge*, PA28 6QE. Tel: (05832) 266.
Campbeltown. *Ardshiel*, Kilkerran Road. Tel: (0586) 52133. *Royal*,
Main Street. Tel: (0586) 52017. **Southend**. *Keil*. Tel: (058683) 253.
Carradale. *Carradale*, PA28 6RY. Tel: (05833) 223.

Total distance 151m.—*7m* **'Rest-and-be-thankful'**.—*14m*
Inveraray.—*24m* **Lochgilphead**.—*4m* **Junction with B8024**.—*30m*
Tarbert.—*5m* **Kennacraig**.—*13m* **Tayinloan (Gigha)**.—*18m*
Campbeltown.—*9m* **Saddell Abbey**.—*17m* **Claonaig**.—*10m* **Tarbert**.

Arrochar (also on Rte 20)—at the head of Loch Long, a bare 2m from
ever popular Loch Lomond and sheltered below the piled heights of
Argyll Forest Park (see Rte 47)—is a lively holiday and touring centre.
A83, rounding the curve of the loch, soon starts to climb **Glen Croe**,
with, reached in *3m* from Arrochar, *Ardgartan Forest Office*, starting
point for some rugged and long forest walks. Ascending below Ben
Arthur (N. 2891ft)—also known as the Cobbler from the Gaelic
meaning forked peak—the modern road in *4m* smoothly breasts the
pass at *'Rest-and-be-thankful'*, a watershed at 860ft earning its name
from a stone so inscribed and recalling the repair of the road by the
army in the 18C. In fact the stone is beside the adjacent old, or
military road, and it was up this far steeper and more hazardous
ascent that—'doubling and doubling with laborious walk'—the poet
Wordsworth and his sister coaxed their horses in 1803.

From 'Rest-and-be-thankful' the road drops through the open
moorland of Glen Kinglas to reach in *4m* the junction with A815
marking the start of Rte 47 into the peninsula of Cowal. Just beyond,
Strone Gardens (April–Sept: Daily, 09.00 to dusk. Tel: 04996-284.
Fee) include a pinetum boasting the tallest tree in Britain, the 'Grand
Fir', c 188ft.

After rounding the head of Loch Fyne A83 changes direction SW,
heading deep into Campbell country with (*10m*) its 'capital' of
Inveraray (1000 inhab. *ECl*. Wed. *Inf*. April–Sept), a pleasant planned
18C town, approached over elegant contemporary bridges crossing
the Aray and Shira and best known for its prestigious castle.

The town originally clustered around its first castle, its fortunes
being those of the castle and its masters, the Campbells—earls,
marquises, and finally dukes of Argyll. When on his succession in
1743 the 3rd Duke decided to build a new castle, he at the same time
planned to move the whole village and thus much improve the
surrounds of his new home. A notable example of 18C town planning,
today's Inveraray dates therefore in concept from 1743, though the
plans were not finalised until the 1750s and it took close on another
100 years to complete town and castle as seen today.

At one end of the main street is the rather severe *Church* (Roger
Mylne, 1794), and at the other the 16C *Cross*, transferred from its
earlier site. A large gateway beside the *Argyll Arms* (John Adam,
1750) admits to an avenue which passes the Episcopalian Church,
known for its *Bell Tower* (Mon–Sat., 10.00 to 13.00. 14.00 to 17.00.

Sun., 15.00 to 18.00. Tel: 0499-2063. Fee for ascent), containing some of Scotland's finest bells, several named after saints and so inscribed.

*Inveraray Castle, a Gothic-revival fairy-tale towered and turreted palace, as tempting externally as it is rewarding within, is open April–June and Sept–mid Oct: Mon.–Sat. except Fri., 10.00 to 13.00. 14.00 to 18.00. Sun., 13.00 to 18.00. July and Aug: Mon.–Sat., 10.00 to 18.00. Sun., 13.00 to 18.00. Gardens open selected weekends. Tel: 0499-2203. Fee.

History (family and castle). Great Colin (Cailean Mor), founder of the fortunes of the powerful but politically not always astute Campbell family, was Sir Colin Campbell of Lochow (Loch Awe). He died in 1296, and all the later chiefs have taken the name MacCailean Mor. His son married the sister of Bruce and his descendants became earls in 1457 and dukes (of Argyll) in 1701. Archibald, 8th Earl (beheaded 1661), leader of the Covenanters, became marquis in 1641. His son, who unwisely supported Monmouth's rebellion, was likewise beheaded (1685). The 8th Duke (died 1900) was a distinguished author and Liberal statesman, and the 9th Duke (died 1914) married Princess Louise, daughter of Queen Victoria (painting by Sydney Hall in the castle's Victorian Room).

The castle, replacing one of the 15C of which some ruins survive, was begun for the 3rd Duke in c 1746 by Roger Morris, assisted by William Adam and possibly using a sketch by Vanbrugh. The splendid decorated interior was completed by Roger Mylne in 1772–82 for the 5th Duke. The top storey and the conical caps to the towers represent rebuilding after a fire in 1877. The castle was again swept by fire in 1975, the roof and the upper floor being destroyed, but restoration began immediately and was completed by 1978.

The castle is known for its magnificently decorated rooms and many treasures; the French-style decorative painting, with grisailles by Guinand and flowers and other work by Girard, can hardly be surpassed. The treasures include 18C Beauvais tapestry; oriental and European porcelain, including Japanese Imari ware (early 18C), Chinese blue and white, Meissen and Derby; fine displays of arms in decorative patterns; and 18C furniture. The distinguished collection of portraits includes works by, amongst many others, Kneller, Raeburn, Hoppner, Gainsborough, Batoni, Ramsay, Cotes, Winterhalter and Gavin Hamilton.

A new feature (1984) is the adjacent *Combined Operations*

Old Castle of Inveraray. Dating from the 15C but now a ruin, this predecessor of today's splendid 18C castle was long the home of the Campbell chiefs.

Museum, recalling that Inveraray was the Second World War's first British Combined Operations training base; a base through which passed over a quarter of a million troops of many nations.

A walk through the castle grounds leads N for 1m to a 17C dovecot (*Carlunan*) and, over 1m beyond, the little *Falls of Aray*. A longer walk ascends the Shira to *Rob Roy's House*, a ruin where the outlaw is said to have lived for some time. From here *Ben Bhuidhe* (3156ft) may be ascended by following the ridge.

In less than *2m* A83 passes the *Argyll Wildlife Park* (April–Oct: Daily, 10.30 to 20.00. Tel: 0499-2264. Fee) where in a setting of woodland, pond and burn the visitor can meet over 100 species of wildfowl, owls, wallabies, feral goats and roe deer.—*4m* **Auchindrain Museum of Farming Life** (April, May, Sept: Daily except Sat., 11.00 to 16.00. June–Aug: Daily, 10.00 to 16.00. Tel: 04995-235. Fee) illustrates life on a typical joint-tenure or strip-system farm, common in the Highlands until the late 18C. Such places were more multiple-tenancy villages than farms, paying a communal rent, in the case of Auchindrain to the Duke of Argyll. The museum includes a display area, as also 18 and 19C crofts and farm buildings, complete with livestock and furnished with contemporary farm and domestic equipment.—*2m* **Furnace**, so called from a now long abandoned 18C iron smelting furnace, historically interesting for having profited from charcoal resulting from Hanoverian government deforestation aimed at removing a ready shelter for Highlander rebels. Today the granite quarries are the important feature here.—*3m* **Crarae Gardens** (Daily, 08.00 to dusk. Tel: 05466-633. Fee) are known for rhododendrons, conifers, eucalyptus and flowering shrubs, all within the setting of a glen.—*6m Lochgair*, with a hotel, is a village pleasantly sited beside an inlet of the same name.

7m **Lochgilphead** (2500 inhab. *ECl.* Tues. *Inf.* April–Sept), an unpretentious local and holiday lochside centre, has a wide main street originally designed to serve as a market and a church containing a window by Burne-Jones. For *Achnabreck Farm*, 1m N, with rocks bearing notable cup and ring markings, as also for Lochgilphead to Oban, see Rte 46.—*2m* **Ardrishaig** is at the start of the *Crinan Canal* which permits small boats to pass from Loch Fyne across the isthmus to the W coast at Crinan. Surveyed by Watt and constructed to Rennie's plans between 1793–1801, the canal, now used mainly by pleasure craft, is interrupted by 15 locks over a distance of nine miles.

In *2m* the junction is reached with B8024. From this point the main A83 reaches Tarbert in 9m, but, though pleasant enough with views across to Cowal, there is nothing of specific interest along this stretch. This Rte therefore chooses the westerly loop provided by B8024 (30m to Tarbert) around the peninsula of **Knapdale**, a much slower road, but more interesting and affording views towards Jura and Islay. For anybody with a feel for very early Christianity, St. Columba's Cave will be incentive enough to opt for this road.

5m Achahoish, from where a small road (for Ellary) rounds the head of Loch Caolisport and in 3m reaches **St. Columba's Cave**, archaeologically proven (in the 19C) to have been occupied as long ago as the Middle Stone Age (c 8000 BC), traditionally associated with St. Columba's arrival in Scotland (6C) and certainly used for Christian ceremony at about that time. There is not, of course, a lot to be seen, and some imagination and sensitivity help here, but there is a rock-shelf with an altar, and, above, carved crosses, while a large basin, perhaps a Stone Age mortar, may have been used as a font. That this place was occupied until at least medieval times is indicated by traces of houses and the ruin of a (? 13C) chapel in front of the cave. Alongside there is a second, smaller cave in which, should the light be just right, it is possible to make out a faint cross on the rear wall.

Running with the shore of Loch Caolisport B8024 in *10m* (from Achahoish) reaches the *Kilberry Stones* (AM; signed, W of B8024), a group of medieval gravestones collected over the last century from various parts of the Kilberry estate. There is also a large boulder reputedly once used for trials of strength.—*3m Carse*, where, on the right just beyond the river bridge, are three standing stones.—Beyond, B8024 completes its loop by turning N to run beside West Loch Tarbert and in *11m* rejoin A83 just N of Tarbert.

1m **Tarbert** (1500 inhab. *ECl.* Wed. *Inf.* April–Sept) is a sheltered small town at the head of the short East Loch Tarbert which is picturesquely overlooked by a ruined castle, built by Bruce in 1325, later rebuilt and known to have been a residence of Robert II and James IV. Today mainly a fishing and yachting centre, Tarbert marks the N tip of the long, narrow peninsula of **Kintyre**, reached by crossing the 'tarbert', the little isthmus, 1m long, which separates East from the far longer and more important West Loch Tarbert. Today, in a car, the isthmus is barely noticed, a matter of two minutes. But it is perhaps worth recalling that this is a historic mile and that others had a more strenuous crossing. That wily Viking, King Magnus Barfud, for instance, who in 1198 negotiated a treaty giving him all the land he could sail around and then, taking the tiller of a galley and hoisting a sail, had himself hauled across so that he could claim Kintyre; or Bruce who dragged his ships across on his way to attack Castle Sween; and indeed, though with more peaceful intent, local fishermen who regularly portaged right up until the opening of the Crinan Canal in 1801.

5m **Kennacraig**, for the car ferry to Islay (see Rte 65), and the junction also with B8001 along which this Rte later returns northward completing the circuit of Kintyre. Affording fine views across West Loch Tarbert and of Knapdale beyond, A83 in *7m* kinks S of *Dunskeig* (reached by minor road from Clachan), a combined dun and hill fort nearly 500ft high and commanding the loch entrance, to descend to (*1m*) **Ronachan Bay**, sometimes called *Seal Bay*. The latter name is well deserved for the rocks offshore are favourites with seals—some of them Atlantic grey seals, Britain's largest wild animal; and, should the seals pall, then there is still the pleasure of fossicking for the dazzling white quartz lying among the profusion of sea pinks. A few yards farther S, and *Corriechrevie Cairn*, one of the largest in Kintyre, overlooks the road, while *1m* farther (not visible from the road, but reached by a short track) will be found the *Ballochroy Stones*, comprising three standing stones, a burial cist and, adjacent to the E, a boulder showing cup markings.

4m Tayinloan, for the car ferry to the island of **Gigha** (crossing 20 minutes. Roughly four crossings daily each way. Caledonian MacBrayne. Tel: 088073-253 or 0475-33755).

History. Standing stones and cairns prove prehistoric occupancy, but in more recent times, by at least the 15C, the owners were the McNeills, related to those in Knapdale. Aggressive action by the Macleans in 1530 decimated the Gigha McNeills and the island was sold to Macdonalds in 1554, who in turn sold it to

Sir John Campbell of Calder. Hector McNeill of Taynish repurchased the island in 1590 and it remained in the family until 1865. The cemetery bears frequent witness to the Gigha McNeills, probably the oldest branch of this clan.

Pronounced, roughly, 'gear'—the name derives from the Norse for God's Island—Gigha covers some six square miles and supports a permanent population of about 200. The principal visitor objective is *Achamore Gardens* (Daily, 09.00 to sunset. Tel: 05835-254. Fee), a large woodland area particularly noted for its rhododendrons and azaleas.

Keeping for the most part close to the shore, A83 skirts (9m) *Bellochantuy Bay*, with a hotel, before turning SE to reach (9m) **Campbeltown** on Kintyre's E coast (6600 inhab. *ECl.* Wed. *Inf.* The Pier). Market and shopping centre for a wide district, and tucked comfortably around the head of its bay, the town has a particularly inviting waterfront.

History. Whether or not, as is sometimes claimed, this place was antecedent to Dunadd (see Rte 46) can safely be left to the visitor's individual judgement. What is certain is that until the mid 17C the town was Kinlochkerran, a name recalling the Irish St. Kieran, contemporary of Columba and Aidan, both so closely associated with Dunadd. The 17C, though, saw the end of the long strife between the Campbells of Inveraray and the Macdonalds of Kintyre, the latter being defeated (finally at Dunaverty, see below) and their lands given to Archibald Campbell, 7th Earl of Argyll, who quickly substituted his own family name for that of the saint. *Castlehill Church*, above the town, was the rallying place in 1684 for the 9th Earl's rebellion in support of Monmouth. In 1774 Flora Macdonald, emigrating with her family to Carolina, set sail from Campbeltown.

Campbeltown Museum (Mon., Tues., Thurs., Fri., 10.00 to 13.00. 14.00 to 17.00. 18.00 to 20.00. Wed. and Sat., 10.00 to 13.00. 14.00 to 17.00. Tel: 0586-52366. Free), in the Library in Hall Street, ranges farther than its name implies and shows geological, archaeological and general cultural material relative to the whole of Kintyre. But perhaps the town's main focus of interest is the 15C *Campbeltown Cross* (facing the harbour), with highly elaborate ornamentation and an inscription to Edward McEachern and his son Andrew. Originally in Main Street, near the town hall, the cross was removed during the last war and later erected on its present site. Also worth a visit is *Davaar Island*, off the entrance to the bay; in fact an island only at high tide, and at other times linked by a shingle bank known as the Dhorlin. In summer there is a ferry service, the objective being a cave in which there is a painting of the Crucifixion, the work (1887) of Archibald Mackinnon, inspired by a dream. In 1934 the picture was retouched by the artist, then aged 80.

TO SOUTHEND AND MULL OF KINTYRE (S and W. c 20m). There is a choice of two roads to Southend on the S coast; the inland road (B842, 10m), or a more scenic, but hilly and winding coastal road (14m). The latter, known as the Learside (leewardside) road and affording views of Ailsa Craig, passes, first, the village suburb of Kilkerran, a reminder of Campbeltown's earlier name, and then the Dhorlin shingle spit across to Davaar.

Southend is a holiday village, immediately S of which is the promontory of *Dunaverty*, once an arrogant stronghold of the Macdonald Lords of the Isles but in 1647 the scene of the bloody close of the Kintyre Macdonald story. Catholic, and supporters of Montrose (who had sided with Charles I), the Macdonalds, some 300 in number, were hunted the length of the peninsula by the Covenanter general, Leslie, and here turned to make their last stand. But, deserted by their Irish allies who sailed away, without water, and led to believe that their lives would be spared, they surrendered. They should have known better, because only two years earlier, at Philiphaugh in the Lowlands, Leslie had shot over a hundred of his prisoners. And here he did the same thing, sparing only one lad.—The island of *Sanda*, 2½m SE, is said to have hidden Bruce in 1306 and is also traditionally associated with St. Ninian after whom a ruined chapel is named (boat in summer from Southend or Campbeltown. Tel: Campbeltown Tourist Information, 0586-52056).

Keil, just W of Southend, claims to be where St. Columba first landed in Scotland, the evidence being footprints in a flat rock at the top of a hillock just beyond a ruined medieval chapel said to be successor of one he founded here.

Beyond Keil Point a minor road across *Mull of Kintyre*, the name given to the peninsula's SW tip, in 6m drops very steeply to Mull lighthouse, built in 1788 and later remodelled by Robert Stevenson. From here Ireland is only 12m distant, the view extending along its N coast, off which lies the island of Rathlin, refuge of Bruce and the strongest claimant to have been the home of the spider from which he drew encouragement.

B842, taken N out of Campbeltown and with increasingly closer views of Arran, in *9m* reaches **Saddell Abbey**, today scanty ruins but once a rich Cistercian house founded in c 1164 by the redoubtable Somerled, said to be buried here. Although his grave is not identified there is an outstanding collection of carved graveslabs showing hounds, stags, galleys, warriors and their weapons and much else. To the N the central mountain is *Beinn an Tuirc* (1490ft), the highest peak in Kintyre. The name means Mountain of the Boar, and traditionally it was here that Diarmuid, a remote ancestor of the Campbells, slew a fierce boar, the origin of the boar's head which appears on the Campbell arms.—*4m Carradale*, a small resort on the approach to which there is a Forestry Commission office providing information on several local forest walks, starting from here or from Grainain picnic site, 3m N.

13m **Claonaig**, for a car ferry to Lochranza on Arran (see Rte 17). At *Skipness*, 2m NE, the large ruined 13C castle has a part contemporary curtain wall with later 13 and 16C extensions, the latter incorporating windows of the original chapel. Adjacent is the ruined (? 14C) church of St. Brendan with early Gothic doorways and windows.—From Claonaig B8001 and A83 reach **Tarbert** in *10m*.

46 Lochgilphead to Oban and Connel

A816 to Oban. A85 to Connel.—Undulating, open and pastoral with seaward and island views. Approaching Oban, some woodland and moor.

SOME HOTELS. **Kilmartin**. *Kilmartin*. Tel: (05465) 244. **Arduaine**. *Loch Melfort*, PA34 4XG. Tel: (08522) 233. **Oban**. *Caledonian*, Station Square. Tel: (0631) 63133. *Alexandra*, Corran Esplanade.

Tel: (0631) 62381. *Great Western*, Corran Esplanade. Tel: (0631)
63101.

Total distance 37m.—*2m* **Cairnbaan (Dunadd)**.—*3m* **Kilmartin**.—*2m*
Carnasserie Castle.—*18m* **Kilninver**.—*7m* **Oban**.—*5m* **Connel**.

For **Lochgilphead**, see Rte 45. A816 runs beside the Crinan Canal to
reach in *1m* *Achnabreck Farm*, where permission can be asked to
walk ½m to find one of the largest known and clearest complexes
of cup-and-ring markings. The markings are incised across two flat
rock faces, the first in a clearing in the wood beyond the top left
corner of the field, the other just beyond.

1m Cairnbaan, a hamlet where B841 and the Crinan Canal bear
W along the northern flank of **Knapdale Forest**, offering forest walks
and two longish scenic drives either side of remote Loch Sween.

KNAPDALE FOREST AND LOCH SWEEN. In 3m W of Cairnbaan, B8025
should be followed S to reach, in 1m at a road fork, *Knapdale Forest
Office* for information and a booklet on a choice of forest walks. The
following, though, are motor roads.

Forest Office to Keillmore (W side of Loch Sween; 10m). This
road passes close to a number of duns, notably a pair either side of
the roughly halfway village of *Tayvallich*. At *Keillmore*, at the road's
end, are a ruined 13C chapel, medieval gravestones and a carved
Celtic cross, perhaps of the 10C. It was along this road that the cattle
herds were driven, coming from Islay and Jura and landing at the
jetty here.

Forest Office to Kilmory Knap Chapel (E side of Loch Sween;
12m). The small and in part winding road in 9m reaches *Castle
Sween*, its keep dating from the 11 or 12C and probably the oldest
stone one on Scotland's mainland. The MacSweens, of Norse origin
(Sueno), were here first, but they lost their title in 1262 to the Earl of
Menteith. In an effort to regain their lands they sided with the English
around 1300–10, as a result losing everything in Scotland and being
forced to find their future in Ireland. In c 1308 Alexander Macdonald
installed himself here, only to be besieged and defeated by Bruce
who achieved surprise by hauling his ships across the isthmus at
Tarbert. Later, in about 1325, Bruce made the McNeills constables
of Sween, a position they held for over 200 years until a McNeill
heiress married a Macmillan, the latter then acquiring the Knapdale
lands and the title of constable. Finally, in 1647, the castle was
destroyed by the royalists. Despite the castle's age and story a
surprising amount survives, primarily, of course, the ancient keep
(unusual in being greater in area than in height), but also some 13C
extensions, the kitchen with oven and storage recesses, and, in the
round tower, what appears to be a large drain or rubbish shaft.

Kilmory Knap Chapel, 3m beyond and dating from the 13C, has
been roofed with glass and shelters a collection of Celtic and later
sculptured stones. Macmillan's Cross (15C), outside the chapel, shows
a hunting scene on one side and a crucifixion on the other.

Just beyond Cairnbaan A816 crosses the little river Add, ahead now
rising the bare and rocky hill of *Dunadd*, on several counts—as the
ancient Dalriadic capital, as a dramatic example of a fort of its period
(c 500–850), for its association, real or guessed, with Aidan, Columba
and original Christian and royal ritual—one of the most evocative
sites in Scotland. And the setting is in tune, too; a rough hump of a

hill set on the bleak Crinan Moss, drained now but otherwise little changed and still carrying the standing stones of an even more ancient people. As the hill is climbed traces of walls and buildings can be made out, but it is at the top that Dunadd has left its tantalising message—a carved boar, for instance, a footprint, a deep basin and even some Ogham writing—all surely playing their part in ancient royal ceremony, perhaps even the first Christian coronation in Britain, when, in 574, Columba officiated at that of Aidan. And tradition goes farther, suggesting that the throne used for this, and possibly earlier ceremonies, was the Stone of Destiny, later moved to Dunstaffnage, then Scone, and finally by Edward I to Westminster.

Dunadd stands on the southern edge of an astonishing concentration of ***Prehistoric Sites**; standing stones, burial cairns, cists, a stone circle, and several of those baffling cup-and-ring clusters, cut not only into cist slabs and standing stones but also covering seemingly random flat rocks. Most of the sites lie just below the W side of A816 between Dunadd and (*3m*) *Kilmartin*, sprinkled along a modest valley which over the later Stone and Bronze ages—millenia before Aidan and Columba performed their ceremonies on Dunadd's platform—must have been of deep and persistent ritual significance.

Most of the sites (all normally with open access) are well signed. First, 1½m N of Dunadd, comes a group of six standing stones, some of them cup-marked, together with *Dunchraigaig Cairn*, in its little wood. Bronze Age, and once 100ft in diameter, evidence has been excavated here of both cremated and uncremated burials. Just beyond, on the left in a field, are the *Baluachraig Rocks*, flat faces profusely carved with cup, ring and other markings. Just beyond again, a left turn should be made on to B8025, followed at once by a right turn along a minor road crossing the Kilmartin burn, this turn rounding a field with another good cluster of standing stones. *Ri-Cruin Cairn* will be found a few yards farther on the left. The next road to the right soon reaches the attractive small *Templewood Stone Circle* which seems to have been used in both the Stone and Bronze ages. Here a burial cist is surrounded by stones, at the base of one of which is an unusual spiral marking. *Nether Largie Cairn South*, across the road from Templewood, is interesting because it is possible to get into the shored-up chamber which has partitions. The cairn is believed to have been used for cremations by Stone Age people, then for uncremated burials by their Bronze Age successors.

A track now heads N for Nether Largie Mid and North cairns, both of the Bronze Age. The former is little more than a pile of stones and an exposed cist, but ***Nether Largie North**, part reconstructed, has been given a glass roof. On the end slab of the cist can be seen axe and other markings, while the capstone alongside bears axe heads and numerous cups.—The last cairn is *Glebe Cairn* (reached from the N end of Kilmartin), associated with two rings of small standing stones, all, however, now covered.

In *Kilmartin* the church gateway forms a pleasing and original style of war memorial, while in the churchyard will be found a 9C cross and also a considerable collection of carved crosses and slabs, mostly medieval. A ruined 16C tower in the N of the village was once that of the rectors, but **Carnasserie Castle**, *2m* N beside A816, is far more rewarding. It was built in the 16C by John Carswell, the first Protestant Bishop of the Isles, a scholar whose translation of Knox's liturgy into Gaelic (1567) was perhaps the first book ever published in that language, and has a number of features of modest architectural interest. Above the entrance, for instance, there are frames for inscribed panels, only one of which, however, survives; there are the string-courses running round the exterior; and traces of the courtyard survive, with, above the gateway, the initials (1681) of Sir Douglas Campbell and his wife, the then owners.

LOCH AWE. Opposite the castle B840 bears NE for (3m) **Loch Awe**, a huge loch cutting for a narrow 23m towards scenery of increasing grandeur and eventually discharging through the river Awe below the lofty mass of Cruachan (see Rte 44B, which describes the N end of the loch). Macarthurs, Macnaughtons, Macdonalds and, above all, Campbells were the principal clans along these shores, and the Campbell slogan 'It's a far cry to Loch Ow' was a defiant boast of the inaccessibility of their fastness. Today, though, roads run with both banks, that along the E being the better and rather more interesting. *Kilneuair Church* (13–16C), reached within the first half mile after the road touches the loch and 200 yards up a path, though now a neglected and overgrown ruin was until the 16C the chief church of this district, noted also for the markets held at its gate. Several late medieval tombs are to be found in the churchyard where there is also a curious little structure which may have been anything from an early penitential cell to an 18C minor folly, or, maybe, both. Less than a mile farther, ruined *Fincharn Castle*, once a Macdonald stronghold, stands on a rock ledge beside the water, but, beyond, the six miles of Eredine Forest must be crossed before the next point of interest, namely *Innis Sherrich Chapel*, dedicated in the 13C to St. Findoc and standing on an islet, perhaps once a crannog and reached still, and only at low water, by rather difficult stepping stones. Just N, and on another islet, ruined *Ardchonnel Castle* (15C) was a lair of the Campbells. Continuing NE, the road reaches Rte 44B in some 16m close to Dalmally.

Forest—first *Inverliever*, then *Inverinan*—is the key feature along Loch Awe's W shore. Within 1m (from Ford, where the lochside choice splits) a massive lone megalith stands in front of Torran Farm, but from here on, for at least the next 8m, the interest is forest walks, picnic sites and view points as far as *Dalavich* where the Forest Office should be visited for advice on the many walks which include the temptingly named Osprey and Otter view points. From just N of Dalavich a scenic small road offers a return route (some 10m) to A816 at Kilmelford by way of Loch Avich.

In *4m* (from Carnasserie Castle) A816 drops to the head of *Loch Craignish*, on the right on the descent being a large standing stone beside the remains of burial cairns.—*8m Kilmelford*, with the small road (see above, Loch Awe) to Loch Avich and Dalavich.—*6m Kilninver*, where B844 diverts to the islands of Seil, Easdale and Luing, all popular day excursions from Oban.

SEIL, EASDALE AND LUING. **Seil** is reached in 4m by way of the delightful, humpbacked *Clachan Bridge*, built in 1791 and popularly known as the Atlantic Bridge. On the island are *An Cala Gardens* (April–Sept: Mon. and Thurs., 14.00 to 18.00. Tel: 08523-237. Fee) with cherries, azaleas, roses and water and rock gardens.—**Easdale**, a tiny island just off the W tip of Seil (ferry, no cars. Crossing 5 minutes. Daily, more or less as required. Tel: 08523-338), boasts a

Folk Museum (April–Oct: Daily, 10.30 to 17.30 or 17.00 on Sun. Tel: 08523-382. Fee), illustrating local domestic and industrial (slate) life on these islands during the 19C.—**Luing**, to the S and the largest of the islands, is linked by car ferry from Seil across Cuan Sound (Crossing 5 minutes. Daily, frequent. Tel: 08523-252). Slate was long the principal industry here, and Luing slate was used to roof Iona cathedral, but farming is now the main activity. From Luing there are summer boat excursions to Mull (Lochbuie); Lunga; Jura and Scarba, with, between them, the whirlpool of Corrievreckan; and the Garvellach Islands, with beehive cells and other early monastic traces (L. MacLachlan, Jubilee Cottage, Isle of Luing. Tel: 08523-282).

4m **Cleigh**, where a minor road to the right leading direct to Connel enables Oban to be avoided. This road soon briefly fringes *Loch Nell*, touching the loch at a point where a crannog islet can be seen and passing, 300 yards farther on the left by a house, the so-called Serpent Mound, an earthwork some 300ft long and thought to be a relic of pagan worship.

Just beyond Cleigh a road (to Kilbride) bears W off A816 and in 1m reaches *Lerags Cross* of 1526; after long lying in three pieces beside the ruined church, it was repaired and erected on its present mound.

3m **Oban** (7000 inhab. *ECl.* Thurs. *Inf.* Argyll Square. Tel: 0631-63122), well situated on the shore and slopes of its bay ,which is protected by the island of Kerrera, combines much of the dignity of the 19C with the needs of modern tourism for which it is a dedicated, if in summer somewhat overtaxed centre. Ferries and cruises are what really count here, an industry born of the development of steam during the 19C and the consequent surge in tourism leading to today's emphasis on sea, road and combined excursions.

Ship services, cruises, excursions. Excursion possibilities from Oban can be bewildering in number, method and choice. Timetables and services are subject to annual alterations, but some of the main possibilities are outlined below.

Caledonian MacBrayne operate car and passenger ferries to Mull (Craignure), Barra (Castlebay) and South Uist (Lochboisdale); also to Mull (Tobermory), Coll, Tiree, Colonsay and Lismore. One of the oldest and most popular excursions is the steamer day cruise via the Sound of Mull and Staffa (close view; weather permitting) to Iona (again, weather permitting) with about an hour ashore. For all the above contact Caledonian MacBrayne Ltd, Ferry Terminal, Railway Pier. Tel: (0631) 62285.

Other local excursions include Duart Castle, Torosay Castle and Grasspoint, all on Mull; Loch Etive; Kerrera; and coach tours to, for instance, Cruachan power station and the islands of Seil, Easdale and Luing. For all these contact Tourist Information or local travel firms.

The main street is George Street, flanking the *Harbour* where seals sometimes contend with ferries for the visitor's interest. Railway Quay forms one arm, North Pier the other, on the latter being *World in Miniature* (April–Oct: Daily. Tel: 0631-66300. Fee), showing around 50 displays of miniature furniture, dioramas, room settings and suchlike. On the hill above two curious, uncompleted buildings attract attention; the circular *McCaig's Tower* is a folly built in 1897 by a local banker anxious to combine easing unemployment with perpetuating his own name, while the other building, to the S and intended as a hydropathic establishment, was abandoned when funds ran out.

In the S part of the town two commercial concerns offer interesting

Dunollie Castle

OBAN

0 yards	300
0 metres	300

Columba Cathedral

Corran Halls
Folk Mus.

A85

CORRAN BRAE

CORRAN ESPLANADE

DUNOLLIE ROAD

BREADALBANE ST

GEORGE STREET

DALRIACH ROAD

ARDCONNEL ROAD

LAUREL ROAD

DUNUARAGAN ROAD

McCaig's Tower

BENVOULIN TERR

NORTH PIER

Harbour

ARGYLL ST

LOCH SIDE ROAD

RAILWAY QUAY

Station

ARGYLL SQ.

ruins (Hydro)

BRIDGE STREET

ALBANY STREET

HIGH STREET

COMBIE ST

GLENSHELLACH TERR

GLEN-BUITEN ROAD

Market

LOCH AVULLIN ROAD

GLENSHELLACH ROAD

GALLANACH ROAD

MILLER ROAD

Oban Glasworks

SOROBA ROAD

MacDonald's
Tweeds

A85

visits. *Oban Glassworks* (Mon.–Fri., 09.00 to 17.00. Also Sat. in summer—shop only—09.00 to 12.00. Tel: 0631-63386. Free), on Lochavullin Industrial Estate and a part of Caithness Glass, enables the crafts of glass-making to be seen. And *MacDonald's Tweeds Ltd*, in Soraba Road, provide an exhibition as also demonstrations of spinning and weaving (April–Oct: Mon.–Sat. Tel: 0631-63081. Free).

To the N, Corran Esplanade skirts the bay, lined by hotels and with also *Corran Halls* which house the small local folk museum (Daily, except Tues. and Sun. Tel: 0631-64211. Free). Beyond come the Catholic *St. Columba Cathedral* (1922, Sir Giles Scott), and the War Memorial, beside which is the *Dog Stone* to which Fingal used to secure his dog Bran. Farther on, on a bluff, stand the ruins of *Dunollie Castle*, once a 12 or 13C stronghold but now reduced to a keep and fragments.

Dunollie has long belonged to the MacDougalls, Lords of Lorne, and their descendant preserves the Brooch of Lorne (see Rte 20) in nearby Dunollie House (no adm). Originally kept at Gylen on Kerrera (see below), the brooch was taken at the burning of Gylen Castle in 1645 and for nearly 200 years hidden in the Campbell house of Braglenbeg in Glen Euchar, 8m SE of Oban. It was returned to the MacDougalls in 1826.

Kerrera, the island protecting Oban's harbour, is reached by frequent ferry (no cars) from Gallanach, 2m S of Oban. Alexander II died on Kerrera in 1249 during an expedition against the Norsemen in the Hebrides, and 14 years later Horseshoe Bay was used by Hakon's fleet on its way S to defeat at Largs. *Gylen Castle*, a MacDougall stronghold at the S end of the island, was destroyed by Cromwell's troops in 1645. The obelisk at the N end honours David Hutcheson, founder of the W coast steamer services.

Leaving Oban A85 in *2m* reaches *Dunbeg*, close to **Dunstaffnage Castle** (AM. Standard, but in winter closed Thurs. afternoon and Fri. Fee), guardian of the entrance to Loch Etive and also, it is said, of the Stone of Destiny, brought here from Dunadd. Thus Dunstaffnage would have been the site of the court of Kenneth Macalpine, first king of the combined Scots and Picts, at any rate until he moved, together with the stone, to Scone. Later the castle passed to the MacDougall lords of Lorne, and, later still, in 1746 when garrisoned by Hanoverian troops, Flora Macdonald was held here for some days.

Seeming almost to spring from the rock platform, the castle—an irregular four-sided ruin with three round towers—dates mainly from the 13C (400 or so years later than when the Stone of Destiny may have been here) and has a contrasting 17C tower-house above its entrance. Features are the walls, in places 66ft high and 10ft thick; the large well with its neat surround with four small turrets; and the ruined chapel which, with 13C lancets, is the burial place of the Campbells of Dunstaffnage, hereditary captains of the castle.

3m **Connel**, see Rte 44B.

47 Cowal

Cowal is the name given to the peninsula bounded on the W by Loch Fyne and on the E by the Firth of Clyde and Loch Long. Pierced from the S by several long, narrow sea lochs, the peninsula hangs like a claw above the island of Bute which, separated by the beautiful waters of the two Kyles of Bute, falls away to the S. Cowal enjoys varied scenery, ranging from the great peaks and forests of *Argyll Forest Park* in the NE to pastoral, forest and sea loch landscapes towards the S. The main town is *Dunoon*, a leading Clyde resort and the scene at the end of August of the Cowal Highland Gathering. It is only this SE corner that can be said to be really populated, though in summer the peninsula's small roads sometimes carry a good deal of touring traffic.

By road Cowal can be reached from A83 near Strone Gardens in the N (Rte 45), the approach chosen by this Rte, which then makes an anticlockwise circuit. Other approaches are the ferries across the Clyde from Gourock to Dunoon or the ferry from Bute.

From near Strone Gardens, A815 to Strachur. A886 and B8000 to Kames. A8003, A886, B836, A815 and A885 across to Dunoon. A885 and A815 back to Strachur.

SOME HOTELS. **Strachur**. *Creggan's Inn*, PA27 8BX. Tel: (036986) 279. **Tighnabruaich**. *Royal*. Tel: (0700) 811239. **Dunoon**. *Enmore*, Marine Parade. Tel: (0369) 2230. *Abbeyhill*, Dhailling Road. Tel: (0369) 2204. *Ardfillayne*, West Bay. Tel: (0369) 2267.

Total distance 75m.—*9m* **Strathur.**—*15m* **Otter Ferry.**—*4m* **Kilfinan.**—*6m* **Millhouse.**—*13m* **Auchenbreck.**—*12m* **Dunoon.**—*4m* **Ardbeg.**—*12m* **Strachur**.

Argyll Forest Park, spread across most of NE Cowal, was the first Forestry Commission Forest Park to be created in Britain (1935) and has since then grown from bare hillsides or infant plantations into one of Scotland's finest expanses of Highland forest. The park, not all of which is afforested, stretches from Strone Point, between Holy Loch and Loch Long, up the shores of Loch Eck and NE across Loch Goil to beyond Glen Croe. Official roads (as opposed to Forestry Commission no-cars roads) serving the park are, towards the S, A880 rounding Strone Point to run up Loch Long to Ardentinny, whence an unclassified road cuts NW across Larach Pass (533ft) to descend to meet A815 which traces the length of Loch Eck (for A815, see the latter part of this Rte); in the N, A83 from Arrochar up to 'Rest-and-be-thankful' (see Rte 45); and, in between and with B828 providing a link from 'Rest-and-be-thankful', B839. This last breaks away SE near the start of this Rte and follows Hell's Glen (719ft)—green, with steep sides and moorland, but scarcely meriting its name—before dropping sharply to *Lochgoilhead* to continue as an unclassified road to pass forest walks and reach (13m from Strone Gardens on Rte 45) *Carrick Castle*, a gaunt keep beside lower Loch Goil, dating mainly from the 15C though it is said to occupy the site of a Norse fort and to stand on 12C foundations. An Argyll stronghold, the castle was burned in 1685 by the men of Atholl.

The park provides a network of forest roads (for walkers only) as also many and varied forest walks. Information from Forest Offices at *Kilmun* on A880 beside Holy Loch (see below) and *Ardgartan* (see beginning of Rte 45).

Leaving A83 near *Strone Gardens* (see Rte 45) A815 in *2m* meets the junction with B839 (see above), a curiosity opposite the junction being white stones in the shape of a heart which mark the traditional wedding place of the Argyll tinkers. Just beyond, on the S side of

A815, is the stone cist of *Ardno Cairn*. Continuing beside Loch Fyne, opposite Inveraray over 1m wide, the road in 7m reaches the junction with A886 which is now followed, A815 representing the return journey. For *Strachur*, a short way along A815, see at the end of this Rte. In another 3m this Rte moves on to B8000 to stay with the coast, while A886 provides a cut across to the head of Loch Riddon, useful for those not wishing to make the complete circuit.

In 4m B8000 touches *Lachlan Bay*, on the right being the humble ruin of a Celtic chapel, standing within a typical large circular stone cashel or enclosure, while across the little river, and in stark contrast, rises ruined *Castle Lachlan*, guardian of this remote bay. A tower of the MacLachlans, in part 12C but mainly early 16C, the castle was razed after Culloden.

8m *Otter Ferry*, where a stop is worthwhile just S of the junction with the road leading E across to Glendaruel. From here, against the skyline to the SE, can be seen the Iron Age hill fort of *Barr Iola* with its tumbled walls, while connoisseurs of chambered cairns will divert 1m E along the Glendaruel road for *Carn Bàn*, the covering of which was removed during the 18C to reveal the stones of the main chamber, still well seen.—4m *Kilfinan*, where the church of 1754 may stand on a Celtic site and certainly does stand within an ancient burial ground, some of the early medieval stones from which have been collected together in the 17C Lamont vault against the exterior N wall of the church.

From (6m) *Millhouse*, where this Rte angles sharply E with B8000, an extended circuit can be made southward, rounding Tighnabruaich Forest to reach Ardlamont Point (Coast of the Lamonts, the clan of southern Cowal) and return beside the western of the Kyles of Bute passing Carry Point, a Forestry Commission picnic site with views of Bute and Arran.—1m *Kames* is a small resort beautifully sited opposite Bute, while Tighnabruaich, 1m farther N, is a similarly sited but larger resort and sailing centre. Beyond Tighnabruaich, and now on A8003, this Rte passes (2m) *Caladh Castle Forest Trail* (1½m with some steep sections) and, travelling high above the water and with frequent parking places, in 8m meets A886 at the head of Loch Riddon, accompanying this road S for 1m to the road junction at *Auchenbreck*. (Here A886 in 4m arrives at *Colintraive*, on the E Kyles of Bute and with a car ferry across to the island. Crossing 5 minutes. Daily, frequent. Tel: 07084-235. A grassy mound in the field near the ferry marks an ancient burial cairn.)

From Auchenbreck B836 loops around the head of Loch Striven, at this point, in front of the farm at *Balliemore*, being two standing stones. Loch Tarsan, soon passed on the N, is a power reservoir with dams in Glen Lean and Glen Tarsan.—7m *Clachaig*, with ruined mills at which gunpowder was made throughout the second half of the 19C.—In 2m B836 joins A815, within the angle being a mound, possibly artificial, on the top of which is a burial place of the Campbells of Ballochyle.

This Rte now heads S for Dunoon. For Holy Loch and A815 northward up Glen Eck, see below after the description of Dunoon.

1m *Sandbank*, where there is a choice of roads, either the direct A885 or the coastal A815. The latter kinks within *Lazaretto Point*, so called from the quarantine station which operated from here during the Napoleonic wars, a stone wall and turret still marking the limits of the station, and then passes *Hunter's Quay*, for the Western Ferries

car ferry to Gourock (Daily, frequent. Tel: 041-3329766). The slightly
more direct inland road runs close to *Adam's Grave*, massive burial
cairn slabs just W of the road on the slope between Ardnadam Farm
and the houses of Sandbank.

2m **Dunoon** (10,000 inhab. *ECl.* Wed. *Inf.* Pier Esplanade. Tel:
0369-3785) is a lively Clyde resort ranking as the 'capital' of Cowal.
The famous Cowal Highland Gathering takes over on the last Friday
and Saturday in August (Secretary, Cowal Highland Gathering, 2
Hanover Street, Dunoon PA23 7AV. Tel: 0369-3206).—Caledonian
MacBrayne car ferry to Gourock (Daily, frequent. Tel: 0475-33755).

History. The town's early history is that of the old castle, traces of which can
still be seen. Built in the 13C, on the site of an earlier stronghold, the castle
was taken in 1296 by Edward I, given by Bruce to the High Stewards,
surrendered to Edward Balliol, then retaken by Robert Stewart who in 1371
became King Robert II. Thus the castle became a royal possession. In 1471 the
Earl of Argyll and his heirs were made hereditary keepers by James III, the
picturesque condition being that they should pay a red rose, should such be
demanded. When the present Queen visited Dunoon in 1958, the Duke of
Argyll's representative, the Captain of Dunstaffnage, duly presented her with
a red rose.

But in the 17C events associated with the castle were anything but
picturesque. In 1646 the Marquis of Argyll, briefly master of Scotland, took the
opportunity to destroy the castle of his Lamont enemies at Toward, 6m to the
S, thereafter bringing some 200 prisoners to Dunoon where they were massacred
and thrown into mass graves. Forty years later, in 1685, the castle's story closed
when the men of Atholl burnt and razed it. Dunoon then relapsed into an
unimportant village until in the late 18C tourism began to grow.

The modern 'castle' (Castle House) was built in 1822 by James Ewing,
Provost of Glasgow, as a 'marine villa', and is now used for municipal
purposes. The remains of the real castle are on *Castle Hill*, above the
pier, at its foot being a statue (1896) of Burns's Highland Mary, born
on the site of the farm of Auchnamore behind the town. To the W of
Castle Hill is the old *Moot Hill*, where once justice was administered.
There had, though, been little justice for the Lamonts in 1646, and
when last century the road round Castle Hill was being built some
of the mass graves were unearthed; the victims of the massacre are
now remembered by a stone Celtic cross erected in 1906 by the Clan
Lamont Society.

To the S of Dunoon A815 skirts the coast to pass ruined Knockamillie Castle
and then, beyond Toward Point, *Toward Castle*, the 15C tower-house of the
Lamonts, destroyed by Argyll in 1646. Beyond, a road continues N beside Loch
Scriven to reach *Inverchaolain* (12m from Dunoon) with many ancient Lamont
graves.—Off Dunoon lie the *Gantock Rocks*, marked by a beacon built by Robert
Stevenson.

This Rte now returns N to reach (*4m* from Dunoon) *Ardbeg* at the
head of **Holy Loch**, traditionally owing its name to the wreck here
of a shipload of earth from the Holy Land destined for the foundations
of Glasgow cathedral. *Kilmun*, 1m S on A880, is worth a visit for both
church and forestry reasons. The church (1841) is by Thomas Burns,
but of the collegiate church founded here in 1441 by Sir Duncan
Campbell only the tower survives. In the vault lies the 8th Earl and
1st Marquis of Argyll, beheaded in 1661; and in the churchyard lies
Elizabeth Blackwell (1821–1910), the first woman to get her name
into the British Medical Register. At Kilmun, too, a Forestry Office

(with an arboretum) provides information on the many forest walks throughout Argyll Forest Park. The road which continues around Strone Point to reach Ardentinny and beyond has already been mentioned under Argyll Forest Park at the beginning of this Rte.

Heading N from Ardbeg, A815 almost at once passes **Younger Botanic Garden** (April–Oct: Daily, 10.00 to 18.00. Tel: 0369-6261. Fee), known for its collection of flowering trees and shrubs, its extensive plantings of many species of conifers, and, above all perhaps, for the spectacular Californian giant redwoods, planted between 1865–70 and providing the entrance avenue. *Glen Massan* (c 5m; dead-end road) ascends NW through scenic country to end on a desolate tract of high moor.

A815 now runs with the E shore of **Loch Eck**, a scenic gash of water, 6m long and only a few hundred yards wide, lined on the E by Loch Eck Forest and on the W by the heights of Benmore, lifting to well over 2000ft. At (*4m* from Ardbeg) *Coylet Inn*, high on the hillside opposite can be seen a deep cleft, long a refuge during times of clan strife and the place where, at the beginning of this century, papers were found relating to the Argyll rising of 1685.—*6m Glenbranter*, just N of the loch's end, was an estate once owned by Sir Harry Lauder, here still standing the memorial he set up to his son, killed during the 1914–18 war.—*2m Strachur*, approaching which the outline of an unusual rectangular motte can be made out in the angle between A815 and the track to a saw mill. In the village the church of 1787 is of interest on three counts; the circular enclosure suggests an early Celtic origin, the church walls incorporate carved stones which came from a chapel nearby, and a little watchman's hut provides a ghoulish reminder of the days of body-snatching.

Just beyond Strachur A815 merges with A886, to complete this circuit of Cowal.

48   Fort William to Mallaig (Also the districts of Ardgour, Kingairloch, Sunart, Morvern, Moidart and Ardnamurchan)

One of several claimants to the title of 'Road to the Isles', A830 runs W from Fort William, bearing N at the coast to reach Mallaig. To the S of this road extends a broken, roughly rectangular peninsula—some 25m broad and stretching 30m southward to the Sound of Mull—embracing the districts of Ardgour and Kingairloch in the E, bordering Loch Linnhe; Sunart in the centre; Moidart and Ardnamurchan in the W; and Morvern to the S. Broken almost into several islands by the long waters of lochs Shiel and Sunart, the whole area is splendidly scenic, country of Highland impact in the N, easing southward into varied mountain and moor, yet still impressive, particularly around the lochs and near the rocky coast with basalt cliffs and views towards the islands.

Rte 48A below describes Fort William to Mallaig; Rte 48B, Kinlocheil to Lochaline through Ardgour, Kingairloch and Morvern;

Rte 48C, Lochailort to Kilchoan through Moidart and Ardnamurchan.

A. Fort William to Mallaig

A830.—Highland grandeur, combining mountains, inland lochs, sea lochs and islands.

SOME HOTELS. **Glenfinnan**. *Glenfinnan House*, PH37 4LT. Tel: (039783) 235. *Stage House Inn*. Tel: (039783) 246. **Lochailort**. *Lochailort Inn*, PH38 4LZ. Tel: (06877) 208. **Arisaig**. *Arisaig House*, Beasdale. Tel: (06875) 622. *Arisaig*. Tel: (06875) 210. **Mallaig**. *Marine*, 10 Railway Road. Tel: (0687) 2217.

Total distance 41m.—*11m* **Kinlocheil**.—*5m* **Glenfinnan**.—*9m* **Lochailort**.—*9m* **Arisaig**.—*7m* **Mallaig**.

The **West Highland Railway** accompanies the road. After a long absence, steam trains now run, in principle on Wed., Thurs., and Sun. during the summer. Leaflet from any principal British Rail Scotland station. Supplement to normal fare. Tel: (0397) 3791.

Leaving **Fort William** (see Rte 49) A830 in *2m* crosses the *Caledonian Canal* (see Rte 51) immediately below Neptune's Staircase, a tight sequence of eight locks, built between 1805–22 and raising the canal by 64ft. There are more locks a short distance below, where the canal enters Loch Linnhe at Corpach, and, just beyond, along the road, stands an obelisk honouring John Cameron of Fassfern who fell at Quatre Bras in 1815, the major skirmish which preceded Waterloo. Continuing W, A830 soon fringes *Loch Eil*—a lovely sheet of water, 8m long, ¾m broad and forming a westward extension of Loch Linnhe—to reach (*6m*) *Fassfern* where the Young Pretender spent a night, four days after raising his standard at Glenfinnan.—*3m* Kinlocheil, just beyond which Rte 48B breaks away.

5m **Glenfinnan Monument and Visitor Centre** (NTS. April–June and Sept—mid Oct: Daily, 10.00 to 17.30. July and Aug: Daily, 09.30 to 19.00. Fee), at the head of Loch Shiel, mark where, on 19 Aug. 1745, the Young Pretender raised his standard, the signal for a venture which, despite victory at Prestonpans and an advance as far S as Derby, would end in April 1746 with disastrous defeat at Culloden.

On 22 June 1745, unknown to his father (the Old Pretender), and optimistically assuming French help, Prince Charles Edward sailed from France with only seven companions. He reached Loch nan Uamh, some 12m W of here, on 25 July, but initially failed to raise any Highland enthusiasm and was in fact criticised for arriving without French backing. However, having gained Macdonald support, and having also shamed the influential Donald Cameron of Lochiel into joining him, he ostentatiously sent his ship away on 4 Aug and fixed a rendezvous for 19 Aug at Glenfinnan. Meanwhile, while the clans were rallied, he waited at Kinlochmoidart (see Rte 48C).

The prince spent the night of 18 Aug with Macdonald of Glenaladale, halfway down Loch Shiel, and the next morning was rowed to the rendezvous. After a slow start men and promises began to pour in, and in the afternoon the standard was raised, the Old Pretender being formally proclaimed King James VIII and the prince his regent.

The *Glenfinnan Monument*, bearing a statue of a Highlander (by John Greenshields), was erected in 1815 by Macdonald of Glenaladale, descendant of that Macdonald whose support had meant so much in getting the venture started, while the NTS *Visitor Centre* vividly tells the subsequent story, large maps showing the progress of the campaign and tracing also the prince's confusing wanderings after Culloden. The Glenfinnan Gathering and Games are held here annually on the Saturday in August nearest to the anniversary.

Loch Shiel reaches over 20m SE to Acharacle (see Rte 48C), here at Glenfinnan, and for over half its length, a scenic sheet of water with rocky wooded sides below mountains approaching 3000ft in height.

Moving into increasingly grand scenery, road and railway split respectively N and S of Loch Eilt and in *9m* from Glenfinnan reach *Lochailort*, where Rte 48C heads S beside the loch of the same name. Next comes islanded *Loch nan Uamh*, beside which a cairn recalls that this otherwise quiet scoop out of the Sound of Arisaig saw both the start and finish of the '45, both the hopeful arrival and the defeated, dispirited departure of its leader. On the latter occasion he had an escort of two French frigates ('Mars' and 'Bellona') which, far too late, had brought money and arms for his cause (see also Rte 51, Loch Arkaig). A small English naval force, one of whose captains was later Earl Howe, engaged the French, but was too weak to hold them.

9m **Arisaig**, sheltered at the head of Loch nan Cealt, itself protected by a barrier of rocks and islets, is a small resort and yachting centre, best known perhaps, together with Mallaig, for Hebridean day cruises to such islands as Eigg, Muck, Rhum, Canna, Mull, Soay and Skye, as also Loch Hourn, Loch Duich, Loch Coruisk and Loch Nevis. Operators include Bruce Watt Cruises, Tel: (0687) 2233 or 2320; and Arisaig Marine Centre, Tel: (06875) 224.

Approaching (*5m*) *Morar* the road crosses a narrow isthmus with the sea on one side and, on the other, Loch Morar, remarkable for its great depth of over 1000ft. It was on the largest of the group of islands near the loch's W end that Lord Lovat was captured two months after Culloden; an intriguer, he had been playing both sides, but was now taken to London and beheaded.

2m **Mallaig** (1000 inhab. *EC1*. Wed. *Inf*. Station Buildings. Tel: 0687-2170. May–Sept), at the end of the road and the end of the railway, is, with Arisaig, important for its ferry and passenger services to Skye and other islands, as also for boat excursions into some of Scotland's most splendid sea loch scenery. Caledonian MacBrayne (Tel: 0687-2403) operate the ferry to Armadale on Skye (see Rte 62; cars only in summer); also services (no cars) to Rhum, Eigg, Muck and Canna (see Rte 63). For other operators, see Arisaig above.

B. Kinlocheil to Lochaline

A861 to Strontian. A884 to Lochaline.—Mountain and sea loch, with distant views across to the heights above Glen Coe.

SOME HOTELS. **Ardgour**. *Ardgour*, PH33 7AA. Tel: (08555) 225. **Strontian**. *Kilcamb Lodge*, PH36 4HY. Tel: (0967) 2257. *Loch Sunart*. Tel: (0967) 2471.

Total distance 53m.—*11m* **Camusnagaul**.—*10m* **Ardgour**.—*5m* **Inversanda**.—*8m* **Strontian**.—*19m* **Lochaline**.

From just W of **Kinlocheil** on Rte 48A, A861 skirts the southern length
of Loch Eil to round the NE point of Ardgour at (*11m*) *Camusnagaul*
with a passenger ferry to Fort William (Crossing 10 minutes. No cars.
Daily, except Sun., roughly every 2 hours. Tel: 0397-3701).—*10m*
Ardgour is on the W shore of the Corran Narrows, crossed by a car
ferry (Crossing 5 minutes. Daily, frequent. Tel: 08555-243), useful for
Glen Coe and other places along both parts of Rte 44.—*5m Inversanda*, where there is a choice between continuing down the coast
to turn inland at Loch a' Choire, or taking the main road W up Glen
Tarbert which, below Garbh Bheinn (N, 2903ft) and Creach Bheinn
(S, 2798ft), two of the higher Ardgour peaks, in *8m* reaches the
pleasant small centre of **Strontian** (pron. Stronteen). Here *Ariundle
Nature Reserve*, to the N, is known for its Atlantic mosses, liverworts
and lichens, while, to the N again, are the long disused lead mines
(care needed), opened in 1722 and in 1790 the source of the discovery
of Strontianite of which Strontium 90 is an isotope. The mines
provided much of the lead used in the bullets fired during the
Napoleonic wars, and were at one time worked by French prisoners.

From Strontian this Rte turns S on A884, while A861 continues W
beside Loch Sunart to reach (8m) *Salen* on Rte 48C.

A884 for a short distance fringes the S shore of Loch Sunart before
bearing S between the districts of Morvern (W) and Kingairloch (E)
to reach in *15m* the hamlet of *Claggan*, just beyond which, at the
head of Loch Aline, is ruined *Kinlochaline Castle*, the 15C square
turreted tower of the chiefs of Clan MacInnes. From here a track
down the E side of the loch leads to a promontory into the Sound of
Mull to which still clings the ruined sentinel keep and broken wall
of *Ardtornish Castle*, built in c 1340 and until the end of the 15C a
principal stronghold of the Lords of the Isles.—*4m* **Lochaline**, known
industrially for its silica quarries (no adm.) used in the manufacture
of high grade optical glass, and by tourists for the car ferry to Fishnish
on Mull (see Rte 64. Crossing 10 minutes. Daily, except Sun., roughly
hourly, but with some gaps. Caledonian MacBrayne, Tel: 0475-
33755).

The road W along the N shore of the Sound of Mull (dead-end
after 10m) passes *Fiunary*, once a home of the Macleods and the
name incorporated in his title by Lord Macleod, founder of the Iona
Community (1938). Beyond, in 2m by the shore, are the ruins of
Caisteal nan Con, another link in the chain of strongholds between
Dunollie (Oban) and Mingary on Ardnamurchan.

C. Lochailort to Kilchoan

A861 to Salen. B8007 to Kilchoan.—At first between the islanded
Sound of Arisaig and the heights of Moidart (nearly 3000ft). After a
flat patch at Acharacle, a scenic run beside Loch Sunart and into
the empty country of Ardnamurchan.

SOME HOTELS. **Glenluig**. *Glenluig Inn*, PH38 4NG. Tel: (06877)
219. **Acharacle**. *Loch Shiel Acharacle*, PH36 4JL. Tel: (096785) 224.
Glenborrodale. *Glenborrodale Castle*, PH36 4JP. Tel: (09724) 266.
Kilchoan. *Kilchoan*. Tel: (09723) 200.

Total distance 34m.—*10m* **Kinlochmoidart**.—*6m* **Acharacle**.—*2m*
Salen.—*6m* **Glenborrodale**.—*10m* **Kilchoan**.

Leaving **Lochailort**, on Rte 48A, A861 for nearly 10m runs through
the rocky coastal scenery of Moidart, below Ross Bheinn (2895ft) and
with panoramic views along the shore and across to Eigg and
Muck.—*10m Kinlochmoidart*, where Old Kinlochmoidart House, now
a ruin, was destroyed by Government troops in 1746 because this
was where the Young Pretender stayed while the clans were rallied
to Glenfinnan. Dalelia, 2m S of here on Loch Shiel, was where the
prince embarked to be rowed up the loch to overnight with his
staunch ally Macdonald of Glenaladale.—*5m Blain*, from where a
small road leads N for (2m) *Castle Tioram*, lone on an islet in Loch
Moidart but accessible at low tide. This was the 13–14C keep of John
of Moidart, but has also a later tower of c 1600. The ancient seat of
the Macdonalds of Clan Ranald, the castle was burnt by its chief in
1715 to prevent its falling into Campbell hands when he joined Mar's
uprising.

The scenery now surprisingly changes as (*1m*) **Acharacle** is
reached, a small centre lying in a patch of oddly open flat country at
the S foot of narrow and snaking Loch Shiel (see also Rte 48A).

2m Salen on Loch Sunart. From here A861 in 8m meets Rte 48B
at Strontian, but this Rte branches W to follow Rte 48B007 along the scenic
northern shore of the loch where seals may often be seen, especially
from a point just W of (*6m*) *Glenborrodale*. Beyond, the road takes a
large inland loop to round Beinn nan Losgann (1026ft) and in *10m*
reach **Kilchoan**, adjacent to which is ruined *Mingary Castle*, a 13C
stronghold of the McIans, a branch of the Macdonald Lords of the
Isles. Standing on a rock promontory and once the formidable
guardian of the entrances both to Loch Sunart and to the Sound of
Mull, Mingary long served the Lords of the Isles but eventually was
witness, too, to their downfall, for here in 1495 James IV received
their submission as also that of other island chiefs. Later, in 1625, the
castle was taken by the Campbells; in 1644—an eventful year—it
was seized on behalf of Montrose, besieged by Argyll, and then
relieved; and in 1745 it suffered the indignity of being garrisoned by
Hanoverian troops who even built a barrack within the walls.

Ardnamurchan Point, 5m NW of Kilchoan and with a lighthouse
of 1846, is the most westerly mainland point in Britain.

From Kilchoan–Mingary there is a ferry (no cars) to Tobermory on
Mull (Crossing 35 minutes. Daily except Sun. Caledonian MacBrayne,
Tel: 0688-2017).

VIII THE NORTH

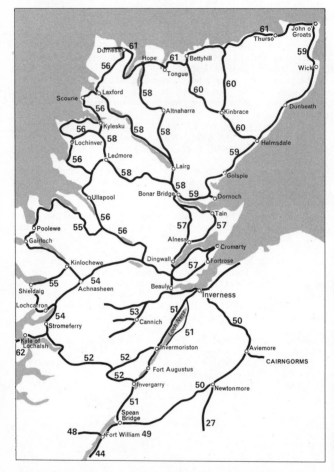

The North, as covered by this section, includes all the mainland beyond the two roads linking Mallaig to Fort William (see Rte 48 in the previous section), and Fort William by way of the Spey valley and the Cairngorms to Inverness (Rte 50). It divides naturally into three zones—the Northern Highlands, that vast empty spread of mountains, lochs, glens, and burns that to many people represents the true Scotland; Inverness and the well-populated and fertile strip to its north; and the Far North, a land of rolling barren moor and bleak peat bog.

THE NORTHERN HIGHLANDS. The visitor to the Northern Highlands, whether as fisherman, yachtsman, walker or motorist, comes in search of space and scenery and these he will find along virtually every road. Indeed over much of the Highlands, bar the occasional castle or broch remnant, there is little else, for until the years following Culloden this was for the most part an untamed land with an untamed people using only primitive communications through the mountains. Today good, though modest and unobtrusive roads, the railway, and local mail and excursion boats bring even remote corners within reach, and the problem for the tourist is now more one of choice than of inaccessibility.

Mention has been made of the remains of brochs, those curious and cunningly constructed defensive towers erected by people of perhaps the 1 and 2C. There are traces of some 500 of these throughout Scotland's North, including the islands, and the practised eye will soon readily pick out the distinctive stone-mounds that tell where a broch once stood. The mainland's two best preserved (the Glenelg brochs) can be seen in *Glen Beg*, not far from Kyle of Lochalsh on the W coast (Rte 52).

The brochs are the marks left by people of 2000 years ago. The inhabitants of more recent times have left none. Yet it is worth reflecting that the peaceful valleys and lower moors, today so empty of anything but sheep, were until the 19C the home of large crofting communities, those Highlanders who for centuries until Culloden had marched out of their mountains to fight for whatever cause their chief was supporting. These people disappeared during the Clearances, leaving virtually no trace of their long presence, though at *Croick Church* in Strath Carron (Rte 57) their names and messages scratched on the glass are a moving reminder of their forced departure.

The principal mountain districts are Ben Nevis, the Cairngorms, Glen Affric, Wester Ross, and Inverpolly.

Ben Nevis, above Fort William (Rte 49), is known more for being Britain's highest mountain (4406ft) than for its scenic merit. Being without a cone or peak, from the roads which run near it the mountain appears simply as a towering, rounded mass and hides the buttresses and corries that are a feature of the N side. Ben Nevis is a walker's and climber's mountain rather than a motorist's. For the latter, though, there is *Glen Nevis*, the wild valley which curves southward round the mountain's foot.

The **Cairngorms** (Rte 50), a mountain mass with six peaks over 4000ft, lie between the Spey valley and upper Deeside, the approach by car being from the former, from *Aviemore*. The magnificent Ski Road (the only road into these mountains) climbs for some 10 miles through *Glen More Forest Park* to end at car parks at 2000ft whence chairlifts take the visitor to within 500ft of the summit of *Cairngorm* (4084ft).—Near Aviemore there are several places worth a visit. These include the Highland Wildlife Park at *Kincraig*; the Landmark Visitor Centre at *Carrbridge*, vividly covering 10,000 years of Highland history; near *Loch Garten* a nature reserve with nesting ospreys; and between Aviemore and *Boat of Garten* the steam line of the Strathspey Railway Association.

The roadless *Monadhliath Mountains* stand between the Spey valley and Loch Ness and the Great Glen, the geological split which cuts clean across northern Scotland. West of Loch Ness is **Glen Affric**

(Rte 53), with its woods, lochs and mountain background one of Scotland's loveliest. A single road ascends the glen to end at *Loch Affric* at its head.

From the Great Glen a scenic road crosses the mountains to *Kyle of Lochalsh* on the W coast, which may also of course be reached by a choice of more northerly roads. North of Kyle of Lochalsh, behind and along the coast, **Wester Ross** (Rte 55) offers exciting mountain and coastal touring country which includes the famous *Torridon* and *Beinn Eighe* range where the pink sandstone is capped with quartzite. Wester Ross can be entered from the S, from Loch Carron, near which a diversion can be made to cross the Pass of *Bealach-nam-Bo* (2054ft), one of the highest roads in Scotland; from the centre, at Achnasheen, passing *Beinn Eighe* and *Loch Maree*; or from the N at the spectacular Corrieshalloch Gorge. A road skirts much of the length of the coast along which are the well-known sub-tropical *Inverewe Gardens* and also *Gairloch*, a popular holiday centre.

The most northerly mountain district is that made up of **Inverpolly Nature Reserve** and adjoining *Glencanisp* (Rte 56), together a confusion of high, isolated peaks, moor and lost lochs, as remote and wild as anywhere in Scotland. By car the best of Inverpolly can be seen from the narrow, winding road which rounds the reserve's S and W sides to reach the village of *Lochinver*.

INVERNESS AND THE COASTAL STRIP. **Inverness** is a crowded town, useful to the visitor if of only limited tourist interest. About 5 miles E are *Culloden* (site of the battle) and *Clava Cairns* (prehistoric site), both places well worth a visit (Rte 43).

North from Inverness there is a well populated fertile coastal strip, largely made up of two peninsulas, *Black Isle* and *Tain*, separated from one another by Cromarty Firth. *Loch Fleet*, N of Dornoch, marks the end of this strip for beyond here the high ground closes in. From the S end at Beauly and from the N at Bonar Bridge fan out all the principal roads across to the W and N coasts.

This strip has little in common with the Highlands that back it, nor is it of particular scenic attraction. Nevertheless it is not without places of interest. Among such are, from S to N, the ruins of 13C *Beauly Priory* and, on Black Isle, those of 14C *Fortrose Cathedral*, with, beyond, the quaint small town of *Cromarty*; above Evanton, the deep cleft of *Black Rock Ravine*; *Tain*, with its ancient church and chapel, and with a foot in history as the place whence in 1307 Bruce's wife and daughter were seized from sanctuary; and finally *Dornoch*, a quiet holiday centre with fine sands, a famous golf course and a cathedral dating from the 13C.

THE FAR NORTH. The Far North includes the former counties, now districts, of *Sutherland* (NW) and *Caithness* (NE), the principal towns being *Dornoch* in the S (see above), and, in the N, *Wick* and *Thurso*, the latter with the car ferry to Orkney. For many the lure of the Far North will be simply that it is Britain's barren and sparsely populated tip, with at one end *John O'Groats*, Pentland and Orkney views, and day excursions to the islands, and, at the other, promisingly named *Cape Wrath*. Yet there is more to the Far North than this. This was the home of some of Scotland's earliest inhabitants; a land in later centuries long under Norse occupation (Sutherland was the 'South Land' for the Norsemen of Caithness); and a place which during the last 150 years has seen events as contrasting as the evictions of the

Clearances and the construction of the nuclear power station at Dounreay.

Scenically Caithness and Sutherland are very different. Caithness, away from its E shore stacks and cliffs, is one third black peat bog and generally flat with fertile coastal strips. Sutherland, by contrast, apart from some wooded and cultivated valleys running in from the coasts, is a land of high, barren moor and bog, broken by numerous lochs and fringed to the W by commanding peaks. As to the coasts, the main road up the E is pleasant enough though not outstanding, while that along the N may prove disappointing because for much of its way it stays inland, giving only occasional views of the sea. Nevertheless the visitor who explores almost any of the many little roads down to the shore will find surprisingly rewarding lost corners with fine beaches and strange cliffs and rocks. Undoubtedly the most scenic road in the Far North is in the NW corner from *Kylesku* to *Durness* (Rte 56). This winds through a forbidding mountain wilderness of rock-strewn glens, glacial boulders and dark lochs, here and there touching a wild and broken coast with many islands. The village of *Scourie*, half-way, provides a break and, as along the other coasts, there are side roads to unexpected corners. One such is to *Tarbet*, with a close view across to the bird sanctuary island of *Handa* (ferry).

The Far North is rich in prehistoric monuments, many easily accessible yet in surroundings where the road, usually small, is the only modern touch. In the E for example, off A9 between Latheron and Wick, the *Grey Cairns of Camster*, with their horned-chamber complex, stand alone out on the peat bog, while not far away in equally unspoilt settings are the 200 or so little stones of the unexplained *Hill o'many Stanes* and the unusual megalith oval of *Achavanich*. Across in the W, beside *Loch Eriboll* (Rte 61), can be found an Earth-house about as intact and as hidden as when it was built in perhaps the 1C; this is just one of the many prehistoric remains in the district around *Durness*. Brochs abound in the Far North more than anywhere else on the mainland, but mostly only as mounds of stones. The best preserved is *Dornadilla* (S of Loch Hope, Rte 58), a small broch, part of the surviving wall of which may still be about its original height. Other recognisable brochs are the two N and S of *Brora* on the E coast.

The Norsemen have left little visible evidence of their years of settlement. Instead this period lives on in place names: 'Lybster' meaning farmstead; 'by', village; 'Wick', bay. Nor is there a great deal from medieval and later times. The principal sites are *Dornoch*, with its cathedral and part of its bishop's palace; a number of castle ruins either side of *Wick*; and some ancient churches between John O'Groats and Dounreay (*Canisbay*; *Dunnet*, with a perhaps 14C saddleback tower; the 12 or 13C St Peter's Church from *Thurso*; and the ruined 12C *Chapel of St Mary*, on the coast 5 miles W). In contrast, just beyond this last, there sprawls the *Dounreay* nuclear power station with its observation room and exhibition.

But the Far North does have its modern ruins, and everywhere the traveller will find abandoned buildings, roofless and crumbling. These do not, as might be thought, date from the Clearances (of that period virtually nothing remains), but are evidence of more recent depopulation throughout this remote region which has little to offer its youth.

49   Fort William and Environs

Tourist Information. Travel Centre, at N end of town. Tel: (0397) 3781.—4200 inhab. *ECl.* Wed., but not in summer.

SOME HOTELS. *Ladbroke Mercury*, Achintore Road. Tel: (0397) 3117. *Alexandra*, The Parade. Tel: (0397) 2241. *Nevis Bank*, Belford Road. Tel: (0397) 2595. *Clan Macduff*, 27 Achintore Road. Tel: (0397) 2341.

Ferry to *Camusnagaul* on Ardgour (Crossing 10 minutes. No cars. Daily, except Sun., roughly every 2 hours. Tel: 0397-3701.—For other loch cruising possibilities, ask Tourist Information).

History. Ignoring nearby Inverlochy Castle (see Rte 50), with a story reaching back to at least the 13C and even, though less probably, to the 10C, Fort William's relatively short history began in 1655 when General Monk built an earthwork fort here. This was replaced by stone during the reign of William III—the settlement being briefly known as Maryburgh in honour of his queen—the new fort achieving the distinction of successfully holding out against the Jacobites during both the '15 and the '45. During the later 19C the fort was pulled down to make way for the railway which, ironically, was to bring tourism, growth and prosperity to a place originally conceived, to quote Dr Johnson, with the purpose of subduing 'savage clans and raving barbarians'.

For Fort William to **Tyndrum**, see Rte 44; to **Mallaig** and the district to the S, see Rte 48; to **Inverness** via the Spey Valley and the Cairngorms, see Rte 50; to **Inverness** via the Great Glen and Loch Ness, see Rte 51.

Today Fort William is as focal for the southern Highlands as Inverness is for the northern. Amid splendid mountain and water scenery, and at the foot of Ben Nevis (Britain's highest mountain), the town is a rail, waterway and, above all, a road hub, a magnet for tourists yet on the whole spacious enough to absorb them.

Of the fort nothing survives, and the visitor in search of the local story should, instead, make for the *West Highland Museum*, in an 18C building in Cameron Square (June and Sept: Mon.–Sat., 09.30 to 17.30. July and Aug: Mon.–Sat., 09.30 to 21.00. Other months: Mon.–Sat., 10.00 to 13.00. 14.00 to 17.00. Tel: 0397-2169. Fee). History, natural history and local ways are the themes here, the scope embracing items as diverse as a crofter's kitchen, early farm implements, Montrose's helmet, a surveying level used by Telford, tartans and, of course, Jacobite relics.

From the tourist point of view Fort William is almost synonymous with Ben Nevis, well explained by means of an exhibition, video and model at the *Ben Nevis Centre*, with also a Scottish Craft Exhibition, in High Street (March– Oct: Daily in summer, otherwise Mon.–Sat., 09.00 to 17.30 but to 22.00 in high season. Tel: 0397-2504. Fee).

Ben Nevis (4406ft) is in fact little seen from the town, and what small part is visible appears as no more than a high, rounded hump. Although Britain's highest mountain, it lacks a definite peak and thus its height and great mass are not readily appreciated. The mountain's main features are the deep Glen Nevis (see below) on the S; the impressive buttresses and gullies on the N, best seen approaching Fort William from Spean Bridge; and the grand corrie on the NE at the head of which a narrow ridge connects the summit with the spur of Cairn More Dearg (4012ft).

The mountain is easily enough climbed by a choice of approaches, but there can be hazards and Tourist Information advice should be

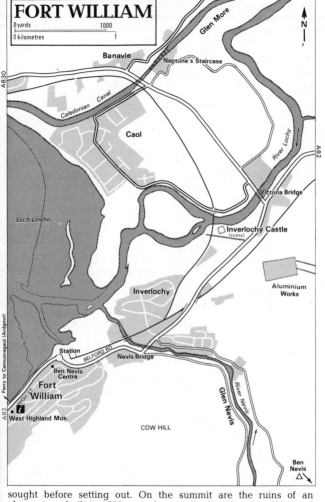

sought before setting out. On the summit are the ruins of an
observatory, built in 1823 to study sunspots but closed in 1904, and
the views, of course, can be immense, except to the NE where the
Cairngorms shorten the horizon. To the S, Loch Linnhe, the Glen
Coe mountains, Ben More on Mull, Ben Cruachan and the Paps of
Jura can be visible, and even, if exceptionally, the coast of Ireland.
To the SE stand Ben Lawers and Schiehallion; to the NE a glimpse
can be caught of Loch Laggan on the approach to the Spey valley.
The line of the Great Glen and its lochs can be traced, while, far to
the W, are the ragged peaks of the Cuillins (Skye), the hills of Rhum
and the Sgurr of Eigg.

  *Glen Nevis, comfortably ascended by car, hooks for a wild and rugged 6m below the western and southern flanks of the mountain. *Glen Nevis House* (no adm.), reached in 1½m, was the headquarters during the '45 of Donald Cameron of Lochiel while he unsuccessfully tried to take Fort William, and the *Old Graveyard*, passed in another mile, is the ancient burial ground of the Glen Nevis Camerons. Beyond, by the farm of *Achriabhach*, the road crosses the river, here tumbling as rapids down a small ravine, and soon ends at a car park, in a highly scenic setting beside a waterslide.—A walk of 1m, in places rough, leads through a gorge to a waterfall, beyond this continuing E over a pass (1320ft) to (another 10m) *Loch Treig* and *Courrour Station*, close to the highest point (1354ft) of the Glasgow to Fort William railway.

50   Fort William to Inverness via Spey Valley and the Cairngorms

A82 to Spean Bridge. A86 to Kingussie. B9152 to Aviemore. A95 and B9153 to Carrbridge. A9 (with diversion along B9154 at Loch Moy) to Inverness.—As far as Loch Laggan, often bleak moor below mountains rising to over 3000ft. Later, as far as Aviemore, down the broad and in part wooded Spey valley, with the Monadhliath Mountains to the N and the Grampians, including the Cairngorms, to the S. Beyond, mixed moor, wood and pastoral land.

SOME HOTELS. **Spean Bridge**. *Spean Bridge*, PH34 4ES. Tel: (039781) 250. **Newtonmore**. *Ard-Na-Coille*, Kingussie Road. Tel: (05403) 214. **Kingussie**. *Royal*, PH21 1HX. Tel: (05402) 236. **Aviemore**. *Post House*, Aviemore Centre. Tel: (0479) 810771. *Badenoch*, Aviemore Centre. Tel: (0479) 810261. *High Range Motel Complex*, PH22 1PT. Tel: (0479) 810636. **Boat of Garten**. *The Boat*, PH24 3BH. Tel: (047983) 258. **Carrbridge**. *Carrbridge*. Tel: (047984) 202. **Tomatin**. *Freeburn Inn*. Tel: (08082) 205.

Total distance 82m.—*9m* **Spean Bridge**.—*26m* **Laggan**.—*7m* **Newtonmore**.—*3m* **Kingussie**.—*6m* **Kincraig**.—*6m* **Aviemore**.—*6m* **Carrbridge**.—*19m* **Inverness**.

For **Fort William**, see Rte 49. For Fort William to *Spean Bridge* by B8004 along the Caledonian Canal, see Rte 51.

Leaving Fort William A82 crosses the Nevis and immediately enters **Inverlochy** with the long pier of the aluminium company, its factory, with its pipes running down the mountain, being to the E of the road. The waters of Loch Treig (E of Ben Nevis), raised 40ft and combined by means of a tunnel-pipe with those of lochs Moy and Laggan, are led by another tunnel beneath Ben Nevis to the aluminium works. *Inverlochy Castle*, on the left just before the junction with A830 (followed by Rte 51) and not to be confused with the 19C hotel of the same name 1m farther, is a large neglected ruin, probably of the late 13C. The impressive remains comprise a walled court with round corner towers, the largest serving as the keep, and two gates, one giving access to the water. A curious legend insists that this was the site of an ancient Pictish city, the king of which, Achaius, is said to have signed a treaty with Charlemagne in 790. More factually this was originally a Comyn stronghold and, later, the scene of three battles, in 1429, 1431 and, more importantly, in 1645 when the Covenanters under Argyll were defeated by Montrose—a

victory which misled Charles I into breaking off negotiations with
parliament, this soon leading to his final defeat.

9m (from Fort William) **Spean Bridge**, where this Rte switches to
A86 while Rte 51 follows A82 from the nearby *Commando Memorial.*
Those Commandos would surely have savoured the scene near Spean
Bridge some two centuries earlier, on 16 August 1745, when a mere
dozen of MacDonald of Keppoch's Highlanders, armed with little
more formidable than bagpipes and blood-curdling cries, routed two
companies of government troops on their way from Fort Augustus to
reinforce the garrison at Fort William. The troops fled back to Loch
Lochy where, meeting more Highlanders, they wisely surrendered
(to become, two days later, enforced spectators at Glenfinnan), while
Spean Bridge achieved its modest mention in history as the site of
the opening skirmish of the '45.

3m **Roy Bridge**, immediately S of which the hamlet of *Keppoch*
was in 1688 the scene of Scotland's last real clan battle, sparked, as
so often, by the fact that the MacDonalds of Keppoch held these
lands by clan tradition, whereas the Mackintoshes had a 'sheepskin
grant'. To settle the matter, and enjoying government support, the
Mackintoshes attacked, only however to be defeated. This, of course,
the government could not accept, and troops were soon sent to finish
off the MacDonalds.—From Roy Bridge a road ascends for 9m up
Glen Roy, on either side of which are the geologically famous *Parallel
Roads*, mountainside terraces left by the slowly sinking waters of the
ice-dammed lake that once filled this valley. The 'roads' are clearly
seen because they date from the comparatively recent geological
time known as the Loch Lomond Advance, a very late Ice Age
build-up of some 10–11,000 years ago. The area is a national nature
reserve (2887 acres) and a Nature Conservancy Council booklet
(normally obtainable from Tourist Information) explains the geology
in some detail.

6m *Loch Moy* (sometimes called Loch Laggan Reservoir), with a
dam 180ft high and 700ft long and occasionally unattractively empty,
is linked by tunnel to Loch Treig, 2m S, whence water flows through
another tunnel under Ben Nevis to the aluminium works at Inverlochy.—Beyond, the road skirts Loch Laggan proper to reach
(11m) *Kinlochlaggan*, between which and *(6m)* *Laggan* the Mashie
is joined by the Spey (N), in the angle between the two rising
Dun-na-Lamb, a hill fort 600ft above the valley.

From Laggan a diversion can be made westward to enjoy a few
miles of the infant Spey and experience, too, some touches of the
Jacobite and Hanoverian stories. For this road (a century later much
used by drovers), though built in 1735 by General Wade for the easier
control of the Highlanders, in fact in 1745 achieved the opposite,
proving a boon for the Young Pretender who advanced SE from
Bridge of Oich through Corrieyarrick Pass and, on reaching
Garvamore (7m from Laggan), seized Cluny Macpherson and
persuaded him and his 400 men to join his cause. The motor road
ends beyond the Spey, but Wade's continues as a track through
Corrieyarrick (2507ft) to descend through Glen Tarff to Fort Augustus
at the S end of Loch Ness.

2m *Cluny Castle* was the home of Cluny Macpherson (see just
above), who, unable of course to return home after Culloden, instead—and despite a large reward offered for his capture—managed
to hide for nine years in a cave in the cliffs of *Craig Dhubh* which

hang above the road about *3m* farther on. Macpherson graves, including those of clan chiefs, will be found in the small burial ground below the castle beside the road, while more about this clan can be learnt at (*2m*) **Newtonmore** (1000 inhab. *ECl.* Wed. *Inf.*, Perth Road. May–Sept) where there is a *Clan Macpherson Museum* (May– Sept: Mon.–Sat., 10.00 to 17.30. Sun., 14.30 to 17.30. Tel: 05403-253. Free). The clan rally and Newtonmore Highland Games are held on the first Saturday in August.—For Newtonmore to *Pitlochry* and *Perth*, see Rte 27.

3m **Kingussie** (1000 inhab. *ECl.* Wed. *Inf.*, King Street. May–Sept) is 'capital' of the historic and sizeable district of Badenoch, bounded by the Monadhliath, Grampian and Atholl mountains and anciently the territory of the Comyns until their defeat by Bruce. Bruce then gave part to Randolph, Earl of Moray, retaining the remainder for the crown, this part later being granted to Alexander, son of Robert II and notorious as the 'Wolf of Badenoch'. But of the medieval stronghold of the Comyns and the 'Wolf' all that survives, just S across the Spey, is an exceptionally large motte, support now for the ruined shell of *Ruthven Barracks*, as stark and ugly visually as is their story. Built in 1718 to control the Highlanders, and in 1734 enlarged by Wade—two years before the poet James Macpherson of Ossianic renown was born in the adjacent village—the barracks were in 1745 at first held successfully against the Jacobites (by Sergeant Molloy and only 14 men) but later fell to the Young Pretender. And it was to this grim Hanoverian outpost that the pathetic remnants of the prince's army rallied after Culloden, only to have such hopes as they may have still held abruptly extinguished by the curt message that every man should seek his safety in the best way he could. So they blew up the barracks and scattered.

More pleasantly, Kingussie is the home of the admirable *Highland Folk Museum* (April–Oct: Mon.–Sat., 10.00 to 18.00. Nov–March: Mon.–Fri., 10.00 to 15.00. Tel: 05402-307. Fee). Founded in 1935 on Iona by Miss I.F. Grant, an authority on Gaelic and clan history, the museum here is now in two parts, open air and indoors. The former shows a 'blackhouse' from Lewis, a click mill, a turf house and a variety of farming equipment, while indoors there is a farming section, a kitchen scene, and a gallery showing Highland furniture and domestic bygones.

Between Kingussie and Aviemore, a distance of 14m, there is a choice of three close and parallel roads, A9 and B9152 keeping N of the Spey while B970 serves the other bank. A9 will be for those in a hurry; a combination of the other two, conveniently linked by a bridge halfway at Kincraig, will provide the easiest approach to several points of interest; B970 will be chosen by those set on exploring the Badenoch mountains' glens of *Tromie* and *Feshie*, the former with a road to Loch An-t-Seilich which plays a part in the Tummel Valley Hydro-Electric Scheme (see Rte 27, Pitlochry).

Leaving Kingussie, B9152 passes the war memorial, interestingly set on a prehistoric tumulus, and then a monument to James Macpherson (see above), builder of the mansion of Balavil (2m from Kingussie) on the site of ancient Raits Castle, once a Comyn stronghold and the scene of a massacre by the Mackintoshes. The story goes that Comyn had invited his Mackintosh enemies to a feast in pretended reconciliation, but had arranged that each Comyn would kill a Mackintosh as soon as the boar's head—long a customary signal for violent death—was brought on. However the Mackintoshes were forewarned and slew the Comyns instead.

6m **Kincraig** is known for its *Highland Wildlife Park* (June– Aug: Daily, 10.00 to 18.00. Spring and autumn: Daily, 10.00 to 17.00 or 90 minutes before dusk if earlier. Tel: 05404-270. Fee), with both drive-through and walk-through sections. The former shows deer, bison and Highland cattle; the latter, wolves, bears, wildcats, eagles and well over 50 other species, while a picnic area and children's farm are among other attractions. *Insh Church*, sitting on a morraine knoll above Loch Insh immediately S of Kincraig, claims that its site was once sacred to the Druids and that it has been continuously used for Christian worship since the coming of Celtic missionaries in the 6 or 7C; a claim supported inside the church by an ancient Celtic bell and a hollow stone said to have been used as a font by St Adamnan.—*3m Alvie*, to the S of which there are three monuments, the most conspicuous being that atop Tor Alvie, a 90ft-high column erected in 1840 to the last Duke of Gordon (died 1836) and bearing inscriptions in Gaelic, Latin and English. Nearby, and more modest, a cairn of 1815 put up by the Marquis of Huntly honours the Highland soldiers who fell at Waterloo, while the third monument, an obelisk nearer the river to the S, remembers Bonnie Jean, Duchess of Gordon (died 1812), who reputedly recruited for the Gordon Highlanders by giving a kiss to those who joined. Another who lived near Alvie, and who is buried here, was Sir George Henschel (1850–1934), the conductor and composer.

In *2m* beyond Alvie, and just short of Aviemore, a road crosses the Spey to reach **Inverdruie**, with three visitor attractions catering for interests as diverse as whisky, a Highland estate and fish, the first two being adjacent. The *Whisky Centre* (April–Sept: Mon.–Sat., 10.00 to 18.00. Sun., 12.30 to 14.30. Tel: 0479-810574) offers a museum, an audio-visual presentation, a tasting room and a shop, while the *Rothiemurchus Visitor Centre* (Tel: 0479-810858) provides an introduction to and facilities for enjoying a large local Highland estate of huge variety—one owned in turn by Comyns, Gordons, Shaws, Mackintoshes and, since 1580, Grants. Away from the centre—with film and slide shows—the attractions include wildlife tours, estate tours, ranger-guided walks and many miles of waymarked walks. Closer to the river will be found the *Fish Farm and Fishing Centre* (April–Oct. Tel: 0479-810395) with myriad trout, a play area and picnic site, and, of course, angling.

The Rothiemurchus estate also includes **Loch-an-Eilean** (2m S of Inverdruie), an exceptionally lovely loch, surrounded by pines below a mountain backdrop and with an island castle, started in the 15C by Lachlan of Mackintosh but later enlarged and passing, as part of the estate, to the Gordons and then the Grants. Until the loch was dammed during the 18C the castle could be reached by causeway, an approach which in 1688 tempted an attack by adherents of James VII/II who, however, reckoned without the spirit of the laird's wife who in her husband's absence put up a successful resistance. A nature trail makes the circuit of the loch and a visitor centre (NCC. May–Sept. Tel: 0479-810477. Free), in a converted croft, tells the story of the local ecology, with particular reference to the pine forest.

1m **Aviemore** (1200 resident inhab. *ECl.* Wed. *Inf.* Main Road. Tel: 0479-810363) has come a long way since it was a settlement beside Wade's military road and, later, with the coming of the railway

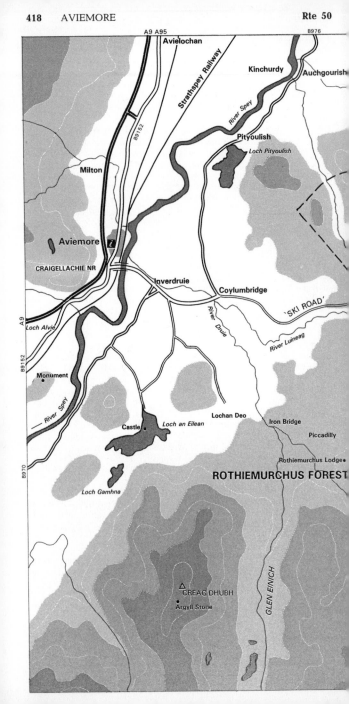

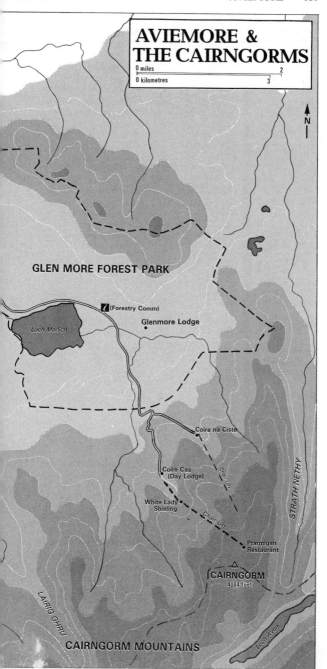

AVIEMORE & THE CAIRNGORMS

0 miles   2
0 kilometres   3

N

GLEN MORE FOREST PARK

i (Forestry Comm)

● Glenmore Lodge

Loch Morlich

● Coire na Ciste

● Coire Cas
(Day Lodge)

Chair Lift

White Lady ●
Shieling

Chair Lift

STRATH NETHY

● Ptarmigan
Restaurant

△ CAIRNGORM
4084 feet

LAIRIG GHRU

Loch Avon

CAIRNGORM MOUNTAINS

in the 19C, an unassuming though stylish small resort.

All this changed during the 1960s with the arrival of the *Aviemore Centre* (Tel: 0479-810624), Europe's first purpose-built leisure and sports centre. Now imaginatively redeveloping, the Centre's many facilities and attractions include a choice of hotels and a Swiss mountain-style chalet motel with self-catering accommodation, a caravan park, a theatre and a cinema, a 'family fun' pub—the Crofter's Inn—and a generous selection of restaurants and shops. Sports facilities (all equipment available for hire) include a giant indoor swimming pool, sauna, solariums, turbo spa, as well as skating, curling, tennis, squash and dry-ski slopes. Additionally a Highland Craft Village is all that its name implies while Santa Claus Land caters for the children. Lastly, the Centre organises a widening choice of excursions, such as, for example, Aviemore's Gilded Bothy Days, aiming to recreate all the distinguished best of a Highland sporting day, and, for the more sybaritic, the Silver Pullman Diner Evening, a journey and a meal recapturing the leisurely elegance of Edwardian rail travel.

Although the Centre inevitably dominates Aviemore, there are other things here, including even a reminder of the prehistoric past in the shape of a few stones of a small ring-cairn off the E of the main road towards the N of the town; while more recent nostalgia is catered for by the steam trains of the *Strathspey Railway* (Services, Easter: Fri.–Mon. Mid April–mid May: Sun. Mid May–mid Oct: Sat. and Sun., with also Mon.–Thurs. in late June–Aug. Timetables from stations. Tel: 047983-692. Fee). Plying between Aviemore (Speyside station) and Boat of Garten, the headquarters of the Strathspey Railway Association (museum), the trains keep alive five miles of a line opened in 1863 and officially closed in 1965. *Craigellachie Nature Reserve* (Nature Trail), immediately W of Aviemore beside A9, provides a mixture of birchwood and moor rising to 1700ft, while geological features include the Craigellachie Rock, historically the rallying place of Clan Grant whose war cry was 'Stand fast, Craigellachie!'. This clan occupied the lands between this Craigellachie and that 37m away at the foot of Strathspey; there are twin Grant mausoleums at Duthill on the road from Carrbridge to Grantown-on-Spey.

Aviemore, together with its Centre, offers a range of year-round special and inclusive holiday arrangements, including winter sports and many other recreations. There are also concessions by British Rail. Write: Aviemore and Spey Valley Tourist Centre, Main Road, Aviemore, PH22 1PP. Tel: 0479-810363.

*Glen More Forest Park and the Cairngorms

Glen More Forest Park lies close to the SE of Aviemore, while beyond lifts the mass of Cairngorm, with the Cairngorms National Nature Reserve. The area is reached by the fine scenic 'Ski Road' (buses) which starts at Coylumbridge, 2m SE of Aviemore and, after crossing the Forest Park, in another 8m reaches the chairlifts at the foot of Cairngorm.

Climbs and Walks. The whole district abounds in possibilities for climbs and walks, ranging from simple, well-marked local nature trails to strenuous undertakings to summits or across the mountains to Braemar (28–30m). Many of the walks trace old drover roads, and many tackle high, wild country which should only be attempted in good weather by those with experience and specialist clothing and equipment. Although in general the walks are public rights of way, and there are no restrictions within the Forest Park, elsewhere there can at certain times of the year be restrictions for reasons of bird protection and deer culling. Advice on the Cairngorms generally, and particularly on climbs and walks, can be obtained from Aviemore Tourist Information, the Forestry Commission Information Centre at Glenmore, or the Rothiemurchus Visitor Centre at Inverdruie.

Glen More Forest Park, covering the NW slopes of Cairngorm, was first known as Queen's Forest, to commemorate the Silver Jubilee of King George V and Queen Mary in 1935, and was given its present name in 1948. With 4000 acres of forest ringed by mountains, the heart of the park is *Loch Morlich* (camping, caravanning, swimming, boating) at the E end of which are the admirable *Forestry Commission Information Centre* and *Reindeer House*, the latter the headquarters of the Reindeer Company which, weather permitting, arranges viewing walks with the herdsman (Daily, assembly 11.00. Reindeer are usually seen within half an hour, but good walkers may join a longer tour. Tel: 047986-228. Fee). The local herd of Swedish reindeer was introduced in 1952, but the animals seen today are Scottish-born descendants. And here, too, a boulder commemorates the Norwegians who trained in this area during the last war.

Leaving Loch Morlich the road climbs first to the *Coire na Ciste* car park at 1800ft (restaurant and facilities) and then the *Coire Cas* car park at 2150ft (Cairngorm Day Lodge, restaurant and facilities), both starting points for two-stage chairlifts serving several ski tows. The westerly view from here is superb and reindeer can often be seen grazing quite close. From Coire Cas the chairlift ascends to the *Shieling* halfway station (restaurant and facilities), then on to the top station at 3600ft with the *Ptarmigan Observation Restaurant*, the highest eating place in Britain. From here a path reaches the summit (4084ft) of *Cairngorm*. (Chairlift from 09.00 to 16.30 or later. Inquiries to Cairngorm Chairlift, Aviemore. Tel: 047986-261.)

The **Cairngorms**, a concentration of splendid mountains lying between Aviemore on the Spey and Braemar on Deeside, represent the highest mountain mass in Britain, with six peaks of over 4000ft. Of granite, the massif is famous for the now rare transparent crystals of brownish quartz, often quite large, known as 'cairngorms'. The *Cairngorms National Nature Reserve* covers some 100 square miles of the southern part of the region. Established between 1954–66, and the largest nature reserve in Britain, it is partly owned by the Nature Conservancy Council but is mainly private estates (Rothiemurchus, Glenfeshie, Glen Avon and Mar Lodge). The reserve has a sub-arctic summit plateau with distinctive arctic-alpine plant and animal communities, and amongst the wildlife that may be seen are mountain hare, wild cat, deer, ptarmigan and eagles. Further information from NCC (NE), 17 Rubislaw Terrace, Aberdeen, AB1 1XE. Tel: (0224) 572863 or (0479) 810477.

Aviemore is left by A95, in *4m* reaching the junction with B9153 (for Carrbridge). Here an eastward diversion may be made to (2m) **Boat of Garten**, so called from the ferry that operated here until the bridge was built in 1898, and today the home of the *Strathspey Railway Association* (see above). *Loch Garten* (2m SE) is a nature reserve established in 1959 to safeguard the first pair of ospreys to breed in Scotland for some 50 years (Mid April—mid Aug: Daily, 10.00 to 20.30. Access only along signposted track to hide). The diversion may be continued for another 4m along B970 to Nethy Bridge, just beyond which, and standing on a motte, is *Castle Roy*, or Red Castle, a ruined curtain-wall stronghold of the Comyns, dating from the 12C and one of the oldest castle ruins in Scotland.

   2m (by B9153) **Carrbridge**, most visited for the imaginative *Landmark Visitor Centre* (Daily, 09.30 to 21.30 in June–Aug; to 18.00 in April, May, Sept, Oct; to 17.00 in Nov–March. Tel: 047984-614. Fee). Here, though the principal attraction is a dramatic multi-screen presentation and exhibition on 10,000 years of Highland history, there is also much else and especially for children; a treetop trail, a pinewood nature trail, a sculpture park, a woodland maze and an exciting adventure playground. Nor should Carrbridge be left without a glance at its picturesque arch of a bridge of 1717, built after two men had been drowned at the ford. Specially designed to be above flood level, the bridge was nonetheless badly damaged by water in 1829, in the same storm which produced that spectacular flood recorded at Randolph's Leap on the nearby river Findhorn. And those with an association with the name Grant may wish to divert the short distance E to Duthill where they will find the family's twin mausoleums.

   This Rte now joins the trunk A9, crossing the Findhorn at (*8m*) *Tomatin*, where the distillery may be visited by prior arrangement (Tel: 08082-234), and in another *2m* branching to the right along B9154 for *Loch Moy*, the heart of Mackintosh territory for over 600 years. The chiefs' island castle was replaced in c 1700 by a mansion N of the loch, this being burnt in 1800 and replaced by two successor mansions, the second, today's Moy Hall (no adm.), dating from 1955. Near here, in February 1746, took place what was to be known as the 'Rout of Moy', an affair remarkably similar to that at Spean Bridge the previous year. Scorning the ambivalence of her husband (the Mackintosh), the lady of Moy (Scott's 'gallant amazon') sheltered the Young Pretender and, on learning that Lord Loudoun, governor of Inverness, was advancing with 1500 men, despatched the Moy blacksmith and six or so men into the night to reconnoitre. Hearing the enemy approach, the blacksmith's band scattered, skirling clan rallies on their bagpipes and yelling Lochiel, Keppoch and their own war cries. Convinced that they had blundered into the main Jacobite army, Loudoun's men turned tail while later, back at Moy, the prince informed the Mackintosh that he must regard himself as his wife's prisoner.

   4m Daviot, where B851 leads NE for Culloden (Rte 43) while this Rte rejoins A9 for (*5m*) **Inverness**, see Rte 51.

51   Fort William to Inverness via the Great Glen and Loch Ness

A82 and A830 out of Fort William to Banavie. B8004 beside the Caledonian Canal to rejoin A82 short of Spean Bridge. A82 (alternative B862 and B852 S of Loch Ness) to Inverness.—
Scenically pleasant, though, for the Highlands, unspectacular, most of the distance being beside the string of lochs (Lochy, Oich, Ness) which fill the Great Glen, the geological split across northern Scotland. The lochs have green and often wooded hilly shores,

with, frequently, mountain background. A82 carries a lot of traffic in summer.

SOME HOTELS. **Invergarry**. *Inn on the Garry*. PH35 4HJ. Tel: (08093) 206. *Glengarry Castle*, PH35 4HW. Tel: (08093) 254. **Fort Augustus**. *Inchnacardoch Lodge*. Tel: (0320) 6258. *Lovat Arms*. Tel: (0320) 6206. **Invermoriston**. *Glenmoriston Arms*, IV3 6YA. Tel: (0320) 51206. **Drumnadrochit**. *Loch Ness Lodge*. Tel: (04562) 342. *Polmailly House*. Tel: (04562) 343. **Foyers**. *Foyers*. Tel: (04563) 216. **Inverness**. *Ladbroke*, Nairn Road. Tel: (0463) 239666. *Kingsmills*, Culcabock Road. Tel: (0463) 237166. *Glen Mhor*, 9–10 Ness Bank. Tel: (0463) 234308. *Caledonian*, Church Street. Tel: (0463) 235181.

Total distance 61m.—*7m* **Gairlochy**.—*16m* **Invergarry**.—*6m* **Fort Augustus**.—Either: *6m* **Invermoriston**.—*12m* **Drumnadrochit**.—*14m* **Inverness**. Or: *14m* **Foyers**.—*10m* **Dores**.—*8m* **Inverness**.

The **Caledonian Canal**, following the Great Glen, links Loch Linnhe in the S with Moray Firth in the N, but only about 22m of its 60m length is true canal, the remainder taking advantage of the succession of lochs. The route was surveyed by James Watt in 1773, construction was begun by Telford in 1803, and the canal was opened in 1822; it turned out, however, to be too shallow and was not finally completed until 1847. For many years it was much used, particularly by sailing boats anxious to avoid the long and often hazardous voyage around Scotland's northern coast. Today, owing to the small capacity of the 29 locks as also the greater seaworthiness of modern ships, the canal is much less active, though it remains popular with pleasure and other small craft.

For **Fort William**, see Rte 49. For Fort William by A82 to *Spean Bridge*, see Rte 50.

This Rte leaves Fort William by A82 but in just over *1m* bears briefly W on A830 (Rte 48), rounding ruined *Inverlochy Castle* (Rte 50) and in *1m*, at *Banavie*, crossing the Caledonian Canal immediately below the tight sequence of the eight locks known as Neptune's Staircase, raising the canal 64ft and representing one of Telford's biggest problems. From Banavie B8004 takes this Rte along the canal's W bank, in *3m* crossing the mouth of *Glen Loy*, down which the Young Pretender marched from Glenfinnan, and in another *2m* reaching *Gairlochy*.

Here a diversion can be made N beside Loch Lochy and then W for a look at **Loch Arkaig**, which, its N shore with a road, cuts westward through the mountains of Lochaber for some 13m. *Achnacarry House* (no adm.), on the isthmus between Loch Lochy and Loch Arkaig and the seat of Cameron of Lochiel, recalls Donald Cameron of Lochiel who, after initial doubts about the Young Pretender's venture, eventually gave his support after being taunted with wishing to stay at home and learn about his prince's fate from the newspapers. He must surely have later rued his decision for he was wounded at Culloden and soon afterwards died in France, while Cumberland destroyed his castle here, now a ruin beside its early 19C successor. *Murlaggan*, at the road's end, was the scene of one of the last Jacobite rallies in 1746, an occasion on which, it is said, treasure belatedly given by the French was cast into the loch to prevent its falling into government hands.

At Gairlochy B8004 carries this Rte back across the canal, here about to lose itself in Loch Lochy, and in *2m* reaches the junction with A82, within the intersection being the *Commando Memorial* (Scott Sutherland, 1952), standing watch above the rough Lochaber land over which the commandos trained during the last war and remembering those among them who lost their lives. From here, too, there is an excellent view of Ben Nevis. For *Spean Bridge*, 1m farther, see Rte 50.

Fringing the E shore of Loch Lochy A82 in *11m* reaches *Laggan*, on the neck between lochs Lochy and Oich and the scene of at least two skirmishes, for the second of which—and it was bloodless—see Rte 50, Spean Bridge. But there was nothing bloodless about the defeat here in July 1544 of Clan Fraser by Clan Macdonald in an affray known as the Battle of the Shirts because both sides discarded their plaids, so hot was the weather. Beyond, beside the road on the W shore of Loch Oich, the *Well of the Heads* (1812)—seven men's heads above a spring—is a bizarre monument to a grim story. In the 17C Keppoch, head of a branch of the MacDonells, sent his two sons to be educated in France but himself died while they were away, leaving the management of his affairs to his seven brothers who, greedy to share these lands, murdered the lads on their return. But the family bard—an improbable but efficient avenger—had the murderers put to death and presented their heads to the chief of the clan at Glengarry, having first washed them in this well where an inscription in Gaelic, English, French and Latin records this 'ample and summary vengeance'.

3m **Invergarry**, where the ruins of *Invergarry Castle* cling on in the grounds of Glengarry Castle Hotel. Successor to earlier castles, this was long the seat of the chiefs of the MacDonells of Glengarry and it would have been here that the Keppoch bard would have made his presentation of the seven murderers' heads. A century or so later, in 1746, there was vengeance on another scale when Cumberland razed this staunchly Jacobite home.—For A87 westward to *Kyle of Lochalsh*, see Rte 52.

If Invergarry Castle, halfway up Loch Oich, recalls the '45's merciless end, *Bridge of Oich*, only *2m* farther N, recalls the high hopes of its beginning, for here—and with strong government forces only just up the road at Fort Augustus—the Young Pretender wheeled southward, to march through the Pass of Corrieyarrick and onward deep into England.

4m **Fort Augustus** (1000 inhab. *ECl.* Wed. *Inf.* Car Park. April—Sept), at the head of famed Loch Ness, offering a choice of onward roads, and home of the Great Glen Heritage Exhibition, comes as an obvious halfway halt along this Rte.

History. That this place was inhabited in very early times is proved by Cherry Island, a loch crannog just offshore to the N of the town, as also by the town's ancient name of Kilcumein, meaning Church of Cumein, a successor of St. Columba. After the '15, Hanoverian government barracks were built here, on the site now occupied by the Lovat Arms Hotel behind which a fragment of barrack still survives. In 1724 Wade made the village his headquarters (for his roads in this district, see below), in 1729 starting the construction of a new fort in a tactically better situation beside the loch. This he named Fort Augustus, after William Augustus, Duke of Cumberland, then only a boy but later to earn such notoriety in these parts. Captured by the Jacobites during the '45, the fort was soon retaken by government troops after Culloden, and it was here that Cumberland was presented with the head of Roderick Mackenzie, a young Edinburgh lawyer who had gallantlly encouraged his captors in their belief that he was the fugitive Young Pretender (see also Rte 52, Glen Moriston). The remains of the by then redundant fort were sold in 1867 to Lord Lovat, who in 1876 presented them to the Benedictine Order for the founding of an abbey and school.

Fort Augustus stands at the crossing of four of *General Wade's Military Roads*. One of these has been followed by this Rte from Fort William. Another, now a footway, leads across to Glen Moriston. A third, now also only a track but the one used by the Young Pretender at the start of his southward march, ascends Glen Tarff to cross Corrieyarrick Pass and reached the Spey. And the fourth, described below, makes for Inverness by way of the SE shore of Loch Ness.

Fort Augustus Abbey (Tours in summer. Tel: 0320-6234. Donation), a boys' school since 1878, is, theologically, successor to two older abbeys; that of St. Adrian and Denys, founded in Hanover in 1645, and that of St. James of the Scots, founded at Regensburg in Bavaria in about 1100 and later an important post-Reformation centre for Scottish Catholics. Architecturally, of course, the abbey represents Wade's fort, the greater part of the ground floor of which has been incorporated into the abbey buildings which range in date from the 19C East Cloister, Chapter House and St. Andrew's Chapel to the nave of 1956 and the porch of 1968. Of particular interest inside are a model of the fort, a curious pagan Roman stone with carvings of the Mother Goddesses, and some finely worked vestments.

The *Great Glen Heritage Exhibition* (May—Oct: Daily, 09.30 to 17.00. Tel: 0320-6341. Fee), beside a sequence of Caledonian Canal locks, illustrates the glen's and the local stories from Pictish to modern times and even includes a Loch Ness monster room.

For walkers there is *Inchnacardoch Forest*, with a trail (4m) starting from the Forest Office (Auchterawe, just SW of Fort Augustus. Booklet obtainable here or from Tourist Information) and combining forest with the bank of the river Oich.

Loch Ness is 24m long, an average of 1m broad, and in places 900ft deep. It has never been known to freeze. Fed by eight rivers and countless streams, the loch's only outlet is by the river Ness into the Moray Firth.

These are the natural facts, to most visitors probably of scant interest compared to the loch's fame as the home of its monster, affectionately known as Nessie. Real or imagined, Nessie is of ancient lineage, recorded by that respected 7C biographer St. Adamnan as having been not only seen but also effectively dealt with by St. Columba. On his way to convert Brude, king of the Picts, Columba ordered a servant to swim across the river Ness and bring back a boat. However, no sooner was the servant in the water than the monster attacked, and the man's life was only saved by the monster's retreat when confronted by Columba's sign of the Cross and shouted invocation. Over the years, and increasingly since the construction of A82 in the 1930s, there have been several sightings and even photographs, and the monster has been the object of serious scientific investigation using the most modern devices, but so far all has been without conclusive result. Meanwhile even the most sceptical find it hard not to scan the loch's enigmatic surface.—Cruises from Fort Augustus and Inverness.

From Fort Augustus there is a choice of roads (both 32m) either side of Loch Ness to Inverness. A82, on the N, is the faster and generally more interesting. B862 and B852, to the S and following the general line of Wade's military road, offer a quieter and rather more scenic alternative.

To Inverness North of Loch Ness

Leaving Fort Augustus Cherry Island crannog is seen just off-shore.—*6m* **Invermoriston** where the northern arm of Rte 52 bears

away W up Glen Moriston.—7m **Balbeg**, beyond which the *Cobb
Memorial* cairn, beside the road and loch and bearing in Gaelic the
words 'Honour to the brave and to the humble', commemorates John
Cobb who lost his life on the loch in 1952 while attempting to break
the world waterspeed record.—3m **Castle Urquhart** (AM. Standard.
Fee), at its most impressive when viewed from the road above, is a
large but battered ruin, less interesting as such than for its theatrical
situation. Successor to an Iron Age fort which once stood on this bluff
(and of which vitrified traces can still be found), and once one of the
largest castles in Scotland, Urquhart was occupied and strengthened
by Edward I, later passing through several hands until 1509 when
James IV gifted it to John Grant of Freuchie. It was he who built
most of the structure seen today, his descendants remaining in
possession until the present century even though the castle was
blown up in 1692 for fear it might fall into Jacobite hands.

While pausing to view the castle visitors may also note that more
monster sightings have been reported from this point than from
anywhere else along either side of the loch.

The road kinks around Urquhart Bay for (2m) **Drumnadrochit**,
home of the *Loch Ness Monster Centre* (Summer: Daily, 09.00 to
21.30. Other periods, check by Tel: 04562-573. Fee) which, with a
shop, restaurant, beer garden and suchlike, offers rather more than
its name implies. From here A831 runs westward up wooded Glen
Urquhart for Corrimony cairn, Glen Affric, Glen Cannich and Strathfarrar, for all of which see Rte 53—14m **Inverness**, see below.

To Inverness South of Loch Ness

Affording view points, B862 climbs to 1162ft before in *11m* arriving
at the junction with B852. Beyond, along B862, Loch Mhor, 5m long,
was formed by joining lochs Garth and Farraline when the river
Foyers was dammed for hydro-industrial purposes. From the road
junction B852 drops sharply to (3m) **Foyers**, beside the loch, on the
descent passing the *Falls of Foyers*, once spectacular enough to earn
praise from Burns but much tamed by hydro-electric projects, first
aluminium smelting (until 1968) and then pumped storage.

2m Inverfarigaig, near which are picnic areas and a small Forestry
Commission visitor centre near the start of a forest trail (1½m and in
places steep; booklet) up to a mountain view point overlooking the
meeting of two river gorges. But there is a reminder, too, that all was
not always peaceful here; Inverfarigaig Fort. Best seen and reached
from the road heading NE out of the village, this Iron Age stronghold
stands atop a rock above the mouth of the river Farigaig and still
shows remains of a thick wall, traces of vitrification and a subsidence
that may indicate the position of a well.

Between Inverfarigaig and (8m) *Dores*, where B862 rejoins from
the high ground, the road—here pretty precisely representing
Wade's—fringes Loch Ness, across the water from Castle Urquhart
and with some inviting picnic spots. Beyond Dores the loch edges
away from the road as it tapers to become the closely parallel river
Ness and Caledonian Canal, the road in *5m* (beyond Sconiport)
reaching a minor road (E) leading in about 1m to the *Knocknagael*
or *Boar Stone*, a rough Pictish block of the 7 or 8C bearing the outline
of a wild boar and also a mirror symbol.—3m **Inverness**, see immediately below.

Inverness (39,500 inhab. *ECl.* Wed. *Inf.* 23 Church Street. Tel: 0463-234353) is a sizeable and busy centre, popularly dubbed 'Capital of the Highlands'. And, administratively, this it certainly is for the town is the headquarters of Highland Region, Scotland's largest local government authority, as also of the important Highlands and Islands Development Board, not to mention lesser bodies. But the tourist anticipating a Highland ambience may well be disappointed for, visually at any rate, the Highlands are at best a distant promise. A road, rail and even air hub (airport at Dalcross, 8m NE), the emphasis here tends to be on administration, commerce and industry. Yet this should not deter the visitor, for Inverness is a town with ancient roots and one which can reward the potterer with some odd corners.

History. According to St. Adamnan, St. Columba visited the Pictish king Brude in about 565 at a castle 'near the Ness'. This may have been Craig Phadrig (see below), site of an Iron and Dark Ages fort. Equally it may have been the early predecessor of Macbeth's 11C stronghold (where Shakespeare placed the murder of Duncan), the site of which is Auld Castle Hill to the E of the present Castle Hill. Macbeth's castle was razed by Duncan's avenger, Malcolm Canmore, and it was either he (in 1057) or David I (c 1140) who founded a new castle on the existing site, the latter also granting the town a charter as a royal burgh.

In the War of Independence, Inverness was three times occupied by the English, and when Bruce retook it in 1307 he followed his usual policy of destroying the castle. In later reigns town and castle alike suffered from the savagery of the Highlanders and were the scene of many assemblies called by Scotland's kings in their attempts to control the clans. In 1562 Mary, Queen of Scots, attempting a northern progress, was refused admission to the castle by Alexander Gordon, son of the arrogant rebel Earl of Huntly, but later the castle surrendered, Mary moved in and Gordon and several others were hanged from the walls. In the following century Cromwell appreciated the town's strategic importance, in 1652–57 building a strong fort, known as 'The Sconce', on the right bank of the Ness beside its mouth, using for the purpose stones from the abbey of Kinloss and the cathedral at Fortrose. This, however, was pulled down at the Restoration.

Inverness Castle was occupied by the Jacobites in 1715, and again in 1745 by the Young Pretender who blew it up, leaving little remaining. The site was finally cleared in 1834 to make way for the present buildings.
Caledonian Canal and Loch Ness cruises in summer. MV 'Scot II' from Muirtown Locks in the Caledonian Canal. Tel: (0463) 233140. Or Jacobite Cruises from Tomnahurich Bridge on the canal. Tel: (0463) 233999.

Inverness is split by the Ness, the main part occupying the right bank. Here, beside High Street, the heart of the town is the *Town House* of 1880, in front of which stands the restored Cross on a base enclosing the Clach-na-Cuddain (Stone of the tubs), a rough block on which women carrying water from the river rested their tubs; a homely, domestic scene not easy to picture alongside today's traffic. The stone is of misty origin and the source of many local tales, one being that it was used as a coronation stone, another that the prosperity of Inverness depends upon its staying where it is. In the Town House are a beam from Cromwell's fort, and some good paintings and heraldic stained glass, while in the Council Chamber are the framed signatures of members of Lloyd George's cabinet which met here in 1921, the first British cabinet meeting held outside London.

Behind the Town House are the castle and the museum. The *Castle*, a dominating 19C structure on the site of that of Malcolm Canmore or David I, is now the home of law courts and local

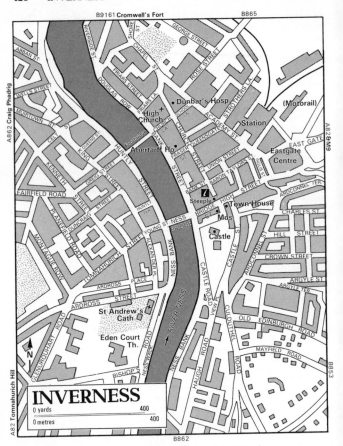

government offices, though a link with the past survives in the courtyard in the form of the well (rediscovered and restored in 1909) while a Jacobite touch is provided on the terrace by a statue of Flora Macdonald. *Inverness Museum* (Mon.—Sat., 09.00 to 17.00. Tel: 0463-237114. Free) illustrates the Highland as much as the Inverness story, themes covered including archaeology and social and natural history and of particular note being the collection of Highland silver.

The principal shopping area is represented by the network of streets generally to the N and NE of the Town House, the focus increasingly being the *Eastgate Centre* near the railway station.

High Street extends W as Bridge Street, on the corner of the latter and Church Street being the lofty *Steeple* of 1791, once the jail. Church Street (with *Tourist Information*) leads to most places of interest in this sector of the town. *Abertarff House*, on the left beyond Fraser Street, dates from 1592 and incorporates a rare example of an old stair-tower; long the town residence of the Lovats, the house was restored by the National Trust for Scotland in 1963 and is now the Trust's Highland office. Beyond, and again to the left, stands the *High Church*, a rebuilding of 1772 but still preserving its 14C tower and with also, in the yard, a curious 17C colonnaded enclosure. Just to the N, in Friars Street, leading off Friars Lane beside the High Church, is *Friars Burying Ground*, on the site of a Dominican priory founded in 1233 and surviving as no more than a broken pillar. And, in Church Street to the E of the High Church, there is *Dunbar's Hospital* (1688; restored), originally an almshouse, now with its row of dormer windows a mellow example of 17C domestic building.

Students of Cromwellian architecture must continue a good half mile northwards—by way of Chapel Street, Shore Street and Cromwell Road—to reach the site of *Cromwell's Fort*, destroyed at the Restoration except for a clock tower.

Across the Ness, to the S beside the river, is *St. Andrew's Cathedral* (1868); a handsome, roseate edifice with an octagonal chapter house and elaborate interior, it serves the see of Moray, Ross and Caithness. The adjacent *Eden Court Theatre*, completed in 1976 and incorporating a 19C house build by Bishop Eden, is a theatre, conference centre and gallery. *Tomnahurich* (Hill of the Fairies), a 220ft-high hill ½m SW of the cathedral, has been beautifully laid out as a cemetery which serves also as a notable local view point, while *Ness Islands* (½m S of the cathedral), linked to one another and the river's banks by footbridges, and even with a miniature railway, form an original public park.

Finally, anyone with a feel for the remote past will make for *Craig Phadrig* (2m W of Inverness, off A9), a 550ft hill bearing a fort, archaeologically dated to about 500 BC but thought also—though 1000 years later—to have been Brude's fastness and the place visited by St. Columba, set on converting the pagan king and citing, it is surely reasonable to surmise, his recent successful brush with the monster of the Ness.

For Inverness E along the coast to **Fraserburgh**, see Rte 43; to **Aviemore** and **Fort William** (via Spey valley), see Rte 50; for the Glens of **Strathfarrar**, **Cannich** and **Affric**, see Rte 53; to **Kyle of Lochalsh**, see Rte 54; to **Ullapool** and **Durness**, see Rte 56; to **Bonar Bridge**, see Rte 57.

52 Invergarry or Invermoriston to Kyle of Lochalsh

A87 from Invergarry, or A887 from Invermoriston joining A87 just short of Loch Cluanie. A87 to Kyle of Lochalsh.—Highland scenery, the approach from Invergarry being the finer.

SOME HOTELS. **Shiel Bridge**. *Kintail Lodge*, IV40 8HL. Tel: (059981) 275. **Dornie**. *Loch Duich*, Ardelve. Tel: (059985) 213. **Balmacara**. *Balmacara*, IV40 8DH. Tel: (059986) 283. **Kyle of Lochalsh**. *Lochalsh*, Ferry Road. Tel: (0599) 4202.—See also **Kyleakin**, Rte 62.

Total distance 46m from Invergarry or 49m from Invermoriston.—*12m* (from Invergarry) or *15m* (from Invermoriston) **Junction A87/A887.**—*14m* **Pass of Stachel (Glen Shiel).**—*5m* **Shiel Bridge.**—*8m* **Eilean Donan Castle.**—*7m* **Kyle of Lochalsh.**

FROM INVERGARRY. Leaving **Invergarry** (see Rte 51), A87 quickly climbs into superb Highland scenery, riding above lochs Garry and Loyne as long views open out westward across lonely, wild country towards Loch Quoich and Loch Hourn. A tempting minor road, breaking away from A87 3m out of Invergarry, traces most of the length of the vista, fringing lochs Garry and Quoich (the latter with a large rock-filled dam) and in 20m ending at *Kinlochhourn* in a savage setting at Loch Hourn's narrow head, still some 12m short of the loch's broader mouth into the Sound of Sleat (for cruises into Loch Hourn, see Rte 48, Arisaig and Mallaig). The return to A87 must be made by the same road, but this matters little for the reversed views are wholly different.—In *12m* from Invergarry the junction with A887 is reached.

FROM INVERMORISTON. From **Invermoriston** on Rte 51, A887 ascends the wooded valley of Glen Moriston beside its tumbling river. In *13m* (about 1m E of Ceannacroc generating station), S of the road and as likely as not rather obscured by bushes, a cairn commemorates the heroic Roderick Mackenzie who, hiding here after Culloden and in appearance not dissimilar to the Young Pretender, was set upon by soldiers and, though mortally wounded, had the presence of mind to cry out 'Ah, villains! You have slain your prince'. The ruse in large measure succeeded, for Mackenzie's head, having first been shown to Cumberland at Fort Augustus, was sent to London where so many people swore that it was that of the prince that, if only for a while, the urgency of the hunt was much relaxed. In rather less than *1m* the road bridges the small river Doe, some 2½m up which there is a cave called *Corriedoe* in which the Young Pretender hid from 24 to 28 August 1746, three weeks after Mackenzie's death in the glen below. In another *1m* A887 meets A87.

After skirting the N shore of Loch Cluanie, A87 starts the descent of **Glen Shiel** through the *Pass of Stachel*, a scenic defile overhung by peaked and jagged mountains rising to well over 3000ft and gashed by gloomy corries. Here (*14m* from the A87-A887 junction) an NTS information panel describes the Trust's wild and mountainous *Kintail* estate and also explains in some detail the skirmish fought here in 1719 during one of the lesser known attempts to put the Old Pretender on the throne.

The Earl of Seaforth, since the '15 a fugitive in France and Spain, in 1719 sailed from Spain with ten ships and 6000 soldiers. However, storms at sea took their toll and only two frigates with some 300 men reached the island of Lewis, where Seaforth raised a few hundred Highlanders (mainly Macraes and Mackenzies) and then crossed to Eilean Donan and Kintail, taking up position across the Pass of Stachel. Attacked by government troops under General Wightman, the Highlanders and Spaniards more than held their own. But when Seaforth was wounded the impetus of the rebellion died, the Spaniards surrendered and the Highlanders dispersed.

Just beyond, the road and the river Shiel together descend below the towering mass (N) of the *Five Sisters*, scenically one of the most dramatic features of the NTS estate, to reach in *5m* **Shiel Bridge**, at the head of Loch Duich and offering a diversion as scenically splendid as it is archaeologically interesting.

DIVERSION TO GLENELG BROCHS (W, 12m. Dead-end unless the car ferry to Kylerhea on Skye is used). Once a military highway, today's unclassified road hairpins spectacularly from sea level up to the *Pass of Mam Ratagan* (1116ft), with a car park and orientation table—an easy enough ascent for a modern car, but one which Johnson and Boswell found daunting as they coaxed their weary horses upwards beside a precipitous edge, Johnson at one point calling out for help as his mount staggered under its rider's ungainly weight. The wide view embraces much of Glen Shiel, defined in part by the great barren wall of the Five Sisters, while, beyond, other vistas open up as—more decorously on this side—the road descends along the flank of Glen More with the mountains of Skye ahead.

At its foot the road forks, the NW prong in 2m reaching the car ferry to Skye (Summer only. Frequent weekday service, 09.00 to 17.00 or 18.00 in July and Aug. Not Sun. Crossing 4 minutes. Tel: 059982-224), while the SW prong at once passes the drab, rectilinear ruin of *Bernera Barracks*, built in c 1722 and until the end of the century this road's military objective.

Less than a mile S from the village of Glenelg a small wooded road turns inland along Glen Beg to reach the two best preserved brochs on Scotland's mainland. These—appearing suddenly as the road leaves the trees—are *Dun Telve* on the right, and, a short way farther on the left, *Dun Troddan*. With walls over 13ft thick at the base and rising respectively to 33 and 25ft, the two combine well to show the main features of broch construction, with massive circular bases, entrance passages, guard cells, parts of the stairway and the typical internal galleries. Leaving these brochs the road continues only for another mile, beyond becoming an inviting track heading for woods and heights and in half a mile arriving at *Dun Grugaig*, a fort of a type which preceded the brochs. Now little more than base wall and tumbled stones, this fort is larger in circumference than the brochs below and semicircular in design with the open side defended by a precipitous drop into a narrow, hidden glen. Along the approach track can be seen traces of another ancient stone and earthwork ring-enclosure.

The coastal road runs for another 9m to *Arnisdale* on the N shore of Loch Hourn.

Beyond Shiel Bridge, and still in grand mountain scenery, A87 rounds the head of Loch Duich, just to the E being the National Trust for Scotland's **Morvich Countryside Centre** (June–Sept: Mon.–Sat., 09.00 to 18.00. Sun., 13.00 to 18.00. Donation), where the Trust's Kintail Estate is described and advice is given on the many climbs and walks, notably—and most strenuously—to the *Falls of Glomach*, some 5 mountain miles to the NE.

Running with the N shore of Loch Duich, A87 in *8m* reaches **Eilean Donan Castle** (April–Sept: Daily, 10.00 to 12.30. 14.00 to 18.00. Tel: 059985-202. Fee), rooted firmly to its islet at the end of a short causeway, guardian of the confluence of three lochs, and picturesque favourite of Scotland's poster designers (the castle is best seen from the old road above). Successor to an Iron Age fort, the castle was built in 1220 by Alexander II to deter Viking penetration, later passing to the Mackenzie earls of Seaforth and in 1719 (see Glen Shiel above) achieving the surely unique distinction of first being garrisoned by Spanish soldiers and then being blown apart by a Hanoverian warship. After 200 years as a ruin, Eilean Donan was rebuilt and now shows Jacobite, Mackenzie and Macrae relics.

Beyond (*2m*), Rte 54 (A890) comes in from the N, while, in another

2m and now beside Loch Alsh, A87 passes *Lochalsh Woodland Garden* (NTS. All year, daily. Fee), with, in the Coach House, a natural history display (Easter–mid Oct: Daily, 10.00 to 18.00).

3m **Kyle of Lochalsh** (700 inhab. *ECl.* Thurs. *Inf.* Easter–Sept), separated from Skye by the narrow Kyle Akin, is the terminus of the railway from Inverness and of this principal road approach to Skye. For *Skye* and the car ferry to the island, see Rte 62.

53 The Glens South West of Inverness (Strathfarrar, Cannich and Affric)

To the SW of Inverness three lovely glens pierce deep into the mountains. These are Glen Strathfarrar, Glen Cannich and Glen Affric, this last being the best known, scenically the most dramatic, and also enjoying the best road with plenty of places to park. Hydro-electric schemes are present in the forms of dams and power stations, but much care has been taken not to mar the magnificent Highland scenery, which indeed many would judge improved by the enlargement of modest lochs into sizeable reservoirs. The glens, all with dead-end roads, (but note that Strathfarrar is a Hydro-Electric Board private road, normally open only to walkers), can be approached from Beauly (on Rte 54, 10m W of Inverness) or from Drumnadrochit (Rte 51) on Loch Ness. The text below assumes the former.

The base road is A831, the village of Struy marking the foot of Glen Strathfarrar, while Cannich is the gateway for the other two.

SOME HOTELS. *Struy*. *Cnoc*, Erchless Castle Estate. Tel: (046376) 264. **Cannich**. *Glen Affric*. Tel: (04565) 214.

Total distance (Beauly to Cannich) 17m.—*10m* **Struy**, for *Glen Strathfarrar* (14m to head).—*7m* **Cannich**, for *Glen Cannich* (9m to head) or *Glen Affric* (9m to head).

From **Beauly** (see Rte 54) A831 ascends the small but picturesque gorge of the river Beauliu, blocked by dams at *Kilmorack* and (*5m*) *Aigas* at both of which the sluices are opened daily to allow fish to make their way upstream (admission to Aigas. July–Sept: Mon.–Fri., at 15.00. Sat. and Sun. at 10.15 and 15.00. Tel: 0463-782412).—*5m* **Struy**, a hamlet at the confluence of the Farrar and the Beauly, the latter here looping SW and now called the river Glass.

GLEN STRATHFARRAR. The road up the glen belongs to the Hydro-Electric Board and is normally open only to walkers. Much of the way wandering through fine woods and past lochs, the road in 4m ends at the large sheet of *Loch Monar*, stretching for 8 narrow miles below mountains, many of which rise to well over 3000ft.

A831, now ascending Strath Glass, in *4m* passes the curious *Well of St. Ignatius*, heavily carved and incorporating a shrine of 1880, and in another *3m* reaches **Cannich**, a scattered hamlet at which Strath Glass, Glen Cannich, Glen Affric and Glen Urquhart all meet. Here a short diversion should be made 3m down Glen Urquhart to *Corrimony Cairn*, a large prehistoric burial cairn, surrounded by a circle of 11 standing stones and with its entrance passage still roofed. When excavated in 1952, evidence was found of a crouched burial.

GLEN CANNICH, thickly wooded with bare mountains looming above, fringes small lochs and, widening in its upper reach, in 9m ends at *Loch Mullardoch* with an impressive dam and a tunnel through which water is fed to Loch Beneveian in Glen Affric. Walkers can explore the narrow length of the loch (9m) below mountains lifting to 3775ft on the N and 3880ft on the S.

*GLEN AFFRIC effectively means *Loch Beneveian*, for the road (9m long, and generous with parking sites from some of which there are forest walks) hugs this wooded, island-studded water for 6m, threading a constant contrast between the dark and light greens of pine and birch and, beyond the dam, riding well above the water and enjoying splendid mountain vistas. Near the start, at *Fasnakyle Switching Station*, display boards explain the hydro-electric scheme; and, at the road's end (770ft), a plaque reminds that Affric was once Clan Chisholm land.

54 Inverness to Kyle of Lochalsh via Achnasheen

A862 to Muir of Ord. A832 to Achnasheen. A890 and A87 to Kyle of Lochalsh.—After leaving the fertile coastal strip at Muir of Ord the road rises gradually across open moorland hills, passing a succession of lochs, Mountains define the W view and the landscape becomes increasingly wild and Highland beyond Achnasheen.

SOME HOTELS. **Beauly**. *Priory*, The Square. Tel: (0463) 782309. **Muir of Ord**. *Ord House*, IV6 7UH. Tel: (0463) 870492. **Strathpeffer**. *Ben Wyvis*. Tel: (0997) 21323. *Highland*. Tel: (0997) 21457. **Garve**. *Strathgarve Lodge*, IV23 2PU. Tel: (09974) 204. **Achnasheen**. *Achnasheen*, IV22 2EF. Tel: (044588) 243. *Ledgowan Lodge*, Ledgowan. Tel: (044588) 252. For **Balmacara** and **Kyle of Lochalsh**, see Rte 52.

Total distance 76m.—*10m* **Beauly**.—*2m* **Muir of Ord**.—*4m* **Marybank**.—*8m* **Garve**.—*17m* **Achnasheen**.—*25m* **Stromeferry**.—*10m* **Kyle of Lochalsh**.

Railway. The railway (British Rail's 'Great Scenic Railway') for the most part follows a similar course to the road. In the E, though, the line continues N beyond Muir of Ord to Dingwall before bearing W. It then climbs a steep and scenic gradient to *Raven Rock* before rejoining the road at Loch Garve. Thereafter rail and road run together as far as Stromeferry, where the railway continues close to the shore to reach Kyle, while the main road cuts across the peninsula. The time from Inverness to Kyle of Lochalsh averages a little over three hours.

Leaving **Inverness** (see Rte 51) A862 crosses the Caledonian Canal (which here joins the sea through a series of six locks) at *Clachnaharry*, meaning Watchman's Stone—the place where the citizens maintained a watch for raiding Highlanders—and then for a while fringes the S shore of Beauly Firth before bridging the Beauly river at the point where A831 carries Rte 53 SW to the glens of Strathfarrar, Cannich and Affric.

10m **Beauly** (1100 inhab. *ECl.* Thurs.) derives its name from the French 'beau lieu', this in turn associated with the now ruined priory, once the 'Monasterium de bello loco'. A pleasant enough small place—though hardly meriting the claim implicit in its name—Beauly is closely associated with the Lovat family, chiefs of Clan Fraser, whose Beaufort Castle (2m S; no adm.) is the 19C successor of their castle destroyed by Cumberland in 1746 (for the fate of the then Lord Lovat, see Rte 48, Loch Morar). In the town square a striking monument commemorates the raising by the 16th Lord Lovat of the Lovat Scouts for service in the South African war, a stirring inscription recording that Lord Lovat 'desired to show that the martial spirit of their forefathers still animates the Highlands today', while, nearby, more modestly at the priory entrance, stands the shaft of the old mercat cross.

Beauly Priory (AM. Standard, but closed Mon. and Tues. morning in winter. Fee) was founded in c 1230 by Sir John Bisset of the Aird for French Valliscaulian monks. Today the most noteworthy features are the three rare and beautiful 13C triangular windows, with trefoils, in the S wall; the window-arcading in the chancel; and the 13C W doorway of the S transept. The N transept (restored 1901) is the burial place of the Mackenzies of Kintail, with a monument to their Sir Kenneth (died 1391), opposite which is the restored tomb of Prior Mackenzie (died 1479). The priory facade, with its three lancets, was built after 1530 by Abbot Reid, later Bishop of Orkney.

2m **Muir of Ord** marks an important crossroads, this Rte here branching NW along A832, while A862 continues N to join Rte 57 at Dingwall.—*4m Marybank*, whence a small road leads W for 22m up lonely Strath Conan, its river dammed but provided with salmon ladders, one of which (Torrachilty; 2m from Marybank. Tel: 09973-223) is open to visitors.

Strathpeffer (1300 inhab. *ECl.* Thurs *Inf.* Visitor Centre. Easter. May–Sept), on A834 3m N of Marybank, comes as something of a surprise. In the 18C sulphur springs were discovered here, the town soon becoming a popular spa, and although those elegant days are now long gone the town's wide street, gardens and many hotels still recall its gracious Victorian past. Today the former *Pump Room*, with a photo exhibition, can be visited in summer; a *Craft and Visitors Centre* (April–Sept: Tel: 0997-21618) shows craftsmen at work in the restored Victorian station; and there is even a *Dolls Museum* at Spa Cottage, The Square (Easter–early Oct: Daily except Tues., 14.00 to 18.00. Tel: 0997-21549. Fee). Finally, for visitors with a feel for clan conflict and legend, there is the *Eagle Stone*, reached by a path (sign, 100 yards) a short way up the road opposite the large Ben Wyvis Hotel. An eagle is the crest of Clan Munro and the stone commemorates a successful affray of 1411 by the Munros against the Macdonalds, while legend is provided by the Seer of Brahan who foretold that ships would tether to the stone should it fall three times; it is said that it has already fallen twice.

Some eighty years later, in 1492, the Macdonalds again came off worst, this time at *Kinellan* (1m W of Strathpeffer) and in a dispute with the Mackenzies. Kenneth Mackenzie accepted Margaret Macdonald as wife, but, on meeting her, found that she had only one eye. So he promptly returned the lady, stressing his point by mounting her on a one-eyed horse, led by a one-eyed groom and accompanied by a one-eyed dog. The slighted Macdonalds attacked, but lost the fight and Margaret's honour remained unavenged.

Castle Leod (no adm.), immediately E of the town, dates from c 1616.—South above the town rises the ridge called *Druim Chat* (Cat's Back), on top of which stands the vitrified fort of *Knockfarrel*, reached by a track by the burn bridge on A834 ½m E of the town.—The mass of *Ben Wyvis* (3429ft) lifts some 10m to the N of Strathpeffer. One approach is by a track starting off A834 to the E of the entrance of Castle Leod.

Beyond *Contin* (*4m* from Marybank) A832 runs through *Torrachilty Forest* (trail; booklet from FC office) and reaches (*2m*) *Rogie Falls* where, in a wooded and rocky setting, a foot suspension bridge leads the visitor over rapids.—*2m* **Garve**, from where Rte 56 bears N along A835 for Ullapool, while this Rte continues with A832 above *Loch Luichart*, the first reservoir in the Highlands to be used for the generation of electricity. In 1955 the railway track here was raised 20ft and a new station built; traces of the old line can still sometimes be traced. From the W end of the loch (*Grudie Bridge, 6m* from Garve), a track ascends for 4½m to Loch Fannich, 9m long and in wild and remote surroundings.

Now in lonely open moorland, A832 heads westward past small lochs and along Strath Bran to reach in *11m* the bleakly sited and scattered hamlet of **Achnasheen** with a station—the railhead for such places in Wester Ross (see Rte 55) as Loch Maree, Gairloch and Inverewe Gardens—at which a double track enables trains travelling in opposite directions to pass. Here, too, this Rte exchanges A832 for A890, the former road now representing one of the approaches to the heart of Wester Ross.

Both westward and southward Achnasheen is the gateway to much of Scotland's grandest Highland scenery, and as this Rte now aims SW towards Loch Carron it is into increasingly wild and broken country, the watershed (634ft) soon being crossed between lochs Gowan and Scaven.

In *18m* the head of **Loch Carron** is reached, a sea loch in two parts, the inner loch (6m long) being separated by a narrow neck from the open outer loch. Just before reaching the loch's head, the road splits, this Rte and the railway fringing the S shore. (For the N shore, see Rte 55. It should be noted that despite the name Stromeferry there is in fact no ferry across Loch Carron's neck.) —*7m* **Stromeferry**, where the main road carries this Rte S to join A87 and approach Kyle of Lochalsh along the shore of Loch Alsh. The railway, though, continues along the S shore of the now open part of Loch Carron, this section of the track having been built in 1897, before which the line ended at Stromeferry. Much of the new track had to be blasted out of the rock and the line represents what was at the time a major engineering achievement.

Dropping S from Stromeferry, A890 in *5m* joins A87, from which point to (*5m*) **Kyle of Lochalsh** see Rte 52.

55   Wester Ross (Loch Carron to Corrieshalloch)

This Rte is concerned with a splendid scenic triangle the apex of which is Garve (Rtes 54 and 56); its base line is the great sweep of broken coast that curves northward from Kyle of Lochalsh to Ullapool. As well as this magnificent coast, the area includes the famous NTS Torridon mountain estate, equally famed Loch Maree, and the well-known sub-tropical Inverewe gardens.

Wester Ross can be approached along any of three principal roads. From the S the entry is from Loch Carron. The central approach comes in from Achnasheen direct to Loch Maree. In the N, close to Corrieshalloch Gorge, A832 forks off A835 to fringe the coast southwards. The road from Garve to Corrieshalloch is described under Rte 56, and that from Garve through Achnasheen to Loch Carron under Rte 54. The description below travels the road from Loch Carron, northward past Torridon, Loch Maree and Gairloch (the only place in the whole area of any size), to Corrieshalloch.

A896 from Lochcarron to Kinlochewe, A832 to Gairloch and Corrieshalloch.

SOME HOTELS. **Lochcarron**. *Lochcarron* IV54 8YS. Tel: (05202) 226. **Shieldaig**. *Tigh-an-Eilean*, IV54 8XN. Tel: (05205) 251. **Torridon**. *Loch Torridon*, IV22 2EY. Tel: (044587) 242. **Kinlochewe**. *Kinlochewe*, IV22 2PA. Tel: (044584) 253. **Gairloch**. *Gairloch*, IV21 2BL. Tel: (0445) 2001. **Poolewe**. *Pool House*, IV22 2LE. Tel: (044586) 272. **Aultbea**. *Aultbea*, IV22 2HX. Tel: (044582) 201. **Dundonnell**. *Dundonnell*, IV23 2QS. Tel: (085483) 204.

Total distance 89m.—*4m* **Kishorn**.—*9m* **Shieldaig**.—*6m* **Torridon**.—*9m* **Kinlochewe**.—*19m* **Gairloch**.—*5m* **Poolewe** (*Inverewe*).—*37m* **Corrieshalloch**.

For *Loch Carron* and its S shore, see Rte 54. On the N shore the straggling village of **Lochcarron** is also known as Jeanstown. *Strome Castle*, 3m SW and on the loch's narrow neck across from Stromeferry, is a small and muddled ruin (NTS) the destruction of which was reputedly caused by the stupidity of the castle women. Long a stronghold of the Macdonalds, the castle was always a thorn in the flesh of the neighbouring Mackenzies. In 1602 Kenneth Mackenzie of Kintail laid siege to this irritant and succeeded in taking the castle and then blowing it up because Strome's women, after drawing water at the well, carelessly emptied it all into the gunpowder vat instead of the water vat and thus rendered the defenders helpless.

Leaving Lochcarron A896 climbs across a peninsula to reach (*4m*) **Kishorn** at the head of the loch of the same name and offering—though only to the confident motorist with a sound car—the opportunity to divert westward into the scenic and interesting Applecross Forest peninsula.

APPLECROSS DIVERSION (c 35m from Kishorn to Shieldaig). Access here in the S is by the difficult but spectacular pass of *Bealach-nam-Bo* (2054ft), narrow, steep and with many hairpins, though the descent to the village of *Applecross* on the W coast is by comparison gentle. In Gaelic the village is known as A Chromraich (Sanctuary), a reminder of a monastery founded here in 673 by St. Maelrubha (died

721), a monk from Bangor in Ireland. The monastery, which soon made this remote place second only to Iona as a Christian centre, was destroyed by the Norsemen, a fate probably also suffered by its founder, though not here but at Skaill (see Rte 60, Strath Naver). Local tradition is that the saint's body came back to Applecross for burial; but see also Loch Maree below.

Southward from the village the road passes largely depopulated hamlets before reaching (4m) *Toscaig*. Northward it rounds the bay beside which is *Applecross Chapel*, the now forlorn and abandoned relic of St. Maelrubha's venture, a remote and evocative corner with an ancient burial ground which may or may not be its founder's resting place. A venerable stone at the entrance commemorates Abbot Macoggie, who left here in 801 to become bishop of Bangor, while inside the chapel there are fragments of a Celtic cross, found beneath the turf here and probably set up in the 8C. Beyond, the road (opened in 1976) follows the coast, first of the Inner Sound with views across to Raasay, and then of Loch Torridon, to rejoin A896 in some 20m at Shieldaig.

9m (direct from Kishorn) **Shieldaig**, off which an island of the same name is an NTS nature reserve almost entirely covered in Scots pine. Here the road turns abruptly eastwards close to the S shore of Upper Loch Torridon to reach (*6m*) the **Torridon Countryside Centre** (NTS. June–Sept: Mon.–Sat., 10.00 to 18.00. Sun., 14.00 to 18.00. Donation. Fee for Deer Museum), a visit to which—with its displays, audio-visual presentation, deer museum, and advice on walks and climbs—is essential for any understanding of the magnificent *Torridon Estate* which looms high above. Formerly owned by the earls of Lovelace, the estate of 16,000 acres came to the National Trust for Scotland in 1967. Bounded on the NE by the summit ridge of Beinn Eighe (3309ft, and combining seven individual summits linked by narrow ridges nearly 5m long), and including peaks such as *Liathach* (3456ft) and *Beinn Allgin* (3232ft), the estate, together with the Beinn Eighe National Nature Reserve (see below) immediately to the N, ranks as one of Scotland's most scenically splendid and naturally interesting mountain masses. a tract as certain to excite the casual layman visitor as it will the naturalist or geologist. For the former the wildlife includes deer, mountain goat, wild cat and eagles; for the latter there are those red sandstone peaks, some 750 million years old, their tops conspicuous with white quartzite, some 150 million years younger.

Much the same might be written about **Beinn Eighe National Nature Reserve** (11,757 acres), across Beinn Eighe on Torridon's north, acquired primarily for the preservation and study of the sizeable remnant of Caledonian pine forest and distinguished for being the first national nature reserve to be declared in Britain. *Aultroy Visitor Centre* (Mid May–mid Sept: Mon.–Sat., 10.00 to 17.00. Tel: 044584-258. Donation), on A832 1m NW of Kinlochewe, shows an excellent illuminated physical model of the district, and leaflets are available for two nature trails, both starting from a car park 2m farther up the road.

Running below Liathach and Beinn Eighe, A896 in *9m* arrives at **Kinlochewe** where A832 comes in from Achnasheen and the E to carry this Rte NW past the Aultroy Visitor Centre and along much of the 12 mile length of *Loch Maree*. Varying in width and with its surprising variety of scenery, this is one of Scotland's loveliest and best known lochs. The name is thought to derive from St. Maree or Maelrubha, the monk who founded the monastery at Applecross and who, tradition claims, was for a while a hermit on the Isle of Maree in the loch's wider part where, dismissing the claims of Applecross, the locals insist that he was buried. The first stretch of the S shore with its Caledonian pine forest is a part of the Beinn Eighe reserve, while farther on, beyond the islands and where the road leaves the loch (*12m* from Kinlochewe), comes the Forestry Commission's *Slattadale Picnic Area*; starting point for forest walks, one of which (short) affords views of Victoria Falls, visited by Queen Victoria when she stayed at the Loch Maree Hotel, while another, the Tollie Path, provides 5m of rough hill walking across to Poolewe. Across the loch the grandest feature is the towering mass of *Slioch* (3260ft), so steep that its corries can be traced from foot to summit.

Leaving the loch A832 cuts across to the sea and (*7m*) **Gairloch** (150 inhab. *ECl.* Wed, but open in summer. *Inf.* Achtercairn), a sizeable village and very popular holiday centre straggling around the broad bay of the same name. The local *Heritage Museum* (Easter–Sept: Mon.–Sat., 10.00 to 18.00. Tel: 044583-243. Fee) provides admirable displays illustrating the long story of these western Highlands.

Beyond Gairloch the road to (*5m*) **Poolewe** passes a view point affording breathtaking vistas seaward across to northern Skye with the mountains of Harris far beyond, and inland up the length of Loch Maree. Poolewe, at the head of Loch Ewe and owing its name to the curious pool formed where the river enters the sea, is best known for **Inverewe Gardens** (NTS. *Gardens.* All year: Daily, 09.00 to 21.00 or ½ hour before dusk. *Visitor Centre.* April–mid Oct: Mon.–Sat., 10.00 to 17.00. Sun., 12.30 to 17.00. Open till 18.30 in summer. Fee). Created by Osgood Mackenzie in 1862, and the property of Scotland's National Trust since 1952, these famous sub-tropical gardens sprawl over a steep promontory jutting into Loch Ewe with its mountain backdrop. Although in the same latitude as icy Labrador and Siberia, the Gulf Stream here makes possible a luxuriance and variety at all times of the year. Among the huge variety of plants are examples from South America and South Africa, Himalayan lilies, and giant forget-me-nots from the South Pacific.

The road beyond Poolewe was once known as 'Destitution Road', a reminder that it was built during the famine of 1851. Although lacking the scenic grandeur of the country around and to the S of Loch Maree, the road nevertheless affords open sea loch views and mountain vistas, the dominating feature being *An Teallach* (the Forge) lifting to 3484ft above the southern shore of Little Loch Broom. *6m Aultbea*, with hotels.—*17m Dundonnell*, with *Ardressie Fisheries* (Easter–mid Oct: Mon.–Sat., 10.00 to 19.00. Tel: 085483-252. Fee), a fish farm at which most aspects of the rearing of trout and salmon can be seen and where the children should enjoy feeding the fish.—In another *14m* A832 joins A835 and Rte 56 at *Corrieshalloch* (Falls of Measach).

56 Inverness to Durness via Ullapool, Lochinver and Scourie

A862 to Muir of Ord. A832 to Garve. A835 through Ullapool to
Drumrunie. Unclassified roads through Inverpolly National Nature
Reserve to Lochinver. A837 and A894 to Laxford Bridge. A838 to
Durness.—Beyond Garve, and increasingly so N of Ullapool, highly
scenic, with the wild grandeur of Inverpolly followed by dark
rock-strewn glens and lochs and a rugged, fretted coast between
Kylesku and Durness.

SOME HOTELS. **Ullapool**. *Ladbroke Mercury Motor Inn*, North
Road. Tel: (0854) 2314. *Royal*, Garve Road. Tel: (0854) 2181.
Lochinver. *Culag*, IV27 4LF. Tel: (05714) 209. *Park House*, IV27
4JY. Tel: (05714) 259. **Kylesku**. *Kylesku*, IV27 4HW. Tel: (097183)
231. **Scourie**. *Scourie*, IV27 4SX. Tel: (0971) 2396. **Kinlochbervie**.
Kinlochbervie, IV27 4RP. Tel: (097182) 275.

Total distance 132m.—*24m* **Garve**.—*20m* **Corrieshalloch
Gorge**.—*12m* **Ullapool**.—*9m* **Drumrunie**.—*20m* **Lochinver**.—*15m*
Kylesku.—*8m* **Scourie**.—*6m* **Laxford Bridge**.—*4m* **Rhiconich**.—*14m*
Durness.

For Inverness to (*24m*) **Garve**, see Rte 54.—In a bleak moorland of
bare, rounded mountains A835 fringes the S shore of *Loch
Glascarnoch*, formed by the damming of the Glascarnoch river and
linked by runnels with Loch Vaitch to the N and the power station
on Loch Luichart to the S. The water divide (915ft) is crossed between
the N end of the loch and the small Loch Droma, to the S of the road
just beyond.

20m (from Garve) *Corrieshalloch Gorge* (NTS. Donation) is a
spectacular mile-long 200ft-deep schist-eroded ravine into which the
Measach Falls plunge 120ft. A suspension bridge just below the falls
was built by John Fowler, engineer of the Forth railway bridge, and
there is a good observation platform a short way farther downstream.
Rte 55 joins here from Gairloch. Just beyond (*2m*) *Lael Forest Garden*
(FC; walks, leaflets), showing some 150 different trees and shrubs
from many parts of the world, borders the E side of the road.

Running now with the E shore of Loch Broom A835 in *10m* enters
Ullapool (800 inhab. *ECl*. Tues., but open in summer. *Inf*. Easter.
May–Sept), a sprawling whitewashed township established in 1788
by the British Fisheries Society, still active with fishing but increasingly important as a lively tourist centre and as the port for the car
ferry (see Rte 66) to Stornoway on the island of Lewis. *Ullapool
Museum* (April–Oct: Mon.–Sat., 09.00 to 18.00. Tel: 0854-2135.
Donation) covers many aspects of Wester Ross, including the
Clearances, geology, crofting and wildlife, while for finer weather
there is a choice of boat excursions, one of the most popular being
to the *Summer Islands*, a scattered and sparsely inhabited group
some 12m to the NW (Islander Cruises, West Argyle Street. Tel:
0854-2264. Mackenzie Marine, Green Pasture. Tel: 0854-2008).

9m Drumrunie, a road junction from which A835, later joining
A837, provides the direct route northward while this Rte bears W for
Inverpolly National Nature Reserve. First, however, it could be
worthwhile to travel 3m N to *Knockan Cliff Information Centre* (NCC.
May–Sept: Mon.–Fri., 10.00 to 17.30. Donation), providing informa-
tion on the reserve and starting point for geological and nature trails

(leaflets). The geological trail is of particular interest because of the break here in the earth's crust known as the Mhoine Thrust and the resultant schists, highly altered rocks not belonging to the local sequence but forced here from perhaps 12m away.

*Inverpolly National Nature Reserve**, with Inverpolly Forest, is a remote and wild confusion of moor, woodland, burns, lochs and lofty, isolated mountain peaks, the reserve in the N merging with *Clencanisp Forest* to form one splendid scenic whole. The principal peaks in the reserve, rising as a half circle around the S end of lonely Loch Sionascaig, are *Cul Mor* (2787ft), *Cul Beag* (2523ft) and the craggy pinnacle of *Stac Polly* (2009ft), while Glencanisp is dominated by *Canisp* (2779ft) and the distinctive sugarloaf of *Suilven* (2399ft).

The unclassified road now followed—narrow, twisting and slow most of the way to Lochinver—first runs below mountains towering high to the right (Cul Beag and Stac Polly) while below on the other side stretch the dark and winding lengths of lochs Lurgainn and Baddagyle. After *8m*, just beyond the W end of the latter loch, a right turn is made to cross the small river Polly and meander northward, often through rowans providing a colourful photographic foreground for shots towards the wall of eastern peaks hanging above the reserve's inner fastness of moor, bog and loch.

12m **Lochinver** (300 inhab. *ECl.* Tues. *Inf.* June–Sept), a largish village, the only place of any size between Ullapool and Scourie and famed for its scenic coast, is a popular objective which can be overcrowded in summer. The best views, and especially that of the dramatic dome of Suilven to the SE, are enjoyed from a boat (Tel: 05714-362 or 291).

Motorists with time may continue by following the northerly loop (some 19m) offered by B869, narrow, twisting, sometimes steep, but generous with its ever varying views along the islanded coast and out into the waters of the Minch or across the breadth of Eddrachillis Bay. This Rte, however, now chooses A837 which soon runs with the shore of *Loch Assynt*, in *10m* from Lochinver reaching the junction with A894, the end-point of the Strath Oykel arm of Rte 58 which describes nearby ruined Ardvreck Castle and Calda House.—*5m* **Kylesku**, where, amid broken and sombre scenery, a fine bridge of 1984 now speeds the motorist across the rocky, islanded confluence of three lochs, Cairnbawn seaward to the W, Glendhu and Glencoul probing E and SE into the mountains. As in so many places, a boat best provides the isolation and the views, excursions here including the three lochs, seal islands, a heronry and, at the head of Loch Glencoul, *Eas Coul Aulin*, claiming to be Britain's highest waterfall (Tel: 097183-239 or 234).

8m **Scourie** (250 inhab.) is a sizeable village and useful stop along several miles of for the most part empty road. From here a boat excursion can be made to *Handa Island* (2m NW), a high-cliffed sanctuary for fulmars, shags, kittiwakes, auks and several other species (R. Macleod, 15 Scourie More. Tel: 0971-2140).

In *3m* A894 makes a neat loop around the NW of *Loch a' Bhagh Ghainmhich*, which is a lot of name for what is little more than a lochan. Here a very minor road, splitting into a diamond and returning to this same spot, affords ever varying island-studded seaward views as it meanders for some 6m through a weird landscape in which there is as much freshwater loch as solid soil and rock. Narrow, twisting, blind and in places abruptly steep, the road serves two places from which boat excursions can be made. One, on the W, is *Tarbet*, another jetty from which Handa Island can be reached (A. Munro, Tel: 0971-2126. Or W. MacRae, Tel: 0971-2156); the other, to the NE, is *Fanagmore*, for cruises into Loch Laxford with its islands, seals and birds (Mr Phillips. Tel: 0971-2319).

3m **Laxford Bridge**, a name deriving from the Norse for salmon. Here the Loch Shin arm of Rte 58 ends, while this Rte continues N along A838 into a strange and forbidding mountain wilderness of dark, rockstrewn glens, perched glacial boulders and black sombre lochs.—*4m Rhiconich* marks the head of grand *Loch Inchard*, flanked on its NE side by a tempting road which rides high above the water to reach the small port of *Kinlochbervie*, a hamlet developed after 1947 for white fish and lobster fishing.

Leaving the sea, now, and aiming NE through a remote and tumbled landscape, A838 in *5m* reaches a surprise in the form of a well beside the road. Dated 1883, it charmingly expresses the gratitude of the surveyor of this road, one Peter Lawson, for the kindness extended to him by the local people—a gentle touch above the rock-strewn wasteland beyond which, to the SE, Strath Dionard emerges from the mountains. Descending, the road in *4m* touches the sandy *Kyle of Durness*, in another *3m* reaching *Keoldale* for the ferry to Cape Wrath, for which, as also for (*2m*) **Durness**, see Rte 61.

57   Inverness to Bonar Bridge

A9 to Tore (for Black Isle). A835 to Dingwall. A962 and A9 to Tain (for Tain peninsula). A9 to Bonar Bridge.—This Rte traverses a fertile coastal-estuaried strip with unexciting seaward views but, inland, hills rising to moor and mountain, notably Ben Wyvis (3433ft). The Rte includes the peninsulas of Black Isle and Tain, the two separated by Cromarty Firth.

SOME HOTELS. **Fortrose**. *Royal*, Union Street. Tel: (0381) 20236. **Cromarty**. *Royal*, Marine Terrace. Tel: (03817) 217. **Dingwall**. *Royal*, High Street. Tel: (0349) 62130. *National*, High Street. Tel: (0349) 62166. **Tain**. *Royal*, High Street. Tel: (0862) 2013. **Bonar Bridge**. *Bridge*, Dornoch Road. Tel: (08632) 204. *Caledonian*, Dornoch Road. Tel: (08632) 214.

Total distance 50m.—*7m* **Tore**.—*5m* **Dingwall**.—*6m* **Evanton**.—*16m* **Tain**.—*15m* **Ardgay**.—*1m* **Bonar Bridge**.

From **Inverness** (see Rte 51) A9, using the interesting low Kessock Bridge of 1980, quickly crosses the narrows linking Beauly Firth to the W and the larger Moray Firth to the E and in *7m* reaches **Tore**, unimportant in itself but at the junction of five main roads and the place from which to start a round of Black Isle.

Black Isle

Black Isle is not in fact an island, but a thick tapering promontory, some 16m long from Tore to Cromarty and up to 8m broad, jutting out NE between Moray Firth on the S and Cromarty Firth on the N. The origin of the name is uncertain, but one suggestion is that it is a translation from the Gaelic Eilean Dubh, itself perhaps a corruption of Eilean Dubhthaich (St. Duthus Isle; St. Duthus, died 1065, Bishop of Ross). A simpler, though almost equally unsatisfactory theory is that, because of the mild climate, the area remains clear when the surrounding landscape is white with snow. A rather lost, quiet district of farm and woodland, there are a number of places of interest, some good beaches, and coastal flats with a variety of seabirds.

The description below makes an anticlockwise circuit of some 33m, but first a diversion to *Redcastle* (2m SW of Tore) may be considered, where the parish church of c 1450, ½m W of the hamlet, was formerly the church of the parish of Killearnan, this name deriving from St. Ierman, a nephew of St. Columba. The ruined castle above the hamlet, originally built in 1178 by William the Lion, was later owned by James Stewart, Marquis of Ormond, son of James III. Also near Tore, beside Allangrange House (1m SE), stand the small ruined remains of a chapel of the Knights Templar.

A832 leads E from Tore to *Munlochy*, just S of which is Drumderfit Hill, scene in 1400 of a Macdonald disaster when the defenders of Inverness first smuggled strong drink into the clan camp and then slaughtered the fuddled Highlanders. Fringing the head of Munlochy Bay, a seabird reserve, the road soon reaches *Avoch*, NW of which is the Rosehaugh estate, during the 17C the property of Sir George Mackenzie, Lord Advocate of Scotland and notorious as the 'bloody advocate' because of his persecution of the Covenanters. Another, and more reputable Mackenzie, Sir Alexander (1735–1821), explorer of Canada and discoverer of the river which received his name, also lived near Avoch, though his home, Avoch House, later burnt down.

Fortrose, though with a population of under 1000, is, with Cromarty, one of the two principal towns of Black Isle. A stone on the golf course marks the spot at which the last witch in Scotland was burnt—a 'distinction' also claimed by Dornoch—but a more worthy objective for the visitor will surely be the *Cathedral*, the small red sandstone ruin of a church founded by David I for the see of Ross, completed in c 1485 by Abbot Fraser, a monk from Melrose, and two centuries later pillaged by Cromwell to provide material for his fort at Inverness. Its otherwise mellow appearance today somewhat marred by a modern steeple perched on the attractive octagonal clocktower, the remains are a mixture of late 14C Dec. work (S nave aisle) and the Perp. style of Melrose. Against the N wall is the badly mutilated canopied tomb of Euphemia, Countess of Ross, builder of this aisle in c 1395, while an arched compartment at the W end is walled off as the burial place of the Mackenzies of Seaforth. Beside the cathedral stands the pleasing, detached 13C Chapter House, complete with sedilia in its lower room.

Adjacent **Rosemarkie**, another charming small place, also enjoys ecclesiastical distinction, having been the forerunner of Fortrose as the seat of the bishopric. Even earlier, though, in the 6C, St. Moluag founded a monastic school and church here—this latter reputedly being rededicated by St. Boniface in 716—and a Pictish stone in the churchyard of the 19C church is traditionally the former's tombstone. The walk NE along the edge of the cliffs will be familiar to geologists through the writings of Hugh Miller, though most visitors may prefer to make for *Chanonry Point*, scenically for the view across the narrow strait to Fort George, traditionally because it was here that Coinneach Odhar, the Seer of Brahan, met his painful end. Required by the Countess of Seaforth to describe what her absent husband was doing, he rashly stated that he was in the arms of a French woman, whereupon the infuriated countess promptly had him burnt to death in a barrel of tar.

With some attractive narrow streets and old cottages, **Cromarty** is a quiet township at Black Isle's tip which marks the S side of the narrow entrance to Cromarty Firth. *Hugh Miller's Cottage* (NTS. Easter. May–Sept: Mon.–Sat., 10.00 to 12.00. 13.00 to 17.00. Also, in June–Sept, Sun., 14.00 to 17.00. Fee), a thatched cottage of 1711 which was the birthplace of the noted geologist (1802–56), is now a museum showing geological specimens and material relating to Miller's work as geologist, writer and stonemason. Also of interest are the *Court House* (1782), the *Cross* (14C; repaired 1744), and the *East Church* with three mid 18C lofts (one for the laird, one for the schoolmaster and his pupils, and the third an investment to raise income from pew rents). And there is also the roofless *Gaelic Chapel*, on a hill above the town, built for the Highlanders who flocked to the cloth mills in the latter half of the 18C; a statue of Hugh Miller (H. Ritchie, 1859) adjoins the chapel and in the churchyard there are tombstones carved by him.

An undemanding road returns westward, providing views across to industrialised Invergordon and farther afield to the wide spread of the mountains. *Udale Bay*, with Nigg Bay across on the N side of the firth, together form a nature reserve, important for its migratory wildfowl as also for the large number of wader species. Farther W (5m), on the shore below B9163, stands the small 15C ruin of *Craig Castle*, an Urquhart stronghold and once also a seat of the bishops of Ross.

From Tore A835 in *5m* reaches the town of **Dingwall** (5000 inhab. *ECl.* Thurs.), a busy centre at the head of Cromarty Firth. The birthplace of Macbeth, the town was colonised by the Norsemen and it is to them that it owes its name ('Thing Volle' meaning Council Place). In 1226 Dingwall was made a royal burgh by Alexander II, but of the old *Castle* only a few stones remain, at the foot of Castle Street, and the principal place of interest today is the *Town House* of 1730 (Easter–Sept: Mon.–Sat., 11.00 to 13.00. 14.00 to 16.00. Tel: 046373-505. Free), providing a small museum of local history in which a special feature is the distinguished military career of Sir Hector MacDonald (1853–1903) who rose from the ranks and fought at Omdurman; he is also commemorated by a monument on nearby Mitchell Hill. An *Obelisk*, on a small mound near the church, stands as a perhaps less worthy but certainly more entertaining memorial. It bears a worn inscription stating that it was 'Erected by George, 1st Earl of Cromartie, who d. 1714 and is buried 3ft 6in to the S thereof'—a curious arrangement apparently chosen by the earl to thwart his wife's declared intention of dancing on his grave. In fact the present obelisk is a small replica (1916) of the original which tapered to 50ft, and, whatever the countess's opinion of her husband, it seems that he was popular enough with other ladies for tradition insists that the mound was raised by the women of Dingwall as a sign of respect for their lamented laird.

Running NE beside Cromarty Firth, the road (A962, becoming A9) passes below (*4m*) *Foulis Castle* (no adm.), seat of the chief of Clan Munro. A condition of the clan's tenure was that a snowball should be presented to the king whenever he visited, a feat apparently possible because the N-facing corries of Ben Wyvis are rarely completely free of snow.—*2m* **Evanton** village is at the foot of *Black*

Rock Ravine, a remarkable cleft—2m long, less than 12ft wide and in places a sheer 200ft deep—through which surges the river Glass. The road up the left bank should be taken for ¾m then a ¼m track which ends close to a footbridge spanning a spectacular section of the ravine. The'*Indian Temple*' crowning Knock Fyrish (1483ft) to the N above Evanton was put up by General Sir Hector Munro (1726–1805) of nearby Novar House as a means of easing local unemployment while at the same time achieving a touch of self-glorification, for the structure is said to represent the gateway to an Indian town taken by him in 1781.

Beyond Evanton (*2m*) A836, avoiding Invergordon and Tain, provides a short cut across high ground, with long views up and down the coast (view indicator on Struie Hill above the descent to Dornoch Firth). This Rte, however, keeps with A9, bypassing the industrial complex of *Invergordon* and in *12m* reaching the junction with B9175, which will be followed for 4m S to *Nigg* by anyone with a feel for old stones and arcane occurrences. At the old parish church a notice describes the various stones and graves, the latter including a tombstone bearing masonry work by Hugh Miller, the stones including two of especial interest. One, showing Pictish and Norse symbols, is in legend associated with that at Shandwick (see below) and thus marked the grave of a shipwrecked Norse prince; the other, the Cholera Stone (a small stone in line with the second window W of the church door), marks the spot where in 1832 the church officer, spotting the plague as a small cloud, courageously caught it and buried it.

2m **Tain** (2000 inhab. *ECl.* Thurs.) is a sturdy small town in which what first strikes the visitor is the attractive 16C (rebuilt 1707) *Tolbooth* with its conical spire and small angle turrets. But while appreciating this, a thought should surely be spared for those simple crofters of the 19C to whom Tain was a notorious centre of the ruthless administration of the Clearances. To them there could have been nothing attractive about the 'sharp-pointed house' from which emanated orders for their dispossession and in which, if they resisted, they were likely to find themselves imprisoned.

But Tain's story reaches way back beyond the Clearances. To Norse days, for the town's name is a corruption of the Norse 'Thing', meaning Council; to its patron St. Duthus, born here in c 1000 and later a distinguished Bishop of Ross; to Malcolm Canmore who granted a charter; to medieval days as a sanctuary, once sought, though in vain, by the wife of Bruce; and to 1587 when a second charter was conferred by James VI. Something of the above is illustrated in Tain's small *District Museum* (Mid May–mid Sept: Mon.–Sat., 10.00 to 12.00. 14.00 to 17.00. Tel: 086286-300. Donation) which serves also as a Clan Ross centre.

Additionally there are a church and a chapel. The latter, *St. Duthus Chapel*, is a small ruin in the cemetery between the town and the golf links. Built between the 11 and 12C, the chapel traditionally both stands on the site of the cottage in which Duthus was born and also houses his bones which are known to have been brought to Tain in 1253 from Armagh in Ireland where he died in 1065. Neither tradition is solidly based, and it may well be that the relics were buried in the ancient church which once stood on the site of today's. The chapel—unusual for not being orientated E–W—was built as a prayer cell with accommodation for a resident hermit charged with guarding the saint's shrine. It stood also within the sanctuary of the Girth of Tain, which, however, was violated on at least two occasions. The first was in 1307 when the Earl of Ross seized Bruce's wife and daughter who had fled here from Kildrummy (see Rte 38); the second was in 1427 when a freebooter, McNeill of Creich, chased an enemy into the chapel, then burning it and all who were inside, though it has been suggested that the offender was in reality a Mackay, masquerading under the name of his McNeill grandmother.

St. Duthus Church, built in c 1360, stands on the site of its early medieval predecessor, traces of which can still be seen in the chapter house. The new church soon became something of a competitor to the chapel on account of the saint's bones—they disappeared in 1560—and was long a place of pilgrimage, among its penitents being James IV who came here each year between 1493 and 1513 in expiation for his part in the death of his father (see Sauchieburn, at the end of Rte 23). Especially noteworthy are the beautiful E window, with five stained glass sections, and other windows depicting two historical events, namely Malcolm Canmore and Margaret conferring their charter, and the Scottish parliament of 1560 adopting Knox's Confession of Faith.

East of Tain

A short way S of Tain B9165 heads E off A9 for *Hill of Fearn*, birthplace and boyhood home of Peter Fraser (1884–1950), Prime Minister of New Zealand from 1940–49, and, just beyond, **Fearn Abbey**.

A Premonstratensian abbey founded in 1221 by Farquhar, 1st Earl of Ross, at Edderton (see below) was removed to Fearn in 1238 because of the greater fertility of the soil here. The young Patrick Hamilton, the first martyr of the Scottish Reformation (burnt at St. Andrews in 1528), was titular abbot, and at his death Fearn was annexed to the see of Ross. Later, the abbey church was converted to parish church, but was the scene of a tragedy in 1742 when the roof fell in, killing 44 people.

Today the again largely restored church embodies the nave and choir of the old abbey church, but the N and S are marked by the roofless remains of small transeptal chapels. In the former S chapel, under a carved canopy, is a much worn recumbent figure of a lady of Clan Mackenzie, while the E end of the chancel is the burial place of the Ross family.

Beyond, on the coast, *Shandwick* has to the S of its bay a red sandstone cliff below which fossils may be found, while above the village stands an ancient and battered cross-slab bearing bosses and animal figures. A more famous stone, now in Edinburgh's Queen Street Royal Museum of Scotland, was found at Hilton of Cadboll, just to the N. Tradition is that these Shandwick and Hilton stones, together with that at Nigg church, mark the graves of three Norse princes lost in a shipwreck on a local reef.

B9165 out of Fearn leads NE towards Tarbat Ness, along which is the village resort of **Portmahomack**, with a small harbour (improved by Telford) and a quaint Victorian iron fountain recording the introduction of 'gravitation water' in 1887. Nearby ruined *Ballone Castle* of the 15–16C was typical Z-plan with diagonally opposed towers; built for the Earl of Ross and later passing to the Mackenzies, the castle was abandoned in the early 19C. *Tarbat Ness*, with one of the highest lighthouses in Britain, guards the S entrance towards Dornoch Firth.

Curving NW out of Tain A9 in *6m* reaches *Edderton*, the original site chosen in 1221 by the Earl of Ross for his abbey, moved a few years later to Fearn. Of this—it was here for only a brief 17 years—nothing of course survives, but, to the N of the village, there is a reminder of even earlier days in the form of a tall stone bearing Pictish symbols and traditionally commemorating a battle with the Norsemen.

9m Ardgay is at the head of Dornoch Firth and at the foot of **Strathcarron**, the latter a strath to be explored to its road's end at Croick (10m) by anybody sensitive to the poignancies of the Clearances. Once this land was the crofting home of the Rosses, but in 1845 the landowner decided that they must make way for more profitable sheep. Quiet roads trace both banks of the brown and boulder-strewn Carron as it drops seawards through lightly wooded and gentle country, but in 1854 the scene at *Gruinards*, on the right bank, was anything but gentle when 70 Ross women stood resolute until, with 20 of their number injured, they were swamped by a small army of eviction agents. Higher up the Strath, Clencalvie too was Ross, and its evicted families, having nowhere else to go, camped beside *Croick Church*, a modest white-pebbled small place built, somewhat surprisingly, to a plan by Telford. Here they scratched their record on the glass of the window, leaving messages still to be read today. 'Glencalvie people was in the churchyard here, May 24 1845'; 'This house is needy refuge'; 'Glencalvie people, the wicked generation'—did they perhaps see their plight as some form of punishment? Nor is this all here, for ·outside the W edge of the churchyard are the collapsed but unmistakeable remains of a broch, a reminder of a refuge of other peoples perhaps 2000 years earlier.

1m **Bonar Bridge** (500 inhab. *ECl.* Wed. *Inf.* June–Sept), on the N side of the head of Dornoch Firth, lies beyond a bridge spanning the channel linking the head of the firth with the loch known as the Kyle of Sutherland; built by Telford in 1812 and rebuilt after a flood of 1892, the bridge has since been widened. It was near *Carbisdale Castle* (Youth Hostel) at the N of the Kyle that Montrose made his final stand in 1650, being routed and then surrendered to his enemies by MacLeod of Assynt (see Rte 58).—For Bonar Bridge to the *North West*, see Rte 58; to *John O'Groats*, see Rte 59.

58 Bonar Bridge to the North West

Three roads, all wandering across remote and open moor, fan NW away from Bonar Bridge. To the W coast (Rte 56) the choice is between Strath Oykel (A837 to Loch Assynt) or Loch Shin (A838 to Laxford Bridge). Scenically, at least by Highland standards, the Strath Oykel road is not outstanding, but its northern part affords good views of the mountains and this road has the advantage that it heads directly for Ullapool and Lochinver and the wild country of Inverpolly and Glencanisp that lies between. The Loch Shin road is pleasant and varied, though not until the end of the loch's rather dreary 16m length.

The road to the N coast (A836 to Altnaharra, then unclassified to

Hope on Rte 61) would be hard to equal for sheer space and remoteness and has also the merit of offering, at Altnaharra, a choice of two other approaches to the N coast.

For all three roads the start is common as far as (4m) Invershin where the Strath Oykel road bears W. The other two split 8m farther N beyond Lairg.

> **Key distances**. Bonar Bridge via Strath Oykel to *Loch Assynt* (junction with A894), 37m.—Bonar Bridge via Loch Shin to *Laxford Bridge*, 45m.—Bonar Bridge via Altnaharra to *Hope*, 49m.
>
> SOME HOTELS (see also Rtes 57, 56 and 61). **Oykel Bridge**. *Oykel Bridge*, IV27 4HE. Tel: (054984) 218. **Inchnadamph**. *Inchnadamph*, IV27 4HL. Tel: (05712) 202.—**Lairg**. *Sutherland Arms*, IV27 4AT. Tel: (0549) 2291.—**Altnaharra**. *Altnaharra*, IV27 4UE. Tel: (054981) 222.

Via Strath Oykel to Loch Assynt

At *Invershin* A837 bears W, after a further 6m merging with a road from Lairg. Soon the little river Cassley is crossed, just beyond being a spot called Tuiteam-Tarbhach (fertile fall of slaughter), site in c 1397 of a bloody affray between the MacLeods of Assynt and Lewis and the Mackays of Sutherland; it was a decisive Mackay victory, only one MacLeod returning to Lewis and he later dying of his wounds.

Beyond Oykel Bridge wooded landscape gives way to moor as gradually the western mountains rise into view, first among them being *Canisp* (2779ft) and to the right *Breabag* (2670ft) and *Ben More Assynt* (3273ft). Beyond Loch Craggie (4m after Oykel Bridge), appear the grand isolated peaks of Inverpolly and Glencanisp Forest; from S to N *Cul Beag* (2523ft) with *Stac Polly* (2009ft) behind, and then *Cul Mor* (2787ft), followed by *Suilven* (2399ft).

A837 is joined by A835 (for Knockan Cliff, 4m SW, see Rte 56), beyond the junction heading due N and in about 4m passing (E) *Inchnadamph Nature Reserve* (3200 acres), an area mainly of specialist geological interest, lying as it does at the W foot of an area of disturbed limestone of Cambrian age and being ringed by the Glencoul, Ben More and Moine thrusts. In the S part of the reserve there are caves and fissures in which prehistoric human and animal bones have been found, while botanists may note that willow scrub found in the peat hollows is of a type common in Scandinavia but rare in Scotland.

As Loch Assynt is approached a memorial on a hillock near the SE corner of the loch commemorates two late-19C geologists (Peach and Horne) who did much to interpret the geology of this part of the Highlands. Beyond, on its promontory, appears the stark fragment of *Ardvreck Castle*, a stronghold (c 1490) of the MacLeods and the grim place in which Montrose was held after his defeat at Carbisdale near Bonar Bridge, while just to the S stand the remains of *Calda House*, a Mackenzie mansion built in the 17C but later abandoned after destruction by a fire.—Here Rte 56 is joined.

Via Loch Shin to Laxford Bridge

A short way N of Invershin the *Shin Falls* (with forest walks) tumble through a rocky gorge, a spot where leaping salmon may sometimes be well seen. Beyond *Lairg* (600 inhab. *ECl.* Wed. *Inf.* June–Sept) A838 angles away NW beside the not very interesting shore of *Loch*

Shin—a narrow hydro-electric reservoir some 17m long—and soon the mountains begin to bar the westward view; *Ben More Assynt* (W, 3273ft), *Ben Leod* (ahead, 2597ft) and *Ben Hee* (N, 2864ft).

Beyond the end of Loch Shin the scenery markedly improves. The hills close in and the road threads a series of lochs and woods between mountains of increasing height, until finally squeezing between the abrupt, quartzite-capped pinnacle of *Ben Stack* (2356ft) and its companion loch to accompany the lovely Laxford river below the great scree face of *Arkle* (2580ft) to the N. Rte 56 is joined at *Laxford Bridge*.

Via Altnaharra and Strath More to Hope

For Invershin to *Lairg*, see above. The road steadily rises across desolate moor to cross the watershed (828ft) at *The Crask*, 1m N of Crask Inn, and reach the remote hamlet of **Altnaharra** at the W end of Loch Naver. Here there is a choice of three roads to the N coast. To the E, B873 skirts part-wooded Loch Naver, beyond joining Rte 60 at Syre; in the centre, A836 continues N across moorland (730ft) before descending to the W shore of *Loch Loyal*, with its extension Loch Creagach forming a lovely sweep of water below (W) the huge granite mass of *Ben Loyal* (2504ft) with its four splintered peaks.

But this Rte turns W along a narrow, unclassified road which after 6m of lonely moor and dark bog meets the watershed at *Loch Meadie* before finding the mountains and dropping into steep-sided green Strath More. Here, in a grand and lovely setting beside the river with *Ben Hope* (3040ft) towering above, there survives a tantalising echo from this valley's Iron Age past; the unusually small broch of *Dornadilla* (or Dun Dornaig), once a home and refuge, today still remarkably well preserved and with the higher part of its wall probably still representing the original height. Just beyond, at *Alltnacailleach*, there is a good waterfall, and, beyond again, the road runs above peaceful Loch Hope to join Rte 61 at *Hope*.

59   Bonar Bridge to John o'Groats

A9.—Generally a narrow coastal strip between the mountains and the sea. At first the coast is flat, but to the N of Loch Fleet it becomes undulating and in places steep, with cliffs. Beyond Dunbeath the mountains ease down to moorland, and from Wick northwards the scene is flat and bleak, though in places with impressive cliffs.

SOME HOTELS. **Dornoch**. *Dornoch Castle*, Castle Street. Tel: (0862) 810216. *Royal Golf*, Grange Road. Tel: (0862) 810283. **Golspie**. *Golf Links*, Church Street. Tel: (04083) 3408. **Brora**. *Royal Marine*, Golf Road. Tel: (0408) 21252. **Helmsdale**. *Navidale House*, KW8 6JS. Tel: (04312) 258. **Wick**. *Ladbroke Mercury Motor Inn*, Riverside. Tel: (0955) 3344.

Total distance 87m.—*14m* **Dornoch**.—*10m* **Golspie**.—*5m* **Brora**.—*10m* **Helmsdale**.—*18m* **Latheron**.—*5m* **Clyth**.—*10m* **Wick**.—*15m* **John o'Groats**.

From **Bonar Bridge** (see Rte 57) the wooded road skirts the N side of Dornoch Firth, passing or running close to a variety of minor sites, some of them prehistoric or nearly so. On the promontory into the firth, 3m out of Bonar Bridge, a search—in summer the undergrowth can be dense—should reveal the remains of a vitrified fort called *Dun Creich*, within it being an unidentified medieval ruin, while at (2m) *Spinningdale*, and more easily seen, a ruin below the road is that of a mill. In a further 2m, opposite *Ospidale House*, a stone column beside the road is said to commemorate the death in battle of a Norse chieftain called Ospis. Next comes *Skibo Castle* (no adm.), built in 1898 by Andrew Carnegie on the site of an old castle to which Montrose was brought after his capture at Loch Assynt and imprisonment in Ardvreck. At *Clashmore*, just beyond, can be seen traces of a chambered cairn in the form of three large stones on a mound W of the school; and there is another chambered tomb in a field S of A9 at *Evelix*. Finally, a lone megalith stands on the right of A949 as this short road approaches Dornoch.

14m (from Bonar Bridge) **Dornoch** (1000 inhab. *ECl.* Thurs. *Inf.* The Square) is a dignified, almost sleepy town, clustered solid around a spacious centre dominated by the squat cathedral, admirably in keeping in local stone. With its miles of sands, golf courses and other amenities this is a popular yet still quiet family resort.

History. Middens discovered at Earl's Cross on the links prove that there were people living here perhaps 3000 years ago. Dornoch's first recorded building, however, was the church of St. Barr which must have stood here in about 600. Later there was a Norse settlement, then in 1224 Gilbert de Moravia (Murray), Bishop of Caithness, started building the present cathedral and Dornoch became the seat of the bishops, who built their castle alongside. In 1570 Dornoch was the victim of a clan feud between the local Murrays and the Mackays of Strathnaver, the town being pillaged and both cathedral and bishop's castle burned. In 1722 the last witch in Scotland was burnt here, a 'distinction' also claimed however by Fortrose; the unfortunate was Janet Horne, condemned for transforming her daughter into a pony, riding her to a witches' coven, and there having her shod by the Devil. In 1942 the Norsemen returned, this time as the Norwegian Brigade which was based here for training and whose stay is recorded by a plaque in the cathedral.

Dornoch Cathedral was begun in 1224 as described above, but after the fire of 1570 all that was left intact was the tower with its spire, the rest being roofless. The choir and transepts were restored in 1616 and the nave in 1634, but major restoration had to wait until that sponsored by the Duchess of Sutherland between 1835–37 and carried out by William Burn—a far too drastic and heavy-handed undertaking which included what was virtually a rebuilding of the nave. A happier restoration was that of 1924, as part of the 700th anniversary commemoration, when the plaster was stripped away to reveal once again the beautiful 13C stonework of the crossing, the choir and the E sides of the transepts. No fewer than 16 earls of Sutherland are said to lie here. At the W end are a statue of the 1st Duke (by Chantrey) who died in 1833 and is even more ostentatiously commemorated by a giant figure high above his Dunrobin Castle (see below), and the mutilated effigy of Sir Richard de Moravia, brother of the cathedral's founder and killed in battle against the Norsemen at nearby Embo (see below).

The town *Cross*, still showing its ancient shaft, is against the N side of the cathedral wall, but all that survives of the once formidable *Castle of the Bishops* is its sturdy tower, now a part of Dornoch Castle Hotel. Also in the Square, in the old jail, is the *Dornoch Craft Centre* (Summer: Mon.–Sat., 09.30 to 18.00. Sun., 12.00 to 18.00. Winter:

Mon.–Fri., 09.30 to 18.00. Tel: 0862-810555. Free) showing crafts and offering a glimpse of 19C prison life.

The northward journey can be continued either by returning direct to A9 or, more interestingly, by taking the minor shore road through Embo and Skelbo. Just outside Dornoch the *Earl's Cross* (see above) stands on the links between the road and the shore, site of prehistoric discoveries but itself probably marking the boundary in the 13C between the lands of the earls of Sutherland and those of the bishop; once it bore on either side their respective arms. At *Embo*, by the entrance to a caravan site, are preserved the scanty, tumbled remains of two prehistoric burial chambers (c 2000 BC), while the caravan site is itself of interest as successor to a Clearances village into which evicted crofters were herded and invited to farm the unpromising, sandy surrounds. Beyond, *Skelbo Castle*, now a small ruin on a grassy mound overlooking Loch Fleet, dates from the 14C but is successor to an older, wooden affair owned by that Richard de Moravia, killed at Embo, whose effigy lies in Dornoch's cathedral. And hither in 1290 came Edward I's commissioners, eager to greet the child Maid of Norway as Queen of Scotland and bride of their king's son, but soon to be shattered by the news of her death at sea.

Immediately beyond Skelbo A9 is rejoined and the head of Loch Fleet crossed by a long causeway raised by Telford in 1815 to carry the new road superseding the ferry that had plied for centuries.—*10m* (from Dornoch) **Golspie**, a long, straggling village closely associated with the Sutherlands, their splendidly carved loft of 1739 being the main feature of St. Andrew's Church, while high above the village on Ben Vraggie (1293ft; sometimes shown as Beinn a' Bhragaich) presides the colossal figure of the 1st Duke, a man as much abused for his Clearances evictions as he was praised for the improvements he sponsored. At Golspie, too, bearing hard round the church along an insignificant road, a high inland loop can be made (c 22m to Brora), first across the shoulder of Ben Horn (1706ft) and up on to a desolate windswept plateau, then by contrast curving northwards and eastwards to drop the length of a glorious open valley, its foot filled by *Loch Brora*, wooded, tranquil and with green meadows creeping into its waters. This is a district rich in cairns, burial chambers, brochs, settlement remains and field systems, the discovery of which should tempt the dawdler armed with a detailed map.

Dunrobin Castle (June–mid Sept: Mon.–Sat., 10.30 to 17.30. Sun., 13.00 to 17.30. Tel: 04083-3177. Fee), from the 13C the seat of the earls, later the dukes of Sutherland, stands on a natural terrace by the sea, once marking the end of the series of ferries which crossed the succession of firths to the S. Said to have occupied the site of a broch, the original castle was a square keep with angle-turrets, built by Robert, 2nd Earl of Sutherland, in c 1275. Over the years this was extended by a tower and hall wing which eventually enclosed a courtyard, until in the 19C Sir Charles Barry carried out the large extension which resulted in today's Scottish Baronial complex. In 1915, when in use as a naval hospital, the castle was damaged by fire, this leading to further reconstruction by Sir Robert Lorimer. Visitors today can still see the massive ancient keep and some of the 19C rooms. (There are plans to convert part of the castle into a hotel with a holiday village in the grounds, but this is not expected significantly to affect viewing.)

Two quite good broch remains can be found beside A9 either side

of (5m) **Brora**, a small town known for the spinning of Shetland wool.
The broch to the S is immediately E of the road just before it crosses
the railway; the other (Cinn Trolla), 3m N and close to the railway,
is better, with an internal diameter of over 30ft, traces of domed
chambers, and outworks about an entrance passage. When excavated
in 1880 two headless skeletons—evidence, surely, of some ancient
unexplained ritual—were found here. Near here, too, a short way
before the Glen Loth road, the last wolf in Scotland was killed in
about 1700, but the stone recording this paradoxically reassuring yet
saddening event tends to move around with road changes.—*10m*
Helmsdale (1000 inhab. *ECl.* Wed. *Inf.* June–Sept) is a grey fishing
township, from which Rte 60 climbs away for the N coast.

Now winding round ravines, A9 climbs to a plateau (750ft) which
ends towards the sea in the bold and rocky *Ord of Caithness*, a place
of ill omen for Sinclairs who prefer not to cross the Ord on a Monday
ever since a large party of the clan marched across on that day on
their way to Flodden, whence none returned. The coastal views are
spectacular, though, and red deer may also be seen. Beside the sea
at *Berriedale* are the scanty remains of a castle, once a fortress of the
earls of Caithness, while at *Dunbeath*, beyond, there is another castle
(no adm.), a large part of which dates to the early 15C. From
Dunbeath, too, a minor road runs 6m W to *Braemore*, near which, at
Eagle Rock, the Duke of Kent (1902–42) lost his life in an air accident.

15m (from Helmsdale) *Laidhay Croft Museum* (Easter–Sept: Daily,
09.00 to 17.00. Tel: 0955-2596. Fee), a croft complex of c 1842 or
earlier, with house and byre together under one roof and an adjacent
barn which is a good example of 'cruck' roof construction, a method
essential here due to the local shortage of timber.—*3m* **Latheron**,
with a *Clan Gunn Heritage Centre* (Tel: 0955-2596) as also, within
the NE angle of A9 and A985, standing stones and a strange hilltop
belfry, sited here so that the summoning bell could be heard
throughout the scattered valleys of the parish.

From Latheron a worthwhile diversion—of prehistoric interest; a
triangle of some 12m back to A9 at Lybster—may be made N along
A985 to *Achavanich*, approaching which Loch Rangag, with broch
remains on a low spit, lies below the road; though little more than a
tumble of stones, the site is of interest for the traces of a ditch and
embankment defence across the neck. The *Achavanich Standing
Stones*, some 40 surviving out of a probable original 60, are just down
the unclassified road which hairpins SE. The oval shape, open to the
SE, is one of only two known sites of this design, and speculation is
added by a once large burial cist just outside the oval's mouth. The
unclassified road meets A9 at *Lybster*, where there is an inscribed
Celtic cross near the N wall of the churchyard.

5m (direct from Latheron) *Clyth*, where prehistoric interest again
suggests a diversion, this time 6m N to the *Grey Cairns of Camster*,
a complex of burial cairns in a remote and desolate peat moorland
landscape that can have changed little since Stone and Bronze Age
peoples brought stones here and erected these massive monuments.
Today well restored and given skylights to help the visitor supple
enough to crawl inside, they include a round and a long cairn, the
former, with complete original passage, being one of the best
examples of its kind on Scotland's mainland. The long cairn—200ft
by 65ft and known as the horned type—has separate chambers as
well as its entrance passage. Human and animal remains, pottery

and stone artefacts have all been found here.

The *Hill o' Many Stanes, on a hillock just off A9 3m beyond Clyth, is a perhaps even more remarkable prehistoric site where no explanation is offered for over 200 small stones painstakingly arranged in 22 rows to form a kind of fan.

In 8m, approaching Wick, the shattered Castle of Old Wick survives from the 12–14C as little more than a clifftop fragment. Originally a Cheyne stronghold, it later passed to the Sutherlands; but the castle's weakness was its lack of a good well, this leading to its surrender after a siege in 1569 and its abandonment a century or so later. There are fine cliffs around here, to the S of the castle being the Brig o' Trams, a stack connected to the shore by a natural arch.

2m **Wick** (8000 inhab. ECl. Wed. Inf. Whitechapel Road, off High Street)—the name deriving from the Norse 'Vik' meaning Bay—is a busy northern centre with an airport and a harbour at the mouth of the river.

History. Wick was mentioned in the sagas as early as 1140 and later became a royal burgh, at which time, though, the place was no more than a scatter of houses and a church on the N bank of the river. In 1808 the British Fisheries Society commissioned Telford to lay out a model village on the S side, this being called, then as now, Pulteneytown. The inner harbour was completed by 1810, the outer by 1831, and there were major improvements as soon as 1868. But the harbour, for various reasons never very successful, declined in importance with the disappearance of the herring and the arrival of the railway; today it is largely used by whitefish boats.

The old town, N of the river, with the narrow, winding High Street and the wider Bridge Street, is the main shopping district. Here the parish church (1830), at the W end of High Street, is adjoined by the older Sinclair Aisle, the burial place of the earls of Caithness. Two main places of interest, however, will be found S of the river, one being the Wick Heritage Centre (limited times. Tel: 0955-2596. Fee), illustrating the fishing industry, and local past domestic and farming life. The other, on Harrowhill a short way farther S, is Caithness Glass (Mon.–Fri., 09.00 to 16.30 or 17.00. Also Sat. in summer, 09.00 to 16.00. Tel: 0955-2286. Free) where glass blowing can be seen and the results purchased.

Noss Head, with a lighthouse, is 3m N of Wick beyond the airport, and from a car park short of the lighthouse a path leads to two adjacent clifftop ruined castles, Sinclair and Girnigoe, the latter of the 15C and the former early 17C. Both were residences of the earls of Caithness, Girnigoe being where the 4th Earl, suspecting that his son (the Master of Caithness) was plotting against him, imprisoned him from 1570–76 and then murdered him. In 1672 the 6th Earl sold his estates to Campbell of Glenorchy, but the sale was disputed by another Sinclair, Sinclair of Keiss (7m N). Campbell thereupon invaded the laid siege to Girnigoe, this being the expedition to which the ballad 'The Campbells are coming' is believed to refer. Both castles were deserted in 1679, soon collapsing into ruin. Ackergill Tower (no adm.), 2m W of the twin castles, dates from the 14–15C.

The stretch of coast between Wick and John o' Groats seems to have been among the earliest inhabited parts of Scotland, and, although nothing can now be seen, excavation during the 19C and more recently has shown that Middle Stone Age people lived here, holding on to their primitive way of life even after more advanced New Stone Age and even Iron Age cultures were flourishing in the more fertile hinterland.

   7m Keiss, with remains on the cliff of its ancient castle, has a small harbour, just to the N of which are clear traces of two brochs. Beyond (*3m*), just S of Ness Head, stands ruined *Bucholy Castle*, built in c 1115 and once the home of Sweyne, a Norse pirate whose story is told in the sagas.—*5m* **John o' Groats**, see Rte 61.

60   Helmsdale to the North Coast

A897 up Strath of Kildonan to Kinbrace. Then choice between A897 via Strath Halladale to Melvich, or B871 via Strath Naver to Bettyhill.—Moor, peat bog and wooded strath, with some mountain backdrop.

SOME HOTELS. See Rte 59 **Helmsdale** and Rte 61 **Bettyhill**.

Total distance to Melvich 37m; to Bettyhill 44m.—*16m* **Kinbrace**. Then either *21m* **Melvich**; or *15m* **Syre**.—*13m* **Bettyhill**.

From **Helmsdale** (see Rte 59) the road, accompanied by the railway, gradually ascends *Strath of Kildonan*, also known as Strath Ullie, a wide valley of slowly rising, mostly open and bald moor, with at its upper end distant mountain views. This parish of Kildonan suffered severely during the Clearances, losing four-fifths of its people (some 2000) between 1801–31, but there was a temporary surge in population when Suisgill and other burns became the scene of gold panning in 1868–69. Cairns and broch remains invite discovery with the help of a large-scale map, and gold panning can still provide entertainment, if with little likelihood of profit.

   In some *12m* the *Suisgill Burn* is crossed, a large broch remain being visible just W of the road a short way beyond.—*4m* **Kinbrace**, a desolate and scattered hamlet at which a choice is offered between A897 along Strath Halladale or B871 up the Helmsdale river and then along Strath Naver. Scenically there is little to choose between the two roads, but that via Strath Naver is wilder, rather more interesting and provides, at Syre, a road W to Altnaharra and Rte 58.

STRATH HALLADALE, green and well cultivated, once defined the boundary between Mackay and Sutherland territory.—*21m Melvich* is on Rte 61.

STRATH NAVER. From Kinbrace to (*15m*) **Syre** in Strath Naver B871 makes its way across wide, open moor affording long vistas, especially S to the mountains which rise beyond the large, bleak lochs that feed the Helmsdale river. Syre, and Skail 2m N, are associated with St. Maelrubha, thought to have been murdered here by the Norsemen in c 722 and a stone is said to mark his grave (but see also Rte 55, Applecross and Loch Maree). Another stone, beside the road towards the N end of the straggling hamlet, recalls the days of Napoleonic danger and the first gathering of the 93rd Sutherland Highlanders on the formation of the regiment in 1800.

Strath Naver has not always presented the tranquil face it does today. At the time when the Sutherland Highlanders gathered at Syre the fertile 10m from the loch to Skailburn was strung with crofter hamlets, the people being Mackays despite their living on Sutherland land. Nineteen years later all the inhabitants had been evicted and their homes burned; many died, and an eye-witness of 1819 has described how on one unforgettable night he counted the flames of 250 crofts, including his own. For the *Strath Naver Museum* at Bettyhill-Farr, see Rte 61.

From Syre B873 bears SE along Loch Naver for Altnaharra on Rte 58. B871 continues N from Syre to reach in *10m* the junction with A836 and (a further *3m*) **Bettyhill**, see Rte 61.

61   John o' Groats to Durness

A836 to Tongue. A838 to Durness.—For much of this Rte the road keeps inland, giving only occasional views of the sea. Rather bleak landscape between John o' Groats and Thurso, along which stretch can be seen, though sadly decreasingly, distinctive local stone slab fences, the only evidence today of an industry which once supplied flagstones for the pavements of cities as far apart as Paris and Melbourne. West of Thurso the scenery gradually changes until W of Melvich the road is winding across mostly bare moor while the coast becomes bolder. The visitor who explores almost any of the many little roads down to the shore will find surprisingly rewarding lost corners, with some fine beaches and strange cliffs and rocks.

SOME HOTELS. **John o' Groats**. *John o' Groats House*, KW1 4YR. Tel: (095581) 203. **Thurso**. *Pentland*, Princes Street. Tel: (0847) 63202. *Royal*, Traill Street. Tel: (0847) 63191. **Bettyhill**. *Bettyhill*, KW14 7SP. Tel: (06412) 202. **Tongue**. *Ben Loyal*, Main Street. Tel: (08005) 216. *Tongue*, IV27 4XD. Tel: (08005) 206. **Durness**. *Parkhill*, IV27 4PN. Tel: (097181) 209.

Total distance 87m.—*11m* **Dunnet**.—*8m* **Thurso**.—*9m* **Dounreay**.—*21m* **Bettyhill**.—*12m* **Kyle of Tongue**.—*8m* **Hope (Loch Eriboll)**.—*18m* **Durness**.

John o' Groats (*Inf.* May–Sept), though not, as often supposed, the northernmost point of Britain's mainland (this is Dunnet Head) is nevertheless the accepted opposite to Cornwall's Land's End, 876m away.

The curious name goes back to one John de Groot, a Dutchman who inexplicably settled in this remote corner during the reign of James IV, a mound with a flagstaff close to the hotel being said to mark the site of his house. In order to avoid family precedence disputes between his eight descendants, the house was octagonal in shape, had eight doors and was centred on an octagonal table; thus each man entered by his own door and could maintain that he was sitting at the head of the table. A more prosaic story is that John worked a ferry across to South Ronaldsay and built a shelter for his waiting customers, with eight recesses to protect them from the wind whatever its direction.

Scattered around an uninviting landscape the village affords seaward views across Pentland Firth and its islands to Orkney (8m away) and, for beachcombers, local small shells known as 'groatie buckies'. In summer there are local boat excursions to, for example, Duncansby Head with its birds and cliff scenery and to the island of Stroma, known for its seals (Tel: 095581-353, -252 or -315) and there is also a summer passenger ferry to Burwick on South Ronaldsay, the excursion including a local bus tour (Two to four times daily. Crossing 45 minutes. Tel: 095581-353).—For John o' Groats S to *Bonar Bridge*, see Rte 59.

Pentland Firth, a name more meaningful in its older version, Pictland Firth, is notorious for its swirling tides and treacherous currents; when the tide is rising the main current sets from W to E, changing direction on the ebb, but the coastal currents run in opposition, forming the dangerous 'roosts' or races. Set in the firth are the island of *Stroma* and, farther E, the group of the *Pentland Skerries*.—From John o' Groats a road runs E (2m) to **Duncansby Head** (210ft), the spectacular NE promontory of Scotland. To the N, at the entrance to the firth, are the *Boars of Duncansby*, a reef the name of which reflects the force of the sea here, while to the S the three *Stacks of Duncansby* rise as obelisks out of the sea.

2m Canisbay, where the church has something from several centuries, though not from as far back as 1222, the year in which a church here is first mentioned. The present church is probably 15C in origin, two aisles being added in the 17C and a new tower in the 18C. On the S end a stone with a large cross records the death in 1568 of Donald Grot (de Groot), son of John. Beyond, in *4m*, the *Castle of Mey* (no adm., though the gardens are open in aid of charity on certain days in July and August), built between 1566–72 and once a seat of the earls of Caithness, was acquired in 1952 by the Queen Mother.—*5m Dunnet* is a scattered village well known for its sands and with an unusual church showing a saddleback tower which may be 14C in origin. Timothy Pont, a noted 17C cartographer, was minister here from 1601–08. *Dunnet Head* (4m N; road), the most northerly point of mainland Britain, is an appropriately bold and lofty (400ft) sandstone promontory. The view seaward to Orkney and in both directions along the coast is splendid, and if, as scholars judge probable, this is the Cape Oreas of the Roman geographer Diodorus Ciculus (c 50 BC), then Dunnet Head can claim to be the first place in Scotland to be mentioned by a writer.—*3m* **Castletown** was where in 1824 the Caithness flagstone industry was founded. The village was built to house the workers, and both village and port flourished until skilfully laid and polished flags were defeated by drab, poured concrete.

5m **Thurso** (9000 inhab. *ECl*. Thurs. *Inf*. Riverside. May–Sept), of Norse origin—the name 'Thors-a' meaning Thor's river—straddles the river of the same name, in the N part being the long, narrow harbour and a pleasant promenade overlooking Thurso Bay.

History. Modest though Thurso is today, this was in medieval times the principal port for the trade between Scotland and Scandinavia and in the 14C of such importance that its weights and measures were adopted throughout Scotland. Later the town became busy with the flagstone industry, while today the ferry service from Scrabster to Orkney and the nuclear power station at nearby Dounreay combine to boost local activity.

From the E the town is entered across Thurso Bridge, ahead being a church (William Burn, 1853), opposite which is a statue, perhaps by Chantrey, of Sir John Sinclair (1754–1835), financier, agricultural writer and economist; he and his daughter Catherine, the latter known as a writer of fiction, lived at Thurso Castle (no adm.) to the NE of the town. Traill Street, bearing right beyond the bridge, soon passes Manson Lane, on the corner being the picturesque small *Meadow Well* from which the townspeople drew their water until well into the 19C and the market too where local fishwives sold their fresh fish.

Farther into the town, at the Town Hall (1872) in High Street, will be found the *Heritage Museum* (Tel: 0847-62371. Fee), serving as a folk museum and as home for a notable collection of stones and fossils, including the bequest of Robert Dick (1811–66), a local baker who made a name as both botanist and geologist. St. Peter's Church, close to the harbour, dates from the 12 or 13C and may have been built by Bishop Gilbert de Moravia, better known for Dornoch's cathedral; rebuilt during the 17C, the church was not used after 1832 and soon became a ruin. The oldest part is the choir, with a semicircular apse within a square end, while the large S gable window with five lights is also noteworthy. *Harald's Tower*, to the NE of the town, built in the early 19C by Sir John Sinclair (see above) as a Sinclair burial place, stands above the grave of Harald, Earl of Caithness, slain in a battle near here in 1196.

On the W outskirts of Thurso A836 passes (left) *Pennyland Farm*, birthplace of Sir William Smith (1854–1914), founder of the Boys' Brigade, while just beyond a fork branches to Scrabster Pier whence the car ferry plies to Stromness in Orkney (see Rte 67). In summer there are twice weekly day excursions combined with an Orkney bus tour (P. and O. Ferries. Tel: 0856-850655).

In rather less than *5m*, at Crosskirk just N of the bridge over the little river Forss, will be found the ruined small *St. Mary's Chapel*, probably of the 12C and with a chancel connected to the nave by an unusual low and narrow doorway. The southward road leads in 5m to *Loch Calder*, the place where St. Rognvald (see introduction to Orkney and Shetland) was murdered in 1158.

4m **Dounreay**, Britain's prototype fast reactor power station with its dome and great spread of buildings, appears as something of a modern shock in a district which seems essentially more attuned to the past than to a technological present (Observation Room and Exhibition. May–Sept: Daily, 09.00 to 16.00. Tel: 0847-62121, Ext. 656. Free). *Reay*, *2m* beyond, the place from which Lord Reay, chief of Clan Mackay, takes his title, has a church of 1739, typical of the local style of that period with a small belfry tower and external stair.—Just short of (*6m*) *Melvich* A897 brings in Rte 60 from Strath Halladale.

13m **Bettyhill** (*Inf.* June–Sept) is named after Elizabeth, 1st Duchess of Sutherland. At the E end of the village the former church of Farr (1774), with a contemporary pulpit and a Celtic cross, has been converted into a *Strath Naver Museum* (Summer: Mon.–Sat., 14.00 to 17.00. Tel: 0862-810400. Donation), a private museum run by volunteer enthusiasts which tells the story of the Strath Naver Clearances (see also Rte 60) and illustrates also the local way of life at and around that period. *Invernaver National Nature Reserve*, across the Naver estuary, contains the finest collection of northern plant communities (of mixed mountain and coastal types) in the N of Scotland, breeding birds also here including the greenshank, ring ouzel and twite or mountain linnet.

Passing the junction with B871 (see Rte 60, via Strath Naver) A836 in *12m* overlooks the **Kyle of Tongue**, a broad, shallow inlet, the tapering head of which lies below the serrated peaks of Ben Loyal and the long E shoulder of Ben Hope. The township of *Tongue*, on this E side, is dominated by ruined Castle Varrich, a 14C Mackay stronghold said to be successor to a Norse fort. Since 1972 crossed by a causeway, the Kyle is part blocked at its foot by Rabbit Island, to which it is possible to walk at low water, while along the Kyle's W side a small road soon loses itself in a quiet corner of sandy beaches, cliffs, curious rocks and islands.

Across the causeway the main road rises to a wilderness of mixed moor and bog known as *A'Mhoine* to reach (*8m*) *Hope* where Rte 58 joins from Altnaharra. Beyond, **Loch Eriboll** fills the scene below, a long, beautiful and very deep inlet which in 1939–45 sheltered assembling Allied convoys and, the war won, saw the surrender of German submarines, thus confirming a prophecy of the Seer of Brahan that a war would end at Eriboll. Here, too, seven centuries earlier, assembled Hakon's Viking galleys, only to sail fearfully away convinced—and rightly so because they were soon defeated at Largs—that an eclipse of the sun was harbinger of disaster. From an even remoter age hut circles can be found here, though not easily amid the bracken. One group lies between two small lochs just N of where the road turns S, a broch remnant also surviving just to the E of the huts; another group awaits discovery to the right of the road about 1m S of Eriboll farm. And on the loch's W side—by a burn bridge just N of the turn to Port Nancon jetty; identified by two modest cairns beside the E verge of the road—there is, hidden in the undergrowth, an intact and wholly unspoilt *Earth-house* complete with curved stair and long passage finishing at a round chamber (torch necessary; may be flooded).

17m (from Hope) *Smoo Cave* is an immense triple-chambered cliff cavern, the outer chamber—some 200ft deep and 120ft high with gaping holes in the roof—being easily accessible from the beach. Access to the second cavern, with a waterfall, is difficult; to the third impossible without special equipment and arrangements.

1m **Durness** (*Inf.* June–Sept), the Scottish mainland's most NW village, is a popular stop along the coastal round, the ending point of Rte 56, and the place at which to arrange a visit to Cape Wrath (see below). It is also interesting to go a mile or so W to *Balnakeil* where a former military camp has since 1964 been a craft village (summer only) with several individual workshops. Balnakeil Bay is a glorious curve of white sand beside which is the now roofless *Durness Old Church*, built in 1619 but on the site of an older church mentioned in Vatican records as having contributed to the third crusade. More tangibly there are two monuments, one of which may mark the grave of Rob Donn (1740–78; born Robert Mackay), a famed local bard. The other—recalling a nice touch of 17C pragmatism—is to Donald MacMurchov, a notorious highwayman who arranged to be buried here in return for his financial help to the then Lord Reay who wished, but could not afford, to rebuild the church; MacMurchov's grave may be in the S wall with a skull and crossbones carving. The large 18C farmhouse opposite the church stands on the site of a summer residence of the bishops of Caithness.

°Cape Wrath—the name has nothing to do with the often wild sea, but comes from the Norse 'hvarf' meaning 'point of turning'—is the 523ft high NW extremity of Britain's mainland, a headland of precipitous gneiss cliffs veined with pink pegmatite. The immense view extends E along the coast and across to Orkney (Hoy, 60m), and W to the Butt of Lewis (45m) and even Harris beyond (80m). Far out to sea may be seen Stack Skerry and Skule Skerry (37 and 42m NE) and the island of Rona (40m NW). The fort-like lighthouse was built in 1828.

Cape Wrath is reached by the Kyle of Durness ferry (no cars) at Keoldale, 1½m
S of Durness (May–Sept: First sailing about 09.00 daily. Tel: 097181-244). The
ferry connects with a minibus service. Bird enthusiasts can leave the bus on
the way and walk about a mile to *Clo-Mor Cliffs*, the highest in Britain. The
road to the cape crosses a bleak moor called *The Parph*, once notorious for
wolves.

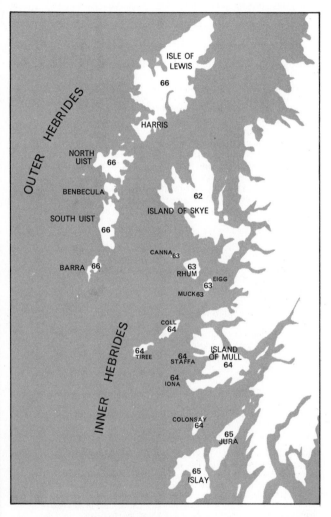

The Hebrides comprise between 40 and 50 islands and innumerable barren islets and reefs. They divide themselves into the Outer and the Inner Hebrides. The latter, which include the large island of Skye, lie, as their name suggests, fairly close to the mainland and stretch some 150 miles from the N of Skye opposite Gairloch to the

S of Islay opposite Kintyre. (Smaller islands, close inshore, are not included here but are described under the appropriate mainland Routes.) The Outer Hebrides straggle 130 miles from the Butt of Lewis in the N to Barra Head in the S. They are separated from the mainland or the Inner Hebrides by the North Minch (40 miles between Lewis and the mainland); the Little Minch (25 miles between Harris or North Uist and Skye); and the Sea of the Hebrides (60 miles from Barra to the mainland).

The **Inner Hebrides** are described below as four Routes: Skye, and then the three groups of islands as served, from N to S, by the ports of Mallaig, Oban and Tarbert (Kennacraig). The **Outer Hebrides** are described as one Route, because it is possible, given careful planning and timing, to motor the length of the group.

Information on communications to and within the islands is given with each island or group of islands. The warning must, though, be sounded that services are seasonal and may be changed at short notice. The principal operator for sea services is Caledonian MacBrayne Ltd, The Pier, Gourock, PA19 1QP. Tel: (0475) 33755. Contact should be made with this headquarters office if plans involve more than one crossing or if information is required on the various cruises and special discounts offered. For air services the operators are British Airways (Highland Division), 85 Buchanan Street, Glasgow. Tel: (041) 3329666; and Loganair, Glasgow Airport, Abbotsinch, Renfrewshire. Tel: (041) 8893181. The main islands are reasonably well served by car ferries. Services can, however, be crowded in summer (advance booking is recommended) and careful planning of both ferries and accommodation, which on some islands is limited, is advisable. This is particularly the case if it is wished to travel the length of the Outer Hebrides where the services from Harris to North Uist and from South Uist to Barra are not daily. Roads throughout the islands are good, if narrow and often winding.

Scenically the Hebrides offer a variety ranging from the barrenness of Barra to the jagged mountains of Skye, while at every turn there seems to be a different kind of coastline. In addition the visitor can enjoy remote places with a way of life noticeably different from that on the mainland, where there is little in the way of 'development', and where the Gaelic culture and language still flourish. It is, however, worth remembering that one aspect of this is that Sunday is strictly observed, few facilities then being available. Prehistoric and early Christian sites will be found on many of the islands, the great ritual site of *Callanish* on Lewis being outstanding among the former while *Iona* is of course a cradle of Scottish Christianity.

History. In the 6C St. Columba and other missionaries came to the Hebrides, preaching to and converting the early tribes. The Norsemen started to arrive in the 8C, first as raiders then as settlers. They called the islands 'Sudreyjar', or 'Southern Islands', a form which has been preserved in the title of the Bishop of Sodor and Man, though the bishops' jurisdiction over the Hebrides ended in the 14C. During the early 12C Somerled, a native chief of Morvern who had married a daughter of one of the Norse kings, rose to power, controlling many of the inner islands. But Norse domination continued elsewhere, not ending until 1266, three years after the Battle of Largs, when Magnus, Earl of Orkney, abandoned all claim. The formal title, 'Lord of the Isles', was first adopted by a descendant of Somerled, John Macdonald of Islay (died 1386). The power of the Lords of the Isles was finally annexed to the crown by James IV. In 1748, with the abolition of heritable jurisdictions, the title vanished. In the early 19C the Hebrides suffered severely under the Clearances, these leading to mass emigration and a decline in population which still continues, today's population being only about one third of that of a hundred years ago. Unemployment is high, though the situation is easing through job creation projects and multi-million-pound investment by the Highlands and Islands Development Board. Hope also focuses, if decreasingly, on the possibilities of oil, and licences have been granted for drilling in the Minch and on the continental shelf.

62 Skye

Skye is both the largest (c 600 sq.m) of the Hebrides, and also the most scenic, in parts wild and lonely, its Cuillin Mountains (c 3000ft) the barest, most precipitous and most impressively awesome in Britain. The coasts, constantly broken by sea lochs, present striking and often strange cliff scenery, and throughout the island there are reminders of its prehistoric and medieval peoples. The island's weak point is its climate, and it is not for nothing that it is known as the Misty Isle.

This is a famed and popular holiday objective. Yet by and large the crowds head for the focal points such as Portree and Dunvegan, and even in summer it is possible to find remote and uncrowded corners.

Tourist Organisation. Isle of Skye Tourist Board, Portree. Tel: (0478) 2137.

Communications. There are three *Car Ferry* services from the mainland:

1. From Kyle of Lochalsh to Kyleakin, this link also serving the train from Inverness. Crossing 5 minutes. All year, daily, frequent (Caledonian MacBrayne. Tel: 059983–282).

2. From Glenelg to Kylerhea. Crossing 5 minutes. Mid May–mid Sept: Mon.–Sat., frequent (M. A. Mackenzie, Glenelg. Tel 059982–224).

3. From Mallaig to Armadale, this link also serving the train from Fort William. Crossing 30 minutes. Summer: Mon.–Sat., up to five services daily. Winter: Restricted service. No cars (Caledonian MacBrayne. Tel: 0687–2403).

Air Services. Glasgow to Broadford. All year, about four days a week (Loganair. Tel: 041–8893181. Or 04712–261).

Internal Bus Services, with seasonal timetables and no Sunday services, are infrequent. In summer there is a choice of day excursions from Portree. Information from Highland Omnibuses, Park Road, Portree. Tel: (0478) 2647. Or, for Post Office services, Tel: (04712) 201, or (031) 2287241.

SOME HOTELS. **Kyleakin**. *Marine and Triton*. Tel: (0599) 4585. **Broadford**. *Broadford*. Tel: (04712) 204. **Ardvasar**. *Ardvasar*. Tel: (04714) 223. **Isle of Raasay**. *Isle of Raasay*, IV40 8PB. Tel: (047862) 222. **Sligachan**. *Sligachan*. Tel: (047852) 204. **Dunvegan**, *Dunvegan*. Tel: (047022) 202. *Misty Isle*. Tel: (047022) 208. **Portree**. *Coolin Hills*. Tel: (0478) 2003. *Rosedale*. Tel: (0478) 2531. *Royal*. Tel: (0478) 2525. **Kensaleyre**. *Macdonald*. Tel: (047032) 339. **Duntulm**. *Duntulm Castle*. Tel: (047052) 213.

History. With early Christian missionaries, Norse occupation and the Lords of the Isles and their long struggle against the crown, Skye's history is that of the Hebrides generally. Thereafter local history is largely one of clan disputes between the Macdonalds (of Trotternish, Sleat, etc.), the Mackinnons (of the E coast), the MacLeods of Lewis (Vaternish and Dunvegan) and the MacLeods of Harris (Duirinish and Minginish).

In 1745 loyalties were divided, but what will always be remembered is that it was from Benbecula to Kilbride Bay just N of Uig that the Skye girl, Flora Macdonald, brought the Young Pretender (disguised as Betty Burke) 'over the sea to Skye'. He remained just under a week, walking first to Portree where—at MacNab's Inn, now the Royal Hotel—he said goodbye to Flora. There followed two nights on Raasay, a return to Skye, and a long walk to Elgol where the Mackinnons gave him a banquet in a cave and a boat to Mallaig on the mainland.

In 1881–85, after a succession of bad harvests and poor fishing seasons, Skye experienced serious crofter riots, the main centres being Loch Sligachan in the E and the Duirinish peninsula in the NW.

*The Cuillin Mountains

The Cuillin Mountains, across the southern part of Skye and with peaks of well over 3000ft, are a tumbled, irregular mass of rough gabbro on basalt, a firm rock affording some of the best climbing in Britain. But these are also Britain's wildest and most difficult mountains and there are few peaks which can be reached without experienced rock climbing or at least a good deal of rough scrambling. Furthermore these mountains can also, and with little warning, disappear within cloud and mist, while for mineralogical reasons the compass is not necessarily reliable. Walking and climbing are therefore only for the experienced and properly equipped, or for others under expert guidance (Cuillin Guides, Stac Lee, Glenbrittle. Tel: 047842–289). *Glen Brittle*, with a road (from near Carbost) all the way to the coast, runs close below the mountains' W flank.

Kyleakin to Broadford

A850. 8m.—**Kyleakin** is a straggling, functional village beside the straits (½m wide) of the same name, this deriving from Norway's Hakon who sailed through here in 1263 on his way to defeat by Alexander III at Largs. *Castle Moil*, a ruin overlooking the straits, once known as Dun Akin and built as a defence against marauding Norsemen, was by the 12–15C a Mackinnon keep. The story goes that one enterprising chatelaine, known as 'Saucy Mary', stretched a chain across the strait and levied a stiff toll from passing shipping.

In 4m Skye's small airport is passed, Glen Arroch from here carrying an unclassified road SE to the ferry at Kylerhea. In another 2m A851 angles away for Ardvasar and the Armadale ferry. **Broadford** (*Inf*. May–Sept), at the junction with A881 for Elgol, is a straggling village beside the bay of the same name and below the red granite mass of *Ben-na-Cailleach* (2403ft).

Armadale to Broadford

A851. 17m.—*Armadale* is simply the ferry terminal, the associated village being **Ardvasar**, just NE of which is *Armadale Castle*, built for Lord Macdonald in 1815–19 by Gillespie Graham near the site of a former house which in 1690 was bombarded from the sea by government forces and burned. Here now is the *Clan Donald Centre* (April–Oct: Mon.–Sat., 10.00 to 17.30. Also Sun. in June–Aug, 13.00 to 17.30. Tel: 04714-227. Fee), with a museum, audio-visual presentation, gardens and an arboretum.

A851 provides the obvious road northwards, but a minor road making a circuit (c 12m) to the NW and rejoining A851 near Knock

Castle is well worth considering as an alternative. Small, twisting and slow through lonely country, this road reaches and for 4m runs with the opposite coast with views across to Elgol and Rhum. Ruined *Dunscaith Castle*, guarding an arm of a coastal bay and seeming to spring from the natural rock, was a 15–16C stronghold of the Macdonalds. But legend is easy to accept here too; that the Irish hero Cuchulainn once came here to learn the art of war from the Amazon Queen of Skye who boasted 100 warriors. Beyond, at *Ord*, this diversion leaves the coast and in 4m meets A851.

Knock Castle is a creeper-clad remnant on the rocky arm of a bay of the Sound of Sleat. Belonging to the Macdonalds of Sleat, it too, like Moil and Dunscaith, has its heroine, a lady dubbed Mary of the Castle after her gallant and successful defeat in the 15C of a siege by the MacLeods. Beyond, *Isleornsay*, with bathing and fishing, takes its name from an island close inshore on which are a lighthouse and the ruin of a chapel. Skirting the small sea loch Loch na Dal, the road heads inland for *Broadford*.

Broadford to Elgol

A881. 14m.—A very scenic run (the most scenic in Skye) towards the southern foot of the Cuillins.

Rounding the foot of Ben-na-Cailleach (2403ft) the road in a little over 2m passes on the right a ruined church (*Cill Chriosd*), traditionally on a site where in the 7C St. Maelrubha had a cell. About 2m farther, on the left within a road fork, *Clach na Annait* is a standing stone the name of which, as also of an adjacent well, is associated with that of a shadowy pagan goddess. Skye marble quarries are now on both sides of the road which loops Loch Slapin to reach the hamlet of *Kilmarie*, a mile or so beyond which, on the shore, is *Dun Ringill*, all that is left of a Mackinnon fort, possibly 9C in origin. Soon after Kilmarie, too, is the start of a path to (3m) *Camasunary* on Loch Scavaig.

From Camasunary a path continues another 3m to Loch Coruisk; this path involves a difficult and even dangerous section known as the Bad Step and is only for the experienced. Beyond Camasunary another path makes for (8m) Sligachan; about halfway, Harta Corrie slices away W, near the corrie's mouth being the so-called Bloody Stone, site of the last clan battle (1601) between the Macdonalds and the MacLeods.

Elgol is a haphazard village scattered around its steep cliff from which there are views across to Rhum and several other islands. It was here that—no longer Betty Burke but disguised as a manservant called Lewie Caw—the Young Pretender was received by the Mackinnons, given a banquet in what is now called *Prince Charles's Cave* (S of the village) and then sent on his way to the mainland. Out of Elgol a road winds E for 1½m to Glasnakille, just above *Spar Cave*, accessible at low tide in good weather and with limestone formations.

Loch Scavaig and **Loch Coruisk* are together in perhaps the wildest setting in Skye. The former is a broad sea loch, its head overshadowed by bare and fretted peaks. Loch Coruisk (or Coire Uisg, Cauldron of Water), beyond across a narrow neck, lies within the very foot of the dark, towering Cuillins and is considerd by many to be Scotland's most dramatic loch (Boat from Elgol, sailings according to demand from 10.30. R. Mackinnon, Tel: 04716–213. J. Mackinnon, Tel: 04716–235). Sailings may also be possible to the island of *Soay*, 4m W off the mouth of Loch Scavaig; the bulk of the

Sligachan Bridge, Isle of Skye, between Kyleakin and Portree.

island's inhabitants moved to Mull in 1953.

Broadford to Sligachan and Dunvegan (Duirinish and Vaternish)

A850 to Sligachan. A863 to Dunvegan. 35m.—With the large island
of Scalpay rising to 1298ft close offshore, the road turns beside Loch
Ainort to pass the *Old Skye Crofter's House* (Daily, 10.00 to 18.00.
Tel: 04712–427. Fee), well illustrating local living conditions in the
early years of the present century. Beyond, at the loch's head, there
is a choice between the main road across the peninsula between
lochs Ainort and Sligachan or, rather more interestingly, the small
road which rounds it. The two roads meet just before *Sconser*, from
where a car ferry serves the island of *Raasay* (Mon.—Sat., about four
crossings daily. 15 minutes crossing. Caledonian MacBrayne. Tel:
0478–2075).

Raasay is some 15m long but uneven in width, with a road serving the length
of the island as far as ruined *Brochel Castle*, long a home of the MacLeods of
Raasay. A staunch Jacobite, the local MacLeod of 1745 joined the Young
Pretender with 100 men, and the following year it was Raasay MacLeods who
sheltered him for two nights. Soon afterwards, government troops landed and
laid waste the estate.—Both Raasay, and the smaller island of *Rona* to the N,
may be visited in summer by excursions from Portree.

Sligachan, at the head of its loch, is at the junction of the roads to
Dunvegan and (10m) Portree, as also of Glen Sligachan up which a
path leads in 8m to Camasunary (see Broadford to Elgol above).
A863, crossing an isthmus, in large part beside the small river
Drynoch, in 6m reaches *Drynoch* at the head of Loch Harport, a deep,
narrow sea loch some 6m long, and from near here the small Glen
Brittle road (see also The Cuillins above) drops southward below the
W flank of the mountains to reach an unexciting shore in 8m.
    Now heading NW above Loch Harport A863 in 4½m passes the

prominent hill fort of *Dun Taimh* before descending to loop around a bay and reach *Struan*, a point at which to pause, for both the best preserved broch on Skye and an earth-house are to the NW nearby. The former (Dun Beag) is on a hill to the right of the road opposite a turning to Ullinish. The latter may be found, though not easily, by taking the Ullinish road for ¼m to a gate on the right; the nearside of the hillock should then be followed round NE for about 400 yards, the earth-house being below the rock outcrop. Beyond Struan, and beyond the head of little Loch Caroy, the road breasts a short rise, at the top (left, opposite a road signed to Upper Feorlig) being the collapsed remains of two chambered cairns.

Dunvegan, the village at the head of the large sea loch of the same name, is best known for its castle. From here, too, there are boat excursions to see the seal colonies on the loch's islets (April–Sept: Mon.–Sat., frequent. Duration c 30 minutes. Tel: 047022–260).

Dunvegan Castle (Easter–mid May. Oct: Mon.–Sat., 14.00 to 17.00. Mid May–Sept: Mon.–Sat., 10.30 to 17.00. Tel: 047022–208 or 0667–53493. Fee) has, since at least 1200, been the seat of the chiefs of Clan MacLeod. The present castle—a massive pile showing almost every building style from the 15 to the 19C—was formerly accessible only from the sea by a small gateway with a portcullis opening on to the rocks but is now entered by way of a bridge across a ravine which once served as a dry moat.

Inside the castle the focus of popular interest is the Fairy Flag, which is shown in the Drawing Room, originally the great hall of the 14C keep. This mysterious silken banner of Middle Eastern origin and dated to somewhere between the 4 and 7C is said to possess the magical property of being able to save the clan from danger. But only on three occasions, two of which though—one being at Trumpan, see below—have already been expended. Legends surround the flag, the most romantic of which is that it came to the MacLeods through the love of a chief for a fairy; forced to part at Fairy Bridge (see below), the fairy presented the chief with the silken coverlet she had drawn over their child. More prosaically, and perhaps more probably in view of the silk's Middle Eastern origin, other tales link the flag with the crusades.

Among much else of interest are, in the Dining Room, the ancient Dunvegan Cup, an Irish drinking vessel of the 10C bearing silver ornamentation of 1493, pictures by Ramsay and Raeburn, and an early charter granted by James IV; just outside the Drawing Room, the Dungeon with its grim oubliette; and many interesting pictures, mementoes of the '45 and letters from distinguished visitors such as Sir Walter Scott and Dr Johnson, a portrait of whom (by Zoffany, after Reynolds) hangs in the Fairy Tower.

Duirinish, a moorland hammerhead immediately W of Dunvegan, is essentially MacLeod, with two prominent hills called MacLeod's Tables and, off Idrigill Point at the peninsula's S tip, three basaltic stacks known as MacLeod's Maidens, a name traditionally honouring a MacLeod chieftain's wife and daughters drowned here in a shipwreck.

B884 traverses the northern area of the irregular peninsula, soon passing the remains of a broch on the left of the road opposite the turn to Uginish. Beyond (4m from Dunvegan) is the *Colbost Folk Museum* (May–Sept: Daily, 10.00 to 19.00. Tel: 047081–213. Fee), an

authentic crofter blackhouse of the 19C. The road breasts a rise,
approaching the crest of which a memorial stands as a reminder that
Duirinish was one of the main centres of the crofter riots of 1881–85,
and then descends to the Glendale *Skye Watermill* (May–Sept:
Mon.–Sat., 10.00 to 19.00. Tel: 047081–213), restored now as a part
of the Colbost Folk Museum and grinding corn as it did a century
ago. The road ends after another 2m at *Milovaig*.

The northward finger of **Vaternish** is soon reached by taking the
Portree road (A850) out of Dunvegan, this in 3m reaching *Fairy
Bridge* (see Dunvegan Castle). From here B886 in 4m kinks into
Stein, scene of an 18C attempt by MacLeod of MacLeod to establish
a fishing industry, defeated by the high cost of salt. Beyond, another
4m of unclassified road ends at *Trumpan*, of interest on three counts,
most notoriously perhaps for the bloody business of 1579 between
the Macdonalds and the MacLeods. While the latter were at worship
a party of Macdonalds landed and burned down the church, all the
MacLeods who were inside perishing. However, on returning to their
boats, the Macdonalds found the rest of the MacLeods waiting for
them, and since the MacLeods had brought the Fairy Flag the fate
of the Macdonalds was sealed and all were killed.

More tangible links with the past are provided here by the Trial
Stone and the grave of Lady Grange. The former long provided a
simple form of justice; accused persons were blindfolded and if they
then succeeded in inserting a finger in the hole they were judged
innocent. The unfortunate Lady Grange (died 1745), though, was
given no option. The wife of a Jacobite Edinburgh judge, she
threatened to reveal a plot (1734) on which she had stumbled,
whereupon her husband promptly packed her off to remote St. Kilda
and left her there until 1742.

From Fairy Bridge A850 crosses 19m of mainly dull moorland to
reach Portree. For *Skeabost* and *Tote*, reached in 13m, see below.

Portree and Trotternish

Portree (1500 inhab. *ECl.* Wed. *Inf.*) owes its name, meaning Port of
the King, to a state visit by James V; previously it was called
Kiltaragleann, the Church at the foot of the glen. The only town on
Skye, and the island capital, this is a picturesque and incidental small
place, though with little of formal interest beyond perhaps the room
at the *Royal Hotel* in which the Young Pretender took his leave of
Flora Macdonald, courteously if optimistically remarking 'For all that
has happened I hope, Madam, we shall meet in St. James's yet'.

In summer, Portree offers a choice of coach, boat and combined
excursions.

Trotternish is a long oval peninsula reaching some 23m northward
from Portree. It provides some good mountain and coastal scenery;
the little port of Uig for car ferries to Harris and North Uist; a croft
museum; Flora Macdonald's grave; and several other sites of varied
interest. The road described starts and finishes at Portree, making a
clockwise circuit of some 55m.

Four miles out of Portree the road forks, the westerly prong (for
Dunvegan) soon bridging the river Snizort at *Skeabost*. Here, on an
island just below the bridge (stepping stones), scanty remains are of
a chapel traditionally associated with St. Columba, while a search
around the tumbled burial ground should reveal three good crusaders'
slabs. Nearby to the N, on the road up to the hamlet of *Tote*, stands

Clach Ard, the Stone on the Hill, bearing a variety of Pictish symbols.

A856 heads N above the E shore of Loch Snizort Beag, home once of prehistoric peoples, for the sizeable hump of a burial cairn survives near Kensaleyre at the head of the loch's nearer arm while, about 1m farther, there are twin small standing stones between the road and the water. Beyond, off to the left, the name *Kingsburgh* recalls the Young Pretender who, having landed farther N, found refuge in the predecessor of the present house. And it was here, too, that Johnson and Boswell met Flora Macdonald. Next, the little river Hinnisdal is crossed, beyond, on the shore, standing the shattered ruin of *Caisteal Huisdean*, stronghold of a 17C pirate, Hugh Gillespie; his end came when he unwisely plotted against his Macdonald lord, the latter then sealing him up in a dungeon at Duntulm (see below) with a piece of salt beef and an empty water jug.

Uig, a neat village at the head of the sheltered bay of the same name, is important as the pier for the car ferries to Tarbert on Harris and Lochmaddy on North Uist (see Rte 66). The N side of the bay is marked by the imposing height of Ru Idrigil, just N of which, by the shore, Skudaborg was an Iron Age fort. From Uig, too, a small road, passing the foot of the The Quiraing (see below), provides a cut across to the E coast.

Along the 2m between Uig and the hamlet of *Linicro* the road again skirts land with Young Pretender associations. He and Flora Macdonald came ashore near Prince Charles's Point (just N of Kilbride Point), Flora then leading her companion to nearby Monkstadt House, home of Sir Alexander Macdonald. Finding, however, that government officers had already quartered themselves there, the pair made their way S to Kingsburgh and Portree.

The road now runs inland along the flank of the hills with lower ground to the left, in part representing *Loch Challuim Chille* (St. Columba's Loch), long drained and reclaimed but once the site of a small Celtic monastery, identifiable today only as a raised area with fragments of a cashel wall, a chapel and a causeway towards the shore.

Next, at Kilmuir, comes the *Skye Cottage Museum* (May–early Oct: Mon.–Sat., 10.00 to 18.00. Tel: 047052–213. Fee), housed in a group of cottages and of particular interest for its collection of old documents and photographs, while just up a side road, in the local burial ground, are the grave and monument of Flora Macdonald (died 1790). Adjacent lies a well preserved crusader slab.

Bearing NE and then E to round the peninsula's tip the road now runs with a cliff-edged, rock-strewn shore with basaltic columns and the gaunt ruin of *Duntulm Castle*, dating from the 17C but on the site of earlier Macdonald strongholds and the place, too, where the pirate Hugh Gillespie met his cruel end. Beyond, at *Floddigary*, the house beside the hotel, was the first married home of Flora Macdonald; she married Allan Macdonald of Kingsburgh in 1750 and her seven children were all born here. *The Quiraing* (1781ft; best approached from the small road across to Uig) now rises on the W above Staffin Bay; here a dramatic complex of towers and pinnacles surrounds a grassy amphitheatre known as the Prison and long used for hiding cattle.

Farther S, after rounding Staffin Bay, the road touches *Loch Mealt* where the distinctive remains of a broch can be seen on a small promontory from the N shore. The loch empties as a little stream, falling 300ft into the sea over a sheer cliff, and from here there is a good view of *Kilt Rock*, so called from the coloured strata and the way in which the basalt column resembles the folds of a kilt (the cliff edge is brittle and dangerous). Beyond, the river Lealt is crossed at a point where the stream cascades by waterfall stages into a ravine, and soon the black obelisk of the *Old Man of Storr* comes into sight at the foot of *The Storr* (2360ft), a cliff fretted with pinnacles and crags and notorious for its treacherously loose rocks. Storr Forest Walk, however, though steep, provides a path towards the Old Man and also views across to Raasay.

Lochs Leathan and *Fada*, below the road, serve as a hydro-electric reservoir, and a cave on the shore E of Loch Fada (accessible only by boat) was the point where the Young Pretender landed from Raasay; he slept in a byre about 2m farther S and walked thence to Elgol. A good hill fort (*Dun Torvaig*) is passed on the left just before the descent to Portree.

63   Inner Hebrides reached from Mallaig (Eigg, Muck, Rhum and Canna)

Tourist Organisation. Fort William and Lochaber Tourist Board, Travel Centre, Fort William, PH33 6EN. Tel: 0397–3781.

Access. No car ferries. For passengers:—1. Caledonian MacBrayne operate a year-round circuit service (also from Armadale on Skye) about four times weekly, though slightly less frequently to Muck which is served by local boat from Eigg. The round trip requires 7 to 8 hours. Tel: 0687–2403.—2. Bruce Watt Cruises operate summer excursions. Tel: 0687–2233.—3. Arisaig Marine (Arisaig, 5m S of Mallaig) also operate summer only cruises and scheduled services. Tel: 06875–224.

Accommodation, where available at all, is modest and limited. For addresses contact Fort William and Lochaber Tourist Board, as above.—**Transport**. Bicycles can be hired.

Eigg (5m by 2½m) is topographically notable for the *Sgurr of Eigg* (1292ft), a strangely shaped hill in the S of the island, a mass of black glassy pitchstone which has assumed columnar forms. The *Singing Sands*, beside the bay of Camus Sgiolaig at the NW, are another, if minor, natural feature, the sand here 'singing' when displaced by walking feet, or even when scoured by the wind, while in *Kildonnan* churchyard a Celtic cross-slab survives as evidence of early Christianity.

Muck, 2m long, at most 1m broad, and with a population of about 25, lies 3m SW of Eigg. The smallest and most southerly of the group, the island is probably best known for its unenviable name, deriving perhaps, and equally unenviably, from a Gaelic form meaning pig, which animal the island was once judged to resemble.

Rhum, 8m by 8m and roughly diamond in shape, rises steeply to a fine volcanic mountain cluster culminating in *Askival* (2659ft), this name and others recall the possible period of Norse occupation. Inhabited since perhaps 6500 BC, the population in the later 18C grew to over 400, but in 1827–28, the time of the clearances, the entire population, at least partly by compulsion, emigrated to America. The island then became the home of sheep, and later (1845) Red deer were re-imported by the sporting Earl of Salisbury. From 1888 to 1957 Rhum was a private estate of the Bulloughs, of Lancashire, who in 1901 built *Kinloch Castle*, now run as a hotel and hostel by the Nature Conservancy Council, the Council having acquired the island in 1957. Today Rhum is a National Nature Reserve and Biosphere Reserve, outstandingly important on several counts—geologically, botanically, ornithologically, for the study of Red deer and for research in woodland re-creation and management.

There are two nature trails for day visitors (at Kinloch) and permission to camp or use bothy accommodation may be obtained from the Reserve Office at The Whitehouse, Rhum, PH43 4RR. Tel: (0687) 2026.

In contrast to Rhum, **Canna** (NTS. 5m by 1¼m) is lowish and fertile, its highest point being under 700ft. The harbour is at the E end, just to the N being *Compass Hill* (458ft), so named because the rich iron deposits in the basalt cliffs are said to distort ships' compass readings. The island offers minor antiquities—the ruin of a tower on a stack between the harbour and Compass Hill is traditionally where a jealous Lord of the Isles confined his beautiful wife; a mutilated sculptured cross represents early Christianity and, nearby, a standing stone recalls even earlier islanders.—The adjacent small island of *Sanday* is reached by a bridge.

64 Inner Hebrides reached from Oban (Mull, Iona, Staffa, Coll, Tiree, Colonsay and Oronsay)

The **Tourist Organisation** covering the above islands is the Oban, Mull and District Tourist Board, Argyll Square, Oban, Argyll. Tel: (0631) 63122.

For **Communications** (see also Rte 46, Oban) and **Accommodation** see under individual islands.

Island of Mull

Access. Caledonian MacBrayne operate car ferry services from Oban to Craignure and Tobermory, and from Lochaline (see Rte 48) to Fishnish. Also a passenger service from Mingary/Kilchoan (see Rte 48) to Tobermory. For detail apply Caledonian MacBrayne, Ferry Terminal, Railway Pier, Oban. Tel: (0631) 62285. Additionally, in summer, several private operators in Oban run excursions to such places as Grass Point, Duart Castle and Torosay Castle (for details apply Tourist Information or local travel firms).

Internal Bus Services. The two principal routes are Tobermory—Salen—Craignure and Craignure—Pennyghael—Bunessan—Fionnphort (for Iona). For details on both these services, Bowman's Coaches, Craignure. Tel: (06802) 313.

Short routes also operate (not Sun.) between Tobermory and Calgary; and Salen, Gruline and Ulva. Tel: (0688) 2220 and (06803) 321.

SOME HOTELS. **Craignure**. *Isle of Mull*, PA65 6BB. Tel: (06802) 351.

Salen (Aros). *Glenforsa*, PA72 6JN. Tel: (06803) 377. **Tobermory**.
Ulva House, Strongarbh. Tel: (0688) 2044. *Western Isles*, PA75 6PR.
Tel: (0688) 2012. **Dervaig**, *Bellachroy*, PA75 6QW. Tel: (06884) 225.
Tiroran. *Tiroran House*. Tel: (06815) 232. **Fionnphort**. *Achaban
House*, PA66 6BL. Tel: (06817) 205.

Mull is an island for coasts; for seaward vistas which are splendid in
virtually every direction. Along the NE the shore as such is relatively
uneventful, lining the narrow Sound of Mull beyond which rise the
heights of Morvern, but elsewhere the coast is so fretted that, while
its total length adds up to some 300 miles, only three miles separate
Salen on the Sound from the Atlantic bay of Loch Na Keal. To the S
of Loch Na Keal the larger Loch Scridain bites in from the W, its
southern arm, with some good cliff scenery, extending far westward
as the Ross of Mull. Beyond waits Iona.

Inland the island scenery is pleasant and varied, that in the
southern part, with the mountain pile of Ben More (3171ft) being the
finest.

The description below—starting at Craignure which is where most
visitors will arrive—heads first for Tobermory and then completes an
anticlockwise circuit of the main island, with, on the way, a diversion
along the length of the Ross of Mull to Fionnphort.

Total distance (excluding Ross of Mull) 84m.—*5m* **Fishnish**.—*6m*
Salen.—*9m* **Tobermory**.—*6m* **Dervaig**.—*5m* **Calgary**.—*12m* **Ulva
Ferry**.—*7m* **Gruline**.—*17m* **Junction with A849** (for **Fionnphort**).—
11m **Strathcoil**.—*6m* **Craignure**.

Craignure is best known for two castles, Duart and Torosay, as also
perhaps for the *Mull and West Highland Railway*, a 10.25 gauge
miniature line linking Craignure with Torosay (Easter–Sept: Tel:
06802–494 or 06803–389).

Torosay Castle (Easter Sat. and Sun. Easter–April and first half of
Oct: Mon.–Fri., 11.00 to 13.00. 14.00 to 16.00. May–Sept: Daily, 10.30
to 17.00. Gardens always open in daylight hours. Tel: 06802–421.
Fee), 1½m S of Craignure, is a 19C Scottish Baronial creation by David
Bryce, surrounded by terraced gardens laid out by Robert Lorimer
and notable for a statue walk with 19 life-sized figures by the 18C
Venetian Antonio Bonazza. The house, largely furnished in
Edwardian taste, shows family portraits by such artists as Sargent
and De Lazlo, and wildlife works by Landseer, Thorburn and Peter
Scott.

Duart Castle (May–Sept: Daily, 10.30 to 18.00. Tel: 0631–63122.
Fee), dramatically guarding Duart Point and well seen from the Oban
ferries, dates from about 1250 and, with one break, has always been
as it still is, the home of the chiefs of Clan Maclean. Burnt by Argyll
in 1691, Duart was confiscated half a century later after Culloden,
but repurchased and restored in 1912 by the then chief, Sir Fitzroy
Maclean. In the keep can be seen the cell in which the officers of
Tobermory's Spanish galleon were held after their ship had been
blown up by Donald Maclean.

5m Fishnish for the car ferry across to Lochaline (see Rte 48).—*4m
Pennygown*, where the ruined chapel is worth a visit for a late Celtic
cross-shaft, bearing a Madonna and, curiously, a ship and a
griffon.—*2m Salen*, the village at the N end of the narrow neck across
to Loch Na Keal and the Atlantic, is traditionally the place where St.
Columba landed on his way to Iona after Aidan of Dalriada had

granted him that island. *Aros Castle*, *1m* N on a shore promontory, is a 13C ruin, thought once to have been a stronghold of the MacDougalls of Lorne, but (*7m*) *Aros Park* (Forestry Commission) is, by contrast, a quiet small country park with a cliff walk, rhododendrons and a picnic and play area.

1m **Tobermory** (800 inhab. *ECl*. Wed. *Inf*. 48 Main Street. May–Sept) clusters cosily and picturesquely around the shore and slopes of its wooded bay, sheltered by the island of Calve. The bay provides one of the safest anchorages along Scotland's W coast and, with its attractive small town, is very popular with yachting visitors.

History. The town was founded as a fishing port in 1788, but though it at first prospered it was unable to survive the competition when the railway reached Oban and the population quickly dropped from 1500 in 1843 to settle at around its present modest figure. It was in the 16C, though, in 1588, that Tobermory Bay earned its niche in history. In that year the 'Florida', a galleon of the Spanish Armada, was driven in for shelter. Although the Spaniards were courteously welcomed and provided with victuals, it soon became clear that they were planning to slip away without paying. Donald Maclean was then sent aboard to claim what was due, only however to be locked up by the Spaniards. Resourcefully he got free, reached the magazine and blew up and sank the ship, thus starting a treasure hunt which continues today, even though, beyond some cannon and a few coins, nothing of great value has so far been salvaged.

There is a small museum, the *Mull and Iona Folk Museum* (April–Oct: Mon.–Fri., 11.00 to 17.00. Tel: 0688–2182. Fee), interestingly housed in a former Baptist church, and the *Well of St. Mary*, from which Tobermory derives its name, is beside a ruined chapel just W of the town. Favourite walks are to Aros Park, mentioned above; and N round the point of Rubha-nan-Gall with a lighthouse to *Bloody Bay*, scene in 1439 of a sea battle between John, 4th Lord of the Isles, and his rebel son Angus. *Ardmore Forest Walk*, just behind and to the N of Bloody Bay, is also popular, a cliff path rounding Mull's northernmost tip and providing splendid sea and island views (motor access by unclassified road via Glengorm Castle).

Tobermory is left by B8073, the start of a generally narrow, twisting and slow road, first across the N of the island and then beside the W coast. After climbing, the road drops briefly to the sea at (*6m*) **Dervaig**, with, near the old cemetery, a group of standing stones. The village is also the home of the *Mull Little Theatre*, Britain's smallest professional theatre (summer repertory. Tel: 06884–267), and there are boat excursions in summer to Staffa, the Treshnish Isles and Coll (Quinish Estate. Tel: 06884–223. Or Penmore Mill. Tel: 06884–242). *Croaig*, 3m NW at the entrance to Loch Cuan, was once a busy port to which drovers brought their cattle from the outer islands before driving the herds across Mull to Grass Point, whence they were shipped, or sometimes swam, to Kerrera and the mainland.

The W coast is reached at (*5m*) *Calgary* (the modest hamlet ancestor of the great Canadian city), just beyond being *Treshnish Woodland Garden* (April–Oct: Daily, reasonable hours. Fee). Here the road curves southward and inland, reaching the sea again in *5m* at *Burg*, with traces of an Iron Age fort just seaward of the road. Just beyond (*1m*), in the burial ground of *Kilninian*, there is a very fine medieval slab, commemorating a chieftain complete with kilt and broadsword, while at *Ballygown*, less than *3m* farther, the quite substantial remains of a broch can be seen by the shore.

Since leaving Burg the road has been fringing Loch Tuath, off the mouth of which lie the **Treshnish Isles**, a string of basaltic rocks rising in terraces. The most southerly island is, from its shape, called the *Dutchman's Cap*, while at the N end of the string rise the cliff islets of *Cairn a' Burgh Mor* and *Beg* with a ruined fortress, besieged in James IV's campaign against the Lord of the Isles and later, in 1690 and 1715, held by Macleans in the Jacobite cause.—Closer in, and forming the loch's S shore, are the larger islands of *Gometra* and *Ulva*, the latter the birthplace of General Lachlan Macquarie (1761–1824), governor of New South Wales and an innovative penal reformer whose enlightened attitude made him so unpopular with the free settlers that he was recalled.

3m Ulva Ferry, whence occasional boat excursions (Tel: 0688–2165) may include Staffa, the Treshnish Isles, Lunga (seabirds), Gometra, Ulva and Iona; some trips pass the Fossil Tree, a 50ft-high petrified tree, perhaps 50 million years old, within the basalt of the cliffs of the Ardmeanach peninsula (see also Burg, below).—Now bearing E beside Loch Na Keal, B8073 in *7m* reaches *Gruline*—at the head of the loch and marking the S end of Mull's narrow isthmus—the road (now B8035) curving SW along Loch Na Keal's S shore below the mass of *Ben More* (3171ft), a mountain thrown up in the same volcanic upheaval that formed Staffa.

Ardmeanach, the fine volcanic peninsula extending Ben More and forming the N shore of Loch Scridain, is separated from the mountain by Glen Seilisdeir which carries B8035 across the peninsula's base. *Inch Kenneth* (private), an island off Ardmeanach's N shore at the mouth of Loch Na Keal, is named after a follower of St. Columba; very fertile, and once serving as granary for Iona, the island was also anciently a stopping place on the way to Iona and, because of the storms which frequently delayed onward travel, it may well have been the enforced burial place of some kings and chiefs. *Gribun Rocks*, near where the road starts to angle across, are an impressive range of overhanging cliffs, while *Mackinnon's Cave*, about 2m down the coast and accessible only at low tide, provides a story. Never fully explored, and believed by some to tunnel clear across the peninsula, the cave takes its name from a piper who undertook to lead a party through the cave but was killed by a witch who had settled here; but she spared the piper's dog which was later seen roaming the peninsula's southern shore.

The road reaches Loch Scridain at (*13m* from Gruline) *Kilfinichan Bay*, whence a small road (to Tiroran), soon becoming a rough track (5m), leads to *Burg*, a National Trust for Scotland remote clifftop property at which the Fossil Tree (see above) can be reached at low water. Limited basic accommodation is available in a restored cottage (Tel: 06815–234).—In *4m* the junction with A849 is reached at the head of Loch Scridain.

TO FIONNPHORT (A849, W. 18m). For most of the way beside the S shore of Loch Scridain, this road travels the length of the Ross of Mull, in 3m reaching *Pennyghael* whence a road crosses the Ross to Carsaig, 4m SW of which along the shore, and accessible only at low water, are the *Carsaig Arches*. Here columnar basalt cliffs (750ft) have been eroded by the sea into astonishing caves and arches. Nuns' Pass, passed on the way, is said to have sheltered nuns driven out of Iona at the time of the Reformation.

Just beyond Pennyghael, at *Pennycross*, a memorial honours the Beatons, physicians for 300 years to the Macleans of Duart; and farther on, in the parish of Ardtun, approaching Bunessan, another memorial stands to the poet Mary Macdonald (1789–1872).

Fionnphort, at the road's end, is a straggling hamlet, notable principally for its huge car park for users of the ferry to Iona, a mile across the sound. In summer there are also excursions to Staffa (Tel: 06817–373).

From the head of Loch Scridain, Glen More carries A849 eastwards, in *11m* reaching *Strathcoil* where there is a memorial to the Gaelic poet Dugald Macphail (1818–87).

From Strathcoil a small road diverges SW for Loch Buie (8m; dead-end), for some of the way closely following the shore of *Loch Spelve*, fanning out from its narrow entrance seen across the water. The grand basalt heights of Ben Creach (2290ft) and Ben Cruie (2354ft) rise above the road as it fringes Loch Uisg to reach the village of *Loch Buie* at the head of its own loch. Here, to the N, is a stone circle and, to the S, the ruined keep of Castle Moy, 15C tower-house of Maclean of Loch Buie. A path continues to Carsaig.

4m Lochdon is at the irregular head of the shallow, meandering sea indent of the same name. The S point of the loch's entrance is *Grass Point*, ferry pier predecessor of Craignure. The small road to the point, branching off A849 just S of Lochdon, represents one of the most ancient ways on Mull, having been first an early pilgrim path and later a drovers' road in the days when Grass Point was the jetty from which the cattle were shipped, or forced to swim, to the mainland.—Passing close to Duart and Torosay castles, for both of which see at the start of this circuit, A849 in *2m* returns to *Craignure*.

*Island of Iona

> **Access**. No cars. The two principal approaches are by excursion from Oban (see Rte 46) or by ferry from Fionnphort on Mull (Crossing 5 minutes. Mon.–Sat., roughly hourly. Restricted service Sun. and in winter. Caledonian MacBrayne. Tel: 06817–203 or 0688–2017).
>
> HOTELS. *Argyll*. Tel: (06817) 334. *St. Columba*. Tel: (06817) 304.

Iona (3m long by 1½m wide) is, after Whithorn, the cradle of Scottish Christianity and rich also in later venerable associations. Austere, bare and often windswept, the island is owned by the National Trust for Scotland, except for the abbey and other sacred buildings and historic sites which are cared for by the Iona Cathedral Trust.

The main sites are all within a short walking distance of the pier and can normally comfortably be seen within the time allowed by excursions. Some of the island can also be toured by horse carriage (April–Oct. Tel: 06814–230).

In summer there are twice daily boat excursions to Staffa (D. R. Kirkpatrick. Seaview Cottage, Iona. Tel: 06817–373).

History. Iona, originally known simply as 'Ia' or 'Hy', was called 'Iova Insula' by Adamnan in his 'Life of Columba', a form transcribed by a careless copyist into Iona. Later it was named 'Icolmkill', 'Island of Columba of the Church'.

Excavation at Dun Bhuirg, on the W coast, has revealed that people lived here during the Iron Age, but it was in 563 that St. Columba left Ireland (where he was born in 521) and, with 12 companions, came to Iona, the nearest land from which he could no longer see his native shores. Here he founded a monastery of which nothing now remains, and hence he set out on those journeys which resulted in the conversion of the northern Picts and the spread of Christianity far and wide over Scotland, and even over Orkney, Shetland and Iceland. As religious head, he confirmed Aidan as King of Dalriada, thus formally establishing the early royal line. Columba died in Iona in 597, shortly after St. Augustine had arrived in Kent to convert the English. He was buried on Iona, but 200 years later, after a Norse raid in which 68 monks were murdered at Martyrs' Bay, his remains are taken back to Ireland (Kells) and all subsequent trace of them has disappeared. (But according to some authorities the bones were brought back to Iona and housed beside the cathedral in what is called St. Columba's Shrine.) Iona, thus hallowed, early became a pilgrim objective, and it was the burial-place of the Scottish kings until superseded by Dunfermline in the 11C. Throughout the Middle Ages the great West Highland chiefs were also brought here for burial.

The Norsemen pillaged the island over and over again during 9 and 10C. In 807 they burned and destroyed the monastery and all belonging to it. In 1203 Reginald, son of Somerled, founded a new monastery for Benedictines, and, a few years later, an Augustinian nunnery. Reginald's monastery, though covering much of its Celtic predecessor, does not coincide with it. The Benedictines' church served as the cathedral of the see of Argyll from 1507 until the dissolution after 1570, and in 1617 it was annexed to the Protestant Bishopric of the Isles. In 1609 the church was the scene of the Statutes of Icolmkill, by which the Hebrides chieftains swore loyalty to the Stuart kings. In 1899 the 8th Duke of Argyll presented the cathedral to the Church of Scotland (Iona Cathedral Trust), restoration beginning soon thereafter. In 1938 the Iona Community was founded by Dr George Macleod and has since undertaken much restoration work in and around the cathedral. In 1979 the island was purchased from the Duke of Argyll by Sir Hugh Fraser, through whose generosity it came in December of that year to the National Trust for Scotland.

Among famous visitors to Iona have been Sir Walter Scott, who found it 'desolate and miserable'; Keats came in 1818 and Wordsworth in 1835, here writing three sonnets. Dr Johnson, another visitor, wrote: 'That man is little to be envied whose patriotism would not gain force upon the plain of Marathon, or whose piety would not grow warmer among the ruins of Iona'.

The main path is followed from the ferry, soon reaching the *Nunnery Church* (c1200, with late 13C additions). It comprises a nave, with an aisle, adjoining which is the Lady Chapel still with some of its vaulting. To the S of the church are the remains of the cloister court, chapter house and refectory. The neighbouring *Church of St. Ronan* (14C) serves as a stones museum. Here can be seen, among other nuns' and priests' tombs, the tomb of the last prioress (died 1543), whose effigy in hood and cloak occupies one half of the slab, the remainder being broken away.—The 15C *Maclean's Cross*, passed farther along the path, is 11ft high and carved with great force and excellence of design. On the left there is a church built by Telford.

In *St. Oran's Cemetery*, or *Reilig Odhrain*, the oldest Christian burial-place in Scotland, 48 Scottish, 8 Norwegian, 4 Irish and 2 French kings are said to rest. The last king buried here was Duncan (1040), murdered by Macbeth, but, sadly, only one of the existing slabs (a plain red stone with a Celtic cross) may be of one of these kings. The many other carved slabs (15C and later) are mainly those of island chieftains, and they were only arranged in their present ridges in 1868. The ashes of Majory Kennedy-Fraser (1857–1930), collector and transcriber of Gaelic songs, were also buried here. Here too lies Dr John Beaton of Mull (died 1657), physician to James VI and last of his famous medical family (memorial at Pennycross on Mull).—*St. Oran's Chapel*, probably on the site of a Celtic cemetery, is a small chamber of Norman style, now restored, said to have been built by Queen Margaret (1080). It is entered by a low, deeply recessed doorway, with chevron mouldings. Inside is the trefoiled canopy of the tomb of Lachlan Mackinnon (died 1489), and here too lie the first two Lords of the Isles (1386 and 1420).

The **Cathedral** is the principal building on the island. In front is preserved a section of the *Street of the Dead*, a roadway of red marble, perhaps of the 13C. Opposite the W facade stands *°St. Martin's Cross* (10C), 14ft high and boldly carved with Runic ornaments and figures; while to the left is the graceful 10C *St. John's Cross*, restored from fragments in 1926 but twice blown down since. Near the well a broken shaft is all the remains of *St. Mathew's Cross*. The restored cell or chapel at the NW angle of the nave is *St. Columba's Shrine* (see History), while *Tor Abb*, a mound just W of the cathedral, has the remains of a cell which may have been that of the saint.

Dating mainly from the early 16C, the cathedral has undergone many later additions and restorations, including those of the present day. Cruciform in plan, its chief external feature is the low square Tower (70ft) above the crossing, with four windows, filled with tracery of elegant design, different in each case. Inside the church the arches supporting the tower and the carved capitals of the columns in the choir should be noticed. In the Chancel are tombs of Abbot Mackinnon (died 1500) on the N, and Abbot Mackenzie (died 1489) on the S. Also on the S side are three sedilia in the Gothic style of the 14C. The elaborate Sacristy doorway (N) dates from 1500. The S transept contains a monument (1912) to the 8th Duke of Argyll (died 1900), who presented the cathedral to the Church of Scotland. From the N transept with Norman arches, the *Cloister* is entered. It incorporates two medieval pillars and has in its centre a group 'The Descent of the Spirit', by Jacques Lipchitz (1960).

Restored monastic buildings include the *Chapter House* (1955), still retaining its Norman doorway and the double arch supporting its vault; the *Refectory* (1949, no adm.); and the *Undercroft* on the W side. To the N are the *Reredorter* (1944) and the *Caretaker's House* (1950), preserving a gable of the old Abbot's House. Two buildings resting on Celtic pre-Benedictine foundations are the small *Michael Chapel* (rebuilt 1960) and the former *Infirmary*, now serving as a museum showing a stone known as Columba's Pillow, perhaps the saint's gravestone; the gravestone (from St. Oran's) of Angus Og (died 1326, an early lord of the Isles); the broken Mackinnon's Cross of 1489; and several other fine stones of chieftains and priors.

The above paragraphs cover the physical sacred aspects of Iona, but there are a number of other places of interest. *Dun-I* (332ft), for instance, towards the N end, not only recalls pre-Columban inhabitants but also provides an all-round survey of the island. On the E shore *Martyrs' Bay* is where 68 monks were killed by Norsemen in 806, while the *White Strand of the Monks* at the NE was the scene of the murder of the abbot and 15 monks as late as 986. On the S shore *St. Columba's Bay*, or, more evocatively, the *Port of the Coracle*, is traditionally the place where the saint landed. Other names are self-explanatory—Otters' Point, Spouting Cave, Meadow of the Lapwings; while yet others—Port of the False Man, Nest of the Red Haired Lad, Field of the Old Woman—simply stimulate speculation.

°Island of Staffa

Staffa may be seen by taking one of the excursions from Oban (Rte 46; no landing) or by boat from Dervaig, Ulva Ferry or Fionnphort, all on Mull (see above; landing sometimes possible). Advance booking is advised.

Staffa (Norse 'Staphi-ey' meaning Island of the Pillars) was virtually unknown
to the outer world before a visit paid to it in 1772 by Sir Joseph Banks, the
explorer, who, on his way to Iceland, had been driven into the Sound of Mull
where he learnt of this extraordinary place from a Mr Leach, an Irish visitor
who had landed there a few days earlier.—Geologically what is now the NW
coast of Scotland was once the scene of violent volcanic action, the subterranean
disturbance finding a vent along a line from Skye to Ireland, the effects of
which can be traced through Staffa, Mull (Ardmeanach), Islay and, in Ireland,
Rathlin and the Giant's Causeway, all basically composed of the liquid basalt
ejected to the surface.

Famous for its great caves and astonishing basaltic formations, Staffa
is little more than 1½m in circumference, with a perpendicular face
(140ft) towards the S and W and a more gradual slope on the NE.
   Should landing be possible the normal place is at the mouth of
Clam Shell Cave, not particularly large, but interesting for the curious
curvature of the basaltic columns. This cave cannot be entered, the
best view being from the boat on landing. The *Great Causeway* runs
to the W, with an islet, about 30ft high, called *Buchaille*; its basalt
columns, visible only at low water, are so distorted as to become
horizontal and even inverted.
   Fingal's Cave is the most famous of Staffa's caverns. It is 227ft
long and the height from the water at mean tide is 66ft, the depth of
the sea within being about the same. The sides at the opening are
vertical and the whole of the sides, ground, and roof are composed
of black pentagonal or hexagonal pillars divided transversely by
joints at nearly uniform distances of 2ft. It was, of course, this cave
that inspired Mendelssohn's 'Die Fingalshöhle', or 'Hebrides Over-
ture'.

Islands of Coll and Tiree

> **Communications**. Both islands are reached by car ferry from Oban.
> 3 to 4 services weekly (Caledonian MacBrayne, Ferry Terminal,
> Railway Pier, Oban. Tel: 0631–62285). Also Air service from
> Glasgow to Tiree, continuing to Barra. Mon.–Sat. (Loganair. Tel:
> 041–8893181 or 08792–309).
>
> On Tiree a Post Office bus serves most places (Tel: 08792–301).
> Bicycles can be hired.
>
> SOME HOTELS. **Coll**. *Isle of Coll*, Arinagour. Tel: (08793) 334.
> *Tign-Na-Mara*, Arinagaour. Tel: (08793) 354. **Tiree**. *Tiree Lodge*.
> Tel: (08792) 368. *Balephetrish House*, Balephetrish. Tel: (08792)
> 549.

Coll is a flat crofting island, 12m long by 3m broad and with about
150 inhabitants, the majority of whom live in the village of *Arinagour*.
Traces of brochs can be found, especially near the island's several
lochs, and there are standing stones at Totronald in the SW part of
the island not far from the airfield. Near here, too, *Breacachadh
Castle* (occasionally open. Tel: 08793–444) is a restored early 15C
tower-house, perhaps built by Angus Og, to whom Bruce granted
Coll, but later belonging to the Macleans.
   Tiree, though low-lying and liable to be windswept—its Gaelic
name means the Land lower than the waves—has a record of
surprisingly sunny weather, statistics showing the longest sunshine
hours in Scotland. Measuring 12m by 3m with some 1000 inhabitants,
the island offers the visitor sandy beaches and a golf course. There
are also scattered dun and broch remains, the best being *Dun Mor*

Vaul in the NE of the island, of particular interest for having started as a timber structure as long ago as the 6C BC before later becoming a stone broch.—*Skerryvore Lighthouse*, 10m SW out to sea, was built in 1843 but has not been manned since 1954.

Islands of Colonsay and Oronsay

Communications. Car ferry from Oban 3 times a week (Caledonian MacBrayne, Ferry Terminal, Railway Pier, Oban. Tel: 0631–62285). The islands may also be reached by excursion boats in summer from Port Askaig on Islay.—*Oronsay* is reached by causeway at low water.

A Post Office bus serves most places (Tel: 09512–323). Bicycles can be hired.

HOTEL. *Isle of Colonsay*, PA61 7YP. Tel: (09512) 316.

History. Colonsay was owned by the Macfies (or Macphies) at least from the 15 to 17C. They were dispossessed by the Macdonalds soon after 1615 and in turn the Campbells ousted the Macdonalds. By a land exchange agreement the McNeills acquired the two islands in 1700 and held them until 1904 when debt compelled sale.

The two islands (combined population some 200) owe their names to St. Columba and his companion St. Oran. But man had made his home here millenia before Christian times and excavations (on Oronsay) have revealed evidence of a Middle Stone Age settlement. Later archaeological traces include Iron Age duns and crannogs and, recalling the Norse years, a ship-burial site. But the emphasis remains early Christian with, on Oronsay, the ruins of a *Priory*, in all probability founded by St. Columba. It survives today as the remains of a 14C Augustinian house, together with crosses and graveslabs, the most notable cross, its head bearing a relief of the Crucifixion, being one commemorating Prior Colin who died in 1510.

Together measuring some 9m from N to S, but barely 2m broad, the islands additionally offer a scenic mix of rocky hills and coastline with sandy beaches, rich bird life, seals, a golf course and *Kiloran Gardens* (daily at reasonable hours; donation) with woodland, rhododendrons and rare shrubs.

65 Inner Hebrides reached from Tarbert/Kennacraig (Islay and Jura)

Tourist Organisation. Mid Argyll, Kintyre and Islay Tourist Board, The Pier, Campbeltown, Argyll. Tel: (0586) 52056.

Access. *Islay* is reached by car ferry from Kennacraig on West Loch Tarbert to Port Ellen. Crossing 2¼ hours. 3 to 4 services daily (Caledonian MacBrayne, Ferry Terminal, Kennacraig. Tel: 088073–253, or, at Port Ellen, 0496–2209). *Jura* is reached by car ferry from Port Askaig on Islay to Feolin. Crossing 10 minutes. Frequent, but less so on Sun. (Western Ferries. Tel: 049684–681).

Scheduled air service from Glasgow to Islay. Mon.–Sat., (Loganair. Tel: 041– 8893181, or, on Islay, 0496–2022).

Internal bus services. On *Islay* the three principal routes are: 1. Portnahaven–Port Charlotte–Bowmore–Airport–Port Ellen–Ardbeg. 2. Port Askaig–Bowmore–Airport–Port Ellen–Ardbeg. (For timings

of both the above, Post Office, Port Ellen. Tel: 0496–2131.) 3.
Portnahaven–Port Charlotte– Port Askaig–Bridgend–
Bowmore–Airport–Port Ellen–Ardbeg. (For timings, Western SMT.
Tel: 049681–292.)

On *Jura* there is a service between the ferry at Feolin and
Craighouse, with occasional onward connection to Ardlussa (Tel:
049682–221).

SOME HOTELS. **Port Ellen.** *Islay.* Tel: (0496) 2260. *White Hart.*
Tel: (0496) 2311. **Bowmore.** *Lochside,* 19 Shore Street. Tel: (049681)
244. **Port Askaig.** *Port Askaig.* Tel: (049684) 245. **Bruichladdich.**
Bruichladdich. PA49 7UN. Tel: (049685) 305.

On *Jura* **(Craighouse)**. *Jura,* PA60 7UX. Tel: (049682) 243.

Island of Islay

Islay is the most southerly of the Hebrides; part arable and part
moorland peat, the island measures some 25m from N to S and 20m
across and has about 4000 resident inhabitants, the chief centres
being Bowmore, Port Ellen and Port Charlotte, with farming, fishing
and whisky distilling the principal occupations. With varied and in
places rugged scenery, beaches, golf, fishing and some prehistoric
and early Christian sites—and renowned too as an ornithological
objective—the island attracts discerning summer visitors, yet is large
and fragmented enough never to appear crowded. Topographically
Islay is almost split into two by the sea lochs Gruinart and Indaal,
the western hammerhead being known as the Rhinns.

Port Ellen to Kildalton Cross and Ardtalla (NE along the coast.
10m). Named after the wife of William Campbell, who started to
rebuild here in about 1821, *Port Ellen* (1000 inhab. *ECl.* Tues.) is a
neat little harbour backed by a genteel crescent of 19C stone cottages.
Immediately to the E a lane bears N for Kilbride, within the farther
angle being a tall standing stone and traces of a chapel. The former,
easily seen, according to one story marks the grave of a Norse
princess named Yula, her name perhaps the origin of this island's.
The chapel—two fields away and not easily recognised because it
survives as no more than a hollow in the turf marked out by a few
rough stones—is dedicated to St. Lasar, an obscure 6C Irish nun, and
is curious for two upright stones with holes through them, perhaps
reminders of some ancient custom (like the Trial Stone at Trumpan
on Skye), perhaps merely serving some prosaic constructional need.

Passing distilleries A846 soon reaches *Lagavulin*, its small bay
guarded by ruined Dunavaig Castle, a tower dating from the 14C
and probably built by John of Islay who in 1386 formally assumed
the title of Lord of the Isles. Beyond, at *Ardbeg*, the road becomes
minor as it fringes *Loch-an-t-Sailein*, the Loch of the Seals, though
without binoculars few seals will be seen as they tend to favour the
outer rocks.

Kildalton Cross, the star among Islay's several Celtic and later
crosses and by many connoisseurs held to be the most beautiful in
Scotland, is 7m from Port Ellen. Dating from c 800 and probably the
work of a sculptor from Iona, the green to grey local stone bears a
wealth of well preserved and intricate patterns and scenes. Nor
should the churchyard of the ruined chapel be ignored, for, though
its stones cannot compare with the cross, they are nevertheless of
interesting enough variety and span from medieval times to the 18C.

Beyond, the road continues a further 3m to *Ardtalla*, from where
a path in another 3m reaches *McArthur's Head*, opposite Jura and

marking the entrance to the Sound of Islay.

Port Ellen to Mull of Oa (W, across the peninsula of The Oa. 7m, but most of the last mile on foot). In 1m from Port Ellen a road bearing N for Kintra should be followed by anyone with a feel for ancient stones, for in 1½m , just before Kintra, *Druim an Stuin* stands on the left beside the road. It is not much of a stone, little more than a large boulder, but it is said to mark the grave of Godred Crovan, a Norse chieftain who drove Fingal out of the Isle of Man and made himself ruler of the western islands until his death here on Islay in 1095.

The peninsula, known for its caves and cliffs and once notorious for smuggling and illicit whisky distilling, rounds off as the *Mull of Oa*. Here a monument, erected by the American Red Cross, commemorates those who lost their lives in 1918 when the American troopships 'Tuscania' and 'Otranto' were lost, the former torpedoed off The Oa, the latter driven ashore on the W coast of the Rhinns.

Port Ellen to Bowmore and Port Askaig (N and NE. 21m). There is in fact a choice of roads, A846 or the parallel B8016, both across dull peat-stacked lowland behind the great sandy crescent of Laggan Bay. A846 runs arrow-straight (its course was originally intended to be a railway), passing the airport and then kinking slightly to reach *Bowmore* (1000 inhab. *Inf.* for the whole island. April–Sept. Tel: 049681–254), a neat, planned 19C township best known for its curious round church of Kilarrow (1767); the design was intended to thwart the Devil by denying him any corners in which to lurk.

At *Bridgend*, 2m beyond Bowmore, the road for the Rhinns bears away W, while A846 continues N for (a further 7m) *Port Askaig* for the ferry crossing to Jura.

The **Rhinns of Islay**, a hammerhead of land almost severed from the bulk of the island by the long bites of lochs Gruinart from the N and Indaal from the S, is in many ways—prehistoric, early Christian and as regards bloody clan strife—the most interesting part of Islay. For touring purposes the Rhinns conveniently divides into two distinct parts; a northern area reached by B8017, 2m W of Bridgend, and a southern district served by a road circuit starting at Port Charlotte.

A standing stone marks the start of B8017 which in 3½m reaches a road junction to the SW of the head of Loch Gruinart. Here a stone, the *Clach Mhic-illean*, stands where a Maclean chief was killed and recalls a vicious clan battle of 1598. The cause was the grant by James VI of land in Islay to Sir Lachlan Maclean of Duart on Mull. This, of course, the local Macdonalds would not accept, so 400 Macleans invaded here, only to lose their chief and suffer a defeat so crushing that only a handful returned to Mull. From this stone an uninviting road heads N, in 2½m reaching the ruined church of *Kilnave*, with a Celtic cross (c 8C) bearing weathered carving. Today a sad ruin across a bleak field, in 1598 this church held hope of sanctuary for a group of defeated and wounded Macleans, a hope, though, that was not realised because the Macdonalds fired the thatch and the Macleans all died beneath its blaze.

B8017, now heading W from the stone, reaches *Loch Gorm*, on a crannog islet near the SE of which are traces of the Macdonald castle which was the objective of the Maclean invasion. *Kilchoman Church*, beyond the SW of Loch Gorm, is more interesting, and especially for its fine Celtic cross, showing a clear Crucifixion and bearing small angels on its arms. Legend, if without evidence, suggests that this cross was erected by John of Islay in memory of his dead Scottish princess, the daughter of Robert II. And here, too, are several tombs showing quaint pygmy-like figures, thought to represent medieval (15–16C) churchmen, though local tradition insists that one stone (the one on which the effigy occupies the most space) was later used to mark the grave here of the luckless Maclean chief.

From Kilchoman it is necessary to return to Loch Indaal and Port Charlotte, a distance of 8m, before embarking on the Rhinns southern circuit.

At *Port Charlotte*, known for Islay cheese, the former Free Church has been converted into a Museum of Islay Life (April–Sept: Mon.–Fri., 10.00 to 17.00. Sat. and Sun., 14.00 to 17.00. Oct–March: Mon.–Fri., 10.00 to 16.30. Tel: 049685–358. Fee), covering the island's story from prehistoric times. Leaving Port Charlotte southward, A847 passes *Ellister Bird Sanctuary* (Rodney Dawson Memorial Trust), with several species of swans, geese and ducks, beyond (7m from Port Charlotte) reaching the twin village-ports of *Portnahaven* and *Port Wemyss*, a picturesque, haphazard corner with cottages reaching tentatively up turf slopes towards the 19C church which, serving both villages, nevertheless offers a separate door for each. A cluster of islands, once shelter for a jostle of fishing boats, marks the broken end of the Rhinns.

The return is made by the minor road which climbs away up on to the Rhinns' desolate, almost treeless central heights. Yet prehistoric people deliberately chose this place, leaving as evidence the great ring of weathered and battered stones known as *Cultoon Stone Circle* (3½m N of Portnahaven and about 100 yards W of the road). Most are prone, and the suggestion has been made that they never were raised, that the project, whatever its arcane purpose, may have been abandoned before completion. Today forlorn sheep are about all that move in a place once thronged first by this circle's builders and then by those who practised its rites.

Nor is *Kilchiaran Chapel* (2m farther, below the hills) without atmosphere, and it is easy enough to accept here that St. Columba did indeed beach his coracle in the sheltered bay, at once building a chapel on the nearest level ground above. Today a ruined medieval successor—dedicated to St. Kieran—shelters an aumbrey, a stoup and a slab bearing one of those pygmy figures found at nearby Kilchoman, while outside a fragment of a Christian cross stands close to a cup-marked stone suggesting that this spot was regarded as sacred perhaps 2000 years before the arrival of Columba.

Curving SE the road in 3m returns to Port Charlotte.

Island of Jura

Although so close geographically to Islay, Jura (28m from N to S by 8m broad) is scenically abruptly and dramatically different, splendidly Highland and with ever-changing seascapes. Halfway along its length the erratic gash of Loch Tarbert all but cuts the island into two; to the S lift the prominent *Paps of Jura*—An Oir, the Mountain of Gold, reaching 2576ft, Siontaidh, the Holy Mountain, reaching 2477ft, and A Chaolais, the Mountain of the Strait, not far below at 2407ft. Red deer, too, are of the essence of Jura, for the island's name derives from the Norse for deer and today the herds still add up to some 5000 animals, most of them in the largely trackless fastnesses of the interior though not infrequently they approach the sparsely populated E coast.

The occasional standing stone proves man's very early presence here, but, at any rate numerically, he now seems in retreat for the 1500 or so inhabitants of the early 19C are now down to around 200, the cattle grazing of the past now superseded by estates given over to rod and gun.

The island's only road runs for 24m, curving within the coast between the ferry at Feolin and Jura's only village, Craighouse, from where—and for much of the way staying scenically high above the water—it follows the E coast past the head of Loch Tarbert to Ardlussa. The drive is essentially one of scenery, seascapes and, with any luck, deer. For the rest, a lone megalith is well seen to the right of the road 3m from the ferry; *Craighouse*, reached in another 5m, is a straggling shoreside village with a pleasant hotel and a distillery; and there are more standing stones near the settlement of *Tarbert*, the point at which Jura is less than a mile wide.

At *Ardlussa* the road ends, deteriorating into a track unsuitable for ordinary cars. This in another 7m reaches *Barnhill*, the house in which George Orwell wrote '1984', while, 3m beyond, Jura's northern tip looks across to the island of Scarba beyond the Strait of Corrievreckan, notorious for its whirlpools and tidal races.

66 Outer Hebrides

From N to S, and spanning 130 miles, the principal islands of the Outer Hebrides (the Long Island) are Lewis, Harris, North Uist, Benbecula, South Uist and Barra. Lewis and Harris are geographically one island; and North Uist, Benbecula and South Uist, linked by a causeway and a bridge, are effectively one. By using the car ferries between Harris and North Uist and between South Uist and Barra it is possible to tour the length of the group. But these ferries, with seasonal timetables, do not run daily, so some planning is necessary.

Each island has its own character. For the most part, though, the scenery tends to be open and bleak, and in this, coupled with their remote situation, lies much of the lure of these islands. Long sandy shores are fretted by countless sea lochs within which are scattered islands and islets. Likewise the often desolate moors are so sprinkled with hundreds of lochs that in many districts there is more water than land. Trees are few, and the scanty soil poor and often difficult to drain, so that farming is limited; lobster and other fishing, the manufacture of tweed and the harvesting of seaweed for the extraction of alginates are some main local activities of a people to whom Gaelic is the everyday language. In the S the population is largely Catholic.

Inhabited by man since earliest times, the islands are rich in prehistoric material.

Tourist Organisation. Outer Hebrides Tourist Board, South Beach Street, Stornoway, Isle of Lewis. Tel: (0851) 3088.

Access. Caledonian MacBrayne operate car ferries as below:

1. To Lewis (Stornoway) from Ullapool. Tel: (0854) 2358.

2. To Harris (Tarbert) from Uig on Skye. Tel: (047042) 219.

3. To North Uist (Lochmaddy) from Uig on Skye. Tel: (047042) 219.

4. To South Uist (Lochboisdale) from Oban. Tel: (0631) 62285.

5. To Barra (Castlebay) from Oban. Tel: (0631) 62285.

6. Between Harris and North Uist. Tel: Uig as above, or (0859) 2444.

7. Between South Uist and Barra. Tel: Oban as above, or (08784) 288.

No Sun. services. Timetables are seasonal. Advance reservation is strongly advised. Intending passengers planning a tour involving two or more routes should coordinate with Caledonian MacBrayne. The Ferry Terminal, Gourock. PA19 1QP. Tel: (0475) 33755, who will also advise on special discounts such as Island Hopscotch or Car Rover.

There are four air services as below:

1. Glasgow and Inverness to Lewis. ⎫
2. Glasgow to Benbecula.   ⎬   B A. Tel: (041) 3329666.

3. Glasgow to Barra.   ⎫
4. Lewis–Benbecula–Barra.   ⎬   Loganair. Tel: (041) 8893181.

Internal Bus Services. See under individual islands.

Accommodation of virtually all middle grades is available. It is prudent, especially in summer, to book. For some hotels, see under individual islands.

Harris Tweed (or 'Clo Mor', big cloth) was originally woven by the islanders only for their own use, but later became much in demand particularly by sporting gentry who visited the islands. In 1909 the Harris Tweed Association was formed to protect the industry against imitators. Genuine Harris Tweed is a tweed made from pure Scottish wool, spun, dyed and finished in the Outer Hebrides and hand woven by the islanders in their own homes. Until the 1930s vegetable dyeing was still normal, the women producing the dyes from lichen, roots, heather, soot and vegetables; today modern dying processes offer a much wider range of colours. There is now a choice of over 5000 designs, and weights vary from 11oz to 6oz. In recent years the industry has declined—due, perhaps, to an increasing preference for lighter clothing—and there are now proposals for revival through small factories and power looms.

Island of Lewis

Bus Services cover virtually the entire island but are operated by several different companies. Routes and information from Tourist Information, Stornoway.

SOME HOTELS. **Stornoway**. *Caberfeidh*, Manor Park. Tel: (0851) 2604. *Seaforth*, James Street. Tel: (0851) 2740. *Royal*, Cromwell Street, Tel: (0851) 2109. **Ness**. *Cross Inn*, Cross. Tel: (085181) 378.

The most northern of the Hebrides and, after Skye, the largest—at its longest and widest some 35m by 30m—Lewis is scenically an interior of moorland and countless small lochs behind coasts which are wildly broken in the S but smooth out as the island tapers towards its northern Butt. The focus is the town of Stornoway, halfway along the E coast, and it is here that the description below starts, before moving out into each of the island's four parishes.

Stornoway (8000 inhab. *ECl.* Wed. *Inf.* South Beach Street) is the island's port and capital, and also the headquarters of the local government Western Isles Area. Founded by James VI, something of the local story is illustrated in the *Stornoway Museum* in the Old Town Hall in Cromwell Street (June–Aug: Tues.–Sat., 14.00 to 17.30. Sept–May: Thurs.–Sat., 14.00 to 17.30. Always open to 19.00 on Thurs. Tel: 0851–3773. Free). Two famous explorers have niches in the town. Alexander Mackenzie (1755–1820), famed in the annals of

Canada, was born here and is remembered by a tablet on *Martin's Memorial Church* in Francis Street; and in *St. Peter's Church*, in the same street, can be seen David Livingstone's prayer book, originally donated to the church of Teamphull Mhor near Butt of Lewis, and a red granite font, brought from the Flannan Islands and one of the oldest in Scotland.

On the W side of the harbour stands *Lews Castle* (1856–63, and now a technical college), presented to the town by Lord Leverhulme (1851–1925) who in 1918 acquired Lewis and Harris and unsuccessfully tried to modernise the methods of farming and fishing. Beyond, it was near *Arnish Lighthouse*, marking the S entrance to Stornoway's bay, that the Young Pretender spent a night (memorial cairn). However his attempt to buy a boat was frustrated by two Lewis ministers. Across the harbour is the rock of *Holm* where on New Year's Day 1919 the troopship 'Iolaire' sank, over 200 soldiers and sailors being drowned.

The **Parish of Point** occupies the small peninsula which, with the airport at its W end, hooks E and NE out of Stornoway. Its only place of interest is the roofless 14C *Chapel of St. Columba*, to be found at the peninsula's base, just N of the E end of the causeway. Said to have been founded by a MacLeod chief, it shelters an effigy which may be that of Roderick MacLeod (15C) as also a cross-slab commemorating his daughter Margaret who died in 1503 and was the mother of the last abbot of Iona.

The **Parish of Barvas** represents much of northern Lewis, the village of *Barvas*, 10m from Stornoway, being reached by A857 across desolate moor. The road SW out of Barvas in 3m reaches the *Arnol Blackhouse* (AM. Standard, but closed Sun. Fee), a traditional crofter dwelling now preserved as a museum. Just beyond, at *Bragar*, there is a curiosity in the form of a whalebone arch with, hanging from it, the harpoon which killed the animal, while, beyond again at Shawbost, the *Folk Museum* (Summer: 09.00 to 19.00. Winter 10.00 to 16.00. Tel: 0851–3088. Donation), illustrating the old way of life in Lewis, is an admirable local school achievement. About 1m W of Shawbost (sign; ½m walk) the same school has restored a Norse watermill.

This road continues into the parish of Uig, soon reaching Carloway Broch and Callanish Standing Stones, for both of which see below.

At Barvas A857 heads NE along the coast, soon reaching two good prehistoric sites. First, at *Ballantrushal*, there is the huge Thrushal Stone (20ft), the tallest monolith in Scotland. Then, half a mile farther N along A857 (E, sign), comes *Steinacleit*, a collapsed burial cairn within a stone circle, an unusual feature here being an irregular outer stone surround.

Approaching Port of Ness the empty moor gives way to a surprisingly green and populated district with several sizeable villages, at *Eoropie*, the last village before the Butt of Lewis, being the church known as Teamphull Mhor, or the Church of St. Moluag, dating from the 12 or 13C and on the site of a much earlier church dedicated to St. Olaf (key from village store). The *Butt of Lewis*, an inhospitable cape with a lighthouse, projects as a confusion of cliffs and rock pinnacles alive with seabirds. *Port of Ness* here is a small harbour from which the Nessmen sail in August and September to collect the 'guga', or young gannets, a favourite local delicacy, from Sula Sgeir, an islet 30m out to the N.

The **Parish of Uig** is reached by A858 leading W, out of Stornoway and in 15m reaching the ****Standing Stones of Callanish**, one of the most astonishing and complete prehistoric sites in Britain, a forest of megaliths planted on the moorland—at first sight apparently haphazard but in fact to a design—and, associated with them, at least one chambered cairn. The central ring of 13 stones has a diameter of 37ft, flattened on the E side. Here there is a central monolith (over 15ft), while a small chambered cairn occupies part of the circle. From the circle radiate rows of stones—four to the E, five to the W, five to the S, and a great avenue of 19 to the N—while just outside the circle stand two seemingly random stones, a tall one to the SW and a short one (re-erected in 1885) to the SE. In all there are 48, generally slim and tall, stones here, set in design and covering a length of 400ft—eloquent yet tantalisingly mute evidence both of the (presumably religious) compulsion that must have driven the builders of this place, as also of the organisation and skills that must have backed them.

Nor does Callanish stand alone, for nearby there are three other stone circles and at least nine, by comparison minor, sites. Two of the stone circles, one showing the remains of a cairn, are readily accessible just S of the main road; the third is a short way down B8011, glimpsed a few hundred yards away up the slope.

There is a road fork here, with B8011 running SW and then NW through some of the best scenery on Lewis as it rounds islanded Loch Roag to reach *Uig*, 18m from Callanish. Near here, in 1831, were discovered the Uig Chessmen (now in the British Museum), a set of walrus-ivory chessmen, hidden perhaps by nuns from a Benedictine house known to have flourished a few miles S down the coast. Nearly 20m out to the W are the *Flannan Islands*, or the Seven Hunters, with remains of Celtic hermits' cells and the scene in 1900 of a never explained tragedy when three light-keepers disappeared without trace.

From Callanish A858 soon reaches *Dun Carloway*, the best preserved broch in the Hebrides, still about 30ft high on one side and occupying a commanding position with a grand seaward view. The road continues into the Parish of Barvas, with, within about 6m, the Shawbost Folk Museum and the Arnol Blackhouse.

The **Parish of Lochs**, traversed by A859 heading S for (30m) Tarbert on Harris, fully lives up to its name. At *Keose*, on the N of Loch Erisort, there is a seaweed alginate factory, and it is of interest to note that some of this was used for fire-proofing astronauts' notepads and thus went to the moon. *Aline Lodge*, at the head of Loch Seaforth, is at the boundary with the island of Harris, and, just beyond, Ardvourlie Bay is where the Young Pretender landed in 1746, thence walking to Arnish near Stornoway.

Island of Harris

Bus Services run N to Stornoway and S to make a round of South Harris (Harris Garage Co, Tarbert. Tel: 0859–2441).

SOME HOTELS. **Tarbert**. *Harris*, Tel: (0859) 2154. *Macleod's Motel*, Pier Road. Tel: (0859) 2364. **Scarista**. *Scarista House*. Tel: (085985) 238. **Leverburgh**. *Rodel*. Tel: (085982) 210.

Harris is split into North and South by the narrow isthmus (½m across) on which is the island's village capital and ferry port of **Tarbert** (*ECl.* Thurs. *Inf.* May–Sept). North Harris is mountainous with peaks of

well over 2000ft. In the E, South Harris is a wilderness of rock and
small lochs, but in the W green downland drops to sweeps of yellow
beaches.

Either side of the isthmus are West Loch Tarbert and East Loch
Tarbert, the latter protected by the small island of **Scalpay** (Car ferry
from Kyles Scalpay. Caledonian MacBrayne. Tel: 085984–220), with
a population of around 500, largely engaged in fishing. During his
wanderings the Young Pretender crossed to Scalpay where he was
hidden by a farmer, Donald Cameron; the Free Church manse now
stands on the site.—The *Shiant Islands*, 12m E of Scalpay, have sheer
cliffs, the home of myriad seabirds (for boat hire from Tarbert or
Scalpay, Tel: 085984–225).

North Harris. One road runs N to Stornoway. Another heads W
between the mountains and West Loch Tarbert, a drive through
lovely coastal scenery with many burns cascading down from above.
Along this road, at *Bunaveneader*, can be seen the slip and other
remains of a whaling station built by the Norwegians in c 1912, later
operated by Lord Leverhulme, but abandoned in 1930. Beyond
Amhuinnsuid Castle (no adm.), built by the Earl of Dunmore in 1868,
the road ends at *Husinish* (14m from Tarbert) opposite the island of
Scarp, now uninhabited but with a modest niche in postal history. In
1934 the island was chosen for an experiment by which mail was to
be delivered by a rocket designed by a German called Zucker. A
special stamp was issued, but the rocket exploded on impact,
damaging most of the mail, and the project was abandoned.

The peninsula of **South Harris** is circled by road, the distance
from Tarbert back to Tarbert being some 36m. The E shore road is
narrow, twisting and slow but runs through rugged, broken coastal
scenery. The western loop is faster, but scenically very different, with
downland and beaches. Along this latter road there are standing
stones at *Nisabost* and *Barvemoor*, while beyond at *Northton*, where
the road curves SE, a track heads for the high nobble of land which
juts out as the westernmost part of Harris. Here, on a little promontory
at the S end, will be found a ruined chapel, of unknown age but
complete with its aumbrey and, whatever its story, a gem in this
setting. *Leverburgh* (formerly Obbe) is where in 1923 Lord Leverhulme tried to establish a large fishing port; the project was
abandoned on his death two years later. For ferry to Berneray and
North Uist, see below.

Rodel Church (c 1500; restored 1787 and 1873), at the peninsula's
S tip, is known for the curious carvings on its tower, these including
strangely tilted figures wearing kilt and plaid. Inside, in the remarkably fine recess of a tomb, is the armoured effigy of Alastair Crotach
(1528), a MacLeod chief from Dunvegan.

Across the strait can be seen the island of *Berneray* (200 inhab;
remains of stone circles), reached by passenger ferry from Leverburgh, the service continuing to Newton Ferry on North Uist (Tel:
08767–230 or 250. The island can also be reached from the S by a
small car ferry from Newton Ferry.

Island of North Uist

Bus Services cover most of the island and run also to Benbecula
airport (Post Office, Lochmaddy. Tel: 08763–330).

SOME HOTELS. **Lochmaddy**. *Lochmaddy*. Tel: (08763) 331.
Locheport. *Langass Lodge*. Tel: (08764) 285.

Vaguely circular in shape, though the geometry is distorted by several promontories, North Uist is scenically an island of high moorland and lochs on the E, while the W is by comparison green and fertile with long beaches. The chief centre is **Lochmaddy** (*ECl*. Wed. *Inf*. May–Sept) on the E coast, apparently taking its name (Loch of the Dog) from the three doglike basalt islets at the harbour entrance. The loch, though only 5m long and with an entrance 1m wide, has a shoreline so tortuous that its length has been calculated to reach 360m.

A road (some 30m) circles the main island, this being described anticlockwise below. Heading NW this road rounds the hill of *Blashaval* to the W, on the lower NW slope of which there are three standing stones known as Na Fir Bhreige, or the False Men. One tradition is that these mark the graves of three spies who were buried here alive; another, more domestic, that the stones represent three men from Skye, turned to stone by a witch as retribution for having deserted their wives. Beyond, B893 leads N to (3m) Newton Ferry with a small car ferry to the island of Berneray and a passenger ferry to Leverburgh on South Harris (Tel: 08767–230 or 250). Continuing along A865 the hamlets of Grenitote and Solas are passed, beside the road, as it curves to travel SE, standing *Kilphedar Cross*, of obscure age and origin but transferred here from a nearby burial ground in 1830. From the road rise here the seaward view can include St. Kilda.

St. Kilda, 45m W, comprises four islands and several islets, the largest, *Hirta*, being 3m long with stupendous cliffs over 1000ft in height. The entire population of 35 were evacuated at their own request in 1930, and the islands are now under the care of the National Trust for Scotland and the Nature Conservancy Council. Each year NTS working parties of volunteers are gradually restoring the village community (details from NTS). The other islands are *Soay* (home of the sheep of that breed), *Boreray* and *Dun*, all being alive with seabirds, these including the world's largest colony of gannets, the largest and oldest colonies in Britain of fulmars, and a large population of puffins.

Farther S, the nature reserve of *Balranald* (warden at Houghharry in summer), known for its variety of breeding birds, lies SW of the road which from here heads SE to reach (6m from Balranald) *Clachan* at a road junction. Here the left fork (A867) returns in 8m to Lochmaddy, but in 2m reaches the round chambered cairn of *Langash Barp*, to the S of the road on the slope of Ben Langash. Though partially collapsed, entry is still possible into a polygonal chamber, while around the exterior base are what appear to be small cists. A track rounds the S of the hill, a short way beyond its end being a prehistoric stone oval known as *Pobull Fhinn*, Finn's People.—*Locheport* (hotel) is 4m E of the Clachan junction.

To the W, some 10m from this road fork, are the *Monach Islands*, uninhabited and a national nature reserve which is a wintering ground for barnacle and white-footed geese. According to old records the Sound of Monach was until the 16C fordable at low water.

Leaving the island circuit, A865 now head S, in 3m reaching Carinish where there is a curious ruin known as *Teamphull na Trionaid* (Trinity Temple), twin church buildings founded on an earlier Celtic site in about 1200 by Beatrix, a daughter of Somerled, and later rebuilt by the wife of John Macdonald of Islay, first Lord of the Isles (she was daughter of Robert II; see also Kilchoman Church on Islay, Rte 65). It is said, too, that this was once an ancient seat of learning, attended by, amongst others, Duns Scotus. More certain is that Carinish was in 1601 the scene of a battle between the MacLeods of Harris and the local Macdonalds.

About a mile beyond Carinish the road breasts a rise, here cutting straight through the clear remains of a stone circle, while to the NE can be seen the distinct outline of a long cairn. Beyond, *North Ford* causeway, taking the road across to the island of Benbecula, was opened in 1960.

Island of Benbecula

> **Bus Services**. For the service to Lochmaddy on North Uist, Tel: (08763) 330. For services to western North Uist (Tigharry, Hosta, Scolpaig), Tel: (08765) 247. For service to Lochboisdale on South Uist, Tel: (08784) 278.
>
> SOME HOTELS. **Liniclate**. *Dark Island*, PA88 5PG. Tel: (0870) 2414. *Inchyra*, PA88 5PY. Tel: (0870) 2176. **Creagorry**. *Creagorry*, PA88 5PG. Tel: (0870) 2024.

Ignoring its many seaward promontories, especially to the E, Benbecula is a rough square, measuring some 5m by 5m and thus the smallest of the main islands of the Outer Hebridean chain. Scenically the island is to a large extent a flat broken area of sea and inland lochs, though on the W side there is a fertile district protected by sand dunes beyond which is beach. The principal village is Balivanich in the NW, alongside being the airport.

The direct road (A865) crosses the island in a little more than 5m, but it is a lot more interesting to make the westward loop provided by B892. This road skirts the airport, ½m SE of which, on a promontory into Loch Dun Mhurchairdh, can be seen *Dun Buidhe*, an Iron Age survival with considerable stone remains and seemingly once a place of some strength. The road turns sharply W to round the airport, just to the S being a small ruin known as *Teampull Challuim Chille*, of unknown origin, but, if only from its name, almost certainly once a chapel. Beyond *Balivanich* the road drops southward, in 1m passing the ruined chapel *Nunton*; dating from the 14C the chapel was once that of a nunnery, wrecked at the Reformation and the nuns massacred. *Borve Castle*, on the left 2½m farther S, though now only a remnant, was a Clan Ranald stronghold until burnt by clansmen who opposed their Jacobite chief and supported George II. Opposite, a short way S of the road, there are traces of a chapel which probably belonged to the castle.

A865 is soon rejoined, about 1½m northwards up this road being *Loch Olavat*, with islets showing evidence of three duns.

It was from the remote district of *Rossinish* in the broken NE of Benbecula that the Young Pretender and Flora Macdonald sailed 'over the sea to Skye'.

Benbecula is linked to South Uist by a bridge across *South Ford*.

Island of South Uist

> **Bus Services**. A service runs the length of the island between Benbecula airport in the N to Ludag in the S (MacAuley Bros, Lochboisdale. Tel: 08784–278).
>
> SOME HOTELS. **Lochboisdale**. *Lochboisdale*, PA81 5TH. Tel: (08784) 332. **Daliburgh**. *Borrodale*. Tel: (08784) 444.

This is a long, thin island (20m by 7m) made up of a W coast of beaches, an interior of peat bog and lochs, and an E side of sea lochs and mountains, the highest being *Ben Mhor* (2033ft) and *Hecla* (1988ft).

Historically South Uist is associated with the Young Pretender's meeting with Flora Macdonald. The prince landed (from Scalpay) on 14 May 1746 in *Corodale Bay* on the E coast below Ben Mhor, thereafter hiding in a forester's hut. From a nearby cave (Prince's Cave) he watched government ships patrolling The Minch, but, though his stay may have been hazardous, it was not without its compensations, for he apparently received many gifts of whisky and brandy and even won an all-night drinking marathon. He was looked after by Neil MacEachain Macdonald and through him met Flora Macdonald, aged 23 and on a visit from Skye to her brother at Milton, her birthplace. MacEachain proposed that she should return to Skye, taking the prince, disguised as a servant girl, with her. At first she refused, on the grounds that this could implicate her friends, but as soon as she met the prince her objections crumbled.

Corodale Bay and Prince's Cave are far from any road, but the island's N–S road passes Milton.

The description below travels the length of South Uist from N to S, starting, just S of the bridge from Benbecula, with the *Eochar Cottage Museum* (Tel: 08784–286), a former blackhouse now showing bygones. Beyond, A865 crosses the large *Loch Bee* by causeway, just beyond the end of which, in Loch Duin Mhoir on the W of the road, there is an islet with clear traces of a dun and its approach. To the E, 1½m farther, stands the 125ft-high granite statue of *Our Lady of the Isles* (Hew Lorimer, 1957). Within less than a mile the road is fringing *Loch Druidibeg*, spattered with islands and stretching over 2m E; a national nature reserve, the loch is the most important breeding ground in Britain of the greylag goose. Another road borders the N shore of the loch to reach the head of Loch Skipport, while in the SW of the loch, on an islet off the S shore (½m from the road), rectangular *Dun Roauill* provides archaeological interest for its unusual shape and as perhaps the best dun on South Uist. Roughly opposite, to the W of A865 and standing in the middle of Loch an Eilean, *Caisteal Bheagram* is the ruin of a small 15 or 16C tower, and at *Howmore*, just to the S, the church offers a rare curiosity in the form of a central communion pew.

Continuing S, A865 passes (2½m from Howmore) below a lone megalith on the slope of Beinn a Charra, beyond, in another mile, reaching the turn (W) for *Ormaclete Castle*, a ruin standing within a farm. Built between 1701–08 for the chief of Clan Ranald, the castle had a short life and an undistinguished end when, in 1715, it was gutted by fire caused by over-enthusiastic celebration of what was prematurely reported to be a Jacobite victory at Sheriffmuir. *Flora Macdonald's Birthplace*, the home too of the brother she was visiting at the time of her meeting with the Young Pretender—today simply a memorial cairn within a low-walled ruin—can be seen up a track to the W of A865 halfway between the turns off to Kildonan and Milton. And opposite the latter turn an eastward track in 1m reaches a chambered cairn, part surrounded by standing stones.

At *Daliburgh* A865 bears E for (2m) **Lochboisdale** (*ECl.* Tues. *Inf.* May–Sept), the island's port and capital. Off the southward road (now B888), in 1m, a road signed *Kilpheder* leads W through this hamlet, beyond, along a track and in the machar-covered dunes, being the remains of an Iron Age wheel-house, or aisled round-house, showing a circular outer wall, radiating dividers and a central hearth.

B888 breasts a rise on which stands a church (1963) containing attractive and unusual Stations of the Cross, the work of a Barra priest, Calum McNeil, beyond, on the S coast, being *Ludag*, a pleasant corner with seaward views of Eriskay, Barra and other small islands. (Vehicle boat to Eriskay. All year: Mon.–Sat., four return trips daily. Tel: 0851–3773 or 08786–223.—Passenger ferry to Eoligarry on Barra. Crossing 40 minutes. Tel: 08784–216).

It was on *Eriskay*, on Prince's Strand on the W shore, that the Young Pretender first set foot on Scottish soil on 23 July 1745. In 1941 the 'Politician' foundered here, carrying 20,000 cases of whisky, a wreck which became the subject of Compton Mackenzie's 'Whisky Galore'.—On *Stack Island*, to the S, the ruined castle was a lair of a notorious local Macneil pirate and wreck plunderer.

Island of Barra

Bus Service. Circuit of the island, including the airport and Eoligarry (Post Office, Castlebay. Tel: 08714–286).

SOME HOTELS. **Castlebay**. *Castlebay*, PA80 5XD. Tel: (08714) 223. **Tangusdale**. *Isle of Barra*, PA80 5XW. Tel: (08714) 383.

Barren, yet with an attraction all its own, Barra owes its name to St. Findbarr, or Barr, said to have converted the island during the 6C. **Castlebay** (*ECl.* Thurs. *Inf.* May–Sept), on the S, is the port and principal centre, on an island in its bay being *Kisimul Castle* (Wed. and Sat., 14.00 to 16.00. Tel: 08714–336. Fee).

History. The history of Barra is essentially that of Kisimul which, started in c 1060, is, in part at least, among the oldest stone castles in Scotland. The main tower dates from c 1120. The castle and the island were owned from 1314 by the Macneils (some put it earlier to 1030), acquired because a member of the clan fought for Bruce at Bannockburn. The castle was virtually destroyed by fire at the end of the 18C, and in 1838 Barra, together with the castle, was sold to John Gordon of Cluny. A century later, in 1937, Kisimul was bought back by the late Robert Lister Macneil (45th clan chief), an American architect. Restoration was completed by 1970 and the castle remains in (American) Macneil ownership.

A road (14m) circles the island, travelling NW out of Castlebay and soon looking down on *Loch Tangusdale*, also known as *Loch St. Clair*, in which the small ruin of Castle Sinclair clings to an islet. The Isle of Barra Hotel (1974) is next passed, soon after which, W of the road opposite the turning to Borve, are two standing stones which, though modest, traditionally mark the grave of a raiding Norse warrior, defeated in single combat by a local champion. Just beyond, the road through *Craigston*—with a local cottage museum (Tel: 08714–336)—leads towards *Dun Bharpa*, a large collapsed chambered cairn part surrounded by standing stones (from the end of the surfaced road the continuing track may be followed for a few hundred yards, after which the cairn is reached by an easy though often wet climb NE).

Along the main road, a mile after the Craigston turn, a small cemetery is reached, a point at which it is worth crossing the dunes to the shore where many seals can normally be seen. Above the cemetery rises *Dun Cueir*, most easily climbed in about 10 minutes from the N and well worth the effort, not only for its commanding position but also because this is a much better preserved dun than many and one which still shows its thick wall and side passages.

At *North Bay* the island circuit should be broken for a diversion of some 4m into Barra's northern tip, the road soon rounding *Traigh Mhor*, the tidal sandy bay which at low water serves as the island's airfield. *Eoligarry*, beyond, is a scattered hamlet at the S end of which is the interesting *Cille-Bharra*, a group of three ruined chapels, perhaps of the 12C. One of these has now been roofed and shelters some weathered, carved graveslabs, probably of the 15–17C though local legend insists that they are Celtic, having been brought from Iona by a local chieftain requiring ballast for his galley; and, indeed, one stone does bear a faint picture of a galley. Compton Mackenzie, the author, is buried here—in sight of Eriskay, the setting for his 'Whisky Galore'—while across the road from the chapels *St. Barr's Well* is the spot where, after coming ashore, the saint struck the ground with his stave and out gushed water. From Eoligarry there is a passenger ferry to Ludag on South Uist (Crossing 40 minutes. Tel: 08784–216).

At North Bay, on an islet in the loch within the E angle of the two roads, stands a figure of St. Barr with his raised stave, the work (1975) of a local artist, Margaret Somerville. In another 4m, at *Brevig*, there are standing stones, beyond, high up on the S shoulder of Heavel (1255ft), standing the *Lady Star of the Sea*, a marble Madonna erected in 1954 by the Welcome Home Fund for Seamen.

A string of small islands runs away to the S, *Vatersay* being the nearest (just over 1m), inhabited, and reachable by regular passenger ferry from Castlebay (Tel: 08714–307). The Annie James Monument, on the shore of West Bay, recalls the site of an emigrant shipwreck.—Boats can sometimes be hired to other islands, notably *Mingulay* whose towering cliffs are famous for nesting seabirds. Here Macphee's Hill is named after a rent collector who, on arriving on the island, found all the tenants dead from the plague; his terrified companions promptly rowed away, leaving Macphee marooned for a year. On *Pabbay* there are Pictish and Celtic Christian stones.

X   ORKNEY AND SHETLAND

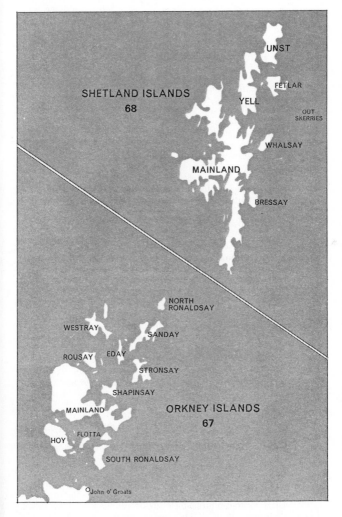

Although often spoken of as one, the two island groups of Orkney and Shetland are (if Shetland's Fair Isle is discounted), in fact separated by some 60m of often wild sea. Both groups are virtually treeless, they largely share a common history, both confusingly call their principal islands Mainland, and they have a common concern with oil. In other respects, though—and certainly from the tourist point of view—Orkney and Shetland are in total contrast; Orkney low-lying, scenically unexciting but offering by far the richest concentration of prehistoric monuments in Britain, Shetland a place of lonely peat upland, countless lochs and ever-present coastal scenery ranging from dark, peaceful inlets to precipitous cliffs alive with seabirds.

Common History. Both Orkney and Shetland were the home during the Stone Age of people of unknown origin; both were colonised by the Picts at about the time of the birth of Christ; both received early Christian missionaries (the frequently found place-name 'Papa' or 'Papil' was the Norse term for the Celtic priests); and both, after perhaps two centuries of Norse raiding and settlement, were annexed in 875 by Harold Haarfagr, who, set on unifying Norway, could no longer tolerate the raids on his coast by Orkney and Shetland-based vikings, or pirates. Thereafter, until 1468, the islands were governed by their own Norse earls of Orkney, the more stirring though not necessarily historically accurate aspects of whose story are told in the sagas, notably the Orkneyinga Saga recording the period from about 900 to 1200.

Some of these earls have left their mark. Thorfinn the Mighty was a virtually independent ruler from 1020–64, his territory including also the Hebrides, a large part of Scotland and a realm in Ireland. He is most associated with Brough of Birsay in Orkney where he had his hall and founded Christ Church. He defeated Duncan of Scotland and later may well have backed Macbeth over Duncan's murder. In the early 12C Thorfinn's grandson Magnus was one of two jointly ruling earls. A gentle man for his times he was murdered in 1116 by his co-earl Hakon. Paul of Orphir ruled next, in turn being supplanted by Magnus's nephew, the remarkable Rognvald, a cultured man and a poet, some of whose verses are in the Orkneyinga Saga. He founded St. Magnus Cathedral in Kirkwall in 1137, Magnus by then having been canonised (probably more on political than religious grounds), and also went on a crusade which took him as far as the Jordan. Later he also was canonised.

Scottish influence, however, gradually took over and from 1230, though still formally bound to Norway, the earls were all Scots. In 1468 Christian I of Norway and Denmark betrothed his daughter, Margaret, to James III of Scotland, and, being unable or unwilling to hand over the agreed dowry, instead pledged the islands, which even today theoretically remain in pawn despite their having been unilaterally annexed by Scotland in 1472. Later the islands were administered on behalf of the crown by stewards, two of these, Earl Robert and his son Earl Patrick, being notorious tyrants. The latter was removed and executed in 1615, from which time Orkney and Shetland became administratively integral with Scotland.

Oil has been the modern event. Yet whatever changes it may have brought to the island way of life, these will be little apparent to the tourist visitor. Orkney's prehistoric sites are unaffected, both as such and in their settings, as is also, except for the one small area of Sullom Voe, Shetland's remote and lonely scenery.

Meanwhile, despite the 500 years since the pledging, Norse is still the source of most place names, the origin of the cadence in the local English speech, an occasional surviving influence in long-house-type building, and even the parent of some legal oddities and local festivals.

Inter-group Communications. Sea link (carrying cars) between Kirkwall in Orkney and Scalloway in Shetland. Crossing 9 hours. Twice weekly in summer; fortnightly in winter. (Wide Firth Ferries, No 2. Horries, Deerness, Orkney, KW17 2QL. Tel: 085674–351.)

British Airways (Highland Division) operate services from Edinburgh and Aberdeen, and from Glasgow and Inverness, to Kirkwall on Orkney and then on to Sumburgh on Shetland. (British Airways, 85 Buchanan Street, Glasgow. Tel: 041–3329666, or departure airports.)

67 Orkney

Its closest island some 6m from mainland Scotland across the Pentland Firth, the Orkney group numbers about 70 islands and islets of which less than one third are inhabited. The largest and most important, with the capital Kirkwall, is called *Mainland*, about 20m long, erratic in shape, and linked in the S by causeways to the islands of Burray and South Ronaldsay. The other islands divide themselves into the North and South groups. With the exception of Hoy (S), all the islands are low-lying or gently rolling agricultural land with few trees. There are scarcely any villages, in their place being dispersed houses and squat farms, the inhabitants largely concerned with the raising of cattle.

To the visitor Orkney is primarily important for its prehistoric monuments, of which the group has by far the richest concentration in Britain. There are sites of importance and interest on most islands, but those on Mainland are the most accessible and best known. All are to the W or N of Kirkwall, the best concentration being close to A965 around the S end of Loch of Stenness. Here, within a radius of less than 2m, are the great cairn of *Maes Howe*, the *Stenness Stones*, the *Ring of Brodgar* and *Unstan Cairn*. Other sites are scattered. The Stone Age village of *Skara Brae* is along the W coast, as is also, farther N, the *Brough of Birsay* archaeological complex (accessible only at low tide), while the best broch, *Gurness*, is on Aikerness to the NE across from the island of Rousay.

In summer there is a choice of Mainland tours, these of course including the principal sites, and there is also a choice of island cruises, island day visits and suchlike (details and bookings through Tourist Information). There are also scheduled bus services (not Sun.) throughout Mainland, but their use for touring the many scattered sites is not really practicable. A hired bicycle is one solution, but a car (own or rented) obviously gives the most flexibility. With a car it would be possible to cover most of Mainland's sites in one day, although this might be rushing places which deserve longer. Two or three days, though, should be ample, these also allowing time for the town of Kirkwall as well as for a run to Scapa Flow, famous as a naval base in the last two wars, and across the Churchill Barrier into South Ronaldsay.

> **Tourist Organisation**. Orkney Tourist Board, Broad Street, Kirkwall, Orkney KW15 1NX. Tel: (0856) 2856.
>
> **Access**. By sea the principal approach is by car ferry from Scrabster

(Thurso) to Stromness. Crossing 2 hours. Basically Mon.–Sat. once
daily in each direction, but with Sun. and extra weekday services
in summer. Advance booking strongly advised. P and O Ferries,
Stromness. Tel: (0856) 850655.—Also (no cars) John o' Groats to
Burwick on South Ronaldsay. Summer only (Thomas and Bewes,
Tel: 095581–353).

By air there are services to Kirkwall from Glasgow, Inverness
and Aberdeen by British Airways (85 Buchanan Street, Glasgow.
Tel: 041–3329666), and from Glasgow, Edinburgh, Inverness and
Wick by Loganair (Glasgow Airport. Tel: 041–8893181).

Inter-island Communications. See under North and South Islands.

SOME HOTELS (Mainland). **Kirkwall**. *Ayre*, Ayre Road. Tel: (0856)
2197. *Kirkwall*, Harbour Street. Tel: (0856) 2232. **Stenness**. *Standing
Stones*, KW16 3JX. Tel: (0856) 850449. **Stromness**. *Stromness*,
Victoria Street. Tel: (0856) 850298. *Ferry Inn*. Tel: (0856) 850280.
Birsay. *Barony*. Tel: (085672) 327. **Dounby**. *Smithfield*, KW17 2HT.
Tel: (085677) 215. **Burray**. *St. Lawrence*, KW17 2SS. Tel: (085673)
298.—Advance booking recommended, especially in summer.

For accommodation on the other islands, book through Tourist
Information when planning the tour.

Kirkwall

Kirkwall (6700 inhab. *ECl*. Wed. *Inf*. Broad Street), the island's capital
and with a busy harbour, is dominated by its solid Cathedral of St.
Magnus, beside which are the ruins of the Bishop's Palace and Earl's
Palace, and also the excellent Tankerness House Museum.

History. Thanks to its harbour and the foundation of the cathedral in the 12C
Kirkwall early became a place of local importance. In 1486 the town was made
a royal burgh by James III, and, later, James V lodged in the Bishop's Palace
and held meetings in Parliament Close, the site of which is now occupied by
the Hydro-Electric Board.

The name Castle Street recalls the old castle. Built in the 14C it was so strong
that its builder, Earl Henry Sinclair, was suspected of receiving help from the
Devil. It was held by Balfour, governor of Orkney, in 1567 against the fugitive
Earl of Bothwell, and was demolished in 1614 after the rebellion instigated by
Earl Patrick (see Earl's Palace, below). The site is marked by a plaque on 1
Broad Street.

In 1650 Montrose mustered 2000 Orkneymen in Kirkwall, but half of them
soon lost their lives by shipwreck.

Kirkwall derives its Norse name (Church Place) from a church
dedicated to St. Olaf, patron saint of Norway; a re-erected remnant
(an arched doorway) of this church's 16C successor can be seen in
St. Olaf's Wynd off Bridge Street. The town's main street is the long,
narrow and irregular Albert Street, locally simply The Street. The
Orkney Library (founded in 1683), in Laing Street, is known for its
collections of books and other material about Orkney, invaluable to
any visitor wishing to study local history and antiquities in any depth.

The ***Cathedral of St. Magnus** is a massive cruciform structure of
grey flagstone and patterned red and yellow sandstone, with a central
tower and spire. The style is a severe and massive Norman.

History. Rognvald III, Magnus's nephew, founded the cathedral in 1137, the
skeleton of the murdered St. Magnus being brought here from Thorfinn's Christ
Church on Brough of Birsay. Two skeletons, one of them with a pierced skull,
found hidden in chests within pillars (see below), are believed to be those of
Magnus and Rognvald, thus making the cathedral unique in Britain for
sheltering the remains of both founder and patron saint. The archbishops of
York tried to claim suzerainty in the 12C, but the see was suffragan to Nidaros

(Trondhjem, in Norway) until Orkney was annexed by Scotland in 1472, when it came under St. Andrews. The building of Rognvald's church apparently went on until well into the 13C, the transepts, with the three W bays of the choir and two E bays of the nave, with interlacing wall-arcades, being the oldest part of the church; the pointed arches supporting the tower are later. By about 1250 the three E bays of the choir were added, and the tower probably also dates from about this time. The steeple replaces a 17C one destroyed by fire in 1671. The church was finally completed in the 14–15C by the W extension of the nave.

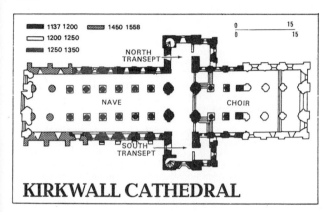

KIRKWALL CATHEDRAL

At the Reformation the cathedral was saved by the townsmen, and it continued to have a succession of seven Protestant bishops. Cromwell's soldiers used the steeple as a prison and as a fortress, also turning the nave partly into a barrack and partly into a stable. After this the building fell into neglect, although the choir was used as the parish church. Major restoration took place in 1912–20.

The cathedral is unusual in that it is owned not by any religious assembly but, by royal charter, by the citizens of Kirkwall.

Lining the *Interior* is a series of tombstones, the earliest (c 1300) being in the N choir aisle. In the S nave aisle is the canopied Paplay tomb (14C) and in the S choir aisle that of Lord Adam Stewart (died 1575), natural son of James V. In the N nave aisle hangs a mort-brod (c 1690) with emblems of mortality, interesting both for itself and as being the sole surviving example of this old type of Orkney memorial. Here also is a plaque commemorating the 833 men lost when HMS 'Royal Oak' was torpedoed in Scapa Flow in 1939. In the fifth bay is a fragment of vault painting.

A beautiful interlaced blind arcade lines the walls near the crossing (the oldest part of the church). The transepts, unlike the nave and choir, are not vaulted. The S rose window is a 19C reconstruction.

The two transeptal chapels (late 12C) are now used as vestries. They contain some 17–18C Communion plate. A dark archway in the S choir wall, above the main arcade, is the entrance to 'Marwick's Hole', a vaulted chamber once used as a prison.

In the raised Choir the massive piers of the central bay contain the remains of St. Magnus (S) and St. Rognvald (N). The contrast between the Norman work to the W and the later work of the E bays is striking.

The fine and unusual E window is ascribed to Bishop Stewart (c 1511), but is probably earlier; the decoration of the three arched recesses below it is notable. On the site of the high altar is the St. Rognvald Chapel (Stanley Cursiter, 1966), with figures (by Reynold Eunson) of the saint, Bishop William the Old (died 1153) and Kol, the Norse master-mason builder of the cathedral. The statue of St. Olaf in the N aisle is a replica (1937) of one in Trondhjem cathedral.

The **Bishop's Palace** (AM. Standard, but closed Fri. afternoon, and Sat. in winter. Fee), is almost entirely a 16C reconstruction on top of the original 12–13C building, of which only some ground floor masonry now remains. It was here, in the lower hall, that in 1263 King Hakon died after his disastrous defeat at Largs in the Clyde. The three great W buttresses were added by Earl Patrick Stewart, whose grandiose plan to join this palace to his own was ended by his downfall and execution. The tower, round outside but square within, bears a small statue, probably St. Olaf but possibly representing Bishop Reid (died 1558), who rebuilt the upper floors.

Across the road stands the more interesting and attractive ruin of the *Earl's Palace (as for Bishop's Palace), built by forced labour for the infamous Earl Patrick between 1600–07. Architecturally this is a gem of the period when castellation was beginning to be used more for ornamentation than defence. The palace is L-shaped, with particularly pleasing angle-turrets, each with its small room, while the enormous kitchens and storerooms and the great hall seem fitting setting for the magnificence and the luxury enjoyed here by the earl and his friends. His initials (P.E.O., for Patrick, Earl of Orkney) stand by the hall's fireplace.

Earl Patrick behaved as a prince, never going out without an escort of 50 musketeers. Such was his behaviour in Orkney (farming out the revenues; imposing forced labour; tampering with the weights and measures) that he spent much of his time from 1609 onwards either imprisoned or on trial. In 1613, learning that his castles had been seized, he sent his natural son, Robert, to Orkney to recapture them. Robert, after some initial success, was defeated and executed. Soon after, Earl Patrick too was executed for having instigated his son's revolt. Although Steward of Orkney and Shetland, and though living in such magnificence, this man was found 'so ignorant that he could scarce rehearse the Lord's Prayer' and was granted a week's stay of execution so that he could 'better inform himself'.

Tankerness House Museum (Mon.–Sat., 10.30 to 12.30. 13.30 to 17.00. Also, in May–Sept., Sun., 14.00 to 17.00. Tel: 0856–3191. Free) houses an admirable presentation of 4000 or more years of Orkney life. The building itself is a beautifully restored example of a 16–18C Orkney merchant laird's home with courtyard and garden.

Northern Mainland

A965 (alternative A964) to Stromness. A967, B9056 and A967 to Brough of Birsay. A966 to Broch of Gurness. B9057 to Dounby. A986 and A965 to Kirkwall.—This circuit visits all the principal prehistoric sites on Mainland.

Total distance 54m.—*10m* **Maes Howe**.—*5m* **Stromness**.—*7m* **Skara Brae**.—*6m* **Brough of Birsay**.—*8m* **Gurness Broch**.—*5m* **Dounby**.—*13m* **Kirkwall**.

There is a choice between Kirkwall and Stromness, the description below following the northerly road. The southern road (A964) offers views across Scapa Flow to the islands of Hoy and Graemsay, and in 9m passes close to *Orphir* where a small apse is all that survives of an 11 or 12C circular church, thought to have been modelled on the Church of the Holy Sepulchre. It was probably built by a crusader or pilgrim as the result of a vow made in the Holy Land, possibly Earl Hakon who made a pilgrimage to Jerusalem as penance for his murder of Magnus. Intact until 1757, the church was then demolished to provide material for a Presbyterian preaching box. The fragment of foundation adjacent is that of the contemporary Earl Paul's hall.—The car ferry to Hoy sails from *Houton*, just beyond.

A965 crosses a causeway, just beyond, to the N, being *Grain Earth-house*, the name being that of a local estate and having nothing to do with the earth-house's possible purpose.—*4m Rennibister Earth-house*, a particularly good example, was discovered in 1926 when a farm vehicle broke through the roof; below there were several human skulls and bones.

To the S along here there are two chambered cairns. One, on *Wideford Hill*, shows a central chamber and three cells, two ring walls and a smaller than usual entrance passage. The other, *Curween*, to the S of (*3m*) Finstown and more easily accessible, is a communal burial cairn of c 1800 BC. Merged into the empty slope of a hill and not much visited, this cairn permits more feel of its ancient past than do some. Human and animal remains were found here, including those of 24 dogs, suggesting that this cairn may have been associated with some hunting ritual.

*3m **Maes Howe* (AM. Standard. Fee)—the first of an astonishing trio of adjacent huge prehistoric monuments—is accepted as the finest chambered tomb in Europe. The roof has been rebuilt, the chamber is artificially lit, and because of the cairn's immense size entry is easy compared to most. The name, Great Mound, is certainly well justified, for this earth and stone hump is 115ft in diameter, 24ft high and over 300ft in circumference with a ditch averaging 45ft in width. Burrowing through the mound, a low, narrow passage, 36ft long, ends at the large inner chamber, off which open burial cells, each roofed and floored by massive single stones. The whole structure is an example of extraordinary strength and skill in the art of dry-stone building, some of the stones used being immense (one weighs over three tons).

Such a place must surely have been built for a line of powerful chiefs, but—and this is the added interest of Maes Howe—their rest was disturbed perhaps 2500 years later by Norsemen, the evidence being 24 runic inscriptions made in about 1150, in their way as fascinating as the mound itself. Many of these were carved by crusaders (probably Rognvald's expedition, known to have wintered in Orkney), one telling that the tomb's treasure was removed in the course of three nights, and another, intriguingly, that it is hidden somewhere to the NW. Yet another provides a very human touch with its record that two of a band, sheltering from a snowstorm, lost their wits and were thus a great hindrance to their companions. There are also 14 personal names, an animated dragon, a walrus or seal, and a knot of serpents.—*Tormiston Mill*, by the car park, is a good example of a large 19C watermill; it now houses a restaurant and a craft shop.

Half a mile to the W the *Standing Stones of Stenness* were perhaps contemporary with Maes Howe, perhaps even at some stage ritually associated with it. Only four stones still stand—thin local flags, one of them 17ft high—but there is evidence of others, including the rock-fill which held them upright. A ditch, cut through the rock but now silted, surrounds the site, and nearby towers the 18ft-high solitary Watch Stone.—Just a mile to the NW, beside B9055, the great *Ring of Brodgar* sits on a bleak moorland isthmus between lochs Stenness and Harray. Of a probable original 60 stones, 27 are still upright within a ditch surround, hacked out of the rock and with two entrance ways.

All around this area are scattered burial mounds, lone stones and other ancient traces, combining to stir speculation as to what compulsions drove prehistoric man and why he chose this corner.

In rather over 2m beyond Maes Howe, *Unstan Cairn*, though a lot more modest, is nevertheless archaeologically important as one of the comparatively few cairns having both stalls and a cell, the former perhaps even being on two levels. Unstan is also important because its excavation in 1844 produced the largest collection of Stone Age pottery found on any Scottish site, this now being in Edinburgh's Royal Museum of Scotland (Queen Street), as also two seated human skeletons below some runic inscriptions.

3m **Stromness** (1800 inhab. *ECl*. Thurs. *Inf*. Ferry Terminal. May–Sept), in marine terms now little more than the dock of the car ferry from Scrabster, as also for local boats serving the S islands, has in the past enjoyed several periods of prosperity. It was long a principal port on the northern sailing routes; for over 200 years, from 1670 to 1891, it was a base for Hudson Bay Company ships; it shared briefly with Kirkwall the North American rice trade; and from 1780 to the beginning of this century Stromness supplied stores and men for the Davis Strait whalers. All this meant that every trader sought to be on the waterfront, the outcome being today's mile-long, straggling narrow main street.

Login's Well, which for so long supplied visiting ships with water, recalls this past, as does also the *Natural History Museum* which, in addition to natural history exhibits, shows material on whaling, fishing, the Hudson Bay Company and even the scuppered German fleet (Mon.–Wed., Fri., Sat., 11.00 to 12.30. 13.30 to 17.00. Thurs., 11.00 to 13.00, and also 15.00 to 17.00 in July and Aug. Tel: 0856–850025. Fee). By way of contrast the *Pier Arts Centre* (Tues.–Sat., 10.30 to 12.30. 13.30 to 17.00. Sun., 14.00 to 17.00. Tel: 0856–850209. Free) combines a permanent exhibition of 20C British art with a programme of temporary exhibitions.

A967, followed in *4m* by B9056, in a further *3m* reaches **Skara Brae** (AM. Standard. Fee), in many ways Orkney's most exciting, and certainly one of the oldest sites. Lying beside the sandy crescent of the Bay of Skaill, this Stone Age settlement of perhaps 3000 BC comes as a welcome change from burial cairns and ritual, enabling the visitor to see something of the everyday domestic life, rather than the death, of prehistoric man. That the village has survived, though, seems to have been because of a natural disaster; because this place was buried in sand and there remained for perhaps 4000 years until revealed by a storm in 1850. This is no scattered settlement, but a small, huddled place in which vague passages link individual 'houses' or rooms, each touchingly personal with its hearth, fish larder-pools, stone beds and other primitive furniture, all fashioned from local flagstone. There is evidence that doors of some kind protected what

Skara Brae. A furnished home of perhaps 3000 BC.

would have been by modern standards minute entrances, and the huts may be pictured as being roofed, perhaps with skins, perhaps with some local thatch.

Much has been found here—in the way of tools, beads, pottery, and stone and whalebone artefacts—all this suggesting several periods of occupation, all based, though, on the economy of the sea.

Heading N, B9056 in *4m* passes to the E of *Marwick Head*, with a clifftop memorial to Lord Kitchener, the 1914–18 war leader who was lost in these waters in 1916 when HMS 'Hampshire', in which he was travelling to Russia, was mined. Beyond, in less than *2m* and just N of the junction with A967, *Boardhouse Mill* (fee) is a watermill of 1873 still grinding the local grain known as 'bere' but pronounced bare. Just NW of here is the ruined *Earl's Palace*, a 16C rebuilding on a site where the earls of Orkney had their palace prior to the rise of Kirkwall in the 12C.

Much more interesting, though, is the early Christian and Norse complex on *•Brough of Birsay* (AM. Standard, but closed Mon., and Tues. morning in winter. Fee), the nearby tidal island reached by foot causeway at low water. The ruins are on the landward slope and, if it is not possible to cross, a distant impression can still be achieved. Brough of Birsay is most associated with Earl Thorfinn (died 1064) and this rather confusing site includes the ruins of his Christ Church, built over the foundations of an earlier Celtic church, with, to the S, the Celtic graveyard partly underlying the Norse. Christ Church was later promoted to cathedral, and to its N are the remains of its bishop's palace, with a cloister. Lower, by the shore, sprawl the quite extensive ruins of Earl Thorfinn's hall, much complicated by the foundations of an earlier hall and what is left of later ecclesiastical buildings. Finally, spreading up the hill, are the outlines of a number of Norse long-houses.

Rounding the northern coast of Mainland, A966 in *8m* reaches the junction with B9057, here also being the short approach to *Gurness Broch* (AM. Standard. Fee) on the shore of stubby, windswept Aikerness across from the island of Rousay. This site shows not only the best preserved broch in Orkney, but also, around and even within the broch, an interesting if highly confused and confusing sequence of other ruins. The broch was probably the primary structure, but over the centuries down to Norse times it became shelter for various domestic buildings, including, inside the tower, partitioned chambers and, outside, cells around a central hearth and also Norse long-houses. The broch tower has two special features. One is the unusual ground-level wall passage; the other is the well, which today's visitor may descend by small rock steps to find at the bottom a stone cistern of clear water. The local pamphlet can be recommended for any detailed understanding of this complex site.

B9057 is now followed SW, in rather over *3m* being a sign to the *Click Mill*, a tiny turf-roofed building which is the last surviving example in Orkney of one of these old horizontal watermills. Built in 1800, the mill is of a type much older in origin.—*2m Dounby*, whence A986 leads SE to pass *Corrigall Farm Museum* (April–Sept: Mon.–Sat., 10.30 to 13.00. 14.00 to 17.00. Sun., 14.00 to 19.00. Tel: 085677–411. Free), a restored Orkney farmhouse of the mid 19C.—In *5m* from Dounby, this circuit is completed at the junction with A965, from which point Kirkwall is *8m* E, the road passing the cairns and earth-houses mentioned on the outward leg.

South Mainland and South Ronaldsay

A960 and B9052 to Churchill Barrier. A961 across Burray and through South Ronaldsay to Burwick.

Total distance 21m.—*3m* **Airport**.—*6m* **Churchill Barrier (N)**.—*4m* **Island of South Ronaldsay**.—*8m* **Burwick**.

3m Kirkwall Airport.—*3m Junction with B9052*, with A960 continuing into Deerness, the peninsula which, reached across a slim isthmus, forms the SE extremity of Mainland. Here, on Brough of Deerness (NE; 1m rough walk), the scanty remains of a chapel, huts and a well recall that this was once a monastery, much visited by pilgrims up until the 17C.—In *3m* B9052 reaches the N end of the *Churchill Barrier*, a series of four causeways linking Mainland to South Ronaldsay across the small islands of Lamb Holm, Glims Holm and Burray and thus sealing off this end of Scapa Flow.

Scapa Flow is the large protected sea area, enclosed by Mainland on the N, then, clockwise, Burray, South Ronaldsay, Flotta and Hoy. Famous as a major fleet base in 1914–18 and 1939–45, Scapa Flow has again become a centre of marine activity with the development of *Flotta* as an oil pipeline landfall and tanker terminal, second only to Sullom Voe in Shetland. In neither war were the defences anything like as impregnable as hoped and in 1917 and 1939 respectively HMS 'Vanguard' and HMS 'Royal Oak' were torpedoed, both with grievous loss of life; the second of these disasters leading to the building of the Barrier. On Germany's surrender in 1918, the greater part of her fleet (70 ships, including 10 great battleships) was ordered to Scapa Flow, and here a few months later they were almost all either beached or scuttled by their crews. Seven remain, lasting magnets for diving enthusiasts.

Crossing the system the wrecks seen on either side are those of the old boom-ships used to secure the entrance to Scapa Flow before the construction of the Barrier. But if these wrecks, however interesting, are ugly, a softer note is early provided by the *Italian Chapel* on Lamb Holm. Inside two drab wartime Nissen huts, this is a beautiful chapel ingeniously and imaginatively built out of scrap metal in 1943 by Italian war prisoners working on the road across the Barrier. The chapel was rededicated in 1960 when restored by the original designer, Domenico Chiocchetti.

The Barrier ends in *4m* on reaching the island of **South Ronaldsay**, close to the village of *St. Margaret's Hope* on the bay into which in 1290 sailed the ship on which the Maid of Norway had died. A more modern context is provided here by the *Orkney Wireless Museum* (April–Sept: Daily, 10.00 to 20.00. Tel: 0856–.2856. Fee), illustrating Scapa Flow's wartime communications and showing also vintage wireless sets.—*8m Burwick*, where, it is said, St. Colon, a disciple of St. Columba, attempted to land. Being refused permission, he returned with a large stone on which he stood and preached. The stone is in the church by the shore, said indeed to stand on the site of a Celtic chapel. Burwick is linked to John o' Groats by summer passenger ferry (see Access above).

South Islands

> **Access**. The South Islands are Hoy, Graemsay and Flotta. *Graemsay* and northern *Hoy* (Moness) can be reached by passenger ferry from Stromness (Tel: 0856–850624). *Flotta* and southern *Hoy* (Lyness and Longhope) can be reached by car ferry from Houton in Orphir, 10m SW of Kirkwall by A964. All year, daily. (Orkney Islands Shipping. Tel: 085681–397).

Hoy is the largest and principal island of the southern group and the only one likely to be of interest to the tourist. Measuring some 12m by 6m, the island has no bus service, but car hire can be arranged. The main centre is *Longhope* in the S, the other car ferry pier being at *Lyness*, 3m to the N and once the headquarters for the Scapa Flow naval base. The entrance to Longhope Bay, separating Longhope from Lyness, is guarded on either side by Martello towers, built in 1813–15 as protection against marauding American privateers.

Hoy is Orkney's only hilly island, with *Ward Hill* in the N rising to over 1500ft. There is also outstanding cliff scenery, notably at the NW with the *Old Man of Hoy* (450ft), a sandstone stack on a basalt base, and *St. John's Cliff* (1140ft), the highest sheer cliff in Britain, this coast well seen from the Scrabster ferry. Archaeologically the island's principal site is the *Dwarfie Stone*, near the Rackwick road 2m from the pier at Moness. Dating from perhaps 3000 BC and unique as the only example in Britain of a rock tomb, this is a sandstone block out of which a passage and two chambers have been hollowed.

North Islands

Orkney's northern islands form a low-lying archipelago some 25m broad and stretching away 30 or more miles N and NE from Mainland. Popular with bird-watchers, they are also rich in prehistoric, Norse

and medieval sites, and arrangements for visiting the islands are
continually improving. Nevertheless some planning is required, not
only to coordinate travel and accommodation but also for visiting
archaeological sites, not all of which are regularly open. There are
no bus services, but bicycles can be hired on many islands. Intending
visitors should first consult the Orkney Tourist Board in Kirkwall.

Access by sea. No car ferries. For passengers there is a choice of
services, the two principal operators being Orkney Islands
Shipping, 4 Ayre Road, Kirkwall. Tel: (0856) 2044; and Wide Berth
Ferries, Horries, Deerness. Tel: (085674) 351. Timetables are
seasonal and sailings in some cases dependent on tides. Below is
an outline.

Shapinsay. All year, Mon.–Sat. At least one crossing daily, with
round trip normally possible (Orkney Islands Shipping).—Wide
Berth Ferries also operate a summer service, on some days with a
package tour including Balfour Castle.

Rousay. Wyre. Egilsay. By Orkney Islands Shipping there is one
return sailing per week from Kirkwall.—There is also a daily round
from Tingwall to Wyre and Rousay, with Egilsay once weekly on
Thurs. Hire to Eynhallow and Gairsay (Flaws Ferries. Tel:
0856–82213 or 82332).

Eday. Stronsay. Sanday. Papa Westray. Westray. Orkney Islands
Shipping operate the following basic schedule: Mon.–Fri., Round
the Islands. Wed., To the islands from Kirkwall. Thurs., From the
islands to Kirkwall.—In summer Wide Berth Ferries also serve the
above islands.

North Ronaldsay. One return service weekly. (Orkney Islands
Shipping).

Access by air. Loganair (Tel: 0856–3457) operate scheduled flights
from Kirkwall to Sanday, Stronsay, Westray, Eday, North Ronaldsay
and Papa Westray. Charters and round trips can be arranged.

Shapinsay (4m by 3m) has little of interest, though as the ferry docks
in Elwick Bay the scene here in 1263 may be pictured for this was
where Hakon assembled his galleys prior to sailing for Largs. Scottish
Baronial *Balfour Castle* here was completed in 1848, and *Quholm*, in
the NE of the island, was the home of the ancestors of the American
writer, Washington Irving, born on a ship bound hence to New York.

Rousay (6m by 5m) is the best island for prehistory, the principal
sites being within 5m of the pier and along the island's S shore.
Nearest, and all within 2m, are three burial cairns, the first being
Taversoe Tuick, with two storeys each with its own entrance passage.
Next comes *Blackhammer*, where the chamber shows seven divisions;
in 1936 two skeletons were found here together with some pottery
and flint artefacts. The last cairn is *Knowe of Yarso*, a stalled cairn
with four compartments. Excavation here in 1934 revealed a large
and baffling collection of bones—of 21 humans, 30 deer, several
sheep and a dog—as also pottery, flint and bone artefacts.

But the best site, *Midhowe, is 3m farther, with, adjacent to one
another, a chambered cairn and a broch. The cairn is an exceptionally
large one of the stalled type, in which the chamber is 76ft long and
7ft wide with 24 burial stalls arranged 12 on each side. The remains
of 25 individuals were found here, together with pottery of the Unstan
type. The adjacent broch, 30ft in diameter, is still in part 14ft
high.—On the nearby island of *Eynhallow* (Norse for Holy Island) the
ruined church probably belonged to a Benedictine monastery of c
1100.

On **Wyre** (3m by less than 1m) stands the ruin of the 12C stronghold of Kolbein Hruga, a Norse robber baron. With a keep and later outworks, this ruin is popularly known as *Cubbie Roo's Castle*. The nearby church was probably built by Hruga's son, Bishop Bjarni, in c 1190.

Egilsay (3m by 1m) is known for its 12C *Church of St. Magnus*, notable architecturally for its lofty round tower (Irish in design, but one of only three such in Scotland) and historically for standing on or close to the site where Magnus was murdered in 1116. Although now roofless, the church was in use until well into the 19C.

Stronsay, erratic in shape but roughly 6m from N to S, is flat and fertile with, at Whitehall in the N, a fish processing factory. On Lamb Head, at the SE tip of the island, there is a small broch, near a stone construction running into the sea which may represent a Pictish or Norse pier.

Sanday, 12m long and shaped like a grotesque fish, is archaeologically best known for *Quoyness Cairn* on the small S shore promontory of Els Ness. It shows a central chamber with six cells.

Eday (8m long) is separated from the small *Calf of Eday* by the narrow Calf Sound, the most scenic passage of the steamer route. A chambered cairn on the Calf is archaeologically of particular interest for being built above an earlier stone structure, perhaps a tomb or perhaps a minute home.

Westray forms a curving 10m from N to S. The island's pier is at Pierowall towards the NE, ½m to the W being the quite extensive ruins of *Noltland Castle* (16C), built by Gilbert Balfour, Master of the Household to Mary, Queen of Scots, but in 1650 burnt by Covenanters. Features here are the hall, the vaulted kitchen and the tiers of gunloops in the wall, reminding that even on a remote island such as this attack could always be expected. There are also two medieval churches on Westray, *St. Mary's* (13C) at Pierowall being historically interesting as successor to the church in which Rognvald heard Mass on his first arrival in Orkney in 1136. The other, and slightly older, church is *Crosskirk* (12C), on the shore near Tuquoy 3m S of Pierowall. Finally, Jacobite days are recalled by the name *Gentlemen's Cave*, to the NW on the S side of Noup Head, a refuge for several survivors of Culloden.

Papa Westray, 4m long and off the NE of Westray, is deeply associated with early Christianity. Not only does the island owe its name to the several hermits who once sought seclusion here, but ruined *St. Tredwell's Chapel*, beside the loch of the same name, is dedicated to that probably legendary saint, also known as Triduana, once believed to have had the power to cure diseases of the eyes (see also Rte 18F, Restalrig). Of unknown age, this chapel is also said to be on the spot at which Christianity first took root in Orkney.

But man was here millenia before the Christian hermits, as evidenced by *Knap of Howar* on the island's W coast. Dated to between 2400–2800 BC these remains of two well-built side-by-side stone houses rank as the oldest still standing dwellings in NW Europe. And prehistoric man even reached the tiny *Holm of Papa*, leaving his mark with two chambered cairns, one a large one with a triple central chamber and several wall cells.

North Ronaldsay, forming a huge crescent 4m long, is Orkney's most northern island. Very low lying, it is surrounded by a dyke outside which the small native sheep live largely on the local rich red seaweed. The remains of a broch, *Broch of Burrian*, guard the island's southern tip.

68 Shetland

The Shetland group, its principal island over 60 miles N of Orkney
and on about the same latitude as the southern point of Greenland,
comprises nearly 100 islands, of which only 12 are inhabited, and
several of these precariously. The principal island, with the capital
at *Lerwick* and the main airport 26 miles S at *Sumburgh*, is called
Mainland; it is some 50 miles long and so indented that it varies in
width from 20 miles to a few yards. The chief other islands are *Unst*,
Yell and *Fetlar* to the NE; *Whalsay*, *Out Skerries* and *Bressay*, off
Mainland's E coast; *Papa Stour* off the W shore; and, far to the S and
W respectively, *Fair Isle* and *Foula*.
  The name Shetland derives from the Norse 'Hjaltland' meaning
'High land', and for the most part the scenery is upland peat bog and
grass or heath moor with countless small lochs, rising at *Ronas Hill*
on Mainland to nearly 1500ft. The coast—and no place in Shetland
is more than 3 miles from the sea—provides continual contrast, being
in places pierced by long, tranquil, winding inlets or voes, and in
places awesome cliffs battered by fierce seas into arches, fissures
and stacks. Trees are rare, cultivation patchy, and almost everywhere
there are sheep, including the distinctive Shetland black and brown,
said to be identical with the wild sheep of Siberia. The small, hardy,
native Shetland ponies will also be seen. Until the early 1970s the
people were mainly fishermen, crofters or those serving local needs,
but with the development of the oil installations much change has
come, especially to Mainland. But the visitor in search of remoteness
and scenery need have no fears since significant oil industrialisation
is confined to the comparatively small Sullom Voe area of Mainland.
  Two archaeological sites (*Jarlshof* and *Mousa*, the latter accessible
only by boat in about May to Sept) are amongst the most important
in Britain. These apart, it is the constantly changing coast that will
most attract the visitor. Special arrangements are necessary for visits
to the distant islands, but car ferries serve Unst, Yell, Fetlar, Whalsay
and Bressay. In summer there are coach tours, but normal bus
services, timed mainly to run from outlying districts into Lerwick in
the morning, returning in the evening, are of little use to the touring
visitor. A car gives most flexibility and is essential if time is a
consideration. Even with a car at least three days should be allowed
if the full opportunities of the coast are to be explored and sites such
as Jarlshof and Mousa given the attention they deserve. Car transport
to Shetland is expensive and the cost should be weighed against that
of hiring; self-drive hire is efficiently organised and cars can be
picked up either at the airport or in Lerwick, but there is heavy
demand in summer and booking is essential.

Shetland knitwear, with its traditional designs, is world famous. The
fine wool is not shorn but plucked or 'roo'ed' from the sheep's neck.
Due though to mainland spinning the local knitwear is to a decreasing
extent made purely of this soft wool. Shops in Lerwick and elsewhere
offer a wide choice of knitwear at surprisingly low prices. In summer

there are exhibitions in Lerwick at Isleburgh Community Centre and in the Town Hall (knitting, carding, spinning).

Birds. Many visitors are attracted to Shetland by the wealth of bird life, the birds dividing roughly into seabirds, northern birds, and migrants. The seabirds include gulls, auks, puffins, storm petrels, shags, guillemots, razorbills, fulmars (who first arrived about 100 years ago), and gannets (first seen in the early years of this century). These birds will be found in their thousands on the cliffs throughout Shetland, but special mention may be made of the nature reserves of Hermaness and Noss. Northern birds, some rare, include the red-necked phalarope, the whimbrel, skuas, and red-throated divers (known in Shetland as rain geese). The migrants are too varied to name. They are most numerous on the E side of the group, and Fair Isle, with its observatory, is internationally famous as a migration station.

Tourist Organisation. Shetland Tourist Organisation, Market Cross, Lerwick, ZE1 0LU. Tel: (0595) 3434.

Access. By sea Lerwick is reached from Aberdeen by overnight car ferry. Three times weekly (P and O Ferries, Orkney and Shetland Services, Jamieson's Quay, Aberdeen, AB9 8DL. Tel: 0224–572615). There is also a car-carrying service between Kirkwall in Orkney and Scalloway in Shetland (Wide Firth Ferries, No. 2 Horries, Deerness, Orkney KW17 2QL. Tel: 085674–351).
  By air there are services to Sumburgh from Glasgow and Inverness via Orkney, and also from Aberdeen (British Airways, 85 Buchanan Street, Glasgow. Tel: 041–3329666). Also to Tingwall from Edinburgh (Loganair, Glasgow Airport. Tel: 041–8893181).

Inter-Island Communications. For ferries see under individual islands. Loganair operate scheduled air services from Tingwall to Fetlar, Unst, Whalsay and Fair Isle; also in summer to Foula and Out Skerries. Tel: (059584) 246.

SOME HOTELS. **Lerwick**. *Thistle*, South Road. Tel: (0595) 2166. *Kveldsro House*. Tel: (0595) 2195. *Grand*, Commercial Street. Tel: (0595) 2018. **Scalloway**. *Scalloway*, ZE1 0TR. Tel: (059588) 444. **Sumburgh**. *Sumburgh*, ZE3 9JN. Tel: (0950) 60201. **Whiteness**. *Westings*, ZE2 9LJ. Tel: (059584) 242. **Walls**. *Burrastow House*, ZE2 9PD. Tel: (059571) 307. **Brae**. *Brae*. Tel: (080622) 456. *Busta House*, Busta, ZE2 9QN. Tel: (080622) 506. **Hillswick**. *St. Magnus Bay*, ZE2 9RW. Tel: (080623) 209.
  On **Yell**. *North Isles*, Sellafirth, ZE2 9DG. Tel: (095784) 293. On **Unst (Baltasound)**. *Baltasound*. Tel: (095781) 334. *Hagdale Lodge*. Tel: (095781) 584.

Lerwick and Scalloway

Lerwick and Scalloway are Shetland's two principal centres.

  Lerwick (7000 inhab. *ECl.* Wed, all day. *Inf.* Market Cross), Britain's most northern town, has a lively harbour and waterfront, home to ships and sailors of many nations, especially Scandinavian and Russian. The town's business and prosperity have much increased as the result of the development of Sullom Voe (20m N) as an oil terminal.

History. The Iron Age and earlier people who lived here are represented by Clickhimin broch; the town's Norse origin by its name, meaning Clay Creek. Bressay Sound was long known as a refuge for seafarers and was an assembly place for Hakon's 200 galleys bound for Largs. But it was the use of the Sound by Dutch fishermen early in the 17C that led to the growth of Lerwick. In 1640 the Dutch fishing fleet's armed escort was attacked here and sunk by French warships. In 1653 a great boost was given to the town's future when 94 ships of Cromwell's fleet arrived, landing troops to build what is now Fort Charlotte, possibly the town's first permanent building. But the Dutch returned in 1673, burning part of the town.

Lerwick's Fire Festival, *Up Helly Aa*, a pagan survival welcoming the return of the sun, is held on the last Tuesday in January. A long procession with flaming torches is headed by a Viking chieftain and a replica of a galley. To end the festival the torches are thrown on to the galley to make a bonfire.

Another touch of the Norse tradition is provided by the '*Dim Riv*', a replica of a Viking longship which takes visitors around the harbour (details from Tourist Information).

Lerwick's main street is Commercial Street, an attractively flagstoned, irregular and sometimes narrow road running roughly parallel with the waterfront. *Fort Charlotte*, near this street's NW end, was built in 1653, burned by the Dutch in 1673, repaired and given a new interior in 1781 when a large barrack block was added, and ranks today as the only intact Cromwellian military structure surviving in Scotland. The ramparts provided splendid views.

Above Commercial Street rises the district of Hillhead, where the *Town Hall* (Mon.–Fri., 10.00 to 12.00. 14.00 to 15.30. Tel: 0595–3535. Free) has some fine stained glass windows illustrating Shetland's story. Opposite, in a modern building, is the admirable *Shetland Museum* (Mon.–Sat., 10.00 to 13.00. 14.30 to 17.00 but closed Thurs. afternoon. Also Mon., Wed., Fri., 18.00 to 20.00. Tel: 0595–5057. Free) showing ship models and navigation instruments; prehistoric and early Christian material, the latter including the delightful Monks' Stone showing a procession of priests, sculptured stones from St. Ninian's Isle and replicas of the treasure found there; Shetland knitting; wireless telegraphy equipment; and articles salvaged from a Dutch East Indiaman wrecked on Out Skerries in 1711.

A reconstructed view of Clickhimin Broch (Crown Copyright: reproduced by permission of Historic Buildings and Monuments, Scottish Development Department).

But *Clickhimin Broch*, on the town's SW outskirts, the massive legacy left by Lerwick's prehistoric and Iron Age ancestors, will for many visitors be the town's most memorable site. Forming an island at the end of a causeway into a small loch, the broch—65ft in diameter and with walls 18ft thick and 15ft high—stands on a great stone platform with a gateway and an enclosure. The broch, though, is no more than the visible survival of one period in the life of a complex site, perhaps occupied from the 6C BC to the 5 or 7C AD and in turn primitive settlement, dun, broch and wheelhouse.

The island of *Bressay* (300 inhab.) is visited from Lerwick (Car ferry. Frequent. Tel: 0595–2024). For many the objective of the visit will be the small island of *Noss* 200 yards off Bressay's E shore, a bird sanctuary (NCC) whose lofty headland of Noup of Noss (592ft) has a cliff-face alive with seabirds, including a colony of gannets. (Mid May–Aug: Daily except Mon. and Thurs., 10.00 to 18.00. Visitors are ferried across by inflatable dinghy, but before leaving for Bressay should confirm with Tourist Information that the weather and sea conditions permit the crossing).

Scalloway (1000 inhab. *ECl.* Thurs.), on the W coast 5m from Lerwick and until about 200 years ago the village capital of Shetland, is now mainly concerned with fish processing, one of the factories (L. Williamson. Tel: 059588–237) welcoming visitors. There is a small museum (Bona Vista), but Scalloway's most prominent feature is the stark ruin of *Earl Patrick's Castle* (Mon.–Sat., 09.30 to 19.00. Sun., 14.00 to 19.00. Key from cottage opposite. Free); built with local forced labour in 1600, in a medieval style already oldfashioned, the castle was abandoned on its owner's execution only 15 years later. In the harbour area a plaque recording a visit here in 1942 by Prince (later King) Olaf recalls that during the last war Scalloway was a base for Norwegian patriots carrying out clandestine operations, and that the expression to 'take the Shetland bus' meant to escape from Norway to Shetland.

Bridges connect Scalloway southwards with the islands of *Trondra* and *Burra* (W and E), their length (6m) served by a scenic if desolate road of moorland and waterscapes. The hamlet of Papil, at the S of West Burra, was an early Christian centre and the place where the Monks' Stone (see Shetland Museum above) was found as also the Papil Stone now in the Royal Museum of Scotland.

South Mainland (Lerwick to Sumburgh Airport and Jarlshof)

A970 (S), with diversion loop along B9122.—South Mainland is a long narrow finger of mixed moor and downland. The road follows the E side, generally running well above the shore and affording good coastal views.

Total distance 27m.—*13m* **Leebitton (Mousa)**.—*5m* **St. Ninian's Isle**.—*5m* **Croft House Museum**.—*3m* **Sumburgh Airport**.—*1m* **Jarlshof**.

Passing *Clickhimin Broch* the road in *3m* reaches *Hollanders' Knowe*, once a Dutch trading point but now marking the junction with B9073 for Scalloway.—*10m* **Leebitton**, below the road, is the pier for visits to the island and broch of **Mousa**, reached in about 15 minutes (Tom Jamieson. Tel: 09505–367 to arrange mutually convenient timing. Summer only). This is by far the most complete of Scotland's more than 500 brochs and also, standing as it does on the shore of an empty island, one of the country's most exciting sites and one, too, with a colourful past. Here, it is said, the local Picts successfully sought refuge from Roman slave hunters; and here, many centuries later, in 1150 if the sagas are to be believed, a Norse nobleman hid with the famous beauty with whom he was eloping. Since then, and even allowing for some careful restoration, structurally and scenically, not a great deal can have changed and Mousa still stands over 50ft in diameter, 45ft high and with walls tapering from 12ft to 7ft in thickness. And within the walls there are still galleries and stairways, by one of which a walkway around the tower's top can be reached.

In 3m after rejoining the main road a worthwhile diversion can be made along the westerly loop provided by B9122, this in 2m reaching the hamlet of *Bigton*. Here a small road drops to the sandy shore where the car may be parked and the isthmus crossed to **St. Ninian's Isle**, its bare and breezy downland, today occupied only by ponies and sheep, once the home of an early Christian monastic settlement. All that stands here now, easily reached and overlooking the isthmus, are the lower courses of a 12C chapel. But excavation in 1958 revealed the remains of a pre-Norse church, and, under a stone slab, a magnificent hoard of 8C Celtic silver, perhaps buried by the monks when faced with the threat of Viking raids. This silver is now in Edinburgh, but good replicas can be seen in the Shetland Museum in Lerwick. About ½m S of the chapel there is a Holy Well, seeping out from the peat as a small crystal clear spring.

In another 4m B9122 rejoins A970 at *Boddam*, just S of which (1m) is the *Croft House Museum* (Tues.–Sun., 10.00 to 13.00. 14.00 to 17.00. Tel: 0595–3434. Fee), convincingly preserving a picture of croft life as it was in the mid 19C. Here are the cottage, barn, byre and stable, all attached to one another and provided with the authentic household utensils of the day, while down the hill, beside a burn, a horizontal watermill, of original Norse design, still turns.

As the road drops to (3m) **Sumburgh Airport** there can be a distant view ahead of Fair Isle, while to the W rears *Fitful Head*, so named from the Norse 'hvitfugla' meaning white birds.

**Jarlshof (AM. Standard, but closed Tues., and Wed. afternoon. Fee) is less than 1m farther, near the hotel beside the S end of the main runway. This fanciful Norse name (an invention by Sir Walter Scott for his book 'The Pirate') is in fact highly misleading because this archaeological complex, accepted as being one of the most important in Britain, dates from at least the Bronze Age and displays the remains of five distinct periods of occupation piled around and on top of one another over perhaps 3000 or more years. The small Museum is well worth a visit, if only for its plan of the site as also for a series of pictures imaginatively illustrating how Jarlshof may have looked at various stages of its occupation.

The ruins, sprawling across a low promontory by the sea's edge, are inevitably confusing, but plaques well identify the various periods. From the Bronze Age there are huts, as well as evidence both of farming (with one of Britain's earliest cattle stalls) and of a metal worker's shop. The Iron Age is represented by two earth-houses, a broch with an outer defence wall (perhaps 1C) and also by rather later (3–8C) wheel-houses. These last, probably family homes, take the form of a number of individual recesses spoked around a central hearth and, with so much still clearly identifiable, are perhaps the most satisfying remains at Jarlshof. Norse settlement here of one kind or another probably spanned some 500 years (9–14C) but the builders of those centuries have left only a confusion of long-house remains. Next come the foundations of a medieval farmstead (14–16C), and then, most recent and most prominent, the walls of the 16C house of earls Robert and Patrick Stewart.

Nearby *Grutness Pier* is used by the boats for Fair Isle, while *Sumburgh Head*, notorious for its tidal races, has a lighthouse (1821, and only in 1975 converted from paraffin to electricity) which may sometimes be visited (Tel: 0950– 60375).

Across the bay, at the tip of its W arm (½m walk), the substantial ruin of *Ness of Burgi* was an Iron Age fort of what is known as the 'block-house' type, believed to have been the immediate predecessor of the brochs.

North Mainland (Lerwick to Esha Ness or Sandvoe)

A970 (N), followed by B9078 to Esha Ness.—Moor, inland lochs and seascapes.

Total distance 36m.—*5m* **Veensgarth**.—*5m* **Loch Girlsta**.—*6m* **Voe**.—*5m* **Brae** (for **Sullom Voe**).—*6m* **A970 split**, followed by *9m* **Esha Ness** or *9m* **Sandvoe**.

3m Bridge of Fitch where a branch of A970 leads off SW for Scalloway.—*2m* **Veensgarth** is a scattered and characterless valley community around a crossroads and Tingwall airfield. From here A971 (see West Mainland, below) heads NW for West Burrafirth and Sandness, while B9074 drops S beside Loch of Tingwall to reach Scalloway. A diversion of 2m as far as the S end of the loch should be made by anyone attracted by Shetland's Norse period because this Tingwall valley is historic as the meeting place of the island's parliament and law court, the Althing. The actual site is believed to have been *Law Ting Holm*, a small promontory, in Norse days an island, jutting into the NW corner of the loch. Beyond, B9074 skirts the loch below (W) Gallows Hill—scene not only of hangings but also in the early 18C of the burning of a mother and daughter, both accused of witchcraft—to reach the foot of the loch where a standing stone reminds that prehistoric man too regarded this valley as important.

More recent times, largely 19C, are recalled by the Shetland bygones shown in the *Tingwall Agricultural Museum* at Veensgarth (Tues., Thurs., Sat., 10.00 to 13.00. 14.00 to 17.00. Tel: 059584–344. Fee), a fascinating clutter covering crofting, fishing and domestic life, all housed in an 18C granary and stables. And something more of this past and local atmosphere can be enjoyed by attending one of the folklore evenings held here on certain days in summer (Bookings and transport arrangements through Tourist Information).

In *5m* A970 runs beside *Loch Girlsta*, tracing its name to that of a Norse maiden, Geirhilda, said to have died tragically and to be buried on an island.

DIVERSION INTO LUNNA NESS (B9075, B9071 and unclassified. NE, 14m to Lunna). B9075 branches E just beyond Loch Girlsta to wind across remote and empty countryside with fine views to reach (9m) *Laxo*, pier for the car ferry to Whalsay. (Laxo can also be reached more quickly if less interestingly by continuing N along A970 for a further 6m beyond Loch Girlsta and then turning E for 2m along B9071). From Laxo B9071, becoming an unclassified road, continues for 5m to *Lunna*, halfway along Lunna Ness. Here the small church (1753) has a leper squint, while, in a more modern context, Lunna House, now a hotel, was during the last war the headquarters of the Norwegian resistance. Lunna is also the place where the Ninian oil pipeline crosses this peninsula, making its landfall at Grut Wick (1½m NE), thence running SW down the promontory to Cul Ness from where it continues below the water to reach Sullom Voe.

From Loch Girlsta A970 heads due N for (*6m*) **Voe**, near which a number of roads meet. B9071 leads E for (2m) Laxo and the car ferry to Whalsay; A968 continues N for (9m) Toft and the car ferry to Yell, and thence to Unst and Fetlar; B9071 wanders SW to meet the West Mainland road (see below) at Bixter.

Beyond Voe A970 skirts *Olna Firth*, once busy as the last whaling station in Shetland.—*5m* **Brae**, where the motorist curious about the Sullom Voe oil terminal should take B9076 which, passing Scatsta airfield, in under 5m skirts the terminal complex, thence continuing for another 4m to reach the Yell car ferry pier at Toft.

Sullom Voe Oil Terminal (visitor facility planned). During the last war Sullom Voe was an active, operational flying-boat base; today oil has taken over, as huge tankers are fed by the North Sea pipelines.

The terminal—Europe's largest, and at present handling some 1.3 million barrels of crude daily—with its tanker jetties, occupies the peninsula of *Calbeck Ness*, now firmly joined to the mainland by reclaimed land, formerly part loch and part tidal pool. To Sullom Voe come the 36-inch Brent and Ninian pipelines, each drawing on neighbouring fields. The Ninian pipeline travels 103m from its field to its first landfall at Grut Wick on Lunna Ness (see above). From Cul Ness, also on Lunna Ness, it again crosses below water, reaches land at Firth Ness, then turns W to run parallel with the Brent pipe across land to the terminal. The Brent pipe starts at the Cormorant field, 93m away. Reaching Shetland it passes well N of Lunna Ness and between the islands of Linga and Samphrey before making landfall in Firths Voe.

In *1m*, at *Mavis Grind*, A970 crosses a short narrow isthmus where the Atlantic and the North Sea—the latter represented by the head of Sullom Voe, the former by a small sea loch—wash within a few yards of one another. Here the road enters the district of Northmavine, probably the most scenic in Mainland, in rather over *5m* reaching a road fork where A970 splits. A useful and very scenic link between this road's westward and northward arms is provided by an unclassified road running from the head of Ura Firth on the westward arm to skirt beautiful Ronas Voe and join the northward arm at this voe's head. Along this road a touch of history is provided by a monument known as the *Hollanders' Grave*, visible on the hill immediately W of Skeo Head Pier, 1m N of Ura Firth. This marks the grave of Dutch seamen killed in 1674 when their Indiaman, the 'Wapen van Rotterdam', sheltered in Ronas Voe where it was found and taken by the frigate 'Newcastle', though not without a fight.

TO ESHA NESS. A970 loops the head of Ura Firth, passing the small road described immediately above, and in *4m* ends at the village of *Hillswick*. Just before the village the westward road becomes B9078, this soon affording good if sometimes distant seaward views of strangely shaped scattered stacks. This road ends in *5m* at *Esha Ness (lighthouse) where, but with caution, the precipitous cliff edge can be approached with its view northward to the *Grind of the Navir* (Gateway of the Giants), a mile's length of awesome eroded cliffs,

stacks and clefts facing the unbroken assault of the Atlantic and alive
with screaming seabirds.

TO SANDVOE. Heading N from the road split, this northward arm of
A970 in under *3m* passes close to the head of Ronas Voe (for the
small road along the voe, see above), the high ground to the NW
here rising to *Ronas Hill* (1475ft), Shetland's highest point. In *3m*,
after skirting Colla Firth, the road reaches the oval *Loch of Housetter*
with, clearly seen a few yards W of the road, two standing stones
and, a short way N, a chambered cairn where, amid the rubble, the
entrance passage can still be traced. Beyond, the road ends at (*3m*)
the hamlet of *Isbister* or, beside its small voe, that of *Sandvoe*, while
Mainland tapers away northward as a promontory ending as the
narrow Point of Fethaland, continued, a mile or so away, by a scatter
of skerries and stacks.

West Mainland (Lerwick to Sandness)

> A970 to Veensgarth. A971 to Sandness.—Beside voes, followed by
> moorland broken by many small lochs.
>
> Total distance 25m.—*5m* **Veensgarth.**—*10m* **Bixter.**—*2m* **Stanydale
> Temple.**—*3m* **Bridge of Walls.**—*5m* **Sandness.**

For Lerwick to (*5m*) **Veensgarth**, see North Mainland above. In *2m*
A971 crosses *Wormadale Hill*, above the head of Whiteness Voe and
affording grand views, before dropping to round the S end of *Strom
Loch*, with, on an islet, fragments of Strom Castle, medieval in date,
though almost certainly on the site of an Iron Age dun. The castle's
story is shadowy, but it was perhaps an early residence of the Sinclair
lords before the building of their castle at Scalloway. *Hjaltasteyn*,
beside A971, shows and sells handcrafted jewellery using Shetland
gemstones (Showroom: Mon.–Fri., 09.00 to 17.00. Sat., 10.30 to 16.30.
Sun., 14.30 to 17.00. Workshop: Mon.–Fri., 11.00 to 12.30: 14.30 to
16.00. Tel: 059584–351). Beyond, in rather over *3m*, the road kinks
round the head of Weisdale Voe, a short way to the N here being
Kergord with the largest stand of trees in Shetland. Weisdale was
the birthplace in 1786 of the remarkable John Clunie Ross who
settled in the Cocos Islands, becoming 'King' and having his sovereignty recognised by Queen Victoria.

5m **Bixter**, from where a road meanders northward for 10m to
meet A970 at Voe. From just beyond Bixter, too, B9071 runs S to
reach (4m, to the E) *Sand*, with fragments of a chapel traditionally,
though apparently without evidence, built by the crew of a Spanish
Armada galleon wrecked here.

In *2m* beyond Bixter an unclassified road leads S to reach in
another 1½m the (probably wet) moorland path to (½m) the intriguing
Stone Age site known as *Stanydale Temple*. Hut remains beside the
path, and scattered generally around, tell that this uninviting and
remote moor was once home to a sizeable Stone Age community,
centred presumably on the heel-shaped 'temple'; called such because
similar ancient buildings in the Mediterranean, and especially in
Malta, are so classified, though it seems equally if not more likely
that this place served some domestic communal purpose. Walls, some
12ft thick, enclose an oval chamber with stalls, and floor holes can
be seen into which roof support poles would have been fitted. And
a further puzzle is provided by the fact that wood traces found here
have been analysed as spruce, a tree believed not to have existed in

Scotland before the 16C, this prompting the suggestion that the
prehistoric builders used driftwood washed across from America.

Along A971, in another *1m*, an unclassified road leads N for (4m)
West Burrafirth for sailings to the island of Papa Stour.—*2m Bridge
of Walls* where A971 splits, the left fork soon reaching *Walls*, for
sailings to Foula. The right fork for some *5m* traverses a district of
continual small lochs before curving through **Sandness**, a name
embracing a group of crofting communities. Papa Stour lies a mile
or so offshore, and Foula, over 20m away, may also be seen.

Islands of Yell, Fetlar and Unst

> The islands of Yell, Fetlar and Unst are linked by car ferries. Toft
> (Mainland) to Ulsta (Yell), 20 minutes crossing. Gutcher (Yell) to
> Belmont (Unst), 10 minutes crossing. Gutcher (Yell) to Oddsta
> (Fetlar), 20 minutes crossing. The service through Yell to Unst runs
> daily, roughly hourly; Fetlar service roughly 4 services daily, but
> fewer on Sun. Advance booking is advised. Tel: (095782) 259 or
> 268.—Air services to Unst and Fetlar from Tingwall (Loganair).
>   There are limited bus services. Timetables from Tourist
> Information.

Yell (17m by 6m; 1200 inhab.) is in large part made up of rolling
peat moor. Between Ulsta (ferry) and Mid Yell there is a choice
between a westerly or an easterly road. The former is rather faster;
the latter more interesting and more scenic, passing crofts and
hamlets and with views across to Out Skerries and Fetlar. Along this
latter road, at Burravoe (4m from Ulsta), *Old Haa of Burravoe*, a large
white crowstepped building dating from 1637 and the oldest building
on the island, is being developed as a local museum and arts and
crafts centre (May–Sept. Tel: 095782–225, 241 or 256. Fee).

A drive northward from Gutcher is worth considering. In 4m,
where the road curves and dips W at Brough, the oval Kirk Loch
comes into view to the N, beside its W shore being the roofless *Kirk
of Ness* (grass path a little farther down the road), a medieval church
dedicated to St. Olaf but abandoned in 1750. Beyond, to the N
between the church and the shore and half lost in sand and grass,
there is an extensive and challenging wilderness of stone fragments,
of (to the layman) unintelligible pattern but thought to represent
perhaps thousands of years of prehistoric and later occupation. The
cliffs here are magnificent, but their rims are brittle and dangerous.

The drive should be continued for another 2m to Gloup where the
Fishermen's Memorial (sign; short walk), on the hillside overlooking
Gloup Voe, really tells its own story. During the 19C this voe was
the home of a substantial fishing community, devastated on 20 July
1881 when in a great storm ten boats and 58 men were lost.

Fetlar (5m by 3m), the name being Norn for Fat Land, is Shetland's
most fertile island. That prehistoric man took advantage of this is
clear from the several cairns, brochs and other remains, while some
ruined chapels represent medieval if not earlier Christianity. But it
is as a nature reserve, and especially as a bird sanctuary—most
popularly for the snowy owl—that Fetlar is best known. Visiting
ornithologists are asked to contact the RSPB warden (Tel:
095783–246).

Unst (12m by 5m), a mix of bleak rolling downland and peat moor
and Britain's northernmost inhabited island, is known for its ponies,
cliff scenery and fine knitted work, though sadly this last is disap-

pearing. The main road (A968) runs virtually the length of the island from the ferry pier at Belmont to the two scattered centres of Baltasound and Haroldswick, but within 2½m from the ferry both eastward and westward diversions should be made.

The first (E) rounds Uyea Sound, soon passes a standing stone and in 3m reaches *Muness Castle* (key at cottage), a desolate ruin in a not much less desolate landscape but interesting for having been built for Lawrence Bruce in 1598 by the same man who designed Scalloway's castle. This Lawrence Bruce was related to, and is reputed to have been almost as evil as, the notorious Earl Patrick, and this castle seems to have lasted not much longer than Scalloway, being burnt down, possibly by French privateers. Nevertheless, apart from the top storey—which was pulled down to provide material for the enclosure wall—the shell is more or less complete, among features being, below the windows, the shot-holes decorated with rings and trefoils; the decorated turrets; and, in the kitchen, the oven and sink, the latter still with its drain.—*Haaf Gruney*, an uninhabited island 2m S of Muness, is a national nature reserve where storm petrels breed amid the remains of a long-disused chromite mine.

The westward diversion (signed to Westing) in ½m reaches a yet smaller road leading down towards the sea and almost immediately passing a large, rough standing stone. Beyond, the road deteriorates into a track, at the end by the shore being the ruined 12C church of *Lund*, in use until 1785. Here will be found the graves of two merchants from Bremen (died 1573 and 1585), today just two names but in their time surely respected representatives of the Hanseatic trade; see also Whalsay, below. The Westing road continues NW, in 1m breasting a rise with, on the left, the grass-covered mound of a broch, notable for the extent of its surrounding earthworks. And in another mile, as the road dips to cross a burn by a stone bridge opposite a ruined house, will be found a restored, horizontal click mill of original Norse design.

A968 crosses a featureless landscape to reach first *Baltasound*, with two hotels to the N of its bay and the airfield to the S, and then the equally scattered community of *Haroldswick*, named after Harald Haarfagr (see Orkney and Shetland, Common History) who in 875 based himself first on Fetlar and then here before annexing the islands. This is Britain's most northern village and the post office willingly franks visitors' letters to this effect.

From Haroldswick a road climbs due N to *Saxa Vord* (936ft), named, it is said, after a Norse giant but today crowned by Ministry of Defence installations and boasting that here, in 1962, was registered the British wind speed record of 177 mph, at which point the anemometer blew away. From here there is a superb view across the deep and beautiful inlet of *Burra Firth*, with a coastguard and lifeboat station at its head and, beyond its mouth, *Muckle Flugga* with its lighthouse. The W side of Burra Firth, between the firth and the open sea, forms *Hermaness National Nature Reserve*, one of Scotland's most important seabird sanctuaries, with skuas breeding on the moorland, and colonies of gannets, puffins, guillemots, kittiwakes and others on the 600ft-high cliffs. The base of the reserve is quickly (2m) reached by B9086 out of Haroldswick, the promontory then stretching over 2m N from the road's end.

Other Islands

Whalsay (5m by 2m; 1000 inhab.), 3m off Mainland's E coast, is reached by Loganair from Tingwall or by car ferry from Laxo (Crossing 35 minutes. Several times daily. Tel: 08066–376 or 259). The island prospers through fishing and fish processing, that this has long been the case evidenced by the so-called *Bremen Böd*, near Symbister pier, a 17C Hanseatic store and trading booth, the only complete surviving example in Scotland; today the building serves as a local interpretive centre for visitors. Nor need interest be confined to this pier area, for in the NE, beyond the hamlet of Isbister, there are the *Standing Stones of Yoxie*, a small complex dated to c 2000 BC and presumably serving some ritual purpose. Adjacent is the so-called *Bunzie House*, also of the Stone Age and, it has been suggested, perhaps serving as a kind of vestry for the priests.

Out Skerries form an island-group some 5m to the NE of Whalsay. Only the two main islands (adjacent and joined by a bridge) are inhabited, the 100 or fewer people living by fishing and fish processing in a modern, mechanised factory opened in 1970.—By sea the islands are reached by twice-weekly boat from Lerwick, the crossing requiring three hours. Tel: (0595) 2024. Air service in summer by Loganair from Tingwall.

Papa Stour, volcanic in origin and with a coast that is all bays, stacks, natural arches and caves, of which it has some of the finest in Britain, measures some 3m by 2m and supports a population of some 40 people. As its name suggests—it means Great Island of the Priests—Papa Stour was associated with the early Christian hermits and missionaries. Later, until the 18C, the islet of *Brei Holm* off the E coast was used as a leper colony. Just off Mainland's W coast opposite Sandness, Papa Stour is reached by boat from West Burrafirth. Crossing 30 minutes. Tel: (059586) 335.

Foula (Bird Island), 20m W of Papa Stour and measuring only 2m square, is a wild, remote island with cliffs 1200ft high, home to countless seabirds including the largest skua colony in Britain. Once 300 people lived here—many of them Norse descendants for the Norn language survived here until about 1800—but their number is now down to about 40.—Air service in summer by Loganair from Tingwall. Sea access is by once to three times weekly boat from Walls. Tel: (03933) 3232, but also consult Tourist Information, Lerwick, because the island can be isolated for lengthy periods by bad weather and visitors must rely on their own supplies.

Fair Isle (3m by 1m; population 80), lying halfway between Shetland and Orkney and since 1954 owned by the National Trust for Scotland, has a name long associated with intricate knitwear patterns, an art which some trace back to Spaniards wrecked here during the Armada of 1588. Today the local Cooperative sells island products worldwide. Otherwise—and increasingly since the establishment in 1948 of the Bird Observatory Trust—it is birds that rule here, the island being an internationally recognised ornithological habitat and an important migratory staging station.—By sea Fair Isle is reached by boat from Grutness. Twice weekly. Crossing three hours. Tel: (03512) 222. For accommodation at the Bird Observatory, apply The Warden. Tel: (03512) 251. Day visits can be made by Loganair from Tingwall.

INDEX

Topographical names are in **bold** print; names of persons in *italics*; other entries, including subsidiary indexes, in Roman print. Where there are two or more page references the more important are in appropriate cases printed **bold**.

Printed in Great Britain by
Fletcher & Son Ltd, Norwich

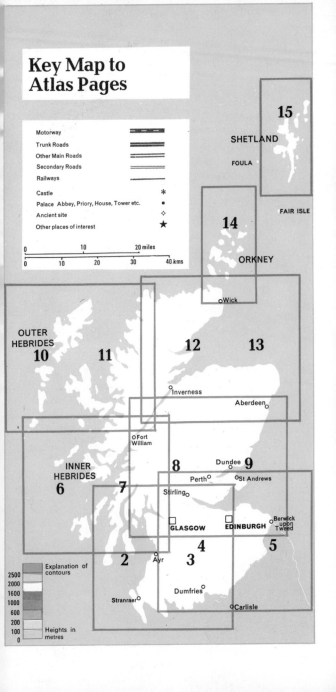

Key Map to Atlas Pages

Motorway	
Trunk Roads	
Other Main Roads	
Secondary Roads	
Railways	
Castle	*
Palace Abbey, Priory, House, Tower etc.	■
Ancient site	◇
Other places of interest	★

0   10   20 miles
0   10   20   30   40 kms

15
SHETLAND
FOULA

FAIR ISLE

14
ORKNEY

○Wick

OUTER
HEBRIDES
10

11

12

13

○Inverness

Aberdeen○

○Fort
William

8

Dundee○ **9**

Perth○   ○St Andrews

INNER
HEBRIDES
6

7

Stirling○

□
GLASGOW

□
EDINBURGH

Berwick
upon
Tweed

5

2   ○
Ayr

3

4

Explanation of
contours
2500
2000
1600
1000
600
200
100
0

Heights in
metres

Stranraer○

Dumfries○

○Carlisle

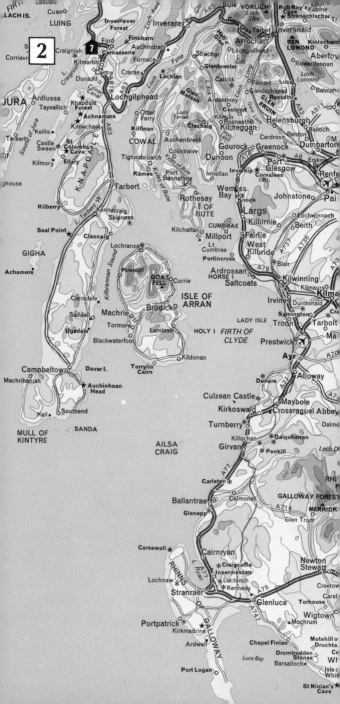

o Bell Rock

bar
BARNS NESS

Cockburnspath Fast   ST ABBS HEAD
Dunglass   Coldingham
bbey   Eyemouth
hans
         Edins Hall   Burnmouth
         Broch   Chirnside   Lamberton
                  Foulden Berwick
Duns   Edrom   han Tweed
        Ladykirk   Norham
                Tweed
Hume   Coldstream
rstain   698
lm   Carham   Wark
Kelso
Eckford   Yetholm
        Morebattle
     Cessford
Oxnam
urgh   Woden
            Law
    Carter Bar

E BORDER

EST PARK

ENGLAND

Newcastle
          Tyne

*Kisimul
VATERSAY

6

MINGULAY

RHUM

EIC

10

MUCK

ARDNAMUR

Kilc

COLL

Tobern

Den

Calgary

TIREE

TRESHNISH
ISLES

GOMETRA

L. Tuath

ULVA

STAFFA

INCH
KENNETH

Burg

IONA

Fionnphort

Loch
Penn

ROSS

COLONSAY

*Kilorar

ORONSAY

L Gruinart

Port Askaig

Kilchoman

RHINNS

Port Charlotte
Bowmore

Loch Indaal

ISLAY

Portnahaven

Kildalton
Port Ellen

THE
OA

BUTT OF LEWIS

Eorop

Ballantrushal

Barvas

Arnol
Bragar
Shawbost
Carloway

GT
BERNERA

L E W I S Stornoway

Uig

Callanish

Keose

SCARP

Husinish Aline

L. Seaforth

Amhuinnsuid *H A R R I S

Tarbert

SHIANT ISLE

SCALPAY

St Kilda →

Leverburgh

Rodel

BERNERAY

Duntulm *

Floddiga
ST

Skye
Mus. QUIRAING

L. Mealt

Udal Newton

Balranald ★ NORTH UIST

Lochmaddy

Trumpan WATERNISH

Uig TROTTERNISH

Stein

Clachan

Carinish

Boreraig Fairy

Kingsburgh

L. Snizort L. Fada

MONACH
ISLANDS

Balvanich Grimsay

Rossinish

Glendale

Milovaig Colbost Dunvegan

Skeabost

Po

BENBECULA

DUIRINISH

S K Y E

WIAY

L. Druidibeg

Struan

A86

A850

IDRIGLL PT.

L. Harport

Drynoch Sco

Howmore SOUTH
UIST

Talisker

Sligachan

THE
CUILLI

L. Cor Ke

L. Scave

Lochboisdale

Pollachar Ludag

SOAY

ERISKAY

BARRA Eoligarry

Sound of Barra

CANNA

6 ↓

PO

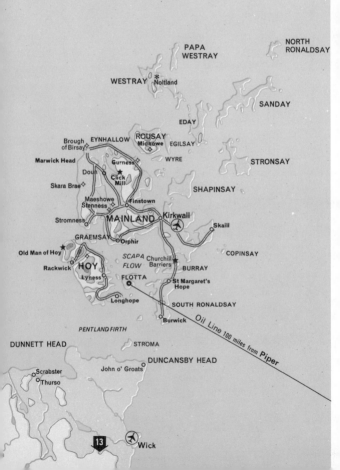

14

NORTH
RONALDSAY

PAPA
WESTRAY

WESTRAY ✳Noltland

SANDAY

EDAY

ROUSAY
Brough EYNHALLOW Midhowe EGILSAY
of Birsay ★

Marwick Head WYRE STRONSAY
Gurness

Doun
Click
Skara Brae◇ Mill SHAPINSAY

Maeshowe
Stenness Finstown

Stromness MAINLAND Kirkwall ✈
Skaill

GRAEMSAY Orphir
COPINSAY
Old Man of Hoy ★ SCAPA
Rackwick HOY FLOW Churchill ★
Barriers BURRAY
Lyness FLOTTA ◇St Margaret's
Hope
Longhope SOUTH RONALDSAY

Burwick Oil Line 100 miles from Piper
PENTLAND FIRTH

DUNNETT HEAD STROMA
DUNCANSBY HEAD

Scrabster John o' Groats
Thurso

13 ✈Wick

15

16

Key to Text sections
with Route numbers
Local Government Boundaries

SHETLAND
ISLAND AREA

Orkney & Shetland
Routes 67 & 68

ORKNEY
ISLAND AREA

WESTERN
ISLES
ISLAND AREA

North
Routes 49-61

HIGHLAND

North East
Routes 36-43

GRAMPIAN

Hebrides
Routes 62-66

TAYSIDE

East Central
Routes 20-35

Argyll
Routes 44-48

CENTRAL

FIFE

LOTHIAN

STRATHCLYDE

19 Glasgow

18 Edinburgh

South East
Routes 1-9

BORDERS

South West
Routes 10-17

DUMFRIES
& GALLOWAY

ENGLAND

N. IRELAND

NOTES

NOTES